The Literature
of the Old Testament

NUMBER V OF THE

RECORDS OF CIVILIZATION: SOURCES AND STUDIES

The Literature
of the Old Testament

By JULIUS A. BEWER

THIRD EDITION

Completely Revised by Emil G. Kraeling

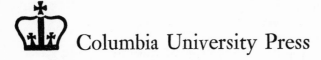 Columbia University Press

NEW YORK AND LONDON 1962

TO MY DEAR MOTHER

IN GRATITUDE AND DEVOTION

RECORDS OF CIVILIZATION
SOURCES AND STUDIES

EDITED UNDER THE AUSPICES OF THE
DEPARTMENT OF HISTORY, COLUMBIA UNIVERSITY

Preface

THIS BOOK was first published in 1922. The second edition, slightly revised, appeared in 1933. New plates being needed it was considered an opportune time for a revision that would take cognizance of progress in this field of study. As I was closely associated with Professor Bewer in the Old Testament department at Union Theological Seminary in New York for twenty-four years, Columbia University Press, through its Executive Editor, Mr. Henry H. Wiggins, inquired of me whether I would be willing to undertake this task. Though engaged in another project, I could not well refuse to perform this service to the memory of the beloved friend and colleague to whom I had dedicated my Papyri publication of 1953.

At the time of giving this consent I did not contemplate making many changes, but I came to the conclusion that a more thoroughgoing revision was needed if justice were to be done those readers who seek guidance in this book concerning the Old Testament as seen by present-day scholarship. Dr. Bewer's main concern was to acquaint the student with the critically interpreted contents of the Old Testament. Alterations in critical judgments, chronological order or arrangement of materials would, I felt, have seemed of slight importance to him in comparison with that objective.

A crucial chapter was that which Dr. Bewer had entitled "Deuteronomistic Historians." As he had come rather close to the view currently held by an increasing number of scholars of the existence of a Deuteronomistic historical work, I drew the full consequences and adopted that position. After making that decision, which had considerable ramifications, I felt less hesitant in making other changes. There have been some rearrangements, especially in the later chapters. The chapter on Chronicles was shortened and the sections on Ezra-Nehemiah and Song of Songs were augmented. In the chapter on Canon and Text the material on sources of error in manuscript transmission was omitted, as of value only to the student of Hebrew, and replaced with material about the Dead Sea Scrolls. Some brief information on the Apocrypha and Pseudepigrapha is given in an Appendix; and a new Bibliography with emphasis on books that have appeared since the first World War has been provided. In spite of my contribution I feel that this is still Dr. Bewer's book in all that matters most.

My thanks are due to the Bewer family for reposing confidence in me; to Mr. Wiggins for his courtesy and consideration; to Mr. Edward McLeroy, Editor, for his patient and painstaking editorial work; and to Dr. Herbert Donner of Göttingen University—of which Dr. Bewer was an honorary member—for a list of criticisms and suggestions. I am indebted to Miss Lisa McGaw for revising the indexes.

EMIL G. KRAELING

Contents

Introduction

THE Old Testament is not a single book but a little library of thirty-nine books as we ordinarily count them. Originally there were even more, for several which were at first distinct and separate are now combined in one; and many more authors were responsible for their production than tradition allows. The Old Testament, as we now have it, is the result of a long literary process in which compilers and editors had a large share. It is in this final form that it has exerted its great influence on ancient and modern civilization alike. But each book, each component part indeed, had its special significance for its own time as well. Some of them were the direct cause of powerful religious and social movements; others contain the soul-stirring addresses that gave new direction to the life of the nation. Like tributary streams which irrigate the land in their individual courses before their waters mingle in the river adding to its greatness and power, so each separate piece of the Old Testament gave refreshment and inspiration to the people before it became united with a particular book or with the collection as a whole, whose greatness and power it now augments.

To trace the origin and development of the individual contributions, to see how they sprang out of the life and thought of the people, how they influenced the cultural development of Israel, and how they in turn were influenced and modified, until finally the one great Sacred Bible resulted, is a fascinating task. If we read the various parts of the Old Testament in the order in which they originated, it takes on a new significance, for the warmly pulsating life of the people and of its leaders is felt much better at its sources. The common folk with their songs and stories, the poets and the prophets, the historians, lawgivers, and sages, all stand before us as we follow in our imagination the various phases of the great development and

try to recapture the different experiences with sympathetic understanding until we feel the power that moved them all and recreate in
our own mind the times of long ago, when the pioneers of the Spirit
blazed new paths for the moral and spiritual development of the
race.

This we will attempt to do, and in order that we may really feel
the throbbing life of this great movement we will take the results of
the special, detailed, and laborious literary investigations regarding
the composition of the individual books, the separation of their
various elements, their date, and authorship for granted and follow
the historical development of the literature of the Old Testament
unencumbered by technicalities. It is true that there are differences
of opinion on the part of critical scholars about the date and composition of quite a few documents, but the main lines of the development are sufficiently clear to warrant our weaving the single literary
results together in a story, which in itself will be a means of judging
their plausibility and validity.

The chronological sequence of the books which literary criticism
has established differs greatly from their order in our Bibles. And
not only is this true of the books as a whole but of their component
parts as well, for most of the books are of composite authorship.
Those who are under the impression that the Pentateuch was written
by Moses, Job in very early times, the Psalms largely by David,
Proverbs, Song of Songs, and Ecclesiastes by Solomon, the Book of
Isaiah in its entirety by the prophet of that name, the Book of Daniel
by the Jew who allegedly held a high post under Nebuchadrezzar
and his successors, will naturally be shocked at this modern picture
of the historical development (see Chronology, Appendix, p. 459 f.).
They will ask: how did this changed view arise?

Only a few landmarks in the history of the Old Testament study
can be mentioned here. The decisive insights for the whole literary
and religious development in Israel were those by which the basic
sources of the Pentateuch were discovered and their proper succession fixed, for this great work covers five hundred years of writing
activity. The famous French physician Jean Astruc in his *Conjectures*
of 1753 (published anonymously in that age of heresy-hunting), saw
in the change of divine names in Genesis—where *Elohim* is used

for God in some passages and the sacred Tetragrammaton, or four letter word, *Jhvh* [1] (in recent English transcription, *Yhwh*) in others —a clue to a compilation of two sources. The insight probably would have remained abortive, like that of a German cleric who expressed the same idea a little earlier, had it not been for its adoption by the great Biblical scholar J. G. Eichhorn in his monumental "Introduction" to the Old Testament, 1781. He held the basic document (*Grundschrift*) to be the one using Elohim and beginning with Gen. 1:1. In later editions he (mistakenly) rejected the idea advocated by K. D. Ilgen in 1798 that there were really two strands using Elohim.

A second high point in Pentateuchal criticism, as seen in retrospect, was M. L. De Wette's recognition in 1805 of the fact that the Book of Deuteronomy was the basis of the reformation of King Josiah that is reported in 2 Ki. 22–23. The full importance of this discovery was not seen at the time. With H. Hupfeld in 1853 it became clear that Ilgen had been right: there were three strands in Genesis, the (supposedly) older Elohist (the author beginning at Gen. 1), a "younger" Elohist and the (allegedly) still younger writer who used the name Yahweh; in addition there was the *Redactor* who had combined these sources and had contributed connecting links and supplementary matter.

But the development of the Hebrew religion remained incomprehensible with this chronological order of the sources. Only those who thought of Moses (the presumable author of the "basic document") as having the highest and purest form of religion, from which there was a decline in later times, could be satisfied. The decisive breakthrough was made by Julius Wellhausen in his *Geschichte Israels*, I, 1878 (in the 1883 edition and in the English translation of 1885 called *Prolegomena to the History of Israel*). He showed that the supposed "earlier Elohist," whom he called the Priestly writer,

---

[1] The Jews frightened by Lev. 24:11 (cf. especially the form this verse has in the LXX), substituted *Adonay* "Lord" for this name wherever it stood, when reading the Bible. In the LXX the word *Kyrios* was substituted for the name. In the vocalized Hebrew Bibles of a later age the vowels of *Adonay* (with a modification of the first one for a good reason) were given to the name *Jhvh*. Christians learning Hebrew in the Renaissance thought this name was to be read *Jehovah*. The true pronunciation had been reported by early ecclesiastical writers. Modern scholars vocalize the name *Jahveh* or *Yahweh*.

or P, instead of being the oldest Pentateuchal author was the youngest, and wrote after the exile. While he was not the first to entertain
this idea he gave it the convincing proof. The oldest Pentateuchal
writer, he held, was the one who used the name Yahweh and hence
could be called Yahwist (Jahvist) or J. After him came the other
writer using Elohim, for whom the name Elohist, or E, was now
reserved; and then came the Deuteronomist or D. Instead of PEJD
the true order of the sources was JEDP.

Now the whole situation became plain. With these main points
fixed it was possible to differentiate the earlier and later elements in
other books and to assign to these their places in the literary history.
A tremendous movement began, in which numerous other scholars
in other lands participated, and within a generation an entirely new
picture of the Hebrew literary and religious development had been
obtained. There have been many refinements and attempts to revise
the basic hypothesis, some of which will be mentioned in due course.
But in the main it has stood the test of time.

Literary criticism was supplemented at the close of the nineteenth
century by a new approach based on the recovery of ancient sources.
Since Wellhausen's time, in which the pre-Islamic Arabs furnished
the chief sphere of comparison for ancient Hebrew life and religion,
the great achievements of Assyriologists and Egyptologists had
opened up knowledge of the literatures and religions of peoples
whose civilizations had dominated the Ancient Near East. The
Babylonian Creation Epic; the Gilgamesh Epic and especially its
flood-story; the Code of Hammurabi; the Tell el Amarna tablets,
containing the correspondence of Asiatic kings with the Pharaohs
Amenophis III and IV; the Assyrian, Egyptian, and Old Persian
historical inscriptions; Egyptian Prophecy and Wisdom literature;
all these and others not mentioned provided completely new information and yardsticks with which to measure Hebrew literature and
to illuminate innumerable passages of the Old Testament. This trend
continued, and new finds constantly broaded the picture. The discovery of the existence of a Jewish colony at Elephantine Island and
its papyri of the fifth century B.C.; the exploitation of Semitic Epig-
raphy (Sinaitic, Phoenician, Aramaic, Moabite, South Arabian,
North Arabian); the recovery of the languages and literatures of

the Hittites and of the North-Canaanitic kingdom of Ugarit (*Rās Shamra*); the cuneiform texts from the Amorite kingdom of Mari on the Euphrates and from that of Alalakh in Syria; the full exploitation of the Sumerian Mythological texts from Nippur; the Hebrew ostraca from Samaria and Lachish; new Aramaic papyri and inscriptions; the Dead Sea Scrolls—all of these have tremendously broadened the horizon of Old Testament research.

Partly stimulated by the archeological movement there arose at the turn of the century a new line of inquiry: that of the study of the development of the Hebrew literary forms, inaugurated by Hermann Gunkel. He sought an answer to the question of what the life-situation (*Sitz im Leben*) was, which produced the particular literary form, and carried this study through for narrative literature in his commentary on Genesis (3rd ed., 1910), and for Hebrew poetry in his commentary on the Psalms (1926–33). He made rich use of the ancient Oriental sources for comparative purposes, but also invoked the study of folklore in dealing with many passages of the Old Testament. In this respect he was continuing stimuli going back to the German poet and scholar Johann Gottfried Herder (1744–1803). A second line deserving mention here is the interest in cult and the discernment of cultic background in Old Testament materials. This was inaugurated by the Norwegian scholar Sigmund Mowinckel in his studies on the Psalms (1921–24), and is currently exercising considerable influence on the subject called "Theology of the Old Testament."

It is not possible in a survey of Hebrew literature such as this to explore all the interesting angles of the Old Testament research. Our main concern is to study the individual literary productions, large and small, in the order in which they arose and in the light of interpretation placed upon them by modern exegetes. The undertaking is strictly historical; but we must not lose sight of the fact that through the action of the Christian Church the Old Testament is part of the Bible—that great book of religious and moral instruction by which western man has been formed to a greater extent than is commonly realized. To see this heritage more clearly and accurately and to evaluate it more correctly, is the task to which we must address ourselves.

ABBREVIATIONS USED IN THE
TEXT AND FOOTNOTES

(For complete information see Bibliography.)

ANET   Pritchard, *Ancient Near Eastern Texts*

APOT   Charles, *Apocrypha and Pseudepigrapha of the Old Testament*

AV   Authorized Version of the Bible

LXX   Septuagint Version of the Bible

MT   Masoretic Text of the Hebrew Bible

RSV   Revised Standard Version of the Bible

I

Early Poems

LONG before any one in Israel thought of writing in literary form, people sang songs and told stories, delighted in riddles and wise sayings, and handed them down from generation to generation in oral tradition. The few of these that have come down to us, embedded as quotations in our prose books, are all in poetry. They had been conceived in enthusiastic moods and had often been recited or sung on festive occasions, when the rhythmic form of some classes like the war songs and paeans of victory was accentuated by dancing and the accompanying clapping of the hands or by crude music. Certain men were especially interested in these folk songs. We read of ballad singers or reciters of poems in early Israel (Num. 21:27) and may be sure that in course of time they felt the need of committing their repertoire to writing. The names of two such early collections we know, the "Book of the Wars of Yahweh" and the "Book of Yashar" or the "Upright." The works themselves, the earliest books of Hebrew literature of which we have any record, are no longer extant, but some of the poems, which are quoted from them in the (later) prose narratives,[1] indicate that they were books of poetry.

Among the ancient poetic material that is still preserved in the books from Genesis to Samuel there are lyric songs, as well as didactic, prophetic, and cultic poems. Unfortunately, it is impossible to

[1] The fragment of the list of stations in Num. 21:14f. is quoted from the "Book of the Wars of Yahweh"; while Joshua's command to the sun and moon (Josh. 10:12f.), David's lamentation over Saul and Jonathan (2 Sam. 1:19–27), and Solomon's dedicatory sentence (1 Ki. 8:12f.) are from the "Book of Yashar."

date them exactly. Though some are very old, not a single song has come down from a time earlier than Moses, and whether any has from his own time is doubtful. One of the oldest, in spirit if not in age or form, is the song of the terrible Lamech with its unquenchable thirst for revenge, its cruel lack of pity, and brutal boastfulness (Gen. 4:23f.). It comes from a primitive civilization in which even the law of blood revenge exerted no restraint. Proudly the reckless warrior utters his boast to his wives,

> Adah and Zillah, hear this voice of mine,
>   wives of Lamech, hearken to this speech of mine:
> I slay a man for wounds of mine,
>   and a young man for bruises of mine.
> If Cain takes vengeance sevenfold,
>   Lamech will truly seven and seventy fold!

The rhythm is perfect and the rhyme, which is rare in Hebrew poetry, enhances the wild beauty of the song. Who can tell how old it is? The form is polished, the contents are savage. But poetic forms are ancient, and primitive savagery among desert tribes may have haunted the Israelites long after they had settled in Palestine. The brutal boast of endless blood feud has many parallels in Arab songs, where it is also addressed to the women.

From Moses' time, it may be, comes the original paean of Miriam after the great deliverance at the Sea of Reeds (Ex. 15:21). It was in just such manner that the ancient Arabs also celebrated their victories. With music and dancing the women, led by Miriam, repeated ever again the exciting refrain,

> Sing to Yahweh,
>   for highly exalted is He,
> The horse and its rider
>   He has hurled into the sea.

It consisted only of these lines, just as the paean of the women on David's victory over the Philistines (1 Sam. 18:7). A much later poet worked it out in more detail, beginning with this same refrain but unfolding its theme at length, and then attributing the whole not to Miriam but to Moses (Ex. 15:1ff.), the greater personality, as often happens in literary history.

There are some other interesting bits of poetry connected with this period. The brief distich which tells of Yahweh's eternal warfare against Amalek,

> A hand on the banner of Yahweh!
> Yahweh has war with Amalek forever (Ex. 17:16),

is our oldest literary witness to the immemorial enmity between Israel and Amalek. But whether it actually comes from this early time, it is impossible to tell.

The ancient cultic formulas with which the ark was addressed, when it was taken into battle and when it returned (Num. 10:35f.), are most probably from the time of the Exodus or of the Conquest. They give us the primitive conception of the ark. In ancient times it was taken into battle, especially when the situation was critical, for in it Yahweh manifested His presence to His people sitting on the ark as on a throne. When it set out at the head of the army these words were spoken,

> Arise, Yahweh,
> that Thine enemies be scattered,
> and they that hate Thee flee before Thee!

when it came back from victory,

> Rest, O Yahweh,
> Thou myriads of regiments of Israel!

For Yahweh was the god of battle, worth myriads of regiments of Israel. He brought victory and then returned to his seat on the ark. The narrator understood these verses as referring to the beginning and the end of the day's march in the wilderness. When the Ark started, Israel broke camp; when it stopped, Israel did so too. Such cultic formulas are frequently reinterpreted by later generations.

A list of names of places through which Israel had passed on its march to Canaan was handed down in poetry. It has its parallels in Arabic poetry where the recitation of lists is often enlivened by a reminiscence of one kind or another. We have only a little fragment of the list and its text is difficult. It is quoted from the Book of the Wars of Yahweh, in which the Exodus from Egypt and the Conquest of Canaan appear to have been celebrated in poetry and song.

The particular point the narrator wished to prove by the quotation was that the Arnon was the border of Moab at that time. In the connection from which this fragment was taken some verb such as "they occupied" preceded the initial place-name.

> Waheb in Suphah and the valleys,
>> Arnon and the cliff of the valleys,
> That slopes down to the dwelling of Ar,
>> And leans on the border of Moab. (Num. 21:14f.)

Perhaps the little song of the well was also taken from this source.

> Spring up, O well; sing in response to it,
>> Well that the princes digged,
> The rulers of the people delved
>> With their sceptres and staves!
>> From the desert a gift! (Num. 21:17f.)

It celebrates the opening of a well in the desert. And just as today Arabs on the borders of Moab, in the region where Israel's song is located, assert that a particular well has been dug by their respective chief and sing songs to the well, so the Israelites claimed that their princes had delved it with their own staffs, although in reality their part was probably nothing but symbolical action. The narrator who inserted this song located its first recital at a place called Beer in Moab, north of the Arnon; that is exactly the neighborhood where Alois Musil found this custom still practiced by the Arabs.[2] The song belongs therefore to this locality, and Beer may be Beer-elim, that is, "the well of the terebinths" which is mentioned in Isa. 15:8.

The taunt song on the Amorites (Num. 21:27–30) belonged to the repertoire of the ballad singers. It is inserted in the narrative to illustrate the assertion that Moab had been conquered by Sihon king of the Amorites. If this is correct, we may see in the song a satire on the Amorites. The Israelites mockingly invite the Amorites to come and rebuild Heshbon, the stronghold of their king

---

[2] Compare the song collected by him:

> Spring up, O well,
>> Flow copiously.
> Drink and disdain not,
>> With a staff have we dug it.
>>>>>> Musil, *Kuseyr Amra*, 1907, p. 298.

Sihon, that mighty victor, who had subdued all Moab. They were
strong enough to conquer Moab in the past, but now they themselves have been defeated by Israel! [3]

> Come to Heshbon, let it be built,
>   let the city of Sihon be restored!
> For a fire went forth from Heshbon,
>   a flame from the city of Sihon,
> It devoured the cities of Moab,
>   consumed the heights of the Arnon.
> Woe to thee, Moab!
>   thou art undone, O people of Kemosh:
> He gave his sons as fugitives,
>   and his daughters into captivity,
>   [to Sihon, king of the Amorites.]
> Their offspring (?) has perished
>   from Heshbon to Dibon,
> And their women (?) . . .
>   . . . unto Medeba (?). (Num. 21:27–30)

The Book of the Upright contained also Joshua's famous prayer
during the battle of Gibeon, in which he begged that the day might
be long enough for a complete rout of the enemies,

> O Sun, stand thou still over Gibeon,
>   and Moon, over the vale of Aijalon!

And similarly the answer,

> And the sun stood still, and the moon stayed,
>   till the people were avenged on their foes.

This was expressed poetically by the author who lived some time
after the conquest had been completed. But the narrator, who quoted
it, interpreted it prosaically: a stupendous miracle was the result!

> And the sun stayed in the midst of heaven, and hasted not to go down
> about a whole day. And there was no day like that before it or after it,
> that Yahweh hearkened to the voice of a man. (Josh. 10:12–14)

[3] This interpretation is not quite certain. Some believe that the song celebrated
Israel's victory over Moab, and date it from the time of Omri (*ca.* 900 B.C.).
But the reference to the ballad singers suggests that it is older. And if our
interpretation is correct, this taunt may come from the time of the conquest
or shortly thereafter and may even be earlier than the Song of Deborah, which
also ends in a taunt.

The finest and most elaborate of all early war songs, and generally regarded as the most ancient too, is Deborah's famous ode which celebrates Israel's victory over Sisera (Judg. 5). Composed either by the great prophetess herself or by some contemporary, the song is as invaluable for the history of the time as it is remarkable for its literary quality and poetic power. It begins with an imposing description of Yahweh's march from Sinai to battle for His people, and a sketch of the conditions of the time. The enthusiastic rally of the tribes who lived in or near the great plain of Esdraelon is then contrasted with the attitude of the more distant ones who kept aloof. A vivid picture of the mighty battle follows, with the flight of Sisera and his inglorious death at the hand of Jael, while a masterly portrayal of the anxious mother of Sisera and her ladies-in-waiting who are anticipating their share in Sisera's spoil, which will never come, concludes the song, to which a reader has added the "pious" wish, "So let all Thine enemies perish, O Yahweh!"

Because the leaders took the lead in Israel,
  because the people freely volunteered,
    bless ye Yahweh!

Hear, O ye kings; ye princes give ear!
  I will sing to Yahweh,
    I will sing praise to Yahweh, the God of Israel.

Yahweh, when Thou wentest forth from Seir,
  when Thou marchedst from Edom's field,
The earth trembled, the heavens also swayed,
  yea, the clouds poured water,
    the mountains quaked at the presence of Yahweh, God of Israel.

In the days of Shamgar the son of Anath,
  caravans ceased,
    and wayfaring men took roundabout ways.
The rural population (?) had ceased,
  in Israel they had ceased,
Until thou didst arise, Deborah,
  didst arise a mother in Israel.

They chose new gods (?),
  then was war in the gates (?).

A shield or spear was not seen
  among forty thousand in Israel.
My heart belongs to the rulers of Israel,
  to those that freely volunteered among the people!

Bless ye Yahweh,
  ye that ride on tawny asses,
Ye that sit on rich carpets (?)
  and ye that walk by the way, sing!
(?) Hark the huzzahing (?) at the watering places!
  there they rehearse the victories of Yahweh,
The victories of his country folk in Israel,
  (how) at that time the people of Yahweh went down to the gates.

Rouse thee, rouse thee, Deborah;
  rouse thee, rouse thee, utter a song:
    arise, Barak, and lead forth thy captors, thou son of Abinoam.
Then marched down for him the nobles,
  and the people of Yahweh marched down for him as heroes.
From Ephraim they came down to the valleys (?),
  after them Benjamin with his hosts;
From Machir came down commanders,
  and from Zebulun they that wield the marshal's staff.
And the princes of Issachar were with Deborah;
  as was Issachar, so was Barak,
    into the valley they rushed forth at his heels.

Among the tribal divisions of Reuben
  were great searchings of heart.
Why didst thou sit still among the sheepfolds,
  to hear the flute calls of the flocks?
Gilead remained beyond the Jordan:
  and Dan sought the protection of (?) ships!
Asher sat still on the shore of the sea,
  and abode by his landings.
Zebulun is a people that jeoparded their lives to the death,
  Naphtali also, upon the heights of the field.

The kings came and they fought;
  then fought the kings of Canaan,
In Tannach by the waters of Megiddo: [4]

  [4] Some scholars think that this implies that Megiddo was uninhabited at this
time and see a clue here to a dating of the events with the help of the Univer-

they took no gain of money.
From heaven fought the stars,
   from their courses they fought against Sisera.
The river Kishon swept them away,
   that onrushing river, the river Kishon.
O my soul, march on with strength (?).
   Then were battered the hoofs of the horses
     by the furious galloping of their chargers.

Curse ye Meroz, said the angel of Yahweh,
   curse bitterly its inhabitants,
Because they came not to the help of Yahweh,
   to Yahweh's help among the heroes.

Blessed above women be Jael,
   blessed above women in the tent.
Water he asked, milk she gave;
   she brought him curd in a lordly bowl.
She put forth her hand to the tent pin,
   and her right hand to the workman's hammer;
And with the hammer she battered Sisera, she crushed his head;
   yea, she shattered and struck through his temple.
At her feet he sank down, he fell, he lay still,
   where he sank down, there he lay slain.

Out of the window leaned Sisera's mother
   and looked through the lattice,
"Why is his chariot so long in coming?
   why tarry the hoof-beats of his horses?"
The wisest of his princesses answered her,
   yea, 'tis she that made reply to her,
"Surely they are finding, dividing the spoil,
   a damsel or two for each man;
Booty of dyed garments for Sisera,
   booty of dyed garments, embroidered,
     a dyed garment, two pieces of embroidered stuff for the neck
      of . . ."

So let all Thine enemies perish, O Yahweh,
   but let them that love Thee be as the sun when he rises in his might.
     (Judg. 5)

_____

sity of Chicago excavations of the mound. There was a break of habitation
between stratum VII and VI. The suggested date for the battle of Taanach
then is 1125 B.C.

This triumphal ode belongs in the judgment of critics to the finest odes in the literature of the world and is not excelled in poetic power by any of the later war poems of Israel. Its significance for our knowledge of the history of Israel greatly enhances its value. In the threatening crisis of a powerful offensive of Canaanite city kings against the Israelite invaders who had consolidated their gains in the mountains south and north of the Great Plain, the tribes Issachar, Zebulun, Naphtali together with Ephraim, Benjamin, and Machir were rallied by Deborah to the standard of Yahweh. Barak of Issachar assumed chief command. The battle itself with its victorious issue for Israel is clearly portrayed, but the further results we must infer. That it helped to weld Israel's tribes together is certain. It is noteworthy that the unifying element is the religion of Yahweh. The conviction that Reuben, Gilead, Dan, and Asher ought also to have followed the summons, and the bitter reproach for their failure to do so, show that in a crisis the feeling that they all belong together pervaded the people. It is all the more significant that Judah, Simeon, and Levi are not mentioned at all; perhaps the author did not consider them as part of Israel. For our knowledge of the conditions of Israel immediately preceding the attack, the power of the Canaanites, their control of the plains with their passes and caravan routes, their military forces with chariotry and cavalry, as well as for the strength of the religion of Yahweh, who comes from His sacred seat far in the south to the rescue of His people, Deborah's song is of singular importance.

Israel delighted also in proverbs, riddles, and wise sayings. Perhaps the oldest proverb that has come down to us in poetic form was once quoted by David.

> From the wicked comes forth wickedness,
> but my hand shall not be upon thee. (1 Sam. 24:14)

Even in his day it was a "proverb of the ancients." Many others must have circulated among the people, but they were not written down or collected at so early a date, and thus they are lost to us.

Riddles too were a favorite pastime of Israel in all ages. We still have the riddle which Samson propounded at his wedding,

> From the eater came forth the meat,
> and from the strong one came forth sweet,

of which the guests gave their solution in the form of another,

> What is sweeter than honey,
> and what is stronger than a lion? (Judg. 14:14, 18)

To this Samson sarcastically replied with a popular rhyme,

> Had ye not ploughed with the heifer of mine,
> ye had not found out this riddle of mine.

Both riddles are older than the stories of which they now form a part, for they originally meant something altogether different, since the real answer to the second was "love." The narrator used it for his story with an entirely new meaning. What the first one originally meant is uncertain; perhaps it was the lion in the sky that brings the harvest.

Samson's taunt,

> With the jaw of an ass
> I smashed them in mass,
> With the jaw of an ass
> I slew a thousand men (Judg. 15:16),

was taken literally by the narrator, while originally the idiomatic phrase "with a jawbone of an ass" suggested that Samson's astounding victory had been won with a most miserable, despicable weapon (cf. Judg. 5:8).

There were also longer didactic poems. The most remarkable of them all is Jotham's fable of the trees' choice of a king, which teaches that the good and useful people have too much to do to accept the office of king; only worthless and dangerous people are willing to become monarchs. Loyalty to them in the hope of gaining protection by them is sheer mockery, and disloyalty involves ruin.

> Hearken to me, lords of Shechem,
> that God may hearken to you!

> The trees went forth on a time
> to anoint them a king,
> And they said to the olive, "Reign over us!"
> But the olive said unto them,

"Should I leave my fatness
    which gods and men prize in me,
And go to sway over the trees?"

Then the trees said unto the fig-tree,
    "Come thou, and reign over us!"
But the fig-tree said unto them,
    "Should I leave my sweetness
And my good fruit
    and go to sway over the trees?"

Then the trees said unto the grape vine,
    "Come thou, and reign over us!"
But the grape vine said unto them,
    "Should I leave my wine
That cheers gods and men,
    and go to sway over the trees?"

Then said all the trees unto the thorn,
    "Come thou, and reign over us!"
And the thorn said unto the trees,
    "If in truth ye anoint
Me as king over you,
    then come, take refuge in my shade,
But if not, fire shall proceed from the thorn,
    and devour the cedars of Lebanon." (Judg. 9)

This bitter judgment of kingship is applied by the narrator to Abimelech, whom the people of Shechem had made king. Whether the author himself composed the fable or whether it was taken from the people's fund of stories either by Jotham or by the author is a matter of debate. The latter seems a little more probable on the whole. The fable appears to voice the feelings of many free Israelites in the period shortly before the introduction of the monarchy. Only dire need made them ready for this new form of government. The fable is of great historical importance, even if it came from a much later time than we have assumed.

Another class of early poems is in the form of prediction: this is merely a literary form; for in reality they did not foretell the future, but explained the present as due to the magically potent word of the ancestor's blessing. These blessings were composed in poetry, because the inspiration of the vision of the future put the ancestors into an exalted mood in which speech assumes rhythmic form. The historian may use these poems as documents of the time which they predict, but not of that of the ancestors themselves, for they were not composed by them, but by the later poets who reflected on the causes of the conditions of their own times and found them in these magically effective blessings. The Blessing of Noah may be the earliest of them, but this is uncertain.

> Cursed be Canaan!
>   Meanest slave shall he be to his brothers!
>
> Bless, Yahweh, the tents of Shem,
>   and let Canaan be his slave!
>
> God enlarge Japheth,
>   and let him dwell in the tents of Shem,
>   And let Canaan be his slave. (Gen. 9:25–27)

The most striking feature is the curse on Canaan, which is reiterated in the blessings of Shem and Japheth. The historical allusions cannot be made out with certainty. But it seems quite probable that they refer to the time after David, when Canaan had been completely subdued and Israel and Philistia dwelt in the tents of Shem, when the recognition of each other's independence and territorial integrity had been finally won in the great Philistine wars, which David had brought to a successful termination.

In the Blessing of Jacob (Gen. 49) the ancestor, not speaking in his own name as an individual but representing the national consciousness of Israel, expresses the verdict on the historical condition and the future of the single tribes, beginning with Reuben and ending with Benjamin. We get here valuable information about the history of the tribes before and during the early monarchy. The various oracles were probably not all composed at the same time; most are earlier than the monarchy, but the blessing of Judah implies the rule of David as an accomplished fact, and the blessing of Joseph seems to date from the time of the divided kingdom, at least in its present form.

JUDAH, thee shall thy brethren praise:
  Thy hand shall be on the neck of thy foes,
  Thy father's sons shall bow down before thee.
Judah is a lion's whelp;
  From the prey, my son, thou art gone up:
He stoops down, he couches as a lion
  And as a lioness; who shall rouse him up?
The sceptre shall not depart from Judah,
  Nor the ruler's staff from between his feet,
Until he come to whom it belongs,[5]
  And whose is the homage of the peoples.
Binding his foal to the vine,
  And his ass's colt to the choice vine;
He washes his garments in wine,
  And his vesture in the blood of the grapes:
His eyes are red with wine,
  And his teeth white with milk. (Gen. 49:8-12)

JOSEPH is a young fruit tree,
  A young fruit tree by a fountain;
  His branches run over the wall (?).
The archers sorely provoked him,
  And strove with him and harassed him:
But his bow remained firm,
  And the arms of his hands were nimble.
By the hands of the Mighty One of Jacob,
  By the name of the shepherd of the children of Israel,
By the God of thy father, who shall help thee,
  And by the Almighty, who shall bless thee,
With blessings of heaven above,
  Blessings of the deep that couches beneath,
  Blessings of breast and of womb.
The blessings of thy father
  Surpassed the blessings of the everlasting mountains,
  The blessings of the everlasting hills,
May they be on the head of Joseph,
  And on the crown of the head of the prince of his brethren. (Gen.
    49:22-26)

[5] The ordinary translation of v. 10 is,
      The sceptre shall not depart from Judah,
        Nor the ruler's staff from between his feet
       Until *Shiloh* come,
        And unto him shall the obedience of the people be.
Shiloh has often been taken as a cryptic name for the Messiah. But it is more

The Blessing of Jacob is rhythmically more regular than the Song of Deborah, which is its companion in the elucidation of early tribal history.

The oracles of Balaam (Num. 23f.) belong here too, only in them a famous non-Israelite seer of antiquity utters those rhythmic verses that have the power to bring about all the glory proclaimed therein. The heathen prophet cannot pronounce a curse, when God has commanded a blessing. He must bless Israel, although Balak wants him to curse it, because in his vision he sees Israel's great future, Saul's victories, and David's splendid reign. These oracles are not real predictions, but poetic descriptions of the time of Saul and of David, during which they were composed. They are put into Balaam's mouth by the same literary device which ascribed the Blessings to the ancestors. The revelation of the divine purposes to a non-Israelite, the manner of Balaam's prophetic inspiration, and his emphasis on God's consistency are as important for our understanding of the development of Israel's religion as the political references are for the history of the early monarchy.

From Aram has Balak brought me,
    The king of Moab from the mountains of the East:
Come, curse me Jacob,
    And come, denounce Israel!
How shall I curse, whom God has not cursed?
    And how shall I denounce, whom Yahweh has not denounced?
For from the top of the rocks I see him,
    And from the hills I behold him:
Lo, it is a people that dwells alone,
    And that reckons not itself among the nations.
Who can count the dust of Jacob,
    Or number the myriads of Israel?
Let me die the death of the righteous,
    And let my last end be like his!

---

probable that we should read "until he comes *to whom it belongs*" (Hebrew: *shellō*), and explain this as a reference to David. Judah will not lose its tribal independence until David comes, who is naturally not mentioned by name in the "prediction"; then David will become the ruler of nations, not only of the tribe Judah! The same result is attained if one translates "until he comes to Shiloh" (hence achieves rule over Ephraim), or if one emends the text to" his ruler (Hebrew: *mōshelō*).

Thy love to me was wonderful,
   passing the love of women.

How are the heroes fallen,
   and the weapons of war perished! (2 Sam. 1:19–27)

This lamentation was taken from the Book of Yashar. The metre is not regular, but whether this was due to textual corruption or to the strong, passionate sorrow that would not be forced into the rhythmic regularity of the lamentation meter, although it sometimes finds utterance in it, we do not know. The somber refrain is full of sadness. The dirge does high credit to the poet as well as the man. David's noble soul shines forth from it in immortal beauty.

   The second dirge, over Abner, is much briefer.

Must Abner die as a fool dies?
Thy hands were not bound,
Thy feet not put in fetters.
As one falls before knaves, so thou didst fall! (2 Sam. 3:33f.)

Its very brevity shows David's sincerity. There is nothing artificial in this lamentation, no love is expressed, only honor for the hero whose foul murder has jeopardized David's secret diplomacy.

   These poems are secular, there is nothing religious in them. But a poet of such high order, as the lamentation over Saul and Jonathan exhibits, and of such profound religious feelings, as we know David to have been, probably composed also religious hymns and psalms.[6] But if any of these are really contained in our Psalter, we can no longer point them out. Even Psalm 18, if it was actually written by him, is no longer in its original form; and Psalm 24:7–10, which is still regarded by some as Davidic, is now a part of a later psalm, whose religion is far in advance of that of David and his time.

   But the beautiful parable of Nathan (2 Sam. 12:1–4) with its remarkable religious lesson we may attribute to David's time, although some believe that it was composed much later. It is not in metric form, but it is highly poetic in its diction and wonderfully effective in its contents. Who can forget the rich man who had so many flocks and herds but who nevertheless—when a guest came whom he had to entertain—rudely seized his poor neighbor's one

[6] Cf. Ch. XX.

Rise up, Balak, and hear;
   Hearken to me, O son of Zippor:
God is not a man that He should break His word,
   Neither the son of man, that He should change His mind.
Should He promise and not do it?
   Or speak and not make it good?
Behold, I have received orders to bless:
   And He has blessed and I cannot reverse it.
He has not beheld calamity in Jacob;
   Nor seen trouble in Israel:
Yahweh his God is with him,
   And the shout for his king is among them.
God who brought them forth out of Egypt,
   Is for him like the horns (?) of the wild-ox.
Now shall it be said of Jacob and of Israel,
   What has God wrought!
Behold, the people rises up like a lioness,
   And like a lion it lifts itself up:
It shall not lie down till it eat of the prey,
   And drink the blood of the slain.

The oracle of Balaam the son of Beor,
   Even the oracle of the man whose eye was opened,
The oracle of him who hears the words of God,
   (And knows the knowledge of the Most High),
Who sees the vision of the Almighty,
   Falling down, and having his eyes opened:
How beautiful are thy tents, O Jacob,
   thy tabernacles, O Israel!
Like valleys are they spread forth,
   like gardens by the river-side,
Like cedars which Yahweh has planted,
   like palms beside the waters.

A man shall come from his seed (?)
   and shall rule over many nations,
And his king shall be higher than Agag,
   and his kingdom shall be exalted.
God who brought him out of Egypt;
   is for him like the horns of the wild-ox:
He shall devour the nations, his adversaries,
   and break their bones in pieces,
   and shatter their loins.

He couched, he lay down like a lion,
   and like a lioness, who shall rouse him up?
Blessed is every one that blesses thee,
   and cursed is every one that curses thee.

The oracle of Balaam the son of Beor,
   Even the oracle of the man whose eye was opened,
The oracle of him who hears the words of God,
   And knows the knowledge of the Most High,
Who sees the vision of the Almighty,
   Falling down and having his eyes opened:

I see him, but not now;
   I behold him but not nigh:
A star has shone forth out of Jacob,
   a sceptre has risen out of Israel,
And it smites through the temples of Moab,
   and the skulls of all the sons of tumult (?).

And Edom shall be a possession,
   while Israel does valiant deeds,
And Jacob shall trample down his enemies,
   and destroy the survivors of Seir. (Num. 23:7-10, 18-24; 24:3-9, 15-19)

The time of David must have been rich in other forms of poetry too. One of the earliest poems of his time, which has been handed down to us, is the song of the women celebrating Saul's and especially David's victory over the Philistines (1 Sam. 18:7; 21:11; 29:5),

Saul has slain his thousands,
   but David his myriads!

It is almost as brief as Miriam's Song, for it consists of only two lines which the women sang in ecstatic joy as they received the returning victor with music and dancing. Over and over again they repeated the simple, expressive refrain.

Almost equally brief, but picturing entirely different emotions, was Sheba's rhythmic call to rebellion in David's old age.

We have no portion in David,
   nor have we heritage in Jesse's son!
Every man to his tents, O Israel! (2 Sam. 20:1)

It is the fierce war cry of a bold, embittered Benjamin the various tribes to forsake their allegiance to King D reestablish the situation that had prevailed before they pl selves under his rule.

David himself is celebrated in tradition as a minstrel and But unfortunately, almost everything he composed is lost two dirges remain; chief among them is the famous lamen over Saul and Jonathan of which at least a nucleus is authentic. the sorrow and love of a great heart are poured out in moving wo of beauty and sincerity.

Thy glory, O Israel, is slain on thy heights,
   how are the heroes fallen!

Tell it not in Gath,
   publish it not in Ashkelon's streets,
Lest the Philistines' daughters rejoice,
   lest the daughters of the uncircumcised triumph.

Hills of Gilboa, no dew nor rain
   be upon you, ye fields of death!
For there lies defiled the shield of heroes,
   the shield of Saul, not anointed with oil.

From the blood of the slain,
   from the fat of the mighty,
Jonathan's bow never turned back,
   nor did empty come back the sword of Saul.

Saul and Jonathan, the beloved and dear,
   in their lives and their death not divided!
They were swifter than eagles,
   they were stronger than lions!

Daughters of Israel, weep ye for Saul,
   who clothed you with scarlet and fine linen wrappers,
   who put ornaments of gold upon your apparel.

How are the heroes fallen in the thick of the battle!
   O Jonathan, slain on thy heights,
I am in anguish for thee, O Jonathan, my brother!
   Very dear hast thou been unto me:

Rise up, Balak, and hear;
  Hearken to me, O son of Zippor:
God is not a man that He should break His word,
  Neither the son of man, that He should change His mind.
Should He promise and not do it?
  Or speak and not make it good?
Behold, I have received orders to bless:
  And He has blessed and I cannot reverse it.
He has not beheld calamity in Jacob;
  Nor seen trouble in Israel:
Yahweh his God is with him,
  And the shout for his king is among them.
God who brought them forth out of Egypt,
  Is for him like the horns (?) of the wild-ox.
Now shall it be said of Jacob and of Israel,
  What has God wrought!
Behold, the people rises up like a lioness,
  And like a lion it lifts itself up:
It shall not lie down till it eat of the prey,
  And drink the blood of the slain.

The oracle of Balaam the son of Beor,
  Even the oracle of the man whose eye was opened,
The oracle of him who hears the words of God,
  (And knows the knowledge of the Most High),
Who sees the vision of the Almighty,
  Falling down, and having his eyes opened:
How beautiful are thy tents, O Jacob,
  thy tabernacles, O Israel!
Like valleys are they spread forth,
  like gardens by the river-side,
Like cedars which Yahweh has planted,
  like palms beside the waters.

A man shall come from his seed (?)
  and shall rule over many nations,
And his king shall be higher than Agag,
  and his kingdom shall be exalted.
God who brought him out of Egypt;
  is for him like the horns of the wild-ox:
He shall devour the nations, his adversaries,
  and break their bones in pieces,
  and shatter their loins.

He couched, he lay down like a lion,
    and like a lioness, who shall rouse him up?
Blessed is every one that blesses thee,
    and cursed is every one that curses thee.

The oracle of Balaam the son of Beor,
    Even the oracle of the man whose eye was opened,
The oracle of him who hears the words of God,
    And knows the knowledge of the Most High,
Who sees the vision of the Almighty,
    Falling down and having his eyes opened:

I see him, but not now;
    I behold him but not nigh:
A star has shone forth out of Jacob,
    a sceptre has risen out of Israel,
And it smites through the temples of Moab,
    and the skulls of all the sons of tumult (?).

And Edom shall be a possession,
    while Israel does valiant deeds,
And Jacob shall trample down his enemies,
    and destroy the survivors of Seir. (Num. 23:7–10, 18–24; 24:3–9, 15–19)

The time of David must have been rich in other forms of poetry too. One of the earliest poems of his time, which has been handed down to us, is the song of the women celebrating Saul's and especially David's victory over the Philistines (1 Sam. 18:7; 21:11; 29:5),

Saul has slain his thousands,
    but David his myriads!

It is almost as brief as Miriam's Song, for it consists of only two lines which the women sang in ecstatic joy as they received the returning victor with music and dancing. Over and over again they repeated the simple, expressive refrain.

Almost equally brief, but picturing entirely different emotions, was Sheba's rhythmic call to rebellion in David's old age.

We have no portion in David,
    nor have we heritage in Jesse's son!
Every man to his tents, O Israel! (2 Sam. 20:1)

It is the fierce war cry of a bold, embittered Benjaminite, calling on the various tribes to forsake their allegiance to King David and to reestablish the situation that had prevailed before they placed themselves under his rule.

David himself is celebrated in tradition as a minstrel and a poet. But unfortunately, almost everything he composed is lost. Only two dirges remain; chief among them is the famous lamentation over Saul and Jonathan of which at least a nucleus is authentic. In it the sorrow and love of a great heart are poured out in moving words of beauty and sincerity.

> Thy glory, O Israel, is slain on thy heights,
>   how are the heroes fallen!
>
> Tell it not in Gath,
>   publish it not in Ashkelon's streets,
> Lest the Philistines' daughters rejoice,
>   lest the daughters of the uncircumcised triumph.
>
> Hills of Gilboa, no dew nor rain
>   be upon you, ye fields of death!
> For there lies defiled the shield of heroes,
>   the shield of Saul, not anointed with oil.
>
> From the blood of the slain,
>   from the fat of the mighty,
> Jonathan's bow never turned back,
>   nor did empty come back the sword of Saul.
>
> Saul and Jonathan, the beloved and dear,
>   in their lives and their death not divided!
> They were swifter than eagles,
>   they were stronger than lions!
>
> Daughters of Israel, weep ye for Saul,
>   who clothed you with scarlet and fine linen wrappers,
>   who put ornaments of gold upon your apparel.
>
> How are the heroes fallen in the thick of the battle!
>   O Jonathan, slain on thy heights,
> I am in anguish for thee, O Jonathan, my brother!
>   Very dear hast thou been unto me:

> Thy love to me was wonderful,
>   passing the love of women.

> How are the heroes fallen,
>   and the weapons of war perished! (2 Sam. 1:19–27)

This lamentation was taken from the Book of Yashar. The metre is not regular, but whether this was due to textual corruption or to the strong, passionate sorrow that would not be forced into the rhythmic regularity of the lamentation meter, although it sometimes finds utterance in it, we do not know. The somber refrain is full of sadness. The dirge does high credit to the poet as well as the man. David's noble soul shines forth from it in immortal beauty.

The second dirge, over Abner, is much briefer.

> Must Abner die as a fool dies?
> Thy hands were not bound,
> Thy feet not put in fetters.
> As one falls before knaves, so thou didst fall! (2 Sam. 3:33f.)

Its very brevity shows David's sincerity. There is nothing artificial in this lamentation, no love is expressed, only honor for the hero whose foul murder has jeopardized David's secret diplomacy.

These poems are secular, there is nothing religious in them. But a poet of such high order, as the lamentation over Saul and Jonathan exhibits, and of such profound religious feelings, as we know David to have been, probably composed also religious hymns and psalms.[6] But if any of these are really contained in our Psalter, we can no longer point them out. Even Psalm 18, if it was actually written by him, is no longer in its original form; and Psalm 24:7–10, which is still regarded by some as Davidic, is now a part of a later psalm, whose religion is far in advance of that of David and his time.

But the beautiful parable of Nathan (2 Sam. 12:1–4) with its remarkable religious lesson we may attribute to David's time, although some believe that it was composed much later. It is not in metric form, but it is highly poetic in its diction and wonderfully effective in its contents. Who can forget the rich man who had so many flocks and herds but who nevertheless—when a guest came whom he had to entertain—rudely seized his poor neighbor's one

[6] Cf. Ch. XX.

little ewe lamb that was as dear to him as a daughter? Who is not
startled by the terrible application "thou art the man!" that Nathan
thundered into David's ears? It is one of the finest poems in prose
that has come down to us from antiquity.[7]

From Solomon we still have his original dedicatory sentences at
the dedication of the temple. They are quoted, the Greek text tells
us, from the "Book of Song," which was probably the same as the
"Book of Yashar." The Hebrew, and therefore the English, text has
omitted the important first line which is preserved by the Greek.

> Yahweh has set the sun in the firmament,
>> but declared He Himself would dwell in deep darkness.
> I have built now for Thee a lofty abode,
>> a place for Thy dwelling forever. (1 Ki. 8:12f.)

From the time of Jeroboam I (932–911 B.C.), if not before, comes
the Blessing of Moses (Deut. 33). It is the Ephraimite counterpart
of the Blessing of Jacob. While Joseph receives a long eulogy and
prediction in the Judean Blessing of Jacob, only little space is given
to Judah in this Ephraimite poem.

> Hear, Yahweh, the voice of JUDAH,
>> and bring him to his people.
> Thy hand contend for him
>> and be Thou a help against his adversaries. (Deut. 33:7)

Contrast this with:

> The precious things of heaven above,
>> and the deep that couches beneath,
> And the precious things of the fruits of the sun,
>> and the precious things of the growth of the moons,
> And the chief things of the ancient mountains,
>> and the precious things of the everlasting hills,
> And the precious things of the earth and its fulness,
>> and the favor of him that dwelt in the bush.
> Let come upon the head of JOSEPH,
>> and upon the crown of the head of the prince of his brethren.
> For the strength of a bull and majesty are his,
>> and his horns are the horns of the wild-ox:

---

[7] The last words of David (2 Sam. 23:1–7) were composed by a later poet
who put these wise sayings about true and successful royal rule into the mouth
of the aged king.

With them he pushes peoples,
    all of them, even the ends of the earth:
These are the myriads of Ephraim,
    and these are the thousands of Manasseh. (Deut. 33:13–17)

In its present form the Blessing of Moses has a much later poetic introduction, which depends on the Song of Deborah, and a late conclusion, which contains the beautiful lines,

The eternal God is thy dwelling place,
    and underneath are the everlasting arms. (Deut. 33:27)

The historical situation of this blessing seems to be slightly later than that of Jacob's. With the change of historical conditions came a new formulation of the single parts. Simeon is not mentioned at all, Reuben is dying out, Levi is no longer a secular but a priestly tribe, the temple is already built. Judah is in difficulties, but Joseph is prosperous and powerful. The form of the poem with its "blessings" for the individual tribes still presupposes a strong tribal consciousness. The theocratic tone of the poem contrasts strikingly with the secular tone of Gen. 49. It is quite likely that a priest of the Northern Kingdom was its author. Again the historian can learn much from this blessing about the time of the early monarchy, but not about that of Moses.

Very different is the impressive Song of Moses (Deut. 32). After calling upon heaven and earth to listen, and after uttering a praise of God and a criticism of the ingratitude of His people, the poet reviews the past in beautiful and vivid words. The initial thought of the Creator's apportioning of the earth is remarkable:

When the Most High gave to the nations their inheritance,
    When he separated the sons of men,
He fixed the bounds of the peoples
    According to the number of the Sons of God.[8]
But Yahweh's portion was His people
    Jacob His allotted heritage. (Deut. 32:8–9)

Each people has its divinely ordained habitat and is under a "Son of God" (Gen. 6:2)—a demotion of the gods of other peoples such

[8] So the Greek, recently confirmed by a Dead Sea Scroll Hebrew fragment of the song published by P. W. Skehan. The traditional Hebrew reads "Sons of Israel."

as Moab's Chemosh or Ammon's Milcom to the rank of lesser divine beings—but Israel is under the immediate care of Yahweh, the Most High. Some scholars hold the poem to be extremely ancient, asserting that it only reviews the history up to the conquest and taking the references of v. 21b to "those who are no people . . . the foolish nation," with which Yahweh will provoke Israel, as referring to the Philistines or other neighbors of early times. However the words "But Jeshurun [*i.e.* Israel] waxed fat and sleek" (v. 15) presuppose the attainment of prosperity such as was not reached in the early days, and the author looks back on military calamities (v. 30). The enemy requires no identification, for the remark is only coined to cap Yahweh's preceding statement and its form is governed by that.

> They have stirred me to jealousy with what was no god,
> They have provoked me with their idols. (Deut. 32:21ᵃ)

The harsh denunciation of the people and the threats of dire calamities to come puts this poem in the neighborhood of prophecy. The defeats suffered fit the Aramaean or Assyrian wars of the eighth century.

In these ancient poems we find the balancing of the lines, called "parallelism of the members," which is characteristic of Hebrew as of Oriental poetry from the oldest times. Rhyme we meet but rarely; the song of Lamech is quite exceptional in this. It is the rhythmic accents of the lines that produce their poetic form. The accents, not the length or number of syllables, are measured. Frequently the first half contains three, occasionally two, beats and is balanced by an equal number.[9] In the so-called Qinah, or lamentation meter, the second half is shorter, the whole line is usually a pentameter. The power of the refrain was also known, as was the effective grouping into strophes. Like their Arab kinsmen the ancient Israelites delighted in lyric poetry and practiced its art. The few poems that have been preserved and some suggestions in later poetry show that there were almost innumerable occasions which lent themselves to song and poetry. The high development of the art of poetic expression which we find in these early poems indicates that a long

[9] The fragment of a scroll mentioned in note 8 provides the first clear example of a text written in a manner to show the poetic form. It was too wasteful of space to be carried through ordinarily in long documents.

training must have preceded the earliest literature. Long before poems were committed to writing, they had been sung and recited orally and thus handed down from generation to generation as true folk poetry. It is greatly to be regretted that not more of them have come down to us. Many more must have been available to the old narrators because tradition, in poetic form, is better remembered, and more exactly passed on to the succeeding generations.

II

Early Narratives

IT IS to be expected that great events experienced by a people will stimulate the rise of a literature. The Hebrew people went through the fire of trial in the struggle with the foreign oppressors and came out of it a nation headed by a great king who governed the land from a city he had wrested from the Canaanites. Under his successor there was a vast rise in prosperity. All at once Israel entered into the elect circle of peoples aspiring to culture. Pride in the past and its heroes led to the desire to record happenings that were still remembered, and thus to the beginnings of literature. Some specimens of this literature have survived, imbedded in a historical work that was compiled by a Deuteronomistic author in the sixth century (see pp. 229f.). For the time of the rise of the nation he included the following four ancient pieces: 1) the story of the ark of the covenant, 1 Sam. 4–6 (continued in 2 Sam. 6); 2) the narratives of Saul's rise, 1 Sam. 9–10:16; 11; 13; 14; 3) the narratives of David's rise, 1 Sam. 16:14; 2 Sam. 5 and perhaps 8; and 4) the narrative of the Davidic succession, 2 Sam. 9–20; 1 Ki. 1–2.

There may have been no real account available of the crisis that led to the rise of a Benjaminite monarchy. For this the compiler had to use a specialized story dealing with the ark of the covenant and what had happened to it in those times. It was apparently composed by a man of priestly mind who saw everything from the vantage point of the cult of the temple at Jerusalem and held the coming of the ark to the city of David to have been an event of paramount importance. For the ancient Judean reader this story provided an impressive and religiously oriented entrance into the exciting chapter of history that was to be rehearsed.

The crisis was brought about by Israel's neighbors to the southeast, the Philistines. This people, coming from Asia Minor and the Mediterranean isles, had invaded Palestine not long after the Hebrews and had made themselves masters of the maritime plain in the south. Very soon they attacked the Israelites in their mountain seats. At this time the Hebrew tribes were only confederated in a loose manner and were beset by tribal rivalries. They had, however, a central sanctuary at Shiloh on Mt. Ephraim where the ark of the covenant, a sacred relic of the Mosaic era, was kept. When a decisive battle became necessary to stop the Philistine invaders, the ark was carried forth; and the Israelite fighting men, believing that Yahweh was invisibly enthroned upon it, hoped for victory through his mighty arm. But instead, Israel was defeated at Aphek and its holy ark was carried off by the victorious Philistines. However, the Philistines were not able to enjoy possession of Israel's palladium.

The overthrow of the statue of Dagon in his temple at Ashdod, where the ark had been placed, as well as a plague of tumors in one city after another whither they brought it, were attributed to Yahweh, and it was decided to send it away to Israel with votive offerings of five golden tumors and five golden mice[1] to pacify Yahweh. After some mishap it was finally quartered at Kiriath-jearim (1 Sam. 4–7:1).[2] While the story is focused on the fate of the ark it vividly illustrates the element most important for history—the formidable Philistine peril.

The danger grew greater. The Philistines conquered the mountains and put garrisons in various strong places. Divided as Israel's tribes were, they could never hope to end their subjection under the Philistines. The situation seemed hopeless. Only in union was there strength enough for the task. To achieve such union a great leader

[1] The custom of presenting as votive offerings images of the members of the body that are afflicted with disease is connected with "sympathetic magic." The mice were symbols of the bubonic plague. The ancients knew already that mice and other rodents are the carriers of this disease.

[2] In 1 Sam. 7:2f. the Deuteronomistic writer's account of a conversion of Israel from idolatry and a victory over the Philistines at Mizpah has been added. It makes Samuel Israel's deliverer. But the older, more dependable versions of the happenings are found in chap. 9f.

was needed around whom all could rally but he did not appear—so an early story relates—until the seer Samuel in the little town of Ramah discovered him in the person of the mighty Saul, whose gigantic stature and wild contagious enthusiasm carried the people with him. In the form of a folktale we are told how Saul went out to seek his father's asses and found a royal crown (1 Sam. 9:1—10:16). This story seeks to give the prophet the role of king-maker and tries to show that Samuel saw the need of the people and provided the leader. But this was a popular rather than a historical account of the events. The occasion which actually showed Saul's capacity for leadership was presented by the Ammonite attack upon Jabesh in Gilead. Saul rose to it of his own initiative and it was this act of inspired leadership that won him the kingship (1 Sam. 11:1-11, 15).

Saul set himself at once to the high task of freeing Israel from Philistine rule. He was ably seconded by his great son, the lion-hearted Jonathan. The latter gave the signal for the war by slaying the Philistine prefect at Geba (1 Sam. 13:1-7a, 15b-18, 23). This originally independent narrative tells one of Jonathan's exploits in detail. Accompanied only by his armor-bearer he climbed up into the Philistine camp, succeeded in killing twenty men in combat, and by this initial success gave to Saul the opportunity for a telling victory which brought many, who had hitherto been fearful, to his side. Saul almost marred the glory of this triumph by insisting that Jonathan should be killed, because he had unwillingly violated the ban that Saul had placed on food that day, by tasting some honey which greatly refreshed him and his aide. But the people saved the victorious hero, "for he has wrought with God this day" (14:1-46, 52).[3]

Well might Israel rejoice over this success, but Saul saw clearly

[3] In this story the Greek version has preserved a longer text, which shows the method of the casting of the lot-oracle, the Urim and Tummim, through which Jonathan's guilt was discovered. After Saul and Jonathan had placed themselves on one side and the people on the other, Saul said, "Yahweh, God of Israel, why hast Thou not answered Thy servant to-day? If the guilt be in me or in my son Jonathan, Yahweh, God of Israel, give Urim; but if Thou say thus: the guilt is in Thy people Israel, give Tummim." And Jonathan and Saul were taken, but the people escaped. And Saul said, "Cast between me and Jonathan, my son! Whom Yahweh will take, he shall die." And the people said to Saul, "It shall not be so!" But Saul prevailed over the people. And they cast between him and his son Jonathan, and Jonathan was taken.

that the power of the Philistines was by no means broken and that
he faced a long struggle. Full of enthusiasm as he was at times when
nobody could resist him and the fanatic power of his inspiring personality, he was also visited by seasons of terrible mental depression.
It was to counteract this that there was brought to him that most
wonderful figure in Israel's history, young David, who by his skillful
playing was able to charm away the dark spirit from Saul's mind.
Therewith begins the narrative of David's rise which was to lead
the shepherd boy of Bethlehem to imperishable glory (1 Sam. 16;
2 Sam. 5:8). At once Saul came under the spell of his fresh beauty
and grace. His music laid its healing touch on Saul's sad spirit. But
in the end the young warrior-minstrel thrust his soul into a deeper
gloom from which none could save him. For David was destined
to put the most celebrated heroes, Saul and Jonathan, in the shade
by his skill, prowess, and success in battle. One story especially
was told of him: how he killed a mighty Philistine giant in single
combat. The tale was elaborated later on, and the Philistine warrior
was identified with the famous Goliath of Gath,[4] whom in reality
not David but Elhanan of Bethlehem had slain—as we know from
2 Sam. 21:19. David's great name attracted this deed to itself and
as so often happens in history the more famous person was credited
with what was accomplished by a lesser man. When the women
came out to meet the returning victors, singing and dancing, they
sang to the accompaniment of timbrels and cymbals over and over
again in antiphony,

> Saul has slain his thousands,
> but David his myriads!

It was only natural that Saul should honor the young hero and wish
to bind him closer to himself and his house. The narrators did not
look at it from this side, but presented David's advancement and
honors and even his marriage to Saul's daughter Michal from the
viewpoint of Saul's later jealousy. But we may be sure that it did
not vitiate Saul's every motive from the outset. It is certainly true
that nobody could withstand the charm of David's personality; Saul

[4] The Greek version already contains this identification of the warrior with
Goliath, but it has the story in a much shorter and earlier form.

and Jonathan, Michal and the people all felt it and responded to it. It was natural that it awakened in Saul a restless spirit of envy. His kingship was too recent, his hold on the people only due to his valor and leadership, and here was a younger man, already put by the people above him as warrior, constantly growing in influence and power. His sick mind felt those sinister forces working. Whether David thought of becoming king, as Saul feared, we do not know. Legendary elements have doubtless entered in here and obscured the true facts. That he should actually have plotted at this time, seems to be excluded by Jonathan's stanch friendship for him. At any rate, in a fit of anger Saul threw his spear at David, who now fled for his life. Jonathan made sure that Saul had actually intended to kill David and then told him in secret.

David now led the life of a fugitive, whom Saul pursued with relentless rigor. Gradually all sorts of lawless elements gathered about him, and he became the captain of this band of outlaws. Finally escape seemed impossible and he resorted to a step which was really high treason: he went over with his men to Israel's merciless foes, the Philistines, and became the vassal of King Achish of Gath! He stayed four months [5] with him. Then came the day when he was summoned to fight against Saul and Jonathan. Nothing is said of the tragic conflict in his soul, when he saw no way of escape. But fate smiled once more upon him; he was spared the crowning shame of battling against his own people by the distrust of the other Philistine princes who refused to have him and his men in their army. So he was sent back. When he arrived at his residence town Ziklag, he was told that the Amalekites had made a raid upon the city during his absence, burned it down, and taken the women and children into captivity, among them David's wives Ahinoam and Abigail. He quickly pursued them, attacked them unawares and defeated them, rescued all the women and children, and returned with much booty. With fine tact he set the precedent for the law of booty, deciding "as his share is that goes down to the battle, so shall his share be that tarries by the baggage: they shall share alike." Then he sent, with much diplomatic skill, portions of the booty to the

---

[5] According to the Septuagint, not one year and four months, as the Hebrew says (1 Sam. 27:7).

princes of the various Judean townships in the Southland in order to
ingratiate himself with them.

Meanwhile the tragedy of Saul had reached its end. One of the
most stirring of ancient stories relates how, on the eve of battle, he
went to the witch of Endor and asked her to conjure up Samuel's
ghost that he might give him counsel. But he only received the
confirmation of his rejection and the prediction of his and his sons'
death and of Israel's defeat in the battle on the morrow. Stunned by
the terror of these words Saul suddenly fell down unconscious. He
was utterly exhausted by this experience and his fast. Hardly could
they persuade him to eat. Then he went away—to his doom. In
the battle on Gilboa's height his sons were slain, and he himself was
severely wounded as he fought his last fight. To escape ignominious
death at the hand of the Philistines he fell upon his own sword.
Thus ended the first king of Israel.

When David learned of the event, he was moved with bitter sorrow, and sang the noble lamentation that has touched so many
generations by its beauty, sincerity, and pain. Sorrow and love
mingled therein, but there is no word of God, no thought of immortality, no hope of ever seeing them again, for Yahweh was considered God of the living; he had no interest in the shades of the
nether world.

After Saul's and Jonathan's deaths, David offered himself to the
Judeans, who chose him as their king at Hebron, the great city of
the South. But the Northerners, more specifically Abner, Saul's
commanding general, set Eshbaal,[6] one of Saul's sons, on the throne.
His residence was on the other side of Jordan at Mahanaim, for the
northern part of Israel to the plain of Esdraelon was in the hands
of the Philistines. After two years of state of war, during which
David in wise self-restraint did not press his advantage, Abner was
murdered by Joab, David's commander-in-chief, as a result of a
blood feud, for he had killed Joab's brother Asahel. Abner's death
came at a most inopportune moment for David, for he had just
made a pact with Abner, which had as its aim the overthrow of

[6] The corruption of Eshbaal (= the man of Baal) to Ishbosheth (= the man
of shame) is due to the later custom of substituting *bosheth = shame* for Baal;
cf. Hosea's prediction that the Baals should no more be mentioned by their
names (Hos. 2:17). The real name is preserved in 1 Chron. 8:33.

Eshbaal. All this was jeopardized, but David succeeded in convincing the people that he was innocent of the crime. Child of luck that he was, he gained his end nevertheless. Two Israelitic captains murdered Eshbaal soon afterwards. Now David was without rival for the throne of all Israel. And all the tribes came and made him their king.

Two decisive political events marked David's early reign, the final, definite defeat of the Philistines and the capture of the strong fortress of Jerusalem, which hitherto had been in the hands of the Jebusites. It was a rare piece of insight that led David to make Jerusalem the national capital. Not only its central situation and natural strength, but also its hitherto neutral character (it had belonged neither to the North nor to Judah) made it the city which would rouse no antagonism and around which all tribes could rally. Most cleverly David made Jerusalem also the religious center of Israel by bringing to it the ark of Yahweh in solemn procession, during which David performed a cultic dance displeasing to his wife Michal. The far-reaching significance of the act of making Jerusalem the political and religious capital of Israel cannot be overestimated (2 Sam. 2–6).

Now comes the most remarkable of the early narratives—the story of the Davidic succession, 2 Sam. 9–20; 1 Ki. 1–2. It begins with Nathan's prediction of the everlasting duration of the house of David—the divine recognition of the founding of the dynasty (2 Sam. 7)—followed by the account of David's magnanimity towards Meribbaal,[7] the son of Jonathan, the last scion of the house of Saul (2 Sam. 9). Then comes the war against the Ammonites and Aramaeans, in which the sad story of David's adultery with Bathsheba and the murder of her husband Uriah is the most famous episode (2 Sam. 10–12). Amnon's rape of his half sister, Tamar, leads off that strange series of events in which one crime was always the cause of another. However strong David may have been as a warrior and king, he was weak as a father. His unwillingness to punish Amnon for the rape of the latter's half sister Tamar led to her brother Absalom's fearful revenge on Amnon; and his later indecision in curbing the political activities of Absalom, who had inherited all of David's personal charm and diplomatic sagacity,

[7] This and not Mephibosheth was his real name; cf. 1 Chron. 8:34, and the note on p. 28.

brought about in the end a rebellion which almost cost David his throne, but which, thanks to the extraordinary diplomacy of the king's old friend and councillor Chushai and Joab's ruthless military measures, ended in Absalom's defeat and death. The spirit of rebellion, once awake, next seized the Benjaminite Sheba, who summoned the northern tribes to secede from David. A quick military expedition under Joab put down this movement which threatened the existence of the union (2 Sam. 13–20). All this is told by a man who had been present in all these situations, with all the variety of graphic and intimate detail that bears the stamp of veracity on its face.

Finally this narrator brings us into the sick chamber of David and tells of the momentous things that were worked out there: Adonijah's and Solomon's struggle for the throne, and the last provisions of David, his testament in which he told his son how to deal with his father's enemies and his friends. The brutal measures by which Solomon established his throne by ridding himself most mercilessly of his opponents bring this story of the founding of the monarchy to a close, shedding at the end a most unexpected light on Solomon, the prince of peace of whom a later age believed that he shed no blood (1 Ki. 1f.).

This story of the Davidic succession is an extremely able literary composition, well rounded and complete in itself. The author told it simply and plainly; he had no theory to propound or to prove, his interest was historical and biographical. The institution of the monarchy was to him a divine blessing in which he rejoiced. He revered David, but was not blind to his faults, and pictured not only the bright but also the dark side of his life. He never had any word of blame for him, or for any of the others; everywhere he withheld his personal judgment. Only in the selection of his material does the author show his own convictions to some extent. It was evident to him that there was a real connection between Amnon's rape of Tamar and Absalom's rebellion. He showed how one led to the other. And he was right in this, but history, even political history, was all a matter of personal history to him. The great nexus of the social movements, the tribal and separatist tendencies in this story and the driving forces in national and international relations were not so important to him as the story of the persons that made the history. That he wove the anecdotal together with the strictly historical was inevitable with such a view of historiography as his. It does not detract from his work, however, for most interesting material, embodying the views of the people of those days, has thus been preserved, illuminating and vivifying the story. That he had no chronological system he could not help, for that was a later achievement. One thing that strikes us in connection with his objective manner is the unobtrusiveness of his religion. The writer was a pious man, to whom God and His righteous rule were realities. Though He did not directly intervene by miracles, He was there nevertheless, in the silent background of all events, unobserved yet real. This makes this author's history so attractive. The fascinating details which he tells so well are all true to life, and therefore so valuable. His sense of reality is refreshing. One seeks in vain among the Babylonians and Egyptians for a historical work of similar power and charm.

A splendid beginning had thus been made for the prose literature of Israel. The first historical narratives were of the highest value. Others were sure to follow. And indeed we learn from 1 Ki. 11:41 that there was a Book of the Acts of Solomon. Well might the splendor, wealth, and power of Solomon call forth an enthusiastic description of his reign. Had he not by his reorganization of the internal administration of the kingdom; his wise utilization of the control of the caravan routes that led from Egypt and Arabia to Phoenicia and Syria; his great commercial undertakings as middleman and carrier; his commercial and political treaties with Egypt and Phoenicia, laid the foundation of the vast national wealth? Had he not strengthened the military power by important fortifications, and given to the world an exhibition of magnificent splendor in the building of the temple and the palaces and in the maintenance of a brilliant court and harem at Jerusalem? Had not his wisdom become famous beyond the frontiers of his country?

Unfortunately, the Book of the Acts of Solomon is lost, and we only know that besides "all that he did" it told of "his wisdom." We may surmise that the author of the Deuteronomistic historical work took some of his material about Solomon's reign from it, but

he worked it over in the interest of his own religious theory, and
we can no longer reconstruct his sources. The story of Solomon's
dream at Gibeon, in which he prayed, "Give Thy servant an understanding heart to judge Thy people, that I may discern between good
and evil, for who is able to judge this Thy great people?"; the famous
Solomonic judgment in which he decided the question to whom the
babe, which two women claimed, belonged by asking for a sword
and commanding, "Divide the child in two, and give half to the one,
and half to the other," thereby infallibly discovering the real mother
by her love, which would rather suffer the loss of the babe than consent to its death; [8] the visit of the Queen of Sheba, and her astonishment at Solomon's wealth and wisdom—which had seemed incredible
to her before—but of which she now confessed, "The half was not
told me"; all these tales the Deuteronomistic historian preserved,
along with the account of Solomon's ever memorable deed of building
the temple, his other building operations, and his internal administration and political activities. Historically, most reliable information
such as Solomon's provincial organization and system of taxation,
his cession of twenty Galilean cities to King Hiram of Tyre, the
rebellion of Hadad, Rezon, and Jeroboam, is thus accompanied
by legends and anecdotes that cluster around his wisdom, wealth,
and power. Some of this material comes from men who still had
first-hand knowledge of Solomon's time. The description of the
temple which shows great familiarity with the details of its construction may have been written by a priestly author or taken from
the Annals of the Temple (cf. p. 48).

[8] This story has numerous parallels and was probably attributed to Solomon
from such floating material.

III

Early Laws

HEBREW tradition attributes to Moses, the great founder of Israel's religion, the authorship of its entire legislation in the Pentateuch. That is impossible, for laws as a rule embody customs and grow gradually in history. As conditions change and insight deepens, customs vary and laws are modified. If a leader like David decides a matter differently from the usual way, and it commends itself to the judgment of the people by its fairness, it becomes henceforth a precedent with all the force of a law. Thus David changed the custom of dividing the booty and made his own arrangement "a statute and ordinance for Israel unto this day" (1 Sam. 30: 21–25; cf. p. 27). And yet in Num. 31:25ff. Moses is credited with this law! Of course, an element of truth underlies the tradition that Moses gave the whole law to Israel. He had given the fundamental principles on which the entire legislation was built: the insistence on the exclusive worship of Yahweh as Israel's only God and on obedience to His will which refers especially to social morality within the nation. The whole subsequent development of religion in Israel presupposes these principles from the beginning.

The most famous formulation of Israelite law is contained in the Decalogue in Ex. 20:2–17 (cf. Deut. 5:6–21). The ten original pithy sayings were later elaborated with commentary material, which is printed here in smaller type. The Deuteronomy version varies slightly in this secondary matter.

I am Yahweh thy God, who brought thee out of the land of Egypt, out of the house of bondage.

Thou shalt have no other gods before Me.

Thou shalt not make unto thee a graven image,

nor any likeness of any thing that is in heaven above, or that is in the earth beneath, or that is in the water under the earth: thou shalt not bow down thyself unto them, nor serve them; for I Yahweh thy God am a jealous God, visiting the iniquity of the fathers upon the children, upon the third and upon the fourth generation of that hate Me, and showing lovingkindness unto thousands of them that love Me and keep My commandments.

Thou shalt not take the name of Yahweh thy God in vain:

for Yahweh will not hold him guiltless that takes His name in vain.

Remember the Sabbath day, to keep it holy.

Six days shalt thou labor, and do all thy work; but the seventh day is a Sabbath unto Yahweh thy God: in it thou shalt not do any work, thou, nor thy son, nor thy daughter, thy man-servant, nor thy maid-servant, nor thy cattle, nor thy stranger that is within thy gates: for in six days Yahweh made heaven and earth, the sea, and all that in them is, and rested the seventh day: wherefore Yahweh blessed the Sabbath day, and hallowed it.[1]

Honor thy father and thy mother,

that thy days may be long in the land which Yahweh thy God gives thee.

Thou shalt not kill.

Thou shalt not commit adultery.

Thou shalt not steal.

Thou shalt not bear false witness against thy neighbor.

Thou shalt not covet thy neighbor's house,[2]

thou shalt not covet thy neighbor's wife, nor his man-servant, nor his maid-servant, nor his ox, nor his ass, nor anything that is thy neighbor's.

Whether Moses formulated an original Decalogue of which this one is a revision, we can neither dogmatically assert nor deny. In their present form these commandments are certainly much later. In any case, Israel seems to have entered upon its historical career with the fundamental obligation of "monolatry," that is, of wor-

---

[1] For this religious reason Deuteronomy has a social reason: "that thy man-servant and thy maid-servant may rest as well as thou. And thou shalt remember that thou wast a servant in the land of Egypt, and Yahweh thy God brought thee out thence by a mighty hand and by an outstretched arm: therefore Yahweh thy God commanded thee to keep the Sabbath day." This is thoroughly in line with the humane character of the Deuteronomic legislation.

[2] Deuteronomy puts the command "thou shalt not covet thy neighbor's wife" before "thou shalt not covet thy neighbor's house," thereby singling out the wife and elevating her from her former position of mere property. This is in line with Deuteronomy's attitude to women and is the result of a long development.

shipping Yahweh alone as its God, and of obedience to the will of God, which was principally social morality.

When they had settled in Canaan and lived in close contact with the Canaanites, whom they had by no means driven out or exterminated, the civilization and religion of Canaan influenced Israel profoundly. They passed from their half nomadic stage to the settled life of agriculture with its different and superior civilization. With the new order came new customs and new laws. Israel had had her own civil laws before, but they did not meet all the new conditions. Here the Canaanites became her teachers. They had been under the sway of a legal tradition which was spread over the entire Near East, and of which the Code of Hammurabi of the First Dynasty of Babylon, is the most famous example. This common legal tradition explains the astonishing parallels that have been observed between Hebrew laws and those of other Oriental peoples—ofttimes, too, not just in the sphere of codified law, but in a kind of common law presupposed in the contract tablets.

The oldest Hebrew code of laws is the so-called Book of the Covenant, Ex. 20:23—23:19. It is particularly instructive to find here a readily recognizable combination of two different styles of legal formulation. There is on the one hand the hypothetical formulation: "if a man does so and so." This is typical of the Babylonian legal tradition since Sumerian times. No doubt the Canaanites received it and used it in their laws, and the Hebrews in turn took over such ordinances. On the other hand, there is another type of legal formulation which is more terse. Sometimes it starts with a participle, *e.g.* "the one striking" (a single word in Hebrew); at other times it starts with an imperative. This may be genuinely Israelitic style, brought along by the nomads. Rules put in the imperative could be joined into a series, as in the Decalogue. According to recent theory they were hammered into the popular mind at religious festivals (cf. Deut. 27).

The law code, which was thus made, was well thought out and carefully planned and arranged according to fundamental subjects. It is especially note worthy that the code was not written from a priestly point of view. Civil law precedes religious law, and takes up by far the largest space (Ex. 21:1—22:17). Of course, just as in

Babylonia Hammurabi was represented as receiving the law from
the sungod Shamash, so in Israel Moses was represented as receiving
the law, both the civil and criminal, directly from God, and giving
it to the people whom he bound by a sacred covenant to obey it.
A thoughtful reading of the law with the supplied headings will
show the careful plan and the systematic carrying out of certain
fundamental legal principles by one controlling purposeful will,
which modified and corrected the ancient customs and laws.

I. LAWS CONCERNING PERSONS

1. *Personal Rights during Slavery*

a. MEN

If thou buy a Hebrew slave, six years he shall serve: and in the seventh
he shall go out free for nothing.

If he come in by himself, he shall go out by himself: if he be married,
then his wife shall go out with him.

If his master give him a wife, and she bear him sons or daughters; the
wife and her children shall be her master's, and he shall go out by himself.

But if the slave shall plainly say, I love my master, my wife, and my
children; I will not go out free: then his master shall bring him unto
God, and shall bring him to the door, or unto the door-post; [3] and his
master shall bore his ear through with an awl; and he shall serve him
for ever.

b. WOMEN

And if a man sell his daughter to be a slave, she shall not go out as the
male slaves do.

If she please not her master, who has espoused her to himself, then shall
he let her be redeemed: to sell her to a foreign people he shall have no
power, because he has dealt deceitfully with her.

And if he espouse her to his son, he shall deal with her after the manner
of daughters.

If he take for himself another wife; her food, her raiment, and her
conjugal rights shall he not diminish. And if he do not these three things
to her, then shall she go out for nothing, without money.

2. *Laws Safeguarding Life and Limb*

a. HOMICIDE, MURDER, KIDNAPING

He that smites a man, so that he dies, shall surely be put to death.

And if a man lie not in wait, but God deliver him into his hand; then
I will appoint a place whither he shall flee.

And if a man come presumptuously upon his neighbor, to slay him
with guile; thou shalt take him from Mine altar, that he may die.

---

[3] Apparently two customs are combined, one places the rite at the sanctuary,
the other in the home.

And he that smites his father, or his mother, shall be surely put to death.

And he that steals a man, and sells him, or if he be found in his hand, he shall surely be put to death.

And he that curses his father or his mother, shall surely be put to death.[4]

b. ASSAULT AND BATTERY

And if men contend, and one smite the other with a stone, or with his fist, and he die not, but keep his bed; if he rise again, and walk abroad upon his staff, then shall he that smote him be quit: only he shall pay for the loss of his time, and shall cause him to be thoroughly healed.

And if a man smite his male or his female slave with a rod, and he die under his hand; he shall surely be punished. Notwithstanding, if he continue to live a day or two, he shall not be punished: for he is his money.

And if men strive together, and hurt a woman with child, so that her fruit depart, and yet no harm follow; he shall be surely fined, according as the woman's husband shall lay upon him; and he shall pay for the miscarriage. But if any harm follow, then thou shalt give life for life, eye for eye, tooth for tooth, hand for hand, foot for foot, burning for burning, wound for wound, stripe for stripe.[5]

And if a man smite the eye of his servant, or the eye of his maid, and destroy it; he shall let him go free for his eye's sake. And if he smite out his man-servant's tooth, or his maid-servant's tooth; he shall let him go free for his tooth's sake.

c. ACCIDENTS AND CONTRIBUTORY NEGLIGENCE

And if an ox gore a man or a woman to death, the ox shall be surely stoned, and its flesh shall not be eaten; but the owner of the ox shall be acquitted.

But if the ox was wont to gore in time past, and it has been testified to its owner, and he has not kept it in, but it has killed a man or a woman; the ox shall be stoned, and its owner also shall be put to death.

If there be laid on him a ransom, then he shall give for the redemption of his life whatsoever is laid upon him.

Whether it have gored a son, or have gored a daughter, according to this judgment shall it be done to him.

If the ox gore a male or female slave, there shall be given to their master thirty shekels of silver, and the ox shall be stoned.

II. LAWS OF PROPERTY

1. *Accidents to Animals*

And if a man shall open a pit, or if a man shall dig a pit and not cover it, and an ox or an ass fall therein, the owner of the pit shall make it

---

[4] This assumes the terrible efficacy of the curse.
[5] This is the classic formulation of the *lex talionis*.

good; he shall give the price of it to its owner, and the dead beast shall be his.

And if one man's ox hurt another's, so that it dies, then they shall sell the live ox, and divide the price of it; and the dead also they shall divide. Or if it be known that the ox was wont to gore in time past, and its owner has not kept it in; he shall surely pay ox for ox, and the dead beast shall be his own.

2. Theft of Animals

If a man shall steal an ox, or a sheep, and kill it, or sell it; he shall pay five oxen for an ox, and four sheep for a sheep.

If the thief be found breaking in, and be smitten so that he dies, there shall be no bloodguiltiness for him. If the sun be risen upon him, there shall be bloodguiltiness for him.

He shall make restitution: if he have nothing, then he shall be sold for his theft.

If the theft be found in his hand alive, whether it be ox, or ass, or sheep; he shall pay double.

3. Damage to Fields and Vineyards

If a man cause a field or vineyard to be burnt, and shall let the burning spread, and it burn another man's field; of the best of his own field, and of the best of his own vineyard, shall he make restitution.

If fire spread, and catch in thorns, so that the shocks of grain, or the standing grain, or the field are consumed; he that kindled the fire shall surely make restitution.

4. Loss of or Injury to Property

a. MONEY OR OTHER PROPERTY HELD IN TRUST

If a man shall deliver to his neighbor money or stuff to keep, and it be stolen out of the man's house; if the thief be found, he shall pay double. If the thief be not found, then the master of the house shall come near to God, to see whether he have not put his hand to his neighbor's goods. For every matter of trespass, whether it be for ox, for ass, for sheep, for raiment, or for any manner of lost thing, of which one says, This is it, the cause of both parties shall come before God; he whom God shall condemn shall pay double to his neighbor.

b. ANIMALS KEPT FOR THE OWNER

If a man deliver to his neighbor an ass, or an ox, or a sheep, or any beast, to keep; and it die, or be hurt, no man seeing it: the oath of Yahweh shall decide between them both, whether he has not put his hand to his neighbor's goods; and its owner shall accept it, and he shall not make restitution. But if it be stolen from him, he shall make restitution to its owner. If it be torn in pieces, let him bring it for witness; he shall not make good that which was torn.

c. BORROWED OR HIRED PROPERTY

And if a man borrow anything of his neighbor, and it be hurt, or die, its owner not being with it, he shall surely make restitution.

If its owner be with it, he shall not make it good, if it be a hired thing, it came for its hire.[6]

d. SEDUCTION OF A VIRGIN

And if a man entice a virgin that is not betrothed, and lie with her, he shall surely pay a dowry for her to be his wife. If her father utterly refuse to give her to him, he shall pay money according to the dowry of virgins.

In the next section (Ex. 22:18–31) Social and Religious Laws are given. The section is a little disarranged. This may be an indication that it was added to the original law code later on, or the dislocation may have been purely accidental. Certainly the religious laws belong together, that is to say, the prohibition of blasphemy should follow the law against sacrificing to any other god. And the law of kindness to the enemy's ox or ass belongs with the social laws. In the following the supposed original order has been restored and the Social and Religious Laws separated.

III. SOCIAL LAWS

1. *Honest Administration of Justice*

Thou shalt not take up (on thy lips) a false report; nor make common cause with him that is in the wrong by becoming an unrighteous witness (on his behalf). Thou shalt not follow a majority to do evil; neither shalt thou bear witness in a cause to turn aside after a majority to wrest justice: neither shalt thou favor a poor man in his cause.

Thou shalt not wrest the justice due to thy poor in his cause.

Keep thee far from a false matter; and the innocent and righteous slay thou not: and do not justify the wicked. And thou shalt take no bribe: for a bribe blinds the open-eyed, and perverts the cause of the righteous.

2. *Justice to the Defenceless Classes*

And a sojourner shalt thou not oppress: for ye know the heart of a sojourner, seeing ye were sojourners in the land of Egypt.

Ye shall not afflict any widow, or fatherless child. If thou afflict them at all, and they cry at all to Me, I will surely hear their cry; and My wrath shall wax hot, and I will kill you with the sword; and your wives shall be widows, and your children fatherless.

3. *Considerate Treatment of the Debtor*

If thou lend money to any of My people with thee that is poor, thou shalt not be to him as a creditor; neither shall ye lay upon him interest. If thou at all take thy neighbor's garment to pledge, thou shalt restore it to him before the sun goes down: for that is his only covering, it is his garment for his skin: wherein shall he sleep? and it shall come to pass, when he cries to Me, that I will hear; for I am gracious.

[6] *Or,* if it be a hired servant, it (the damage) goes to his hire.

4. *Kindness to the Enemy's Animals*

If thou meet thine enemy's ox or his ass going astray, thou shalt surely bring it back to him again. Thou shalt not see the ass of him that hates thee lying under his burden, and forbear to help him; thou shalt surely help him.

The conditions to which this law corresponds are those of the premonarchic period. Israel was settled in Canaan and had passed on to the stage of agriculture; they raised of course also cattle and asses and sheep. The land was not communal but individual property. Workmen hired themselves out, and cattle also were rented for agricultural purposes. Money was not yet the common means of exchange, although it was used; natural products were given and taken as a rule. The king is nowhere mentioned. The judicial function lay in the hands of the community of all free citizens. There were no professional judges, usually the elders or members of the aristocracy served as arbiters. The law warns against intimidation or bribery by the rich and powerful, and favoritism towards them, but also against partiality for the poor.

There were no police or prisons in those days. The punishment was either corporal or the imposition of a fine. The execution of the judgment was left to the winning party. In cases of murder the *goel* or next-of-kin was obliged to secure vengeance. Revenge in its ancient, unrestricted form, as we saw it in the Song of Lamech (p. 2), has given way to the so-called *lex talionis*, the law which decrees like for like, "an eye for an eye," etc. The right of asylum is granted to the man slayer but refused to the murderer, who may even be torn from the altar. Some fines are fixed by the injured party, but in some cases arbitration is resorted to, in order that an excessive fine be avoided. If any cases could not be decided by evidence or testimony, they were settled by an oath of the accused at the sanctuary. The efficacy of the oath or curse (for an oath involved cursing oneself in case of guilt) was not doubted by anyone. The curse was believed to have terrible power. He that cursed his father or mother was put to death, for he had set free forces that would accomplish the desired end in a magic but very real way.

It was not necessary to state expressly what would be done to a man who refused to accept the judicial verdict, because he could not remain in the fellowship of the community. The band of outlaws of whom David became captain was composed of such fugitives from justice. They could not be apprehended and thrown into prison, because there were no prisons, but they had punished themselves by their flight and their self-imposed excommunication.

It is significant that such social laws as those of kindness to debtors or justice to and kind treatment of widows, orphans, and strangers were left to the individual conscience. The only sanction behind them is religious: Yahweh is the protector of these defenceless classes. There is nobody else to enforce such laws. Yet they belong to the finest parts of the entire law code, especially the prohibition against taking interest on loans from poor fellow Israelites. This was not due to sentimentalism, for the consistent upholding of this law also in the later law codes of the Old Testament shows that Israel was deliberately opposed to the custom of taking interest from fellow tribesmen. It is therefore not an indication of the primitive stage of civilization in which all tribesmen are brothers and as such obliged to help each other in need.

In their marital relation, however, the Israelites were on a low plane. The fact that the marital law in this code is immediately joined to the slave law is in itself significant. There was only one distinction between selling a girl to a man as a wife or as a slave, for the latter was expected to share his couch too. It was that the man could sell the slave again to other Israelites, but not the wife, whom he could divorce at any time he pleased but not sell. A wife was part of a man's property, which he acquired by buying. The deflowering of a virgin is therefore treated in connection with offences against property. The seducer must either pay the dowry and marry her, or if the father refuse, he must simply pay the dowry, as a compensation of the lessened value of the girl! [7]

The final piece (Ex. 23:10–19) forms an appendix which contains the religious laws. The laws dealing with idolatry and the altar, which are now prefixed to the Book of the Covenant in 20:23–26,

---

[7] This indicates the immense progress that was made by Deuteronomy in treating the wife not as a part of a man's property but as a person, when it put the commandment "thou shalt not covet thy neighbor's wife" by itself (cf. p. 135).

belong with these. It is significant that they are now so arranged as to frame the code on either side, so that the religious laws enclose the others. But that was not the intention of the original codifiers. In the parallel, Ex. 34:17ff. the prohibition of making molten gods is directly connected with the cultic laws (cf. also 23:13).

IV. RELIGIOUS LAWS

1. *Images*

Ye shall not make other gods with Me; gods of silver, or gods of gold, ye shall not make to you.

2. *The Altar*

An altar of earth thou shalt make for Me, and shalt sacrifice thereon thy burnt-offerings, and thy peace-offerings, thy sheep, and thine oxen: in every place where I record My name I will come unto thee and I will bless thee. And if thou make Me an altar of stone, thou shalt not build it of hewn stones; for if thou lift up thy tool upon it, thou hast polluted it. Neither shalt thou go up by steps to Mine altar, that thy nakedness be not uncovered thereon.

3. *Sorcery, Perverseness, Sacrifices to other Gods, Blasphemy*

Thou shalt not suffer a sorceress to live.

Whosoever lies with a beast shall surely be put to death.

He that sacrifices to any god, except to Yahweh only, shall be banned.

Thou shalt not revile God, nor curse a ruler of thy people.

4. *Cultic Laws*

a. FIRSTFRUITS AND FIRSTBORN

Thou shalt not delay to offer the firstfruits of thy threshing floor and of thy winepress.

The firstborn of thy sons shalt thou give to Me.

Likewise shalt thou do with thine oxen, and with thy sheep: seven days it shall be with its dam; on the eighth day thou shalt give it to Me.

b. UNCLEAN FOOD

And ye shall be holy men to Me: therefore ye shall not eat any flesh that is torn of beasts in the field; ye shall cast it to the dogs.

c. THE SABBATH YEAR

And six years thou shalt sow thy land, and shalt gather in its increase: but the seventh year thou shalt let it rest and lie fallow, that the poor of thy people may eat: and what they leave the beast of the field shall eat. In like manner thou shalt deal with thy vineyard, and with thy oliveyard.

d. THE SABBATH

Six days thou shalt do thy work, and on the seventh day thou shalt rest; that thine ox and thine ass may have rest, and the son of thy handmaid, and the sojourner, may be refreshed.

5. *Monolatry*

And in all things that I have said to you take ye heed: and make no mention of the name of other gods, neither let it be heard out of thy mouth.

A parallel to the concluding laws (Ex. 23:14–19) which is found in Ex. 34:10–26 is hardly as Goethe thought the original version of the decalogue. It is commonly regarded as the Jahwistic equivalent of Ex. 20, and referred to as "the cultic decalogue." Quoted below is the first section of it, and where it parallels Ex. 20 the materials are placed side by side. Probable expansion of the text by later commentary is given in smaller type.

Ex: 34:10–17: And He said, Behold, I make a covenant: before all thy people I will do marvels, such as have not been wrought in all the earth, nor in any nation; and all the people among which thou art shall see the work of Yahweh; for it is a terrible thing that I do with thee.

Observe thou that which I command thee this day: behold, I drive out before thee the Amorite, and the Canaanite, and the Hittite, and the Perizzite, and the Hivite, and the Jebusite. Take heed to thyself, lest thou make a covenant with the inhabitants of the land whither thou goest, lest it be for a snare in the midst of thee: but ye shall break down their altars, and dash in pieces their pillars, and ye shall cut down their Asherim,

for thou shalt worship no other god:

for Yahweh, whose name is Jealous, is a jealous God; lest thou make a covenant with the inhabitants of the land, and they play the harlot after their gods, and sacrifice unto their gods, and one invite thee and thou eat of his sacrifice; and thou take of their daughters for thy sons, and their daughters play the harlot after their gods, and make thy sons play the harlot after their gods.

Thou shalt make thee no molten gods.

Ex. 23:14–19: Three times thou shalt keep a feast unto Me in the year:

The feast of unleavened bread shalt thou keep: seven days thou shalt eat unleavened bread, as I commanded thee, at the time appointed in the month Abib, for in it thou camest out from Egypt.

Ex. 34:18–26: The feast of unleavened bread shalt thou keep. Seven days thou shalt eat unleavened bread, as I commanded thee, at the time appointed in the month Abib; for in the month Abib thou camest out from Egypt.

All that opens the womb is Mine; and all thy cattle that is male, the

And none shall appear before Me empty:

and the feast of harvest, the first-fruits of thy labors, which thou sowest in the field: and the feast of ingathering, at the end of the year, when thou gatherest in thy labors out of the field.

Three times in the year all thy males shall appear before the Lord Yahweh.

Thou shalt not offer the blood of My sacrifice with leavened bread; neither shall the fat of My feast remain all night until the morning.

The first of the firstfruits of thy ground thou shalt bring to the house of thy God.

Thou shalt not boil a kid in its mother's milk.

firstlings of cow and sheep. And the firstling of an ass thou shalt redeem with a lamb: and if thou wilt not redeem it, then thou shalt break its neck. All the firstborn of thy sons thou shalt redeem.

And none shall appear before Me empty.

Six days thou shalt work, but on the seventh day thou shalt rest: in ploughing time and in harvest thou shalt rest.

And thou shalt observe the feast of weeks, even of the firstfruits of wheat harvest, and the feast of ingathering at the year's end.

Three times in the year all thy males shall appear before the Lord Yahweh, the God of Israel.

For I will cast out nations before thee, and enlarge thy borders: neither shall any man desire thy land, when thou goest up to appear before Yahweh thy God three times in the year.

Thou shalt not offer the blood of My sacrifice with leavened bread; neither shall the sacrifice of the feast of the passover be left unto the morning.

The first of the firstfruits of thy ground thou shalt bring to the house of Yahweh thy God.

Thou shalt not boil a kid in its mother's milk.

The sentences immediately following (Ex. 34:27–28) have been the cause of the never ending search for the original decalogue in the foregoing, although in the nature of the case there can be no agreement on the ten laws which are believed to constitute it.

And Yahweh said to Moses, Write thou these words: for after the tenor of these words I have made a covenant with thee and with Israel.

And he was there with Yahweh forty days and forty nights without eating bread or drinking water. And he wrote upon the tables the words of the covenant, [the ten commandments].

The final words "the ten commandments" are a later addition by one who believed that it was the decalogue that was originally written on the two tables of stone and not, as the author of Ex. 34 held, the Book of the Covenant.

The law against image worship may originally have been intended as a protest against the golden bulls which Jeroboam made for the temples at Bethel and Dan, and the law of the primitive altar against the more elaborate altars in Solomon's temple. But it is equally possible that the laws are earlier, for the temptation to idolatry and to the making of better altars was present from the beginning of Israel's stay in Canaan.

The Canaanites influenced the religion of Israel as well as their civilization. Some of their customs and beliefs Israel could not accept. But they took over from them the various sacred places, where the diety was believed to dwell and which had been hallowed by agelong worship, together with the paraphernalia of worship, and the great annual agricultural festivals: the feast of Unleavened Bread at the beginning and the feast of Weeks at the end of the grain harvest in the spring and early summer—Easter and Pentecost, and the feast of Tabernacles at the end of the vintage and fruit harvest in the fall—the great thanksgiving feast. Only the first, the Massoth festival, is reinterpreted in our code and connected with the exodus from Egypt, when the haste of the departure prevented the Israelites from leavening their bread. Originally the unleavened bread had nothing to do with this; it was the first fruit of the new harvest eaten before God. The new barley must not be mixed with any leaven of the old because there must be no trace of decay in the new gift of life.

The law of the altar, given above as the second of the religious laws (p. 42) is of fundamental importance for the true understanding of the development of Israel's religion. There was at first not one single sanctuary which alone was legitimate, but there were many local sanctuaries, which were called "high places" and which everybody frequented. They had formerly been the sacred places of the

Canaanites; now they belonged to Israel, who worshiped Yahweh there. In spite of these borrowings of Canaanite religious elements the religion of Yahweh remained victorious; it assimilated Canaanite religion as far as it was not altogether incompatible with Yahwism; the rest it rejected and overcame. It was too strong to be conquered in this fight between the two religions. This ancient cultic law is evidence of its triumphant strength.

IV

The Growth of

Historical Literature

THE establishing of a royal and national government necessitated the keeping of the records of all important events. This already may have begun under Saul, and was certainly in vogue under David and Solomon. After the division of the kingdom, Israel and Judah kept separate annals. The author of the history, of which the Books of Kings like those of Samuel were a part, made use of them and incorporated a number of excerpts from them in his work. He refers the reader to them for further information (cf. 1 Ki. 14:19 and 14:29 etc.).[1] These annals recorded the events of the various reigns from year to year, very much like the Assyrian and Babylonian chronicles. The style was that of the actuary, dry, careful, and reliable, as the following extract from the Annals of Judah indicates:

And it came to pass in the fifth year of King Rehoboam, that Shishak king of Egypt came up against Jerusalem; and he took away the treasures of the house of Yahweh, and the treasures of the king's house; he even took away all: and he took away all the shields of gold which Solomon had made. And King Rehoboam made in their stead shields of brass, and

---

[1] Perhaps he also took from them such materials as the summary of the wars of David in 2 Sam. 8. From a "court calendar" like the one of Nebuchadrezzar he may have derived the catalogue of his generals and courtiers in 2 Sam. 20:23–26; 21:15–22; 23:9–39. The list of his wives and sons in 2 Sam. 3:2–5; 5:13–16 must have come from genealogical records kept at the palace. For Solomon and the other kings there were similar lists and brief summaries of the important events. On the historical work mentioned see ch. XV.

committed them to the hands of the captains of the guard, who kept the door of the king's house. And it was so, that, as oft as the king went into the house of Yahweh, the guard bore them, and brought them back into the guard-chamber. (1 Ki. 14:25–28)

The collection of such facts in these annals was not historical literature, but it supplied sources for the historian. It enabled him to grasp the trend of the history of successive periods and provided the materials for a chronology which had hitherto been lacking.

It is not impossible that a parallel set of official records was kept by the priests of the temple in Jerusalem, for the temple stood in the center of the religious life of the nation; all great undertakings and especially all wars were consecrated here, trophies were brought to it, and it suffered loss whenever disaster befell the nation. However, as the existence of such records in Israel and Judah is not demonstrable one may assume that priestly authors were moved to write down what they knew of great happenings. Certain stories in the Books of the Kings reveal such intimate knowledge of the temple that they can only be ascribed to the men who were most deeply interested in it: the stories of the building of the temple by Solomon (1 Ki. 6f.); of the rebellion in the temple against Athaliah (2 Ki. 11); of the repairs of the temple under Jehoash (2 Ki. 12:4–16); of the new brazen altar which Ahaz imported from Damascus (2 Ki. 16:10–18); and probably that of Josiah's reformation (2 Ki. 23:3ff.).

Extremely valuable as the Royal Annals and priestly narratives were, they did not treat of all the phases of the life of the people. They probably did not even mention the religious crisis of the ninth century about which a prophetic author wrote in the Elijah Stories some time after the death of the great prophet.[2] And yet this crisis was the result of politics and was destined to lead to the overthrow of the dynasty of Omri. The stories themselves are of great significance. Ahab had married the princess Jezebel of Tyre in order to cement the political and commercial relations between Israel and Phoenicia. It was an act of political wisdom. But Jezebel, a woman

[2] They are now incorporated in 1 Ki. 17–19, 21; 2 Ki. 1. In 1 Ki. 20 and 22 stories of Ahab have been introduced. The beginning of the Elijah stories has apparently been dropped.

of strong personality, had not given up her native religion, but had brought Baal priests and prophets with her in order that she might worship the Baal of Tyre in her accustomed manner in the sanctuary which Ahab erected for her in Samaria. As a considerable part of the population was of Canaanitic stock in this area (Judg. 1:27f.) Baal worship had a great appeal. It seems likely that the erection of a Baal sanctuary was not due to weakness on Ahab's part, but was considered policy: to give the Canaanite element in the kingdom a religious center at Samaria, such as the Israelite elements had at Bethel and Dan (1 Ki. 12:26–29). But that Jezebel made her royal husband an apostate from the religion of Yahweh, as the author of the Books of Kings would have us believe, is unlikely.

With the introduction of the powerful Baal of Tyre, a religious crisis came that Ahab may not have foreseen, for in view of the ambivalent attitude of the kings it meant that either the Tyrian Baal or Yahweh must prevail in the end. This was at least the conviction of the champion of Yahweh, whose very name Elijah (*Yahweh is my God!*) rang out the challenge and embodied the watchword of the fight. Suddenly he appeared before Ahab and in the name of Yahweh, the God of Israel announced a drought that would last three years. As abruptly as he had appeared, he vanished. The drought actually came and reduced the land to terrible straits. From the point of view of the reader of these narratives this in itself was a sign of Baal's impotence, for if he really were God, and more especially the God of Fertility, he could have averted the calamity.

The decisive occasion is skillfully retarded by interesting tales about Elijah's experiences and acts during the three years of drought: his feeding by the ravens at the brook Cherith; his reward of the widow at Zarephath in Phoenicia by a miracle providing that "the jar of meal did not waste nor the cruse of oil fail"; and his raising of her son who had died during the prophet's stay at the widow's home. Such miracle tales do not add for us anything to the moral and spiritual grandeur of Elijah, but they show how the people of his time were impressed by the tremendous power of his personality: to this man of God nothing was impossible, he could even restore the dead to life; God worked His miracles through him and for him! When the drought was nearing its end, Elijah met King Ahab, who

greeted him with the words, "Is it thou, thou troubler of Israel?"
but did not dare to touch him although he had tried for three years
to apprehend him! Brushing aside this accusation, Elijah proposed
that all Israel and the four hundred and fifty prophets of Baal (and
of Asherah, Baal's consort) should meet on Mount Carmel.[3]

What followed is told with such dramatic power that only the
ancient narrator's own words can do justice to it. When the people
were all assembled, Elijah reproved them:

How long go ye limping between the two sides? If Yahweh be God,
follow Him; but if Baal, then follow him. And the people answered him
not a word. Then said Elijah to the people, I, even I only, am left a
prophet of Yahweh; but Baal's prophets are four hundred and fifty men.
Let them therefore give us two bullocks; and let them choose one bullock
for themselves, and cut it in pieces, and lay it on the wood, and put no
fire under; and I will dress the other bullock, and lay it on the wood,
and put no fire under. And call ye on the name of your god, and I will
call on the name of Yahweh: and the God that answers by fire, let him
be God. And all the people answered and said, It is well spoken.

And Elijah said to the prophets of Baal, Choose one bullock for yourselves, and dress it first; for you are many; and call on the name of your
god, but put no fire under. And they took the bullock, and they dressed
it, and called on the name of Baal from morning even until noon, saying,
O Baal, answer us! But there was no voice, nor any that answered. And
they limped [4] about the altar which they had made.

And it came to pass at noon, that Elijah mocked them, and said, Cry
aloud; for he is a god: either he is musing, or he is gone aside, or he is
on a journey, or peradventure he sleeps and must be awaked.

And they cried aloud, and cut themselves after their manner with
swords and lances, till the blood gushed out upon them.[5] And it was so,
when midday was past, that they raved in prophetic ecstasy until the
time of the offering of the evening oblation; but there was neither voice,
nor any to answer, nor any that regarded.

And Elijah said to all the people, Come near to me; and all the people
came near to him. And he repaired the altar of Yahweh that was thrown
down. And with the stones he built an altar in the name of Yahweh; and

[3] Originally the story of the divine judgment on Mt. Carmel may have had
no connection with the story of the drought, in which it now provides the
climactic scene.

[4] They performed a cultic dance.

[5] A primitive rite in which the suppliant offers of his own blood to the
deity whether as a substitute for human sacrifice, or to come into more intimate union with the deity, or to awaken pity depends on the circumstances.

he made a trench about the altar, as great as would be sown with two measures of seed. And he put the wood in order, and cut the bullock in pieces, and laid it on the wood. And he said, Fill four jars with water, and pour it on the burnt-offering, and on the wood; and they did so. And he said, Do it the second time; and they did it the second time. And he said, Do it the third time; and they did it the third time. And the water ran round about the altar; and he filled the trench also with water. And it came to pass at the time of the offering of the evening oblation, that Elijah the prophet came near, and said, O Yahweh, the God of Abraham, of Isaac, and of Israel, let it be known this day that Thou art God in Israel, and that I am Thy servant, and that I have done all these things at Thy word. Hear me, O Yahweh, hear me, that this people may know that Thou, Yahweh, art God, and that Thou hast turned their heart back again. Then the fire of Yahweh fell, and consumed the burnt-offering, and the wood, and the stones, and the dust, and licked up the water that was in the trench. And when all the people saw it, they fell on their faces: and they said, Yahweh, He is God; Yahweh, He is God! And Elijah said to them, Take the prophets of Baal; let not one of them escape. And they took them; and Elijah brought them down to the brook Kishon, and slew them there.

And Elijah said to Ahab, Get thee up, eat and drink; for there is the sound of abundance of rain. So Ahab went up to eat and to drink. And Elijah went up to the top of Carmel; and he bowed himself down upon the earth, and put his face between his knees. And he said to his servant, Go up now, look toward the sea. And he went up, and looked, and said, There is nothing. And he said, Go again. And the servant went seven times. And it came to pass at the seventh time, that he said, Behold, there arises a cloud out of the sea, as small as a man's hand. And he said, Go up, say to Ahab, Make ready thy chariot, and get thee down, that the rain stop thee not. And it came to pass in a little while, that the heavens grew black with clouds and wind, and there was a great rain. And Ahab rode, and went to Jezreel: and the hand of Yahweh was on Elijah; and he girded up his loins, and ran before Ahab to the entrance of Jezreel. (1 Ki. 18:21–46)

Yahweh had triumphed. The fundamental principle of the time of Moses was here reiterated with extraordinary power and effectiveness: Yahweh alone is to be worshiped in Israel! But not only because He is Israel's God, but because He alone demonstrates His reality by His activity. This had become clear to Elijah by contrasting Yahweh and Baal. The question of other gods besides Baal did not present itself to him. If it had, we may be sure that his answer would have been the same: they are impotent. Thus Elijah had passed beyond Moses. He was well on the way to monotheism, although he did not yet reach it.

The next story is not a sequel but really a parallel to this, although it is at present connected by Jezebel's threat to Elijah that she would kill him for his slaughter of Baal prophets.[6] The great man fled for his life and hastened to Mount Horeb to seek Yahweh where He had appeared of old to Moses. There was no trace of victory in his soul, only utter despair. In the strength of miraculously provided food he walked through the wilderness forty days and nights until he came to the cave on Mount Horeb, and stood upon the mountain.

And, behold, Yahweh passed by, and a great and strong wind rent the mountains, and broke in pieces the rocks before Yahweh; but Yahweh was not in the wind: and after the wind an earthquake; but Yahweh was not in the earthquake: and after the earthquake a fire; but Yahweh was not in the fire: and after the fire the sound of a soft stillness. And when Elijah heard it, he wrapped his face in his mantle, and went out, and stood in the entrance of the cave. And, behold, a voice came to him, and said, What doest thou here, Elijah? And he said, I have been very jealous for Yahweh, the God of hosts; for the children of Israel have forsaken Thy covenant, thrown down Thine altars, and slain Thy prophets with the sword; and I, even I only, am left; and they seek my life, to take it away. (1 Ki. 19:11–14)

The tempest, earthquake, and fire were the heralds of Yahweh, the awe-inspiring, terrible God. The deep calm that ensued was not symbolic of the gentleness of God, for He spoke to Elijah not kindly, gentle, gracious words of love but words of fearful import that were far more like the tempest, earthquake, and fire than like the gentle stillness.

And Yahweh said to him, Go, return on thy way to the wilderness of Damascus: and when thou comest, thou shalt anoint Hazael to be king over Syria; and Jehu the son of Nimshi shalt thou anoint to be king over Israel; and Elisha the son of Shaphat of Abelmeholah shalt thou anoint to be prophet in thy room. And it shall come to pass, that him that escapes from the sword of Hazael shall Jehu slay; and him that escapes from the sword of Jehu shall Elisha slay. Yet will I leave seven thousand in Israel, all the knees which have not bowed to Baal, and every mouth which has not kissed him. (1 Ki. 19:15–18)

[6] The Greek version may have preserved the original beginning, "If thou art Elijah, I am Jezebel!"

Yahweh is terribly jealous, He will not tolerate the worship of Baal. He will punish His apostate people unsparingly through Hazael, Jehu, and Elisha, until only a faithful remnant is left. The loyalty of His people is more important to Him than its power and prosperity. Moreover, to this prophet's thought Yahweh's dominion is not confined to Israel. Thus Elijah broke down part of the national limitations of Yahweh. He sees the God of Israel using as His instrument Aram or Syria, where His agent is to be enthroned. To Elijah, Yahweh directs the movements of history and not only those of Israel. But God's purpose has not yet been achieved, Elijah—contrary to the impression given by 1 Ki. 18—has not yet won a decisive victory for Him, nor will this prophet be the instrument of victory after all. Nevertheless in the end the divine purpose will be accomplished, and Elijah is to summon the human agents needed to complete the work. On his return from Horeb he met Elisha ploughing with twelve oxen and threw his mantle over him, thereby compelling him as by magic power to follow him. Elisha could only say good-by to his parents and eat a farewell meal with his people of the oxen which he had slaughtered, before he left everything and everybody dear to him and became Elijah's servant. Renunciation of family ties was a prerequisite for his discipleship! The story is not fully preserved for it must then have related the "anointing" of the other two agents of destruction, Hazael and Jehu. These acts were left out because the Deuteronomistic editor wanted to include stories in which they were attributed to Elisha (2 Ki. 8:7–15; 9:1f.). Indeed it may well be that the story of the call of Elisha is taken from the Elisha cycle and is not that of the old Elijah narrative.

In another story Elijah appears as the champion of social justice. Naboth, a prominent citizen of Jezreel, had a vineyard adjoining the royal palace. Ahab wanted it but could not prevail upon Naboth to sell or exchange it, because it was an ancient family possession. Jezebel, with diplomatic skill and coldhearted cruelty, had the elders of Jezreel proclaim a fast, put Naboth at the head of the people, accuse him through bribed witnesses of blasphemy against God and the king, and stone him to death, so that Ahab could confiscate the vineyard for the crown. Just as the king was about to take possession of it, Elijah appeared, the incarnate conscience of Israel, the Spokesman of Yahweh. Impatiently Ahab exclaimed, "Hast thou found me, o mine enemy?" And he answered, "I have found thee! Hast thou killed and also taken possession? Thus says Yahweh, In the place where dogs licked the blood of Naboth shall dogs lick thy blood, even thine." [7] Yahweh's demand of righteousness is absolute, it is binding on king and peasant alike. That was a principle which had been written into the very foundation of the Yahweh religion.

The other principle that Yahweh was to be worshipped alone, Elijah once more reiterated, when King Ahaziah sent to the famous deity of healing, Baal-zebub [8] the god of Ekron for help after he had fallen through the window of his upper chamber. Elijah met the messengers with the stern command,

> Go, turn again to the king that sent you, and say to him, Thus says Yahweh, Is it because there is no God in Israel, that thou sendest to inquire of Baal-zebub, the god of Ekron? therefore thou shalt not come down from the bed whither thou art gone up, but shalt surely die.[9] (2 Ki. 1:6)

All these Elijah stories are legends which the people told about this spiritual hero, whom tradition ranks only second to Moses among all the great ones of Israel. That does not mean that they were simply invented, for they contain many historical elements, although it is often difficult to draw the line between fact and fiction, and they give us perhaps a truer picture of the greatness of the prophet than a strictly historical, matter-of-fact presentation could have done. Here the impression that this moral and spiritual giant made upon his people is given; their enthusiasm and admiration have idealized, heightened, and enlarged his personality, and yet their

[7] This brief prophecy was later expanded (1 Ki. 21:20b–26) to include the whole family of Ahab, and a still later hand added that Ahab humbled himself before Yahweh and that therefore this threatened extermination occurred not in Ahab's but in his son's days.

[8] Baal-zebub was the god of flies, as his name shows (baal = lord, zebub = fly). Flies, just as mice (cf. p. 24), already were regarded by the ancients as carriers of diseases. The fly-god brought them on or drove them away, he brought diseases and healed them. It is controversial whether Beel-zebul, prince of the demons, Matt. 12:24, is to be connected with this Philistine deity.

[9] A later hand may have added the strange story of Elijah's sending fire upon two companies of fifty soldiers with their captains who had been despatched to apprehend him. The third captain implored him for his own and his soldiers' lives, whereupon he went with him and told the king the same that he had told the messengers.

interpretation showed the deepest insight, because it was born out
of affection and awe. Such was the prophet as he lived in their memories. And truly, the moral and spiritual insight revealed in these tales,
the emphasis on exclusive worship of Yahweh, who in contrast to
Baal was the only real God; the insistence on the demand of social
justice as absolute; and the enlargement of the dominion of Yahweh,
who directs history and uses even foreign nations for His purposes,
these truths belonged to the master before the disciple wrote them
down. We may be sure that the pupil was not greater than his
teacher.

Some decades later a collection of Elisha Stories was made which
is now incorporated in 2 Ki. 2–8; 13:14–21. In the first of these
Elijah has grown to almost superhuman stature. He was too great
to die! Elijah and Elisha were walking for the last time together.

> And Elisha said, I pray thee, let a double portion of thy spirit be upon
> me. And he said, Thou hast asked a hard thing: nevertheless, if thou see
> me when I am taken from thee, it shall be so unto thee; but if not, it
> shall not be so. And it came to pass, as they still went on, and talked, that,
> behold, there appeared a chariot of fire, and horses of fire, which parted
> them both asunder; and Elijah went up by a whirlwind into heaven.
> And Elisha saw it, and he cried, My father, my father, the chariots of
> Israel and the horsemen thereof! (2 Ki. 2:10–12)

Elisha asked for two-thirds (cf. Deut. 21:17) of his spirit, and Elijah
made the divine granting of this request conditional. If he saw Elijah's
removal from the earth he would know that he (Elisha) had received
it. Elisha had seen and had become chief heir! The mantle of Elijah
was his too, and with it he smote the waters of Jordan so that he
could pass through! To the other prophets who saw him do it, this
was proof enough that Elijah's spirit rested on Elisha.

With a miracle Elisha had begun his career and soon one followed
upon another. Endowed with heavenly power, he walked among the
people who told story after story of this great man of God: how he
healed the water at Jericho by throwing salt into it, saying, "Thus
says Yahweh, I have healed these waters: there shall not be from
thence any more death or miscarrying"; how he punished young
lads, who had called after him, "Go up, thou bald head!" by bringing

two she-bears upon them out of the woods through his curse; how
he helped a poor widow from the fate of having her two children
sold because of her debts by miraculously filling vessel after vessel
with the oil of a single pot; how he rewarded the childless Shunamite
woman for her hospitality to him by promising her a son and later
by restoring the little lad to life when he had died from sunstroke;
how he averted death from some sons of the prophets, who had
eaten poisonous pottage, by throwing some meal into the pot; how
he fed a hundred men with but twenty loaves of bread; how he
healed Naaman the Aramaean general from his leprosy; how he
helped some disciples of his to recover an axhead that had fallen
into the Jordan by making the iron come to the surface; how horses
and chariots of fire protected him from the Aramaean soldiers who
had been sent to apprehend him and how upon his request Yahweh
smote the Aramaeans with blindness so that he could lead them into
a trap; how he foresaw and magically influenced the future when
he told King Jehoash to shoot arrows and to stamp upon the ground
and how the king smote only three times when he should have done
so five or six times, with the result that he could now defeat Aram
only three times but not completely and decisively; and finally how
even after his death, when men in their sudden fright of Aramaean
raiders threw a corpse that they were going to bury into the grave
of Elisha, the life-giving power of the prophet's bones was so great
that the man at once revived. Miracle upon miracle! He was won-
derland indeed! It is as if we were reading the story of the life
of one of the saints, including all the legends and miracle tales that are
so similar the world over, whether the saint be Jew or Christian,
Buddhist or Mohammedan. Some of these stories had been told of
Elijah also. They are invaluable for the history of popular religion
in Israel. But we learn nothing of Elisha's message from them. His
personality is pictured in these tales as kindly, gentle, humane, always ready to help in time of need, but conscious of his power and
insistent on the honor due to him as a prophet of Yahweh.

Fortunately, some materials of great historical value supplement
the legendary picture of the times. They are narratives dealing with
the rise and fall of the Dynasty of Omri. They have not all been
preserved, because not all of them fitted in with the scheme of the

author of the Books of Kings. Although their writers were interested in the part the prophets played, they were concerned primarily with the political movements and wrote from a political point of view and subordinated, without underestimating, the prophets. It is, however, a source of some perplexity that they do not mention Elijah or Elisha.

The story of Omri himself, except for a few brief but important items, is lost. This is all the more to be regretted, because Omri was a really great king, as the Assyrian inscriptions show when they still call Israel "the (land of the) house of Omri" a century after its fall. But the story of Ahab's Aramaean wars is probably preserved in 1 Ki. 20, 22 (if we may trust the mention of his name in 20:2 and 22:20). Aram, as the Syrian kingdom of Damascus was then called, was at that time in its period of power. It was pushing westward to gain access to the sea and to control the great caravan routes. Omri, Ahab's father, had been defeated by Benhadad I, had lost a number of Israelite cities in the northern Transjordan territory, and had been compelled to grant to the Aramaeans a city district in his newly founded capital Samaria with commercial privileges. We may surmise that it was to counteract this strong Aramaean power that Omri had entered into family relations with Phoenicia, and arranged the marriage of his son Ahab with the Tyrian princess Jezebel. The author of the story does not speak of this, but only of the siege of Samaria by Benhadad II and his defeat by "the king of Israel," presumably Ahab. He says nothing of the reason for the resumption of warfare by Aram, but tells of the advice of an unidentified prophet of Yahweh, which brought victory to the king of Israel.

The renewal of the war in the following year was also predicted by the prophet, and so was the crushing defeat of Benhadad, before the battle had commenced. After the decisive victory it was again a prophet who denounced the lenient terms which the king of Israel had imposed on Benhadad; for he only demanded the return of the cities which his father had lost and commercial privileges in Damascus, such as the Aramaeans had gained in Samaria. This prophet voiced here the people's indignant dissatisfaction with the treaty of peace (1 Ki. 20). One does not gain the impression that the ruler was an apostate who would have nothing to do with Yahweh; on the contrary the prophets of Yahweh play an important role in his decisions. It is obvious that if the ruler was Ahab we here receive an entirely different idea of him than in the Elijah stories.

It soon developed that the king of Israel was not able to compel the execution of the terms of the treaty with Aram. So he decided to resort to force by attacking Ramoth in Gilead. His vassal king, Jehoshaphat of Judah, had to go with him. But before embarking on a campaign they inquired of Yahweh's oracle from his prophets. They all declared, "Go up; for Yahweh will deliver it into the hand of the king." When Jehoshaphat asked whether there was not another prophet (of repute), Ahab replied there was still one other, "Micaiah the son of Imlah, but I hate him, for he does not prophesy good concerning me, but evil." However, he sent for him. Meanwhile the leader of the other prophets, Zedekiah, brought two horns of iron and said, "Thus says Yahweh, with these shalt thou push the Aramaeans until they are destroyed." And all joined him in saying, "Go up to Ramoth Gilead and prosper, for Yahweh will deliver it into the hand of the king."

The messenger who had gone to fetch Micaiah asked him to give a good oracle, but the prophet replied, "As Yahweh lives, what Yahweh says to me, that will I speak." But he repeated at first to the kings the message of the other prophets, in a sarcastic tone we presume, for the king of Israel rebuked him and demanded that he tell nothing but the truth. Then he said,

> I saw all Israel scattered on the mountains,
>   as sheep that have no shepherd:
> And Yahweh said, "These have no master,
>   let them return every man to his house in peace." (1 Ki. 22:17)

It was a dramatic picture of the defeated people and their slain king in the characteristic poetic form which is so common with the great literary prophets. In explanation of the discrepancy between his oracle and that of the other prophets Micaiah continued,

> Therefore hear thou the word of Yahweh: I saw Yahweh sitting on His throne, and all the host of heaven standing by Him on His right hand and on His left. And Yahweh said, Who shall entice Ahab, that he may go up and fall at Ramoth-gilead? And one said on this manner; and another said on that manner. And the spirit came forth and stood

before Yahweh, and said, I will entice him. And Yahweh said to him, Wherewith? And He said, I will go forth, and will be a lying spirit in the mouth of all his prophets. And He said, Thou shalt entice him, and shalt prevail also: go forth, and do so. Now therefore, behold, Yahweh has put a lying spirit in the mouth of all these thy prophets; and Yahweh has spoken evil concerning thee. (1 Ki. 22:19–23)

The prophet Zedekiah full of rage struck Micaiah on the cheek, exclaiming, "Which way went the Spirit of Yahweh from me to speak to thee?" To which he replied, "Behold, thou shalt see on that day, when thou shalt go into an inner chamber to hide thyself," and to the king who sent him back to prison till his return he said, "If thou return at all in peace, Yahweh has not spoken by me." Then the king of Israel went into battle. He disguised himself, but in the battle an arrow sent at a venture mortally wounded him. In spite of his wound, he stayed with his chariot in the fight till evening, when he died. Who can withhold his sympathy from so brave and noble a king and warrior? The story is important not only in correcting our estimate of Ahab (if he, indeed, is the king meant) but also in giving us the remarkable episode of the prophet Micaiah. His picture of the catastrophe is exquisitely phrased in metric language and his view of prophetic inspiration does not doubt either the sincerity or the actual inspiration of the opposing prophets, but carries back their false prophecy to a deception by Yahweh Himself, who in a solemn heavenly council had decided to lead Ahab astray through a spirit of falsehood! For a true historical understanding of the professional prophets Micaiah's judgment of them is as important as his view of inspiration is valuable for the development of religious reasoning. Jeremiah judged his opponents more sharply and explained the discrepancy between their message and his own quite differently (Jer. 23). Jeremiah's theology may be better, but the fairness of Micaiah's judgment is noteworthy.

After Ahab's death, Moab under its king Mesha revolted against Israelite suzerainty. In Mesha's famous memorial monument [10] details about the revolt are given. But Ahab's son and second successor Jehoram (called Joram in most cases) tried to restore Israelitic

[10] In "The Moabite Stone," erected by Mesha at Dibon on the Arnon, this ruler tells of his wars with Israel. An English translation is given in *ANET*, p. 320.

supremacy. An Elisha story in 2 Ki. 3 relates how Jehoram with his vassals, the kings of Judah and of Edom, advanced against Moab from the south through Edom and how the prophet Elisha, who reappears here, obtained water for the suffering army by making use of his knowledge of the country in which the rain water is retained under the surface of the soil by the rocky substratum and is procured by the digging of trenches. It is of great interest to learn that Elisha induced his prophetic ecstasy by the music of a minstrel. We never find that the great prophets used external stimulants in order to transport themselves into the trance, but of the prophets of Baal we learned in the Elijah stories that they danced and raved and shouted and cut themselves with knives till the blood gushed forth and of the Israelitic prophets who roved in companies through the land in Saul's time we may assume the same. The dervishes today still use the same means. Elisha gave to the kings also the prediction of victory over Moab. When on the next morning "the sun shone upon the water, the Moabites saw the water against them as red as blood: and they said, "This is blood; the kings are surely destroyed, and they have smitten each man his fellow: now therefore Moab, to the spoil!" This was the Israelite view. We may be sure that the Moabites were not deceived by those pools of water or by their red color, for both were familiar sights to them. But they were defeated and their land was devastated. Then, as his last resort, King Mesha took his eldest son, the crown prince, and offered him upon the wall of his capital as a burned offering to his god Kemosh. It was a desperate means to gain help, but it succeeded. "And there was a great wrath [of Kemosh] against Israel, and they departed from him, and returned to their own land." Moab remained free, Jehoram's attempt to subdue it again had proved vain. This is in accord with Mesha's inscription. The Israelites, we see, still believed in the real existence and power of the god of Moab. We hear of no protest by Elisha either.

In the next story (2 Ki. 6:24—7:19) Elisha is also opposed to Jehoram, but again he gives him a hopeful prediction. Benhadad of Damascus besieged Samaria in his time—if the placement of the story, which does not give his name, can be trusted—until a famine raged whose terror is brought home to the reader by the experience of the king as he inspected the wall. A woman called out to him for help and said in answer to his question,

> This woman said to me, Give thy son, that we may eat him today, and we will eat my son tomorrow. So we boiled my son, and ate him: and I said to her on the next day, Give thy son, that we may eat him; and she has hidden her son. And it came to pass, when the king heard the words of the woman, that he rent his clothes as he was standing upon the wall; and the people looked, and, behold, he had sackcloth within upon his flesh. Then he said, God do so to me, and more also, if the head of Elisha the son of Shaphat shall stand on him this day. (2 Ki. 6:28-31)

Why Elisha was held responsible for the distress, we are not told. From the sequel we may deduce that he had counseled the king not to capitulate, but to trust in the help of Yahweh. Elisha knew instinctively, the author states, that the king had planned his death and told the elders who were with him, "See ye how this son of a murderer has sent to take my head?" So they bolted the door against the assassin. When the king himself appeared soon afterwards and said, "Behold, this evil is of Yahweh; why should I wait for Yahweh any longer?" Elisha declared in an oracle of Yahweh that by this time tomorrow the famine in Samaria would be at an end, and warned the king's aide, who doubted the truth of this, "Behold, thou shalt see it with thine eyes, but shalt not eat thereof." Meanwhile the Aramaeans had received news of the intended invasion of a powerful confederation of enemies. The author speaks of the Hittites and the Egyptians, but that was the mistaken popular notion; in reality the Assyrians were menacing Damascus. Four famishing lepers, who had gone to the camp of the Aramaeans to get food, discovered that it was forsaken, and after eating and drinking and taking spoil they told the people of Samaria the good news, which seemed to them too good to be true. They investigated and then all poured out of the city to plunder the Aramaean camp. The press at the gate was so great that the king's aide, who was the officer in charge there, was trampled to death, as the prophet had foretold.

In the next two stories Elisha is the executor of Elijah's testament. In Damascus he told Hazael, who inquired about the outcome of Benhadad's serious illness,

Go, say to him, Thou shalt surely recover; howbeit Yahweh has showed me that he shall surely die. And he settled his countenance stead-fastly upon him, until he was ashamed: and the man of God wept. And Hazael said, Why does my lord weep? And he answered, Because I know the evil that thou wilt do to the children of Israel: their strong-holds wilt thou set on fire, and their young men wilt thou slay with the sword, and wilt dash in pieces their little ones, and rip up their women with child. And Hazael said, But what is thy servant, who is but a dog, that he should do this great thing? And Elisha answered, Yahweh has showed me that thou shalt be king over Syria. (2 Ki. 8:10–13)

The next day Hazael murdered Benhadad and became king in his stead.

The narrator shows exquisite tact in this fateful interview: the prophet was on a terrible errand, his heart was full of grief and tears streamed down his cheeks, he had to tell Hazael; but he did not tell him directly, he only suggested, and Hazael understood the suggestion all too well. Did Elisha actually show such delicacy? Or was this only his disciple's way of telling the terrible tale?

The anointing of Jehu follows (2 Ki. 9, 10). Jehoram had been wounded in a fierce battle for the capture of Ramoth Gilead against the Aramaeans and had gone home to nurse his wounds. Elisha took this opportunity of sending one of his disciples to anoint Jehu, whom Jehoram had left in command of the army. He was at once pro-claimed king by his fellow officers when they learned what "this mad fellow" had done. This epithet shows what impression the ecstatic behavior of these prophets made in more worldly circles. Jehu—perhaps only for political reasons—must have been one of the fanatical Yahweh party, whom Elisha could use for his purpose of overthrowing the dynasty of Omri which was religiously too toler-ant of other cults and not enthusiastic enough for Yahweh. The wars with Aram, in which questions of political power and commer-cial control were decided, had pushed aside for these rulers the great religious matters which concerned the prophetic party. Ahab had incurred their hatred for his marriage with Jezebel, and for his judicial murder of Naboth. Jehu now rode at a furious pace to Jezreel and murdered his king and the visiting Judean king Ahaziah. He felt himself to be the avenger of Naboth and the fulfiller of Elijah's oracle to Ahab. After killing Jehoram,

He said to Bidkar his adjutant, Take up, and cast him in the portion
of the field of Naboth the Jezreelite; for remember how that, when I and
thou rode together after Ahab his father, Yahweh uttered this oracle
against him: Surely I have seen yesterday the blood of Naboth, and
the blood of his sons, says Yahweh; and I will requite thee in this plot,
says Yahweh. Now therefore take and cast him into the plot of ground,
according to the word of Yahweh. (2 Ki. 9:25f.)

Queen Jezebel too, who defied the regicide, he commanded to be
thrown out of the window; seventy royal princes in Samaria were
executed at his suggestion, although he later disclaimed all responsibility for this; forty-two royal princes of Judah he slew on
their way to a visit of the princes of Israel. The horror of it all
sent a shudder through both countries, yet none dared to resist the
brutal usurper, who knew so well how to cloak his acts with religious
devotion. He invited Jonadab, the son of Rechab, to ride with
him in his chariot in order that he might be seen with the head of
the fanatic Yahweh party called the Rechabites, who in their violent
opposition to Baal worship rejected not only the religion but also
the civilization of Canaan with its vine culture and its cities (cf.
Jer. 35:2ff.).

The final stroke, by which Jehu exterminated the adherents of
Baal, was struck at a feast of Baal which they were all compelled to
attend, and where they were all cut down. The words "Thus Jehu
destroyed Baal out of Israel," end the story which is so dramatically
told in this on the whole reliable document. The author approved
of Jehu, though he does not say so outright, but a hundred years
later the prophet Hosea shuddered as he foretold the fall of Jehu's
dynasty because of these cruel crimes. Conscience had a history in
Israel as elsewhere. What Elisha's conscience approved, Hosea's condemned!

The Elisha of these two narratives is quite different from the
kindly and humane man of God in the other Elisha stories. But this
presentation is more historical. Even so we do not gain the impression that he had a double portion of his master's spirit or that he was
at all comparable to Elijah in personal greatness or historical significance. But we learn that his political activity and importance were
considerable. The religious ideas attributed to him in the stories do

not contain any thought that was higher than the thought of the people about him.

The Narratives of the Rise and Fall of the Dynasty of Omri are among the most valuable historical sources of Hebrew history. They may have been recorded in the reign of Jehu (845–818 B.C.) by writers who, in spite of a predilection for the prophets, had no prejudice against the dynasty, but described Ahab so as to evoke our deep interest in him, if not our admiration for him. They awaken, too, our sympathy for Jehoram, in spite of Elisha's opposition to him. These authors maintained the standard of fairness and objectivity set by those who wrote about the early history of the founding of the monarchy.

V

The Yahwist

LEGENDS of a more remote past than those dealt with in Chapter IV had been handed down from age to age in Israel with astounding tenacity of memory. Some had come from hoary antiquity, repeated by one generation to another. The priests had recited the stories connected with their particular sanctuaries; the shepherds had told their tales of pastoral life, the peasants of agricultural, the city dwellers of urban life. They were all at first single stories, complete in themselves, independent of others. Minstrels and story-tellers had collected and narrated them to the people in camp or at the festivals, and the parents had told them in turn to their children. Yet, in course of time, with the development of settled life the need for writing them down came to be felt, and certain groups of stories were thus preserved. It was inevitable that by the time we come to literate records, the tales should have been more or less modified in the long oral process of tradition. Stories that were originally not Israelitic but Canaanitic or Babylonian had been made Israelitic. Thus religious tales, originally connected with the Canaanitic god Baal or the Babylonian god Marduk or with some other deity, were now told of Yahweh. In the time of the great kingdom of David and Solomon, the first period of the flowering of Hebrew literature, or perhaps a little later (*ca.* 900), the Judean author whom scholars call the Yahwist or J (see p. xiv), because he uses the name Yahweh for God, gathered the various stories and narrative cycles together for a great work, in which he told the story of the people from its origin to the conquest of Canaan, and showed how and why his people came into possession of the land.[1]

He went back to the beginning of time and of man's creation; how Yahweh had formed him from the dust of the ground and breathed the breath of life into his nostrils, then placed him in the garden of Eden and built a companion for him from one of his ribs. That is the reason, he observed, why "a man leaves his father and his mother and cleaves to his wife and they become one flesh"; they belonged originally together! "And the man called his wife's name Eve, because she became the mother of all living." Deep questions of never-ceasing interest to the human mind are answered in these early tales. The golden age lay at the beginning. Men were happy and carefree in the wonderful garden of Eden. Why did it not last? Why did misery come into this world and all pain and suffering and labor? Because of man's disobedience! Yahweh had forbidden them to eat of the fruit of a tree in the midst of the garden, but, tempted by the wily serpent, they transgressed this command and were punished, the woman with the fearful pain of childbearing and her ever renewed desire with its ever following pangs; the man with hard and endless labor for the fruit of the soil, which had hitherto been his without work. The serpent too was cursed, that is why it now crawls on its belly and why there is perpetual enmity between it and man! A variant story had told also of the tree of life, by the eating of whose fruit man would become immortal. Israel in common with other nations believed that knowledge and eternal life could be procured by the eating of certain food. Our author took from this latter tale the motivation of man's expulsion from the garden of Eden, of which the other story had said nothing. Yahweh feared that man might eat from the tree of life also, so He drove him out and barred the way to the garden by Cherubim and an ever turning glittering sword.

[1] It is widely believed that there were two Yahwistic authors who are labeled J[1] and J[2]. The latter may have incorporated the former. This refinement of the basic theory of Wellhausen (see Introduction, p. xiii) was introduced by Karl Budde (1883), though for the early chapters of Genesis only. Rudolf Smend (1912) held that J[1] and J[2] were separate Yahwistic strands running through the Hexateuch. Otto Eissfeldt carried this through in his "synoptic" arrangement of the narrative materials of the Hexateuch in his *Hexateuch-Synopse* (1922), and has maintained it in his *Einleitung in das Alte Testament* (2nd ed., 1956). He gives J[1] the letter L (lay source). Robert H. Pfeiffer in his *Introduction to the Old Testament* (1948) substitutes S. See notes 14, 16.

The Eden story was originally told by a man who looked upon agriculture as the normal occupation. Quite unconcerned about its origin, the author, who had told of man's first disobedience, now followed it with a story of the first murder, which was originally told by a shepherd, for Cain the murderer was "a tiller of the ground" and his cereal offering was not acceptable to Yahweh, but Abel was "a keeper of sheep" and "Yahweh had respect to Abel and to his offering." To our author this was of no significance any more; to him the reason for Yahweh's nonacceptance of Cain's gift was moral, for Yahweh, who sees the heart, warned Cain,

> Why art thou wroth? and why is thy countenance fallen? If thou doest well, shall it not be lifted up? and if thou doest not well, sin couches at the door, and unto thee is its desire; but do thou rule over it. (Gen. 4:6)

Nevertheless Cain slew Abel, but was punished with a fearful curse which drove him away from his home "a fugitive and wanderer in the earth." As a protection against murder Yahweh gave him a sign, the tribal sign of the Cainites, by which he was recognized everywhere as a member of a tribe which was famous for its terrible blood revenge. Our author placed this early institution of law at the beginning of human history, quite unconcerned that in reality it came much later and that with all its terrors it was a great step in advance, safeguarding life through family or tribal action before a strong government could take the execution of justice in hand. That this story presupposed the existence of many people besides Adam and Eve and their sons, did not trouble our author either.

He then proceeded to speak of Cain's building of the first city and of his descendants who were the ancestors of the nomadic cattle raisers, of the musicians, and of the smiths, and he incorporated here the terrible song of Lamech which celebrated his brutal, unrestrained blood feud (cf. p. 2). Civilization had advanced through Cain and his descendants, but so had murder and sin! Side by side with the Cain line the author shows how in the Seth line religion arose. After the birth of Seth's son Enosh, "men began to call upon the name of Yahweh." [2]

He next told of the fabulous giants of old, "the Nephilim," the offspring of heavenly beings and fair daughters of men; but gave

[2] *I.e.,* worship of the deity was inaugurated.

only a fragment of what must have been a longer story, for Israel, like other peoples, had tales about such demigods. As the brief reference to them now stands, it seems to have been intended to serve as an illustration of the growing sinfulness in the world. For directly afterwards we read, "And Yahweh saw that the wickedness of man was great in the earth, and that every imagination of the thoughts of his heart was only evil continually," wherefore He determined to destroy mankind.

The means chosen for this judgment was a deluge. Only "Noah found favor in the eyes of Yahweh," and was saved in an ark which he had made, with his family and seven pairs of every clean and two pairs of every unclean beast. In the terrible flood which Yahweh brought on by a rain lasting forty days and forty nights man and beast perished. When Noah after landing on the mountains of Ararat and going forth from the Ark offered burnt offerings,

> Yahweh smelt the sweet savor, and Yahweh said in His heart, "I will not again curse the ground any more for man's sake, for the imagination of his heart is evil from his youth; neither will I again smite any more everything living as I have done.
> > While the earth remains,
> > > seedtime and harvest, and cold and heat,
> > > and summer and winter, and day and night
> > > shall not cease. (Gen. 8:21f.)

This fact of the ineradicability of human sinfulness is at once illustrated in the shameful behavior of Canaan towards his father Noah who had drunk too much of the wine which he had been the first to make. Noah's curse on Canaan and his blessing of Shem and Japheth (see p. 12) contains the theme of J's whole history, Canaan is to be subject to Shem and Japheth. This is the program of the future, whose realization J traces through the succeeding ages, until Israel (Shem) becomes at last the lord of Canaan. The curse and the blessing of the ancestor have, according to ancient belief, a magic potency to set free forces that work for their fulfillment. In spite of all obstacles that may ever again rise to frustrate the great hope, the final outcome is assured.

With this end clearly in view, J proceeds to tell the remarkable story. After quickly giving a genealogy of the sons of Noah, in

which he showed how they repeopled the earth, and telling of the
tower of Babel that men built in their overweening pride and for
which they were scattered over all the earth,[3] J commenced the
story of Abraham, the father of the chosen race. At the beginning
he placed the great promise,

Now Yahweh said to Abram, Get thee out of thy country, and from
thy kindred, and from thy father's house, to the land that I will show
thee: and I will make of thee a great nation, and I will bless thee, and
make thy name great; and be thou a blessing: and I will bless them that
bless thee, and them that curse thee will I curse: and in thee shall all the
families of the earth be blessed. (Gen. 12:1–3)

But this was for the distant future. Obediently Abraham went forth,
without knowing his destination, until he came to Shechem in
Canaan, where the divine promise was made, "to thy seed will I
give this land."

But soon afterwards a severe famine compelled him to leave this
promised land and to seek food in Egypt. There the beauty of his
wife Sarah brought them into a perilous situation, but they emerged
safely from it and returned to Canaan with the great wealth which
the Pharaoh had given him. But again the reader is kept in suspense,
for Abram almost lost the promised land through his generosity—
as would actually have happened if Lot had not chosen the marvelously fertile territory of Sodom (which later, through a judgment of God, was turned into a desolation on account of the city's
fearful wickedness). At Hebron, where Abram now settled, Yahweh
gave him the promise of a son, but Sarah was barren! The promise
seemed unfulfillable. He was not even to see the child of Hagar, the
handmaiden Sarah had given him as a concubine, for she fled into
the wilderness because of the intolerable harshness of the jealous
Sarah. At last, when he and his wife were so old that they could no
longer expect children, Yahweh promised a son to them as a reward
for their hospitality on His visit with two angels at Abram's tent.[4]
And true enough, at the predicted time Isaac was born!

When the boy had grown up, Abram sent his trusted steward to

[3] The primeval story of J is in Gen. 2:4b—4:25; 5:29; 6:1–8; 7:1–5, 7–10, 12,
16b, 17b, 22f.; 8:2b, 3a, 6–12, 13b, 20–22; 9:18–27; 10:8–19, 21, 24–30; 11:1–9.
[4] J's story of Abram is in Gen. 11:28–30; 12 (except 4b, 5); 13:1–5, 6b, 7–11a,
12b, 13, 18; 15:1–11*, 17, 18a; 16:1b, 2, 4–8, 11–14; 18:1–16, 20–22a; 19 except 29.

his homeland in Mesopotamia that he might procure for him a wife from the daughters of his kinsmen, for he should not marry a Canaanite maiden. After a successful trip the steward came back with Laban's sister, Rebekah, whom Isaac gladly took as his wife.[5] But she also was barren! And only after Isaac's earnest entreaty did Yahweh grant to her children, the twin brothers Jacob and Esau. While still in her womb, they struggled together. The oracle of Yahweh interpreted this as prophetic of the strife of the two nations, Israel and Edom, whose ancestors they would be, and the prediction was given, "the elder shall serve the younger." The full significance of this appeared, when Esau = Edom was born first, and Jacob = Israel second. The first-born should ordinarily be the heir. But Jacob had the promise! J also included another explanation of the superior role of the younger son: by fraud he obtained his father's potent blessing, which had been intended for his favorite elder son, Esau.

Yet in spite of all this, the fulfillment seemed again impossible, for Jacob had to flee from Esau's vengeance. But it turned out to be his good fortune. He went to Laban, his mother's brother, married Laban's two daughters, Leah and Rachel, and came back with immense wealth—which he had gotten by his work and by his cleverness—accompanied by his wives and twelve sons, most of whom he had by Leah, whom he had at first not wanted! All obstacles such as Laban's pursuit and Esau's encounter, however threatening they were at the time, were removed and Jacob settled once more in Canaan. The time for the possession of the promised land seemed to have come.[6]

But again his favorite son, Joseph, was carried away from the land, sold to Egypt as a slave, and thrown into prison. From there he rose to the position of viceroy, and at a time of great famine was able to save his aged father and his brethren. Jacob with all his sons left the land too and emigrated to Egypt, where he died after blessing his sons (cf. pp. 12f.). Once more the promise seemed frustrated.[7]

[5] J's story of Isaac is in Gen. 21:1a, 2a, 7, 33; 22:20–24; 24; 25:1–5, 11b, 18a; 26:1–33*.

[6] J's story of Jacob and Esau is in Gen. 25:21–26a, 28; 27:1–10, 14f., 17, 18a, 20, 24–27a, 29b–32, 35–39a, 40a, 41–45; 28:10, 13–16, 19a; 29:2–14, 26, 31–35; 30:9–16, 20b, 21, 24b, 25, 27, 29–40ac, 41–43; 31:1, 17, 18a, 25, 27, 31, 43f., 46, 48, 51–53; 32:3–7a, 13b–22a, 23b–29, 31f.; 33:1–17a; 34*; 35:21f.; 36:15–19, 31–39; 38.

[7] J's story of Joseph is in Gen. 37:3f., 12, 13a, 14b, 18b, 21, 23a, 25–27, 28b, 31a, 32f., 35; 39:1ac, 2ff.; 42:2, 4b–7, 27, 28a, 38; 43:1–13, 14b–23a, 24–34; 44; 45:1a, 2,

In Egypt the descendants of the sons of Jacob became a very numerous people, and part of the promise was being fulfilled. This growth
filled the Egyptians with anxiety, so they oppressed and enslaved
them, and all male children were killed. A champion arose for them
in Moses, who had been spared through being adopted by Pharaoh's
daughter, but he had to flee after killing an Egyptian who had slain
a Hebrew. Once again this apparent misfortune turned out to be of
a decisive significance for Israel's fate. For in Midian, whither Moses
had fled and where he had married the priest's daughter, Zipporah,
Yahweh appeared to him and said that He had heard the cry of His
people in Egypt and that Moses must go there as His agent to effect
their release, and for this He endowed him with miracle-working
power. On Moses' return to Egypt with his wife and son, Yahweh,
for no reason given, attacked him at a lodging place in the wilderness, but Zipporah saved him by applying the magically potent
blood of her son whom she had circumcised.

In Egypt the mission to Pharaoh was at first unsuccessful and
only resulted in harsher oppression of the people.[8] But by a series of
plagues,[9] which Moses announced in Yahweh's name, Pharaoh was
finally compelled to let the people go in order that they might celebrate the feast to Yahweh at the sacred mountain in the wilderness.
At the last they could not leave Egypt too quickly for him. In great
haste, without having time to leaven their dough, they departed in
the month Abib (later called by the Babylonian name *Nisan:* about
April). As a memorial of this exodus Moses ordered that they should
keep the feast of unleavened bread every year in Abib, and give to
Yahweh the first-born males, animal and human. The great throng
of 600,000(!) men, besides children and a mixed crowd of foreigners, went southward, Yahweh marching before them in a pillar
of cloud by day and of fire by night.

But suddenly the whole deliverance was endangered, for Pharaoh
had changed his mind and pursued them with his chariotry. There

---

4b, 5a, 9–11, 13f., 19, 28; 46:1a, 28–34; 47:1–5a, 6b, 12–27a, 29–31; 48:2b, 8a, 9b,
13f., 17–19; 49:2–27, 33a*; 50:1–11, 14, 18, 21, 24.

[8] Ex. 1:6, 8–12, 14a; 2:11–23a; 3:2–4a, 5, 7–9a, 16–18; 4:1–16, 19, 20a, 24–26, 29–
31; 5:3, 5–23; 6:1.

[9] J has seven plagues, 1. the Nile was made foul (Ex. 7:14, 16, 17a, 18, 21a,
24f.); 2. frogs (8:1–4, 8–15a); 3. flies (8:20–32); 4. murrain (9:1–7); 5. hail
(9:13, 17f., 23b, 24b, 25b–29a, 33f.); 6. locusts (10:1a, 3–11, 13b, 14b, 15ac–19,
24–29); 7. death of the first-born (11:4–8).

seemed to be no way of escape, but Yahweh "caused the sea" (which apparently extended at that time far inland and hindered the Israelites from crossing to the wilderness) "to go back by a strong wind all night, and made the sea dry land" and thus enabled them to pass through safely, while the pursuing Egyptians stuck fast with their chariot wheels in the soft ground and were miserably overtaken and drowned by the incoming tide. A mighty deliverance had been granted! Full of joy Israel sang to Yahweh,

> I will sing to Yahweh,
>   for He has triumphed gloriously,
> The horse and its rider
>   has He hurled into the sea.

This was the foundation of all their great historical experiences, a never-to-be-forgotten deed of Providence. Yahweh had defeated the Egyptians. He had shown that He could save His people from all perils.[10]

In the desert He cared for them and provided them with water and food, in spite of their ungrateful murmurings. In the great vision Yahweh had told Moses that He would bring them out of Egypt to the fertile land of Canaan, and this destination he constantly kept in mind.[11]

Moses secured his brother-in-law Hobab as a guide. At last they were at the border of the land and sent spies to reconnoiter the southern part. When they returned and reported that the land was indeed flowing with milk and honey, but that the inhabitants were strong, some of them veritable giants in stature, and that their cities were fortified, the people were afraid and refused to attempt the invasion. So near their destination, so near the fulfillment of the prophecy, and again it had to be postponed! Yahweh declared that the present generation would not see it.[12]

---

[10] Ex. 12:21a, 27b, 29–34, 37–39; 13:3a, 4, 6, 10–13, 21f.; 14:5f., 10a, 11–14, 19b, 20b, 21b, 24a, 25, 27b, 28b, 30; 15:1.

[11] Ex. 15:22–25a, 27; 17:3, 2b, 7ac; 18:7, 9–11. Certainly it is not to be obtained as to whether J told of happenings at the mountain of God. If he did then very little is preserved. The following are ascribed to him by some scholars: Ex. 19:9, 11–13 (setting bounds); 24:9–11 (the covenant-meal); 33:1–4, 12–23 (the departure). But views differ widely on the source criticism here.

[12] Num. 10:29–33; 11:4–13, 15, 18–24a, 31–35; 12:16; 13:17b, 18b, 19, 22, 27a, 28, 30f.; 14:1c, 3, 8, 9b, 31, 41–45.

When they finally attempted to invade Canaan from the East, they attacked and defeated the Ammonites and Amorites who blocked their way. King Balak of Moab, fearing invasion and defeat by Israel, sent for the famous prophet Balaam, the son of Beor, that he might curse Israel and thus destroy it. But when he came, he could not curse, because Yahweh compelled him to bless. And in his oracles (cf. pp. 14f.) he foretold not only the future prosperity of Israel, but also the coming of David "the star out of Jacob—the sceptre out of Israel," and his conquest of Moab and Edom. The horizon of the ancient prediction was widened and it was sure to be fulfilled. Moab was not attacked. Indeed some Israelites joined the Moabites in sacrificial festivals in honor of their gods, but Yahweh demanded in great anger that the ringleaders should be hanged for this. With the account of the occupation of the East Jordan territory by the Manassites the J material of the Pentateuch comes to an end.[13] Perhaps the so-called "negative account" of the conquest included in Judg. 1:1—2:5 still belongs to it. According to this account, Israel conquered the land, but not all of it; especially the cities and the plains remained in the hands of the Canaanites, because the cities were too strongly fortified, and in the plains Israel could not prevail against their chariotry. The Canaanites were therefore neither completely driven out nor exterminated. Israel settled among them and learned the art of war from these experienced warriors (Judg. 3:2). Nevertheless (in the end) the Canaanites "became subject to taskwork." The great prediction of Gen. 9:26 had been fulfilled: Canaan was Israel's slave. Here J may well have concluded his story.[14] The supposition that he must have carried it further is not convincing. The Priestly document, as we shall see, did not do so either; and in general the epics of the ancient peoples, to which J bears some resemblance, had a limited period in history for their theme.

[13] Num. 21:16-20, 24b, 25-32; 22:3b, 4, 5ac-7, 11, 17f., 22-36a, 37b, 39; 23:28; 24; 25:1b, 2, 3b, 4; 32:39-42.
[14] The belief that JEP run through Joshua and JE, perhaps even through Judges and 1 Samuel, still has its advocates but is being increasingly abandoned in favor of the view first put forward by Martin Noth, *Überlieferungsgeschichtliche Studien*, I, 1943, that the historical books from Joshua through 2 Kings were handed down in a Deuteronomistic work (see pp. 229ff.). The duplications and inconsistencies in their narratives then are explained differently than in Genesis, where the combination of parallel strands is clear.

Even if it ran only to the end of the conquest it was a wonderful work, this story of J. It was the first comprehensive history that had ever been written; even the Greeks had nothing like it till centuries later. The early history of Israel was set in the framework of the history of the world! The vast horizon which takes in the nations of the earth, insofar as the author knew of them, and gives them their place in the descent from earliest mankind, was a historiographical achievement of the first order. And equal in importance was the marshaling of the whole movement of history under one great idea which is stated in the blessings of Noah and Abraham and realized in spite of all sorts of obstacles that retarded and often threatened to frustrate it—because it was a divine idea. Here a deeply religious mind was at work, which thought of history as the working out of the purpose of God. For He was behind the great movements and He ordered events according to His plan. That the worldwide horizon was not maintained all through the story lay in the nature of the author's task. Later when the great world-shaking movements inaugurated by Assyria, Babylonia and Persia came, the prophets, especially the so-called Deutero-Isaiah, thought in universal terms. But the beginning was made by J, who deeply influenced this great prophet of the exile. Of course, he had the material for his history before him, partly in oral, partly in written form. But he ordered it as we have it now.

The historical value of J's material varies. In the primeval period J had of course only myths and legends, for nobody had been present at the creation, and the story of the deluge was ultimately derived from the Babylonian Gilgamesh epic,[15] as a comparison demonstrates. We expect no history in this first period, but stories woven by the poetic imagination. The story of the creation and of the deluge likewise came originally from Babylonia or Assyria, perhaps also the story of the tower of Babel; whether they had come to Israel through the mediation of the Canaanites or more directly when Solomon opened the avenues of commercial and intellectual

[15] The Gilgamesh epic describes the friendship and adventures of the famous ancient heroes Gilgamesh, an early king of Erech (cf. Gen. 10:10), and Engidu, and Gilgamesh's search for eternal life after the death of his friend, in the course of which he comes to his translated ancestor Ut-napishtim, the Babylonian Noah, who tells him the story of the flood in Tablet XI. See *ANET*, 72ff.

intercourse with the East, is not of great importance. In the second or patriarchal period we are still in the epic period. The stories embody valuable reminiscences of tribal history, but these are not always easy to extract. The whole period is described in legends and it is often impossible to reconstruct any real history from them. J brought order into the stories by arranging them as he did, making Abram the ancestor, Isaac his son, Jacob his grandson, and Joseph his great grandson. In the Mosaic period there is more historical foundation and we may say that the oppression in Egypt, the deliverance by Moses, and the marvelous escape at the Sea of Reeds are historical facts, although the history is interwoven with legend.

J was not only a master in planning, arranging, and grouping the whole material, but also in the narration of the individual story. His literary art is exquisite. He gives fresh, lifelike, concrete, and graphic portraiture; the stories move swiftly and are full of interest. No wonder that they have delighted the readers of more than two millennia. We must not forget that the stories as J had received them in oral or written form had been polished for generations, but nevertheless he impressed his literary stamp upon them. In their present form they are his property.[16]

More important than this literary art was the transformation of the popular tales into truly Israelite narratives in which the spirit of the religion of Yahweh dwelt. One of the best illustrations of the molding and transforming activity of the Israelite mind is the story of the deluge, for a comparison with its Babylonian prototype shows not only the remarkable similarity of the two, even in details, but also the striking difference. In the Hebrew story every trace of polytheism and mythology is omitted; it is a moral and monotheistic tale. If we understand J correctly, he was not only a superb his-

[16] Current criticism is inclined to follow Gerhard von Rad in regarding J as dependent on summary formulations made for cultic use, praising the God of Israel for a series of mighty deeds, which gave J the outline for what he narrated in detail. The oldest example of such historical summaries is the so-called "Little Creed" (Deut. 26:5–10). The Psalms 78; 105; 136, provide further instances. J merely needed to follow the topics Exodus, Desert Wanderings, and Occupation of Canaan on which the summaries dwell. He prefaced them with the Patriarchal history and the primeval history. With due recognition of his own contribution he nevertheless stands in a literary tradition leading from the old historical summaries to the completion of the Pentateuch. See von Rad, *Das formgeschichtliche Problem des Hexateuchs*, 1938.

torian and a wonderful literary artist, but also a great teacher of religion. He taught by means of his stories. Yahweh was to him the
one great God, the Creator, the only God for Israel. Yahweh controlled the forces of nature, as the creation and deluge stories show,
and also the forces of history, as the whole trend of J's tales proves.
He is a moral God who demands righteousness, rewards faith and
kindness, innocence and unselfishness, but punishes wickedness and
oppression, and this not only in Israel, but on the whole earth, in
Babel, in Egypt, etc. Such is Israel's God and to Him the people must
be loyal; for He had done everything for them, so that they have
finally become a great and prosperous nation.

It is noteworthy that in telling the ancient stories J did not reject
the various Canaanite elements that had been introduced into Israel's
religion, but he transformed them. Thus the ancient local sanctuaries
of the Canaanites were sacred to Israel not because Baal had lived
and received his worshipers' homage there, but because Yahweh
had appeared there to the ancestors, who then had built altars to
Him there. The sacred places were not the only places where
Yahweh dwelt and worked, for He was not bound to them. He
dwelt in heaven. The sacred trees were not God's dwelling place,
but some were planted by Abram, and the sacred wells were dug by
Isaac. The deity did not live in them, as the Canaanites thought.
When Yahweh appeared to Abram at Hebron, He did not come out
of the tree; nor out of the well at Beerlahairoi when he appeared to
Hagar. The sacred pillars of stone were not Bethels or houses of
God, but memorial or grave stones. But there was no open fight
against these paraphernalia of Canaanite worship—only a quiet reinterpretation, which displaced their old meaning and made them
harmless. Of course, unassimilable ideas were discarded, *e.g.* poly-
theistic notions and female deities. In the story of the visit of the
three men to Abram, anthropomorphic as it is, there are no longer
three deities, as there must have been in the older narrative, but
Yahweh and two angels.

It is not surprising to find that occasionally J did not quite succeed in eliminating every non-Israelite trace. In the story of the
temptation the serpent is no longer a deity, but something uncanny
still clings to it so that even to the modern reader it is not quite like

a mere serpent; in the marriage of the angels with human women the mythical is still shining through. In the jealousy of God lest men become immortal (Gen. 3:22); in His fear that men might become too powerful in their union (Gen. 11:6); in Jacob's wrestling with God (Gen. 32:24f.); in Yahweh's sudden attack upon Moses in the wilderness lodging place (Ex. 4:24); in all these there are elements which cannot easily be harmonized with J's exalted idea of God. But after all, how very little there is of all this, and what a wonderful energy and success in the tranformation of religious ideas are manifest all through J's work!

That J deepened the purely Israelite ideas in these stories is also manifest, e.g., in the story of Cain, where the older conflict between the nonacceptability of cereal sacrifices and the legitimacy of animal sacrifices is thrown into the background entirely, and the moral idea of harboring sinful thoughts and the subsequent mastery of sin in the heart are emphasized, together with man's social obligation of being his brother's keeper. It is true that there is a very pronounced anthropomorphism in some stories, e.g., when God walks in the garden, or visits Abram in the tent and eats a meal there. This does not easily conform to the grand conception of the Creator. But it is a question whether J felt an incongruity here, and we must not forget that anthropomorphic ideas are often a sign of vital religion. More serious is, to our mind, that J did not disapprove of Abram's lie; that he told with evident relish the stories of Jacob's deception of his father and his fraudulent tricks upon Laban; and that he did not omit the story of Lot's incest. True enough, these are elements which belong to a lower level of ethics according to our ideas. But they are quite incidental and cannot dim the glory of this man, to whom we owe admiration and gratitude as historian, literary artist, and religious teacher.

Later some variant or new traditions of the Yahwistic type were inserted in suitable places, so the story of Rebekah in the harem of Abimelech in Gen. 26 and of Judah and Tamar in Gen. 38. More especially certain religious additions were made to heighten the religious quality of a story. Thus the promise was repeated to Abram in Gen. 13:14–17 and to Jacob in Gen. 28:13–16, 19a; in the story of the plagues a series of insertions was made which showed that

they were manifestations of Yahweh's power and designed to prove
His deity and make His name known in all the earth.[17] The most
beautiful of these additions are Jacob's prayer at the river Jabbok
(Gen. 32:10–13) and Moses' intercession in Num. 14:11–24, where
some of the finest religious convictions are expressed. The most significant of them all are Abram's plea for Sodom, in which the problem of solidarity of responsibility and the saving effect of even a
small remnant receives consideration,[18] and the story of the stay at
Sinai and the giving of the law.[19]

[17] Ex. 7:17a; 8:6b, 18b; 9:14–16, 29b; 10:1b, 2.   [18] Gen. 18:17–19, 22b–23a.
[19] Ex. 19:11b–13, 18, 20–25; 24:1f., 9–11; 32:25–29; 33:1, 3, 4a; 34:1–5, 10a, 14,
17, 18a, 19–23, 25–28.

VI

The Elohist

IN the northern kingdom a work quite similar to the Yahwist's great history was prepared, perhaps at the beginning of the eighth century. Here a man of prophetic mind wrote the early Hebrew story from a northern point of view, emphasizing the Israelitic tradition more strongly than the Judean, and presenting it from the standpoint of a believer in theocracy. He did not have the vast sweep of J, nor did he give his story the universal setting in which J had so effectively placed his history of Israel, but he made it more definitely the vehicle of his religious ideas. His name is lost, but he is now generally known as the Elohist, or E, because he used Elohim [1] for God and avoided the proper name Yahweh until the time of Moses, for he believed that it was first revealed to Moses and had been altogether unknown to the patriarchs.

E's story is parallel to J's, but it apparently began with Abram, and did not have the account of early mankind.[2] In three stories which are preserved of Abram we discern at once the peculiar character of E. There is a distinct advance in his theological and ethical views. The story of Sarah in Pharaoh's harem as told by J had left an unfavorable impression of Abram upon the reader. E corrected this in his version (Gen. 20:1–17), which placed her in the harem

---

[1] *Elōhīm* is a plural in form and can mean "gods," as in Ex. 20:3; but the Heb. plural ending *īm* was originally a collective or abstract ending, and so it commonly means "deity." The singular form of Elohim is Eloah. It occurs frequently in Job. The earliest instance is Deut. 32:15.

[2] One prominent scholar, Sigmund Mowinckel, has argued that there is E material, instead of a younger stratum of J, in Gen. 1–11. Several others, Wilhem Volz and Wilhem Rudolph, have denied that E represents a continuous strand, but that too has remained a minority view.

of King Abimelech at Gerar and emphasized that nothing had happened to her, because God had warned the king early enough in a
dream. From J's story it appeared that Abram had told a lie when he
said that Sarah was his sister. E pointed out in his version that he
had not really lied, because Sarah was indeed his sister, the daughter
of Abram's father, though not of his mother. Again, the present
which Abram received from the king is here definitely declared to
be for Sarah's vindication in the eyes of all who are with her. Abram
is thus cleared of every stain, and even declared to be a prophet, at
whose intercession Abimelech and his harem were healed! In J's
story of Hagar's flight Abram had not acted admirably either. E
therefore showed in his version (Gen. 21:8–21) how much Sarah's
demand to expel Hagar and her son pained the patriarch; how he
was comforted by God, who told him to obey Sarah and promised
that He would greatly bless Hagar's son; and how Abram gave
Hagar a bottle of water and bread for the journey when he sent her
away! The finer feeling of E shows itself also in the moving way in
which he describes Hagar's despair in the desert, when the water was
gone and the boy cried, and she did not know what to do. This same
quality of sympathy is also manifest in E's wonderful story of the
sacrifice of Isaac (Gen. 22:1–14, 19). But most important here is the
teaching that while God demands absolute obedience, even if it involves the sacrifice of the dearest that a man possesses, He will not
have human offerings at all. His demand of Abram that he sacrifice
Isaac was only for the purpose of testing him. For the redemption
of the first-born sons He had provided an animal substitute. The
story clearly opposes the inhuman practice of sacrificing the first-
born son, which seems to be presupposed even in the ancient law in
the Book of the Covenant, Ex. 22:29. E was a teacher who knew
the effectiveness of a well-told story in religious education.

Of Isaac E seems to have had no special tales besides the sacrifice
and his part in the Jacob and Esau stories. But here we note again
revision of the earlier tradition on ethical grounds. In J Jacob and
Esau had struggled even in their mother's womb, Jacob trying to
get the upper hand in order to become the first-born. E told instead how Esau sold his birthright to Jacob, who thus became legally
the first-born (Gen. 25:29–34)! In J the eating of the aphrodisiac

mandrakes had enabled Rachel to conceive. But E said it was due
to God's favor (Gen. 30:22). E could not tolerate the sharp practices of Jacob which J had told so gleefully and as a result of which
Jacob had become so wealthy. So he took pains to point out that
it was God's special blessing which took the sheep from Laban and
gave them to Jacob, and even had Leah and Rachel testify that they
were fully convinced of this (Gen. 31:4–16). How honest Jacob
was! and with what righteous indignation he could scold Laban as
a consequence! Yet here a contrary motive, stronger than the desire
to present the ancestors in the purest light, led E to tell of a deception that Rachel practiced upon her father (Gen. 31:19, 32–35).
She had stolen her father's teraphim! And when he later demanded
them back from Jacob and searched for them all through the camp,
Rachel sat on them and excused herself for not rising by saying that
she was menstruating! Here E wanted to throw contempt on these
household gods, which a woman had stolen and upon which she
sat in her supposed condition of ritual impurity! The humor of the
situation was effective. Having laughed over the teraphim that had
thus been treated, the reader could no longer take them quite so
seriously as before. One of the most effective arguments, humor,
was thus used by E, when it served his end. Though Rachel had
stolen and lied, E has no word of censure for her. As for Jacob,
before he came to Bethel, he collected all the idols and amulets in
his camp and buried them under the oak near Shechem (Gen. 35:
1–4). E had no antagonism to the local sanctuaries. Jacob set up a
pillar at Bethel and poured oil upon the top of it (28:18) and later
built an altar there (35:7). He buried Deborah under the oak below
Bethel (35:8). But pillars and trees or posts were only memorials
for E, he did not believe that they were the seats of the deity. God
to E dwelt in heaven, His angels ascend to it by a stairway (28:12).
E wanted to supersede the popular belief by his own higher view.
We perceive his method of teaching and admire him for it.

E's masterpiece is his version of the Joseph story. It is a well-knit
tale, utilizing materials of tradition and popular lore. The theme
is stated in the words of Joseph to his brothers,

Ye meant evil against me, but God meant it for good, to bring to pass,
as it is this day, to save much people alive (50:20). And now be not

grieved, nor angry with yourselves, for God sent me before you to preserve life. For these two years has the famine been in the land: and there are yet five years, in which there shall be neither ploughing nor harvest. And God sent me before you to preserve you a remnant in the earth, and to save you alive by a great deliverance. So now it was not you that sent me hither but God. (45:5–8)

This is a fine statement of belief in the silent activity of God in the affairs of men, guiding and controlling all in accordance with His purpose. God's providence rules and overrules in the life of the individual, for to E Joseph was here an individual; he was not the tribe, even though tribal memories are contained in the story.

In the Moses story E preserved a number of traditions that J did not give. After the recital of God's overruling providence which saved the child Moses from certain death and put him into the care of Pharaoh's daughter (Ex. 1:15—2:10) the most significant story is told of God's self-revelation to Moses at Horeb, the mountain of God in Midian, where Moses for the first time learned the name of the God who had chosen him as His agent in the deliverance of Israel from Egypt.[3] To E the Yahweh religion of Israel began with Moses; he did not believe that the fathers had worshiped Yahweh before. In this he was probably correct; their religion had been an "El" religion or polydemonism. With Moses the religion of Yahweh commenced. To J, as we saw, Yahweh worship had begun with Adam's grandson Enosh. We have here the differing traditions of the Leah and of the Rachel tribes. Judah had known Yahweh from of old, Joseph learned to know Him through Moses.

On his way to Egypt Moses met his brother Aaron, who became his associate in the work of deliverance according to E (4:27f.; 5: 1, 2, 4). At the time of his first vision Yahweh had given to Moses a miracle-working rod, which he used in bringing on the plagues and for the crossing of the Sea of Reeds,[4] where E ascribed the song of Moses to Miriam, Aaron's sister (15:20f.) whom J had not mentioned. At Horeb Moses smote the rock with his rod and procured water for the people, and at Rephidim he held his rod in his hand during the entire battle against the Amalekites until Joshua, who

[3] Ex. 3:1, 4b, 6, 9b–15, 19–22; 4:17f., 20b.
[4] Ex. 7:15, 17b, 20b, 23; 9:22, 23a, 24a, 25a, 31, 35; 10:12, 13a, 14a, 15b, 20–23, 27; 11:1–3; 13:17–19; 14:7, 9a, 10b, 15a, 16a, 19a, 20a, 24b.

was the commanding general here and who also elsewhere in E is of great importance, had won the victory. Aaron and Hur had steadied Moses' arm. There was no word of intercession spoken, the miracle-working rod alone had won the victory! [5]

At the Horeb encampment Moses' father-in-law, Jethro, visited him, offered sacrifices to Yahweh, shared in the communion meal with Moses, Aaron, and the elders, and on the next day showed Moses how to organize the administration of justice (Ex. 18 except 8, 9–11). This is one of the most important traditions of E, and especially noteworthy in that it admitted that judicial organization in Israel went back ultimately to a Midianite priest, and not to Moses. Immediately following this is E's story of the great legislation at Mount Horeb and the giving of the Decalogue. The code of laws embodied in the Book of the Covenant on the basis of which the people made a solemn covenant with Yahweh (Ex. 20:22—23:19) was probably not in the original story of E, but only inserted later.

In the story of the Golden Calf, which Aaron fashioned from the golden earrings of the people, E made splendid use of the opportunity of showing the heinousness as well as the folly of worshiping gods made with hands and of attributing to such a calf the great act of deliverance from Egypt (Ex. 32:1–6, 15–24). In his anger Moses broke the sacred tables of the law and E has no word of rebuke for this, because his anger was justified. E's keen sense of irony is seen in the answer of Aaron to Moses,

> Let not the anger of my lord wax hot, thou knowest the people that they are set on evil. For they said to me, "Make us gods, which shall go before us: for as for this Moses, the man that brought us up out of the land of Egypt, we know not what has become of him." And I said to them, "Whosoever has any gold, let them break it off." So they gave it me, and I cast it into the fire, and there came out this calf. (Ex. 32:22–24)

The *naiveté* of this explanation of Aaron is significant. Again as in the case of Rachel the readers or hearers must have laughed, and having once laughed at the golden calf, they found it hard to take the golden calves in the temples at Bethel and Dan as seriously as before. E's humor had spoiled their sacred significance for them, and that was his intention!

[5] Ex. 17:1b, 2a, 4–6, 7b*, 8–16.

Sent away from Mount Horeb by the indignant God, the people
were led by the ark of Yahweh in which His presence manifested
itself. E has preserved the ancient signals used with it (Num. 10:
33–36; cf. p. 3). Murmurings of the people were punished at Ta-
berah (Num. 11:1–3) and the rebellion of Miriam and Aaron was
visited terribly, at least upon Miriam, but on Moses' intercession her
leprosy was removed (12:1, 9–15).[6]

After cravenly hesitating at first to invade Canaan on the report
of the spies, but stung by the reproof of Yahweh, who declared
that none of the present generation except Caleb would see the
land, the people attacked the Amalekites and Canaanites against
Moses' command and suffered a disastrous defeat (Num. 14:39–45).
Obedience to Yahweh and to His prophet is one of E's important
teachings. Dathan and Abiram also with all their families suffered
death, because they dared to rebel against Moses' authority (Num.
16).[7] Israel's request for permission to pass through Edom's territory was refused, so they turned south to skirt the land of Edom
(20:14–18, 21a, 22a). On the way from Kadesh fiery serpents were
sent among them because of their murmurings against God and
Moses. But Moses interceded for them, when they repented, and
was instructed to make a serpent of brass, which would bring healing to everyone who looked at it when he was bitten (21:4b–9).
This was a case of healing by sympathetic magic, a practice well
known among many peoples. The significant part of the story however is that E here tried to counteract the worship of the brazen
serpent, an ancient idol which had found its place in the temple at
Jerusalem, by reinterpreting its meaning. It was indeed quite old,
he admitted, for it went back to Moses. But he only made it as a
symbol. It was not divine, nor did it represent a god. Yahweh used
it as a means of healing those that had been bitten by serpents in the
wilderness. There was therefore no reason whatever to pay homage
to it. E's reinterpretation did not have the desired effect, it still
permitted the people to look upon it in the expectation of being
healed from their present ills, and they continued to offer incense to

[6] Originally Aaron must have been punished too, but that is now omitted because of his eminence among the priests.

[7] The analysis of J and E in this story is not certain. Probably vv. 1b, 2a, 12,
14b, 25, 27b, 32a, 33b, 34 are from E.

it. The spell was broken only by its destruction under King Hezekiah (2 Ki. 18:4).

For the story of Israel's march E gave extracts from the Book of
the Wars of Yahweh (cf. p. 1) and told of the defeat of Sihon,
King of the Amorites, and the occupation of his country; and of
Balak's fruitless attempt to destroy Israel through the prophecies
of the famous Balaam (Num. 21–24 in part). In the punishment of
those that had taken part in Moabite sacrificial festivals, E demanded
that every one who had joined himself to Baal Peor, not only the
ringleaders, should be executed (25:3a, 5). E's loyalty to Yahweh
was intense, his antagonism against other gods most bitter.

It is controversial whether E's account of the death of Moses and
the appointment of Joshua is preserved in the closing chapters of
Deuteronomy. These, as noted above, are now more generally ascribed to the Deuteronomistic historical work. A high opinion of
Moses written in the spirit of E but probably not by E himself,
and comparable to that of Deut. 34:10 appears in the story of
Miriam's and Aaron's rebellion:

> Hear now My words;
> If there be a prophet among you,
> I Yahweh make Myself known to him in visions,
> I speak with him in dreams.
> My servant Moses is not so;
> He is entrusted with all My house,
> With him I speak mouth to mouth,
> Plainly, and not in dark speeches,
> And the form of Yahweh he beholds. (Num. 12:6ff.)

Quite in line with this is the story of the seventy elders who received something of the spirit of Moses and began to prophesy,
and of the two elders that had remained in the camp and prophesied
too. The ideal of E is voiced by Moses, "Would that all Yahweh's
people were prophets, that Yahweh would put His spirit upon
them" [8] (Num. 11:16f., 24b–30).

As in the case of the Yahwist it is doubtful whether the Elohist's

---

[8] Since this story tells of Moses' installing these elders as judges at the command of Yahweh, while E himself had told of the judicial organization as
introduced by Moses at the suggestion of Jethro his father-in-law, it was
probably inserted later.

strand continued beyond Numbers. Scholars are currently much divided in this matter. One thing is certain: the editing of the Books of Joshua, Judges, Samuel is of a different nature than that of Genesis, Exodus, Numbers. Much that was formerly assigned to the Elohist can perhaps be attributed to the Deuteronomist.

Even if one confines E's strand to the Pentateuch he was a wonderful teacher.[9] Like J he was an ardent worshiper of Yahweh and a thorough believer in Israel's obligation of exclusive loyalty to him. That spirit he wished to inculcate in his readers too. He attacked the worship at the local sanctuaries as little as J, and accepted the various festivals and cultic practices, and all sorts of Canaanitic institutions. He was quite friendly to the priesthood, as his interest in Aaron, their legendary ancestor, shows. In the transformation of the ancient narrative material, however, he went further than J. His moral consciousness was more sensitive and refined, so he qualified Abram's deliberate lie and explained Jacob's wealth as not due to his sharp practices but to the blessing of God. His more advanced theology made him shun the naive anthropomorphic methods of God's revelation that J still used in his stories. In E, therefore, God no longer appeared in person, but revealed Himself in a vision or a dream, or by one angel or more. He had His special organs of revelation. Abram was a prophet, Miriam a prophetess, the seventy elders were endowed with the spirit of prophecy. But the greatest of them all was Moses, with whom God alone spoke face to face; there was none like him. To E there was a progress of divine revelation in history. The forefathers beyond the River were idolaters. Abram became God's prophet. But the full revelation of God was not given until Moses, to whom God revealed for the first time His name Yahweh. Thus E did not use this name before Moses. In this he held fast the memory of the polydemonistic character of the religion before Moses. He told history not merely for its own sake, but as a means of religious instruction; he made it more definitely than J the vehicle of religious truth and inserted therefore more of a distinctly religious character and more of the miraculous. He was a

[9] Perhaps the credit belongs not to E as a person but to the prophetic school of which he is a representative. Realization of the broader basis behind this approach relieves one of the necessities of supposing that such a chapter as 1 Sam. 15 must have been written by E.

thorough believer in the theocratic form of government and showed the inherent wickedness of the monarchy. Great teacher that he was, E used not only the story but also the direct method of command and prohibition by law, and the argumentative and hortatory method of prophetic address. If only he could instill the truth in his people's minds, if only he could make his people more loyal to Yahweh!

E prepared his work about 750 B.C. After the fall of the Northern Kingdom in 722, Judah fell heir to Israel's name and literary treasures. For E the Judeans had their own parallel Yahwistic history. But E had so much additional material and especially such a strong prophetic tendency that it was felt that it must be preserved by all means. So it was decided, perhaps around 700 B.C. or a little later, to combine them in a single history JE, which was given a pan-Israelitic slant. Scholars have recently begun to give the redactor of this compilation, hitherto called R^{JE}, a special designation: *the Jehovist*. For the period from the creation to Abraham there was only the Judean document. From Abraham on both documents were woven together. For the Abraham stories J served as the basis and the E stories were inserted; but as the redactor proceeded he made more and more use of E; thus in the Joseph story E is the basis, and while in the Exodus story J and E are at first almost equally used, E becomes more and more predominant in the Sinai sections. This was only natural, for the prophetic element is stronger in E and its pedagogic value seemed to the Jehovist to be greater than that of J. The work of compilation was done with great skill. Sometimes both stories were placed side by side without abridgement as, *e.g.*, the stories of Sarah's peril and Abraham's deception (Gen. 12 J; 20 E); sometimes they were woven together into a single story, now J now E forming the basis into which the variant traditions were worked as, *e.g.*, in the story of how Joseph came to Egypt (Gen. 37). Occasionally it was necessary for the redactor to add certain sentences of his own in order to make room for the variant story or to harmonize both, *e.g.*, Gen. 16:9 in J's story of Hagar's flight, for Hagar had to be brought back in order to fit into E's story (Gen. 20). Again, the Jehovist added matter of his own in order to emphasize certain ideas, *e.g.*, by reiterating the promise of Israel's great future (Gen. 22:15–18; 26:3b, 4f.). But for all this he treated the stories both of J and of E with much reverence and left them pretty much as they had been handed down. This is fortunate for us and remarkable for him, for his own religious ideas were in several respects more advanced even than those of E. If he had radically revised the stories in the interest of his own higher religious conceptions, many valuable and interesting survivals of earlier stages of religious development would have been altogether lost to us.

VII

Amos and Hosea

A NEW epoch not only in literature but in religion began
with the rise of the literary prophets, for they did not merely produce a new class of literature, but ushered in the greatest movement
in the spiritual history of mankind. It was a great day for religion,
when at a harvest feast in Bethel, in the reign of Jeroboam II, about
760 B.C. Amos surprised the festive throng by chanting a funeral song
of Israel:

> The virgin Israel is fallen,
> she shall no more rise,
> Prostrate she lies on her ground,
> none raises her up. (Amos 5:1)

Nothing could have been more startling to his listeners than the
announcement, which he then made, that Yahweh Himself would
deal the deathblow to His people. How could He, who was so completely bound together with Israel that His very existence depended
on that of His people, destroy them? It would have meant His own
destruction too, for He would no longer be known and worshiped,
His religion would be extinct with Israel's death. But Amos asserted, with irresistible spiritual authority, that in spite of her national prosperity under Jeroboam's splendid reign Israel was doomed
by Yahweh Himself.

How did Amos gain this conviction? He was not a professional
prophet but a plain shepherd in Tekoa, some ten miles south of
Jerusalem in Judah. He also practiced tending sycamore trees, per-

haps in the Jericho neighborhood.[1] His mind was wonderfully clear,
his moral nature finely developed, his spiritual sensitiveness singularly alert. He lived on the rim of the dreadful wilderness of Judah.
In the silence of the desert he may have meditated on the future of
the northern kingdom, pondered till a great fear came upon him, a
dark presentiment of impending disaster; he brooded over it until
he was in the ecstatic state, where his feelings crystallized into a
vision of a locust plague, which threatened to destroy Israel by caus-
ing starvation. He interceded with Yahweh, and Yahweh relented.

Thus the Lord Yahweh showed me: and, behold, there was a brood
of locusts in the beginning of the shooting up of the latter growth; and
lo, it was the latter growth after the king's mowings. And it came to pass
that, when they were about to devour completely the herbage of the
land, then I said, O Lord Yahweh, forgive, I beseech Thee: how shall
Jacob stand? for he is small. Yahweh repented concerning this: It shall
not be, said Yahweh. (7:1-3)

Again it came, his fear would not be quieted: another vision of
destruction! Once more it was averted by his intercession.

Thus the Lord Yahweh showed me: and, behold, the Lord Yahweh
called to contend by fire; and it devoured the great deep, and would
have eaten up the land. Then said I, O Lord Yahweh, cease, I beseech
Thee: how shall Jacob stand? for he is small. Yahweh repented concerning this: This also shall not be, said the Lord Yahweh. (7:4-6)

Such intercession already reveals the consciousness of a special
relation to Yahweh, as in the case of Abraham, when he interceded
for Sodom (Gen. 18:22f.). But when Yahweh reveals himself in
visions it is for a purpose. Amos does not relate at what occasion he
was given a direct command to go to Israel to prophesy; but he al-
ludes to it in 7:15, and once speaks of the compulsion that rests upon
a prophet.

> Does a lion roar in the forest,
>   when he has no prey?
> Does a young lion cry out of his den,
>   if he has taken nothing?

[1] Sycamores do not grow in the high altitude of Tekoa, but require the
warmer climate of the Jordan valley (Luke 19:4). Presumably Amos sought
seasonal employment there. The tending involved slitting of the fig-like fruit
to hasten its ripening.

Does a bird fall upon the earth,
   where no trap is set for it?
Does a snare spring up from the ground,
   and has taken nothing at all?
Is the trumpet blown in the city,
   and the people are not afraid?
Does evil befall a city,
   and Yahweh has not done it?
The lion has roared,
   who will not fear?
The Lord Yahweh has spoken,
   who can but prophesy? (3:4–6, 8)

Amos went to the northern kingdom, and what he saw there, at
Samaria and elsewhere, showed him the reasons for Yahweh's anger.
He saw the fearful social corruption of the people, the oppression
of the poor, the revelries of the rich, the debasing immoral practices
carried on in connection with the worship of Yahweh at the various
sanctuaries, and with it all a sense of shamelessness and arrogance.
He castigated men in the name of Yahweh for these sins.

Three further visions of Amos are reported. It seems probable
that he received them during his sojourn in the northern kingdom.
The finality in the conviction of the coming judgment suggests
that experience of the unrepentant attitude he encountered elicited
them. The first uses the figure of the wall built out of plumb.

Thus He showed me: and, behold, the Lord stood beside a wall made
by a plumb-line, with a plumb-line in his hand. And Yahweh said to me,
Amos, what seest thou? And I said, A plumb-line. Then said the Lord,
Behold, I am setting a plumb-line in the midst of My people Israel; I
will not again pardon them any more; and the high places of Isaac shall
be desolate, and the sanctuaries of Israel shall be laid waste; and I will rise
against the house of Jeroboam with the sword. (7:7–9)

As a wall that is crooked *must* fall, so a nation that is corrupt *must*
perish. The same refusal of Yahweh to exercise further patience is
expressed in the vision of the basket of fruit.

Thus the Lord Yahweh showed me: and, behold, a basket of summer
fruit. And He said, Amos, what seest thou? And I said, A basket of summer fruit. Then said Yahweh to me, The end is come upon My people
Israel; I will not again pardon them any more. (8:1f.)

In the Hebrew this involves a pun based on the close similarity of
the words "summer-fruit" (*qayiṣ*) and "end" (*qēṣ*).

The last vision was clearly seen at or after a visit to an Israelite
temple—no doubt the one at Bethel.

I saw the Lord standing beside the altar: and He said, I will smite the
capitals, that the thresholds shake; and I will kill with a crash all of them;
and I will slay the last of them with the sword: there shall not one of
them flee away, and there shall not one of them escape. Though they dig
into Sheol, thence shall My hand take them; and though they climb up
to heaven, thence will I bring them down. And though they hide themselves in the top of Carmel, I will search and take them out thence; and
though they be hid from My sight in the bottom of the sea, thence will I
command the serpent, and it shall bite them. And though they go into
captivity before their enemies, thence will I command the sword, and
it shall slay them: and I will set Mine eyes upon them for evil, and not for
good. (9:1–4)

Here the destruction of the temple by Yahweh himself is foreseen.
If Amos related this vision in the temple in addressing the public
one cannot be surprised at what the brief piece of a biographical report relates:

Then Amaziah the priest of Beth-el sent to Jeroboam, king of Israel,
saying, Amos has conspired against thee in the midst of the house of
Israel: the land is not able to bear all his words. For thus Amos says,
Jeroboam shall die by the sword, and Israel shall surely be led away captive out of his land. Also Amaziah said to Amos, O thou seer, go, flee
thou away into the land of Judah and there eat bread, and prophesy there:
but prophesy not again any more at Beth-el; for it is the king's sanctuary,
and it is a royal house. Then answered Amos, and said to Amaziah, I am no
prophet, nor prophet's son; but a herdsman, and a dresser of sycamore-
trees: and Yahweh took me from following the flock, and Yahweh said
to me, Go, prophesy to My people Israel. Now therefore hear thou the
word of Yahweh: Thou sayest, Prophesy not against Israel, and drop not
(thy word) against the house of Isaac; therefore thus says Yahweh:
  Thy wife shall be a harlot in the city,
  And thy sons and thy daughters shall fall by the sword,
  And thy land shall be divided by line;
  And thou thyself shall die in a land that is unclean,
  And Israel shall surely go into exile away from his land. (7:10–17)

The high priest Amaziah thus drove Amos from Bethel, but the message lived because it was vindicated in 721. Perhaps he recorded the

revelations he had received himself; but more probably, faithful followers made several collections which later were combined.

It is a short book: clear, easily understood, arranged in three sections. After the brief motto comes the prophecy of Yahweh's judgment of the neighboring nations and of Israel—a rhetorical masterpiece of great power (ch. 1f.). The middle section (3–6) contains a series of oracles, grouped according to identical introductions, "Hear this word" and "Woe to," all dealing with Yahweh's absolute righteousness and Israel's certain doom on account of her social corruption. The last section (7–9:8a) gives a record of his visions and of his experience at Bethel, besides various other utterances.[2]

We note with astonishment the excellence of Amos' literary style. All his addresses are in clear rhythmic lines, usually grouped in strophes. This is characteristic of all the great prophets, not only of Amos. In the exaltation of the prophet's spirit the words flow from his lips in rhythmic regularity. It is a well-recognized fact not confined to the Hebrews, that there is a kinship between the prophet and the poet. In Amos poetic power was combined with rhetorical skill. In his great address against the foreign nations he used solemn and impressive refrains at the beginning and the end of each strophe. He began with the hostile neighbors, scored their sins, and predicted punishment to one after another, when suddenly, after intoning the same terrible opening refrain, he turned on Israel, denounced her social corruption, and foretold her certain doom:

> *Thus says Yahweh,*
> *For three transgressions of* ISRAEL,
>   *yea for four, I will not revoke the punishment:*
> Because they have sold the righteous for silver,
>   and the needy for a pair of shoes, etc. (2:6)

Amos grasped with singular clearness a truth of fundamental importance: the righteousness of God. This brought him into conflict with popular religion along several lines. In the first place there was his emphasis upon upright conduct as opposed to mere

---

[2] Later the book received several nonauthentic additions, an oracle against Judah among the oracles against the nations (2:4f.); a series of "doxologies" celebrating Yahweh's rule in nature (4:13; 5:8f.; 9:5f.); and a prediction of the glorious future of Judah (9:8b–15).

cult. The priests and the people believed that Yahweh's requirement was the cult and that He would be pleased with them, if they
fulfilled this. Amos insisted that God's sole requirement was social
justice. God had never required any sacrificial cult from His people at all—only righteousness, nothing else! As for the cult,

> I hate, I despise your feasts,
>   and I take no delight in your solemn assemblies.
> Yea, though ye offer Me your burnt-offerings
>   and meal-offerings, I will not accept them;
>   neither will I regard the peace offerings of your fat beasts.
> Take away from Me the noise of thy songs,
>   for I will not hear the melody of thy viols:
> *But let justice roll down as waters,*
>   *and righteousness as an overflowing stream!*
> Did ye bring unto Me sacrifices and offerings in the wilderness
>   forty years, O house of Israel? (5:21–25)

The answer is, of course, No! Even in the wonderful days of the
early relationship between Yahweh and Israel no sacrifices were
brought. Well, then, Yahweh cannot be found in mere external
worship with all its magical devices. His grace can be only experienced in the steady pursuit of the moral ideal. The emphasis is altogether on law and righteousness. "Seek *good*, and not evil, that ye
may live" stands side by side with "Seek ye *Me* and ye shall live."

This extreme attitude toward the entire cult was rooted in the
polemical nature of Amos' prophecy. The question never occurred
to him how, from his point of view, religion should be organized.
He saw the injustice and oppression, the greed and brutality, the
luxury and debauchery, in short, the violation of the common moral
law by a people who were most zealous in the performance of all
religious rites and ceremonies, giving much to God in order to get
much from Him. He revolted against this practice and attacked the
cult which had benumbed the moral feeling and perception of the
people. Not gifts to God, but justice to men! was his cry. How can
men be so bare of all feeling of delicacy and shame as the father and
son are who carry on their debauch in the name of religion at the
cost of the suffering poor (2:7f.)? How can Yahweh endure a
nation whose sleek rich women spur their husbands on to oppress the

poor and to grind out of them the means for frivolous and luxurious banquets (4:1–3)? Yahweh is righteous and punishes injustice with relentless anger.

The second point in Amos' message was that Yahweh's requirement of righteousness is universal. Not only Israel but all the nations of the world must heed his will; else they will be punished by the righteous Yahweh, who visits everywhere the violations of the moral law. Yahweh is not only Israel's God, but the God of the whole world and interested in all the nations.

> "Are ye not as the children of the Ethiopians unto me,
>   O children of Israel?" says Yahweh.
> "Have I not brought up Israel out of the land of Egypt,
>   And the Philistines from Caphtor
> And the Aramaeans from Kir?" (9:7)

The national history of Israel's hated enemies also has been guided by Yahweh! We note with glad amazement how broad Amos' idea of God has become. Moab, he declared, would be punished, because they had "burned the bones of the king of Edom into lime" (2:1). A nationalist would have rejoiced over this brutality that violated deep-rooted instincts of humanity, for Edom was Israel's enemy. Of course, Amos ran counter to the cherished popular belief in Israel's peculiar connection with Yahweh. He knew it well. But assuming for a moment that "you only have I known of all the families of the earth," he drew this startling consequence, *"therefore I will visit upon you all your iniquities"* (3:1). If Israel claims the prerogative of special intimacy, it must bear special responsibility. The relation between Yahweh and Israel is entirely moral and will be dissolved, if the moral conditions are not fulfilled.

In the third place, along with this universal outlook went Amos' reaction against the popular hope of the "Day of Yahweh." Ardently the people looked for the day, when Yahweh Himself would triumph over all His and Israel's enemies. Amos rudely shattered this belief.

> Woe to you that desire the day of Yahweh!
>   Wherefore would you have the day of Yahweh?
> It is darkness and not light! (5:18)

There is a sternness in Amos which was born out of moral indignation. He was a man of steel, whose indomitable spirit no opposition could break. But we must not forget that he pleaded twice with Yahweh for little Jacob (7:2, 5). And we may well ask whether he actually had no hope for Israel, although his messages contain nothing but unrelieved doom. Only once he refers to the possibility that a few might perhaps be saved.

> Hate the evil, and love the good,
> and establish justice in the gate:
> *it may be* that Yahweh, the God of hosts,
> will be gracious to *the remnant* of Joseph. (5:15)

Did he ever elaborate on this hope? It may be! But if he did so his predictions of such a nature have not survived. It is most probably to a later age that we owe the conclusion (9:8b–15) which now follows upon his messages like the dawn upon the gloomy night.

Amos may justly be called the prophet of righteousness, for that expresses his great contribution to religion. The moral character of Yahweh had, of course, been recognized before. Amos himself did not believe that he had said anything new. He assumed the knowledge of the divine law in all men, and its implications as well. But nobody had ever seen so clearly what it involved or dared to be so thoroughgoing in the application of this truth. It is the outstanding feature of Amos' practical monotheism. Not because Yahweh is almighty, nor because He is the one great Cause behind the phenomena of the world, but because He is righteous and visits unrighteousness everywhere, did He come to be regarded as the one God.

Only a few years after Amos, Hosea began to prophesy. Since he lived in Israel, the dating by Judean kings given in the opening verse must be due to later hands. The belated mention of Jeroboam II of Israel may be original, but incomplete; it indicates that he began to prophesy under that ruler. Continuance to the time of Hezekiah is improbable.

Gentle and tender, warm-hearted and loving, Hosea stood in sharp contrast to the rugged, mighty prophet of the South. But he ranks with him among the greatest by reason of his spiritual insight. He also was a prophet of doom. The dynasty of Jehu, founded on blood, will fall! Yahweh will no longer pity His people but reject them forever! Thus he proclaimed, in harmony with Amos. Alongside this runs a hopeful line of prediction. It grows out of the story of his marriage.

When the collection of Hosea's prophecies was made, the subject matter dealing with or reflecting his marriage was put in three important chapters at the head of the book. Perhaps this was even the original nucleus of the book to which the other prophecies of ch. 4–14 were then added. The first chapter speaks of him in the third person and thus seems to be biographical; the second contains a group of oracles born out of his experience; the third is composed in the first person and thus is autobiographical.

The relation of the autobiographical chapter to the biographical chapter is controversial. The present text makes this a second marriage (by adding the word "again"). But this seems most improbable, since the whole symbolism requires monogamy. To suppose that ch. 3 is a sequel to ch. 1 and concerns Hosea's disciplining of the mother of his children is to disregard the clear statements about a marriage in v. 2. Chs. 1 and 3 are parallels.

The first person report is that of Hosea himself, but relates only the initial stage of the marriage. He was told to wed a woman who was living in fornication and who would be an adulteress. He married her knowing what she was, and the first prophetic sign was that he quarantined her for a time from any sexual intercourse. The final words of v. 3 require a restoration of two words in the Hebrew "And morever I [will not come in] unto thee." This treatment is given the woman as a sign of what Yahweh is going to do with his people:

> For many days shall the children of Israel dwell
>   Without king and without captain,
> Without sacrifice and stone pillar
>   Without ephod and without teraphim.[3]

The third-person account of ch. 1 is written from a later perspective. The original sign of 3:4 having served its purpose, other, more recent signs loomed larger; the first required no retelling since it had already been written down by the prophet. This biographical

[3] Verse 5 is a later addition. Cf. note 6.

account, however, gives the name of the woman Hosea married
and records the birth of her children, at the same time implying that
she lived in adultery. It must be borne in mind that the prophet
was acting on Yahweh's orders in wedding that kind of a woman to
symbolize Israel, which was that kind of a people—disloyal to
Yahweh. It is Yahweh, too, who commands that the three children
receive those ominous names, which made them living embodiments
of warning.

And she conceived, and bore him a son. And Yahweh said to him, Call
his name Jezreel; for yet a little while, and I will avenge the blood of
Jezreel upon the house of Jehu, and will cause the kingdom of the house
of Israel to cease. And it shall come to pass at that day, that I will break
the bow of Israel in the valley of Jezreel. And she conceived again, and
bore a daughter. And He said to him, Call her name Lo-ruhamah,[4] for I
will no more have mercy upon the house of Israel, that I should in any
wise pardon them. Now when she had weaned Lo-ruhamah, she conceived, and bore a son. And he said, Call his name Lo-ammi,[5] for ye are
not My people, and I will not be your God. (1:2a, 3–6, 8)

The second chapter is born out of the prophet's experience, yet
does not deal directly with it. One may, perhaps, legitimately infer
that Hosea loved his wayward wife. But the concern of his prophesying is with Israel, figuratively imagined as an adulterous spouse
and Yahweh imagined as husband. In the powerful oracle of 2:2ff.
MT 2:4ff.) where the children are called upon to contend (not
"plead") with their mother, the thought is hardly of Hosea's children but of the children of Israel, for the mention of what the lovers
give the mother shows the national background. The lovers are the
Baals to whom disloyal Israel is attributing her grain, wine, and oil.
The passage reflects on 3:3 but imaginatively pursues that situation
further to a repentance of the spouse and a return to the husband.
It is particularly significant that an element of hope enters in. After
a period of punishment Yahweh will lure Israel into the wilderness
and there, where they had spent the time of their first love, will
He woo her once more, and when she turns to Him again and really

---

[4] This means, she that has not obtained mercy. Later postexilic editions added
v. 7.
[5] This means "not My people." Postexilic editors added v. 10f. (in the Hebrew, 2:1–3).

comes to know Him and to see how vain and empty her love for others has been, He will restore her to her own land, and a wonderful fertility of it will accompany the reestablishment of the love relationship between Yahweh and Israel. Hosea still believed in the necessity of punishment; Israel will have to go into exile, but it will not be due to Yahweh's vindictiveness but to His redemptive purpose: her sin will not merely be punished, but inwardly conquered. The stern prophet of doom has become the prophet of love, a love that is faithful in spite of the loved one's faithlessness, a love that punishes, but does so in order to redeem and restore. Perhaps he entertained a similar hope of gaining the undivided love of his wife, and that hope may have led him to the further step of hope for Israel.

In the second part of the book (4–14) there is a collection of further utterances of Hosea.[6] They are mostly brief pieces, put together without any definite scheme of arrangement. In one of the most moving passages he does not shrink from transferring the terrible struggle of his own heart to the heart of Yahweh:

> How shall I give thee up, Ephraim?
>> how shall I cast thee off, Israel?
> How shall I make thee as Admah?
>> how shall I set thee as Zeboim? [7]
> My heart is turned within Me,
>> My compassions are kindled together.
> I will not execute the fierceness of Mine anger,
>> I will not return to destroy Ephraim:
> For I am God, and not man,
>> the Holy One in thy midst, and not mortal. (11:8f.)

The whole second part of the book of Hosea is poetry. His imagination is vivid, his style most picturesque. At times he moves us by the exquisite tenderness of his feelings, at times he carries us away in his passionate anger, again he startles us by the originality

[6] We have the book of Hosea in a Judean edition. Two Judean editors made slight modifications and additions. The earlier one made the messages to apply to Judah as well as to Israel (5:10, 12, 13, 14; 6:4, 11; 8:14; 10:11; 12:2). The later one added hopeful words for Judah (1:7, 10) and some favorable references (3:5 "and David their king," 4:15a; 11:12b).

[7] Admah and Zeboim are closely linked with Sodom and Gomorrah, cf. Deut. 29:22.

and unexpected beauty of his thought and diction. There is a rest-
lessness of spirit in the book, a nervousness, and an ever-present
sadness. But at the end the yearning hope finds rest in the divine
promise of harmony and restoration.

Hosea conceived the relation between Yahweh and Israel after
the analogy of the marital relation. Israel is Yahweh's spouse. He
had fallen in love with her in the wilderness and had given her
blessings of every sort. But she, in base ingratitude, became faithless
and turned to other lovers, the local nature deities of the Canaanites,
the so-called Baalim, from whom she claimed to have received the
blessings of agriculture. In wild and shameful cult she gave them her
love. The Israelites themselves did not look upon their worship thus;
they thought they were worshiping Yahweh in this cult—they
called Him their Baal, their owner, possessor, husband. But while
they might think that it mattered not whether they followed this
nature cult, Hosea perceived that it imperiled the purity of the
religion of Yahweh and negated the very basis, which according to
time-honored tradition, it had received in the period of the desert
sojourn. Its base, licentious practices deadened the moral and
spiritual sensibility of the people. So he fought against it with all
his might, and no less against the image worship which went with it.
With bitter sarcasm he scorned the idols as the work of men's hands
and ridiculed the practice of kissing the calves, those images in the
sanctuaries that were to represent Yahweh! As if Yahweh, the
spiritual deity, could be represented by an image at all! Hosea
did not succeed in his determined attack upon the local shrines.
He incurred the enmity of the priests and of others. They taunted
him, "The prophet is a fool, the man that has the spirit is mad."
Passionately he retorted, "For the abundance of thine iniquity, and
because the enmity is great" (9:7). But his work was not in vain,
a century later his principle won out in the great reformation of
Josiah (cf. Ch. IX).

Although Hosea laid most stress on the religious corruption of
the people, he did not overlook the moral iniquities, which he condemned no less than Amos (4:1ff.). He agreed with the Judean
prophet that God demanded righteousness, not sacrificial cult. He
also went into the political field that Amos had not touched; he

attacked the monarchy and showed the folly of making alliances. He foresaw the clash between Assyria and Egypt, warned the pro-Assyrian as well as the pro-Egyptian party, and showed that Yahweh's plan would be carried out, no matter what these politicians might do to hinder it. For the political history of the last years of the Northern Kingdom Hosea's book, with its invaluable information and its keen judgment, is as important as for the religious.

Religiously, socially, politically the people had been faithless to Yahweh. Unfaithfulness was their fundamental sin. The keen reader of the human heart probed more deeply. Unfaithfulness was grounded in ignorance. If the people only knew Yahweh, they would not worship Baal or confound Yahweh with Baal or worship images; they would not commit the terrible social sins and violate all the moral law; they would not choose kings or enter political alliances with foreign nations, for Yahweh is spiritual and moral and the only real saviour. Oh, if Israel but knew Yahweh! But "my people perish for lack of knowledge." There rings through these words all the pathos of Hosea's sad heart. He knew the value of the knowledge of God, he knew it is life indeed. Righteousness and love and trust, all spring from it. And thus says Yahweh:

> I desire loving kindness and not sacrifice,
>> and the knowledge of God rather than burnt offerings. (6:6)
> Therefore turn thou to thy God,
>> keep kindness and justice,
>> and wait for thy God continually. (12:6)

Hosea knew that sin had become a habit with the people, a tendency, from which they could not free themselves. And yet he hoped that through the awful suffering, which they would have to undergo, they would come to know Yahweh, repent with all their hearts, and be restored again.

We miss in Hosea the idea of God as found in Amos, with its universal implications. He was interested in his own people, he wanted to bind Yahweh and Israel together in a union of whole-hearted affection. Never before had the relation between God and Israel been filled with such strong emotion. Love is the keynote of this relation. Yahweh alone for Israel, and Israel alone for Yahweh. Hosea deepened and intensified religion, but he also narrowed it in this exclusive possession of one by the other. The spiritualization and refinement of religion is his great contribution. His joining of love with righteousness also in the relation of man to man meant much for social ethics, for the healing of society is possible only by righteousness and love. His profounder interpretation of the nature of sin, and his union of hope with moral discipline by his faith in the love of God as a redeeming and regenerating power exerted great influence on religious thought, while his insistence on the knowledge of God as absolutely essential points forward to his spiritual kinsman John, who wrote, "This is life eternal that they might know Thee the only true God, and him whom Thou didst send, even Jesus Christ."

VIII

Isaiah and Micah

WHILE Hosea was still prophesying in the North, there arose in Judah the most majestic of the prophets, Isaiah of Jerusalem. For forty years or more he was God's spokesman to his people, *ca.* 738–700 B.C. or even later. The splendor of his diction, the wealth of his imagery, the amazing variety of his style, now grand and majestic, powerful and sweeping, now gentle and sweet, moving as if full of silent tears, mark him out as the prince of Hebrew orators. But he was greater than his style and his words. He had penetrated through outward appearances to the underlying reality, had seen the One who directs all movements of history, had understood His character and purpose, and thus was enabled to interpret Him to his people and to unfold His plan in the events of the nations.

One day in the year that King Uzziah (short for Azariah, 2 Ki. 15:1) died (735), Isaiah was in the temple in deep meditation; we can but imagine his thoughts, his hopes, and his fears, for he does not tell us of them. Suddenly his inner eye was opened and there came to him the vision that burnt itself indelibly into his soul and ever after controlled his thought and life. He saw the divine King on His throne. Filled with awe, he only dared to look at the vast flowing garment that filled the temple, and at the mysterious winged seraphim, from whose lips pealed forth the mighty antiphonal song that expressed to him ever after the true nature of Yahweh:

> Holy, holy, holy is Yahweh of hosts,
> the whole earth is full of His glory.

At the vision of holiness Isaiah was shaken by fear. In the swift realization of his own and his people's sinfulness he cried out in utter dismay. He had seen the divine mystery, he knew he must die. But a seraph flew to him and purified his lips with a burning coal from the altar and pronounced him clean. By this act of consecration Isaiah was enabled to appreciate the true significance of the scene and to hear Yahweh Himself as He asked, "Whom shall I send, and who will go for us?" In quick, glad readiness Isaiah cried, "Here am I, send me!" At once he received his commission. He must go and speak to "this people," as they are scornfully called, he must continually make clear to them Yahweh's will, continually interpret to them the true significance of all events; but they shall never grasp the inner meaning of his words, and as they hear without understanding and without following the light thus revealed, they will grow more and more callous, lose their spiritual sensibilities and their very capacity of repentance and moral recovery, and thus they will be prepared for destruction—by Isaiah's ministry:

> Go, and tell this people:
> Hear ye continually, but understand not,
>   and see ye continually, but perceive not!
> Make the heart of this people fat
>   and their ears heavy, and shut their eyes,
> Lest they see with their eyes, and hear with their ears,
>   and understand with their heart, and return and be healed!

When Isaiah, full of anguish, asked, "Lord, how long?" Yahweh replied,

> Until cities are waste without inhabitant,
>   and houses without man,
>   and the land becomes utterly waste,
> And Yahweh has removed men far away,
>   and the forsaking be great in the land.
> And if there be yet a tenth in it,
>   it also shall in turn be consumed,
> As a terebinth and as an oak
>   whose stump has remained after they are felled. (Isa. 6:9–13a)

Their destruction is to be complete. If a remnant should be left in the awful visitation, it too shall be destroyed, until nobody remains of all the sinful people.[1] No prophet ever received a more

---

[1] The addition at the end "a holy seed is its stump" expresses the later conviction (of Isaiah?) regarding the remnant that is to be converted and saved. The

terrible commission. But Isaiah performed it in the strength of this vision of God's holiness, which dominated henceforth all his thought.

God's holiness, His physical majesty, had to him as its corollary man's insignificance. It behooves man to be humble before the high God. In his earliest prophecies (2:6ff.) Isaiah described how Yahweh, in His hatred of everything proud, would sweep in a fearful tornado on His great day over the country, breaking the cedars of Lebanon, shattering the oaks of Bashan, tearing down every high building, crashing into the ships on the ocean, leaving wreckage and ruin in His path, while above it all there rings out the triumphant refrain, "And Yahweh alone shall be exalted in that day!" With this is joined another prophecy of the Day of Yahweh, in which Isaiah turns upon sorcery and wealth, horses and chariots, and the idols made by men's hands, all of which alienate men from God, and warns his people in the refrain,

> Go into the caverns of the rocks,
>   and into the clefts of the ragged rocks,
> From before the terror of Yahweh,
>   and from the glory of His majesty,
> When He arises to shake mightily the earth!

Isaiah's eyes were sharpened by his prophetic activity among the people. He had witnessed the downfall of Jehu's dynasty that Hosea had prophesied. He knew that Zechariah's murderer, Shallum, had in turn been assassinated by Menahem and that intolerable conditions prevailed in the country. He came to foresee a revolution in Judah too, for here also social conditions were unbearable, the king was a child and a tool in the hands of the women. The revolution was to be the judgment of Yahweh. The injustice and grinding oppression of the people by the leaders and princes, and the haughty, coquettish wantonness of the Jerusalem women were the reasons why He must intervene (3:1—4:1; 32:9–14).

Isaiah made quite an impression on the people, though not of the kind he wanted. For they seem to have avoided the dark prophet of woe. So, one day, he appeared in the market place as a minstrel,

---

Dead Sea Isaiah Scroll has suggested new but unconvincing translations of the last line quoted above. See Burrows, *More Light*, pp. 147ff.

for he wanted the people to listen to his message. He began by singing in melodious rhythm concerning something that had been experienced by his "beloved," *i.e.*, friend.

> I will sing now of my beloved,
> a love-song concerning his vineyard.

Since vineyard was a term that could be used figuratively for one's mistress (Song of Songs, 8:11f.), people must have expected a recital of a romantic nature. He sang of how the friend had done everything he could for his vineyard, only to be bitterly disappointed at the harvest. Here the singer stopped and asked his hearers to judge between the two. But as nobody replied, he went on to tell of the severe but just treatment that he would mete out to it. His hearers all agreed, not thinking of anything extraordinary until he said, "I will also command the clouds that they rain no rain upon it." No mere man could say that. The "friend" meant was God. But before they could recover from their astonishment, Isaiah had thundered the application of his love song into their ears,

For the vineyard of Yahweh of hosts is the house of Israel,
and the men of Judah his pleasant plant:
And He looked for justice (*mishpat*), but behold oppression (*mispaḥ*);
for righteousness (*ṣedhaḳah*), but behold a cry (*ṣeʿaḳah*). (5:1–7)

The play on words in the Hebrew constituted a particularly effective conclusion. Perhaps Isaiah at this occasion also pronounced his series of woes, that have come down the avenues of time with none of their power lost: the woes upon them that buy up houses and fields until they alone are in possession of the land; upon the drunkards; the frivolous mockers; the swindlers; the self-conceited; and the unjust judges (5:8–24). Woe to them all, their punishment is certain, for

> Yahweh of hosts is exalted in justice,
> and God the Holy One shows His holiness in righteousness.

At another time Isaiah mourned over the deterioration of Jerusalem in the characteristic rhythm of the dirge.

> How is the faithful city become a harlot!
> she that was full of justice!
> Righteousness lodged in her,
> but now murderers.

The princes and judges are companions of thieves, grafters, and perverters of justice. But Yahweh will avenge Himself on them all. He will remove the wicked elements and thoroughly purge the city.

> And I will restore thy judges as at the first,
>   and thy counsellors as at the beginning:
> Afterward thou shalt be called,
>   The city of righteousness, a faithful town. (1:21–26)

All of a sudden a ray of hope had come into Isaiah's message! The punishment is only for the wicked; after their removal the ancient righteousness of Zion will once more be restored by Yahweh Himself, not by introducing a new system but by installing righteous men as office-holders.

From now on Isaiah's message was no longer unrelieved gloom. His words had fallen on fruitful ground. A group of earnest and repentant people had gathered about him. It must have been at this time that he gave the significant name "Shearjashub" to a son who was born to him, in the hope that after all "a remnant shall return" to Yahweh and be saved.

So far Isaiah had not yet mentioned the Assyrians, although the advance of Tiglathpileser against Aram had already begun and King Menahem of Israel had been forced to pay tribute to him in 738 (cf. 2 Ki. 15:20). The Aramaeans perceived the fateful danger, and under the leadership of Rezin of Damascus a confederacy was effected between the erstwhile enemies, Damascus and Samaria. It was of the utmost importance that this alliance be strengthened. When King Ahaz of Judah refused to join it, the confederates were so deeply concerned about it that they resolved to compel Judah by force of arms to overthrow Ahaz and to join them.

It was at the beginning of this Syro-Ephraimitic war (735), when Ahaz went out to inspect the fortification of the city in view of the impending siege, that Isaiah met him in one of the most memorable interviews of history.[2] He had been instructed by Yahweh to take his little son Shearjashub with him, for the latter's name was symbolic of his message. With intense conviction the prophet assured the king in the name of God Himself that he need not fear

---

[2] It is questionable whether the picture this story gives of the patriotic prophet can be reconciled with that which is to be drawn of him from his assuredly authentic oracles, above all Isa. 6:9ff.

the contemptible confederacy of Syria and Ephraim; God's plan
was to frustrate its purpose. Let Ahaz believe and rely on Yahweh,
for "if ye will not believe, surely ye shall not be established!" To
Isaiah who had seen the great vision of the Heavenly King it was
easy to believe that He was the sole ruler and director of all the
affairs of men, that He alone controlled all the movements of history, and that His will alone mattered. He had declared that the
allies' plan would be frustrated, and of course it would. If Ahaz believed, Yahweh would do the rest. But Ahaz did not reply; he did
not believe. Isaiah, desperate in his desire to win him, offers to him
any sign in heaven or hell in confirmation of his message. But the
king evades with a pious phrase, whereupon Isaiah burst forth full
of indignation,

> Hear ye now, O house of David: Is it a small thing for you to weary
> men, that ye will weary my God also? Therefore the Lord Himself will
> give you a sign: behold, a young woman shall conceive, and bear a son,
> and shall call his name Immanuel [*i.e.* with us is God]. For before the
> child shall know to refuse the evil, and choose the good, the land of
> whose two kings thou art so terribly afraid shall be forsaken. (But) curds
> and honey shall he eat, when he knows to refuse the evil and choose the
> good. (For) Yahweh will bring upon thee, and upon thy people, and
> upon thy father's house, days such as have not come, from the day that
> Ephraim departed from Judah. (7:1–17) [3]

This is the sign: the young woman (the Hebrew does not use the
special word virgin) who now becomes pregnant shall cry out
in giving birth "*Immanuel* = with us is God," and so name her
new-born babe. Whether this means the prophet's wife or a wife of
Ahaz or some as yet unknown person [4] is uncertain. In any case

[3] "Curds and honey" (v. 15) belongs not to the hopeful but to the threatening
part of the announcement. The country of Judah will be devastated, there
will be no harvests and the inhabitants will have to eat the food of nomads
at that time. Isaiah makes this meaning plain in 7:21:
"And it shall come to pass in that day, that a man shall keep alive a young
cow, and two sheep; and it shall come to pass, that [because of the abundance
of milk which they shall give] he shall eat curds: for curds and honey shall
every one eat that is left in the midst of the land." The bracketed material has
been added. This is no description of a golden age, but of one of meager
existence.
[4] In Mic. 5:3 the allusion is to this passage and the woman is understood to
be the mother of the ideal king of the future. The Septuagint translation in
rendering "young woman" as "virgin" introduced a new thought which Matt.

when the event takes place the divine deliverance already will be manifest, and in two or three years the countries of the enemies will be devastated. Ahaz will remember this hour in which God offered His grace to him in vain, but the name "Immanuel" will not be to him pure joy, for the result of his unbelief will be that Judah also will have to pass through an unprecedented calamity (7:1–17). For Ahaz this hour meant little, for mankind it was of incalculable value, for it put faith into the center of religion, and this interview has therefore been called the natal hour of faith, which for Isaiah was the conviction of the reality and supremacy of the spiritual world, of God.

Isaiah brought these messages also to the people. In a spectacular manner he wrote upon a large tablet in legible letters "*Maher shalal hash baz* = the spoil speeds, the prey hastens," in the presence of two unimpeachable witnesses of high rank. And to a son who was born at this time he gave this strange name Maher-shalal-ḥashbaz, in order to have a double attestation that he foretold at this time that "the riches of Damascus and the spoil of Samaria shall be carried away before the king of Assyria" (8:1–4; cf. 17:1–6). In his high ecstasy he even defied the whole world,[5]

> Know, ye peoples,
> and give ear all ye of far countries:
> Gird yourselves, and be broken in pieces!
> Gird yourselves, and be broken in pieces!
> Take counsel together, and it shall be brought to nought,
> speak the word, and it shall not stand,
> *for with us is God!* (8:9f.)

He did not conceal from the people the danger for Judah in the invasion of Israel by Assyria. He judged Ahaz's policy rightly; it would not bring deliverance in the end. He foresaw that the clash between Egypt and Assyria would take place in Palestine and engulf Judah too, since the people had not put their trust in the softly flowing waters of Siloam, *i.e.*, in Yahweh's silently working power. With God no confederacy of human forces could prevail against them, without Him they were lost (7:18–25; 8:5–8).

1:23 was to utilize. Matthew's "they shall call" is paralleled by the Isaiah Scroll's "one shall call."

[5] The authenticity of such nationalistic utterances is not certain. See note 2.

During the exciting days of the Syro-Ephraimitic war Isaiah the patriot felt the strong power of the war psychosis from which the people suffered. When they denounced men as traitors and conspirators, aiding and abetting the enemy, he felt like joining them in patriotic fervor but Yahweh held him "with the strong pressure of the hand," by an irresistible psychic constraint, and warned him that there was only one plotter to be taken into account—Yahweh Himself, the arch-conspirator who was planning the ruin of His people (8:11–15).

Soon Isaiah found himself in such fatal opposition to the king and the people that he withdrew from his public ministry and devoted his attention to the training of his disciples. Quietly he worked, conscious that also for the public he and his children with their symbolical names were still witnesses of Yahweh, although silent for a time. Patiently he would wait for a better time, for his hope was in Yahweh who dwelt in Mount Zion (8:16–18).

Events moved too quickly to permit him to be quiet very long. In 733 the most northern and the East Jordan tribes had been carried into Assyrian captivity, Israel had become a vassal; in 732 Damascus had fallen. And now after the death of the great conqueror Tiglathpileser in 727, Israel, under King Hosea, revolted against her new sovereign Shalmaneser V. Isaiah predicted what was bound to come. Yahweh had tried to save them by discipline after discipline, but all in vain, they did not repent; after the recital of each act Isaiah concluded with the refrain,

> For all this His anger is not turned away,
> and His hand is stretched out still,

until he announced the final punishment, the end, in the famous description of the Assyrian advance.

> And He will lift up an ensign to the nation from far,
> and will hiss to it from the end of the earth,
> And, behold, it comes swiftly with speed,
> none is weary or stumbles among them,
> none slumbers nor sleeps.
> The girdle of their loins is not loosed,
> nor the latchet of their shoes broken;
> Their arrows are sharp,
> and all their bows bent;

> Their horses' hoofs are accounted as flint,
>   and their wheels as a whirlwind.
> Their roaring is like a lioness,
>   they roar like young lions;
> Yea, they roar, and lay hold of the prey,
>   and carry it off safe, and there is none to deliver. (5:26–29)

The same social iniquities of which Judah was guilty are the cause of Israel's doom. The Assyrians are the instrument of punishment in the hand of Yahweh, who controls all nations in His righteous rule (9:7—10:4; 5:25–29; 28:1–4).

In 722–721 Samaria was taken and Israel was carried into captivity. Above the fallen city we seem to hear again the dirge which Amos had sung some thirty years before:

> The virgin Israel is fallen,
>   she shall no more rise.

And in its empty streets and places the heart-breaking words of Hosea seem once more to sound with all their mingled sternness and grace, their justice and love, awaking a wistful yearning in us, a hope which can never be fulfilled. For Israel had gone into exile, never to return.

In the next decades there were repeated attempts by the subject nations to throw off the Assyrian yoke. In an oracle dated in the year of the death of Ahaz (716?), Isaiah addressed the following warning to them (we may infer that they had sent ambassadors to the new ruler of Judah, Hezekiah, to seek his cooperation against Assyria, which at this time may have been heavily involved in the northern regions and had but small forces in the west):

> Rejoice not, O Philistia, all of thee,
>   because the rod that smote thee is broken,
> For out of the serpent's root shall come forth an adder,
>   and his fruit shall be a fiery flying serpent.
> And the first-born of the poor shall feed,
>   and the needy shall lie down in safety;
> And I will kill thy root with famine,
>   and thy remnant shall be slain.
> Howl, O gate; cry, O city!
>   thou art melted away, O Philistia, all of thee;
> For there comes a smoke out of the north,
>   and there is no straggler in his ranks!

To the question directly put to him by the people Isaiah replied,

> What then shall one answer the messengers of the nation?
> That Yahweh has founded Zion,
>   and in her shall the afflicted of His people take refuge! (14:28-32)

Trust in Yahweh alone, not trust in any political alliance, is the guarantee of salvation; it alone can insure national permanence.

In 713-711 popular opinion in Jerusalem was strongly in favor of joining the Philistines, who now were aided by Egypt. Isaiah perceived the folly and peril of it, and for three years he walked in the streets of Jerusalem like a prisoner of war "naked and barefoot" in order to give weight to his impassioned warnings. Thus all the Egyptians and Ethiopians (who at that time ruled Egypt) would be carried away into exile by the Assyrians, if they rebelled against them; Judah would be bitterly disappointed if she trusted the allies (20:1-6). This time Isaiah succeeded, Judah remained neutral. All through the following years he tried in many addresses to convince his countrymen of the profound truth that their national salvation could only be secured through faith in Yahweh, but without avail. When Sennacherib ascended the throne of Assyria in 705, the whole country was in rebellion. Popular enthusiasm had been inflamed. King Hezekiah was unable to resist the pressure and joined the anti-Assyrian alliance, especially as it was certain that Egypt would this time support the movement with all her strength. Isaiah never receded from his position. Here also he saw more clearly than the others and denounced the pact with Egypt as bringing only disappointment and woe.

> Woe to them that go down to Egypt for help,
>   and rely on horses,
> And trust in chariots because they are many,
>   and in horsemen because they are very strong,
> But they look not to the Holy One of Israel,
>   neither seek they Yahweh! (31:1)

There is only one real helper, Yahweh! All human and material forces are of no avail, the battle is between the spiritual and the material world.

> The Egyptians are men, and not God;
>   and their horses flesh and not spirit:

And when Yahweh shall stretch out His hand,
both he that helps shall stumble and he that is helped shall fall,
And they shall all be consumed together. (31:3)

On another occasion Isaiah summed up his counsel in the great
words

In returning and rest shall you be saved,
in quietness and confidence is your strength. (30:15)

Isaiah repeated his warnings so often that the people grew tired
of them. When he appeared one day in the temple just as sacrificial
meals were celebrated and the participants, priests and prophets
included, were so intoxicated with strong drink that "all tables were
full of vomit and filthiness so that there was no place clean," he
was greeted with scornful derision:

Whom will he teach knowledge?
and whom will he make to understand the message?
Them that are weaned from the milk,
and drawn from the breasts?
For it is "precept upon precept, precept upon precept;
line upon line, line upon line;
here a little, there a little."

To which Isaiah retorted, that since they would not listen to God's
plain message by which they could gain rest and refreshment, His
word would be to them "precept upon precept" with the fearful
result that they would "go and fall backward and be broken, and
snared and taken." He then continued:

Therefore hear the word of Yahweh, ye scoffers,
that rule this people that is in Jerusalem:
Because ye have said,
"We have made a covenant with death,
and with Sheol are we in agreement,
When the overflowing scourge shall pass through
it shall not come unto us;
For we have made lies our refuge,
and under falsehood have we hid ourselves":
Therefore has the Lord Yahweh said thus,
"Behold, I lay in Zion for a foundation a stone,
a tried stone, a precious corner-stone of sure foundation:
He that believes shall not be removed!

> And I will make justice the line,
>> and righteousness the plummet;
> And the hail shall sweep away the refuge of lies,
>> and the waters shall overflow the hiding-place.
> And your covenant with death shall be annulled,
>> and your agreement with Sheol shall not stand.
> When the overflowing scourge shall pass through,
>> then ye shall be trodden down by it."
> As often as it passes through,
>> it shall take you;
> For morning by morning shall it pass through,
>> by day and by night:
> And it shall be nought but terror
>> to understand the message.
> For the bed is too short for one to stretch himself on,
>> and the covering too scanty for one to wrap himself in.
> For Yahweh will rise up as in mount Perazim,
>> He will be wroth as in the valley of Gibeon;
> That He may do His work, His strange work,
>> and bring to pass His act, His strange act.
> Now therefore be ye not scoffers,
>> lest your bonds be made strong!
> For a decree of destruction have I heard
>> from the Lord Yahweh of hosts
>> upon the whole land. (28:7–22)

The most significant sentence in this strong address has been printed in italics. Isaiah penetrated through the outward events to the underlying spiritual realities. Faith was to him the eternal foundation. "He that believes shall not be removed," for he is allied with the mightiest power in the whole world, with God Himself. But the people did not see what Isaiah had seen and they did not believe. In a remarkable passage he has preserved a picture of the popular mood at that time. It was on a day when Jerusalem celebrated some little ephemeral triumph, perhaps the bringing in as prisoner of war of the pro-Assyrian King Padi of Ekron, mentioned by Sennacherib, or a temporary lifting of the Assyrian siege of 701. The people were on the roofs to see the joyful spectacle, living only in the present, blind to the future. Their own ruin was impending, and they were celebrating a festival of joy!

> What ails thee now that thou art wholly
>> gone up to the house-tops?

> O thou that art full of shoutings, a tumultuous city,
>> a joyous town;
> Thy slain are not slain with the sword,
>> neither are they dead in battle;
> All thy rulers fled away together,
>> they fled afar off;
> All thy mighty men are captured,
>> captured without their bows!

As this terrible picture stood before Isaiah's mind, it filled him with such uncontrollable grief that he implored the people,

> Look away from me,
>> Let me weep bitterly;
> Labor not to comfort me
>> for the destruction of the daughter of my people!
> For it is a day of discomfiture, of treading down and perplexity
>> from the Lord, Yahweh of hosts,
> In the valley of decision a breaking down of walls,
>> and a crying to the mountains.
> And Elam has lifted up the quiver,
>> and Kir has uncovered the shield.
> Thy choicest valleys are full of chariots,
>> and the horsemen set themselves in array at the gate,
> And He has taken away the covering of Judah.

The measures which the people had taken for such a crisis were without avail, because they had not turned to Him who sends judgments upon the evil-doers. They had not appeased Him with earnest repentance, but conducted themselves with incredible lightheartedness and frivolity.

> The Lord, Yahweh of hosts, called
>> on that day
> To weeping and mourning and baldness,
>> and to girding with sackcloth:
> And, behold, joy and gladness,
>> slaying of oxen and killing of sheep,
> Eating of flesh and drinking of wine:
>> "Let us eat and drink, for to-morrow we shall die!"
> And Yahweh of hosts revealed Himself in mine ears,
>> "Surely this iniquity shall not be forgiven you till you die." (22:1–14)

Events moved relentlessly onward. Sennacherib appeared in Judah and devastated the country. Egyptian help proved inadequate. At last the capitulation of Jerusalem was demanded (36:4ff.).

Then Isaiah rose to the height of his great conviction. Although he appears to contradict himself,[6] he was nevertheless true to his fundamental faith in the holiness of God and the obligation of humility on the part of men. The Assyrian had been Yahweh's instrument again and again. He had used him also against His own people, but now he had overstepped the limits of his commission. Isaiah had long observed that the Assyrian was not conscious of being Yahweh's servant, that it was sheer lust of conquest that carried him on. But now when he dared to boast in reckless arrogance that he would overthrow the city of Yahweh *and Yahweh Himself*, Isaiah replied with scornful irony,

> Shall the axe boast itself against him that hews therewith?
>   shall the saw magnify itself against him that wields it?
> As if a rod should wield them that lift it up,
>   or as if a staff should lift up him that is not wood! (10:15)

The Assyrian can no longer be regarded as Yahweh's instrument, but must be punished. He shall not take Jerusalem, but will himself be broken by Yahweh.

---

[6] Defenders of the story of Isa. 36–37 may argue that Isaiah himself refuted any charge of inconsistency in the remarkable passage in which he showed that different conditions require different treatment, as may be learned from the farmer. This may be construed as first of all an answer to his own questionings:

Give ear, and hear my voice;
  hearken, and hear my speech!
Does the plower continually plow for the sowing?
  does he (continually) open and harrow his ground?
When he has levelled its surface,
  does he not cast abroad dill and scatter cummin,
And put in the wheat in rows, and the barley in the appointed place,
  and the spelt in its border?
For his God instructs him aright
  and teaches him.
For dill is not threshed with threshing-sledges,
  neither is a cart wheel turned about upon cummin;
But dill is beaten out with a staff,
  and cummin with a rod.
Is bread-grain crushed?
  nay, he will not be always threshing it;
And though he drive the wheel of his cart over it,
  he scatters it, but does not crush it.
This also comes forth from Yahweh of hosts,
  who is wonderful in counsel and excellent in wisdom (28:23–29).

Surely, as I have thought, so shall it come to pass;
   and as I have purposed, so shall it stand:
That I will break the Assyrian in My land,
   and upon My mountains tread him underfoot:
Then shall his yoke depart from off them,
   and his burden depart from off their shoulders.
For this is the purpose that is purposed upon the whole earth,
   and this is the hand that is stretched out upon all the nations.
For Yahweh of hosts has purposed, and who shall annul it?
   and His hand is stretched out, and who shall turn it back? (14:24–27)

According to the account in 37:36ff., the incredible happened.
Sennacherib was compelled to march away, apparently a pestilence
decimated his army. If that is what happened it was a great deliverance for the Jews, and constituted one of the most significant events
in Judean history. Unfortunately it does not agree with Sennacherib's own account of the happenings.[7] To reconcile them some
scholars postulate a second campaign of Sennacherib between 689
and 686 and hold that it was then that Sennacherib suffered the reverse related in the Biblical story. The real attitude of Isaiah in 701
is portrayed in the great oracles that now stand at the beginning of
the book (1:2–20) and which show that at that time he certainly
did no nationalistic prophesying. The description of the situation
after Sennacherib's campaign fully confirms the Assyrian ruler's
claims. Zion was "left as a lodge in a cucumber field"; the kingdom
was reduced to Jerusalem and its environs (1:4–9).

In a powerful attack on existing religious practice, Isaiah rejected
the cult as strongly as Amos had done, including new moon and
sabbath and prayer, summoned the people to a life of social justice,
and pleaded with them,

Come now, and let us reason together, says Yahweh,
   Though your sins be as scarlet,
      they shall be as white as snow,
   Though they be red as crimson,
      they shall be as wool. (1:18)

One would like to believe that it was this message that set Hezekiah
to work in reforming the cult of Judah (2 Ki. 18:3–6). That Isaiah
influenced him there can be no doubt.

[7] See *ANET*, pp. 287f.

In view of the attitude taken by Isaiah in the authentic oracles
the question of whether and when he uttered the great Messianic
prophecy of ch. 9 is difficult to answer.[8] That he foresaw a gleam of
hope for the future is revealed by his prediction that Jerusalem
would be called the city of righteousness (1:26). If Hezekiah undertook reforms, anticipating to some extent those of Josiah a century
later, one can imagine Isaiah as having spoken that prophecy under
the impression of Judah's repentance. The words are so beautiful
that they still are music to our ears.

> The people that walked in darkness have seen a great light,
>> on them that dwelt in the land of deep gloom has the light shined.
> Thou hast multiplied gladness, increased joy,
>> they joy before Thee according to the joy in harvest,
>> as men rejoice when they divide the spoil.
> For the yoke of his burden, and the staff of his shoulder,
>> the rod of his oppressor Thou hast broken as in the day of Midian.
> For all the armor of the armed man in the tumult,
>> and the garments rolled in blood,
> shall be for burning, for fuel of fire.
> For unto us a child is born, unto us a son is given;
>> and the government shall be upon his shoulder:
> And his name shall be called Wonderful Counsellor,
>> Mighty God, Everlasting Father, Prince of Peace.
> Great shall be his government, and of peace there shall be no end,
>> upon the throne of David and upon his kingdom,
> To establish it and to uphold it
>> with justice and with righteousness from henceforth even forever.
> The zeal of Yahweh of hosts will perform this. (9:2-7)

In another poem Isaiah described the endowment of the king with
the spirit of God by which he would be enabled to rule as an ideal
monarch in an age of peace:

> And there shall come forth a shoot out of the stock of Jesse,
>> and a branch out of its roots shall bear fruit.
> And the Spirit of Yahweh shall rest upon him,
>> the spirit of wisdom and of understanding,

---

[8] It is possible that the prophecy began with 8:23, as it does in the Vulgate.
In Matt. 4:15 something of 8:23 is likewise combined with 9:1. If so, the
prophecy may have been elicited by the calamity to the Israelite territory
brought about by Tiglathpileser's invasion in 733-732. It would then belong to
the early period of Isaiah.

The spirit of counsel and might,
  the spirit of the knowledge and fear of Yahweh.
He shall not judge after the sight of his eyes,
  neither decide after the hearing of his ears;
But with righteousness shall he judge the poor,
  and decide with equity for the meek of the earth;
And he shall smite the tyrant with the rod of his mouth
  and with the breath of his lips shall he slay the wicked.
And righteousness shall be the girdle of his waist,
  and faithfulness the girdle of his loins.
And the wolf shall dwell with the lamb
  and the leopard shall lie down with the kid;
And the calf and the lion and the fatling together;
  and a little child shall lead them.
And the cow and the bear shall feed,
  their young ones shall lie down together;
And the lion shall eat straw like the ox,
  and the sucking child shall play on the hole of the asp,
  and the weaned child shall put his hand on the adder's den.
They shall not hurt or destroy in all My holy mountain,
  for the earth shall be full of the knowledge of Yahweh,
  as the waters cover the sea. (11:1–9)

In another poem (32:1–8, 15–20) the ideal reign is still further described. Isaiah had a childlike faith in the importance of the personality of the king. He expected an ideal age from the rule of the ideal monarch and the administration of righteous office holders. The golden age was to him the purification and glorification of the old order. That had been his hope in the early years of his ministry (1:25f.), but he had not painted it with the glowing colors of his riper age. Social justice and social peace, however, always remained fundamental with him.

As he worked out his hope of the future his vision grew larger. He saw the time coming when many nations, attracted by Judah's glory, would come to Mount Zion to inquire of the oracle of Yahweh about the conditions of national happiness and peace, and would bring all their international disputes to the arbitership of Yahweh and abide by His just and impartial decisions:

And it shall come to pass in the latter days,
  that the mountain of Yahweh's house shall be established

On the top of the mountains,
  and shall be exalted above the hills.
And nations shall flow unto it,
  and many peoples shall go and say,
"Come ye, and let us go up to the mountain of Yahweh,
  to the house of the God of Jacob;
And He will teach us of His ways,
  and we will walk in His paths!"
For out of Zion shall go forth the law,
  and the word of Yahweh from Jerusalem.
And He will judge between the nations,
  and will decide concerning many peoples;
And they shall beat their swords into ploughshares,
  and their spears into pruning-hooks;
Nation shall not lift up sword against nation,
  neither shall they learn war any more. (2:2–4)

A vision of universal peace! Thus did the aged prophet look forward with longing eye into the future and formulate a hope for all mankind that makes men's hearts still beat faster, for these words still express humanity's longing for peace.

It is no wonder that these so-called Messianic passages have been regarded for many centuries as the most important contribution of Isaiah. As a matter of fact, this is not so; he was primarily the prophet of faith, and his greatest and most significant contribution was his teaching of faith in the holiness of God, which meant to him faith in His physical and moral majesty and supremacy, in His overwhelming reality and righteous rule of the world and in His direction of all history. If he wrote the messages of hope at all, which is seriously questioned, he gave them only to his disciples.

Isaiah was a man of affairs and an orator, not primarily a writer. It was due to the opposition he encountered that he felt impelled to write down his messages. The first little book (6–8) he probably wrote at the time of his withdrawal from the public ministry under Ahaz. Around this as a nucleus other early oracles were added (2:6ff.; 3:1—4:1; 5:1–24 and 9:7—10:4; 5:25–29). Another little book Isaiah wrote during the time of Sennacherib, when the people would not hear any more of his attacks upon the Egyptian alliance. Yahweh commanded him then,

> Now go, write it before them on a tablet,
>   and inscribe it in a book,
> That it may be for the time to come
>   for ever and ever. (30:8)

Those messages are contained mainly in ch. 28–31. We owe them in a sense to Isaiah's opponents.

The Book of Isaiah now contains many passages which are not from him. Not only the whole second part, ch. 40–66, most of the oracles against foreign nations in ch. 13–23, the so-called apocalypse in ch. 24–27, the biographical material in ch. 36–39, but a good many other passages were added later, so that we now have a great collection of oracles in his book, of which Isaiah's own are not even the largest part.[9]

Besides the majestic Isaiah the figure of his contemporary Micah appears small. But in reality he was one of the great prophets. He belonged to the plain people in the little Judean town of Moresheth-Gath near the Philistine border. Of his family and of his profession we know nothing. He left no record of the experiences that made him a prophet, for he scorned all external attestations of his authority and relied solely on the manifestation of the Spirit and of Power. Like another Amos he came, in the last decade of North Israel (730–722–1), and announced the certain fall of Samaria. Even then he feared that Jerusalem would be involved too (1:3–7). This became a certainty to him during Hezekiah's reign. With burning passion and scorching words of terrible power he arraigned the leaders of his people for all their moral iniquities and predicted the impending destruction. He was the spokesman of the poor, who were suffering in dumb submission from outrageous oppression and shameless perversion of justice. Princes, priests, and prophets, all were guilty,

---

[9] Tentatively one may arrange leading passages chronologically as follows. From his call to the Syro-Ephraimitic war (738–735): 6; 2:6–18; 3—4:1; 32:9–14; 5:1–24; 1:21–26, 29–31. During the Syro-Ephraimitic war (735–734): 7; 8; 17:1–6, 9–11. After the war but before the fall of Samaria (734–721): 9:8–10; 4; 5:25–30; 28:1–4. In the year that Ahaz died (716): 14:28–32. During Sargon's siege of Ashdod (711): 20. Before and during Sennacherib's invasion (701): 10:5ff.; 14:24–27; 17:12—18:6; 22; 28:7–29; 29:1–4, 6–16; 30:1–17, 27–33; 31. After the invasions: 1:2–20; 9:1–7; 11:1–9; 32:1–8, 15–20; 2:2–5. However, all anti-Assyrian oracles, notably 10:5–15; 14:24–27 which were quoted on pp. 116ff., are of doubtful authenticity according to many scholars.

greed and avarice possessed them and poisoned the whole social and religious life of the nation.

Therefore shall Zion for your sake be ploughed as a field,
   and Jerusalem shall become heaps,
   and the mountain of the house of the high places of the forest. (3:12)

A hundred years later this prophecy was still remembered, so great had been its impression (cf. Jer. 26:18f.).

Perhaps the first three chapters (except 2:12f.), in which were collected Micah's memorable addresses, and the threatening passages in ch. 4 are all that has come down from him, especially if he did not prophesy after Hezekiah's reign. But it is likely that he lived and worked also during the time of Manasseh. If he did, the great passages in ch. 6:1—7:6 may have come from him too. It is true that there is an unexpected tenderness in the poem in which the prophet interprets the awful practice of child sacrifice, to which the people had been driven in their despair in Manasseh's time, as a sad mistake in their deep craving for reconciliation with God. He represents the people asking with great concern:

Wherewith shall I come before Yahweh,
   and bow myself before the high God?
Shall I come before Him with burnt-offerings,
   with calves a year old?
Will Yahweh be pleased with thousands of rams,
   with ten thousands of rivers of oil?
Shall I give my first-born for my transgression,
   the fruit of my body for the sin of my soul?

He answers,

He has showed thee, O man, what is good,
   and what does Yahweh require of thee,
But to do justly, and love kindness,
   and to walk humbly with thy God? (6:6–8)

What a wonderful passage this is! What insight it reveals! It gives the classical definition of prophetic religion. With what tenderness it is expressed! Age had mellowed the stern prophet. He understood and pardoned. But in his early ministry also Micah had shown how deeply he himself was moved by the prospect of Israel's certain destruction:

> For this will I lament and wail,
>   I will go stripped and naked;
> I will make a wailing like the jackals,
>   and a lamentation like the ostriches. (1:8)

He had known quite well even then that Yahweh was kind. "Do not My words do good to him that walks uprightly?" (2:7) But the social iniquity of the people necessitated their punishment. And that was his conviction still. With all the fire of his youth he scored the social wrongs. But it is not so exclusively the leaders that he now charged. Deceit, violence, injustice were rampant in all classes. Conditions were now worse than they had been before. "The godly man has perished out of the land, there is none upright among men. The best of them is a brier which is only straighter than the others in a hedge" (7:2, 4). Nobody may trust his closest relation and dearest friend. "A man's enemies are they of his own house" (7:6).

If Micah, directly following this arraignment of the general deterioration of the people, uttered the words,

> But as for me, I will look unto Yahweh,
>   I will wait for the God of my salvation:
> My God will hear me (7:7),

we may ask whether he carried this hope silently in his heart or whether he published it. Were not some of the hopeful passages of his book written with reference to North Israel (2:12f.; 4:6f.)? And does not Micah's characteristic preference for the country as opposed to the city appear in the addition to the famous prophecy of universal peace (4:1-4) and in the prediction of the coming of the ideal king from the country town of Bethlehem (5:2-4)? If we only knew! It seems rather that later writers inserted all the hopeful passages in his book. He himself was convinced that he was a prophet of doom. In sharp contrast to the venal professional good-weather prophets of his time he had exclaimed,

> But as for me, I am full of power
>   and of judgment and of might,

> To declare to Jacob his transgression,
> and to Israel his sin. (3:8)

As such Micah lived in the memory of the people. Not even Amos excelled him in his terrible arraignment of social ills. He shared Hosea's conviction about the demoralizing local cult, but went beyond him by predicting the extermination of the sacred pillars and posts (5:13), and prepared thus even more directly the Deuteronomic reformation.

IX

Deuteronomy

WHATEVER may be the historical facts of the reformation of Hezekiah, whether 2 Ki. 18:4 is correct in saying that "he removed the high places, and broke the pillars and cut down the Asherah," [1] or whether it was in the main a purification of the temple and the local sanctuaries from all their idolatrous paraphernalia, in any case it was short-lived. A reaction set in directly under his son and successor Manasseh (692–638 or 696–642), under whom Assyrian influence became dominant in Judah not only in politics and civilization but also in religion. The introduction of Assyrian worship, the cults of the sun, moon, and stars, especially of Ishtar, the queen of heavens (Venus), came inevitably with Assyrian suzerainty. Altars for these cults were built in both courts and on the roof of the temple, while horses and chariots of the sun were placed at the entrance, and other cultic implements were provided. With this went a recrudescence of the old forms of superstition, witchcraft, necromancy, and the like, and of the familiar worship of Baal and his consort Asherah in the especially heinous form of Moloch [2] worship with its—perhaps only symbolical—human sacrifices at the Topheth in the valley of Hinnom on the south side of Jerusalem. Manasseh himself is said to have caused his son to pass through the fire (2 Ki. 21:3–7; 23:4–6, 10–12). It must not be supposed, however, that all this meant the giving up of Yahweh

[1] Cf. also the words of the Assyrian officer to the people in 2 Ki. 18:22.
[2] The original pronunciation was Melech = King. The Masoretic editors wrote it with the vowels of *bosheth* = shame.

worship by Manasseh and his subservient priests. Yahweh retained
His place—only not exclusively. In His holy temple there were
now a number of other gods too, but not necessarily as His rivals,
for we must assume that the priests interpreted Yahweh as the God
of heaven who was supreme over all the other deities, the God of
gods, the Lord of lords. We may be sure that this did not pass
without vigorous protest. The Deuteronomistic historian who wrote
2 Ki. 21:10ff. speaks of prophets who announced doom to Manasseh,
and v. 16 says in retrospect that he "shed very much innocent blood,
till he had filled Jerusalem from one end to another." The words of
Jeremiah, "Your own sword has devoured your prophets like a
destroying lion" (2:30), perhaps show that this meant not simply
judicial murders by a high-handed government, which copied the
despotic methods of Assyria, as Ahab and Jezebel had done with
those of Tyre (Mic. 6:16; 7:1–6), but religious persecution and
martyrdom.[3] But the blood of the martyrs is ever the seed of the
church.

Similar conditions must have prevailed in the territory of the
northern kingdom, which since 722–721 B.C. had become an Assyrian
province. Scholars incline increasingly to the belief that it was here,
rather than in Judah, that the original nucleus of the Deuteronomic
program was evolved in anticipation of a possible restoration.[4] One
must then suppose that a copy of this northern draft came into the
hands of the Jerusalem priesthood, and lay unheeded for a while in
the temple archives (that is, if 2 Ki. 22:8 can be trusted).

Who the original proponents of this program were is a question
that naturally arises in this connection. It certainly required men of
priestly training to set up a legislation of this stamp. If it arose in
the north it must have been produced by religious leaders, who felt
that drastic means were necessary to reestablish the Israelite community as people of Yahweh. The role assigned to the "Levitic
priests" in the ceremonies at Mounts Ebal and Gerizim near
Schechem (27:9, 14) seemingly reflects their importance in the

---

[3] A later legend tells of the sawing asunder of the prophet Isaiah under
Manasseh, cf. the pseudepigraphic *Ascension of Isaiah*, 5:11, in *APOT*, vol. II.
The author of Hebrews, 11:37, evidently knew the story.

[4] Northern origin of the Code was first advocated by A. C. Welch (1924),
but coupled with an attempt to date it very early.

whole project. If this be so it is one of the ironies of history that it worked out to their disadvantage, when taken up by the Judeans (cf. p. 133, note 6).

The first and basic principle of the reform movement was the purification of religious practice. Yahweh's worship was not to be atomized like that of the Canaanite Baal and carried on "on every hill and under every green tree." All foreign cults were to be exterminated, and Yahweh's own cult was to be purged of all images and other heathen elements, however much they may have become part of Israel's worship. The high-places, those breeding spots of idolatry with its debasing rites, must be destroyed. A second principle helped clinch the first. Yahweh must have only one sanctuary where he might be worshiped and His oracle consulted. This was not so astounding an idea as it seems in the light of later needs, for the area for which this was projected—especially if north Israelitic— was very small. The planners, though imbued with prophetic spirit in many respects, believed that a cult was necessary and for this not only a stated place, a sanctuary, but also certain rules and regulations, ceremonies, and offerings were needed. But this worship must be pure, whole-hearted, and sincere, based on a true moral life, and free from all impure heathen elements. Thus these men, who had the interest of true religion at heart were convinced that the great end they had in view could be gained not by putting away all external forms of religion but by purging and regulating them.

They emphasized, therefore, as their third cardinal principle the requirement of true social morality. The combination of whole-hearted worship, in accordance with a purified sacrificial system, constituted a distinct compromise between the prophetic and the priestly views.

The Deuteronomic program, however, also had a political aspect. It was a strong-willed attempt to make a people pull itself up by the bootstraps in the face of a disintegrating world order that seemed to present possibilities for a great new future. Moses is speaking to the men of to-day; it is as though the whole history since his time were wiped out and Israel again stood in the plains of Moab with its future before it. The drums roll through this program; the mood is set for the kind of warfare that the stories of the book of Joshua relate of conquest days. Presumably this would involve the liquidation of all pagans left in the land—certainly that of priests of idolatry (see 2 Ki. 23:20).

The present book of Deuteronomy is not a unified production. We must seek its nucleus in the area of chs. 12–26. Around this central section there are two layers: the inner one, chs. 4–11 and 27–30; and the outer one, chs. 1–3 and 31–34. This outer layer is composed of the narrative with which, as many now believe, the Deuteronomistic historical writer (*Dtr*) began his work (see p. 229). He allegedly incorporated chs. 4–30 in it and thus preserved the whole for posterity. The inner layer, chs. 4–11, 27–30, is mainly hortatory. There is in it a shifting back and forth from second person singular address to second person plural address (discernible in the *AV*). Some use this as a criterion for parceling out this material to two different hands.

The central section, chs. 12–26, is a law code in which the demands of religion and life are formulated. Since it is supposedly Moses who is promulgating this law, we may speak of "the lawgiver." It is inherently probable in any case that an individual drafted the legislation. He believed that he was giving the people nothing but the great principles of Mosaism. He thought he was only expounding these and bringing them out more clearly and in a more modern form. Much of the substance of his work was really quite old. The basis of the new code was the Book of the Covenant (pp. 35ff.), which it sought to replace, and other existing legal rules, oral or written. The lawgiver arranged his materials in a systematic carefully planned *corpus iuris*, as the following summary will show.

I. Religious Laws 12:2–16:17
  1. The one legitimate sanctuary 12:2–28
  2. Against the worship of other gods 12:29–13:18
    Against heathen mourning customs 14:1, 2
    Against eating unclean food 14:3–20
    Against eating fallen animals 14:21
    Against boiling the kid in its mother's milk . . 14:21
  3. Tithes 14:22–29
    Year of Release: *a*. of debts, *b*. of slaves 15:1–18
    Firstlings 15:19–23
    Three yearly festivals: Passover, Weeks,

* This really belongs here; it may be displaced in the Bible.

The arrangement on the whole is clear, but some laws are not in their logical places now (as 16:18ff.; 12:1ff.) and some groups are not arranged properly according to their subject-matter. No. VI contains three groups not related to each other and the whole section intervenes awkwardly between V and VII. No. IX is not well arranged, and No. XI not at all. Some laws of No. IX belong with X. The lack of orderly grouping and arrangement in these sections is all the more striking, because in the greater part of the code it has

been carried out so well. Whether this is due to the fact that the
author found those laws partly arranged and partly not, or whether
some were inserted later, we do not know.

At the beginning stands the law of the single sanctuary, which
involved the destruction of all other sanctuaries and the centralization of all worship in one place. It is unlikely that the man who
coined the words about "the place which Yahweh your God shall
choose" was thinking of Jerusalem. If he was an Israelite, as suggested above, he must have thought of a northern sanctuary, probably Bethel. But indubitably the Jerusalem priesthood interpreted the
words as applying to Jerusalem. The ordinance was so important
that we have it in three slightly different formulations in ch. 12, all
of them saying the same as the first one which we quote:

Ye shall surely destroy all the places wherein the nations that ye shall
dispossess served their gods, upon the high mountains and upon the hills,
and under every green tree: and ye shall break down their altars, and
dash in pieces their pillars, and hew down their Asherim; and ye shall
burn with fire the graven images of their gods; and ye shall destroy their
name out of that place. Ye shall not do so to Yahweh your God. But
to the place which Yahweh your God shall choose out of all your tribes,
to put His name there, shall ye resort, and thither thou shalt come; and
thither ye shall bring your burnt-offerings, and your sacrifices, and your
tithes, and the heave-offering of your hand, and your vows, and your
freewill-offerings, and the firstlings of your herd and of your flock: and
there ye shall eat before Yahweh your God, and ye shall rejoice in all
your undertakings, ye and your households, in which Yahweh thy God
has blessed thee. (12:2–7)

True Yahwism had been defiled by contact with the Canaanites and
their religion. If Israel in the period of the conquest had obeyed the
command of Yahweh to exterminate them and to destroy all their
sanctuaries and instruments of worship, this would not have happened, for then Israel would not have been tempted to fall away
from Yahweh. But the high places with their altars, sacred posts and
pillars could be demolished now; and all worship of other gods, not
only of Baal and Asherah, but also of the sun, moon, and stars, and
all the licentious and superstitious practices connected with it could
be done away with. Deuteronomy would have nothing to do with
them and ordered therefore the strict regulation of clean and unclean food, as well as of other things that were related to foreign

worship, *e.g.*, the mixture of wool and linen in weaving, mourning customs, etc., in order that the worship of Yahweh might be pure, uncontaminated by any heathen element.

The reformers perceived quite well what was involved in the radical abolition of the local sanctuaries and advocated the measures directly necessitated by it. If all festivals, even the Passover, had to be celebrated at the central sanctuary and all sacrifices had to be brought there, it was no longer possible to sacrifice an animal at the local shrine for banqueting purposes. Sacrifice and secular slaughter had to be separated and the latter was allowed anywhere, only the blood must not be eaten.

When Yahweh thy God shall enlarge thy border, and thou shalt say, I will eat flesh, because thy soul desires to eat flesh; thou mayest eat flesh, after all the desire of thy soul. If the place which Yahweh thy God shall choose, to put His name there, be too far from thee, then thou shalt kill of thy herd and of thy flock, which Yahweh has given thee, and thou mayest eat in thy home town, after all the desire of thy soul. Even as the gazelle and as the hart is eaten, so thou shalt eat of it: the unclean and the clean may eat of it alike. Only be sure that thou eat not the blood: for the blood is the life; and thou shalt not eat the life with the flesh. Thou shalt not eat it; thou shalt pour it out upon the earth as water. Thou shalt not eat it; that it may go well with thee, and with thy children after thee, when thou shalt do that which is right in the eyes of Yahweh. (12:20-25)

Similarly tithes could not easily be brought to a distant central sanctuary. It was therefore permitted to convert them into money and to buy with it other material at the sanctuary.

And if the way be too long for thee, so that thou art not able to carry it, because the place is too far from thee, which Yahweh thy God shall choose, to set His name there, when Yahweh thy God shall bless thee; then shalt thou turn it into money, and bind up the money in thy hand, and shalt go to the place which Yahweh thy God shall choose: and thou shalt bestow the money for whatsoever thy soul desires, for oxen, or for sheep, or for wine, or for strong drink, or for whatsoever thy soul asks of thee; and thou shalt eat there before Yahweh thy God, and thou shalt rejoice, thou and thy household. (14:24-26)

Again, the altars of the local sanctuaries had served as places of asylum for the man-slayer. After their removal cities of refuge were to be designated where one who had unintentionally killed someone might flee from the avenger of blood. But only such a one, not the intentional murderer, should find refuge there (19:1–13). In place of the priests, who could no longer officiate at the local shrines in judicial cases as dispensers of the oracle, lay-judges had to be appointed in the various places. If these felt unable to decide a case, it was referred to the priests at the central sanctuary, who with a lay-judge were to form the supreme court of the land (17:8ff.).[5]

Of the local priests (Levites, cf. Judg. 17:7ff.), who had lost their places and their income, care had to be taken. The lawgiver decrees,

> And if a Levite come from any of thy gates out of all Israel, where he sojourns, and come with all the desire of his soul to the place which Yahweh shall choose; then he shall minister in the name of Yahweh his God, as all his brethren the Levites do, who stand there before Yahweh. They shall have like portions to eat, besides that which comes of the sale of his patrimony. (18:6–8)

But Deuteronomy in its final form admonishes the people again and again to take care of the Levites, since in consequence of the reformation they had fallen among the poor and dependent classes (e.g., 12:19; 14:27, 29; 16:11, 14).[6]

In all these matters the spirit of fairness and humaneness which characterizes the entire legislation is apparent. Righteousness and love are to be shown to all. The great prophetic teaching of social justice is applied in detail. The ideal for the lawgiver was that there should be no poor in the land:

> Howbeit there shall be no poor with thee (for Yahweh will surely bless thee in the land which Yahweh thy God gives thee for an inheritance to possess it), if only thou diligently hearken to the voice of Yahweh thy God, to observe to do all this commandment which I command thee this day. For Yahweh thy god will bless thee, as He promised thee: and thou shalt lend to many nations, but thou shalt not borrow; and thou shalt rule over many nations, but they shall not rule over thee. (15:4–6)

But he knew that this was utopian, and therefore he tried to inculcate the spirit of justice and kindness in the treatment of the poor.

---

[5] Since of old the administration of justice was in the hands of the local aristocracy; the priestly oracle had only been the last resort.

[6] These passages reflect the fact that the law quoted could not be carried through owing to the opposition of the Zadokite priesthood of Jerusalem (cf. 2 Ki. 23:9).

If there be with thee a poor man, one of thy brethren, within any of thy gates in thy land which Yahweh thy God gives thee, thou shalt not harden thy heart, nor shut thy hand from thy poor brother; but thou shalt surely open thy hand to him, and shalt surely lend him sufficient for his need. Beware that there be not a base thought in thy heart, saying, The seventh year, the year of release, is at hand; and thou be grudging against thy poor brother, and thou give him nothing; and he cry to Yahweh against thee, and it be sin in thee. Thou shalt surely give him, and thy heart shall not be grieved when thou givest to him; because for this thing Yahweh thy God will bless thee in all thy work, and in all that thou puttest thy hand to. For the poor will never cease out of the land: therefore I command thee, saying, Thou shalt surely open thy hand to thy brother, to thy needy, and to thy poor, in thy land. (15:7–11)

The orphan, widows, and resident foreigners (sojourners), to whom the Levites also are sometimes added because they belonged to the dependent classes, are to be dealt with justly and kindly (24:17; 27:19). The gleanings in the fields are to be left for them (24:19–21; cf. Ruth 2:2ff.). At the great festivals they are to be made happy at the sacrifices (16:11, 14). The tithes of the third year are for their benefit, for they are Yahweh's clients (14:28f.; 26:12–15). The poor are to be assisted in every way. Money or victuals are to be lent to them without any interest in a spirit of glad helpfulness:

Thou shalt not lend upon interest to thy brother; interest of money, interest of victuals, interest of anything that is lent upon interest. (23:19)

Things absolutely necessary for the daily life must not be taken from them in pledge, e.g., the mill or even the upper millstone (24:6). And when pledges must be exacted, great consideration for the feelings of the debtor was to be shown.

When thou lendest thy neighbor any manner of loan, thou shalt not go into his house to fetch his pledge. Thou shalt stand without, and the man to whom thou lendest shall bring forth the pledge without to thee. And if he be a poor man, thou shalt not sleep with his pledge; thou shalt surely restore to him the pledge when the sun goes down, that he may sleep in his garment, and bless thee: and it shall be righteousness to thee before Yahweh thy God. (24:10–13)

Every seventh year was to be "a year of release," when the collection of all loans was forbidden, and an opportunity was afforded to the poor for material rehabilitation (15:1–11). The difficulties connected with such a law were felt by the lawgiver, and he knew no other way to enforce it than by moral and spiritual appeal.

The laborers are to be treated justly and kindly too; they are to be paid promptly in the evening of the working day.

Thou shalt not oppress a hired servant that is poor and needy, whether he be of thy brethren, or of thy sojourners that are in thy land within thy gates: in his day thou shalt give him his hire, neither shall the sun go down upon it (for he is poor, and sets his heart upon it); lest he cry against thee to Yahweh, and it be sin to thee. (24:14f.)

For the slaves also there is to be justice and kindness. A runaway slave must not be returned to his owner (23:15f.). In the seventh year, when the Hebrew slaves were released, they were to be sent away not empty-handed but provided with all sorts of products to enable them to make a fresh beginning in their new freedom (15:13f.). Deuteronomy went beyond the older law by specifying that this related also to women. In another connection D enjoined astonishingly humane consideration for a female prisoner of war (21:10–14). The hard fate of Israelite women carried off by the Assyrians had shown the desirability of such a law.

This is in harmony with D's advanced conception of woman as a person. To him she was no longer merely a part of man's property. In his recension of the Decalogue she is singled out and separated from man's household (5:21). The law against kidnaping (24:7) applies not only to the male, as it did in Ex. 21:16. Deuteronomy defends the bride that has been unjustly accused, by punishing the man not only by a money fine but by public chastisement (22:18f.); the man who rapes a betrothed girl in the open country where her cries for help bring no rescue is to be put to death, and the seducer of an unbetrothed virgin must pay her father fifty shekels and marry her, but has forfeited the right of divorcing her (22:25–29). It was not sentimentalism but the sense of justice that actuated the lawgiver in this, for if the woman was guilty, she was to suffer just punishment as well as the man.

In the family relation too the lawgiver had the social values at heart. He regulated divorce (24:1–4); restricted the custom of the Levirate marriage to brethren who lived together and safeguarded the observance of the law (25:5–10); separated the inheritance of the first-born from sentiment and based it on justice (21:15–17); and limited the father's right to punish his disobedient son (21:18–21).

The administration of justice was ordered by the appointment of lay-judges in the various towns and of the supreme court in Jerusalem (16:18–20; 17:8–13). Justice was to mark all proceedings.

Thou shalt not wrest justice: thou shalt not respect persons; neither shalt thou take a bribe; for a bribe blinds the eyes of the wise, and perverts the words of the righteous. That which is altogether just shalt thou follow, that thou mayest live, and inherit the land which Yahweh thy God gives thee. (16:19f.)

The rights of the accused were carefully guarded. A full trial was to be made; nobody could be condemned save on the testimony of at least two witnesses.

One witness shall not rise up against a man for any iniquity, or for any sin, in any sin that he sins: at the mouth of two witnesses, or at the mouth of three witnesses, shall a matter be established. (19:15)

In cases of capital punishment the witnesses had to be the first to lay hand on the condemned criminal in order that they might bear the full responsibility in case he had been condemned unjustly (17:4–7). To counteract the tendency to false testimony Deuteronomy decreed,

If an unrighteous witness rise up against any man to testify against him of wrong-doing, then both the men, between whom the controversy is, shall stand before Yahweh, before the priests and the judges that shall be in those days; and the judges shall make diligent inquisition: and, behold, if the witness be a false witness, and have testified falsely aganst his brother; then shall ye do to him, as he had thought to do to his brother: so shalt thou put away the evil from the midst of thee. And those that remain shall hear, and fear, and shall henceforth commit no more any such evil in the midst of thee. And thine eyes shall not pity; life for life, eye for eye, tooth for tooth, hand for hand, foot for foot. (19:16–21)

The distinction between murder and manslaughter was strongly emphasized in connection with the establishment of cities of refuge (19:1–10). Blood revenge was limited to the actually guilty person and the responsibility of the other members of his family repudiated.

The fathers shall not be put to death for the children, neither shall the children be put to death for the fathers: every man shall be put to death for his own sin. (24:16)

This was one of the most significant advances in criminal law. The discovery of the value of the individual and of his separate rights and obligations was responsible for this. Although the execution of the blood feud still lay in the hands of the family, the community was strong enough to limit its extent. The next step must be that the community itself becomes the executor of the punishment. Deuteronomy was almost ready for this, but did not yet take it.

The spirit of humaneness and of regard for the personal dignity of the other appears also in the law which orders that the punishment of flogging must take place in the presence of the judge and must not be carried to such an extent that it degrades the "brother" too deeply (25:2f.).

In the concluding ritual formularies the one about the first fruits holds a particular interest, because it contains the so-called "Little Creed." In bringing the offering the individual was supposed to repeat the words:

A wandering Aramaean was my father; and he went down to Egypt and sojourned there, few in number; and there he became a nation, great, mighty and numerous. And the Egyptians treated us harshly, and afflicted us, and laid upon us hard bondage. Then we cried to Yahweh the God of our fathers, and Yahweh heard our voice, and saw our affliction, our toil and our oppression; and Yahweh brought us out of Egypt with a mighty hand and an outstretched arm, with great terror, with signs and wonders; and he brought us to this place and gave us this land, a land flowing with milk and honey. And behold now I bring the first fruit of the ground which thou, Yahweh, hast given me. (26:5–10)

Some scholars hold that this was set up with an eye to the Israelite sanctuary Shechem in the original Deuteronomic program. The words priest and Levite are used interchangeably in this connection. The recapitulation of national history given in this creed is held to reflect the cultic interest that allegedly produced the detailed accounts of the early history.

Justice and love, equity and humanity pervade the Deuteronomic code of laws.[7] And these qualities are directly connected with God,

[7] But note that the humanitarian laws are for Israelites, not for foreigners, (15:3 23:20). The resident foreigner (the sojourner) was included in Deuteronomy's large heartedness and the Israelites were urged to love him. But this does not refer to all foreigners; some are excluded forever from citizenship in Israel (23:1–8). There is no thought of sharing the blessings of Israel's wonderful religion with others.

for He is impartial and just, merciful and loving. Therefore Israel is to be like Him. Here we come upon the conviction which underlies everything else in Deuteronomy. It was not possible to bring this out fully in the laws, but in the introduction Moses exhorts the people with great warmth and urgency to love Yahweh and to do His will.

This introduction, as stated above, is composed of chs. 4–11, giving discourses of Moses. When the Deuteronomistic historian prefixed his opening chs. 1–3 the original beginning of the received work was disturbed, for it must have a suitable start. As matters now stand Moses is giving a discourse, urging the people to hear the laws and statutes and to obey them. Such obedience will raise them in the eyes of the nations.

Behold, I have taught you statutes and ordinances, even as Yahweh my God commanded me, that ye should do so in the midst of the land whither ye go in to possess it. Keep therefore and do them; for this is your wisdom and your understanding in the sight of the peoples, that shall hear all these statutes and say, Surely this great nation is a wise and understanding people. For what great nation is there, that has a god so nigh unto them, as Yahweh our God is whensoever we call upon Him? And what great nation is there, that has statutes and ordinances so righteous as all this law, which I set before you this day? (Deut. 4:5–8)

Let them remember that Yahweh is a spiritual being, that they saw no form of Him at Mount Horeb, and that they must therefore never make an image of Him nor worship the sun, moon or stars. The nations may serve them, for Yahweh has allotted these to them, but Israel He has made His own people, and He is quite jealous of their affection. If they are not faithful, they will not long remain in the promised land, for

Yahweh will scatter you among the peoples, and ye shall be left few in number among the nations, whither Yahweh will lead you away. (Deut. 4:27)

The exile of Israel is predicted here, and the author now adds with a strong hopefulness the promise.

And there ye shall serve gods, the work of men's hands, wood and stone which neither see, nor hear, nor eat, nor smell. But from thence ye shall seek Yahweh thy God, and thou shalt find Him, when thou searchest after Him with all thy heart and with all thy soul. When thou art in tribulation, and all these things are come upon thee, in the latter days thou shalt return to Yahweh thy God, and hearken to His voice; for Yahweh thy God is a merciful God; He will not fail thee, neither destroy thee, nor forget the covenant of thy fathers which He swore to them. (Deut. 4:28–31)

No other people ever had such wonderful experiences with God as Israel,

> Know therefore this day, and lay it to thy heart, that Yahweh is God in heaven above and upon the earth beneath; there is none else. And thou shalt keep His statutes, and His commandments, which I command thee this day, that it may go well with thee, and with thy children after thee, and that thou mayest prolong thy days in the land, which Yahweh thy God gives to thee for ever. (Deut. 4:39f.)

A situation description (4:45–49), which might well have formed the opening of the book as received by *Dtr*, leads to a discourse in which Moses tells Israel of the covenant at Horeb, and restates the Decalogue given there; the people were too terrified to hear anything more. Yahweh, therefore, communicated the laws to Moses privately. They were of course the ones he is now going to give them in chs. 12–26. Deuteronomy ignores the Book of the Covenant (Ex. 20:23—23:19), which it is seeking to replace.

With another fresh beginning (ch. 6) Israel is told that these are the laws that are to be observed, and is urged to do this for its own benefit. Then follows the famous *Shema* (hear).[8] In later times when the language of v. 8 was taken literally instead of figuratively (as in Ex. 13:16) it led to the development of "phylacteries" (Matt. 3:5) worn at the prayer season (and hence called *tephillin*).

> Hear, O Israel: Yahweh is our God, Yahweh alone:[9] and thou shalt love Yahweh thy God with all thy heart, and with all thy soul, and with all thy might.

[8] Shema (hear) is the opening word of 6:1 and so became the name of this prayer. Jesus quoted 6:4–5 as the first and greatest commandment (Mark 12:28f.). But the Jewish Shema was extended with other passages: 11:13–21; Num. 15:37–41 and a few praises. It was a kind of creed the Jew recited twice daily (Josephus, *Antiquities*, IV, viii, 13). In the phylacteries found at Qumran the Shema scripture selections differed and the phylacteries themselves were not made according to later rules. The selections used were Deut. 5:1—6:9; 10:12—11:21; Ex. 13:1–10, 11–16. Since 6:4–5 did not stand at the beginning it was hardly called the Shema at the time of Christ. Indeed, this explains why Jesus' picking out of that sentence was not so self-evident and could elicit the admiration of the scribe.

[9] The translation of these words is debatable. The meaning may be: Yahweh our God is one Yahweh (not divisible into local manifestations).

And these words, which I command thee this day, shall be upon thy heart; and thou shalt teach them diligently unto thy children, and shalt talk of them when thou sittest in thy house, and when thou goest on a journey, and when thou liest down, and when thou risest up. And thou shalt bind them for a sign upon thy hand, and they shall be for frontlets between thine eyes. And thou shalt write them upon the door-posts of thy house, and upon thy gates. (6:4–9)

Similarly at a later juncture the requirements of Yahweh are summarized in a form with which we are familiar from Mic. 6:8:

And now, Israel, what does Yahweh thy God require of thee, but to fear Yahweh thy God, to walk in all His ways, and to love Him, and to serve Yahweh thy God with all thy heart and with all thy soul, to keep the commandments of Yahweh, and His statutes, which I command thee this day for thy good? Behold, to Yahweh thy God belong heaven and the heaven of heavens, the earth, with all that is therein. Only Yahweh had a delight in thy fathers to love them, and He chose their seed after them, even you beyond all peoples, as at this day. Circumcise therefore the foreskin of your heart, and be no more stiffnecked. For Yahweh your God, he is God of gods, and Lord of lords, the great God, the mighty, and the terrible, who regards not persons, nor takes reward. He executes justice for the fatherless and widow, and loves the sojourner, in giving him food and raiment. Love ye therefore the sojourner; for ye were sojourners in the land of Egypt. Thou shalt fear Yahweh thy God; Him shalt thou serve; and to Him shalt thou cleave, and by His name shalt thou swear. He is thy praise, and He is thy God, that has done for thee these great and terrible things, which thine eyes have seen. (10:12–21)

The conclusion of the inner layer of material that has been laid about the code (chs. 27–30) is likewise most impressive. The law is to be recorded on steles, and an altar is to be erected on Mt. Gerizim (27:4) [10] and sacrifice brought there. Furthermore the tribes are to be stationed in two groups on Ebal and Gerizim and the Levites are to pronounce twelve curses on those who break certain basic rules. This is followed by further exhortation by Moses in chs. 28–30.[11] The two ways are set before the people: the one leading to an existence in the favor of Yahweh and enjoying all the benefits

[10] The *MT* has Mt. Ebal, but the Samaritan Pentateuch has preserved the correct reading. Jewish bias against the Samaritans and their sanctuary produced the change.

[11] There has been an accumulation of materials in this area. Thus 28:64–68 are hardly understandable before 320 B.C. (cf. Josephus, *Antiquities*, Bk. XII, i, 1).

he will bestow, and the other to an existence in his disfavor with all the punitive hardships and disasters that will entail.

Deuteronomy is written most impressively in an "urgent and sonorous" style, one of the most distinctive in the Old Testament. It is the style of a preacher. The rhythm of its language, the particular phraseology of its well-formed sentences, and the distinction of its vocabulary are impressive. And the whole is pervaded by such a warm tone, the author's solicitude is so sincere, that the reader who has come under the spell of this great reform preacher is filled with admiration. His style and thought influenced many writers, among them Jeremiah, and the whole devotional language of the people, as the Psalter and the prayers in the books of Nehemiah (1:5–11; 9:6ff.) and Daniel (9:4–19) prove. Anyone who has once felt the charm and understood the quality of this style will never forget it and will always be able to detect it in other books with ease.

In view of its nationalistic, one might even say militaristic, spirit it is apparent that this book if written in the time of Manasseh—whether in Israel or Judah—could not be published immediately. Not only was Israel's territory composed of Assyrian provinces, Judah too was completely subservient to Assyria. But when after Amon's short reign Josiah became king (641–609 B.C.), the situation gradually grew more favorable, for with the passing of Ashurbanipal in 626 Assyria went into swift decline. The prospect of a restoration of Israel under the leadership of Judah now became a realistic possibility. A religious reformation, it could be hoped, might make Yahweh more favorably inclined toward his people in the future.

This was the moment of opportunity for Jewish leaders to act. In 621 the new law book was placed in the hand of King Josiah, Hilkiah, the chief priest, had "found" it in the temple and gave it to the chancellor Shaphan, who had been sent by the king on an errand to the temple. On his return Shaphan read it before Josiah. "And it came to pass when the king had heard the words of the book of the law that he rent his clothes" (as a sign of grief). After Hilkiah, Shaphan, and three others at the command of the king had secured the divine attestation of the book through an oracle, which Huldah the prophetess gave to them, Josiah at once began to institute a reformation of the cult in accordance with the demands of the

Deuteronomic law.[12] In a convocation of the entire people at the temple the king and the people adopted in a solemn covenant this code as the fundamental law of the state. The temple now was cleansed of everything connected with foreign worship; the sanctuaries outside of Jerusalem were destroyed and defiled; all through the land idolatry and superstition were put away; and the Passover was celebrated in Jerusalem as had been directed in this law (2 Ki. 22f.).[13] It was the most radical reformation imaginable and it was carried out with relentless zeal.

Deuteronomy itself had left the identity of the central sanctuary subject to future definition, and had merely spoken in vague terms of "the place which Yahweh your God will choose out of all your tribes to put his name and make his habitation there[14] (Deut. 12:5, etc.). The original formulators may have thought of the cult center of the premonarchic tribal confederacy—in all probability Shechem (cf. 11:29f.). But Josiah and his supporters viewed Jerusalem as the chosen central sanctuary, and by winning acceptance for the Deuteronomic law set in motion effects that were far-reaching. Religion now had an authoritative book around which it centered more and more, even making it possible to dispense with the temple. It could be taught. Men were exhorted to study it day and night, to think of it at home and abroad, to teach it to their children. Religion was a reasonable thing. There was nothing mysterious about it. One need not go far to know it, as a Deuteronomist phrased it,

For this commandment which I command thee this day, it is not too hard for thee, neither is it far off. It is not in heaven, that thou shouldest say, Who shall go up for us to heaven, and bring it unto us, and make us to hear it, that we may do it? Neither is it beyond the sea, that thou shouldest say, Who shall go over the sea for us, and bring it to us, and

---

[12] It is probable that Josiah had already initiated some reforms prior to the discovery of Deuteronomy.

[13] We may note in this connection that the more precise relationship of Deuteronomy to the reformation of Josiah is still one of the foremost problems of Old Testament research. The law book found in the temple was hardly identical with the code in 12–26 as we have it. But theories as to an original Deuteronomy or of separate editions later combined have failed to convince.

[14] This distinctive Deuteronomic idea is an interesting compromise between the more ancient view that Yahweh was personally present in his temple and a belief in his transcendence. His "name" is hypostasized and serves as his earthly representative.

make us to hear it, that we may do it? But the word is very nigh unto thee, in thy mouth, and in thy heart, that thou mayest do it. (30:11-14)

With Deuteronomy thus began the movement by which the religion of Israel became the religion of a book. In this respect we feel the effect of Deuteronomy to this day, both in Judaism and Christianity.

The reformers apparently gained their ends. But though they had insisted on wholehearted devotion to Yahweh, they concentrated their efforts on securing this in and through the cult. They tried to effect a spiritual reformation by the change of the cult, whereas it can be accomplished only by a change of the heart. With the best intentions and the purest enthusiasm they had failed. The critic had already risen in the person of the prophet Jeremiah. But before dealing with him we will treat of his three lesser contemporaries.

X

Zephaniah, Nahum,

Habakkuk

TWO prophets who lived in the time of Josiah, Zephaniah, and Jeremiah (presumably in the earliest phase of his prophesying), predicted a great catastrophe at the hand of a northern foe. It has been customary to seek a contemporary justification for such a fear in the report of a Scythian invasion, which allegedly passed down the Palestinian coastal plain to the border of Egypt in the reign of Psamtik I, 663–609 B.C. (Herodotus, Bk. I, 103–6). This remains an uncertain quantity, and should not be credited until Assyro-Babylonian sources turn up the true facts. The new Babylonian Chronicle texts (cf. p. 147) do not mention the Scythians for 626–623 B.C., and the "Manda people" who do appear in 612 are the Medes. It may be, however, that the earlier migration of Scythians and Cimmerians in the northern theater provided the imaginative stimulus for the prophets mentioned, as well as for the authors of Isa. 5:26–30 and Deut. 28:49ff.

Not only is Zephaniah's father's name mentioned, but also his grandfather's—a fact suggesting some pride of descent. The grandfather was a Hezekiah, but hardly the king of that name. The prophet sensed the coming of the Day of Yahweh, the awful day which Amos had painted as a day of darkness and judgment; and Isaiah predicted as a day of earthquake and tornado. It was approaching with ominous speed; horror and fright seized the heart of the prophet, and with compelling words of terrifying effect he described it to his people:

> The great day of Yahweh is near,
>   it is near and hastes greatly.
> Hark! the day of Yahweh;
>   the mighty man cries bitterly there.
> That day is a day of wrath,
>   a day of trouble and distress,
> A day of wasteness and desolation,
>   a day of darkness and gloom,
> A day of clouds and thick darkness,
>   a day of the trumpet and alarm,
> Against the fortified cities,
>   and against the high battlements.
> And I will bring distress upon men,
>   that they shall walk like blind men,
> And their blood shall be poured out as dust,
>   and their flesh as dung.
> Neither their silver nor their gold
>   shall be able to deliver them
> In the day of Yahweh's wrath,
>   in the fire of His zeal.
> For He will make an end, yea, a terrible end,
>   of all them that dwell in the earth. (1:14–18)

It was this passage whose terror inspired the mediaeval hymn, *Dies irae, dies illa,* of which the English counterpart is still found in hymnals:

> *Day of wrath, O day of mourning!*
> *See fulfilled the prophets' warning,*
> *Heaven and earth in ashes burning!*

To Zephaniah the day will be the day of universal judgment,

> I will utterly consume all things,
>   from off the face of the ground,—says Yahweh.
> I will consume man and beast,
>   I will consume the birds of the heavens,
>   and the fishes of the sea.
> I will cause the wicked to stumble,
>   and I will cut off man
>   from off the face of the ground,—says Yahweh. (1:2–3)

The judgment will come especially upon Judah because of her social and religious corruption, the religious and moral indifference and materialistic scepticism of her people. Zephaniah singled out Philistia, Ethiopia, and Assyria too,[1] but he turned again his bitter accusations upon the oppressing and rebellious city with her corrupt princes and judges, prophets and priests, whom he knew so well. He recognized in the poor people the hope of Israel. He had studied not only Amos and Micah but also Isaiah and knew the latter's teaching of the pious remnant, on whom the hope of the future was built. So he called these "humble of the land" to repentance and moral renewal in order that they might escape from the fearful judgment. The Day itself can no longer be averted, it must surely come, but "it may be that you will be hid in the day of Yahweh's anger" (2:3). Later this hope became a certainty to him and he prophesied,

> I will leave in the midst of thee
>   an afflicted and poor people,
>   and they shall take refuge in the name of Yahweh.
> The remnant of Israel shall not do iniquity,
>   nor speak lies;
> Neither shall be found in their mouths
>   a deceitful tongue;
> For they shall feed and lie down,
>   and none shall make them afraid. (3:11–13)

Faith, social justice, and peace characterize this plain and somber picture of the future. It lacks Isaiah's brilliance and beauty, but it is quite in keeping with Zephaniah's sober, unadorned style. The religious community, independent of the political state, is here predicted by him who foresaw the destruction of the state and all its organization.

It may be that Zephaniah held out a similar hope to the nations, although this is doubtful. Was the final outcome of their judgment merely punishment and annihilation or was it also purification, as in Israel's case? If Zephaniah thought only of punishment (3:8), a

---

[1] An exilic reader added the Moabites and Ammonites in 2:2–11, and inserted in 2:7 the political hope, "and the coast shall be for the remnant of the house of Judah," and "for Yahweh their God will visit them and bring back their captivity."

later editor with wider vision and universal sympathies saw what
Zephaniah did not see and what was yet inherent in his message, and
added

> For then will I turn to the peoples a pure language,
> that they may all call upon the name of Yahweh,
> to serve Him with one consent. (3:9f.)

Another editor with national interest in mind sometime during the
Exile felt the need of adding something expressing the hope of Israel's
restoration, which Zephaniah had treated so soberly. He therefore
supplied a poem of joy and hope so that the book now ends with
a song (3:14–20).

At the time of the death struggle of the Assyrian empire, which
took on much greater vividness through the publication of a neo-
Babylonian Chronicle text in 1923,[2] a prophet named Nahum seems
to have prophesied. The book attributed to him has a twofold title:
"The Burden Concerning Nineveh," and "The Book of the Vision
of Nahum the Elkoshite." The first may have been the title of the
actual oracle against Nineveh before the book was expanded. He is
called "the Elkoshite," which presumably means a man from a town
named Elkosh. As no such place is known in Palestine the belief that
it was somewhere in Mesopotamia, and that Nahum was a descend-
ant of Israelite captives has some plausibility.

The book shows traces of editing at the beginning. A partially
preserved psalm, a so-called alphabetic acrostic, in which each line
or verse begins with a letter of the Hebrew alphabet, was put at
the head, but only goes as far as the eleventh letter (k) in v. 8,
though attempts at reconstruction are sometimes made with the
material in vv. 9–10 to get a couple of additional letter beginnings.
Some hopeful prophetic sayings have been injected in vv. 11–12,
2:1 and 3 (2:1 evidently being drawn from Is. 52:7). The assuredly
genuine Nahum material only begins with 2:2 and continues in v. 4.

Nahum was a nationalist, and his heart was filled with vengeance
for his country's foe. Full of enthusiasm, he welcomed Assyria's

---

[2] See *ANET*, p. 303. The publication of C. J. Gadd, *The Fall of Nineveh*
(1923), established the fact that Nineveh fell in 612, not 606 as previously
supposed. This text has been republished in J. D. Wiseman, *Chronicles of the
Chaldean Kings* (1956), along with important new material (see p. 166, note 5).

imminent fall. At last the brutal despot will be overthrown. All the known world has had to bear his sinful tyranny. At last his cruelty and rapacity, his lying diplomacy are to be requited. Yahweh, the God of history, will judge him. He taunts the city of Nineveh, with its mighty fortifications,

> Art thou better than No-Amon
>   that sat by the Nile
> With water around her,
>   her rampart a sea
> and water her wall? (3:8)

Thus reminding it of the fate of Thebes, which Ashurbanipal had destroyed in 663. Yahweh has ordered the affairs of the world to Assyria's undoing. No other judgment will ever be needed. This one will be final. He seems to have had the satisfaction of seeing this nation's full destruction, which came about soon after the fall of Harran in 610, for he describes the resultant situation and the exultation of the world:

> Thy shepherds (i.e., rulers) slumber
>   O king of Assyria
>   thy nobles sleep.
> Thy people are scattered on the mountains
>   and no man gathereth them.
> There is no assuaging of thy hurt,
>   thy wound is grievous.
> All that hear the report of thee
>   clap their hands over thee,
> For upon whom has not thy wickedness
>   passed continually? (3:18–19)

Nahum was a great poet. His word-pictures are superb, his rhetorical skill is beyond praise. In the description of the attack, destruction, and plundering of the city he exhibits a vivid imagination and a great power of poetic expression. In the history of religion, however, he holds an inferior place. Were it not that the feelings of oppressed humanity found voice in him and that he was conscious of it, his message would have been one of unrelieved nationalism.[3]

[3] Among the Dead Sea Scrolls there is a commentary on Nahum, which seeks to interpret the prophecy as relating to events of the time of the commentary's author. A rendering of the preserved fragment thus far pub-

Nahum witnessed the triumph of righteousness in Nineveh's fall. But justice was not always victorious, and the experiences of life could not always be harmonized with faith in God's moral government of the world. The problem of theodicy sorely troubled Nahum's greater contemporary Habakkuk. He is expressly called a prophet (1:1; 3:1), and thus had made prophesying his occupation. His Assyrian name reflects the fact that he was born in the era of Assyrian control of the land. It was an axiom of religion that Yahweh is righteous. But in Judah a condition of social injustice and oppression had set in under Jehojakim (608–597) and Yahweh did not interfere.[4] Did He not care? That could not be! But why, oh why did the righteous God tolerate such wickedness in the world? In words whose pathos still moves the reader's heart Habakkuk complained and appealed to Yahweh.

> O Yahweh, how long shall I cry,
>   and Thou wilt not hear?
> I cry out unto Thee "violence!"
>   and Thou wilt not save.
> Why dost Thou show me iniquity,
>   and look upon perverseness?
> For destruction and violence are before me,
>   and there is strife, and contention arises.
> Therefore the law is slacked,
>   and justice never goes forth;
> For the wicked compasses about the righteous;
>   therefore justice goes forth perverted. (1:2–4)

Habakkuk neither doubted nor denied the reality or the righteousness of God, but he could not understand His silence in the presence of these terrible conditions. His faith was baffled by his experience. Ten thousand times his cry has been repeated by men whose anguish was deeper than his own and whose faith had given way to doubt. The problem of God's righteous government had grown too dark, their hearts were full of despair, and no reply ever came back from

---

lished is to be found in Millar Burrows, *More Light on the Dead Sea Scrolls* (1958), p. 404.

[4] Some scholars think that the evildoers referred to are the Assyrians rather than Jehoiakim and his supporters. The words of 1:15–17; 2:5 are then applied to them rather than to the Chaldeans. That view would necessitate dating Habakkuk soon after 626 B.C., when the Chaldean rise began.

a leaden sky. But Habakkuk's appeal was answered. The solution
came to him in the advance of the Chaldeans whom Yahweh had
raised up as His instrument to establish justice in the world.[5] Like
Isaiah he interpreted the historic movements of his time as guided
and controlled by Yahweh, and from this great predecessor and
teacher he took the features of his vivid description of the foes
whom he had never seen.

But after the Chaldeans had come under Nebuchadrezzar, the
problem came back with redoubled force, for Habakkuk saw that
their victory could not be the final answer, for they had turned out
to be brutal and self-sufficient, caring naught for God or man. Without regard for Yahweh they overthrew and plundered nation after
nation and "made their own might their god." The cruel injustice
of the situation was even more glaring now than before. Again
Habakkuk appealed to Yahweh,

O Yahweh, Thou hast ordained him for judgment,
   and Thou, O Rock, hast established him for correction.
Thou that art purer of eyes than to behold evil,
   and that canst not look upon perverseness,
Wherefore lookest Thou upon the treacherous and art silent,
   when the wicked swallows up the man that is more righteous than he?
    (1:12f.)

The problem was harder than ever. It could not be solved in the
same manner as before, for in the political constellations of the time
there was no ray of hope. The Chaldeans were impregnable in the
strength of their empire. But Habakkuk could not give up his faith
in Yahweh's righteous government of the world; that was too deeply
ingrained in the fiber of his religion. His only hope was in Yahweh
and it was not disappointed, for the illumination apparently came to
his troubled mind in a vision of God.

But the fulfillment of the vision tarried. Yahweh did not intervene.
Conditions remained as before or grew worse. Once more the
prophet sought an explanation:

[5] Some scholars have argued that "Chaldaeans" should be corrected to
"Kittaeans" (cf. Dan. 11:30; 1 Macc. 1:1; 8:5 where the word is used for
"Greeks."). The Habakkuk scroll (cf. below) interprets "Chaldeans" as
"Kittaeans" but confirms the textual reading "Chaldeans."

> Upon my watch tower I will stand,
>   and take my place upon the rampart,
> Will wait to see, what He will say to me,
>   and what answer I shall get to my plea.

Patiently he waited till the answer came,

> Write the vision, and make it plain upon tablets,
>   that he may run that reads it.
> For the vision is yet for the appointed time,
>   and it hastes toward the end, and shall not lie:
> Though it tarry, wait for it,
>   because it will surely come, it will not delay. (2:1–3)

The vision which he had seen is true and will certainly be fulfilled. Let Habakkuk publish it abroad, using such large letters that a runner can read it without pausing. Yahweh is in control of this world. His righteousness will surely be vindicated at the appointed time, all appearances to the contrary notwithstanding. Do not doubt, only believe! Be steadfast in your allegiance to Yahweh and in your faith in His righteousness, for "The righteous shall live by his faith"! (2:4b).[6] After this Habakkuk could wait, and in the confident assurance that the vision would be fulfilled "at the appointed time" he pronounced his woes upon the Chaldean oppressor. His problem had been solved for him.

Among the Dead Sea Scrolls was found a commentary on the prophecy of Habakkuk which ends with chapter 2. This lends some support to the idea that the present third chapter was supplied later, and was taken from a collection of psalms in which the poems were ascribed to Biblical personages in particular situations where such utterances seemed appropriate. If Habakkuk failed to relate his vision an editor may have supplied a suitable one. However, many scholars defend its authenticity. It is a majestic theophany description. Yahweh appears as in times of old in all His awe-inspiring splendor and terrifying power to accomplish the deliverance of His people and the destruction of their foes. The contents fit most remarkably the requirements of Habakkuk's book.[7]

---

[6] Faith here means faithful adherence to God and his word. The one who has such faithfulness will survive.

[7] A legend about Habakkuk is found in the Apocrypha in the piece from the Greek Daniel called *Bel and the Dragon*, vv. 33–38.

If Habakkuk prophesied between 625 and 590, as seems probable, the fulfillment of his vision tarried for several generations, for Babylon did not fall until 539. Nor was its fall so impressive as that of Nineveh. Much greater destruction was wrought there later when it rebelled against the Persians.

How great Habakkuk's influence was upon his contemporaries we do not know, but a single line of his was to have a far reaching effect. Though he was but a spiritual disciple of the great prophet of faith, Isaiah (and by no means as great as he), the formulation of the result of his profound soul-struggles was so simple and striking that six centuries later Paul of Tarsus could adopt it as most adequately expressing the answer to his own deep problem (Rom. 1:17; Gal. 3:11); and after another fifteen centuries Martin Luther could find in it, on the basis of Rom. 1:17, the light that liberated his soul from the torment of hell and led it to the peace of God. To each in his own way the words of the ancient prophet became a shining beacon:

The righteous shall live by his faith.

XI

Jeremiah

ABOUT 650, during the reign of Manasseh, Jeremiah was born as the son of a priestly family in the little country town of Anathoth, about four miles northeast of Jerusalem. He grew up well versed in the traditions of his people, especially of his exiled northern countrymen, for his family belonged to the North, to Benjamin rather than to Judah. He reveals a deep spiritual kinship with northern Israel's prophet Hosea. By nature shy and sensitive, gentle and loving, with a fine poetic imagination, keen moral insight, and profound religious devotion, Jeremiah was uniquely fitted for his task. When he was called to be a prophet he shrank at first from this high calling and pleaded his youth, but Yahweh persuaded and consecrated him in the great spiritual experience which gave him a consciousness of prophetic mission unparalleled among the prophets. It was revealed to him that he had been predestined and prepared for this office even before he was born (1:4–10). One may suspect that such visions are the result of long preparation, and that great experiences of this nature come to a climax in sudden inner-illumination. But we know nothing of the preparation that led to Jeremiah's vision.

The occasion for the beginning of his prophetic activity seems to have been the gathering storm on the world horizon. It brought to mind the Scythian and Cimmerian migrations of the recent past (p. 144). Anxiously Jeremiah looked to the north; in a second vision it became plain to him that a fearful calamity would break in on his people from there, that Yahweh had summoned northern armies to attack Jerusalem and the other Judean cities, because they had "forsaken Yahweh, burned incense to other gods and worshiped the work of their hands." Jeremiah must go and announce this to his people. He knew that it would not be easy, that it would bring him into sharp conflict with the leaders and the nation itself. But emboldened and empowered by Yahweh's own assurance of help, he spoke his message courageously in the face of persecution and death (1:13–19). In a series of vivid, and picturesque oracles he announced the coming of the wild northern hosts. The impression they made on him was profound. He heard them coming, saw them galloping irresistibly onward over Palestine's hills. He had no rest and peace, his visions tormented him, his auditions tortured him until he cried out in the despair of his soul,

> My anguish, my anguish, I am pained
>   at my very heart,
> My heart is disquieted within me,
>   I cannot hold my peace;
> Because thou hast heard, O my soul, the sound of the trumpet,
>   the alarm of war.
> Destruction upon destruction is reported,
>   for the whole land is laid waste:
> Suddenly are my tents destroyed,
>   and my curtains in a moment.
> How long shall I see the standard,
>   and hear the sound of the trumpet? (4:19–21)

He looked at the fields and mountains, saw them in all their glory, listened to the birds and to the songs of men and of women, and— all of a sudden they had vanished!

> I beheld the earth, and, lo, it was waste and void,
>   and the heavens, and they had no light.
> I beheld the mountains, and, lo, they trembled,
>   and all the hills moved to and fro.
> I beheld, and, lo, there was no man,
>   and all the birds of the heaven were fled.
> I beheld, and, lo, the fruitful field was a wilderness,
>   and all its cities were broken down. (4:23–26)

The astonishment is made vivid by the repeated "I beheld" and the following "and, lo." As if he could not trust his eyes, he looked from one to the other: desolation round about and utter loneliness, even the birds had fled. Ah, destruction comes, it is inevitable, bringing desolation, ruin, and death. And why? It comes from Yahweh Himself, because of the terrible religious corruption of Judah. The northern hosts are but the agents of the offended deity.

Jeremiah had seen the fearful religious corruption at the local shrines and was deeply offended by the base practices of the people. He knew that was the reason for the awful ruin that was so sure to come. He warned his people, pleaded with them to repent and avert God's anger in this way. But their repentance must be wholehearted,

> Break up your fallow ground,
>   and sow not among thorns.
> Circumcise yourselves to Yahweh,
>   and take away the foreskins of your heart! (4:3f.)

It meant breaking with the past, beginning a new life; it meant doing away with all the shameful practices at the local sanctuaries, giving up the Baalim, whom Judah still worshiped, and turning with heart and soul to Yahweh (2:1–13, 20–35). It meant also renouncing the foolish policy of seeking international alliances with Egypt or Assyria, which had brought nothing but national humiliation. The only helper, the real saviour was Yahweh. And Him they had forsaken (2:14–19, 37f.).

Apostasy from Yahweh had been the reason for North Israel's national ruin. Judah should have learned the lesson, yet she had not returned to Yahweh "with her whole heart, but feignedly." As Jeremiah pondered on the fate of Israel, he felt sure that she had by now repented and would therefore be called back (3:6–13, 19–25; 4:1f.).

The prophet's longing for the restoration of his more immediate countrymen found utterance in some poems that have been gathered in a what was once a separate booklet—chs. 30–31. They are among the most exquisite things he wrote. This is saying a good deal, for he was a divinely appointed poet from whose soul came words that still haunt the memory by their beauty, and still woo the heart by their grace.

> The people that were left of the sword
>   have found favor in the wilderness,

Israel goes to his rest.
        Yahweh appeared to him from afar:
        "Yea, I have loved thee with an everlasting love,
            therefore with loving-kindness have I drawn thee." (31:2f.)

These last two lines belong to the most wonderful sayings of the whole Bible. The glory of the Gospel is in them, proclaiming the everlasting love of God. Jeremiah's own soul stood forth in these words. He proceeds: Israel shall be restored, Samaria be rebuilt,

    For there shall be a day, that the watchmen shall cry
        upon the hills of Ephraim,
    "Arise ye, and let us go up to Zion
        unto Yahweh our God!" (31:6)

In another poem Jeremiah starts with a description of how in Ramah, quite near his home, the buried Rachel,[1] the ancestress of north Israel, was mourning over the exile of her children.

    Hark! in Ramah is heard lamentation
        and bitter weeping,
    Rachel is weeping for her children;
        she refuses to be comforted.

But now Yahweh's answer flows like balm into her wounded heart,

    Refrain thy voice from weeping,
        and thine eyes from tears,
    For thy work shall be rewarded,
        and they shall come again from the land of the enemy. (31:15f.)

In still another poem Jeremiah represented Yahweh soliloquizing,

    I have surely heard
        Ephraim bemoaning himself thus,
    "Thou hast chastised me and I was chastised,
        as a calf unaccustomed to the yoke:
    Let me come back, that I may return,
        for Thou art my God!
    Surely after I was punished, I repented,
        and after I was instructed, I smote upon my thigh:

_____

[1] Her tomb was in the tribal territory of Benjamin, Gen. 35:16; 1 Sam. 10:12. Later it was imagined as near Bethlehem in Judah. A gloss to that effect was added in the Genesis passage; cf. Matt. 2:18; and Christian tradition.

> I was ashamed, yea, even confounded,
> > because I did bear the reproach of my youth."

This penitent appeal touches Yahweh's heart. He is still musing but the father's love is aroused,

> Is Ephraim My dear son?
> > is he a darling child?
> For as often as I speak of him,
> > I do earnestly remember him still,
> Therefore My heart yearns for him:
> > I will surely have mercy upon him. (31:18–20)

Who does not think of the Prodigal Son and his father's longing and yearning? In a separate poem, the prophet calls Israel home.

> Turn again, O virgin of Israel,
> > turn again to these thy cities!
> How long wilt thou go hither and thither,
> > O thou backsliding daughter? (31:21)

This hope was never fulfilled. Later prophets adopted it, but none gave to it such moving and beautiful expression as Jeremiah had done. That was because his heart reached out in these words to his exiled brethren, his whole being longed for their return.

But the endeavor of Jeremiah's life, as it lies before us, belonged to the people of Judah. For them he lived and worked with all his might. His vigorous, radical preaching earned him the enmity of many, even among his friends and nearest relatives. They determined to do away with him. Jeremiah was so guileless that it was to him a real providence when Yahweh gave him knowledge of it (11:18—12:6).

Jeremiah apparently left Anathoth at this time and went to Jerusalem to carry on his prophetic activity in the very heart of the nation.[2] He found an almost incredible corruption there. As he mingled freely among the people in the streets, he failed to discover a single upright man among them.

> Run ye to and fro through the streets of Jerusalem,
> > and see now and know,

[2] It is not certain that he had not preached in Jerusalem in the first period of his activity, or at what time the utterances that follow were spoken.

> And seek in her broad places,
>   if ye can find a man,
> If there be any that does justly,
>   that seeks truth,—
>   and I will pardon her.
> But though they say, "As Yahweh lives!"
>   surely they swear falsely.

At first he thought that only the poor and uneducated were so degraded, but he was to learn that the upper class people were no better.

> And I said, Surely these are the poor,
>   they are foolish;
> For they know not the way of Yahweh
>   nor the law of their God:
> I will go to the great men,
>   and will speak to them;
> For they know the way of Yahweh
>   and the justice of their God.
> But these with one accord have broken the yoke,
>   and burst the bonds! (5:1-5)

How can Yahweh pardon such people? He must punish them all for their wickedness. But Jeremiah's conscience was exceedingly sensitive. There might be some righteous persons after all among these sinners. He must investigate again. He felt that Yahweh had made him "an assayer and tester among My people, that thou mayest know and assay their way." But test as he might, no precious metal was found in the crucible (6:27-30). And when Yahweh said to him once more,

> Thoroughly glean as a vine
>   the remnant of Israel,
> Turn again thy hand as a grape gatherer
>   upon the shoots,

he replied,

> To whom shall I speak and testify,
>   that they may hear?
> Behold, their ear is uncircumcised,
>   and they cannot hearken:
> Behold, the word of Yahweh has become to them a reproach,
>   they have no delight in it. (6:9f.)

As he thinks of these rebuffs, indignation burns in his heart. In vain
he tries to hold back, against his will he pours out those scorching
words which set free the forces that will sweep the people into ruin.

> I am full of the wrath of Yahweh,
>   I am weary with holding in;
> I will pour it out on the children in the street,
>   and upon the gathering of youths together:
> Yea, even the husband with the wife shall be taken,
>   the aged with him that is full of days.
> And their houses shall be turned unto others,
>   their fields and their wives together;
> For I will stretch out My hand
>   upon the inhabitants of the land,—says Yahweh.
> For from the least of them even unto the greatest of them
>   every one is given to covetousness;
> And from the prophet even unto the priest
>   every one deals falsely.
> They have healed the wound of My people
>   slightly, saying, "Peace,
> Peace," when there is no peace! (6:11–14)

He reiterated his announcement of the northern foemen, who will
be Yahweh's agents, and depicted them and their advance upon Jerusalem most graphically and dramatically (5:6, 15–17; 6:1–8, 22–26;
8:14–17). But the coming catastrophe filled his heart with grief.

> Oh that I could comfort myself against sorrow!
>   my heart is faint within me.
> Behold, the voice of the cry of the daughter of my people
>   from the land wide and broad:
> "Is not Yahweh in Zion?
>   Is not her King in her?"—
> "Why have they provoked Me to anger with their graven images,
>   and with foreign vanities?"—
> "The harvest is past, the summer is ended,
>   and we are not saved!"—
>
> For the hurt of my people am I hurt,
>   I mourn, dismay has taken hold on me.
> Is there no balm in Gilead?
>   is there no physician there?
> Why then is not recovered
>   the health of the daughter of my people?

Oh that my head were waters,
and mine eyes a fountain of tears,
That I might weep day and night
for the slain of the daughter of my people! (8:18—9:1)

In this mood he composed those poems which, in the judgment of literary critics, belong to the finest in the literature of the world. First the dirge over the country,

For the mountains will I take up
a weeping and wailing,
And for the pastures of the wilderness
a lamentation,
Because they are burned up,
so that none passes through;
Neither can men hear
the voice of the cattle:
Both the birds of the heavens and the beasts
are fled, they are gone.
And I will make Jerusalem heaps,
a dwelling-place of jackals;
And I will make the cities of Judah a desolation,
without inhabitant. (9:10f.)

Then the lamentation over the people,

Consider ye, and call
for the mourning women,
And send for the skillful women
that they may come!
And let them make haste and take up
a wailing for us,
That our eyes may run down with tears,
and our eyelids gush out with waters.
For a voice of wailing is heard out of Zion:
"How are we ruined!
We are greatly confounded,
because cast down are our dwellings!" (9:17–19)

And the most moving of all, his oracle to the women,

Hear the word of Yahweh, O ye women,
and let your ear receive the word of His mouth;
And teach your daughters wailing,
every one her neighbor lamentation:

> "Death is come up into our windows,
>   it is entered into our palaces,
> To cut off the children from without,
>   the young men from the streets.
>
> "The dead bodies of men shall fall
>   upon the open field,
> As the sheaves after the harvestman;
>   and none shall gather them." (9:20–22)

It is a gruesome picture that is painted here of the grim harvester, death, which appears here for the first time in literature to haunt the imagination of men ever after.

Whether Jeremiah's hearers were much impressed is doubtful. They were too set in their ways; as a rule they would not hearken, they would not repent. This seemed unnatural to the prophet. He saw with sorrow that they would not follow the deepest instincts of their being.

> Yea, the stork in the heavens
>   knows her appointed times;
> And the turtle dove and the swallow and the crane
>   observe the time of their coming;
> But my people know not
>   the law of Yahweh. (8:7)

Of course, they were religious in their way. They brought many sacrifices and were even intent on perfuming the odor of the offerings in order to make them still more acceptable to Yahweh. But Jeremiah was sure that Yahweh had never commanded any sacrifices, and had required from the fathers nothing but obedience to the moral law: that was His sole requirement now (7:21–26).

> To what purpose comes there to Me
>   frankincense from Sheba,
> And sweet cane from a far country?
> Your burnt-offerings are not acceptable,
>   nor your sacrifices pleasing to Me. (6:20)

He called the people back to the ways of the good old time, for they alone could lead men to their true goal.

> Stand ye in the ways and see,
>   and ask for the old paths,

> Where is the good way, and walk therein,
> *and ye shall find rest for your souls.* (6:16)

Centuries later Jesus used these same words in his immortal appeal
(Mt. 11:29), not as a conscious quotation, but as something that once
heard was unforgettable and had become his own by spiritual ap-
propriation and been deepened by his personal experience. To Jeremiah religion was a matter of the soul. Each man has longings that
can find their satisfaction only in God, and the way to God is by
repentance and social righteousness. But preach to his people as much
and earnestly as he might, he found no response, till finally life
among them seemed to him unbearable.

Jeremiah must have been in sympathy with some of the objec-
tives of the reformation of Josiah. It has often been observed that
his prose speeches have a kinship with the style of the Deuteronomists. This can be interpreted as the work of reporters who were
of that class; one might compare the Jeremiah of the poems and the
Jeremiah of the prose addresses with the Jesus of the first three
Gospels and the Jesus of John. But there is every reason to believe
that Jeremiah welcomed the reformation which did away with such
fearful heathen abuses as the *Tophet* (7:31f.; 19:6, 11ff.; cf. 2 Ki.
23:10). It seems unavoidable to identify the "words of the covenant"
of which he speaks in 11:1–17 with the Deuteronomic law, and to
concede that he was endorsing it in the face of bitter opposition
which it received in rural quarters, where the closing of the sanctuaries created economic loss. But it is also clear that the nationalistic
and militaristic spirit of Deuteronomy was as foreign to him as its
legalism. Jeremiah had always insisted on a change of heart, for
religion was not a matter of cult to him so much as a matter of
character and life. To him the stress laid on sacrifices had always
been obnoxious. Now that the reformation was accomplished, he
quickly perceived that it had brought only an outward change.
External conformity was easier to attain than moral renewal, but it
was useless.

Soon Jeremiah found himself in sharp opposition to the religious
leaders. When they appealed to the law-book for their justification
and applied its test of prophetic authenticity (Deut. 18:21f.) to
Jeremiah whose prediction of doom through the northern foe had

not been fulfilled; when they challenged his authority and rejected
the living word of God that he had given, Jeremiah attacked them
bitterly and charged them with fraud:

> How do ye say, "We are wise,
>   and the law of Yahweh is with us"?
> But, behold, the false pen of the scribes
>   has made of it falsehood.[3]
> The wise men are put to shame,
>   they are dismayed and taken:
> They have rejected the word of Yahweh,
>   and what manner of wisdom is in them? (8:8f.)

How could they be wise and at the same time reject the word of
Yahweh spoken by the prophet? He found reassurance in the vision
of an almond tree (shāqēd) which brought to his mind the words
of Yahweh "I will watch (shōqēd) over My word to perform it"
(1:1f.). And it was not many years before it was fulfilled.

With the reformation in force and the heathen abuses abolished
or driven underground Jeremiah seems to have had little occasion
to prophesy until historical world events moved to their great climax.
Josiah and those about him felt the approach of a great hour of
opportunity for reestablishing a strong state by invading the Assyrian
province of Samaria, after the fall of Nineveh, or of Harran. We
learn of his going up to Bethel and the cities of Samaria, killing the
priests of the high places and destroying the heathen installations
(2 Ki. 23:14–20). The author of these items is only interested in
such cultic matters. He says nothing about his installing adminis-
trators in the region.

One circumstance could give Josiah pause: the fact that Egypt,
the world power closest to Judah, was lending support to Assyria
in the struggle that took place after the fall of Nineveh. It therefore
is possible that Josiah's undertaking was a mere excursion of a token
nature and that he sought an interview with Pharaoh Necho, when
the latter passed through the plain of Esdraelon, to obtain recogni-

---

[3] It is impossible to date Jeremiah's early oracles with any assurance, therefore
one can only regard it as highly probable that "the law of Yahweh" is the
Deuteronomy of Josiah's reformation. The statement about the scribes has
been taken to mean that Jeremiah considered the "discovery" of the book of
the law in the temple (2 Ki. 22:8) a fraud. But it may refer to the sophistries
of interpretation in the administration of the law.

tion for an annexation of the region. There could be no doubt but that if Necho saved Assyria the latter kingdom would have to yield him Palestine, to which Egypt had claims since time immemorial. The brief report we have is tantalizing:

In his (Josiah's) days Pharaoh Necho king of Egypt went up against [4] the king of Assyria to the river Euphrates. King Josiah went to meet him; and Pharaoh Necho slew him at Megiddo when he saw him. (2 Ki. 23:29)

The "Battle of Megiddo" is an invention of legend, as given by the Chronicler (2 Chron. 35:20ff.); the 2 Kings account tells the truth. Josiah must have sought an audience with Necho to gain recognition for his seizure of Samaria. The Egyptian ruler immediately stabbed him.

The death of Josiah must have been a severe blow to the elements in Judah that had brought about the Deuteronomic reformation. Here was a righteous king, and Yahweh had forsaken him. The whole effort to rebuild a united nation crumbled before the might of world powers, which in due time would regulate the shape of the future as the outcome of their struggles gave them the opportunity. Josiah was succeeded by his son Jehoahaz, but the latter was deposed by Necho after three months and taken to Riblah on the Orontes River in Syria, evidently Necho's headquarters. The people were still mourning over Josiah. But Jeremiah now told them,

Weep not for the dead,
nor bemoan him;
But weep sore for him that goes away!
for he shall return no more,
nor see his native country. (22:10–12)

Those were days full of national uncertainty and darkness. Nobody knew what the future might bring. But the inviolability of the temple at Jerusalem had become a dogma, and in their perplexity the people knew that this at least was certain, whatever else might come: Jerusalem could never be taken, because the temple of Yah-

[4] Either a scribal error or an error of understanding on the part of the Hebrew writer is responsible for this preposition. The Babylonian Chronicle texts show Egypt on the side of Assyria. See p. 147, note 2.

weh was in it. But Jeremiah did not share this common faith and felt driven to shatter it in the name of truth. He appeared in the temple court at a time when pople from all over Judah were assembled for worship, and with ringing words he denounced their trust in Yahweh's temple as unwarranted (7:1ff.). "Amend your ways and your doings, and I will cause you to dwell in this place. Trust not in lying words, saying, This is the temple of Yahweh, the temple of Yahweh, the temple of Yahweh." Only if you repent and lead righteous lives, will you be saved. Else "I will do to the house which is called by My name, as I did to Shiloh" whose temple had been destroyed in the Philistine wars. "And I will cast you out of My sight, as I have cast out all your brethren, even the whole seed of Ephraim." This was a most daring speech, but Jeremiah's spiritual courage ever rose to the height of the occasion, if he was sure that Yahweh spoke through him. It sounded like blasphemy to his hearers and in their wrath they demanded his death. According to the parallel account of this occasion in ch. 26, only the intervention of the princes who recalled Micah's similar prophecy (Mic. 3:12) and Hezekiah's attitude to it, and the powerful aid of his friend Ahikam, a son of Josiah's chancellor Shaphan, saved him from certain death. Another prophet, Uriah, who had also prophesied very much like Jeremiah, had to flee for his life to Egypt, but was extradited and executed in Jerusalem.

Jehoiakim, at the beginning of whose reign this happened, had been made king by Pharaoh Necho. He was entirely different from his father Josiah. Jeremiah gives a striking character sketch of him, in which he compares his luxurious building activities and oppressive treatment of the people with Josiah's plain but righteous life:

> Woe to him that builds his house by unrighteousness,
>   and his chambers by injustice;
> That uses his neighbor's service without wages,
>   and gives him not his hire;
> That says, I will build me a wide house
>   with spacious chambers,
> And cuts him out windows; and it is ceiled with cedar,
>   and painted with vermilion.
> Shalt thou reign, because thou strivest
>   to excel in cedar?

> Did not thy father eat and drink,
> and do justice and righteousness?
> He judged the cause of the poor and the needy,
> then it was well with him.
> Was not this to know Me?
> says Yahweh.
> But thine eyes and thy heart are not
> but for thy covetousness,
> And for shedding innocent blood,
> and for oppression and violence, to do it. (22:13-17)

When Jeremiah said this, he had had opportunity to know and to judge him by his deeds, which led to this severe condemnation:

Therefore thus says Yahweh concerning Jehoiakim, the son of Josiah, king of Judah:

> They shall not lament for him,
> "Ah my brother! or Ah sister!"
> They shall not lament for him,
> "Ah lord! or Ah his glory!"
> He shall be buried with the burial of an ass,
> drawn and cast forth
> beyond the gates of Jerusalem. (22:18f.)

Jehoiakim was Necho's vassal till May or June, 605, when the Egyptian army was defeated by the Babylonian crown prince Nebuchadrezzar at Carchemish.[5] The Egyptians withdrew before him. Says the Chronicle:

He accomplished their defeat, and to nonexistence he beat them. As for the rest of the Egyptian army which had escaped from the defeat so quickly that no weapon had reached them, in the district of Hamath the Babylonian troops overtook and defeated them so that not a single man escaped to his own country.

This is the authentic commentary on Jer. 46:1-12. The impression the event made is reflected in the concluding words of this poem.

> The nations have heard of your shame
> and the earth is full of your cry:
> For warrior has stumbled against warrior;
> they have both fallen together.

[5] For this event the brief item of Jer. 46:2 has been, until recently, the only authority. But the new Babylonian chronicle texts, Wiseman, *Chronicles of the Chaldean Kings* (1956), have now brought the authoritative information. The passage quoted is given in Wiseman's translation.

We can well believe that Nebuchadrezzar at that time received the submission of all Syria and of Palestine, including that of Judah. The death of his father Nabopolassar necessitated his return to Babylon and his own accession (September, 605), but he came back again to the West in February, 604 to collect tribute. There was one holdout: Ashkelon, then apparently the leading city of Philistia. Nebuchadrezzar marched against it and late in that year destroyed it—an event which was in prospect in the oracle Jer. 47:1–7 (erroneously labeled "before Pharaoh smote *Gaza*"). It now was fully true

And the king of Egypt did not come again out of his land, for the king of Babylon had taken all that belonged to Egypt from the brook of Egypt to the river Euphrates. (2 Ki. 24:7)

Jeremiah foresaw that Jehoiakim would not remain a loyal subject of the king of Babylon. He announced in an oracle dated in 604 that Nebuchadrezzar was the servant of Yahweh who would carry out His purpose of punishing Judah for its disobedience (25:1–11). In a grand vision Yahweh gives to Jeremiah the cup of wrath which he must present to Judah, to all the surrounding nations, and to Egypt in order that they should drink, become intoxicated, and fall into a stupor from which they should never rise again (25:15–29).[6] Jeremiah knew the temper of these nations and of Judah too well to believe that the clash with Nebuchadrezzar could be averted. He could not hope that his people would heed his warning. Too long and too persistently had they resisted his message. They had lost the very capacity of repentance.

> Can the Ethiopian change his skin,
>   or the leopard his spots?
> Then may ye also do good,
>   that are accustomed to do evil. (13:23)

This is the classical formulation of the profound psychological and religious truth, which Hosea had seen before Jeremiah. He had no

---

[6] This passage was worked over by interpolators who believed it referred to a universal judgment. They inserted therefore a number of nations which they thought should be included and made v. 26 to read "and the king of Sheshach (= Babylon) shall drink after them" showing that they misunderstood the historical situation altogether. Some of the additions were not yet in the Hebrew text used by the Greek version. The list that remains after they are removed consists of Judah, Egypt, Philistia, Edom, Moab, Ammon, Dedan, Teman, Buz, and the mixed tribes that dwell in the desert.

hope of the king either. He knew his pride and vanity. He warned
him and the people, to humble themselves and not embark on dangerous adventures.

> Hear ye, and give ear;
>   be not proud;
> Give glory to Yahweh your God,
>   before it grow dark,
> And before your feet stumble
>   upon the mountains of twilight,
> And while ye look for light,
>   He turn it into the shadow of death,
>   and make it gross darkness.

He knows that they will not hear,

> My soul weeps in secret for your pride,
>   and mine eyes weep sore,
> Because Yahweh's flock is taken captive. (13:15-17)

By his plain speech Jeremiah incurred the king's displeasure, and
could no longer appear in public as freely as before. The result was
that he dictated the prophecies that he had given so far to his scribe
Baruch, and on a fast-day in 604 he sent Baruch to read the scroll to
a vast assembly in the temple. It made a great impression. A hearer
informed the council members of it, and they sent for Baruch, who
read it to them. After telling him that he and Jeremiah should hide
themselves, they took it to the king and Jehudi, evidently a member
of the council, read it to him. But he cut it in pieces with his pen-
knife and threw them one by one into the fire, in spite of the prot-
estation of some of the councilors. Jeremiah and Baruch he commanded to be apprehended, but they had hidden themselves too well.
Jeremiah thereupon dictated his prophecies again to Baruch, "and
there were added besides to them many like words" (36:22).

Jeremiah had always been a man of prayer; with intense earnestness he interceded again and again for his people. Some of his prayers
are preserved; they are of touching simplicity and beauty, as the
following shows:

> Though our iniquities testify against us,
>   work Thou for Thy name's sake, O Yahweh;
> For our backslidings are many,
>   we have sinned against Thee.

O Thou hope of Israel,
   its Saviour in time of trouble,
Why shouldst Thou be as a sojourner in the land,
   and as a wayfaring man that turns aside to tarry for a night?

Why shouldst Thou be as a man affrighted,
   as a mighty man that cannot save?
Yet Thou, O Yahweh, art in the midst of us,
   and we are called by Thy name,
Leave us not! (14:7–9)

But these prayers were in vain, Yahweh could not accept them, for the people's penitence was not sincere.

Though Moses and Samuel stood before Me,
   yet My mind would not be toward this people.
Cast them out of My sight, and let them go forth. (15:1)

Of particular interest are the so-called "Confessions of Jeremiah" (11:18–23; 12:1–6; 15:10–21; 17:12–18; 18:18–23; 20:7–18). They have been influenced by the lamentation style developed in psalmody and reveal something of the inner struggle in the soul of the prophet. In one of these we find him utterly despondent:

Woe is me, my mother, that thou hast borne me
   a man of strife and a man of contention to the whole earth!
I have not lent, neither have men lent to me,
   yet every one of them does curse me.
Because I am called by Thy name,
   O Yahweh, God of hosts.
I sit not in the assembly of them that make merry or rejoice;
   I sit alone because of Thy hand,
   for Thou hast filled me with indignation.
Why is my pain perpetual,
   and my wound incurable,
   refusing to be healed?
Thou hast been to me as a deceitful brook,
   as waters that fail! (15:10, 16d–18)

His grief had carried him too far: he had charged Yahweh with untrustworthiness! He knew that he had greatly offended and that he was no longer worthy of being Yahweh's prophet. But there came to his soul in that dark hour Yahweh's earnest message, in which He called the prophet himself to repentance:

If thou return, I will let thee come back,
    that thou mayest stand before Me;
And if thou wilt take forth the precious from the vile,
    thou shalt be as My mouth.
They shall return to thee,
    but thou shalt not return to them.
And I will make thee to this people
    a brazen fortified wall;
And they shall fight against thee,
    but they shall not prevail against thee;
For I am with thee to save thee
    and to deliver thee, says Yahweh.
And I will deliver thee out of the hand of the wicked,
    and I will redeem thee out of the hand of the terrible. (15:19–21)

What an hour this had been to Jeremiah! Humbly he reports it too in his utter truthfulness. It is as if he wanted to purge his soul by his confession. He had many such times when he came to Yahweh with his plea, driven by his desperate need. The unexpected depths of his heart that were revealed to him in such seasons of despair led him to meditate on the inscrutability of the human heart. And it was a comfort to him that God knows the heart, and that He can heal it.

Heal me, O Yahweh, and I shall be healed,
    save me, and I shall be saved,
    for Thou art my hope.
As for me, I have not hastened
    after Thee for evil,
Neither have I desired the woful day,
    Thou knowest.
That which came out of my lips
    was before Thee.
Be not a terror to me,
    Thou art my refuge in the day of evil. (17:14–17)

Jeremiah's life was full of persecution not only by the king but especially by the priests and the professional prophets. After one of his addresses, in which he had attacked them, they said,

Come, and let us devise devices against Jeremiah,
    for the law shall not perish from the priest,
Nor counsel from the wise,
    nor the word from the prophet.

> Come, and let us smite him with the tongue,
>   and let us give heed to all his words,

in order that they might trap him and bring about his undoing. Earnestly Jeremiah prayed to Yahweh not to recompense evil for good,

> Remember how I stood before Thee
>   to speak good for them,
>   to turn away Thy wrath from them. (18:18–20)

Another of these experiences is recorded in 20:7–10. It contains the famous confession, which throws much light on the life of Jeremiah's soul,

> As often as I speak, I cry out,
>   I cry, "Violence and destruction!"
> Because the word of Yahweh is made a reproach to me
>   and a derision, all the day.
> And if I say, "I will not make mention of Him,
>   nor speak any more in His name,"
> Then there is in my heart as it were a burning fire
>   shut up in my bones,
> And I am weary with forebearing,
>   and I cannot contain.

But the most terrible of all is Jeremiah's curse of his birth, it is full of the blackness of despair:

Cursed be the day wherein I was born,
   let not the day wherein my mother bore me be blessed, etc. (20:14ff.)

Not even the bold author of the Poem of Job dared to take over this desperate curse without modification (Job 3).

These "confessions" cannot be dated with certainty, for Jeremiah suffered persecution not only during Jehoiakim's rule. Probably some of them belong to the reign of Zedekiah. The last two stand at present directly after the story of the shameful insult that had been offered him by Pashhur the priest who had put him in the stocks after his object-lesson with the potter's earthen flask, which he had broken before the people as a sign of how they would be broken by Yahweh (19:1—20:6). It may well be that the burning sense of this public humiliation occasioned Jeremiah's sad complaint and his outbreak of despair. But he always conquered himself in his intimate communion with God, who came to be his only friend. And he was always ready to go out again and proclaim the unwelcome truth.

What Jeremiah had foreseen came about. For three years (since paying tribute in 604?) Jehoiakim remained quietly Nebuchadrezzar's vassal, but then he rebelled. The new Babylonian Chronicle text provides the explanation for his seemingly unwise decision.[7] In 601 Nebuchadrezzar had attempted to invade Egypt—an undertaking that may have elicited Jer. 46:13–24 and 46:25–26—but had been thrown back in a fierce battle by Necho. Egyptian authority must immediately have been reconstituted in the south, and Jehoiakim may have been more afraid of what Necho could do to him than of Nebuchadrezzar's return. He therefore gave up his loyalty to the Babylonian.

Nebuchadrezzar did not come to the western regions in the following year (600). The Chronicle says that he gathered together chariots and horses in great number. He had evidently decided to revert to this type of armament, which had been so important a thousand years earlier but had been largely abandoned in favor of cavalry by the Assyrians. It naturally took time to train horses and men for this warfare and Nebuchadrezzar gave them an easier task than the Egyptian campaign in 599—he marched against the Arabs. These, when subjected, were evidently encouraged to harass Judah (2 Ki. 24:2).

In December, 598 B.C. Nebuchadrezzar, according to the Chronicle, marched to Palestine and encamped against the city of Judah. From the book of Jeremiah we learn that at his approach a group of Rechabites had sought refuge in Jerusalem. One day Jeremiah took them into one of the chambers of the temple and placed bowls full of wine and cups before them and told them to drink. But they refused. Their ancestor Jonadab had strictly commanded them to live as nomads in tents, to abstain from agriculture and especially viticulture, and never to drink any wine. It was the protest of fanatic Yahwism against Baalism. These Rechabites had always been true to it; they had entered the city only because they had fled before Nebuchadrezzar. In what striking contrast their loyal obedience to

[7] See note 5.

their father's command stood to Judah's shameful disobedience to Yahweh! Let the people take note of it, for they will be punished for their unfaithfulness, while the Rechabites will be rewarded for their fidelity, their family will never be completely extinct (ch. 35).

Hardly had the siege of Jerusalem begun when Jehoiakim died. He was not "buried with the burial of an ass, drawn and cast forth beyond the gates of Jerusalem," as Jeremiah had predicted, but slept honorably "with his fathers" (2 Ki. 24:6). His son Jehoiachin, or Coniah as Jeremiah called him, succeeded as king. The situation in Jerusalem became more critical. Jeremiah tried against hope to bring the people to repentance. He made a special appeal to Jehoiachin and his mother:

> Say thou to the king and the queen mother,
>   Humble yourselves, sit down,
> For your headtires are come down,
>   even the crown of your glory.
> The cities of the South are shut up,
>   and there is none to open them:
> All Judah is carried away captive,
>   it is wholly carried away captive. (13:18f.)

It was all in vain. Soon Jeremiah proclaimed,

> As I live, says Yahweh,
>   though Coniah were
> The signet upon My right hand,
>   yet would I pluck thee thence. (22:24)

The king and his mother shall go into exile never to return. Jehoiachin had been king only three months when Jerusalem was taken [8] and he with the *élite* of his people was carried into captivity to Babylon, where he died long afterwards.[9] After they had gone Jeremiah said,

---

[8] According to the new Babylonian Chronicle text (note 5) Jerusalem fell on the 2 day of Adar 597 B.C. (March 16).

[9] A trace of the captive Jehoiachin has turned up in Babylon in the ruins of a vaulted building near the Ishtar Gate. Tablets reporting the issuance of rations (according to Ernst F. Weidner, *Mélanges syriens offerts à M. René Dussaud* [1939], vol. II, p. 923), list *Yaukin* king of *Yahud* and other Judean captives as recipients. At this time he evidently was not incarcerated. One tablet mentioning him is dated 592 B.C.

> Is this man Coniah a despised broken vessel?
> is he a vessel wherein none delights?
> Wherefore are they cast out,
> he and his seed,
> And are cast into a land
> which they know not? (22:28)

After this first band of captives had been carried away, Jeremiah found his work in Jerusalem still harder. The people who had remained appeared to him wholly evil while the exiles, at least in comparison with the people in Judah, seemed to him so much better that he gradually began to conceive a hope of their restoration. In a vision both groups were compared to two baskets of figs, the one very good, the other very bad: Yahweh looks with favor upon the exiles and will bring them back to their home; the people in Judah, however, will be exterminated, they are so bad. Just as in his early days Jeremiah had believed that the experience of the exile had turned the heart of the Israelites to Yahweh, so now he hoped that the Jewish exiles would learn to know Yahweh. It is true, they had lost the capacity of repentance, but Yahweh said,

> I will give them a heart to know Me,
> that I am Yahweh:
> And they shall be My people,
> and I will be their God,
> For they shall return to Me
> with their whole heart. (24:7) [10]

When Zedekiah sent an embassy to Nebuchadrezzar, Jeremiah wrote a letter to the exiles in Babylonia in which he admonished them to give up their hope of an immediate return and to settle down

[10] This is very much in the vein of Hosea. If Jeremiah entertained a hope of this kind there seems little reason to deny him the prophecy of a restoration of the house of David.
"Behold, the days come, says Yahweh, that I will raise up unto David a righteous Branch, and he shall reign as king and deal wisely, and shall execute justice and righteousness in the land. In his days Judah shall be saved and Israel shall dwell safely; and this is his name whereby he shall be called: Yahweh our righteousness." (23:5-6)
In 33:14-16 there is a repetition of this prophecy, which then is amplified in vv. 17ff. Not only is David never to lack a man to sit upon the throne of the "house of Israel," but there is never to be any lack of Levitic priests. A further oracle in 33:23-26 reenforces the restoration idea. All of 33:14-26 is missing in the *LXX* text.

in Babylonia to the ordinary pursuits of life. Let them not be deceived by any prophets who predict the speedy restoration. They
must first learn the bitter lessons of the exile; not until they seek
Yahweh with their whole heart will they be permitted to return.
Religion was to Jeremiah a spiritual matter, it was not bound to the
temple or the country. What a wonderful truth this was, the people
did not perceive; it was an epoch-making contribution to the development of religion. Religion could be practiced in Babylonia as
well as in Judah. One of the exiles, Shemaiah, wrote back indig-
nantly to the priest Zephaniah in Jerusalem, inquiring why he had
not put Jeremiah in the stocks and in shackles. Zephaniah read the
letter in the hearing of Jeremiah, whereupon the latter uttered a
prediction that Yahweh would punish Shemaiah (ch. 29).

In Jerusalem also Jeremiah aroused much opposition by the stand
that he took in national affairs. To him they were a religious concern. Yahweh had appointed Nebuchadrezzar as His servant and had
given him dominion over the various nations. Rebellion against him
meant rebellion against Yahweh's will and would be punished. That
was Jeremiah's position to the end. When in 593 ambassadors came
from Edom, Moab, Ammon, Tyre, and Sidon to persuade Zedekiah
to join their alliance against Babylon, he appeared with bonds and
bars upon his neck and told them in unmistakable sentences that any
nation that would not put its neck under the yoke of the king of
Babylon would be destroyed by Yahweh. To Zedekiah he gave the
same warning. Hananiah, a prophet, vehemently opposed Jeremiah
and announced that Yahweh would break the yoke of the king of
Babylon within two full years and restore the sacred temple vessels
and the exiles to Jerusalem. In confirmation Hananiah took the bar
from Jeremiah's shoulder and broke it. Jeremiah could only reply at
the first moment, "Amen: Yahweh do so!" But he added, sig-
nificantly enough, that the former prophets had always prophesied
calamity, that the presumption was therefore always in favor of the
prophet of doom, and that a prophet of peace must first be au-
thenticated by the fulfillment of his prediction. With this he left. But
soon afterwards he returned and announced with absolute clearness
of conviction, "Thus says Yahweh: Thou hast broken the bars of
wood; but thou hast procured in their stead bars of iron." The

Babylonian yoke cannot be broken. To Hananiah himself Jeremiah predicted that he should die within a year, "because thou has spoken rebellion against Yahweh." And he died the same year in the seventh month (ch. 27f.).

It is possible that Jeremiah at this time gave special oracles of doom for Edom (49:7f., 10f., 22), Moab (48, now much revised), and Ammon (49:1-5). The alliance was not made; perhaps Jeremiah had impressed the king with his earnestness and sincerity. But Zedekiah appears to have had to go to Babylon in order to clear himself of suspicion. It is said that Jeremiah wrote on a scroll a prophecy of Babylon's destruction, gave it to one of the king's companions, Seraiah, a brother of Baruch, in order that he should read it aloud in Babylonia, then bind a stone to it, cast it into the Euphrates and say, "Thus shall Babylon sink and shall not rise again because of the evil that I will bring upon her" (51:59-64). It is difficult to believe that Jeremiah did this, for he was still firmly convinced that Nebuchadrezzar was Yahweh's servant and that opposition to him was rebellion against Yahweh.

At length Zedekiah was unable to resist the force of popular sentiment and Egyptian diplomacy, and joined the anti-Babylonian alliance. Soon a Babylonian army besieged Jerusalem. Jeremiah knew that his prediction of 27:10 would wholly be fulfilled and told two messengers of the king that Yahweh would give the city into the hand of the king of Babylon (21:1-10). But Zedekiah could not act in accordance with this warning. So the siege continued and grew severe. In this crisis all Hebrew slaves, male and female, were freed under a solemn covenant. But lo and behold as soon as the enemy turned his main attention to the capture of the Judean cities in the South, they were again put in bondage. Jeremiah denounced this treachery and foretold the return of the Chaldeans and the capture and sack of Jerusalem (ch. 34). This seemed to be in doubt, and we may imagine his adversaries as jubilant, when the Chaldeans had to raise the siege entirely because an Egyptian army was advancing in the South.[11] But Jeremiah was sure that they would soon return.[12]

---

[11] For Egypt Jeremiah had a threatening oracle too (46:13-26).

[12] The Lachish ostraca (*ANET*, p. 321) may reflect this situation of the campaign in the south. They mention the letter of a prophet, but do not give his name.

During this interval Jeremiah wanted to go to his native town Anathoth to receive his share of an inheritance. As he was leaving the city, he was made prisoner by the captain on duty at the gate on the charge that he was falling away to the Chaldeans. He was taken before the princes, flogged, and imprisoned in the house of the pit belonging to Jonathan the scribe. While he was there, King Zedekiah sent for him to ask for an oracle; he gave it, it was always the same, "Thou shalt be delivered into the hand of the king of Babylon." At the same time he implored the king not to send him back to the house of Jonathan lest he die there. He was therefore committed to the court of the guard, where he received a loaf of bread every day until it was all spent (ch. 37). Even here he reiterated his Cassandra messages of the certain fall of the city and counseled the people to fall away to the Chaldeans. Then the princes demanded his death from Zedekiah, who consented against his better judgment. They threw him into a dungeon which was full of mire and where he would have perished miserably, if the Ethiopian eunuch Ebedmelech had not rescued him with the help of three men whom the king had given to him for this purpose.

From the court of the guard where the prophet was put again, Zedekiah summoned him once more for a secret council. Jeremiah advised him that his only way of escape was to go out to the king of Babylon and capitulate, and he need not be afraid of the Jews that had fallen away to the Chaldeans. But if he would not heed this advice, he would be carried into captivity and the city would be burnt. The king was well-meaning but weak; he asked Jeremiah not to tell the princes anything of this conversation, but to put them off when they inquired by saying that he had asked the king not to send him back to Jonathan's house. This the prophet did, to save the unhappy king from his own courtiers (ch. 38).

While he was in the court of the guard, an event of great importance happened to him. His cousin Hanamel—evidently impoverished by the plundering Assyrian soldiery—came from the country and asked him to buy his field at Anathoth from him, because he was his nearest kinsman and as such obliged to help. It seemed preposterous. Jeremiah had predicted for many years the ruin and desolation of the land, and now, when the Chaldeans were in the country and the fulfillment of his prophecies was at hand, there came this strange request. But its very strangeness showed to Jeremiah that Yahweh was behind it. He bought the field (with funds deposited in the temple, or borrowed from friends at court?), and in his soul the glad hope was born, "Houses and fields shall yet again be bought in this land" (32:6–15). But Jeremiah's thought went beyond that. As he looked into the future, he foresaw the time when Yahweh would make a new covenant with Israel, not as the old one that had been written on tables of stone,

> I will put My law in their inward parts,
>   and in their hearts will I write it;
> And I will be their God,
>   and they shall be My people.
> And they shall no more teach
>   every man his neighbor,
> And every man his brother, saying,
>   "Know Yahweh!"
> For they shall all know Me,
>   from the least of them unto the greatest of them:
> For I will forgive their iniquity,
>   and their sin will I remember no more. (31:31–34)

By it the ideal relation between God and man will be introduced, true religion will prevail. It consists essentially in the knowledge of God and implies communion with Him and true morality as the result of it. The law will then be, what it ought always to have been, the natural expression of the heart. With what infinite sadness had Jeremiah exclaimed that the birds know the law of their coming and going, "but my people know not the law of Yahweh" (8:7). In the time to come they will follow the deep, inward law of their being, the instincts of their hearts, they will ever do God's will and thus be in true fellowship with Him.

Jeremiah has no wonderful descriptions of the future glory. His outlook is somber outwardly, because to him the glory was all within: the greatest thing is the knowledge of God and the doing of His will. So he could see the awful destruction of Jerusalem and the captivity of his people without being heartbroken. He had seen all this before, he had suffered anguish for it in his soul, but when the fall came he looked into the future full of hope. The nation had perished, the temple lay in ruins, but true religion had not perished. It would find its home again in a new city whose people would know and obey Yahweh.

After the fall of Jerusalem in 586 B.C., Jeremiah was left in the country with Gedaliah, who had been made governor of the province. But when Gedaliah was murdered by the fanatic prince Ishmael, Jeremiah was taken by the people, who feared the vengeance of Nebuchadrezzar, to Egypt, against his vigorous protest. In Tahpanhes (Daphne) in Egypt he was seen one day carrying great stones to the plaza before the royal palace and making a base. To the astonished Jews he explained that Yahweh would send His servant Nebuchadrezzar to Egypt and upon these stones would he set his throne and spread his pavilion, for he would conquer Egypt, destroy its temples, and carry away its idols (ch. 43). Their flight to Egypt had not taken the fugitives out of Nebuchadrezzar's reach! But neither the symbolic object-lesson nor the address made any impression upon them.

To Jeremiah's utter dismay the Jews began their old idolatrous worship again, especially the women, and when Jeremiah rebuked them, they answered that as long as they had served the Queen of Heaven (prior to Josiah's reformation) it had been well with them and they would serve her again. He replied by predicting their virtual extermination, and as a sign of the truth of this prediction he announced to them the certain defeat which Pharaoh Hophra would suffer at the hand of his enemies (ch. 44).

This is the last we hear of him who was in many ways Israel's greatest prophet. He grasped with deep insight the fundamental elements of religion and stated them with great clearness. In him all the best of Amos, Hosea, and Isaiah was brought to full fruition. He spiritualized religion by separating it from all outward institutions, even from the nation. They all perish, but religion remains: the soul in fellowship with God. Religion is a matter of the individual heart. Like Hosea, to whom he was so similar, Jeremiah incarnated his message. He must be solitary and alone, he must not marry, nor have children, because all parents and children would soon perish in the terrible catastrophe. He must not go into a house of mourning to express his sympathy, because men would soon die and not be buried and lamented. He must not be glad with happy people, because the voice of gladness and mirth would soon be hushed in the land (16:1–9). Despised, forsaken, persecuted, he was a man of sorrows. Yet ever did he do his work bravely and faithfully, although his heart would soon break. Oft times he was ready to despair, but always the strong voice came to him that had come in the great hour when he first knew that he was Yahweh's prophet, "Fear not, for I will be with thee!" And he conquered, and though his people treated him shamefully during his lifetime, he won the homage of their hearts in the end: to them be became "The Prophet," and Deutero-Isaiah may have had him in mind as the type of the true servant of Yahweh, in a prediction only fulfilled in the man on Calvary (Is. 53). Greater honor can hardly be given to any man than was thus given to Jeremiah of Anathoth, the prophet of the heart.

Jeremiah first collected his oracles, as we saw, in 603 when he dictated them to Baruch. After the destruction of this roll he wrote a second enlarged edition. The sentence "and there were added besides to them many like words" (36:32) may refer not only to this time but to successive additions, for his book now contains oracles from him as late as 586. There are three elements to be distinguished in our present edition: 1. Jeremiah's own work, 2. Baruch's biography of Jeremiah, 3. Later additions. If we arrange Jeremiah's own work according to chronology, we may group as follows:

During the reign of Josiah 1–6; 7:21—12:6 (except 10:1–16); and 31:2–6, 15–21.
During the reign of Jehoiakim 7:1–20; 12:7—13:17; 13:20—20 (except 17:19–27); 22:1–23; 25:1–24 (worked over).
During the reign of Jehoiachin 13:18f.; 22:24–30.
During the reign of Zedekiah 21; 23:1f., 9ff.; 24.
After the fall of Jerusalem 31:31–34.

There is much difference of opinion whether the oracles against the nations (46–51) go back to Jeremiah,[13] but we have seen that several of them were certainly written in his time.

---

[13] These oracles against the nations circulated at first as an independent book. When they were inserted in the Book of Jeremiah, some manuscripts had them

Baruch was not only Jeremiah's scribe but also his friend; he was an educated man of a noble family, a man of character and great personal influence. He was Jeremiah's intimate from the reign of Jehoiakim on, he visited him in prison and accompanied him to Egypt. He loved and revered the great prophet with all his heart and set him a monument in a biography. That is the reason why we know so much more of Jeremiah than of the other prophets. We are indebted to this biography for much valuable history. Parts of it were later on connected with Jeremiah's oracles. They are now found in 19:1—20:6; 26–29; 32; 34–45. To the time of Jehoiakim refer 19:1—20:6; 26; 35; 36; to Zedekiah's 27–29; 32; 34; 37f.; to the time after the fall of the city, 39–44. Baruch ended his book with a prophecy which Jeremiah had given to him personally in 604. In view of the terrible crisis which was so soon to come upon his people, Baruch must ask nothing for himself. Yahweh will spare his life. That great boon must suffice. The little oracle formed, as it were, a seal upon Baruch's book.

Both Jeremiah's and Baruch's books were subjected to much revision. A great many passages appear twice, some even three times. In the Greek Version a number of these repetitions and other additions do not yet occur, indeed its original Hebrew text had some 2700 words less than our Hebrew text, a clear indication that the latter text was expanded in places by later scribes. Literary criticism suggests that the diffuseness of style, which is at times wearisome, was not due to Jeremiah but to copyists and editors.[14]

---

at the end (46–51), others, represented by the Greek Version, had them in a different order between Jer. 25:13 and 25:14.

[14] A fragment of an early Jeremiah scroll, dating from *ca.* 200 B.C., was found in Cave IV at Qumram. Where preserved it follows the shorter text represented by the Septuagint.

XII

Ezekiel and

the Holiness Code

AMONG the exiles carried to Babylonia in 597 was Ezekiel, a priest who was destined to become one of the most influential prophets. The group to which he belonged was settled at Tel Abib (more phonetically written Tel Aviv, now the name of the capital of the new state of Israel). It seems likely that this name was originally Babylonian: *Til-abūbi*, "mound of the flood," a designation for ancient ruined sites popularly believed to have been destroyed by the Deluge. Ezekiel refers to his being at the river Chebar. It was a thrilling discovery when the Assyriologist H. V. Hilprecht announced in 1903 that the name of this river had been found in business documents of the fifth century B.C. from the Babylonian city of Nippur.[1] This was made all the more plausible by the fact that these texts contained many Hebrew names—evidently those of the descendants of Jewish exiles living at or near Nippur in the Persian era.

"In the thirtieth year, the fourth month, on the fifth day of the month" there occurred the experience that made Ezekiel a prophet. This kind of dating follows Babylonian style, but something is missing: the basic chronological starting point.[2] There seems to be a

[1] The river is not mentioned on the Nippur map, which was not elucidated until 1956. Cf. Samuel Kramer, *From the Tablets of Sumer,* 1956, p. 271. It thus was outside the city area and only could have been a canal. The phrase in which it occurs, describing a property between Nippur and the *nār Kabari,* suggests only a small distance. For Hebrew names at Nippur see A. T. Clay, *Light on the Old Testament from Babel,* 1907, p. 444; map, p. 293.

[2] Many scholars take this to mean the thirtieth year of Ezekiel's life (cf. Num. 4:30), but the Babylonian dating pattern is evident. When fully given

parallel dating in v. 2 in which the month number is lost: "The fifth year of the exile of Jehoiachin [593–592], the fifth day of the month." In 593 the fourth month of the Babylonian year began on our July 27, in 592 it began on July 17.

In a trance he saw the throne of Yahweh in a great storm cloud that came from the north and flashed lightning in all directions. Four mysterious beings, looking like men but each with four heads, that of a man, a lion, an ox, and an eagle, and with four wings, shining in unearthly brilliance, bore aloft the throne which had four glittering wheels whose rims were covered with eyes.[3] As they approached with a deafening roar, Ezekiel saw that

> Upon the form that looked like the throne was something like the appearance of a man upon it above. And I saw something like shining metal from what looked like his loins and upward; and from what looked like his loins and downward I saw an appearance like fire, and there was brightness round about it. As the appearance of the bow that is in the cloud in the day of rain, so was the appearance of the brightness round about. This was the appearance of the likeness of the glory of Yahweh. (1:26–28)

Ezekiel saw, of course, in a flash, what takes so long to tell. Overwhelmed by the power of the vision, Ezekiel fell down on his face, but heard at once the voice of Yahweh commanding, "Son of man, stand upon thy feet, and I will speak with thee!" The Spirit entered into him so that he could stand up to be commissioned as

the dates in the chronicle texts have year, month, and day. In the Wiseman text the day is usually omitted, but cf. the long known chronicle text starting with the accession of Tiglathpileser III. The second date given in Ezekiel would not necessarily have to agree with the first, but is probably correct. A dating by the thirtieth year of Nebuchadrezzar would make this vision too late (574). But at Nippur there may have been a continuation of popular dating by an event of local interest. The Wiseman chronicle mentions events at Nippur (which had been an Assyrian outpost), for 623, which would be thirty years before 593. Unfortunately the tablet is broken here, but it seems possible that Nippur was liberated in that year by Nabopolassar. This would have been an occasion to date from. Such a dating as "in the thirtieth year of the liberation of Nippur by Nabopolassar" might readily have been damaged at the beginning of a scroll, or have become incomprehensible and dropped.

[3] The prophet's imagination creates unnatural imagery in the attempt to make the object express ideas. Eyes on the rims of wheels are peculiar; but the starting point of the idea may have been the ornamental rosette on the hub of chariot wheels, as shown on Assyrian sculptures. These rosettes have a circle in the middle.

Yahweh's prophet to his people: he must go and give to them God's messages without fear; whether they will hear in their rebelliousness or not, in any case they will know that a prophet has been among them. What he must say was given him in a scroll written on both sides, containing "lamentations, and mourning, and woe." This he had to eat, "and it was in my mouth as honey for sweetness." Jeremiah also had "eaten" Yahweh's words and they had been the joy and rejoicing of his heart. Like Isaiah Ezekiel was to have no success, like Jeremiah he would have to face much opposition. But

Behold, I have made thy face hard against their faces, and thy forehead hard against their foreheads. As an adamant harder than flint have I made thy forehead: fear them not, neither be dismayed at their looks, though they are a rebellious house. (3:8f.)

As the glory of Yahweh departed with the sound of a great rushing, Ezekiel was lifted up by the Spirit. "And I went in bitterness, in the heat of my spirit; and the hand of Yahweh was strong upon me." It was the natural feeling of resentment against the psychic pressure that held him enthralled. "Then I came to them of the captivity at Tel Abib . . . and I sat there overwhelmed among them seven days." He was completely stunned by the awful experience of the vision.

How strongly Ezekiel was influenced by his predecessors, especially by Isaiah and Jeremiah, is apparent at once. But he took almost three chapters (1:4—3:15) to tell his inaugural vision, while Isaiah told his in thirteen verses, suggesting rather than minutely describing, but arousing in the reader the feeling of deep reverence which had filled him in those moments of awe. Ezekiel was a theologian and his theological interest was prominent even in his inaugural vision, as we shall see.

A week after his call, the prophet was made a kind of minister to the exiles in a message that reveals his highly developed sense of personal responsibility for each individual soul entrusted to his care.

Son of man, I have made thee a watchman to the house of Israel: when thou hearest a word at My mouth, give them warning from Me. When I say to the wicked, Thou shalt surely die; and thou givest him not warning, nor speakest to warn the wicked from his wicked way, to save his life; the same wicked man shall die for his iniquity; but his blood will I require at thy hand. And if thou warn the wicked, and he turn not from his wickedness, nor from his wicked way, he shall die for his iniquity; but thou hast delivered thy soul. Again, when a righteous man turns from his righteousness, and commits iniquity, and I lay a stumblingblock before him, he shall die: because thou hast not given him warning, he shall die for his sin, and his righteous deeds which he has done shall not be remembered; but his blood will I require at thy hand. But if thou warn the righteous man, that he sin not, and he do not sin, he shall surely live, because he took warning; and thou hast delivered thy soul. (3:17–21)

As he went forth to fulfill his mission, he used every means at his disposal to impress the people with the one great truth which he had to deliver: the certainty of the imminent destruction of Jerusalem and Judah. As a result of the terrible impression the vision of Yahweh had made upon him, leaving him stunned for a week, his nervous system was so severely shaken that he was subject to cataleptic attacks. But he came to see in a vision that they were one of God's ways of speaking through him to the people.

Go, shut thyself within thy house. But thou, son of man, behold, I will lay bands upon thee, and bind thee with them, and thou shalt not go out among them: and I will make thy tongue cleave to the roof of thy mouth, that thou shalt be dumb, and shalt not be to them a reprover; for they are a rebellious house. But when I speak with thee, I will open thy mouth, and thou shalt say to them, Thus says the Lord Yahweh: He that will hear, let him hear; and he that will forbear, let him forbear: for they are a rebellious house. (3:24–27)

In the course of a series of object-lessons which he enacted at the divine command his cataleptic tendency was made an impressive vehicle of prophecy. In the first object-lesson he pictured the impending siege of the city.

Thou, son of man, take thee a tile, and lay it before thee, and portray upon it a city, and lay siege against it, and build forts against it, and cast up a mound against it; set camps also against it, and plant battering rams against it round about. And take thee an iron pan, and set it for a wall of iron between thee and the city: and set thy face toward it, and it shall be besieged, and thou shalt lay siege against it. This shall be a sign to the house of Israel. And thou shalt set thy face toward the siege of Jerusalem, with thine arm uncovered: and thou shalt prophesy against it. (4:1–3, 7)

In the second object-lesson Ezekiel portrayed the plight of the besieged and the rationing of foodstuffs and water.

Take thou also unto thee wheat, and barley, and beans, and lentils, and millet, and spelt, and put them in one vessel, and make thee bread thereof. And thy food which thou shalt eat shall be by weight, twenty shekels a day: from time to time shalt thou eat it. And thou shalt drink water by measure, the sixth part of a hin: from time to time shalt thou drink. Moreover he said to me, Son of man, behold, I will break the staff of bread in Jerusalem: and they shall eat bread by weight, and with fearfulness; and they shall drink water by measure, and in dismay: that they may want bread and water, and be dismayed one with another, and pine away in their iniquity. (4:9a, 10f., 16f.)

Between these two now stands the object-lesson of the length of the exile of Israel and of Judah, which was enacted in two long cataleptic spells.

Moreover lie thou upon thy left side, and bear the punishment of the house of Israel; according to the number of the days that thou shalt lie upon it, thou shalt bear their punishment. For I have appointed the years of their punishment to be to thee a number of days, one hundred and ninety days: so shalt thou bear the punishment of the house of Israel. And, when thou hast accomplished these, thou shalt lie on thy right side, and shalt bear the punishment of the house of Judah: forty days, each day for a year, have I appointed it to thee. And, behold, I lay bands upon thee, and thou shalt not turn thee from one side to the other, till thou hast accomplished the days of thy straits. (4:4-6, 8)

To an object-lesson illustrating the suffering in a foreign land belongs the preparation of unclean food, such as the people will have to eat in exile. It is now interwoven with the object-lesson of the scarcity of bread during the siege.

Take thou also unto thee wheat, and barley, and beans, and lentils, and millet, and spelt, and put them in one vessel, and make thee bread thereof; [according to the number of the days that thou shalt lie upon thy side, even one hundred and ninety days, shalt thou eat thereof.] And thou shalt eat it as barley cakes, and thou shalt bake it in their sight with dung that comes out of man. [And Yahweh said, Even thus shall the children of Israel eat their bread unclean, among the nations whither I will drive them.] Then said I, Ah Lord Yahweh! behold, my soul has not been polluted; for from my youth up even till now have I not eaten of that which dies of itself, or is torn of beasts; neither came there abominable flesh into my mouth. Then He said to me, See, I have given thee cow's dung for man's dung, and thou shalt prepare thy bread thereon. (4:9, 12-15)

With these and similar symbolic actions (compare, *e.g.*, 5:1–12; 12:1–20; 21:18–23), all of them intensely interesting and of deep significance, Ezekiel announced the coming catastrophe of Judah and Jerusalem.[4] The reason for it was the idolatry and moral iniquity of the people. In a vision of great historical value Ezekiel described the idolatry in the temple of Jerusalem. A bright angel took him by a lock of his hair to Jerusalem and showed him the image which provoked Yahweh's jealousy, the cult of the mysteries, the lamentation for Tammuz or Adonis, and the worship of the sun, all of them in the temple (ch. 8).

But this religious corruption was not all. The moral iniquity of "the bloody city," of kings and princes, priests and prophets and people cried to heaven (7:23; 9:9; 11:6ff.; 22; 24:6f.; 34:1–10). Ezekiel put moral and religious sins on the same basis. The whole history of Israel from the beginning was one of blackest unfaithfulness to Yahweh. Judah was worse than Israel, even than Sodom (ch. 16; 23). The inevitable result of such wickedness must be fearful punishment. Ezekiel heard in his vision how the destroying angels were summoned, and saw how one of them set a mark upon the foreheads of the pious in Jerusalem before the terrible slaughter of the inhabitants began and before the angel scattered heavenly fire over the city (ch. 9f.). "And the glory of Yahweh went up from the midst of the city, and stood upon the mountain which is upon the east side of the city" (11:23). That was a prerequisite, for the city could never be destroyed as long as Yahweh was in it!

The judgment was coming; "that they may know that I am Yahweh" was Ezekiel's constant refrain. It was not to be disciplinary and redemptive but strictly punitive. His holy name had been profaned, Yahweh must vindicate His holiness by justice.

In this connection Ezekiel worked out a severe theory of individual retribution. Religion was to him a matter of the individual.

---

[4] Some scholars holding all this to be out of place in Babylonia assume that Ezekiel returned to Jerusalem from the exile and carried on a ministry there. Another view is that he was not carried off at all in 597, but that his book was later edited to make it seem that he was. G. Hölscher (1924) held only the poetic sections of the book to be authentic; similarly W. Irwin (1943). C. C. Torrey considered it a pseudepigraph of the third century B.C. For a detailed account of this debate see H. H. Rowley, "The Book of Ezekiel in Modern Study," *Bulletin of the John Rylands Library*, vol. 36, pp. 146ff.

Reward for righteousness or wickedness was strictly individual too.
Over against the complaint of the people, which voiced itself in the
bitter irony of the proverb, "The fathers have eaten sour grapes,
and the children's teeth are set on edge," Ezekiel insisted that each
one is rewarded or punished for his own deeds not for those of another, "the soul that sins shall die," "Yahweh is righteous and will
judge every one after his own ways," every single individual! And
only for what he himself has done will he be held responsible. There
is no indiscriminate punishment, no suffering for the sins of others,
no hereditary guilt. Neither will the goodness of another have any
vicarious influence. Nobody will be saved by the righteousness of
another.

> Though these three righteous men, Noah, Daniel, and Job, were in it
> (the city), they should deliver but their own souls by their righteousness,
> says the Lord Yahweh. (14:14–20)

Every man stands or falls by himself. The solidarity of society,
which had hitherto been emphasized so strongly, is here broken up.
There is no organic social relation among its individual personalities.
They are each independent entities. Ezekiel carried this principle
still further by separating the moral life of the individual into single
separate acts. Life was to him not an organic whole, but composed
of countless single acts. Character was not taken into account. This
has been called the atomism of the moral life, for life is divided into
atoms in this theory. If a righteous man sins, his whole life of
righteousness is not counted. If a wicked man repents and does
justly, his whole life of wickedness is not counted.

> As I live, says the Lord Yahweh, I have no pleasure in the death of the
> wicked; but that the wicked turn from his way and live: turn ye, turn
> ye from your evil ways; for why will ye die, O house of Israel? (33:11)

This theory is elaborated upon especially in chs. 18 and 33.

The extremes of Ezekiel's position were due to the practical
exigencies of the situation. He needed to emphasize the truth that
God would accept the sinner, if he sincerely repented, no matter
what his past life of sin had been. That he also at times predicted
the indiscriminate extermination of the righteous and the wicked in
the destruction of the city is seen from 21:3,

Behold, I am against thee, I will draw forth My sword out of its sheath, and will cut off from thee the righteous and wicked.

As teacher Ezekiel could not merely emphasize the negative side of his doctrine of retribution, but must show to men an ideal of piety which was attainable. And this he did. God had given them a law. To keep it ensures life (20:11–13). The spirit of Deuteronomy was strong in Ezekiel.

As spiritual counselor of the exiles he had to deal also with practical problems which the elders proposed to him. One was in connection with the manner of worship from which all idolatrous elements are to be banished (14:1–11). Another had to do with the question of erecting a sanctuary to Yahweh in Babylonia. Ezekiel frowned upon it, in the spirit of Deuteronomy. Learn the lessons of history: it was your idolatry, your worship on the high places, that ruined you. Yahweh wants only one place, Jerusalem, as His sanctuary.

For in My holy mountain, in the mountain of the height of Israel, says the Lord Yahweh, there shall all the house of Israel, all of them, serve Me in the land: there will I accept them, and there will I require your offerings, and the first-fruits of your oblations, with all your holy things. With the sweet savor will I accept you, when I bring you out from the peoples, and gather you out of the countries wherein ye have been scattered; and I will be sanctified in you in the sight of the nations. And ye shall know that I am Yahweh, when I shall bring you to the land of Israel, to the country which I sware to give to your fathers. And there shall ye remember your ways, and all your doings, wherein ye have polluted yourselves; and ye shall loathe yourselves in your own sight for all your evils that ye have committed. And ye shall know that I am Yahweh, when I have dealt with you for My name's sake, not according to your evil ways, nor according to your corrupt doings, O ye house of Israel, says the Lord Yahweh. (20:40–44)

Underlying all of Ezekiel's teaching was his belief in the awful holiness of physical majesty and absolute power of Yahweh. This had been wrought into every fiber of his being in the awe-inspiring visions of Yahweh. Beside Him there was no other god, *i.e.*, no real god. The gods of the nations were to Ezekiel only angels. In the inaugural vision the four throne bearers and the heavenly throne symbolized the gods of the four corners of the world and the sky with its countless stars (eyes): Yahweh was enthroned above them all, the other gods were but His ministers or parts of His throne! And again, the seven destroying angels in ch. 9, representing as they most probably do the gods of the seven planets,[5] were no longer rivals of the omnipotent Yahweh. The beginning of the later highly developed Jewish angelology is here made. As yet Yahweh Himself spoke to Ezekiel, but the angels performed the various deeds, they tended to become intermediaries between the transcendent God and weak, mortal man ("the son of man"). This must not be taken to mean that Ezekiel entertained a more spiritual conception of God by emphasizing His transcendence. He merely stressed the holiness of God, which Isaiah had proclaimed so strongly. And he emphasized it in such a way that the God of Jeremiah with His tenderness and solicitude, coupled with His great moral earnestness, seems quite different from this God whose passion is His own holiness and who punishes with relentless wrath. God's interest in the nations, according to Ezekiel, was only to compel the recognition of His holiness by His almighty power: "They shall know that I am Yahweh, when I shall lay My vengeance upon them." Again and again this idea is expressed. This acknowledgment of His holiness is all that Ezekiel was interested in. He never thought of a conversion of the nations or of the establishment of intimate relations with them. The universal implications of monotheism he never understood. To him Yahweh and Israel belonged together; Jerusalem was the center of the world, where Yahweh dwelt. He held this not as a traditional doctrine, but as a vital element of his faith. We find therefore with him a universal God but not a universal religion.

Up to the fall of Jerusalem in 586 Ezekiel remained the prophet of doom; in varied manner he proclaimed the end of Judah and Jerusalem. He enacted strange object-lessons, narrated remarkable visions, delivered searching addresses, allegories, and parables until the catastrophe came. On the day that Nebuchadrezzar began the siege his wife was taken from him, and this became the occasion of an object-lesson.

[5] Compare especially the heavenly writer with the inkhorn with the Babylonian god Nabu, the scribe of the gods.

The word of Yahweh came to me, saying, Son of man, behold, I take away from thee the desire of thine eyes with a stroke: yet thou shalt neither mourn nor weep, neither shall thy tears run down. Sigh, but not aloud, make no mourning for the dead; bind thy headtire upon thee, and put thy shoes upon thy feet, and cover not thy beard, and eat not the bread of mourners. So I spoke to the people in the morning; and at even my wife died; and I did in the morning as I was commanded. (24:15–18)

When the people asked him why he behaved so strangely, he told them that soon the temple, the desire of their eyes, would be profaned and the children they had left behind in Jerusalem would be slain. Then they would do as Ezekiel was now doing (24:19ff.). For Tyre and Egypt against whom Nebuchadrezzar also warred, he had oracles predicting their ruin (chs. 26–30).

One night in January, 585, half a year after Jerusalem had fallen, Ezekiel felt the hand of Yahweh upon him; the terrible presentiment that something awful had happened struck him dumb with fear. The next day the news came, "The city is smitten." Then his mouth was opened again so that he could speak.[6] He was no longer dumb. The great tension under which he had been was over. The crisis had passed. His predictions of doom had been fulfilled (33:21f.).

A new period began for him. Soon he looked forward into the future, and became a prophet of restoration. He reasoned as follows. The fundamental principle that controlled all actions of Yahweh was His holiness. The profanation of His holy name by Israel had necessitated their punishment, "that they may know that I am Yahweh." But now after they had been taken into exile, it was the nations that profaned it by ridiculing Israel and Yahweh, who had been impotent to save His people: "These are the people of Yahweh! and they are gone forth out of His land!" To vindicate His holiness before the whole world Yahweh must show His absolute power in order that all should know that it was not due to His impotence but to His judgment that Israel had been carried into captivity. Thus He will punish the nations that surrounded Judah and restore His people to its own land (ch. 36). Ammon, Moab, Edom, and Philistia will suffer, "that they may know that I am Yahweh."

---

[6] The "pathological" aspect of Ezekiel's personality has engaged various writers, including Karl Jaspers (1947).

Therefore say to the house of Israel, Thus says the Lord Yahweh: I do it not for your sake, O house of Israel, but for My holy name, which ye have profaned among the nations, whither ye went. And I will sanctify My great name, which has been profaned among the nations, which ye have profaned in the midst of them; and the nations shall know that I am Yahweh, says the Lord Yahweh, when I shall be sanctified in you before their eyes. (36:22f.)

Israel will be restored. Her political resurrection is foretold in the famous vision of the Dry Bones which are revivified by the Spirit of God (37:1–14). Yahweh, the good shepherd, will gather all His scattered flock from all countries and bring them back to their homeland (34:11ff.). But only the righteous will be permitted to return; in a cleansing judgment in the Syrian desert all rebels and sinners will be removed (20:34–39; 34:17–22). To the remnant Yahweh will give a new heart and a new spirit, and His own Spirit will dwell in them making them loyal and obedient.

And I will sprinkle clean water upon you, and ye shall be clean: from all your filthiness, and from all your idols, will I cleanse you. A new heart will I give you, and a new spirit will I put within you; and I will take away the stony heart out of your bosom, and I will give you a heart of flesh. And I will put My Spirit within you, and cause you to walk in My statutes, and ye shall keep Mine ordinances, and do them. Then shall ye remember your evil ways, and your doings that were not good; and ye shall loathe yourselves in your own sight for your iniquities and for your abominations. (36:25–27, 31)

In all this Yahweh takes the initiative. He cannot wait for Israel's repentance. But Ezekiel believed that it would inevitably come as a result of Yahweh's wonderful grace. The prophets before him had maintained that repentance must precede forgiveness and restoration. Ezekiel believed that "we love God because He first loved us." This renewed people will return to Palestine, both Israel and Judah, and there they will be united under one Davidic king, a strong and numerous nation, blest with fertility and peace.

The word of Yahweh came again to me, saying, And thou, son of man, take thee a stick, and write upon it, "Judah, and the children of Israel attached to him": then take another stick, and write upon it, "Joseph, the stick of Ephraim, and all the house of Israel attached to him": and join them for thee one to another into one stick, that they may become one stick in thy hand. And when the children of thy people shall speak to thee, saying, Wilt thou not show us what thou meanest by these? say to them, Thus says the Lord Yahweh: Behold, I will take the stick of Joseph, which is in the hand of Ephraim, and the tribes of Israel attached to him; and I will put them with it (with the stick of Judah) and make them one stick, and they shall be one stick in the hand of Judah. And the sticks on which thou writest shall be in thy hand before their eyes. And say to them, Thus says the Lord Yahweh: Behold, I will take the children of Israel from among the nations, whither they are gone, and will gather them on every side, and bring them into their own land: and I will make them one nation in the land, upon the mountains of Israel; and one king shall be king to them all; and they shall be no more two nations, neither shall they be divided into two kingdoms any more at all; neither shall they defile themselves any more with their idols, but I will save them from all their backslidings, wherein they have sinned, and will cleanse them: so shall they be My people, and I will be their God.

And My servant David shall be king over them; and they all shall have one shepherd: they shall also walk in Mine ordinances, and observe My statutes, and do them. And they shall dwell in the land that I have given to Jacob My servant, wherein their fathers dwelt; and they shall dwell therein, they, and their children, and their children's children, for ever: and David My servant shall be their prince for ever. Moreover I will make a covenant of peace with them; it shall be an everlasting covenant with them; and I will set My sanctuary in the midst of them for evermore. My tabernacle also shall be with them; and I will be their God, and they shall be My people. And the nations shall know that I am Yahweh that sanctifies Israel, when My sanctuary shall be in the midst of them for evermore. (37:15–28)

Ezekiel based his hope for the future entirely upon the exiles. The people who had remained in Palestine after the catastrophe of 586 felt themselves the true heirs of the nation. But Ezekiel strongly opposed them, they were idolaters and murderers, and Yahweh would surely exterminate them (33:23–29). Similarly, the Edomites, who had occupied Judean territory, would be driven out, their own country would be devastated or they themselves would be destroyed (ch. 35).

In order to remove any doubt that the new condition of happiness and peace would prevail forever, and in order that Yahweh should be recognized the world over, Ezekiel introduced an entirely new element into the prophetic thought of the future. After the restoration, the northern enemy who had been predicted by former

prophets will come. Gog of Magog as the head and representative
of united heathendom will attack Israel with a vast army, but Yahweh Himself will fight against him with the forces of nature. The
immense multitude of the slain will be a prey to the ravenous birds
and beasts, and it will take more than seven months to bury the
remains. The mass of weapons will be so great that they will serve
as fuel for fire for seven years, for they will not be needed for war
any more (ch. 38f.).

To these great hopes of political and moral restoration Ezekiel
added the ecclesiastical. The restoration could be perfect and lasting only if Yahweh dwelt in the midst of His people forever. In
586 before the destruction took place, He had left Jerusalem because His holy name had been profaned. He will come again and
the very name of the city will be "Yahweh is there." But to ensure
His perpetual presence every profanation of His holy name must be
made impossible. Ezekiel meditated long on this problem. He believed it could be solved by the sharp antithesis between the sacred
and profane. This was the basic principle of his plan, which he completed early in 573 and which he had worked out so thoroughly
that it stood objectively before him in a vision (ch. 40–48).[7] He
was carried in the trance to Jerusalem, where an angel appeared
as his guide and instructor and showed him the new order.

The first point of importance was that the new sanctuary should
be guarded against every profanation. Yahweh, he believed, would
alter the topography to suit the needs of the future. He saw that
this had been done by isolating the temple on the top of a high hill,
which was situated in Judah in the middle of a strip of territory comprising 25,000 square cubits. It was walled in and surrounded by two
courts. From the open space which surrounded the outer wall Ezekiel
ascended a stairway to one of the four gates of the outer court;
passing through it, he ascended another stairway to one of the four
gates of the inner court, in the middle of which stood the sanctuary
on a still higher level, up to which a stairway led, with only one
entrance from the east. It was divided into the entrance hall, the

[7] The authenticity of this section of the book of Ezekiel has been subject to
much doubt. But there is increasing confidence that at least a nucleus of this
material comes from the prophet's pen. The introduction 40:1–4 can hardly
be discounted and demands this kind of a continuation.

holy place, and the holy of holies. Ezekiel was told, "Son of man, this is the place of My throne, and the place of the soles of My feet, where I will dwell in the midst of the children of Israel forever." The isolation of the temple was complete.

The royal palace no longer adjoined the temple nor did the royal graves defile it, and the city was about one and a half miles south of it. Immediately surrounding the temple was an open space. At a distance of 50 cubits, surrounding the temple precincts, was an area of 10,000 by 25,000 cubits where the priests would live. Adjoining them in the north, the Levites had an equally large district. The city was south of the priests, but separated from them by 500 cubits. The sanctuary was thus well protected, at least externally, against defilement.

But the sanctifying principle was carried still further. East and west of the sacred square, extending to the Jordan and Dead Sea and to the Mediterranean, respectively, were the royal domains. To the north the tribe of Judah, to the south the tribe of Benjamin immediately adjoined, for they were the most faithful; the others lived to the north or south of them each in an equally large district. The whole land was sacred, to be inhabited only by Yahweh's people. In their midst, safeguarded on all sides against defilement, Yahweh dwelt in His temple. The people had access only to the outer court. The priests alone could minister in the house. The holy of holies not even the priest Ezekiel entered in his vision: only the angel went in.

The second point of importance in the sharp antithesis between the sacred and profane was the personnel of the temple. The foreign temple slaves were abolished. In the former temple they had performed the menial tasks, "uncircumcised in heart and uncircumcised in flesh." But no longer may any uncircumcised foreigner enter the temple; his presence would defile it. Their places were to be taken by the Levites, who did not belong to the sons of Zadok, the Jerusalem priests. They were the priests of the ancient sanctuaries outside of Jerusalem which had been abolished in 621. The Deuteronomic law (18:6–8) had provided that they should participate in the cult at Jerusalem. But the Zadokites did not permit them to share their rich income. Ezekiel ordered therefore that while they should gain their living in the temple at Jerusalem, they might do so only as priests of an inferior class, they should be watchmen and butchers and do all the other menial tasks that the old temple slaves had formerly done.[8] He justified this "degradation of the Levites" as a penalty for their idolatrous service on the high places.

Thus says the Lord Yahweh, No foreigner, uncircumcised in heart and uncircumcised in flesh, shall enter into My sanctuary, of any foreigners that are among the children of Israel. But those Levites that went far from Me, when Israel went astray, that went astray from Me after their idols, they shall suffer punishment. They shall be ministers in My sanctuary, having oversight at the gates of the house, and ministering in the house: they shall slay the burnt-offering and the sacrifice for the people, and they shall stand before them to minister to them. Because they ministered to them before their idols, and became a stumblingblock of iniquity to the house of Israel; therefore have I lifted up My hand against them, says the Lord Yahweh, and they shall suffer punishment. And they shall not come near to Me, to execute the office of priest to Me, nor to come near to any of My holy things, to the things that are most holy; but they shall bear their shame and their abominations which they have committed. Yet will I make them keepers of the charge of the house, for all the service thereof and for all that be done therein. (44:9–14)

The Zadokites, the Jerusalem priests, alone may perform the real priestly functions, they alone may officiate in the inner court and the sanctuary. In order that even they may not defile the temple, strict orders were given: they should wear only linen garments in the temple lest they perspire, and they must put them off when they leave the inner court lest they communicate holiness to the people by their touch. They must not drink wine when they go on duty; they dare not marry a widow, except the widow of a priest, nor a divorced woman; nor may they go into the presence of a dead person, unless it be the nearest relative.

The third point on which Ezekiel concentrated his attention was the cult. It was necessary to devise a cultic system for the continual renewal of the fellowship between Yahweh and Israel by removing any accidental profanations. Through the cult, especially through the sin-offerings, atonement was made, the sanctuary cleansed, Yahweh pacified. These sin-offerings were to be brought especially

[8] This development merely legalizes a situation that had already developed in the preexilic temple after Josiah's reform (see p. 133).

on New Year's Day, on the Passover, and on the fifteenth of the seventh month. The prince must provide for these sacrifices. Definite regulations for the daily as well as the Sabbath and New Moon sacrifices are given. The cult becomes of central importance in the life of the restored community.

The political side was minimized in this plan of the new constitution of Israel. Its land was confined to the region west of the Jordan, from Hamath in the north to Kadesh and the Egyptian frontier in the south—boundaries Israel had only attained for a brief period under David. Rather strangely no claim was made to any territory east of the Jordan. But western Palestine shall belong to Israel in its entirety. No Philistines or Edomites will be there, for they will be destroyed. Only Israel shall live there and such foreigners as have been received into full citizenship. It seems as if the political status of the Davidic king was also lowered. He is called not king but "prince," and his main business appears to be to provide for the maintenance of the cult from the taxes which he receives from the people. But Ezekiel may have avoided the term king as a matter of caution. And in 45:8–12; 46:18 he refers to the social and political administration and the duties of a just government, although, according to his principle, the people in the restored community would all be holy and righteous. His sense of reality here was stronger than the ideal. It was just the opposite in the apportionment of the territories of the different tribes, for each gets an equal strip of land from the Mediterranean to the Jordan or the Dead Sea, irrespective of all demands of history or topography.

The program was essentially particularistic. Ezekiel never thought of the conversion of the nations and their participation in the blessings of the new era. The wonderful river flowing out of the sanctuary (ch. 47) is neither literally nor figuratively a blessing for the whole world. The desert and the Dead Sea are impossible in the holy land where Yahweh dwells and where everything is fruitful. The blessings of the river were material not spiritual. The trees were for food and for medicine. Strikingly enough, some salty marshes which served the purpose of obtaining salt (a taxed item in 1 Macc. 10:29) were to remain. Ezekiel's practical sense shines through in this provision.

Ezekiel stood between the priestly and prophetic movements; more priestly than Deuteronomy he was still a prophet, who at the transition of one age to another worked for the transformation of the older, freer, national ideas into the newer, stricter, ecclesiastical ideals and institutions. He therefore has been well called the Father of Judaism. He was extremely influential. His pronounced individualism and particularism; his emphasis on the transcendence of God with its accompanying angelology; his teaching concerning the future, Gog of Magog and the reign of blessedness until his onslaught,[9] the new Jerusalem and the wonderful river; but especially his subordination of the political state to the religious community and his emphasis on the cult influenced both Catholic and Protestant thought and ecclesiastical life profoundly.

The book of Ezekiel is very clearly arranged—a circumstance to be attributed to his editors rather than to the prophet himself—and in the main in strict chronological order with definite dates. The first part contains prophecies of judgment (chs. 1–24), the second prophecies of hope, involving negatively the punishment of the nations (chs. 25–32) and positively the restoration of Israel (chs. 33–48), of which the plan of a new constitution forms the end (chs. 40–48). Some passages of hope which really belong to the second part now appear in the first part. The prophet did not hesitate to make changes in his former utterances. On New Year of 571 he corrected an oracle against Tyre (29:17–20) which he had given in 586 and in which he had predicted its capture by Nebuchadrezzar. After the Babylonians had been obliged to raise their 27 years' siege, Ezekiel promised to Nebuchadrezzar the conquest of Egypt as a compensation for Tyre.

Ezekiel's style shows no distinction. He was prosaic even when he wrote poetry. Not that he lacked imagination; he delighted in allegories and symbolic expressions (which sometimes offend our taste) and he could visualize things and situations sharply, but he had no poetic talent. He was a thinker and knew how to write lucidly. But he loved and never wearied of reiteration.[10] Still, not

[9] Ezekiel did not specify the length of this period, but here is the germ of what later became the millennium. Cf. Rev. 20.

[10] The repetitiousness of Ezekiel may, however, be due to later commentary and expansion of text. The editing of this book was evidently very different from that of other prophetic books.

all repetitions come from him, many are due to a poorly edited text, and the occasional obscurities are the work of bad copyists. His book deserves much study not for its literary qualities but for its significant contributions. He may not be so attractive as Jeremiah, but he was more immediately influential.

Another writer among the exiles gave proof of this by compiling the little law book in Leviticus 17–26, which is appropriately called the Holiness Code, and abbreviated H.[11] He is akin to Ezekiel in spirit, thought, and expression. In spite of the great catastrophe that had broken upon the Jews, he could not let go of his belief that Yahweh would not cast them off forever, that there must be a future for them, if they repented. And so he worked in the midst of the exile for the restoration. He was not a man of thrilling visions, but his conviction burnt in his soul like a steady flame and made him work out—with the help of older materials which he simply took over—the norms of the future community in this law book. It occupies an intermediate place between Deuteronomy and the later Priestly Code, in which it was afterwards incorporated. But it can still easily be distinguished by its characteristic phraseology and the concluding remark,

These are the statutes and ordinances and laws, which Yahweh made between Him and the children of Israel in Mount Sinai by Moses. (Lev. 26:46)

His controlling thought was the holiness of Yahweh and the obligation of the people to be holy also. One of his formulas is, "Ye shall be holy for I, Yahweh your God, am holy" (Lev. 19:2; 20:7, 26; 21:8), another is the ever repeated "I am Yahweh (your God)," to which there is added several times "who sanctifies you" (or "them" or "him"). This holiness was primarily physical, it was not moral perfection but especially the separation from everything tabooed by the religion of Yahweh. Holy to Yahweh meant separate from any other god and whatever belonged to his cult, it implied avoidance of everything that defiled, it referred to ritual sanctity. Its characteristic meaning is brought out in Lev. 20:26,

You shall be holy unto Me, for I, Yahweh, am holy, and have set you apart from the peoples that you should be Mine.

[11] First recognized as separate and so named by A. Klostermann in 1877.

The first law of H, at least in the order in which we have the code now, is a prohibition of secular slaughter. Deuteronomy had permitted it, because after the centralization of the cult in Jerusalem it would have been impossible to compel the people to go to the temple for every animal that was to be slaughtered. There had been no distinction between sacred and secular slaughter before; every slaughter was a sacrifice. When now the distinction was made, the ordinary man did not always remember that there was such a distinction, his slaughter was to him a sacrifice, and it was easy enough to regard it as brought to the local demons. To guard against this, H forbade the practice of secular slaughter altogether:

> To the end that the children of Israel may bring their sacrifices, which they sacrifice in the open field, even that they may bring them to the priest, and sacrifice them for sacrifices of peace-offerings to Yahweh. And the priest shall sprinkle the blood upon the altar of Yahweh and burn the fat for a sweet savor to Yahweh. And they shall no more sacrifice their sacrifices to the he-goats, after which they play the harlot. (Lev. 17:5-7)

If H thought at all of the practicability of this law in combination with the centralization of worship in Jerusalem, he must have expected the restored community to occupy only a small territory about Jerusalem. Closely connected with slaughter was the prohibition of eating the blood which was sacred to Yahweh, for it is the seat of life,

> I have given it to you upon the altar to make atonement for your souls, for it is the blood that makes atonement by reason of the life. (17:11)

In ch. 18 laws are given regulating the sexual life, forbidding marriage among very near relatives and certain sexual abominations which were practised by the Egyptians and Canaanites. For the Jews they were all defiling and punishable by death.[12] How seriously concerned H was about these matters appears from his insertion of a parallel list in ch. 20, where the punishment for each crime is

---

[12] An advance on earlier customs appears in the prohibition of the marriage of brother and half-sister (contrast Gen. 20:12; 2 Sam. 13:13), of a man and his brother's wife (contrast the "Levirate" marriage of Deut. 25:5f.), and of a husband and his wife's sister during the lifetime of the wife (contrast Leah and Rachel, Gen. 29).

added and an exhortation to holiness concludes the whole. Moloch worship is condemned in both chapters, witchcraft is stamped as a moral crime at the end of ch. 20.

A law containing certain food taboos was also found in H, for in 20:25 we read,

Ye shall therefore make a distinction between the clean beast and the unclean, and between the unclean fowl and the clean: and ye shall not make your souls abominable by beast, or by bird, or by anything where-with the ground teems, which I have separated from you as unclean. (Lev. 20:25)

A specified list appears in Lev. 11, in which vv. 43–45 are according to style and thought quite certainly from H—the rest being later material.

The whole emphasis in these laws is on cultic purity, and the same is true of the laws for the priests and high priests, and the right quality of sacrificial animals (Lev. 21f.) as well as of the laws concerning the holy days and festivals, Sabbath, Unleavened Bread, Feast of Weeks and of Booths (23:1–3, 9–12, 15–20, 39–44). The ancient agricultural meaning of the great harvest feasts is still preserved, but the Feast of Booths is already interpreted (in addition to the Feast of Unleavened Bread) as a memorial of the Exodus from Egypt.

How strong H's cultic interest was, may be seen from a comparison of the law of the Sabbath year in Deut. 15 with Lev. 25. This is quite significant, for the Sabbath year was originally a social and economic institution designed for the amelioration of the lot of the poor. In H,

The seventh year shall be a sabbath of solemn rest for the land, a sabbath unto Yahweh: thou shalt neither sow thy field, nor prune thy vineyard. (25:4)

H declares that during the Exile the land enjoyed its Sabbaths and "the rest which it had not in your Sabbaths, when ye dwelt in it" (26:34f.). The land belongs to Yahweh, He alone is the owner, His people are only His tenants. Part of the time the land is to be left to Him alone, it is to be allowed to rest from its production, to keep a Sabbath unto Yahweh.

But H had also the social and moral interests of the people at heart. The holiness in which he was interested is not wholly cultic. In ch. 25 he adds laws against taking unfair advantage of the poor, makes provisions for the buying back of property that had to be sold because of the poverty of the owner, and gives admonitions to aid the impoverished fellow Jews, to charge no interest on loans to them, and not to treat them as slaves with rigor, if they had been compelled to sell themselves, for they are the slaves of none but Yahweh (25:14, 17-25, 35-40a, 42f., 47-49, 53, 55).

Perhaps the supreme contribution of H. is the famous ch. 19 with its great social laws, among which vv. 17f. easily take first rank:

> Thou shalt not hate thy brother in thy heart: thou shalt surely warn thy neighbor, and not incur sin because of him. Thou shalt not take vengeance nor bear any grudge against the children of thy people; but thou shalt love thy neighbor as thyself: I am Yahweh.

This is the highest point in the ethics of the Old Testament, where the inner disposition, the heart, not only the outward deed counts. Jesus regarded it as the commandment which must be joined directly to the greatest commandment, love of God and love of the neighbor. It is true, that "neighbor" meant to H the fellow Jew and therein his limitation appears. But he did not confine it wholly to them, for a little later he says,

> The stranger that sojourns with you shall be to you as the native among you, and thou shalt love him as thyself; for ye were strangers in the land of Egypt: I am Yahweh your God. (19:34)

The spirit of the finest sections of Deuteronomy is seen in such laws. D's influence appears also in H's concluding exhortation (ch. 26) which is modeled on D's. Here however the phraseology of Ezekiel is so apparent that Ezekiel has sometimes been regarded as the author of this chapter. Indeed some have proposed him as the author of the entire Holiness Code. Though that is no longer held, it is clear that Ezekiel was the spiritual kinsman of H. Both worked for the future restoration, impelled thereto by their unconquerable faith in God, who would yet save His people.

After describing the experiences of the exile which have come to

Israel because of its disobedience to the divine laws, H looked forward to the future:

And they shall confess their iniquity, and the iniquity of their fathers, in their trespass which they trespassed against Me, and also that, because they walked contrary to Me, I also walked contrary to them, and brought them into the land of their enemies: if then their uncircumcised heart be humbled, and they then accept of the punishment of their iniquity; then will I remember My covenant with Jacob; and also My covenant with Isaac, and also My covenant with Abraham will I remember; and I will remember the land. The land also shall be left by them, and shall enjoy its Sabbaths, while it lies desolate without them: and they shall accept of the punishment of their iniquity; because, even because they rejected Mine ordinances, and their soul abhorred My statutes. And yet for all that, when they are in the land of their enemies, I will not reject them, neither will I abhor them, to destroy them utterly, and to break My covenant with them; for I am Yahweh their God; but I will for their sakes remember the covenant of their ancestors, whom I brought forth out of the land of Egypt in the sight of the nations, that I might be their God: I am Yahweh. (Lev. 26:40–45)

Ezekiel and H were destined to play a large part in the legal development of religion which culminated in the so-called Priestly Code and in the reign of legalism.[13] Fortunately there were poets and prophets both during the exile and after, to whom the other aspects of religion were more important.

[13] We do not have H in its original form. When it was incorporated in the great Priestly Law Code it was revised and later priestly elements were added, especially the priestly calendar of the festivals (Lev. 23:4–8, 13, 14, 18b, 19a, 21–38), the law of jubilee (Lev. 25:8–12, 15f., 26–34, 41, 44, 50–52, 54), the prescriptions regarding the golden candlestick and the shewbread (Lev. 24:1–9), and the story of the blasphemer who was stoned to death (Lev. 24:10–15a, 16b, 22a, 23). A few sections appear to have been separated from it and put elsewhere (Ex. 31:13–14a; Lev. 11:43–45; Num. 15:37–41).

XIII

Exilic Poets

and Prophets

SHORTLY after the fall of Jerusalem in 587 B.C. the dirges now combined in the Book of Lamentations were composed. A tradition already attested to by the Septuagint attributed them to Jeremiah. But they do not represent the viewpoint of this prophet. Nor is it likely that they are the work of a single poet. The two lamentations which are preserved in the second and fourth chapters are the most closely related ones, and were no doubt composed by men who had experienced the city's destruction. The terrible scenes of the famine, the pitiful cry of the infants for nourishment, the ghastly sight of faces black and withered from suffering, and the horror of mothers eating the flesh of their own children were unforgettable.

The tongue of the sucking child cleaves
   to the roof of his mouth for thirst:
The young children ask bread
   and no man breaks it to them.
They that are slain with the sword are better
   than they that are slain with hunger;
For these pine away, stricken through,
   for want of the fruits of the field.
The hands of the pitiful women
   have boiled their own children;
They were their food
   in the destruction of the daughter of my people. (Lam. 4:4, 9f.)

The fate of the priests and prophets, the anxious, fruitless waiting for relief from Egypt, and the flight with Zedekiah were before the poet:

> Our pursuers were swifter
>   than the eagles of the heavens:
> They chased us upon the mountains,
>   they laid wait for us in the wilderness.
> The breath of our nostrils, the anointed of Yahweh,
>   was taken in their pits;
> Of whom we said, "Under his shadow
>   we shall live among the nations." (4:19f.)

With a bitter prediction to Edom that her punishment also will come very soon ch. 4 closes.

The second chapter is quite similar and gives us vivid and valuable touches of the siege of Jerusalem. It ends with the moving appeal,

> See, O Yahweh, and behold
>   to whom Thou hast done thus!
> Shall the women eat their fruit,
>   the children that are dandled in the hands?
> Shall the priest and the prophet be slain
>   in the sanctuary of the Lord?
> The youth and the old man lie
>   on the ground in the streets;
> My virgins and my young men
>   are fallen by the sword:
> Thou hast slain them in the day of Thine anger;
>   Thou hast slaughtered, and not pitied.
> Thou hast called, as in the day of a solemn assembly,
>   my terrors on every side;
> And there was none that escaped or remained
>   in the day of Yahweh's anger:
> Those that I have dandled and brought up
>   has mine enemy consumed. (2:20–22)

The author took the characteristic lamentation meter with its longer first and shorter second half lines to express the sorrow of his heart. He also made use of an alphabetic acrostic, beginning each strophe with a new letter in the order of the alphabet (cf. above, p. 147), and did it so well that the artificial side is quickly forgotten by the reader.

It was probably another survivor of the great catastrophe who
wrote perhaps a little later in Palestine a prayer which is now the
fifth chapter of the Book of Lamentations. He put the cruel sufferings of the people before Yahweh and implored Him for mercy and
help. He did not write in lamentation meter or in acrostic form,
but his poem would be of especial value if we could be sure that he
was one of the people that had been left in the land. But this is
uncertain, and for all we know he may have been the same as the
author of chs. 2 and 4, even though he did not use the acrostic and
the lamentation meter.

The writer of ch. 1 did use them, but his mood was different from
that of the others; he was full of deep penitence. He painted Zion's
sad condition after 586 and let the unhappy one speak herself later
on,

> Is it nothing to you, all ye that pass by?
>   behold and see,
> If there be any sorrow like unto my sorrow,
>   which is brought upon me,
> Wherewith Yahweh has afflicted me
>   in the day of His fierce anger. (1:12)

Zion knows that her troubles are due to her sins against Yahweh,
she has deserved her punishment, but she prays that her enemies
also may soon get their desert.

All four of these lamentations are now grouped around the long
acrostic psalm in ch. 3. This is composed in lamentation meter and
the acrostic is accentuated, so that not only the first but every line
of each strophe begins with the same letter of the alphabet. The
artificiality of this is apparent. The poem is less vivid than the others
and seems to be further removed from the catastrophe. It begins
with,

> I am the man that has seen affliction
>   by the rod of His wrath,

and it was probably responsible for the early but untenable tradition
that Jeremiah was the author of the Book of Lamentations. The
one who collected the lamentations in this book did not yet ascribe
them to Jeremiah, but simply called them "Lamentations." The

Greek translation however prefaced the book as follows, "And it
came to pass, after Israel was led into captivity and Jerusalem laid
waste, that Jeremiah sat weeping, and lamented with this lamentation over Jerusalem, and said." The other versions followed this
lead. It was quite natural that these poems should have been ascribed
to Jeremiah,[1] for he was the only inspired author of that period
whose name was handed down to posterity; the names of the real
authors were unknown.

The feelings of many Jews in their Babylonian exile, their sorrow
and homesickness, their love for Jerusalem and their hatred for their
enemies, the Babylonians and the shameless Edomites, who had
gloated over Judah's fall, found expression in Ps. 137, which attracts
us by the beauty and pathos of its beginning and repels us by the
savage cruelty of its conclusion.

> By the rivers of Babylon,
> There we sat down, yea, we wept,
> When we remembered Zion.
> Upon the poplars in its midst
> We hanged up our harps.
> For there our captors required of us songs,
> And mirth our tormentors:
> "Sing us one of the songs of Zion."
>
> How shall we sing Yahweh's song
> In a foreign land?
> If I forget thee, O Jerusalem,
> May my right hand be forgotten.
> May my tongue cleave to the roof of my mouth,
> If I remember thee not;
> If I set not Jerusalem
> Above my chief joy.
>
> Remember, O Yahweh, against the Edomites
> The day of Jerusalem;
> Who said, "Rase it, rase it,
> Even to its foundation!"
> O daughter of Babylon, thou destroyer,

[1] Passages like Jer. 8:21 and 2 Chron. 35:25 may have helped to produce this
supposition.

> Happy shall he be, that rewards thee
> As thou hast served us.
> Happy shall he be, that takes and dashes
> Thy little ones against the rock.

We shudder at this final imprecation and turn with a feeling of relief to the beautiful prayer which is preserved in Is. 63:7—64:11. The author wrote in the early part of the Exile, most probably in Palestine, where he saw not only the ruins of the city and the temple, but also the incredible influence of the Chaldean occupation.

> 'Tis only a little while that they have possessed Thy holy people,
>   that our adversaries trod down Thy sanctuary,
> And we have (already) become as they over whom Thou never borest rule,
>   as they that were not called by Thy name. (Isa. 63:18)

The present was hopeless. So our author turned to God's dealings in the past in order to revive his hope for the future.

> I will recall the loving kindnesses of Yahweh,
>   the praises of Yahweh,
> According to all that Yahweh has bestowed on us,
>   and the great goodness toward the house of Israel. (63:7)

The great time of the beginnings of the nation came into his mind with all the romance woven about it by gratitude and love, how Yahweh had made them His own and placed His trust in them and had said,

> "Surely, they are My people,
>   children that will not deal falsely."
> So He was their Saviour
>   in all their affliction.
> Not a messenger and an angel,
>   His own presence saved them.[2]
> In His love and in His pity
>   He redeemed them,
> And He bore them and carried them
>   all the days of old.

---

[2] The translation "in all their afflictions He was afflicted," etc., which carried with it the profound truth of divine fellowship and sympathy in suffering, if not of God's own atoning suffering, is not supported by the Septuagint. The Hebrew text must be restored according to the latter.

> But they rebelled and grieved
>   His holy Spirit;
> Therefore He was turned to be their enemy,
>   and Himself fought against them. (63:8–10)

Unwittingly the poet has come here to a point from which he can derive no inspiration. So he breaks off this line of thought and decides once more to recall the days of Moses and God's wonderful deeds in that golden age of Israel's past. This kindles his hope anew and he breaks forth into the passionate prayer,

> Look down from heaven, and behold
>   from the habitation of Thy holiness and of Thy glory!
> Where are Thy zeal and Thy mighty acts,
>   the yearning of Thy heart and Thy compassions?
> Do not restrain Thyself!
>   for Thou art our Father,
> Though Abraham know us not,
>   and Israel do not acknowledge us,
> Thou, O Yahweh, art our Father,
> "Our Redeemer" from of old is Thy name. (63:15f.)

The second part of the prayer is similar, but the consciousness of sin is more strongly in the foreground of the poet's thought. He sees the disheartening and demoralizing effects of the fearful calamity. Despair and doubt are twin brothers, and doubt gives way to denial, and denial to indifference.

> O Yahweh, why dost Thou make us to err concerning Thy dealings,
>   and hardenest our hearts against Thy fear? (63:17)

The people cannot understand God's dealings, and the result is that though it is but a short time ago that this terrible thing happened they have lost their faith and do not feel that they have anything to do with Yahweh any more. Oh, that Yahweh would only come down and interfere as in the days of old! The poet is conscious of the sins of the people and of the justice of God's punishment.

> But now, O Yahweh, Thou art our Father:
>   we are the clay, and Thou our potter;
>   and we all are the work of Thy hand.
> Be not wroth very sore, O Yahweh,
>   neither remember iniquity forever:
>   behold, look, we beseech Thee, we are all Thy people. (64:8f.)

A penitent plea for help, not without hope but full of sadness and without certitude.

In 562 Nebuchadrezzar had died, his son Amel-Marduk (the Evil-merodach of 2 Ki. 25:27) had freed King Jehoiachin from prison and allowed him to live at his court.[3] It was the first ray of hope for the Jews. Soon greater things happened. Cyrus entered upon his brilliant career. At first, king of a small dependency of Media, he became in quick succession king of Persia and Media, and in 547–546 attacked and defeated Croesus of Lydia taking the well-nigh impregnable Sardis which he annexed to his realm and wealth. Nabonidus, or Nabonedos as the Greeks called him, the last king of Babylon, was Croesus' ally. Cyrus now turned against him. The details of the war are unknown, only of the final stage are we fully informed by contemporary inscriptions. In 539 Babylon fell into the hands of the Persians.

Several prophets eagerly watched these movements and, years before Babylon fell, they predicted its doom. Their utterances are found in Isa. 13 and 14:4–21. The former is a prophecy. Yahweh has stirred up the Medes against Babylon. He is mustering them for battle. They are His consecrated agents on the Day of Yahweh when He punishes "the world for its evil and the wicked for their iniquity." Following the pattern of Zephaniah, the prophet pictured the awful day, when the sun shall grow dark in the morning, the moon and the stars shall not shine, the earth and the heavens will shake "by the wrath of Yahweh of hosts." But few will escape. "I will make a man more rare than fine gold."

> Every one that is found shall be thrust through;
>   and every one that is taken shall fall by the sword.
> Their infants also shall be dashed in pieces before their eyes;
>   their houses shall be rifled, and their wives ravished. (Isa. 13:15f.)

Babylon shall be completely overthrown, never to be built again. The ghastly desolation and utter desertion of the once glorious city are graphically described. The author was a poet of great dramatic power.

---

[3] See p. 173.

In the second poem the emotion rises still higher. The author sings a song full of gruesome beauty, describing the descent of the king of Babylon to Sheol. At last the oppressor has ceased, his staff is broken "that ruled the nations in anger, with a persecution that none restrained. The whole earth is at rest" and rejoices; even the cedars of Lebanon exult because they will no more be felled. The fall of the tyrant stirs even Sheol.

> Sheol from beneath is moved for thee
> > to meet thee at thy coming;
> It stirs up the dead for thee,
> > even all the chief ones of the earth;
> It has raised up from their thrones
> > all the kings of the nations.
> All they shall answer
> > and say unto thee,
> "Art thou also become weak as we?
> > art thou become like unto us?
> Thy pomp is brought down to Sheol,
> > and the noise of thy viols:
> The worm is spread under thee,
> > and worms cover thee."
>
> How art thou fallen from heaven,
> > O day star, son of the morning!
> How art thou cut down to the ground,
> > that didst lay low the nations!
> And thou saidst in thy heart,
> > "I will ascend into heaven,
> I will exalt my throne
> > above the stars of God;
> And I will sit upon the mount of congregation,
> > in the uttermost parts of the north;
> I will ascend above the heights of the clouds;
> > I will make myself like the Most High."
> Yet thou shalt be brought down to Sheol,
> > to the uttermost parts of the pit. (Isa. 14:9-15)

Full of astonishment all shall look upon the slain tyrant, whose body shall not rest in an honorable grave but will be cast forth and trampled under foot,

>   Because thou hast destroyed thy land,
>   thou hast slain thy people. (Isa. 14:20)

His sons also shall be slain "that they rise not up and possess the earth and fill the face of the world with cities."

These two poems were later connected by an editor who supplied a reference to Israel's restoration and lordship over the nations (14:1–4a). He probably added also two verses at the end in which the complete ruin of Babylon is predicted.

These poems, though tremendously impressive, are not of high religious or moral value, because they are charged with the spirit of triumphant hate. The authors were nationalist prophets like Nahum.

Totally different was the prophet whose oracles are preserved in Is. 21:1–15. He was not a great poet but a true seer; he lived in Palestine not in Babylonia; no word of hate or of triumph over the fallen foe fell from his lips. In his day he appears to have been noted, for inquirers came to him even from Edom. In the evening twilight, ordinarily his season of refreshment, he had an experience which filled him with anguish and fear. He had seen a terrific storm, such as sweeps through the desert south of Judah, and had heard in an audition the terrible words,

>   The robber is robbing, the destroyer destroying!
>   Go up, O Elam, besiege, O Media!
>   Make all the sighing to cease! (Isa. 21:2)

Quickly the vision changed. He saw a banquet hall with the (Babylonian) princes at a feast. All of a sudden the cry rang out, "Rise up, ye princes, anoint the shield!" This vision had thrown the prophet into a terrible excitement. Now, very much like Habakkuk, he got ready for God's answer. We note a most interesting thing for the psychology of prophecy. He fell into a trance and set up his second self as a watchman, ordering it to see and remember so as to be able to report later on. It was also suggested what he would see: "a troop, horsemen in pairs, a troop of asses, a troop of camels." The seer cried,

> O Lord, I stand upon my watch-tower
>   continually by day,
> And am stationed at my post
>   whole nights.

Then suddenly he saw,

> And behold, here comes a troop of men,
>   horsemen in pairs,

and heard the message,

> Fallen, fallen is Babylon;
> And all the graven images of her gods
> Are broken unto the ground! (Isa. 21:8f.)

Thereupon he turned to his people that had so long been threshed and beaten and gave them the word of relief from Yahweh Himself, but added no word of exultation or revenge!

The Edomites heard of this prophet and came to ask his advice. "Watchman, what of the night?" How late is it? What is the present situation in this world crisis? Does this struggle of the Chaldeans with the Medes and Persians mean for us day or night, freedom or merely a change of overlord? The watchman did not know. Now it was like morning, now like the night. Everything is still uncertain. But come again, he tells them, perhaps a definite answer can be given then. We note with surprise the uncertainty of this prophet, but with delight the absence of any trace of hatred for the Edomites, Israel's bitter national foes (Isa. 21:11f.).

His humane feeling appears also in his last oracle, in which he is solicitous for the welfare of Arabian caravans in their flight from the war zone. The attack of Cyrus had begun. Babylon was doomed! (Isa. 21:13–15)

But there was still another anonymous prophet who predicted the fall of that mighty city; some call him the greatest of the Old Testament prophets. To him a separate chapter must be devoted.

XIV

Deutero-Isaiah

NOBODY had watched the marvelous victories of Cyrus more eagerly than a man, whose name is unknown, but who is now generally called the Second or Deutero-Isaiah, because his book was affixed to Isaiah's.[1] His heart began to stir with a great hope, which soon grew into a firm conviction. He had a prophet's insight and interpreted events in the light of the fundamental prophetic conviction that Yahweh was the supreme director of all movements of history. Yahweh must be behind these glorious triumphs of Cyrus; the great Persian's career was explicable only on this supposition. What then was Yahweh's plan? What did He intend to accomplish through this wonderful conqueror? He could not doubt, he knew it all too well. From about 546 on he proclaimed to his people— perhaps more through written oracles than through public speaking —their deliverance and restoration. He had a poet's wondrous language, and the music of his words stole into their sad hearts almost against their will as he began,

> Comfort ye, comfort ye My people,
>   says your God.
> Speak ye comfortably to Jerusalem,
>   and cry unto her,
> That her warfare is accomplished,
>   that her iniquity is pardoned,
> That she has received of Yahweh's hand
>   double for all her sins. (Isa. 40:1-2)

[1] First established by Eichhorn in 1785. Since Bernhard Duhm's commentary on Isaiah (1892) Deutero-Isaiah has been generally considered as limited to chs. 40-55. He called Isa. 56-66 Trito-Isaiah; cf. pp. 258ff

He heard in an audition how the heavenly beings were at work in
the desert, preparing a miraculous highway for Yahweh, because He
would go straight through the Syrian desert at the head of his exiled
people, leading them home to Jerusalem and Judah.

> Hark! one is crying, "In the wilderness
>   prepare ye the way of Yahweh;
> Make level in the desert
>   a highway for our God!
> Every valley shall be exalted,
>   and every mountain and hill shall be made low,
> And the uneven shall be made level,
>   and the rough places a plain:
> And the glory of Yahweh shall be revealed,
>   and all flesh shall see it together." (Isa. 40:3–5)

How the vision inspired the prophet! He came back to it again and
again, and it was ever more marvelous to him. His thoughts flew
to Jerusalem and he called upon the city to watch for the coming of
Yahweh.

> O thou that tellest good tidings to Zion,
>   get thee up on a high mountain;
> O thou that tellest good tidings to Jerusalem,
>   lift up thy voice with strength,
>   lift it up, be not afraid;
> Say unto the cities of Judah,
>   "Behold, your God!"
> Behold, Yahweh comes as a victor,
>   and His arm has ruled for Him.
> Behold, His reward is with Him,
>   and His recompense before Him.
> He will feed His flock like a shepherd,
>   He will gather the lambs in His arm,
> And carry them in His bosom,
>   and will gently lead those that have their young. (Isa. 40:9–11)

It was all so certain to our prophet that he saw it already accomplished. He knew that Babylon would fall and sang her funeral
dirge.[2] Cyrus was Yahweh's agent, he would set the exiles free, send

---

[2] Perhaps Deutero-Isaiah's indefatigable insistence, perhaps a growing insight into the political situation roused other prophets also to predict the fall
of Babylon. A whole anthology of such prophecies is gathered in Jer. 50:2—

them home and command that Jerusalem and the other cities be rebuilt. What a bright hope this was! Again and again the poet broke forth into song because of the joy that this message brought to his soul. If he could only inspire the people with his faith! But most of them were too weary and had ceased to hope. In the great Babylonian civilization they constantly felt the tremendous power of the Chaldean empire. Its mighty armies, gigantic buildings, and great material wealth had crushed all hope out of their hearts: Babylon was far too mighty, far too powerful to be overthrown. But the prophet had heard a voice in which sounded the power of eternity:

> Hark! one said, "Cry!"
> and I said, "What shall I cry?"
> "All flesh is grass,
> and all its goodliness is as the flower of the field.
> The grass withers, the flower fades,
> when the breath of Yahweh blows upon it;
> The grass withers, the flower fades,
> but the word of our God shall stand forever." (Isa. 40:6–8)

All human power is ephemeral, "surely the people is grass." Empires crumble to pieces and fall, but the word of our God is eternal: the fall of Babylon and the deliverance of the exiles are sure.

> For as the rain comes down
> and the snow from heaven,
> And returns not thither,
> but waters the earth,
> And makes it bring forth and bud,
> and gives seed to the sower
> and bread to the eater;
> So shall My Word be,
> that goes forth out of My mouth:
> It shall not return unto Me void,
> but it shall accomplish that which I please,
> and it shall prosper in the thing whereto I sent it. (Isa. 55:10f.)

With mighty words the prophet proclaimed the omnipotence of Yahweh. Let the people think of the really tremendous things in the world of nature and ask but the question, who can do them?

51:58. The collection was made at a later time, but the historical background of the single oracles is that of the last few years of the Babylonian exile.

Can the nations do any of them? Compare them with Yahweh and
see how insignificant they are: mortal men that perish in a moment!

> Who has measured the waters in the hollow of his hand,
>> and meted out heaven with the span,
>> and comprehended the dust of the earth in a measure,
>> and weighed the mountains in scales,
>> and the hills in a balance?
> Who has directed the Spirit of Yahweh,
>> or being His counsellor has taught Him?
>> with whom took He counsel, and who instructed Him,
>> and taught Him the right path,
>> and showed Him the way of understanding?
> Behold, the nations are as a drop of a bucket,
>> and are accounted as the small dust of the balance,
>> behold, He takes up the isles as a very little thing,
>> all the nations are as nothing before Him,
>> they are accounted by Him as less than nothing and vanity.
> "To whom then will ye liken Me,
>> that I should be equal to him?" says the Holy One.
> Lift up your eyes on high,
>> and see, who has created these,
> That brings out their host of number,
>> and calls them all by name;
> Because of the greatness of His might and the strength of His power
>> not one is lacking. (Isa. 40:12–15, 17, 25f.)

None can be compared to Yahweh. There is no other God besides
Him, He alone is God.

Deutero-Isaiah was the protagonist of monotheism and the first in
Israel's history to express it in clear-cut terms. In majestic imagery
he summoned the nations with their idols before the tribunal of
Yahweh: here let them prove their deity, here let them show their
power! Have they ever predicted anything that they were going to
do? and have they ever done it? They cannot reply, and the obvious
conclusion is,

> Behold, ye are of nothing,
>> and your work is of nought;
>> an abomination is he that chooses you. (Isa. 41:24)

Deutero-Isaiah ridiculed the worship of images. He identified the
gods with their idols and showed the supreme folly of worshiping a

piece of wood overlaid with silver and gold, and fastened with nails
lest it fall apart. In all the world there is only one God: Yahweh!
He alone has shown Himself to be God. He it was that called Cyrus
and set him on his victorious career. For who was it that had predicted his victories? Surely not the idols, whose worshipers he has
come to overthrow! No one else but Yahweh, who has directed the
history of the world from the beginning and will do so to the end,
the eternal, omnipotent God, the creator and ruler of the world. The
prophet never tired of emphasizing this conviction, he was mastered
and inspired by it. One feels that it was something that had come
with all the force of an original discovery to him, although he
thought that everybody had known it from childhood.

> Have ye not known? have ye not heard?
>> has it not been told you from the beginning?
>> have ye not understood from the foundations of the earth? (Isa. 40:21)

Not only was he the first to declare monotheistic belief, he was
also the first to expound it, to reason about the unity of God. How
profoundly he had grasped this truth is seen especially in his answer
to the objection against Yahweh's use of the foreigner Cyrus as His
"anointed one," His Messiah.

> Does one strive with his maker?
>> a potsherd with the potter?
> Does the clay say to him that fashions it,
>> "What makest thou?
>> And thy work has no handle?"
> Does one say to a father, "What begettest thou?"
>> or to a woman, "With what travailest thou?"
> Thus says Yahweh,
>> the Holy One of Israel and his maker:
> "Do you ask Me of the things that are to come; concerning My sons,
>> and concerning the work of My hands will you command Me?
> I have made the earth,
>> and created man upon it:
> I, even My hands, have stretched out the heavens,
>> and all their host have I commanded.
> I have raised him up in righteousness,
>> and I will make straight all his ways:
> He shall build My city,
>> and let My exiles go free,

Not for price nor reward,
   says Yahweh of hosts. (Isa. 45:9–13)

Yahweh uses as His instrument whom He wills. The creature has no
right to give orders to the creator; Yahweh is absolutely sovereign;
He created the world and orders it according to His plan. He has
chosen Cyrus as His instrument, and Cyrus will carry out His plans.

The unity of God was the one pole of Deutero-Isaiah's teaching of
God. The other, which he emphasized just as strongly, was Israel's
special relation to Him. In gracious, kindly, and endearing words he
spoke of Yahweh and His love for His people. Some of the most
charming passages are devoted to it. Immediately after his powerful
exposition of Yahweh's omnipotence he proceeded to dispel doubts
concerning His care for His people.

Why sayest thou, O Jacob,
   and speakest, O Israel,
"My way is hid from Yahweh,
   and the justice due to me is passed away from my God?"
Hast thou not known?
   or hast thou not heard?
An eternal God is Yahweh,
   the creator of the ends of the earth;
He faints not, neither is weary;
   there is no searching of His understanding.
He gives power to the faint;
   and to him that has no might he increases strength.
Even the youths shall faint and be weary,
   and the young men shall utterly fall:
But they that wait for Yahweh shall renew their strength;
   they shall mount up with wings as eagles:
They shall run and not be weary;
   they shall walk and not faint. (Isa. 40:27–31)

The power of religious hope has seldom been more beautifully
expressed. The prophet's own experience, his own optimism and
enthusiasm shine through here. His mission was to comfort, and
he comforted indeed. With exquisite tenderness he answered Mother
Zion's complaint, for he knew so well her doubt and the weariness
of heart it brings:

Zion said, "Yahweh has forsaken me,
   and the Lord has forgotten me."

> Can a woman forget her sucking child,
>   that she should not have compassion on the son of her womb?
> Yea, these may forget,
>   yet will not I forget thee. (Isa. 49:14f.)

The pathos and power of these lines are unsurpassed. Mother Zion,
who has been bereaved of her children, will suddenly have them
again, and many more than she ever had before, when the exiles
return (49:16–21). Compare at least one other of these exquisite
poems, 51:17ff. or 54:4–8. In the latter Israel is the wife of Yahweh,
now forsaken and grieved in spirit, but really a wife of youth, whom
He had loved with all the passion of His first love, and whom He
will not cast off forever.

> For a small moment have I forsaken thee;
>   but with great mercies will I gather thee.
> In overflowing wrath I hid My face from thee for a moment,
>   but with everlasting lovingkindness will I have mercy on thee,
>   says Yahweh, thy Redeemer. (Isa. 54:7f.)

The point that is emphasized in all these passages is the love of
Yahweh for Israel, His special relation to her, He can never forget
her, for she is peculiarly His own. The influence of Hosea seems
patent here.

The two ideas of Yahweh, the God of the whole world and the
God of Israel, may exclude each other, if either is stressed too much.
Their relation constituted a real problem. If there is only one God,
who rules the world and guides the affairs of the nations, He must
be the God of all and be interested in all. But could the long historic
connection between Yahweh and Israel be given up? That was un-
thinkable. Deutero-Isaiah found a reconciliation between the two
ideas in the belief that Yahweh had chosen Israel as His servant in
order that through him the knowledge of the one God and of true
religion might be mediated to the nations. The salvation of the world
is God's purpose, Israel's restoration is only the means to this end.
Cyrus is the anointed instrument who prepares the conditions which
will make the establishment of the true universal religion of Yahweh
possible. That is why it is given to him to overthrow the nations,
who are adherents of false religions, and to restore Israel, the possessor of the true religion. Cyrus himself will come to know and

worship Yahweh as the only true God, and the nations through
him, for Yahweh had girded him,

> That they may know from the rising of the sun
>   and from the west,
> That there is none beside Me:
>   I am Yahweh, and there is none else. (Isa. 45:6)

The fall of Babylon and the deliverance of Israel in which the
victories of Cyrus must culminate, together with the spectacular
homeward march of the exiles will attract the attention of the whole
world, "and all flesh shall see it together." Yahweh will call "the
escaped of the nations," will ask them whether all this is not proof
of His sole deity, and will invite them all:

> Look unto Me, and be ye saved,
>   all the ends of the earth;
> For I am God, and there is none else.
>   By Myself have I sworn,
> The word is gone from My mouth
>   in righteousness, and shall not return,
> That unto Me every knee shall bow,
>   every tongue shall swear. (Isa. 45:22f.)

A universal God and a universal religion are the crown of history,
the goal of the world! Heaven and earth may perish; in and above
this perishing world there is an eternal reality, the salvation of true
religion.

> Attend unto Me, O My people,
>   and give ear unto Me, O My nation:
> For a law shall go forth from Me,
>   and My justice for a light of the peoples.
> I will bring near in a moment My righteousness,
>   My salvation is gone forth,
>   and Mine arm shall judge the peoples;
> The isles shall wait for Me,
>   and on Mine arm shall they trust.
> Lift up your eyes to the heavens,
>   and look upon the earth beneath;
> For the heavens shall vanish away like smoke,
>   and the earth shall wax old like a garment,
>   and they that dwell therein shall die like gnats:

> But My salvation shall be forever,
> and My righteousness shall not be abolished. (Isa. 51:4–6)

No prophet had ever expressed so clearly the sum of Israel's religion. It is true that at times Deutero-Isaiah laid undue stress on Israel's glory, although this was really only incidental to the attainment of the higher glory of universal religion. It is true that he made fellowship with Yahweh dependent on the individual's becoming a member of Israel (44:5), that he foretold that the Davidic king would be "a prince and commander to the peoples" (55:3–5), and that the Egyptians, Ethiopians, and Sabeans would go to Israel in chains, fall down and supplicate,

> Surely, God is in thee, and there is none else,
> there is no God.
> Verily, with thee God hides Himself,
> the God of Israel, the Saviour. (Isa. 45:14f.)

It is true he said that Yahweh would give nations as a ransom for Israel (43:3f.), that Israel should thresh the peoples and beat them to pieces (41:15f.), that kings and queens should attend the returning exiles, and that in abject humiliation

> They shall bow down to thee with their faces to the earth,
> and lick the dust of thy feet. (Isa. 49:23)

But all this is so entirely out of harmony with his prophecies of universal religion, that it seems incredible that Deutero-Isaiah should have written it. Yet it is not impossible that even he was carried away to appeal to Israel's pride by his desire to inspire them with new hope at times when the higher truth found no response. One wishes that he had not yielded to the temptation, or that he had at least not put these words into Yahweh's mouth. He stimulated thereby, quite unwittingly, the national and religious arrogance of the later Jews, and made it easy for them to miss the really great truths which he proclaimed.

But all this cannot cloud the glory of his essential message, which is so great that we are still thrilled by it. It reaches its high-water mark in four poems of singular beauty and power, the so-called "Songs of the Servant of Yahweh" (Isa. 42:1–4; 49:1–6; 50:4–9;

52:13—53:12),[3] which we have not touched upon so far. Here a profound interpretation of the people's travail is given in the light of its mission. The problem of innocent suffering is solved by fixing the attention upon its purpose, not upon the reason for it. Israel is personified as the servant of Yahweh.[4] He is now despised and crushed, without national existence, far from his own land, in exile. But he is still Yahweh's servant, through whom true religion is to be established in all the world. It seems impossible. All his work in exile must be in vain; it means but suffering and shame. But no, this very suffering is part of Yahweh's plan! Through it His purpose for the world will be accomplished. For He is about to restore Israel to such marvelous glory that the nations and kings of the world will be astounded and come to a true understanding of Israel's suffering. Yahweh Himself calls upon them:

> Behold, My servant shall prosper,
>   he shall be exalted and lifted up and very high!
> Just as many were astonished at him,
>   because his visage was so marred that it was not that of a man,
>   and his form so that it was no longer human;
> So shall many nations wonder,
>   kings shall shut their mouths at him:
> For that which had not been told them shall they see,
>   and that which they had not heard shall they consider.

[3] These were first isolated by Duhm, who considered them later insertions.

[4] The theory here espoused that the servant is Israel finds support in the fact that Israel is called servant outside the above passages (43:10; 44:1; 45:4). However, the servant of the songs has a task to perform *for* Israel (42:6f.; 49:5). What is said of him in the fourth song does not readily lend itself in all particulars to fit a collective entity. Duhm who had in 1875 taken the servant of the songs to be the *ideal* Israel, in 1892 switched to an individual interpretation. He held that the servant of the songs was a teacher of the law who was smitten with leprosy (53:3 *MT*) and thus despised as under the judgment of God. Deutero-Isaiah considered this man's sufferings vicarious and foresaw his vindication. Thus began a flood of individual interpretations; persons such as Jeremiah, Jehoiachin, Zerubbabel were suggested as candidates. The thought that Deutero-Isaiah was speaking of himself (cf. Acts 8:34) was also sponsored by prominent scholars. This was modified subsequently by the view that the fourth song was composed by Trito-Isaiah, celebrating his teacher Deutero-Isaiah as Teacher-Messiah. Latterly the idea of "corporate personality" has been invoked to effect a compromise between collective and individual interpretation. For a detailed account see H. H. Rowley, *The Servant of the Lord* (1952).

The heathen themselves now speak: [5]

> Who could have believed that which we have heard?
>   and to whom had the arm of Yahweh been revealed?
> For he grew up before Him as a tender plant,
>   and as a root out of a dry ground:
> He had no form nor comeliness, that we should look at him,
>   nor beauty, that we should desire him.
> He was despised and forsaken of men,
>   a man of sicknesses, and acquainted with disease,
> And as one from whom men hide their face
>   he was despised, and we esteemed him not.

This had been their natural explanation of Israel's suffering and bitter fate. But now in the light of his glorious restoration they see the real meaning of his suffering: Israel had suffered for their sake. Sorrowfully they confess,

> Surely, he has borne our sicknesses,
>   and carried our sufferings,
> While we esteemed him stricken,
>   smitten of God and afflicted.
> But he was wounded for our transgressions,
>   he was bruised for our iniquities;
> The chastisement of our peace was upon him,
>   and with his bruises we are healed.
> All we like sheep have gone astray,
>   we have turned every one to his own way:
> And Yahweh laid upon him
>   the guilt of us all.

In this confession of Israel's vicarious suffering for them the heathen appropriate inwardly its fruit. The prophet agrees with them and now dwells on the servant's patience in all his affliction.

> He was oppressed, yet he humbled himself,
>   and opened not his mouth,
> As a lamb that is led to the slaughter,
>   and as a sheep that before its shearers is dumb.
> By oppression and judgment he was taken away,
>   and as for his generation, who considered?

[5] It is equally possible to hold that in 53:1 the prophet himself is speaking of the revelation he has received. The same Hebrew word here rendered "that which we have heard" is rendered "message" in Is. 28:9, 19, "tidings" in Jer. 49:14 by the *RSV*.

> For he was cut off out of the land of the living,
>> for our transgressions he was smitten to death.
> And they made his grave with the wicked,
>> and with a rich man in his death,[6]
> Although he had done no violence,
>> neither was any deceit in his mouth.

But this innocent suffering was in accordance with Yahweh's plan, which the prophet proceeds to reveal. Without it the light of true religion would never have come to the heathen.

> Yet it was the will of Yahweh to bruise him
>> and he pierced him; [7]
> When he makes himself an offering for sin
>> he shall see offspring, he shall prolong his days;
>> the will of Yahweh shall prosper through his hand.
> On account of the travail of his soul
>> he will see light and be satisfied.

Yahweh himself holds out to the servant the victor's crown for his willing, vicarious suffering.

> Through his knowledge shall the righteous one, my servant,
>> make many righteous, and bear their iniquities.
> Therefore will I divide him a portion with the great,
>> and he shall divide the spoil with the strong:
> Because he poured out his soul unto death,
>> and was numbered with the transgressors,
> Yet he bore the sin of many,
>> and made intercession for the transgressors. (Isa. 52:13—53:12)

The glorification of Israel is not an end in itself but the means to the end. It is incidental to something far greater, far more wonderful: the conversion of the whole world to the one and only God, Yahweh. It was one of the greatest things that Deutero-Isaiah did that he enunciated this clearly and unmistakably.

> And now Yahweh did say,
>> He that formed me from the womb for His servant:

[6] The Dead Sea Isaiah Scroll has "and with rich men his high place." This abnormal use of "high place" reflects the later custom of making prominent mortuary monuments, such as those of the Maccabees at Modein (1 Macc. 13:17–20). The text may originally have read "doers of evil."

[7] MT "he made him sick." The Isaiah Scroll offers this more plausible reading. Verses 10-11 are particularly difficult and have probably suffered corruption.

> That He would bring Jacob again to Him,
>   and Israel should be gathered unto Him,
> And I should be honored in the eyes of Yahweh,
>   and my God had become my strength;
> And He said, "The raising up of the tribes of Jacob
>   and the restoration of the preserved of Israel
> Are less significant than thy being My servant;
>   so I will give thee for a light to the Gentiles,
> That My salvation may be
>   to the end of the earth." (Isa. 49:5f.)

The servant's mission is to mediate universal salvation. Upheld by Yahweh and empowered by His Spirit, he will enter upon the active part of his work. As he goes forth to bring true religion to the heathen, the hearts of the peoples meet him, they know that he has the true knowledge of God, which alone will satisfy their deepest cravings. Yahweh is not longing alone, they long for Him too.

> Behold, My servant, whom I uphold,
>   My chosen, in whom My soul delights:
> I have put My Spirit upon him,
>   he will bring forth justice to the Gentiles.
> He will not cry, nor lift up his voice,
>   nor cause it to be heard in the street.
> A bruised reed will he not break,
>   and a dimly burning wick will he not quench.
> He will bring forth justice in truth.
>   He will not fail nor be discouraged,
> Till he have set justice in the earth;
>   and the isles shall wait for his instruction. (Isa. 42:1-4)

Justice is here equivalent to the true moral religion; its universal establishment is the divinely appointed goal of the history of the world. Israel as God's missionary servant and prophet is commissioned to win all nations for this end.

Deutero-Isaiah presented here the ideal which he had for his people. He knew that the reality was totally different, Israel was "a people robbed and plundered, snared in holes, and hid in prison houses," a "deaf" and "blind" servant (42:18-22). They had not taken this suffering upon themselves with willing patience. The prophet had idealized them in his poems. He wanted to rouse them by holding up before them this high ideal of their world-wide mission. He knew how wonderful his message was, and that the people might not believe it.

> For My thoughts are not your thoughts,
>   neither are your ways My ways, says Yahweh.
> For as the heavens are higher than the earth,
>   so are My ways higher than your ways,
>   and My thoughts than your thoughts. (Isa. 55:8f.)

The wonder of it filled the poet himself with such joy that he must sometimes break forth into song, and all through his book there are such lyrical outbursts as this,

> Sing unto Yahweh a new song,
>   and His praise from the end of the earth, etc. (Isa. 42:10–12)

Deutero-Isaiah was the most enthusiastic of the prophets. He had wonderful truths to proclaim, but he never attempted to convince men by the force of his logic alone; he placed himself on the highest level and by the contagious power of his enthusiasm and of his own profound belief he tried to inspire them with new hope and courage, with new loyalty and trust. How well he knew the human heart! How he touched every chord by the music of his words! He carried the people away by his own enthusiasm to see his vision and to hope with him. He had passages of exquisite beauty; as with the touch of a mother's tenderest caress he comforted, as seldom a man has comforted, for he was one of the greatest comforters of the race. No preacher could excel him in the moving power of his appeal, "Ho, every one that thirsts, come ye to the waters" (55:1–3); no saint could surpass him in his certitude,

> For the mountains may depart,
>   and the hills may be removed;
> But My lovingkindness shall not depart from thee,
>   neither shall My covenant of peace be removed,
>   says Yahweh, that has mercy upon thee. (Isa. 54:10)

This prophet wrote only in poetry. That is why some critics cannot regard 44:9–20, in which the folly of idolatry is ridiculed with

biting irony, as coming from him, for it is entirely in prose.[8] There
are some who believe that the Poems of the Servant of Yahweh were
not composed by him either, because they are said to be unrelated
to their context and to differ in their ideas from Deutero-Isaiah's.
But the latter point we have attempted to disprove, and the former
is not a serious argument, for Isa. 40–55 is not a single poem but a
collection of poems, and there is no reason to expect a close connection between them and the adjoining passages. Indeed, the understanding of the book is deepened and its literary attraction is enhanced, if the individual units are separated and read and enjoyed
by themselves; else even this author may become monotonous, although his rhythmic language is melody to the ear. Deutero-Isaiah
is surpassingly gentle when he comforts, overpowering when he describes Yahweh's omnipotence, clear and forcible when he reasons,
compelling when he sets forth his hope or calls to repentance, always
beautiful, never dull or commonplace. His style is so finely wrought
and so clearly marked that it can never be forgotten when its pe-
culiarities have once been perceived. Many later poets and prophets
show the influence which his style had upon them. But his finest
and deepest thoughts were understood by but few, until He came
who embodied the ideal of the Servant of Yahweh in himself: Jesus
of Nazareth.[9] To Christians the Book of Deutero-Isaiah is so dear
for that reason, and because it is so evangelical. We still delight in
calling him the Evangelist of the Old Testament.

[8] This was a favorite theme of later writers. In Jer. 10:1–16 one of them
inserted an attack upon the worship of idols quite in the manner and style of
Deutero-Isaiah.

[9] Given the views of Old Testament prophecy as supernaturally predictive of
the Messianic times (so also the Dead Sea Scrolls Community), it was natural
that the servant passages should have a tremendous value for early Christianity.
Isa. 53 gave the interpretation of the confessional formula of 1 Cor. 15:3–4.
Whoever believes in divine providence will not quarrel with it for having
produced Christian insight by now antiquated means.

XV

Deuteronomistic

Historiography

THE prophets had been profoundly interested in history, because to them God was the import of all history and the goal toward which it tended. They saw Him at work behind all events, weaving at the loom of time. His will controlled all and was destined to be carried out with all the terrors of retribution. History thus became more significant than ever, for here God's work was manifest. The prophets viewed it on a wide horizon, for God was working everywhere. He used the Aramaeans, the Assyrians, the Babylonians and others as His instruments. In Deutero-Isaiah the petty national limits were cast aside, and a prophet had arisen who unfolded the divine purpose for all the nations. This conviction of the victory of God's righteousness was for the prophets not the result of historical study but came out of the prophetic tradition and was confirmed by their own inner experience.

To one of the Deuteronomists the whole history of his people illustrated the great lessons of Deuteronomy and the reformation of Josiah. During the exile, but after 561 B.C. and apparently in Palestine, this individual wrote the story. His heart was filled with the hope that his people might learn from this history that only wholehearted allegiance to Yahweh and exclusive worship at Jerusalem could secure salvation and national permanence. It is now widely held that his work, for which *Dtr* [1] is used as abbreviation, was divided

[1] The older critical view assumed that J and E continued at least through Joshua and ascribed the Deuteronomic elements in the following historical

into four great sections: 1. the end of the Mosaic era and the period of the conquest (Deut. through Josh.); 2. the period of the Judges (Judg. through 1 Sam. 7); 3. the rise of the monarchy (1 Sam. 8 through 1 Ki. 11); 4. the Divided Kingdom (1 Ki. 12 through 2 Ki. 25). The history of about seven centuries was viewed in the light of one great religious principle.[2] Every hero and king was tested by the norm of whether he had been exclusively loyal to Yahweh. It was a religious philosophy of Hebrew history. It assured mastery of the material and in that respect was an achievement. Our author was not, however, so much interested in history for its own sake, but only in so far as it afforded him illustrative material. He was a teacher of religion, who used history as his object lesson; it taught with convincing power the great truths in which he was interested. If we judge his work from the side of modern historiography our admiration for him is greatly lessened, for then we cannot see in it an advance but rather a retrogression. It was the beginning of that development which subordinated history to religion, and led to the undue assumption that man can understand the ways of God.

The Deuteronomistic historian drew on older sources. He could not use everything, so he made his selections and arranged them for his purpose. It cannot be asserted that in his use of the sources he ever deliberately changed the facts in order to conform them to his dogma, even though he understood and interpreted the entire history in its light. But by selecting his material, omitting the non-usable or non-tractable, skillfully arranging the suitable, and imposing his own point of view upon it, he actually did present a historical construction which was different from the real history itself. Fortunately, however, much that contradicted his own view survived, because he used or excerpted his older sources literally. He

---

books to editors. But it is strange that there is no Deuteronomistic editing in Genesis-Numbers. The thesis that an author-editor compiled a work governed by his thought was set forth by Martin Noth in 1943. See p. 73, note 14.

[2] Of course, since the temple had not been in existence before Solomon, the Deuteronomic principle of the centralization of worship could not be used as the dominating idea in the light of which the whole history could be understood and presented. But it was only one aspect of the larger idea of wholehearted loyalty to Yahweh and exclusive worship of Him. And this larger idea became the master key that unlocked the true meaning of history.

furnished them with introductions and conclusions of his own, and frequently added observations in his characteristic Deuteronomistic style, but the excerpts themselves he did not change. In one sense this shows that he was not a master of historiography, else he would have told the entire history in his own words and thus have made the whole consistent throughout. It is fortunate that he wrote as he did, for this enables us to disengage his own material from that of his sources and thus to recover the more original and historical presentation of antecedent books, which would otherwise have been completely lost. Perhaps the most uncertain thing about the Deuteronomistic historical work is its beginning, since that is involved with the problem of Deuteronomy. Not all scholars who accept the *Dtr* thesis agree that the work opened with the introductory address of Moses when he gave the people the Deuteronomic law (Deut. 1–3). However, a more suitable beginning is hard to find, and so we shall begin there.

Reviewing the events from Horeb on, Moses in the plains of Moab showed how the people's quarrelsomeness had been too great a burden for him alone so that he had to appoint judges to help him in his work; how the people's disobedience and lack of faith had prevented them from entering the land long ago; how they had fared with the Edomites, Moabites, and Ammonites; how they had conquered the East Jordan country; and how Yahweh was angry with Moses because of the people and would not allow him to enter the promised land. He then incorporated the Deuteronomic law with its framework discourses (Deut. 4–30) and thereupon proceeded to relate the final events of the Mosaic era: how Moses appointed Joshua as leader for the conquest (as foreseen in Deut. 3:28), and exhorted him; how he wrote down the law, and commanded its reading every seventh year at the autumn festival; how he bade the priests deposit it beside the Ark (containing the tables with the commandments, of which the Deuteronomic law is imagined as the authoritative interpretation); and finally how Moses died. These chapters however were subject to expansion, interpolation and final compilatory activity when Deuteronomy was cut off from Joshua–2 Kings and the priestly account of the death of Moses combined with that of *Dtr* interpolation had perhaps already brought in the Song of Moses (Deut. 32), which has been provided with a framework (31:27b–30; 32:44–45) and a secondary introduction (31:16–22). The blessing of Moses (Deut. 33) was injected without any effort to provide transitions, and so perhaps was done very late. The original *Dtr* element in these chapters thus is to be sought in 31:1–15, 24–26; 34:1–6, but has been expanded and worked over.

In Joshua 1 the Deuteronomistic historian continues with the story of Joshua's address to the tribes before the invasion of western Palestine. For the actual account of the happenings he had available a series of stories dealing with the conquest in the territory of the tribe of Benjamin, with a small amount of material about Judea and the taking of Hazor in Naphthali—an unusually large city by Palestinian standards, as its site and the excavations recently conducted there have shown. In the address of ch. one the picture of the occupation has been generalized and nationalized. The person of the Ephraimite Joshua had apparently been injected by previous tradition into the individual narratives, which are mostly local legends. Nevertheless he must have been a figure of wider interest in view of the role that is ascribed to him in Josh. 17:14–18 where he advises the Joseph tribe, which feels slighted in the land apportionment, as to what it should do. In the geographical section, ch. 13–21, *Dtr* seems to have used a list of the cities and towns dating from the time of King Josiah. He himself contributed 1; 8:30–35; 12; 23. In ch. 23 Joshua delivered his farewell address to the people, in which he demanded of them careful observance of the law (of Deuteronomy) and strict segregation from the heathen whom Yahweh had driven out before them, lest they become a snare to them, and Israel be quickly expelled from the country which Yahweh has given them. Therewith this historian's account of the conquest ends. Ch. 24, the gathering of the tribes at Shechem, was added later. It is composed of a valuable report of the Elohistic type (pp. 79ff.).

For the second part of his work, the story of the Judges, *Dtr* took his material from older hero tales (such as those of Ehud, Gideon, Jephthah, and that of the villain Abimelech), and a list of the so-called Minor Judges, who gave legal instruction and acted as appellate judges where local decisions did not satisfy (Judg. 10:1–5;

12:8–15).[3] He furnished each story with a framework in which his characteristic point of view was fully expressed. If Israel had remained wholly true to Yahweh, they would have enjoyed the full blessings of His theocratic rule. But after Joshua's death they sinned.

The Israelites did that which was evil in the sight of Yahweh, and served the Baalim; and they forsook Yahweh, the God of their fathers, who brought them out of the land of Egypt, and followed other gods, of the gods of the peoples that were round about them, and bowed down to them: and they provoked Yahweh to anger. And the anger of Yahweh was kindled against Israel, and He delivered them into the hands of the spoilers that despoiled them, and He sold them into the hands of their enemies round about, so that they could not any longer stand before their enemies. Whithersoever they went out, the hand of Yahweh was against them for evil, as Yahweh had spoken, and as Yahweh had sworn to them: and they were sore distressed. And Yahweh raised up judges, who saved them out of the hand of those that despoiled them. And when Yahweh raised them up judges, then Yahweh was with the judge, and saved them out of the hand of their enemies all the days of the judge: for it repented Yahweh because of their groaning by reason of them that oppressed and vexed them. But it came to pass, when the judge was dead, that they turned back, and dealt more corruptly than their fathers, in following other gods to serve them, and to bow down to them; they ceased not from their doings, nor from their stubborn way. (Judg. 2:11f., 14–16, 18f.)

It was a constant cycle of defection, punishment, and deliverance, ever repeated. According to this principle the stories of the greater judges were retold and by an artificial chronology made to appear in historical sequence.

The story of Othniel may serve as a sample of the application of this philosophy; it is entirely from the Deuteronomist's pen and may contain no historical element at all beyond the name of Othniel.

And the Israelites did that which was evil in the sight of Yahweh, and forgot Yahweh their God, and served the Baalim and the Asheroth. Therefore the anger of Yahweh was kindled against Israel, and he sold them into the hand of Cushan-rishathaim king of Aram Naharaim: and the Israelites served Cushan-rishathaim eight years. And when the Israelites cried unto Yahweh, Yahweh raised up a saviour to the Israelites,

[3] The designation "judge" may have been transferred from these Minor Judges to the military heroes by *Dtr*—perhaps because one of them, Jephtha, happened also to have been a judge (12:7).

who saved them, even Othniel the son of Kenaz, Caleb's younger brother. And the Spirit of Yahweh came upon him, and he judged Israel; and he went out to war, and Yahweh delivered Cushan-rishathaim king of Aram Naharaim into his hand: and his hand prevailed against Cushan-rishathaim. And the land had rest forty years. And Othniel the son of Kenaz died. (Judg. 3:7–11)

In the following verse the next cycle begins,

And the Israelites did that which was evil in the sight of Yahweh, and Yahweh strengthened Eglon the king of Moab against Israel, because they had done that which was evil in the sight of Yahweh. (Judg. 3:12)

In this manner the whole period is treated. One may not withhold his admiration for this kind of solemn, impressive, and effective presentation. How grandly the conviction of the righteous and merciful God of Israel is brought out in the history of His people! And yet from an historical point of view how distorted and wrong this presentation is! It has altogether modified the actual significance of the Judges. Dogma rules again. The political and economic forces are entirely subordinated. Secondary causes are neglected. Religion is the sole cause of all: God is jealously watching over the fidelity of His people and punishes or delivers in accordance with Israel's behavior. Moreover, everything is magnified to national proportions. The sufferings affect the entire nation, the Judges are deliverers of the whole people, and the theocratic rulers of all Israel.

Parts of the Book of Judges as we now have it were not included in the Deuteronomistic historical work, for they show no traces of its customary editing. They are: the summary of the conquest of Canaan with its special references to parts not conquered (Judg. 1:1—2:5), which may have formed the conclusion of the work of the Yahwist; the story of Samson (Judg. 13–16); the stories of Micah and the Danites (Judg. 17f.) and of the atrocity committed at Gibeah (Judg. 19–21). They must have been added later at the appropriate points by editors who thought they were too interesting to be lost.

The story of 1 Sam. 1–7 was really part of the story of the Judges, and traces of the particular framework that marks the Book of Judges appear in it too. Here also the Deuteronomist incorporated older source material. It did not need much redaction, because the narrators had already pointed out the great lessons of theocratic religion in which the Deuteronomist was interested.

The third part of the Deuteronomist's work related the rise of the Hebrew monarchy (1 Sam. 8—1 Ki. 11). Here the ancient sources which he incorporated were augmented by him with the account of the activity of Samuel at Mizpah, of his victory over the Philistines, of the request of Israel's elders that he appoint a king for them (1 Sam. 7:2; 8:22) and of the carrying out of that request (1 Sam. 10:17–27), as well as with Samuel's farewell discourse (1 Sam. 12). From there on the received materials prevail. For the history of Solomon (1 Ki. 1–11), our author used besides the David story (1 Ki. 1f.) the Book of the Acts of Solomon, to which he definitely refers in its conclusion (1 Ki. 11:41), and most probably the Royal and the Temple Annals, although he does not mention either by name. He grouped the whole narrative around the building and dedication of the temple.[4] That was to him the natural center. Before and after it he put the stories which celebrate Solomon's wisdom, might, and wealth.

In 1 Ki. 8:14—9:9 the Deuteronomist has provided a pious blessing of Israel by Solomon, followed by a long prayer and an account of the feast held by the great assembly of the whole realm, as well as a further appearance of Yahweh to Solomon with endorsement of the king's pious sentiments and suitable warnings and promises. Solomon's disregard of this divine instruction is reported in 1 Ki. 11:1–13, 28–43. Clearly, if he had obeyed God wholeheartedly, the disasters that happened would not have come, for these were always, according to the teaching of Deuteronomy, the result of sin. Thus, directly after Solomon's death his kingdom was split in two. What was the reason for this catastrophe? Our author had read in his sources,

King Solomon loved many foreign women, and he had 700 wives, princesses, and 300 concubines. . . . Then Solomon built a high place for

[4] From Temple Annals or a story of the temple must have come the chronological speculation of 1 Ki. 6:1 that it was built in Solomon's fourth year—480 years after the Exodus.

Chemosh, the god of Moab, in the mount that is before Jerusalem, and for Milcom, the god of the Ammonites. (1 Ki. 11:1a, 3a, 7)

This gave him a clew on which he could elaborate.

It came to pass, when Solomon was old, that his wives turned away his heart after other gods; and his heart was not perfect with Yahweh his God, as was the heart of David his father.

And Solomon did that which was evil in the sight of Yahweh, and went not fully after Yahweh, as did David his father.

And Yahweh was angry with Solomon, because his heart was turned away from Yahweh, the God of Israel, who had appeared to him twice, and had commanded him concerning this thing, that he should not go after other gods: but he kept not that which Yahweh commanded. Wherefore Yahweh said to Solomon, Forasmuch as this is done of thee, and thou hast not kept My covenant and My statutes, which I have commanded thee, I will surely rend the kingdom from thee, and will give it to thy servant. Notwithstanding in thy days I will not do it, for David thy father's sake: but I will rend it out of the hand of thy son. Howbeit I will not rend away all the kingdom; but I will give one tribe to thy son, for David My servant's sake, and for Jerusalem's sake which I have chosen. (1 Ki. 11:4, 6, 9–13)

Then the rebellions of Hadad, Rezon, and Jeroboam are told, and the impression is created that they had been sent as a punishment for Solomon's apostasy in his old age, although they really belonged to the beginning of his reign as the excerpts from the sources themselves show (cf. 11:21, 25, 27). This is an illustration of how history may be distorted in the interest of a theory without modifying the facts, by simply rearranging and viewing them from a doctrinal standpoint. In the story of the beginnings of the rebellion of Jeroboam the author expanded the prediction of the prophet Ahijah in his characteristic manner by supplying the reason for the division of the kingdom and inserting, as in Solomon's case, the condition for Jeroboam's permanent success (11:32–39), filling thereby the reader's mind with mingled hope and fear, and preparing him for the worst.

The fourth part of the Deuteronomistic historical work contains the history of Israel and Judah.

Our writer here used valuable sources, though with obvious omission of most of that precise and realistic information that we would so much rather have than all his moralizing. He refers to "Chronicles

(literally: Book of the Events of the Days) of the Kings of Israel"
or "of Judah," meaning royal annals, or literary works of earlier
historians based on them. These books were familiar and accessible
to our writer, as well as to his readers. He himself had taken from
them valuable historical material. He also used unspecified sources:
stories based on Temple Annals or a work concerned with happenings
at the temple; cycles of stories about the prophets Elijah, Elisha, and
Isaiah; also such works as the narrative of the Davidic succession and
other materials.

The order is chronological, but with this restriction that for the
period up to the destruction of the northern kingdom the author
told the story of each king by itself, before beginning that of a king
or kings who had reigned in the other kingdom in the meantime.
This is sometimes awkward, *e.g.*, since Ahab of Israel came to the
throne before Jehoshaphat of Judah, Ahab's whole story, in part of
which Jehoshaphat was an important figure, was told before Jehoshaphat's accession to the throne was mentioned. That was reported
after the story of Ahab had been completed. The histories of the
two kingdoms are thus interlocked.

The author no doubt got his chronological information regarding
the length of the reigns and the various years in which certain important things had happened from the Royal Annals. But for the
whole there was as yet no era. So our author connected the histories of the two kingdoms by synchronisms, in which he computed
in which year of the reigning king of the one kingdom a king came
upon the throne in the other. The years of the reigns he had from
official sources and they are therefore reliable. Unfortunately the
figures given for the chronology by different scholars rarely agree.
This is due to adjustments made in the received figures in various
ways. Fortunately the new Babylonian Chronicle text of Wiseman
(p. 147) makes possible the clarification of the chronology of the
period from Josiah to the fall of Jerusalem. The following gives a
chronology conforming to recent insight in this field.*

* Since the chronology given in previous editions of this work is close to
that of Edwin R. Thiele, *The Mysterious Numbers of the Hebrew Kings,*
1953, we have substituted the latter's figures, with some changes.

Israel		Judah	
Jeroboam (22) . . .	931–910	Rehoboam (17) . . .	931–913
Nadab (2)	910–909	Abijam (3)	913–911
Baasha (24)	909–886	Asa (41)	911–870
Elah (2)	886–885		
Zimri (7 days)			
†Omri (12)	885–874		
Ahab (22)	874–853	†Jehoshaphat (25) . .	870–848
Ahaziah (2)	853–852		
Joram (12)	852–841	†Joram (8)	848–841
		Ahaziah (1)	841
Jehu (28)	841–814	Athaliah (7)	841–835
Jehoahaz (17) . . .	814–798	Jehoash (40) . . .	835–796
Joash (16)	798–782	Amaziah (29) . . .	796–767
†Jeroboam II (41) .	782–753	†Azariah (52) . . .	767–740
Zechariah (6 months)			
Shallum (1 month)			
Menahem (10) . . .	752–742	†Jotham (12)	740–736
Pekahiah (2) . . .	742–740	Ahaz (16)	736–716
†Pekah (20)	740–732		
Hoshea (9)	732–723		
		Hezekiah (29) . . .	716–687
		†Manasseh (55) . . .	687–642
		Amon (2)	642–641
		Josiah (31)	641–609
		Jehoahaz (3 months)	
		Jehoiakim (11) . . .	609–598
		Jehoiachin (3 months)	
		Dec. 598—Mar. 597	
		Zedekiah (11) . . .	597–587

At the beginning of the reign of each king the author gave an introduction containing the date of his accession, its length, and a comprehensive judgment of the king; in the case of the Judean kings also the age of the king at his accession and often the name of his mother. Take as an example for the Judean kings Abijam:

Now in the eighteenth year of King Jeroboam the son of Nebat began Abijam to reign over Judah. Three years reigned he in Jerusalem: and his mother's name was Maacah the daughter of Abishalom. And he walked in all the sins of his father, which he had done before him; and his heart was not perfect with Yahweh his God, as the heart of David

† May have been co-regent.

his father. Nevertheless for David's sake Yahweh his God gave him a lamp in Jerusalem, to set up his son after him, and to establish Jerusalem; because David did that which was right in the eyes of Yahweh, and turned not aside from anything that He commanded him all the days of his life, save only in the matter of Uriah the Hittite. (1 Ki. 15:1-5)

Or the somewhat longer introduction of the "reformer" Asa:

And in the twentieth year of Jeroboam king of Israel began Asa to reign over Judah. And forty and one years reigned he in Jerusalem: and his mother's name was Maacah the daughter of Abishalom. And Asa did that which was right in the eyes of Yahweh, as did David his father. And he put away the sodomites out of the land, and removed all the idols that his fathers had made. And also Maacah his mother he removed from being queen, because she had made an abominable image for Asherah; and Asa cut down her image, and burnt it at the brook Kidron. But the high places were not taken away: nevertheless the heart of Asa was perfect with Yahweh all his days. And he brought into the house of Yahweh the things that his father had dedicated, and the things that himself had dedicated, silver, and gold, and vessels. (1 Ki. 15:9-15)

For the Israelite kings take as an example Baasha:

In the third year of Asa king of Judah began Baasha the son of Ahijah to reign over all Israel in Tirzah, twenty and four years. And he did that which was evil in the sight of Yahweh, and walked in the way of Jeroboam, and in his sin wherewith he made Israel to sin. (1 Ki. 15:33f.)

Or the longer introduction of the "sinful" Ahab:

And in the thirty and eighth year of Asa king of Judah began Ahab the son of Omri to reign over Israel: and Ahab the son of Omri reigned over Israel in Samaria twenty and two years. And Ahab the son of Omri did that which was evil in the sight of Yahweh above all that were before him. And it came to pass, as if it had been a light thing for him to walk in the sins of Jeroboam the son of Nebat, that he took to wife Jezebel the daughter of Ethbaal king of the Sidonians, and went and served Baal, and worshipped him. And he reared up an altar for Baal in the house of Baal, which he had built in Samaria. And Ahab made the Asherah; and Ahab did yet more to provoke Yahweh, the God of Israel, to anger than all the kings of Israel that were before him. (1 Ki. 16:29-33)

The standard of the judgment is the Deuteronomic law. The verdict is based on the king's fidelity to Yahweh and especially, in the case of an Israelite king, on whether he had worshiped the golden calves introduced by the archsinner Jeroboam I, and in the case of a

Judean king on whether he had worshiped on the high places or not. All the northern kings were condemned, and even such godly Judean kings as Asa and Jehoshaphat, who were zealous adherents of Yahweh and exterminators of heathen cults, did not altogether escape the author's censure, because they had not removed the high places (15:14; 22:43). These judgments were so stereotyped that they were applied even to a king like Zimri who reigned only 7 days (16:19)!

At the conclusion of each reign the author also used a regular formula, in which he referred his readers to other historical works for the study of the secular aspects of the king's reign and then stated as a rule, the place of his burial and the name of his successor,

> And the rest of the acts of Abijam, and all that he did, are they not written in the Book of the Chronicles of the Kings of Judah? And there was war between Abijam and Jeroboam. And Abijam slept with his fathers; and they buried him in the city of David: and Asa his son reigned in his stead. (1 Ki. 15:7f.)

The work of the author is easily distinguishable from the excerpts of his sources. The account of the division of the kingdom under Rehoboam (1 Ki. 12:1–20) he gave entire. It is of priceless historical value. But of his own accord he added that the prophet Shemaiah sent the army of 180,000 (!) Judeans and Benjamites home, because the schism of the kingdom had been intended by Yahweh (12:21–24). He wove around a few facts in his sources a complete story of Jeroboam's apostasy, which is so important to him for the understanding of the whole history of the Northern Kingdom. His own work is printed in italics:

> Then Jeroboam fortified Shechem in the hill-country of Ephraim, and dwelt therein; and he went out from thence, and fortified Penuel. *And Jeroboam said in his heart, Now will the kingdom return to the house of David: if this people go up to offer sacrifices in the house of Yahweh at Jerusalem, then will the heart of this people turn again to their lord, to Rehoboam king of Judah; and they will kill me.*
> Whereupon the king took counsel, and made two calves of gold; and he said unto the people, It is too much for you to go up to Jerusalem: behold thy gods, O Israel, which brought thee up out of the land of Egypt. And he set the one in Beth-el, and the other put he in Dan. *And this thing became a sin; for the people went before the one, even unto Dan. And he*

made houses of high places, and made priests from among all the people,
that were not of the sons of Levi. And Jeroboam ordained a feast in the
eighth month, on the fifteenth day of the month, like unto the feast that
is in Judah, and he went up unto the altar which he had made in Bethel,
to sacrifice to the calves that he had made: and he placed in Bethel the
priests of the high places that he had made. And he went up to the altar
which he had made in Bethel on the fifteenth day in the eighth month,
even in the month which he had devised of his own heart: and he or-
dained a feast for the children of Israel, and went up to the altar, to burn
incense. (1 Ki. 12:25–33)

In narrating the visit of Jeroboam's wife to the prophet Ahijah for
the purpose of asking Yahweh's oracle regarding her sick son (14:1–
18) the author put into the prophet's mouth the condemnation of
Jeroboam and of Israel on account of his defection from Yahweh.

The invasion of Judah by Pharaoh Shishak under Rehoboam
(14:25–28) was to him a punishment for the religious transgressions
of Judah. Here again we must distinguish the facts, derived from
his sources, and his religious interpretation of them. This is necessary
all the way through. The conspiracy of Baasha against Nadab and
the assassination of the king and of the whole house of Jeroboam
were predicted by Ahijah as the inevitable result of Jeroboam's sin
(15:25–32). But the new king walked in Jeroboam's way too! And
quite promptly the prophet Jehu announced to him also that he
would not be allowed to found a dynasty. His son Elah was murdered by Zimri (15:33—16:14) who reigned but seven days when
he perished at the capture of Tirzah by Omri, also for no other
reason than that he had worshipped the golden calves! For this he
could hardly have found much time during his brief reign, as he
was besieged by Omri directly after his regicide (16:15–20).

Of the reign of Omri, one of the greatest kings of Israel, the author tells nothing but that he built Samaria, the famous capital of
Israel, a significant accomplishment indeed, but only one. The Moabite king Mesha has told us in his monument the so-called Moabite
Stone [5] that Omri conquered the whole East Jordan country; and
the Assyrians still called Israel "the house of Omri" a hundred years
after the downfall of his dynasty! But to our author his reign yielded
no illustrative material of any value, so he passed it with his stereo-

[5] See *ANET*, p. 320.

typed phrases which would never suggest Omri's importance for
the history of the Northern Kingdom. Of Ahab, his son, we know
more, because the author here used the stories of Elijah. He left the
excerpts which he made from them practically untouched; only
Elijah's prediction of the complete extermination of his house he expanded (21:20b–26, 27–29) and noted its fulfillment (22:38). The
Elisha stories also contained enough religious material so that our
author did not have to add anything to them. But in the Jehu story
he inserted a repetition of his prophecy to Ahab by Elijah in the
words of the young prophet who anointed Jehu as king (2. Ki.
9:7–10a).

The story of the revolution in Jerusalem under Athaliah and the
restoration of the temple under Joash (2 Ki. 11:1–20; 12:4–16) was
perhaps taken from the Temple Annals. For the following reigns the
author derived but little narrative material from his sources, the
defeat of Amaziah by Jehoash of Israel whom he had challenged
presumptuously (2 Ki. 14:8–14) is the most important of them. For
Jeroboam II of Israel and Azariah of Judah there are only the usual
stereotyped phrases, and nothing of signal importance, and yet their
reigns were the most splendid after Solomon. A single hint of this is
contained in the brief reference to Jeroboam's successful wars against
Hamath and Damascus. But he who wants to know about them may
read the Book of the Acts of the Kings of Israel! Our author had
but little use for them.

The story of the last two decades of Israel, with its revolutions
and regicides, was quickly told, always with the same punctilious
introduction and conclusion and a few extracts from the annals. In
Ahaz's reign the Syro-Ephraimitic war was described in the words of
this source, while Ahaz's setting up of a brazen altar made after the
pattern of an altar in Damascus may have been taken from the
Temple Annals. Then the end of Israel came. In 722 Samaria fell into
the hands of the Assyrians after a siege of three years. The people
were carried into exile. Naturally here was the point where the author could show that their sin, especially the sin of Jeroboam, had
caused this terrible disaster. But he also sees how Judah was in-
fected. In his review of the reasons which led to the fall of the
Northern Kingdom (2 Ki. 17:7–17) he says at the end:

Also Judah kept not the commandments of Yahweh their God, but walked in the statutes of Israel which they made. And Yahweh rejected all the seed of Israel, and afflicted them, and delivered them into the hand of spoilers, until He had cast them out of His sight. (2 Ki. 17:19f.)

From now on only Judah was left, and our historian next relates its story from Hezekiah to Josiah (2 Ki. 18:1—23:25a). For Hezekiah, he had a longer introduction than usual, for he regarded him as a great reformer and attributed to him the destruction of the high places, thus making him anticipate Josiah's great reformation in 621 B.C., whether rightly or not is questionable.

He removed the high places, and broke the pillars, and cut down the Asherah: and he broke in pieces the brazen serpent that Moses has made; for unto those days the Israelites burned incense to it; and it was called Nehushtan. (2 Ki. 18:4)

The great invasion of Sennacherib was told in three accounts: 1) in 18:13–16 which came from the annals; 2) in 18:17; 19:8, 9a, 36f.; and 3) in 19:9b–35. The stories of Hezekiah's sickness and of the embassy of Merodachbaladan (2 Ki. 20:1–19) were probably taken from Isaiah, for he is the central figure in them. Most of the story contained in 2 Ki. 18:13—20:19 is also found in the Book of Isaiah (chs. 36–39). The most valuable historical information is always that which was derived from the Annals.

Of Manasseh, who reigned for 55 long years, the author has nothing to say except of his apostasy and his shedding much innocent blood in Jerusalem. In the description of the sinfulness of this ruler he supplied vivid touches and told how the prophets predicted that Jerusalem and Judah also would be completely destroyed, because they had been seduced by Manasseh to commit worse sins than the Amorites.

Therefore thus says Yahweh, the God of Israel, Behold, I bring such evil upon Jerusalem and Judah, that whosoever hears of it, both his ears shall tingle. And I will stretch over Jerusalem the line of Samaria, and the plummet of the house of Ahab; and I will wipe Jerusalem as a man wipes a dish, wiping it and turning it upside down. And I will cast off the remnant of Mine inheritance, and deliver them into the hand of their enemies; and they shall become a prey and a spoil to all their enemies; because they have done that which is evil in My sight, and have provoked

Me to anger, since the day their fathers came forth out of Egypt, even unto this day. (2 Ki. 21:12–15)

The same ominous threat he inserted in Huldah's oracle (2 Ki. 22:15–20).

Thereupon he turned to a bright spot in history: Josiah's reformation, which had averted the anger of Yahweh for a brief time. His encomium on this king, who came to the throne after his father Amon's reign was cut short by assassination, is noteworthy:

And like unto him was there no king before him, that turned to Yahweh with all his heart, and with all his soul, and with all his might, according to all the law of Moses. (2 Ki. 23:25a)

As chief sources for Josiah's reign he used an account of the discovery of the Book of the Law in the temple and excerpts from the Annals of the Kings of Judah concerning the reform measures taken. It must have been a puzzle to him how this just ruler could come to such a sad end as was reported in the Annals (1 Ki. 23:28f.), but he overcame such thoughts by the consideration that on account of the sins of Manasseh, Yahweh had determined to cast off Jerusalem (1 Ki. 23:26–27).

He then told of the last unhappy kings of Judah, and the events connected with the fall of the city and the captivity (2 Ki. 23:25b—25:30), utilizing in the main the Annals of the kings of Judah, but inserting his own remarks at appropriate places.

After reading the history of the chosen people, slanted in this manner, the reader had to conclude that Judah as well as Israel had deserved their fearful fate! The whole book thus became a great confession of sin. And indeed, to this penitent frame of mind the author wished to bring his people by this revised history. If only they would clearly see the spiritual causes of their national disaster, and repent! Then Yahweh might hear in heaven, His dwelling place, and forgive, as Solomon had prayed, and the little ray of light that recently had pierced the gloom in the liberation of King Jehoiachin from prison by Evil-merodach of Babylon (2 Ki. 25:27–30) might be the herald of the coming dawn, the beginning of salvation.

Magnificent as it was in many ways, the Deuteronomistic historical work could not dislodge the Jehovist or compilation of J and E (see p. 87) in the affection of the people, for it had become not only dear to them by long use, but was invested with a certain authority. Besides, it carried the history back to the patriarchs, even to the creation, and related the Egyptian sojourn and the liberation. The two entities were bound to attract each other. Of that development something will be said later (pp. 290f.).

XVI

The Earlier

Postexilic Prophets

WHEN after the fall of Babylon a company of Jewish exiles returned to Judah, nothing but disappointment awaited them. None of the glorious events predicted by Deutero-Isaiah had come true on their homeward march. And in Judah itself a weary struggle for existence resulted. Few in number and poor in means, they found it hard to cope with the difficulties. Drought and failure of the crops aggravated their distress, till finally, disillusioned and disappointed, they were in danger of losing their faith in Yahweh. He had not returned to them; He was still angry with them; there was no hope. Then a man of plain speech but of much practical sense and enthusiasm roused their religious faith by summoning them to work for the Lord. Haggai, "the prophet," agreed with the people that Yahweh had not come back to Jerusalem, but maintained that it was their own fault. For how could He dwell among His people, if they provided no home for Him? They had built their own houses, but the house of God was still in ruins. Yahweh had sent the hard seasons in order to bring them to their senses. But so far they had not understood God's purpose. Let them but build the temple and all will be changed.

Haggai's appeal, made on the first day of the sixth month of the second year of Darius (August 29, 520 B.C.) met with instant response.[1] Headed by Zerubbabel the governor and Joshua the high

[1] Unlike Ezekiel, the exile, who was not willing to date by the years of

priest, the people began the work at once (1:2–12, 14). On the twenty-fourth day of the same month (our September 22) the foundation was laid, and Haggai urged the people again with his speech; let them but mark this day well, it is the turning point in their fate; from this day Yahweh will bless them (1:15, 13; 2:15–19). Four weeks later, when it appeared that the building would be poor in comparison with the splendid temple of Solomon, Haggai met the discouragement with some brave words of hope (2:1–9): Yahweh is with us, and that is after all more important than anything else. Never fear, He will provide for the beauty and splendor of the temple Himself.

For thus says Yahweh of hosts: Yet a little while, and I will shake the heavens, and the earth, and the sea, and the dry land; and I will shake all nations; and the precious things of all nations shall come; and I will fill this house with glory, says Yahweh of hosts. The silver is Mine, and the gold is Mine, says Yahweh of hosts. The latter glory of this house shall be greater than the former, says Yahweh of hosts; and in this place will I give peace, says Yahweh of hosts. (Hag. 2:6–9)

It may be that the news of the great revolution in the north and east of the Persian empire, which had shaken its very foundations but had been successfully put down by Darius, had awakened the hope that Yahweh would shake the nations again and compel them to bring immense tribute into His temple.

Thus encouraged, the people worked on and did so well that two months later, on the twenty-fourth day of the ninth month (December 19, 520) the Samaritans asked permission to join them in building the temple. But Haggai, fearing that this "unclean" element would contaminate the new temple, strongly opposed their request. He insisted that contact with holiness could not sanctify the unclean, but contact with uncleanness infallibly defiled.

So is this people, and so is this nation before Me, says Yahweh; and so is every work of their hands, and where they come near, it is unclean. (Hag. 2:10–14)

Nebuchadrezzar, Haggai dates in Babylonian fashion, much like the Chronicle texts, except that he uses month numbers instead of month names. For the conversion of dates see Richard A. Parker and Waldo Dubberstein, "Babylonian Chronology 626 B.C.–A.D. 75," *Brown University Studies*, XIX, 1956.

That he carried his point, we know from Ezra 4:1–4. On the same day Haggai prophesied to Zerubbabel, who was of Davidic descent, perhaps out of gratitude for his aid in this matter, which had convinced Haggai that he was worthy of becoming king of Judah.

Speak to Zerubbabel, governor of Judah, saying, I will shake the heavens and the earth; and I will overthrow the throne of kingdoms; and I will destroy the strength of the kingdoms of the nations; and I will overthrow the chariots, and those that ride in them; and the horses and their riders shall come down, every one by the sword of his brother. In that day, says Yahweh of hosts, will I take thee, O Zerubbabel, My servant, the son of Shealtiel, says Yahweh, and will make thee as a signet ring; for I have chosen thee, says Yahweh of hosts. (Hag. 2:21–23)

Haggai was strongly influenced by Ezekiel in his view of the importance of the temple for the new community and his fear of its profanation by foreigners, and like him he combined priestly and prophetic interests. He was no great prophet, but by his practical initiative he rendered a genuine service to his people. His eagerness and enthusiasm are still refreshing.

His book was probably put together by one of his disciples. Like Ezekiel's it is in prose and its sections are carefully dated by the day, month, and year. It is small and simple, without any passage of power and beauty. But for the history of the time it is of the highest value. There is a small dislocation in our present text, for 2:15–19 originally must have followed 1:15a.

Haggai had begun his work on the first day of the sixth month of the second year of Darius (August 29, 520). Two months later, on the first of the eighth month (October 27), Zechariah, who is also called "the prophet," but seems to have been a priest as well,[2] joined him and called the people to repentance. He reiterated the message of the former prophets from whom he had learned and on whom he consciously depended in his thought and speech. Like Haggai he indulges in a conspicuously frequent repetition of "says

[2] Cf. Neh. 12:16. He is called Zechariah son of Berechiah son of Iddo in 1:1, but in Ezra 5:1; 6:14 Zechariah son of Iddo. This has an exact parallel in an Aramaic papyrus (no. 15 in Kraeling, *The Brooklyn Museum Aramaic Papyri*, 1953), where Anani son of Haggai son of Meshullam is called Anani son of Meshullam. If a father died early or was of less consequence than the grandfather this is quite understandable.

Yahweh" (it occurs five times in two verses 1:3f.). He evidently encountered much doubt and disbelief regarding his mission. Four times he felt the need of appealing to the fulfillment of his predictions for his vindication, "and ye shall know that Yahweh of hosts has sent me to you" (2:9, 11; 4:9; 6:15). In the night of the twenty-fourth day of the eleventh month of the same year (January 23, 519, according to our reckoning) he saw eight visions in which the pressing problems of his day were solved in a remarkable manner. In the first vision (1:7–17) he saw the heavenly patrol of four horsemen, who on their swift steeds—each a horse of a different color—had traversed the earth that day in different directions, and heard them report to their superior, the angel of Yahweh,

> We have gone to and fro through the earth, and behold, all the earth sits still and is at rest.

The mighty political revolutions that had been stirring the Persian empire had all been put down. Another hope was destroyed. And the angel of Yahweh, who had Israel's fate at heart, voiced the great disappointment in his plea,

> O Yahweh of hosts, how long will Thou not have mercy on Jerusalem and on the cities of Judah, against which Thou hast had indignation these seventy years?

Yahweh replied with "comforting words" to the angel who acted as Zechariah's guide and interpreter in these visions, and he in turn told him,

> Cry thou, saying, Thus says Yahweh of hosts: I am jealous for Jerusalem and for Zion with a great jealousy. And I am very sore displeased with the nations that are at ease; for I was but a little displeased, and they helped forward the affliction. Therefore thus says Yahweh: I am returned to Jerusalem with mercies; My house shall be built in it, says Yahweh of hosts, and a line shall be stretched forth over Jerusalem. Cry yet again, saying, Thus says Yahweh of hosts: My cities shall yet overflow with prosperity; and Yahweh shall yet comfort Zion, and shall yet choose Jerusalem. (Zech. 1:14–17)

In the second vision (1:18–21) he saw four horns and four smiths. The angel interpreted the horns as symbols of the enemy nations and the smiths as their executioners. The prophet was sure that Yahweh's

purpose of punishing the nations, which was an indispensable prerequisite of the coming age of glory, would be carried out. As far
as he could see, there was no human power that Yahweh was using.
But He does not depend on human forces, He sends His heavenly
ministers to execute His will. We come here upon a characteristic
trait of the apocalyptic seer in contradistinction to the prophet:
lacking the great historical agents on earth, he unveils the secrets of
heaven and shows the activity of the angelic beings in the great
movements on earth. To enhance the mystery and impressiveness of
the revelation the apocalyptic writer uses allegory as a favorite means
of presentation.

In the third vision (2:1–13) an angelic surveyor went forth to
measure the area on which Jerusalem should be rebuilt and to mark
the line of the wall. He was young, not initiated into the counsel
of God. The interpreting angel therefore told another angel,

Run, speak to this young man, saying, Jerusalem shall be inhabited as
villages without walls, by reason of the multitude of men and cattle
therein. For I, says Yahweh, will be to her a wall of fire round about, and
I will be the glory in her midst. (Zech. 2:4f.)

Any movement of refortifying Jerusalem by building a strong city
wall is frowned upon here, but not avowedly for political reasons,
although the prophet must have known that the Persians would not
have tolerated it. To him Yahweh's own protection was more than
enough and besides, he looked forward to a large increase of the
population which at present was so small and so poor. He therefore called upon the exiles that were still in the land of the north to
flee and come home with the wealth of the nations, for Yahweh had
sent His angel "after glory" (i.e., riches) "to the nations which
plundered you." None will dare to hinder you, "for he that touches
you, touches the apple of His eye." Afterward many nations will
join themselves to Yahweh, when he dwells among His people in
Zion.

In the fourth vision (3:1–8; 4:6b–10a; 3:9f.) Joshua the high priest
stood before the angel of Yahweh in the soiled garments of an
accused person. At his right was his accuser, the Satan, a heavenly
being, who, according to the prologue of the Book of Job, went all
over the earth to observe people and make complaint to Yahweh

about their sins. Here he accused Joshua and with him the people, whose representative the high priest was. But the angel of Yahweh would not listen to him, for were they not like "a brand plucked out of the fire," had they not but just escaped from captivity? He therefore ordered that Joshua's soiled garments be taken off and fresh ones be put on him as a sign that the sins had been forgiven. Then he had a clean turban put on his head, and told him that if he would faithfully discharge the duties of his office, he would always have access to the heavenly court, as mediator between Yahweh and His people. Moreover, Joshua and his fellow-priests were a sign that the restoration would surely be carried out: they would minister in the new sanctuary. In confirmation of this he placed the beautiful top-stone which should crown the temple at its completion before Joshua. Then the sin of the land would be removed by Yahweh and the golden age would arrive.

In a passage which has accidentally been displaced (4:6b–10a) the significance of the "sign" is made clearer. Great difficulties had arisen which threatened to hinder the completion of the temple. From Ezra 4 we know of the enmity of the Samaritans; from Ezra 5 of the interference of the Persian satrap Tattenai. Was the work after all to be frustrated? The Jews already talked of resorting to force. But the prophet, who had opposed the refortification of Jerusalem before, replied,

This is the word of Yahweh to Zerubbabel, saying, Not by might nor by power, but by My Spirit, says Yahweh of hosts. Who art thou, O great mountain? before Zerubbabel a plain; and he shall bring forth the top stone with shoutings of Grace, grace to it. The hands of Zerubbabel have laid the foundation of this house; his hands shall also finish it; and ye shall know that Yahweh of hosts has sent me to you. For he that has despised the day of small things shall rejoice, and shall see the plummet in the hand of Zerubbabel. (Zech. 4:6b–10a)

After this vision Zechariah fell asleep. But the angel came again and waked him to show him four other visions. In the fifth vision (4:1–6a, 10b–14) he saw a golden candlestick with seven lamps and beside it two olive trees. The angel explained the seven lamps [3] as

[3] After omitting the Zerubbabel oracle, which does not belong here, the connection between v. 6 and v. 10 is as follows, "Then he answered and spoke to me, saying, These seven are the eyes of Yahweh."

"the eyes of Yahweh, which run to and fro through the whole earth," and the two olive trees as "the two anointed ones, that stand by the Lord of the whole earth," the representatives of the political and of the religious government. This meant that the new community was to be a theocracy, with the king and the high priest as the representatives of the real Ruler in heaven.

In the sixth vision (5:1–4) Zechariah saw how the thieves and perjurers among the people were to be exterminated by a terrible curse which was written on a huge flying roll. Its magic power would destroy them all and, besides, it would enter into the house of every one of them and utterly demolish it.[4]

In the seventh vision (5:5–11) the very principle of wickedness was removed from the country. The prophet saw how a woman was thrust into a large container which was then closed by a leaden lid, and how two other women with the wings of a stork carried her through the air to Babylonia, where she belonged and where she could carry on her wickedness. She had no place in the new community in Judah!

In the eighth vision (6:1–8) the prophet saw the heavenly patrol-guard riding forth on the work of the new day that had dawned. After a while the interpreting angel shouted the welcome news to him, "behold, they that go toward the north country have placed My Spirit in the north country." There among the Jewish exiles in Babylonia (cf. 2:6) the Divine Spirit was at work, arousing their love for their homeland.

As a direct evidence of this Zechariah was commanded by Yahweh on the same day to go to the house of a certain Josiah and receive there gold and silver from some Jews who had just come from Babylonia, and to make a crown. This he should place on Zerubbabel's head, for

He shall build the temple of Yahweh and bear the glory and shall sit and rule upoon his throne, and Joshua shall be priest at his right hand, and the counsel of peace shall be between them both.

[4] This presupposes the existence of magic texts written on scrolls. Jews must have learned about such in Babylonia, where long magic texts such as the *Maqlû* series were well known. These were in cuneiform, but Aramaic and Hebrew equivalents on papyrus or leather were no doubt made in this era.

The crown was to be preserved in the temple as a memorial of the donors. Others also would come and aid in the building of the temple (6:9–15). Like Haggai, Zechariah was sure that Zerubbabel was destined to be king. But he believed also that the high priest should be his peer, on the same level of authority, representing the religious side of the theocracy. As far as Zerubbabel was concerned, this dream was never fulfilled. What happened to him we do not know. Whether he was removed or even executed by the Persians, who may have learned of this royalist movement, we cannot tell. But the Persians never appointed another Davidic governor of Judah. The high priest now became the sole native alongside of a Persian prefect. Somebody, mindful of this, changed the crown of Zerubbabel to crowns for Joshua, and the clause, "and Joshua shall be priest at his right hand" into "and he shall be a priest upon his throne," so that our present Hebrew text is a prophecy of the rule of the high priest! Fortunately, the "correction" was not consistent and left some tell-tale marks, and the Greek translation was made from a manuscript, which had not yet corrected the prophecy in order to make it conform to history.

On the fourth day of the ninth month of the fourth year of Darius (December 8, 518), an inquiry was made of the priests and the prophets whether the fast-day that commemorated the destruction of the temple should still be kept. To this Zechariah replied that the people had not fasted for Yahweh's benefit on that day or on the day that commemorated the murder of Gedaliah either. Yahweh was interested not in fasting but in social justice, as the former prophets had preached. The fathers' refusal to listen to them had brought the judgment upon them. Yahweh was now intensely in earnest about Zion's restoration, and desired that Jerusalem should become "the city of truth" and the temple hill "the holy mountain." He was going to repeople the city with returning exiles so that old men and women and young boys and girls should fill the streets with their gracious presence and their joyful mirth. This would all come when the temple was completed. Let the people work diligently on its reconstruction, and they will experience Yahweh's favor in rich harvests. Let them be truthful and peaceable, and abstain from fraud, theft, and perjury. They may be sure that these fast-days, and the others too that commemorated the beginning of the siege of Jerusalem and the day of its capture, will be turned into festivals of joy. And moreover,

Thus says Yahweh of hosts: It shall yet come to pass, that there shall come peoples, and the inhabitants of great cities; and the inhabitants of one city shall go to another, saying, Let us go speedily to entreat the favor of Yahweh, and to seek Yahweh of hosts: I will go also. Yea, many peoples and strong nations shall come to seek Yahweh of hosts in Jerusalem, and to entreat the favor of Yahweh. Thus says Yahweh of hosts: In those days it shall come to pass, that ten men from the nations of every tongue shall take hold of the skirt of a Jew, saying, Let us go with you, for we have heard that God is with you. (Zech. 8:20–22)

Only the first eight chapters of the Book of Zechariah come from this prophet; the rest is of later origin. That which distinguishes him among the prophets is his series of visions. Here we discover his originality, for they are really a little apocalypse. Zechariah was one of the first apocalyptic writers, although not the first, for Ezekiel preceded him in this also. His great dependence on his predecessors, his fusion of priestly and prophetic interests, his love of allegory, his belief in magic, all show that he was not a great prophet, but he is most interesting for all that. His writings are in prose and, the visions excepted, not in remarkable prose. Like Haggai, he dated sections of his book in Babylonian style, several times even giving the month names.

To this period of reestablished life at Jerusalem may be assigned the last portion of the book of Isaiah, chs. 56–66, sometimes ascribed to one author, a third or Trito-Isaiah. The question then is whether Trito-Isaiah is not identical with Deutero-Isaiah and merely represents a later stage in the latter's development.[5] But chiefly in one section (chs. 60–62) is one really reminded of Isa. 40–55, and even here the highest thoughts of the prophet of those chapters are not found. Most scholars incline to the belief that Isa. 56–66 is a compilation of materials composed by several authors. The problem is one of the most difficult and controversial in Old Testament research.

[5] Duhm's Trito-Isaiah was a contemporary of Malachi; K. Elliger's (1928) of Haggai and Zechariah; L. Glahn (1934) denied the separation of Isa. 56–66 from 40–55, holding that Deutero-Isaiah wrote 56–66 a little later (536–530). C. C. Torrey (1928) also maintained the unity of 40–66, and considered Isa. 34–35 to be by the same writer. The parceling out to various authors goes back to Eichhorn.

We have already dealt with the prayer found in Isa. 63:7—64:11, which comes from the time immediately after 587 B.C. (pp. 208f.). Perhaps one may find three other contributors in this section: a warner and reprover; a Torah teacher; and a prophet of hope and consolation for whom the term Trito-Isaiah seems appropriate.

The warner and reprover was a man of deep spiritual insight, whose work is preserved in Isa. 56:9—58:12; 59:1–15a; 65:1–16; 66:1–6, 5–18a, 24. He was opposed to the building of a temple, whether at the time of Haggai and Zechariah or at a previous occasion when such a project had been brought forward (538? cf. Ezr. 1:2f.). He declared, quite in the spirit of the greatest of the earlier prophets,

> Thus says Yahweh, "Heaven is My throne,
>   and the earth is My footstool.
> What manner of a house will ye build unto Me?
>   and what place shall be My rest?
> For all these My hand made,
>   and so they all came to be, says Yahweh.
> But to this man will I look, to him that is poor
>   and of a contrite spirit, and that trembles at My word.
> He that kills an ox is as he that slays a man,
>   he that sacrifices a lamb as he that breaks a dog's neck,
> He that offers an oblation as he that offers swine's blood,
>   he that burns incense as he that blesses an idol!" (Isa. 66:1–3a)

You must prepare a house for Yahweh indeed, but not a temple made with hands. Prepare your hearts for Him, for He makes His home with people of contrite and humble spirit. The whole sacrificial system is worse than useless. Only obedience to His will can prevent the coming of the calamities you fear. If he prophesied in 520 B.C., this bold word may have earned him much enmity and hate. For Haggai and Zechariah had persuaded the leaders and the people to their views. But our prophet also had adherents, who "trembled at His word." They were abused, even excommunicated! But he encouraged them,

> Hear the word of Yahweh, ye that tremble at His word:
> Your brethren that hate you have said,
>   they that cast you out for My name's sake,
> "Let Yahweh be glorified,
>   that we may see your joy."
> But it is they that shall be put to shame! (Isa. 66:5)

The prophet could not prevent the building of the temple. But he
did not give up prophetic mission after it was built. Like Micah
of old he had heard the divine call,

> Cry aloud, spare not,
>   lift up thy voice like a trumpet,
> And declare unto My people their transgression,
>   and to the house of Jacob their sins. (Isa. 58:1)

And he did. He told them that Yahweh was anxious to come to His
people, but they must prepare the way and remove all obstacles,

> For thus says the high and lofty One,
>   that inhabits eternity, whose name is Holy:
> "I dwell in the high and holy place,
>   and with him that is of a contrite and humble spirit,
> To revive the spirit of the humble,
>   and to revive the heart of the contrite." (Isa. 57:15)

But for the wicked there is no peace (57:14ff.). Let the people not
say that Yahweh is either unable or unwilling to help them, for it
is nothing but their moral corruption that prevents Him.

> For your hands are defiled with blood,
>   and your fingers with iniquity;
> Your lips have spoken lies,
>   your tongue mutters wickedness.

> Therefore is justice far from us,
>   neither does righteousness overtake us:
> We look for light, but behold darkness,
>   for brightness but we walk in obscurity, etc. (Isa. 59:1–15)

Their social iniquity went hand in hand with much zeal for worship
and external ordinances, especially fasting. On the very fast-days
they fought and quarreled and exacted work from their laborers.

> Is such the fast that I have chosen?
>   the day for a man to afflict his soul?
> Is it to bow down his head as a rush,
>   and to spread sackcloth and ashes under him?
> Wilt thou call this a fast,
>   and an acceptable day to Yahweh?

> Is not this the fast that I have chosen:
>   to loose the bonds of wickedness,
>   to undo the bands of the yoke,

To let the oppressed go free,
  and that ye break every yoke?
Is it not to deal thy bread to the hungry,
  and that thou bring the poor that are cast out to thy house?
When thou seekest the naked, that thou cover him,
  and that thou hide not thyself from thine own flesh?

Then shall thy light go forth as the morning,
  and thy healing shall spring forth speedily;
And thy righteousness shall go before thee,
  the glory of Yahweh shall be thy rear-guard.
Then shalt thou call and Yahweh will answer;
  thou shalt cry, and He will say, "Here I am!" (Isa. 58:5–9a)

The spirit of the old prophets was still living, for this is prophetic religion. If the people will but do away with oppression, perjury, and lying, if they will but show mercy and kindness, the great and wonderful restoration will surely be accomplished. But only then!

The prophet knew that the leaders were largely responsible for the poor condition of the people. They should have been its spiritual guides, but they were so negligent and selfish that they had lost all spiritual discernment and did not see the dangers that invaded the community (56:9—57:2). There was a party, against whom these leaders did not take strict measures; they were addicted to rank religious apostasy and practised all the abominable rites of the ancient nature, Moloch, and mystery cults. The prophet had no hope for them. It seemed useless to him to call these people to repentance. They would be exterminated. He heard in his spirit the fearful tumult in the temple, Yahweh was about to destroy them with fire and sword (Isa. 66:6, 15–18a, 24).

To the hand of a Torah teacher may be attributed two sections which are now closely connected with the work of the warning prophet (Isa. 56:1–8; 58:13f.). We saw in Haggai the tendency of exclusiveness toward any persons who might profane the sanctuary. It was the spirit of Ezekiel that grew stronger all the time. The holiness of the people, which was an imperative condition for Yahweh's return, could be maintained only by excluding all foreigners and all eunuchs [6] from the temple. The prophet who wrote

[6] Eunuchs were excluded by Deut. 3:1. Many Jews who became servants of the Babylonian royalty were castrated. Among the returned exiles there must have been such men.

Isaiah 56:1–8 protested strongly against this narrow attitude. There is no reason whatever to exclude these eunuchs and these foreigners, if they fulfill the fundamental obligations of the religion of Yahweh, for fellowship with God is not a matter of blood or of bodily perfection. If the eunuchs keep the moral law, observe the Sabbath, and hold fast the covenant,

> I will give to them in My house
>   and within My walls a memorial and a name
> Better than of sons and of daughters,
>   I will give to them an everlasting name,
>   that shall not be cut off.

And "the foreigners that join themselves to Yahweh, to minister to Him, and to love the name of Yahweh to be His servants" and that observe those three basic requirements,

> I will bring them to My holy mountain,
>   and make them joyful in My house of prayer:
> Their burnt-offerings and their sacrifices
>   shall be accepted upon Mine altar;
> For My house shall be called
>   a house of prayer for all peoples. (Isa. 56:1–8)

The strong emphasis on the Sabbath is striking. During the exile it had become one of the distinguishing signs of Judaism. Ezekiel already had said, "Moreover also I gave them My Sabbaths, to be a sign between Me and them, that they might know that I am Yahweh than sanctifies them" (Ezek. 20:12). In Isaiah 58:13f. keeping the Sabbath by cessation from work and pleasure and idle talk, in hearty conformity with the spirit of the sacred day, is declared to be one of the conditions of the future greatness of Israel. A believer in the blessings of true Sabbath observance for the nation inserted a long passage in the Book of Jeremiah (17:19–27). All of these authors were living in the period when the priestly writer celebrated the Sabbath as the crown of creation in Gen. 2:1–3 (cf. ch. XVII).

The third contributor to Isa. 56–66 is that of a prophet of hope and consolation. We seem to hear Deutero-Isaiah's voice again, sweet and melodious, full of joy and comfort, charming the hearer by its beauty. It was probably one of his disciples who had caught the master's style and melody, though not his highest ideas. We may call him the Third or Trito-Isaiah, and ascribe to his pen Isaiah 59:15b—63:6; 65:17-25; 66:7-14, 18b-23. He felt that he was sent on the same mission as his master, to comfort the people and to inspire them with faith in the coming of the glorious restoration. In a passage that Jesus later on could use with reference to himself he expressed the consciousness of his prophetic mission.

> The Spirit of the Lord Yahweh is upon me,
>   because Yahweh has anointed me;
> To preach good tidings to the meek, He has sent me,
>   to bind up the broken-hearted,
> To proclaim liberty to the captives,
>   and the opening of the prison to them that are bound;
> To proclaim the year of Yahweh's favor,
>   and the day of vengeance of our God;
> To comfort all that mourn,
>   to appoint to them that mourn in Zion,
>   to give to them a garland for ashes,
> The oil of joy for mourning,
>   the garment of praise for the spirit of heaviness;
> That they may be called trees of righteousness,
>   the planting of Yahweh, that He may be glorified. (Isa. 61:1-3)

He was sent to a disheartened people, who felt still forsaken by Yahweh (62:4), for though the temple had been erected, it was a poor house without splendor and glory, and Yahweh had not taken up His abode in it. Jerusalem and the cities of Judah were not yet built up, the walls were still in ruins, and only a few people lived there. Trito-Isaiah faced this condition and voiced the wonderful hope of Deutero-Isaiah in words almost as beautiful as those of his master.

> Arise, shine, for thy light is come,
>   and the glory of Yahweh is risen upon thee.
> For, behold, darkness shall cover the earth,
>   and gross darkness the peoples;
> But Yahweh will arise upon thee,
>   and His glory shall be seen over thee.
> And the nations shall come to thy light,
>   and kings to the brightness of thy rising. (Isa. 60:1-3)

Let Jerusalem but look up, great caravans are coming, bringing back her exiled children and untold treasures, the wealth of the

nations. From everywhere they come with silver and gold, frank-
incense and flocks for the temple of Yahweh, which will be glorified
thereby. Full of ecstasy Trito-Isaiah foresees the time when foreigners shall build up Jerusalem's walls and kings shall minister to
her.

> Thy gates also shall be open continually,
>   they shall not be shut day or night,
> That men may bring unto thee the wealth of the nations,
>   and their kings led captive. (60:11)

> And the sons of them that afflicted thee
>   shall come bending unto thee,
> And all they that despised thee
>   shall bow themselves down at the soles of thy feet. (Isa. 60:14)

Jerusalem will be the mistress of the peoples. Any nation that will
not obey her will be destroyed (60:12). Not only will foreigners
build up the ruined cities, but

> Strangers shall stand and feed your flocks,
>   and foreigners shall be your ploughmen and your vine-dressers.
> But ye shall be named the priests of Yahweh;
>   men shall call you the ministers of our God. (Isa. 61:5f.)

How the thought of lordship fills this prophet's mind! There is never
a thought of Israel's servantship as with Deutero-Isaiah, nor does
the idea of the priesthood of Israel imply spiritual mediatorship; it
is only another way of expressing the lordship of the Zadokites.
Trito-Isaiah missed the highest glory of his ideal. Nevertheless not
only this external splendor, wealth, fertility, and lordship, but also
moral and spiritual glory will crown the golden age of Zion.

> I will also make thy officers peace,
>   and thine exactors righteousness.
> Violence shall no more be heard in thy land,
>   desolation nor destruction within thy borders;
> But thou shalt call thy walls Salvation,
>   and thy gates Praise.
> The sun shall be no more thy light by day,
>   neither for brightness shall the moon give light to thee,
> But Yahweh will be to thee an everlasting light,
>   and thy God thy glory.

The sun shall no more go down,
  neither shall the moon withdraw itself,
For Yahweh will be thine everlasting light,
  and the days of thy mourning shall be ended.
Thy people also shall all be righteous,
  they shall inherit the land forever,
The branch of My planting,
  the work of My hands, that I may be glorified.
The little one shall become a thousand,
  and the small one a strong nation,
I, Yahweh, will hasten it in its time. (Isa. 60:17-22)

The prophet was full of eager anticipation. He was constantly interceding with Yahweh in passionate prayer to perform His act of restoration.

For Zion's sake will I not hold my peace,
  and for Jerusalem's sake I will not rest. (Isa. 62:1)

I have set watchmen
  upon thy walls, O Jerusalem,
They shall never hold their peace
  day and night.
Ye that are Yahweh's remembrancers,
  take ye no rest,
And give Him no rest,
  until He establish,
And till He make Jerusalem
  a praise in the earth. (Isa. 62:6f.)

But he knew that the prerequisite for the political restoration and glorification of Jerusalem was the collapse of the heathen powers. And thus he announced that Yahweh Himself would intervene against His enemies. The great upheavals in the Persian empire had passed. There was no one like Cyrus who could be Yahweh's agent in His final judgment of the nations. So Trito-Isaiah showed in splendid imagery, how Yahweh Himself put on His armor for the battle with His foes (Isa. 59:15b-21), and in a dramatic poem that was to find an echo in Julia Ward Howe's *Battle Hymn of the Republic*, he described Yahweh's return from the judgment.

Who is this that comes stained red,
  with garments dyed redder than a grape-gatherer's?

> Who is this that is glorious in his apparel,
>   marching in the greatness of his strength?
> "I that speak in righteousness,
>   mighty to save."
> Wherefore art Thou red in Thine apparel,
>   and Thy garments like his that treads in the vinepress?
> "I have trodden the winepress alone;
>   and of the peoples there was no one with Me:
> Yea, I trod them in Mine anger,
>   and trampled them in My wrath,
> And their lifeblood is sprinkled upon My garments,
>   and I have stained all My raiment.
> For the day of vengeance was in My heart,
>   and the year of My redeemed is come.
> And I looked, and there was none to help,
>   and I wondered that there was none to uphold.
> Therefore Mine own arm brought salvation to Me.
>   and My wrath, it upheld Me.
> And I trod down the peoples in Mine anger,
>   and made them drunk in My wrath,
> And poured out their lifeblood on the earth." (Isa. 63:1–6)

Yahweh's terrible judgment on the nations now forms the prelude
and the postlude to Trito-Isaiah's poems. Two other poems of his
describing the glory of the future are now placed in Isa. 65:17–25;
66:7–14, 18–23, while the beautiful exilic prayers of Isa. 63:7—64:12
are appended to the main stock of poems, most appropriately indeed,
for they still had their profound meaning for this later time. In
Isa. 65:17ff., the creation of a new earth and a new heaven is foretold.
The significant point in it is the undisturbed joy and peace of the
people.

> I will rejoice in Jerusalem
>   and joy in My people;
> And there shall be heard in her no more
>   the voice of weeping and the voice of crying.
> There shall be no more thence an infant of days
>   nor an old man that has not filled his days,
> For the child shall die a hundred years old,
>   and the sinner shall be accursed. (Isa. 65:19f.)

Men will grow old as in primeval days in order that they may taste
to the full the happiness of the new age. It is not yet immortality

that is hoped for, but it is a stage on the way to it. Universal peace will prevail even in nature. Quoting the First Isaiah our prophet concludes,

> The wolf and the lamb shall lie down together
> and the lion shall eat straw like the ox;
> and dust shall be the serpent's food.
> They shall not hurt nor destroy
> in all My holy mountain, says Yahweh. (Isa. 65:25)

In the last section (Isa. 66:7–14, 18–23) the only new thought is that Yahweh will miraculously repeople the country and choose Levitic Priests from the returning exiles. The small number of the inhabitants had troubled Zechariah too. For the new temple many more priests were needed. But they will come!

These great hopes Trito-Isaiah proclaimed. He fell short of Deutero-Isaiah's highest vision, but who will maintain that his activity was not of utmost importance? Did he not put new hope into the hearts of his people? Did he not ever impel them to look beyond the sordid cares of the present and the disheartening pettiness of the day, forward to the golden future where life would be glorified, sorrow and care forgotten, joy and peace never ending? Surely, to fill men's hearts with a divine discontent with the present, an ardent hope for the future, and a firm belief in God and the certain fulfillment of His purpose was a task worthy of a prophet.

The feeling that Yahweh had not yet taken up His abode in the temple distressed many, and while spiritual leaders sought the explanation in the moral condition of the community, others believed that there might be some external reason for it. Some were troubled by the loss of the ark which had been Yahweh's throne in the holy of holies of the former temple. It had perished in 586, and it had not been restored in 516. Was it not likely that this was the cause of Yahweh's delay in returning to His people? A nameless prophet answered this question in an oracle which has been inserted in the Book of Jeremiah (3:14–18):

And it shall come to pass, when ye are multiplied and increased in the land, in those days, says Yahweh, they shall say no more, The ark of the covenant of Yahweh; neither shall it come to mind; neither shall they remember it; neither shall they miss it; neither shall it be made any more. At that time they shall call Jerusalem the throne of Yahweh; and all the nations shall be gathered unto it, to the name of Yahweh, to Jerusalem: neither shall they walk any more after the stubbornness of their evil heart. (Jer. 3:16f.) [7]

In Isaiah 34–35 we have two prophecies which sound as if they had been written by Trito-Isaiah or, if not by him, by another disciple of Deutero-Isaiah. The miraculous transformation of the desert and the wonderful highway through it are portrayed in Deutero-Isaiah's phrases. It is a glowing picture whose brilliance is enhanced by the dark background upon which it is painted, for the first of the two prophecies deals with Edom's punishment (Isa. 34). Impressively the prophet begins with the judgment of Yahweh on the nations and on heaven and earth. The heathen armies will be slaughtered,

> And the mountains shall be melted with their blood,
>   and all the host of heaven shall be dissolved,
> And the heavens shall be rolled together as a scroll;
>   and all their host shall fade away,
> As the leaf fades from off the vine
>   and as a fading leaf from the figtree. (Isa. 34:4)

But all this is but the beginning. To our prophet the world-judgment was of far less importance than the fate of Edom, for he hated Edom with a terrible hatred and attributed his own vindictiveness to Yahweh, who would avenge Jerusalem by destroying Edom so fearfully that it would become a veritable hell, peopled only by all manner of unclean animals. That he degraded God to the level of his own cruelty, never entered this prophet's mind.

It is true, the Edomites had given the Jews just cause for revenge. When Jerusalem fell, they had taken the enemies' part, had entered and plundered the holy city with them, had jeered at the Jews, had cut off the fugitives at the crossroads and delivered them to the Chaldeans. Is it any wonder that the Jews exulted when the news came that Edom was hard pressed by the Arabians and that they were driven out of their country? Obadiah, a man of passionate spirit and an ardent patriot, exultantly issued a terrible poem of

---

[7] The possibility that this is an authentic oracle of the prophet Jeremiah cannot be entirely discounted.

hate. He used an older oracle of Edom's fall as text (vv. 1–4, 8f.) and showed most vividly, partly in the words of the older oracle (vv. 5–7), how it had been fulfilled (Ob. 1–14, 15b),

> As thou hast done,
> it shall be done to thee,
> Thy dealing shall return
> upon thine own head.[8]

Another writer, whose prophecy was incorporated later in the Book of Jeremiah (49:7–22), also used the older oracle for his own prediction of Edom's punishment. But there was at least a redeeming touch of pity for the helpless Edomite widows and children in his words,

> Leave thy fatherless children,
> I will preserve them alive;
> And let thy widows trust in Me.

This note of sympathy is still more pronounced in the fine prophecy of Isaiah 15f. against Moab, which was also threatened by the Arabian invasion. Not only is Judah here called upon to give refuge and protection to the fugitive Moabites, but the prophet himself weeps bitterly for the country and its capital.

> My heart sounds like a harp for Moab,
> and mine inward parts for Kir-heres. (Isa. 16:11)

One feels that bonds of sympathy and friendship knit the author to Moab, perhaps even marital ties. Rarely did a prophet exhibit such feeling of compassion for an enemy country in time of distress. The author of the book of Ruth had similar consideration for the Moabites.

In this same period a prophetic editor added the conclusion to the Book of Amos (9:8b–15) which made that dark book of judgment end in a golden vision of hope and light. After the exiles, thoroughly sifted of all their wicked elements, have returned to their homes, the Davidic dynasty will be reestablished; Edom and all territories that at any time had belonged to Israel will be reconquered; and wonderful fertility will prevail.

---

[8] The rest of the little book vv. 15a, 16–21 comes from a later time.

> Behold the days come, says Yahweh,
> That the ploughman shall overtake the reaper,
>   and the treader of grapes him that sows seed;
> And the mountains shall drop sweet wine,
>   and all the hills shall melt. (Am. 9:13)

The exiles will all participate in the work and the fruits of the restoration, and never again will they be deported from their home. It is quite possible that this writer added the oracle against Edom in the famous address which opens the Book of Amos (1:11f.).

Edom had not been the only guilty one in the fateful year of 586. Moab and Ammon also had mocked and reviled the unhappy Jews. Ezekiel had already pronounced terrible judgment upon them. An editor of the Book of Zephaniah inserted a prophecy against them in 2:8-11, predicting perpetual desolation to their lands because of their scornful behavior toward the Jews who will become their lords.

> The residue of My people shall make a prey of them,
>   and the remnant of My nation shall inherit them. (Zeph. 2:9b)

In the prophecy against Philistia (Zeph. 2:4-7) the editor interpolated the lines,

And the coast shall be for the remnant of the house of Judah (2:7a)
For Yahweh their God will visit them, and bring back their captivity. (2:7c)

National vengeance and national aggrandizement are the keynotes of these hopes. But joined with them is a high note:

> Yahweh will be terrible to them,
>   for He will famish all the gods of the earth;
> And men shall worship Him, every one from his place,
>   even all the isles of the nations. (Zeph. 2:11)

Unfortunately, this note is absent from the other prediction which is now inserted in Isaiah 11:11-16, where the return of the exiles from all quarters of the earth and their conquest of Philistia, Edom, Moab, and Ammon are foretold.

After the dedication of the temple the people had been zealous in the performance of their cultic duties. But it was not long before difficulties arose, which the early enthusiasm had easily overcome.

The maintenance of the temple and its cult was expensive, the people were poor, and no king or government paid for the cost of the temple and its clergy. Bad seasons and heavy taxes made it still harder for the people, so that they sometimes delayed or withheld their tithes or substituted inferior animals for the perfect ones that they had vowed. The priests either did not have the heart or the authority to compel them to stricter observance of their religious duties, and their own position and influence suffered inevitably thereby. Sorcerers, however, reaped a good harvest, for as always in bad times simple-minded people were easily led astray into trying to better their fortunes by magic or to revive their hopes by clairvoyance. For religious purity and devotion the growing custom of intermarriage with foreigners constituted another serious problem. Living among the descendants of the population which had occupied the land after 586, the Jews had mingled and intermarried with them. Their children sometimes spoke the dialect of their mothers rather than Hebrew. The purity of Jewish blood was vitiated, and the devotion to Yahweh undermined. Men were divorcing Jewish wives to wed aliens. All sorts of social wrongs, too, were rampant. The rich oppressed the laborers and the poor defenceless classes—the widows, orphans, and strangers. There was much lying and stealing, blasphemy and perjury. And as so often the wicked prospered, while the righteous suffered hardship of every kind. It is no wonder that many began to doubt God's love and justice, and ask whether religion was after all worth while. Such were the conditions that Malachi faced.

His real name we do not know, for "Malachi" which means "my messenger" was due to a wrong interpretation of his prophecy, "Behold, I send My messenger" (3:1), which was taken to refer to the prophet himself. This led to prefixing of the title "Oracle of the word of Yahweh through the hand of his messenger" (so the *LXX*). In the *MT* "my messenger" became standard, and this word (Heb. *Malachi*) was then taken as a name. About 460 this prophet arose and in a manner very different from any predecessor argued with the people, presumably in the temple, in earnest debate about these problems, taking them up point by point, stating the people's position and then giving his answer. First, at least in the present arrangement of his book, he insisted on Yahweh's love for Israel and proved it to those who had challenged him to point out an evidence of His love, by calling their attention to the terrible catastrophe that had befallen Edom.

Was not Esau (the ancestor of Edom) Jacob's brother? says Yahweh: yet I loved Jacob, but Esau I hated, and made his mountains a desolation. (Mal. 1:2f.)

The punishment of Edom filled Malachi and his hearers with joy and satisfaction and was indeed to them a sign of Yahweh's love for Israel. It was a telling argument, especially as it was followed by the prediction that all attempts at recovery by Edom would be frustrated by Yahweh's eternal wrath against them. To us the joy over Edom's fall is quite intelligible, but to attribute it to God's hatred is repugnant. Excessive anthropomorphism was responsible for this.

Malachi next took up the question of inferior sacrifices, and charged the priests with treating the obligation of perfect offerings with contempt.

When ye offer the blind (animal) for a sacrifice, (ye say) it is no evil! and when ye offer the lame and the sick, it is no evil! Present it now to thy governor; will he be pleased with thee? or will he accept thy person? says Yahweh of hosts. (Mal. 1:8)

How much less than a mere governor can Yahweh be pleased with it,

For I am a great King, says Yahweh of hosts, and My name is feared among the Gentiles! (Mal. 1:14)

Full of indignation the prophet exclaimed,

Oh, that there were one among you that would shut the doors (of the temple), that ye might not kindle fire on Mine altar in vain! I have no pleasure in you, neither will I accept an offering at your hand. (Mal. 1:10)

Yahweh has no need of the Jerusalem temple.

For from the rising of the sun even to its setting My name is great (honored and feared) among the Gentiles, and in every place incense and a pure offering are offered to My name, for My name is great among the Gentiles, says Yahweh of hosts. (Mal. 1:11)

According to this the heathen bring all their sacrifices to Yahweh, since He is the sole reality behind all the gods that are worshiped,

and their sacrifices are purer and more acceptable than those of the
Jews. After Deutero-Isaiah it is not surprising that a prophet should
draw this conclusion.[9] Its significance must however not be exaggerated, for Malachi never thought of the conversion or redemption of the heathen and according to him Yahweh "hates" Edom.
He was intent on bringing out the truth that Yahweh has no need of
the unclean sacrifices in the Jerusalem temple, He receives offerings
enough, and pure ones too, all over the world! It is noteworthy that
to Malachi the cult is so important. The preexilic prophets had rejected the whole sacrificial system, Malachi believed in its efficacy
and value. He insisted, however, on true sacrifices and pressed
back of the unfit offerings to the spirit that prompted them, irrev-
erence, deceit, avarice. Rather than this kind he will have none at all
and close the temple altogether.

It almost seems as if Malachi was himself a priest, for when he
now turned upon the priests, none could be sharper in his judgment,
but was it not only because none had a higher ideal of the priesthood?

My covenant was with him: life and peace I gave to him, with (true)
fear he feared Me, and stood in awe of My name. The direction of truth
was in his mouth, and unrighteousness was not found in his lips: he walked
with Me in peace and uprightness, and turned many away from iniquity.
For the priest's lips keep knowledge, and men seek direction at his mouth;
for he is the messenger of Yahweh of hosts. (Mal. 2:5-7)

Because the priests do not come up to his ideal, they have become
"contemptible and base in the sight of all the people."

The problem of the marriages with foreign women is opened by
the prophet with the question,

Have we not all one father? has not one God created us?

[9] It is noteworthy to find him saying "in every place incense is offered to
My name." From v. 14 it is quite clear that this means that it is the heathen
that fear His name, for He is a great King. The Jews, *i.e.,* the priests whom
Malachi addressed, despised Yahweh's name, the heathen honored it. Ever since
it became known from the papyri that the Jews had a temple at Elephantine
in southern Egypt (see p. 300), many have held that Malachi meant the Jews
in the dispersion, who in every place offered incense to Yahweh's name and
a pure offering. But then Malachi would have exaggerated very much, for
they did not have temples or altars where they could offer "in every place."
He was hardly in sympathy with a decentralization of the cult. The widespread
worship of the "God of heaven" in the Persian era made possible his identifica-

We expect that he will proceed with this brotherhood of all to sanction the custom of intermarriage with the nations. But far from it, Malachi continued,

Why do we deal treacherously every man against his brother, profaning the covenant of our fathers? (Mal. 2:10)

It is the brotherhood of all Jews not of all men that he had in mind, and the obligation of mutual fidelity among the Jews is deduced from it. Some Jews had violated the holiness of Yahweh by marrying "the daughter of a foreign god" and treacherously divorcing the wives of their youth. They had not cared to get "godly seed," children from wives of their own race and religion. True enough, of some it could be said,

Not one has done so who had a residue of the spirit. And what is it with the one? He sought a godly seed. Therefore take heed to your spirit, and let none deal treacherously with the wife of his youth. For I hate putting away (divorce), says Yahweh, the God of Israel. (Mal. 2:15f.)

Next came the question of God's justice. The people said, "Every one that does evil is good in the sight of Yahweh, and He delights in them"; or "where is the God of justice?" The answer to this was the prediction of the impending judgment of Israel, in which the priesthood will be purged of all its base elements and restored to its true ideal, and the wicked will be punished.

Behold, I send My messenger, and he shall prepare the way before Me and the Lord, whom ye seek, will suddenly come to His temple; and the messenger of the covenant, whom ye desire, behold, he comes, says Yahweh of hosts. But who can abide the day of His coming? and who shall stand when He appears? for He is like a refiner's fire, and like fullers' soap: and He will sit as a refiner and purifier of silver, and He will purify the sons of Levi, and refine them as gold and silver; and they shall offer to Yahweh offerings in righteousness. Then shall the offering of Judah and Jerusalem be pleasant to Yahweh, as in the days of old, and as in ancient years.

And I will come near to you to judgment; and I will be a swift witness against the sorcerers, and against the adulterers, and against the false

tion with Yahweh, and an idealization of certain lines of gentile worship (seen at a distance). Some scholars doubt that Malachi was capable of this thought and think it has been added by another hand.

swearers, and against those that oppress the hireling, the widow, and the fatherless, and that turn aside the sojourner from the right and fear not Me, says Yahweh of hosts. (Mal. 3:1-5)

This is not the judgment on the nations but on His own people, and a sharp distinction is made between the individual righteous and wicked. Yahweh is tired of the complaint that He makes no such distinctions.

After dealing once more with the question of the withheld tithes and promising great fertility and divine protection of the harvest, if they bring the tithes into the temple, Malachi came back again to the complaint of the people that religion is not worth while.

Ye have said, It is vain to serve God; and what profit is it that we have kept His charge, and that we have walked mournfully before Yahweh of hosts? and now we call the proud happy; yea, they that work wickedness are built up; yea, they tempt God, and escape. (Mal. 3:14f.)

Malachi noted that "they that feared Yahweh" talked the matter over among themselves, and Yahweh listened and had "a book of remembrance" written for them and promised to spare them on the day when all the wicked will be burnt up root and branch:

To you that fear My name shall the sun of righteousness arise with healing in its wings; and ye shall go forth and gambol as calves of the stall. And ye shall tread down the wicked; for they shall be ashes under the soles of your feet on the day when I act, says Yahweh of hosts. (Mal. 4:2f.)

Then they will know that God makes a distinction between the righteous and the wicked, and that it is worth while to serve Him! The allusion to the sun of righteousness and its wings [10] provides an unusually fine touch in this prophetic oracle.

There is a freshness in the lively debates of the little book that makes it interesting reading. It is written in prose which sometimes has the rhythmic swing of poetry. How much impression the intense earnestness of this priestly prophet made on the people we do not

[10] This poetic thought was no doubt inspired by familiarity with the emblem of the winged solar disk, which Hittites, Assyrians, and Persians used each in their own adaptation—the original stimulus having come from Egypt. In its Persian form the god Ahuramazda is combined with the disk. He holds a ring in his left hand, and his right hand is slightly extended. The gesture of the right hand could have suggested healing to Malachi (cf. Acts 4:30).

know. The economic forces that he opposed were too strong. More than the preaching of a prophet was needed to change these conditions. Outside help was necessary. It came with Nehemiah and Ezra and the large body of earnest Jews who came with them from Babylonia. But Malachi had prepared the way for them.

XVII

The Priestly Document
and the Priestly Editors

THE changed estimate of the temple and its worship on the part of the early postexilic prophets was due to the spirit of the age. Ezekiel had seen that the restoration of Israel and its religion must center around the temple. When the Jews came back from captivity, they found that this was true: the temple was the rallying ground of the new community. Prophets and priests alike believed that zeal for the temple and its worship would kindle enthusiasm for Yahweh, that the spirit of true religion could best be quickened and nurtured by ritual religion. Moreover, now that Judah was no longer a nation but a Persian province, its only hope of independent and effective organization lay in religion, with which the Persian government as a rule did not interfere. Judah must therefore be organized as a theocracy, which was to be symbolized and realized in a hierocracy. The priests must be the leaders, the high priest, as God's direct representative, the visible head of the people.

Ezekiel and the compiler of the Holiness Code had already begun to preserve the temple ritual. Others followed them, compiling, systematizing, and reforming laws and usages in accordance with Judah's changed conditions. The result was the Priestly Code, abbreviated P, in which a fifth-century priestly author gathered the fruits of this work and presented it to the people. Since he provided the law with a historical background and setting the whole is best called the Priestly document. It now forms one of the four great documents of the Pentateuch (JEDP) and is easily recognized by its style, its manner of presentation, and its point of view. Its style is formal, precise, dry, full of phraseological mannerisms which distinguish it sharply from the other documents. Lists and genealogies, exact measures, and chronological dates abound. Its presentation and point of view are controlled by priestly and legal interests. Yet the author wrote for the people not for the priests, desiring to teach them the authority and the importance of the religious institutions of Israel, in order to move them to repentance and to a wholehearted acceptance of the entire cultic apparatus through which alone, to his mind, salvation could be achieved. History was entirely subordinated to this end.

P began with the creation of the world in a wonderfully impressive and majestic story. His priestly interest at once appears, for the climax of the whole creation is the Sabbath. God "rested on the seventh day from all His work which He had made, and God blessed the seventh day and hallowed it." The Sabbath was embedded in the very constitution of the world; it is one of its foundations! In the summary form of a genealogy P carried the history of the world quickly down to Noah, where he tarried to tell the story of the deluge, because it culminated in the so-called Noachian laws which prohibited murder and the eating of blood for all mankind. In the table of the nations he summarized the period from the deluge to Abram [1] and then gave a brief history of Abram [2] which is fuller only in the stories of the origin of circumcision (Gen. 17) and of the acquisition of the burial place at Hebron (Gen. 23). Circumcision, like the Sabbath, was one of the most significant religious institutions of Israel for P, because during the exile and in the dispersion both were distinguishing signs of the covenant, by which the Jew could be recognized. The buying of the burial ground was so important to P, because thereby Israel was bound to Canaan; here was its home, for here its ancestors were buried. For Isaac P had only a genealogy (25:19f, 26b). In the story of Jacob he emphasized the imperative duty of the purity of the blood and voiced his opposition to inter-

[1] Gen. 1:1—2:4a; 5 (except v. 29); 6:9–22; 7:6, 11, 13–16a, 17a, 18–21, 24; 8:1, 2a, 3b–5, 13a, 14–19; 9:1–17, 28f.; 10:1–7, 20, 22f., 31f.

[2] Gen. 11:10–27, 31f.; 12:4b, 5; 13:6a, 11b, 12a; 16:1a, 3, 15f.; 17; 19:29; 21:1b, 2b, 3–5; 23; 25:7–11a, 12–17.

marriage with the Canaanites. Jacob was sent to his kinsmen in Syria to marry among his own people (28:1–9). By contrast Esau's marriages with foreign women are mentioned (26:34f.); aside from these only his settlement on Mount Seir and his genealogy are given of Esau (36:6–8, 40–43). Jacob's further history, his death in Egypt, and his burial at Machpelah were told in a few verses. It is woven into the Joseph story.[3]

The succeeding events were treated in the same manner. After a brief account of Israel's oppression in Egypt, P told of the call of Moses, to whom was revealed for the first time the name of Yahweh and with it the complete and the final revelation of His will; he continued this with Moses' commission to Pharaoh and the story of the plagues.[4] At the exodus from Egypt P's interest centered in the institution of the Passover (Ex. 12:1–14, 28). A rapid sketch of the exodus, in which only the passage through the Sea of Reeds and the giving of the Manna are elaborated,[5] brings us to Mount Sinai in less than a dozen additional sentences.[6] Here Moses ascended the mountain (24:15–18a) and the great law sections begin.

The laws of the sanctuary with all its paraphernalia, and of the institution of the priesthood are given first (Ex. 25–29) and their execution is narrated in the groundwork of Ex. 35–40 and in Lev. 8f. Yahweh had sanctioned only one sanctuary. P believed therefore that it must have existed even at the time of Moses in the tabernacle. Again, Yahweh had consecrated as His legitimate priests only Aaron and his sons, more specially Eleazar and Ithamar. In the story of the sons of Aaron, Nadab, and Abihu, P told how these priests were exterminated for their unauthorized offering of incense (Lev. 10:1–5). The portion of the meal-offering which belonged to the priests was definitely determined (Lev. 10:12–15), and a calendar of sacred days and festivals was fixed by the days of the month (Lev. 23:4–8, 13f., 21, 23–38, 39aβ).

Then the narrative is resumed. The people were numbered, their

---

[3] Gen. 29:24, 28b, 29; 30:22a; 31:18b; 33:18b; 35:6a, 9–13, 15, 22b–29; 37:1, 2ac; 41:46a; 46:6f.; 47:6ac, 7–11, 27b, 28; 48:3–6; 49:1a, 28b–33; 50:12f.

[4] Ex. 1:1–5, 7, 13, 14b; 2:23b–25; 6:2–12; 7:1–13, 19, 20a, 21b, 22; 8:1–3, 12–15; 9:8–12.

[5] Ex. 14:1, 2, 4, 5a, 8, 9, 10c, 15ac, 16b, 17f., 21ac, 22f., 26, 27a, 28a; 16:1–3, 9–14, 15b–17, 21a, 31a, 32, 34, 35a.

[6] Ex. 12:37a, 40f., 51; 13:20; 17:1a; 19:1, 2a.

places in the camp and on the march were assigned, the Levites also were numbered and given their various duties.[7] After the departure from Sinai the stories of the spies with the refusal of the people to invade the country; of Korah's and his company's rebellion; and of the divine approval of Aaron's priesthood as shown in the budding of his staff were told at length.[8] Laws concerning the duties and rights of priests and Levites were appropriately inserted at this point.[9] After the miraculous issuing of the water from the rock, the death of Aaron, and the investiture of Eleazar, the people reached in three stages the steppes of Moab.[10] Here Moses assigned to Reuben and Gad their territories, defined the limits of the territory of all Israel, named the chiefs who were to distribute the land, and set apart the cities of refuge.[11] Then Moses ascended Mount Nebo and died, and was mourned for thirty days. Joshua became his successor.[12]

Therewith the Priestly document probably reached its end. Its high-water mark was the erection of the Tabernacle in the wilderness and the institution of a legitimate cult already in the time of Moses. The account of the division of the land in Josh. 13–21 that was formerly attributed to P is now generally regarded as of earlier origin. To what extent the legal materials now found in P were included in it from the beginning remains a matter of debate.

It is apparent that P used history merely for the purpose of teaching the origin and the sanctity of the various rites and institutions. He had learned from the Babylonians about the four world-epochs but he viewed them from his priestly angle: at the creation the Sabbath was instituted; after the deluge the prohibition of eating blood was imposed; in Abram's time circumcision; in Moses' time the Passover and the legitimate cult. These four periods were four stages in the revelation of God's will; the last marked the climax, for to Moses was revealed the final revelation, the perfect law of God.

[7] Num. 1:1–47; 2:1–16, 18–31, 34; 3:14–39.
[8] Num. 10:11f.; 13:1–17a, 21, 25, 32a; 14:1aα, 2, 5–7, 10, 26, 29, 34–38; 16:1a, 2b–7a, 18, 19b–24a, 35; 17:6–28.
[9] Num. 18:1–15, 17–21, 24–32.
[10] Num. 20:1a, 2, 3b, 4, 6, 7b, 10, 12, 22–29; 21:10, 11a; 22:1.
[11] Num. 32:1a, 2b, 4a, 18f., 28–32; 34:1–12, 16–29; 35:9–29.
[12] Deut. 34:1a, 7–9.

The Priestly Code in its original form was a program for postexilic Judaism. When it was adopted by the solemn assembly of the people under the leadership of Ezra (Neh. 8–10) as a part of the fundamental law of the church-state of Judah, the Holiness Code (Lev. 17–26) had perhaps already been incorporated in it with characteristic modifications, of course, and additions to bring it altogether into harmony with P. Whether Ezra himself was responsible for its insertion, or for any part of the composition of P, we do not know. A beginning had been made and soon after Ezra a great many additions were introduced. It was a time of great interest in such matters. The temple with its worship stood in the center of the people's life, and with it the care for the ritual holiness of the people.

Some of this work of supplementation is easily discerned. A collection of laws concerning sacrifices had been prepared (Lev. 1–7) and another on ritual cleanness (Lev. 11–15). In course of time these were incorporated in P, for they were part of the priestly law. Similarly, the laws for the Nazirite (Num. 6), concerning a suspected adulteress (Num. 5:11–31), and the purification by the ashes of a red heifer (Num. 19) were readily inserted. When the day of atonement became the climax of the great system of expiation, the ritual concerning it was introduced too (Lev. 16). The late institution of the year of jubilee was connected with the Sabbath year, at the end of a cycle of seven Sabbath years, as the fiftieth year.[13] There were moreover a number of points which were in need of additional legislation. Thus the law on sacrifice in Num. 15:1–31 was added as a supplement to Lev. 1–3; the law on trespass in Num. 5:5–10 to Lev. 5:20–26; and the law in Num. 28f. containing directions for the sacrifices on the feasts, to the calendar of feasts in Lev. 23. A detailed treatment of vows and tithes was supplied in Lev. 27 and Num. 30. Certain cases not foreseen in the law had to be decided by additional legislation: e.g., what was to be done if one happened to be unclean or on a journey at the time of the Passover festival (Num. 9:1–14)? or what course was to be pursued with the inheritance, if there was no male heir in the family? could daughters inherit? (Num. 27:1–11). The interest in the sanctuary

---

[13] Lev. 25:8–13, 15, 16, 26–34, 40b, 41, 44–46, 50–52, 54.

was responsible for many other additions and elaborations, both in
the laws of the sanctuary (Ex. 25–29) [14] and in the description of
their execution (Ex. 35–40).[15] The interest in the priesthood led
to the incorporation of the prohibition for the priests of drinking
wine or other intoxicants before the services in the temple (Lev.
10:6–11), and of several regulations concerning the Levites.[16] They
were introduced at various times and by various priestly writers.
The tendency of the time was towards heightening the ritual, which
necessitated all this supplementary legislation that modified the older
law, applied it to new conditions, or harmonized the differences. It
is quite natural that the narrative sections were not greatly augmented. A few genealogies and lists; the stories of the stoning of a
man for blasphemy and of another for Sabbath breaking; [17] the
order of the march; additions to the Korah story; the stories of the
zeal of Phineas and of the raid against Midian; the record of Israel's
journeyings; and the assignment of territory to the sons of Machir
by Moses [18]—these are the main additions to P's narrative.

There was, unfortunately, no intelligent scheme employed in
the process of incorporating all these additional elements. In a number of cases it is quite manifest why a particular section was inserted just where it now is. Thus, *e.g.*, the sacrificial code in Lev.
1–7 was introduced before Lev. 8, because in the consecration of
Aaron and his sons certain sacrifices were mentioned which made
prior information about their character appropriate. But nevertheless Lev. 1–7 breaks the original connection between Ex. 40 and
Lev. 8. In many cases we do not understand the reason why an
insertion was made just at a particular point. The result is that the
clear arrangement of the original P has given way to a conglom-
erate one, and the incorporation of so much priestly matter has also
tended to obscure the fact that P intended his book not for the
priests but for the people as a popular manual of religious rites and
institutions.

[14] Ex. 27:20f., 28:42f.; 29:9b, 21, 26–30, 33, 35b–42; 30:1—31:17.
[15] P had treated this quite summarily in Ex. 35:4–8, 10f., 20–27, 29; 36:8; 39:32,
33a, 43; 40:1f., 16f., 33b, 34.
[16] Num. 1:48–54; 3:5ff.; 4; 8:5–26; 16:1aβ, 7c, 8–11; 17:1–5.
[17] These are precedents for the judges, and therefore really legal passages too.
[18] Gen. 36:1–5, 9–30; 46:8–27; Ex. 6:14–25; Num. 10:13–28; 16:1aβ, 7c, 8–11;
17:1–5; 25:6–18; 31; 33.

The style of all this priestly literature is quite uniform and stereotyped like that of a school. It is dry and prosaic, as a rule, given to specific formulas and precise systematic statement. In the story of creation this very quality enhances the dignity of the narrative so that it rises to majestic grandeur, but this is an exception. The style is so well marked that it is quite easy for even a beginner to single out the priestly work. P's desire for preciseness and accuracy is well illustrated in the exact dates and figures which he gives. But however accurate they may seem to be, they turn out to be altogether unreliable. The whole chronology of the Pentateuch is due to a definite artificial system. The exact age of the antediluvians was, of course, not handed down by any reliable tradition but was an adaptation of an early Babylonian chronological scheme, which P used in such a way that the constantly decreasing number of the years of their lives served as an indication of the constantly increasing sinfulness of mankind. For long life was always connected with piety; the more pious a man was, the longer he was likely to live. Again, it can hardly be assumed that Noah kept a logbook in which he noted on certain definite days the measurements of the log. Quite cleverly these dates are used to show that the flood lasted an entire solar year! It seems probable, too, that P arrived at the exact number of 603,550 for all Israel in Num. 1:46 by the artificial, favorite scheme of figuring called gematria: the numerical value of the consonants of *rōsh kol benê Yisra'el* = "the sum of all the children of Israel" was added up, *rōsh kol* = 551, *benê Yisra'el* = 603; the latter was then multiplied by 1000 = 603,000, and 551 (= *rōsh kol*) was added = 603,551; in a round figure 603,550.

The spirit pervading P is no less marked than the style. The whole of life is viewed from a religious, or rather priestly, standpoint. The writers were priests, and their ideal was the theocracy with the implied hierocracy. Their theological ideas were far in advance of JE. One has but to compare the two creation stories (Gen. 1-2:4a, P; Gen. 2:4b-24, J) to see this. The naive stories of God's appearances, so marked in J, were no longer possible. God was too highly exalted. The long process of purging the ancient tales of all heathen and inferior ideas was brought by P to a successful completion. Many things had to be rejected as incompatible with P's theology and ethics. But it is noteworthy that the victory over the lower and foreign religious practices was not won by radical rejection, but by thorough reinterpretation. In this P followed JE's lead, rather than D's.

P was especially interested in instruction in the law. But though the law was both moral and ritual, P in its complete form did not work out the moral side, because his primary concern was ritual. Not that he regarded the moral as nonessential; he presupposed it. The incorporation of the moral and social laws of Lev. 19 (H) and the institution of the year of jubilee (Lev. 25) show that social values were by no means neglected by P. That most difficult problem of the concentration of the landed property in the hands of a few, against which the prophets had fought with all their might, albeit without success, the priestly writers tried to solve by the legal establishment of the year of jubilee, at the end of seven Sabbath years, that is, in every fiftieth year, in which all landed property had to be returned to the original owner and all Hebrew slaves had to be set free. The magnificent conception that Yahweh alone is the owner of the land and of its produce and the inhabitants are only His tenants, who are to share equally in the blessings of the land and to whom their particular portion is to be restored in the fiftieth year, if for some reason a family has had to part with it, is combined with the similar idea that Yahweh alone is the lord and master of the Israelites, that they can therefore never be the real slaves of another, and that they and their children must be given their liberty in the fiftieth year, if they had been compelled to sell themselves into servitude. This is a heightening of the Sabbath year, which H had already included. The priestly interest is apparent in the figuring out of the year; it comes at the end of seven Sabbath years. But the social interest must not be denied, although the year of jubilee remained a priestly utopia. In spite of this solemn law, it was never carried out in practice.

The priests had ultimately the same aim as the prophets. They wanted to make the people acceptable to God. But while the prophets insisted that this could be done only by righteousness and trust in Yahweh, the priests believed it could best be accomplished by ritual holiness. In and through the cult they sought to educate the people in obedience to Yahweh; by regulating their whole life through many ceremonial precepts they hoped to discipline them to constant remembrance of Yahweh. Obedience was to them, as to the prophets, the all important concern, but it was obedience to all these outward regulations, which they imposed on the people as the direct command of Yahweh. "Ye shall be holy, for I Yahweh, your God, am holy" was their underlying principle. This holiness was mainly cultic, external; it was gained by avoidance of all idolatrous and superstitious practices and by observance of all the laws concerning ritual cleanness, food, sacrifices, and festivals. Religion was a matter of the cult. The earlier prophets had violently protested against such a conception of religion and rejected the entire cultic apparatus as contrary to the will of God. But they had not succeeded in the long run. When the question of the organization of religion in the light of the prophetic ideals was attempted, it was seen that a prophetic religion was too high and exacting for the mass of the people. External forms were necessary, worship had to be carried on. How could this be done so as to be acceptable to Yahweh? Above all else by removing every heathen element from the cult! Deuteronomy had seen this, and in Josiah's reformation all heathen paraphernalia were relentlessly put away; the many local high places, the breeding spots of impure cults, were destroyed and all legitimate worship was centralized in Jerusalem. Although a reaction against this reform set in after Josiah's death, the principle of the one legitimate sanctuary was so firmly established that P could take it for granted.

According to P there had always been only one legitimate place of worship, even in the days of the wilderness wanderings, for at God's command Moses had prepared the tabernacle, the tent of revelation, where all worship was carried on. P carried therefore his ideal back into the past, and what had been accomplished only after a long historical development he presented as existing from Moses' time on. The tabernacle was the pattern of the later temple at Jerusalem, and all cultic worship was possible only there. That is why the patriarchs in P's own story never sacrificed. P was altogether unconcerned about the historical possibility of such an elaborate tabernacle in the wilderness, as he described in Ex. 25–30. The ideal, to him, was actually realized in the past.

This involved also the establishment of the hierocracy by Moses. The whole long development of the priesthood was simply ignored. The differentiation of the Levites from the Aaronite or Zadokite priests and their degradation, which Ezekiel still had to justify, were for P facts from the beginning. The struggle of the Levites for priestly rights he placed in the wilderness period, where Korah and his company reached out for them with such tragic results (Num. 16).[19] The office of the high priest too, which took so long to evolve, was instituted already by Moses according to P. He alone may enter the holy of holies; at his installation he is anointed with the sacred oil and is really the visible head of the theocracy. He wears the purple and the tiara. For a king there is no place. The ideal, we see, was intended for the postexilic people, whom P would win by his fictitious presentation of its origin in ancient history and the divine commands through which it was established.

The whole cult too had been instituted by Moses, P taught. It was the means of securing and insuring the ritual holiness of the people, by which alone Yahweh's continued dwelling among His people could be guaranteed. By the cult any sin which might be upon the people or any individual could be removed; willful sins, real crimes however were not included, because they could only be removed by the death or the excommunication of the sinner. Only ordinary offenses were removed by ritual atonement. The whole cult, according to P, was designed for the expiation of sin. The object of every sacrifice was atonement; the mysterious, atoning efficacy of the blood was experienced in every such act. Animal sacrifices with their blood were therefore specially valuable and numerous. The expiatory character of the cult also dominated the festivals. In P they had lost their character of gratitude and joy to a large extent. They were now freed from all connection with nature and its seasons, in order that nothing might remind one of their original connection with the Canaanite land and its religion. They were now fixed definitely by the days of the month.

---

[19] The story of Nadab and Abihu, who offered a sacrifice of incense which Yahweh had not commanded and who were therefore punished by lightning (Lev. 10), is another instance of P's method of projecting the later struggle of certain priestly families (from the local sanctuaries?) for priestly rank and office in Jerusalem into the wilderness period.

The great festivals were now framed by two solemn days of holy convocation at the beginning and the end. They were no longer occasions of joy, but feasts of reconciliation. The old joyous cult, with its harvest festivals and sacrificial meals and inner parties, had become a serious solemn affair. The cult was no longer the spontaneous expression of the religious mind, but the definite form in which one must approach Yahweh in order to gain atonement.[20] The ancient meal-offering with its rejoicing in the sanctuary had no real place among the sacrifices; secular slaughtering and eating had supplanted it.

The diminution of the personal participation of laymen in the sacrifices is striking; not only was the killing and offering all done by the Levites and the priests, to whom the laymen had only to supply the material, but the presence of the community at the sacrifices was not necessary. They were efficacious also without them; they bound in a mysterious yet real manner the deity together with the people. Here an external, mechanical, magical conception of the sacrifices threatened to drive out the importance of personal, moral, spiritual participation in them. The burnt-offering which was given entirely to the deity (the so-called "peace offering," Lev. 3), became more and more prominent; it was the great offering. Also the sin-offering, which before the exile was virtually unknown, assumed remarkable importance. It was really a private, penitential act and, like the related trespass-offering, it was brought in order to gain forgiveness from Yahweh. Transgressions, whether ritual or moral, could be expiated only if a sin offering was brought, for Yahweh had connected forgiveness with the cult.

That the stress laid on the outward offering might easily obscure the need of inward repentance is apparent. Even a careful observer of the ritual might, for one reason or another, forget or neglect to perform the rite prescribed for the various situations in life, and thus bring uncleanness upon himself and by contact upon others, and Yahweh might leave His people. In order to avoid this a sin-offering was added to the other offerings on every holy day, from New Moon upwards, and a special day, the climax of the whole

---

[20] Fortunately, the practice varied considerably from this somber theory, cf. pp. 366ff.

system, was finally instituted. Once a year, on the tenth day of the
seventh month (Tishri = Sept.–Oct.), on the great Day of Atonement the high priest entered the holy of holies and removed the uncleanness of the priests, the sanctuary, and the people by the special
ceremonies of the day. Here the private cult was connected with
the public cult: the sin-offering of the Day of Atonement atoned
for the omissions of sin-offerings on the part of individuals (Lev.
16; 23:26–32).[21]

The ritual of the Day of Atonement is instructive.

And Yahweh spoke to Moses, after the death of the two sons of Aaron,
when they drew near before Yahweh, and died; and Yahweh said to
Moses, Speak to Aaron thy brother, that he come not at any time into
the holy place within the veil, before the mercy-seat which is upon the
ark that he die not: for I will appear in the cloud upon the mercy-seat.
With this shall Aaron come into the holy place: with a young bullock
for a sin-offering, and a ram for a burnt-offering. He shall put on the holy
linen coat, and he shall have the linen breeches upon his flesh, and shall
be girded with the linen girdle, and with the linen turban shall he be
attired: they are the holy garments; and he shall bathe his flesh in water,
and put them on. And he shall take of the congregation of the children of
Israel two he-goats for a sin-offering, and one ram for a burnt-offering.
And Aaron shall present the bullock of the sin-offering, which is for
himself, and make atonement for himself, and for his house. And he
shall take the two goats, and set them before Yahweh at the door of the
tent of meeting. And Aaron shall cast lots upon the two goats; one lot
for Yahweh, and the other lot for Azazel. And Aaron shall present the
goat upon which the lot fell for Yahweh, and offer him for a sin-offering.
But the goat, on which the lot fell for Azazel, shall be set alive before
Yahweh, to send him away for Azazel into the wilderness.
And Aaron shall present the bullock of the sin-offering, which is for
himself, and shall make atonement for himself, and for his house, and
shall kill the bullock of the sin-offering which is for himself. And he shall
take a censer full of coals of fire from off the altar before Yahweh, and
his hands full of sweet incense beaten small, and bring it within the veil:
and he shall put the incense upon the fire before Yahweh, that the cloud
of the incense may cover the mercy-seat that is upon the testimony, that
he die not: and he shall take of the blood of the bullock, and sprinkle
it with his finger upon the mercy-seat on the east; and before the mercy-
seat shall he sprinkle of the blood with his finger seven times.

[21] The Day of Atonement was probably not yet in the law book of Ezra, else
its observance would have been mentioned in Neh. 8f.

Then shall he kill the goat of the sin-offering, that is for the people, and bring his blood within the veil, and do with his blood as he did with the blood of the bullock, and sprinkle it upon the mercy-seat, and before the mercy-seat: and he shall make atonement for the holy place, because of the uncleannesses of the children of Israel, and because of their transgressions, even all their sins: and so shall he do for the tent of meeting, that dwells with them in the midst of their uncleannesses. And there shall be no man in the tent of meeting when he goes in to make atonement in the holy place, until he come out, and have made atonement for himself, and for his household, and for all the assembly of Israel. And he shall go out to the altar that is before Yahweh, and make atonement for it, and shall take of the blood of the bullock, and of the blood of the goat, and put it upon the horns of the altar round about. And he shall sprinkle of the blood upon it with his finger seven times, and cleanse it, and hallow it from the uncleannesses of the children of Israel.

And when he has made an end of atoning for the holy place, and the tent of meeting, and the altar, he shall present the live goat: and Aaron shall lay both his hands upon the head of the live goat, and confess over him all the iniquities of the children of Israel, and all their transgressions, even all their sins; and he shall put them upon the head of the goat, and shall send him away by the hand of a man that is in readiness into the wilderness: and the goat shall bear upon him all their iniquities into a solitary land: and he shall let go the goat in the wilderness.

And Aaron shall come into the tent of meeting, and shall put off the linen garments, which he put on when he went into the holy place, and shall leave them there: and he shall bathe his flesh in water in a holy place, and put on his ordinary garments, and come forth, and offer his burnt-offering and the burnt-offering of the people, and make atonement for himself and for the people. And the fat of the sin-offering shall he burn upon the altar. And he that lets go the goat for Azazel shall wash his clothes, and bathe his flesh in water, and afterward he shall come into the camp. And the bullock of the sin-offering, and the goat of the sin-offering, whose blood was brought in to make atonement in the holy place, shall be carried forth without the camp; and they shall burn in the fire their skins, and their flesh, and their dung. And he that burns them shall wash his clothes, and bathe his flesh in water, and afterward he shall come into the camp. (Lev. 16:1–28)

The removal of sin by placing it upon the goat that was sent to the demon Azazel in the wilderness was a survival of ancient polydemonism. In other cases the priests, who ordinarily rejected all heathen elements, got rid of them by assimilation and reinterpretation. Thus in the law of the purification of the unclean with the ashes of a red heifer (Num. 19) an original sacrifice to the dead was reinterpreted and incorporated. The tassels, which every Israelite was to wear and which had formerly been nothing but amulets, were to serve as reminders of the law of Yahweh and as safeguards against sinning (Num. 15:37ff.). The golden bells of the high priest's garment had also originally been amulets which protected him against demons; and even in P they still served to shield him when he went in and out of the presence of Yahweh in the holy place "that he die not" (Ex. 28:34f.).

There is much primitive heathenism in the cult, for the cult was not the distinguishing element of Yahweh's religion, indeed Israel had that in common with the other nations who rendered such worship also to their gods. Exclusiveness and rejection of everything that belonged to a foreign religion characterized many priestly laws on ritual purity. The laws concerning clean and unclean animals (Lev. 11) are not to be explained as due to hygienic reasons or to natural aversion but mostly to the fact that these animals were sacred to other gods. The various laws of ritual cleanness were worked out very methodically by the priests. Sexual relations, diseases, death, or other defiling matters were carefully noted and directions for purification were given. The degree of the defilement varied, and so did the degree of purity. For the priests its requirements were more stringent than for the laymen. The closer one is to God, the purer one must be. But everybody must be clean.

The disciplining of the whole life by all these cultic regulations was not an easy task. It was a heavy yoke for many. The economic burden which the cult involved was not light either. The cost of the entire establishment of the temple with its sacrifices and the clergy had to be borne by the people. The public sacrifices alone consumed a large number of animals and other materials.[22] A tax of half a shekel yearly was imposed upon every one "for the service of the tent of meeting" (Ex. 30:11ff.; cf. Matt. 17:24). The support of priests and Levites was costly too; they received not only their

---

[22] It has been figured out that the daily and other public sacrifices alone required every year 1093 lambs, 113 bullocks, 37 rams, 32 goats; 150.6 ephahs of fine flour (= 5487.86 liters), 342.08 hins of wine, and also of oil (= 2076.43 liters). Besides these, oil for the light, spices for the anointing oil and for the sweet incense, and fine flour for the shew bread had to be furnished.

definite portions of the sacrifices, but all the first-fruits and the first-born (for which in the case of men and unclean animals a sum of redemption had to be paid), and the tithes (Num. 18, Lev. 27:30–33), and part of the booty of war (Num. 31:28ff.).

The expenses for the people grew larger as the system developed and all sorts of extra requirements were demanded. Trespass-offerings are an illustration. While formerly trespass was purely a matter of civil law (Ex. 22:7–15), it was now taken into the cultic system and the offender must not only restore in full plus one fifth of the value to the owner, but he must also bring a ram without blemish as a trespass-offering to the temple, for the offence was not only against the neighbor but also against Yahweh and He forgives only if an offering is brought to Him (Lev. 6:1–7). Trespass-offerings were required for a number of things, especially "if any one sin, and do any of the things which Yahweh has prohibited, though he knew not, yet he is guilty, and shall bear his punishment," and bring a trespass-offering, for "he is certainly guilty before Yahweh" (Lev. 5:17ff.). If we consider in addition the freewill offerings and especially the vows, whose payment was rigidly enforced (Num. 6, 30; Lev. 27), we shall get an idea of the heavy economic burden which the maintenance of the cultic system entailed and shall find it not surprising that the priests felt it necessary to stimulate the people's willingness and joy of giving by telling them of the glad and enthusiastic giving of the fathers for the construction of the sanctuary in the wilderness, for which they were so eager to give that soon more than enough was brought and Moses had to command that they cease giving more (Ex. 35 and esp. 36:2–7). Thus did the fathers; could the children do less? Should they not willingly take upon themselves this burden?

To many the law was no burden at all, either economically or religiously. They found in the fulfillment of its commands the way to God and, as we shall see later on in the Psalter, to many it was a joy, a means of fellowship with God. There was no speculation about the reason for the various commands and how they could effect reconciliation; God had commanded them and connected salvation with them. That was enough, obedience was all that was needed for forgiveness.

The ideal of holiness which P had for Israel was inherently exclusive. It necessitated the removal and avoidance of everything that was defiling. This meant not only all sorts of impurities and too obviously heathen practices but also heathen people. In the patriarchal story, intermarriage with foreigners was deprecated: only defilement could come from it. This may be seen in the story of the son of an Egyptian father and an Israelite mother who in a strife with an Israelite blasphemed Yahweh, thus committing a sin for which he had to pay with his life (Lev. 24:10–14). It appears still better in the story of the Israelite who had married a Midianite woman and brought her into the camp, for Phinehas who in his zeal killed both of them was greatly rewarded (Num. 25:6–13), and the extermination of the Midianites was ordered and executed as a result of this defilement (Num. 31). Contact and intercourse with heathen are defiling,[23] and Israel must be clean. Strictly speaking, they should have nothing to do with foreigners. That was however impossible in real life. Foreigners lived among them in Palestine, and they could not be driven out. But certain obligations could be imposed upon them, which they must fulfill. There were certain laws that God had given to all mankind. The Sabbath had been written into the very foundation of the world, it should, therefore, really be observed by all men, although this is not definitely stated. At the time of Noah all men were prohibited to murder and to eat blood; that was definitely meant for all. Now of foreigners who resided among them Israel had required even before the exile that they obey these universal laws, but had not seen fit to impose any special religious duties upon them besides the keeping of the Sabbath. For P this was not enough, for he was intent on removing all impurity from Israel; if therefore one of these resident foreigners had become unclean, he must purify himself, for the impurity was contagious. The comparison of a preexilic law with its exilic formulation illustrates this different point of view:

[23] It is interesting to note in this connection how strongly P himself was influenced nevertheless by foreign ideas and practices. He used Babylonian cosmology in the story of creation, Babylonian history with its four ages of the world, Babylonian chronology and geography, yes even Babylonian cultic elements in his ceremonial law. But it must be observed too that they were all so completely assimilated that they were not felt as foreign at all.

Ye shall not eat of anything that dies of itself: thou mayest give it to the sojourner that is within thy gates, that he may eat it; or thou mayest sell it to a foreigner: for thou art a holy people to Yahweh thy God. (Deut. 14:21)

And every soul that eats that which dies of itself, or that which is torn of beasts, whether he be a native (Israelite) or a resident stranger, he shall wash his clothes, and bathe himself in water, and be unclean until the evening, then shall he be clean. But if he wash them not, nor bathe his body, then he shall bear his punishment. (Lev. 17:15f.)

The general law in P is this: "Ye shall have one manner of law, as well for the sojourner as for the native," *i.e.*, Israelite (Lev. 24:22; Num. 15:15f., 29). But this has reference only to "the stranger that sojourns among them," the resident foreigner, the client, not to others. Here was the basis for the later, less exclusive, view, that religion and not birth was the real characteristic of the true Jew, that membership in Yahweh's congregation depended on the fulfillment of the law, not on Jewish parentage. But P did not draw this conclusion, his attitude still was narrow and exclusive. He did believe in monotheism but not in its universal applications; his conception of God was in many ways exalted and spiritual, but in others limited and particularistic. He had no missionary zeal, no love for the heathen. The precious prophetic heritage of the world was lost in P, for to him the Jews were the people of the law, separate from the nations, without any sense of obligation to bring the true religion to the peoples of the world.

In one direction P led to an altogether unintended liberal result. Although he emphasized the cult at the one legitimate place (Jerusalem) most strongly, he nevertheless showed how Jewish religion could be practised without sacrifices. Certain laws could be kept anywhere, especially the Sabbath and circumcision, which were "signs of the covenant" also in foreign lands. The Jews in the dispersion could not sacrifice, but they could observe many laws of ritual cleanness. On the face of it, it would seem impossible for them to celebrate their festivals anywhere else but in Jerusalem. But P paved the way for the later development by making the Passover once more a family festival, which need not be celebrated at Jerusalem, as D had insisted. The killing of the lamb was not a sacrifice but a secular act, and thus it was possible anywhere. P said nothing of this kind about other festivals, but the tendency had been introduced and it led ultimately to the belief in and to the practice of a religion without sacrificial cult. The only kind of religion left to the Jews after the final destruction of the temple was not the spiritual religion of the prophets but the religion of the law without the sacrificial cult: orthodox Judaism. It is one of the paradoxes of history that the one who insisted more strongly than any other on the absolute importance of the sacrificial cult through which the direct connection between God and His people was maintained should be the one who showed that Jewish religion could exist without it.

Although the Priestly Code was adopted under the leadership of Ezra as the fundamental law of Israel, it was not the only sacred book of the Jewish church. The law of Deuteronomy in the deuteronomistic historical work was of fundamental authority too, and could not be superseded by P. These writers felt that they were continuators of this same work. They had laid more stress on the priestly and ritual elements, it is true, but Deuteronomy claimed to go back to Moses, and they themselves believed that they did so too, for they were merely elaborating the Mosaic religion. There was also the Jehovistic compilation of J and E (JE), beside which P's historical account seemed meager. It is believed that Priestly editors first came to the conclusion that P must be joined with the Jehovist in one composite work. In this fusion, which they promptly undertook, they showed great skill. They felt that they had to exercise wide tolerance for the divergent traditions of the older work. They could not agree with them, and yet they could not remove them altogether, because they were sacred. The task was difficult, but they accomplished it; and when it was finished, they had stamped the entire book with their own spirit. The Priestly document now gave to the whole its own distinctive tone; it was the basis of the compilation, the ground work supplying the frame and order. In its clearly marked divisions the appropriate parts of the Jehovist were inserted. Only rarely did the redactors ($= R^p$) deviate from

P's order in favor of that of the Jehovist. Usually they gave both P's and the other stories side by side, e.g., the story of creation (Gen. 1—2:4a, P; Gen. 2:4b–24, J) or the story of Abraham's covenant (Gen. 15, JE; Gen. 17, P) or the story of Moses's call (Ex. 3, JE; Ex. 6, P). Sometimes they wove both together into a single story, as in the stories of the deluge (Gen. 6–8), of Israel's flight from Egypt and the passage of the Sea of Reeds (Ex. 14), of the Manna and the quails (Ex. 16), the genealogy of Noah's sons (Gen. 10). In this interwoven work P predominated. When the redactors gave only one story, they took P's and omitted the Jehovist's. Thus they left out the latter's accounts of the birth of Ishmael and the death of Abram, and retained only a few fragments of J's genealogies of Seth (Gen. 4:25f.; 5:29). Sometimes the combination of the sources necessitated editorial additions and changes, in order to connect or harmonize the various sections. Thus, in Gen. 27:46 the editors connected most cleverly the older story of Jacob's flight to Haran with P's. In Gen. 32:29—35:10 they changed Israel to Jacob on account of Gen. 35:10 (P).

But there was also the Deuteronomic historical work embracing the Deuteronomic law-code. It seems to have been a second step in the activity of the Priestly editors to cut off Deuteronomy from Joshua–2 Kings, and insert it into the JEP compilation. Only 34:1a, 7–9 come from the original account of the death of Moses.

The result of the combination was a great success. Here was a great historico-legal work,[24] compiled from various sources but held together in a remarkable unity by a grand purposeful plan. All history is directed by God and illuminated by a great plan which runs through all its phases: the purpose of God to bring all the nations to a true knowledge of Himself. This universal conception has its limitations in that for the heathen resident in the Jewish community it involved integration, and for the nations: subjection to Israel. Not the history but the law and the cult were the essential elements—

[24] This opinion holds even if one regards much of the legal material as having been built-in secondarily. That P was originally a purely narrative work, as some scholars have held, seems unlikely; the goal was the setting up of a cult according to Priestly ideal and this presupposes legislation. There is much repetition and inconsistency in P, and this led G. von Rad to seek two strands in the work. The view has not found wide-spread acceptance. See his *Die Priesterschrift im Hexateuch*, 1934.

the revelation of God which regulated the ideal state; and *torah* or law became the official name of the book. But its real significance and greatness is in its universal aspect, not in its limitations. Long before any Greek or Roman historian applied the universal idea to history it was done in Israel, though in a religious form: the history of the world was held to be governed by God.

The book was certainly completed by 330 B.C., the time of the coming of Alexander the Great, for the Samaritans who seceded from the Jews and built their own temple on Mount Gerizim had the Pentateuch in substantially the same form as the Jews.[25] That minor changes were still made even after this time we know from a comparison with the Greek, *LXX*, version which was made about 250 B.C. It is in this final form that the Pentateuch exerted an influence upon Judaism, Christianity, and Islam which is unparalleled in history. Here the sum of the development of ages, embodying religion and cosmology, ethics and jurisprudence, was combined in an imposing form. The whole was attributed to Moses, the founder of Israel and of its religion. It was the great Book, the Bible, for the people.

[25] The preservation of so much material from JE and D about the holy places of Israel is believed by some scholars to have had the purpose (at the time of the editing of the final Pentateuch) of preventing the Samaritans from starting a new cult-center of their own. In the fully edited Pentateuch the central sanctuary is portrayed as alone legitimate for the people established in Palestine and in possession of Jerusalem.

XVIII

Postexilic Historians
and Narrators

AFTER the Jews had returned from captivity, the times were not such as to induce one to write a history of them. Any historical interest that existed was directed to the past. The only contemporary, authoritative sources for the period directly following the exile are to be found in the prophetic books (cf. ch. XVI).

We have seen that in the course of time there had arisen some great historical compilations: that of the Jehovist, or compiler of J and E; that of the Deuteronomistic Historian; and that of the Redactor or Redactors of the present Pentateuch. One more major historical effort was to be made (perhaps around 300, or a little later): that of the Chronicler, as the author of 1–2 Chronicles is commonly called. Ezra-Nehemiah originally were the concluding part of the Chronicler's work, as may be seen from the fact that the close of 2 Chronicles is repeated in the beginning of Ezra.[1] What interests us at this point, however, is that the Chronicler included older sources in Ezra-Nehemiah. Aside from some lists there

[1] The remainder of a column of writing was left when the Chronicler's scroll was cut to detach Ezra-Nehemiah and add it to the Canon. This remainder was recopied for the beginning of the canonical Ezra-Nehemiah. Chronicles only became canonical somewhat later. The manuscript from which Ezra-Nehemiah was cut was used or recopied with the duplicate passage. Ezra-Nehemiah stand before Chronicles in the Hebrew Bible. Furthermore Ezra-Nehemiah were treated as one book in Hebrew Biblical manuscripts until the Middle Ages. In the *LXX*, Ezra-Nehemiah are also one book called Second Esdras, and follow Chronicles, but with an earlier translation, 1 Esdras, intervening. See pp. 461f.

are three discernible major entities: 1) An extract from an Aramaic historical work, dealing with events at Jerusalem in the period of the reestablishment of the city. 2) The Memoir of Nehemiah. 3) A probable Ezra Memoir, which, however, was much rewritten by the Chronicler. While the Aramaic narrative may be younger than the Nehemiah and Ezra Memoirs we shall deal with it first because the preserved portion relates to a time antedating these.

The Chronicler leads over to the Aramaic source material with a Hebrew section Ezra 1:1—4:5. The opening incident, dealing with the edict of Cyrus (cf. 6:3–5) and the delivery of the vessels of the temple to the "prince of Judah" Sheshbazzar, has been combined with a tradition of a return from Exile by the heads of families, priests, and Levites. This is followed in ch. 2 by a list of the returners *under Zerubbabel* of which a duplicate is found in Nehemiah 7. We then hear in ch. 3 of the start of temple worship and of the actual beginning of temple building under Zerubbabel and Jeshua (Joshua in Haggai and Zechariah). This however, is contradicted by the Aramaic narrative in 5:16, according to which Sheshbazzar laid the foundation of the temple.[2] Then follows the objection of the adversaries of Judah and Benjamin, thwarting further building during the remainder of the reign of Cyrus to the time of Darius. One must suspect that Zerubbabel was a new appointee of Cambyses or Darius. This opens the possibility that the returners of ch. 2 came after the time of Cyrus, whose appointee was Sheshbazzar.

In Ezra 4:6—6:13, the Aramaic narrative is utilized. The beginning of it (vv. 6–7) was evidently translated into Hebrew in order to start the Aramaic text at a point where the change of language would seem more natural to the reader. The label *arāmīth* (in Aramaic) signaled the change. There is, however, a serious misplacement of material in the Aramaic narrative: the author first relates hindrances made to rebuilding the temple in the time of Xerxes and Artaxerxes (I), and then comes to its building under Darius. In that

---

[2] Sheshbazzar is the Babylonian name *Shamash-abu-uṣur* (not as generally asserted *Shamash-apal-uṣur*). There is no likelihood of his identity with Zerubbabel, for this is also a Babylonian name, *Zer-Babili*. It occurs on tablets from Nippur (near which was Ezekiel's river, p. 182), published in 1933. They are not dated, but are from this era. None of the persons has a Hebrew name. The texts are to be found in Erich Ebeling's, *Neubabylonische Briefe*, 1949, numbers 284, 287.

connection he tells of the role played by Haggai and Zechariah (see pp. 246ff.). Thus, there can be do doubt that the Darius meant is Darius I Hystaspes (521–485). Xerxes (485–465) and Artaxerxes I (465–424) succeeded rather than preceded Darius. The story related in 5:1—6:15 therefore belongs *before* 4:6–23.

We learn in 5:1ff. how Tattenai,[3] the governor of the province "Beyond the River" (a name coined from the Babylonian point of view and hence meaning Syria-Palestine), interfered with the newly begun building activity. The Jews claimed to have received permission from Cyrus and suggested that this be verified at Babylon. Thereupon Tattenai sent a report to Darius about the matter. A search was made and the edict [4] of Cyrus was found at "Ahmetha the fortress" (Ecbatana in Media). Tattenai was then ordered to let the Jews proceed with their work, and to furnish funds from the provincial treasury to finance the building of the temple as well as to provide sacrifices at the Jewish altar for the king and his sons. Where the governor of the province had his seat is not clear. It may have been at Hamath in Syria, or at Tripolis on the Phoenician coast.

The rebuilding of the temple then is reported, with some mention of the role of the prophets Haggai and Zechariah, and the story is carried chronologically beyond the time reflected in their books— to the completion of the temple on the third day of the month of Adar in the sixth year of Darius (March 11, 516). The festival of dedication is described but not dated, perhaps because it coincided with the Babylonian New Year's festival.

[3] Tattenai has been found mentioned in a document published in 1907 from tablets dug up at Babylon. It is dated June 5, 502 and refers to a slave of Ta-at-tan-ni, governor of Beyond the River. He was evidently a subordinate of "The governor of Babylon and of Beyond the River," a title held by a man named Ushtanni in 521-20.

[4] The edict of Cyrus has been much assailed as a historical fraud. It is not unreasonable, however, in view of Cyrus' policy of reestablishing temples and cults which were destroyed by the Chaldeans. One must start from the Aramaic text of 6:3f. The question of a return of exiles must be separated from that of the edict. It is not mentioned in it, but only in the Chronicler's version in Ezra 1:3. It is highly improbable that there could have been any large scale return at that time. The list that follows in ch. 2 speaks of those who returned with Zerubbabel. Perhaps the Jewish migration was a gradual one. The time of the revolution after the death of Cambyses, when Babylon set up an independent king, Nidintu-Bel, may have led many Jews to flee from there (cf. Zech. 2:10f.).

In the piece of the narrative relating to the times of Xerxes and Artaxerxes I (4:6–23), there is first a brief mention of a complaint made to Xerxes against the inhabitants of Judah and Jerusalem. The complainants named were presumably the officials at Samaria. The complaint is not quoted but no doubt was similar to the one made by a new set of officials to Artaxerxes I. In their letter, the temple is not an issue at all; the Jews are accused of rebuilding the *walls* of Jerusalem. The king is warned of the dangerous possibilities this raises and is advised to look into previous history concerning the rebellions that had taken place there. This complaint brought an order from Artaxerxes I to put a stop to the Jewish activities. It was immediately carried out with a show of military force. Therewith the Aramaic narrative breaks off. It doubtless continued to tell how the fortifications were later completed by royal permission. But this sequel has not been preserved; the story of Nehemiah now takes its place.[5]

The second and major source used by the Chronicler for this post-exilic period was the Memoir of Nehemiah. This is something new in Hebrew literature: a responsible political leader recording his *res gestae*—on a minor scale a parallel to Darius' great story on the rock of Behistun. Nehemiah was one of those Jews who had succeeded in attaining high office under the Persians. He was the king's cupbearer, but such positions often led to posts of greater responsibility. The Nehemiah Memoir, in which the first person was used throughout, has however been edited by the Chronicler who, as many scholars now believe, befuddled the historical situation by injecting Ezra and his promulgation of the law into the Nehemiah story.

The first part of the Memoir has been secondarily expanded with a prayer (1:5–11); a valuable list of those who built the walls of Jerusalem (3:1–32); and a list of the returners from captivity (7:5b–73) already found in Ezra 2. No doubt a divergent list of the returners was given in the Memoir, in which certain people

[5] If the Chronicler rearranged 4:6–23 and 5:1—6:15 what was his reason? Was it because it seemed to give a documentary explanation of why the temple was not rebuilt, as ordered by Cyrus (so the previous edition of this book, p. 286)? Or was it in order to project the animosity of the Samaritans back into the past, as a more recent view suggests?

were not mentioned or in which some were mentioned who had best
be forgotten. The list of Ezra 2 thus was substituted for the original
record. Neh. 7:4-5 reaches over to 11:1ff. for its continuation. In
chs. 8-9, the Chronicler has placed material from the Memoir of
Ezra, which once must have stood between Ezra 8:32-36 and Ezra
9:1, according to the date given. He has, however, turned the first
person of the Ezra Memoir into a third person account, and has
injected Nehemiah into it in Neh. 8:9. In Neh. 10 there is no mention of Ezra—Nehemiah is the leader—but this chapter is probably
not from the Nehemiah Memoir itself. It has been put here by the
Chronicler from another source as a generally suitable sequel to
chs. 8-9. Chronologically, it actually belongs after Neh. 13:31. In
12:36 the Chronicler has artificially injected the presence of Ezra.

The dating at the beginning of the Nehemiah Memoir has been
damaged (much as we found it in Ezek. 1:1, where only the year
number remained): here we have month and year. The king's name
can, of course, be easily supplied from the next date in 2:1. But Nisan
is the first month of the year while Kislev is the ninth. Thus, there
may be an error either in the first date, which should then be the
nineteenth year, or in the next date which could be the twenty-
[first] year.

Nehemiah relates how his brother Hanani came from Judah and
gave him a depressing account of the situation there. The root of
the trouble, we gather, was the defenselessness of the city. This
made it possible for the hostile neighbors to plunder the helpless
population. Nehemiah grieved so much over the matter that the
king spoke to him about his appearance. Placing his hope in God
Nehemiah spoke of what was troubling him: his desire to see the
city, where the graves of his fathers were, rebuilt. The king gave
him an opportunity to make a request, and Nehemiah asked to be
sent to carry out the project. The king asked how long he would be
gone, and Nehemiah mentioned the period of time needed.[6] Re-

---

[6] It is difficult to believe that he could have stayed away for years. He was
not of the Persian nobility like Arsames, the satrap of Egypt who could stay
away from his post for long periods, as shown by the Aramaic documents
published by G. R. Driver. See the abridged and revised edition, *Aramaic
Documents of the Fifth Century* B.C., 1957. The Chronicler preserved only one
mention of absence (13:6) in 433.

ceiving consent, Nehemiah requested letters addressd to the gover-
nors in which they were requested to allow him to pass through to
Jerusalem; also to the overseer of the forests (*i.e.*, Lebanon) to
provide him with the lumber he needed for the walls, the gates, and
for the house he would build for his own residence. In the favorable
action of the king he piously saw the hand of God. Artaxerxes even
gave him a military escort, so he reached Jerusalem safely. His
arrival, he notes, angered Sanballat the Horonite, the Ammonite
"servant," Tobiah (2:10), and doubtless Geshem the Arabian (6:1).[7]

After three days he made a secret nocturnal inspection—no doubt
in the full of the moon—of the walls of Jerusalem. He had revealed
to no one the purpose of his coming. Now however, on having
surveyed the state of affairs, he set the situation before the leaders,
and urged the rebuilding of the walls so that the Jews would no
longer be the object of mockery. He informed the leaders of the
authority given him. The decision was taken and the preparations
were begun. The enemies, hearing of this, mocked the undertaking,
but Nehemiah answered that God would let the Jews succeed, and
that outsiders had no portion or right of memorial in Jerusalem.

It may have taken years to procure the lumber, and the actual
building activity *must* have been long, as is revealed in 5:14-19. The
Chronicler gives the impression that everything was done speedily
and so makes it more interesting.

When the actual raising of the walls was proceeding, Sanballat
and Tobiah held a public mockery of the Jews before the armed
forces at Samaria. To the news of this Nehemiah responded with
an appeal to God to punish them for this sin.

After the wall had been raised to half its height the same foes,
augmented by the Ashdodites (inhabitants of Philistaia, of which
Ashdod was now the leading city), conspired to attack the Jews.
Nehemiah made defense preparations of such a nature that the adversaries thought better of it. But thereafter only half of the men
worked while the other half remained under arms.

---

[7] Sanballat (in Babylonian pronunciation, *Sin-uballiṭ*) was the governor of
Palestine; no doubt Nehemiah's appointment gave him the status of a commissar
in control of affairs in Judah, and independent of Sanballat. Tobiah is the
ancestor of the Ammonite family of the Tobiads. In spite of Nehemiah's words
they continued to have rights in Jerusalem (cf. 13:4). Geshem the Arabian is
perhaps identical with Gashmu the father of king Qainu of Qedar, who gave
votive bowls with his inscription to an Egyptian temple.

When the wall was completed but the gates not yet set in, Sanballat sought a meeting with Nehemiah in a village west of Jerusalem. Nehemiah, however, suspected foul play. Indeed, when repeated invitations were turned down treachery was attempted against him in the city. But Nehemiah, familiar with intrigue from his life at the Persian court, saw through all the schemes. The efforts of the adversaries continued however; and there were many traitors among the Jews.

The gates were now put in place and the defense of the city organized. Nehemiah made his brother Hanani commandant of the city, and another particularly religious and reliable man commander of the fortress. The city area was large and the population sparse, so Nehemiah formulated a plan to draft men from all villages and communities to come and live there. In this manner Jerusalem at once assumed a new importance and became unassailable.

One would expect to hear of a celebration soon after the walls were completed, but perhaps this had to wait until a festival date. The account of the celebration in 12:27–43 does not mention what date was chosen. The possibility that the celebration was delayed until the next Babylonian New Year in Nisan must be considered, for Nehemiah was an official of the Persian king as king of Babylon and its ancient realm. Thus the drafting of the population could have taken place before the festival.

A serious situation of discontent arose among the people, according to the misplaced ch. 5, when they had to borrow money at usurious interest rates. Nehemiah brought about a cancellation of debts. He shamed the creditors by pointing out that out of fear of God he had served without support for twelve years, and together with his brothers had fed a large company. He expected them, too, to bring sacrifices for the restoration of their country.

In the final preserved piece of the Memoir, Nehemiah speaks of his having gone to the king in the thirty-second year of the ruler's reign (433). After his return he found that the high priest Eliashib had given Tobiah (the Ammonite) a chamber in the outer courts of the temple—a room hitherto used for temple purposes. In the Greek era the Tobiads were the Rothschilds of Palestine, and had a strong position in Jerusalem. It may well be that the reason for giving Tobiah this room was to provide a place for the conduct of financial matters. But Nehemiah disapproved of this and overruling the high priest threw out Tobiah's furnishings. He saw to it that the Levites and musicians, who had quit for lack of pay, were brought back and received support. He rebuked the nobles for allowing markets on the Sabbath outside Jerusalem; to stop this traffic, he ordered the city gates to be closed on the Sabbath. He was horrified to find the children of mixed marriages unable to speak the Hebrew language. He drove out a grandson of Eliashib, who was married to a daughter of Sanballat.[8]

In his Memoir, Nehemiah's personality stands out quite clearly. His ability and fearlessness, his devotion and unselfishness shine through his story. He wrought for his people and his God. All through his book his prayer goes up like a refrain, "Remember this, O God, for good," as though he had consciously spread the record of his work before his maker. The anxiety for remembrance is, however, partly due to the fact that he was a eunuch, like all such Persian court officials, and thus had no offspring. The prayer must be read with Isa. 56:4–5 in mind.

There is no record of what became of Nehemiah. The reign of his sovereign continued until 424, and it is possible that his governorship lasted until then. Late in the reign of Darius II (423–405) we find Judea under the Persian governor Bagoas, to whom the Jews of the Elephantine colony addressed their letter of the summer of 407 B.C., appealing for the restoration of their temple of Yahweh.[9] They also wrote to the sons of Sanballat. The reply their messenger took along to Egypt was given in the names of Bagoas and Delaiah, one of the sons of Sanballat. These men were thus at Jerusalem and exercising influence there.

The third narrative used by the Chronicler for this period was the Memoir of Ezra. It may have been written in the first person in imitation of that of Nehemiah. It was utilized by the Chronicler in

[8] Josephus, *Antiquities*, XI, viii, 2, confuses this incident with one that took place a century later, thereby making Sanballat a contemporary of Alexander the Great. The theory that his Sanballat was a grandson of the one of Nehemiah's time has little probability.

[9] See Kraeling, *Brooklyn Museum Aramaic Papyri*, 1953, pp. 21–127, for a full account of the Elephantine colony. A brief survey is given by the same author in "New Light on the Elephantine Colony," *The Biblical Archaeologist Reader*, edited by D. N. Freedman and G. E. Wright, 1961, pp. 128–144.

Ezra 7–10, but he transferred another piece which, as we have already noted, may have originally stood after Ezra 8:32, to the book of Nehemiah where it now forms ch. 8. From a purely literary angle this was an excellent thing to do, for it closely joined the work of the two men most responsible for Judea's reconstruction, into one grand climax. At an age which was less interested in the accurate reporting of history than the propagandistic use of it, this is quite understandable.

According to his narrative Ezra undertook his journey with royal favor under "Artaxerxes king of Persia," in that ruler's seventh year. This has generally been taken to refer to Artaxerxes I and would make the year of this journey 458 B.C. But the new Elephantine papyri of the Brooklyn Museum have shown that no differentiation was made in the datings between Artaxerxes I and II; in either case plain "Artaxerxes" is used. It was thus quite natural for the Chronicler in utilizing a similarly dated Ezra Memoir to think of the more prominent Artaxerxes I, and then to link the activity of Ezra and that of Nehemiah in the manner now appearing in the book of Nehemiah. Many implausibilities are resolved when the coming of Ezra is put in the reign of Artaxerxes II (404–358). The journey then took place in 398 B.C.[10]

Ezra was given a royal decree—written in Aramaic—authorizing him and any Jews who wished to accompany him to go to Jerusalem bearing moneys donated by the king, and also moneys they might collect from the Jews in the province of Babylon, to investigate conditions there on the basis of "the law of God which was in his hand." Ezra left Babylon on the first day of the first month (April 4).[11] A place of rendezvous had evidently been appointed at

[10] Some scholars, in an effort to defend the contemporaneousness of Ezra and Nehemiah in accordance with the Chronicler's presentation, would correct the date of Ezra 1:8 to the *thirty-seventh* year of Artaxerxes I (428). But the Elephantine Jews could still appeal for restoration of their temple in 407; and a son of Sanballat is apparently residing at Jerusalem and is consulted in the matter. All this would be very strange had the reforms of Ezra already been carried out.

[11] This was a good day to leave the city for the great festival of Marduk the god of Babylon, which must still have been celebrated even though on a smaller scale than formerly, began on that day and lasted until the *eleventh*. This shows why Ezra did not leave the gathering place until the *twelfth*: Babylonian religious fanaticism had to be considered.

"the river that comes into Ahavah" (an as yet unidentified geographical name). There were no Levites among those assembled and the departure had to be postponed until such were rounded up, for they had been mentioned in the decree. Ezra was clearly intending to expand the temple services and thus had to provide the personnel. It is characteristic of the religious spirit of the undertaking they were about to embark on that Ezra can say:

> Then I proclaimed a fast there by the river of Ahavah, that we might humble ourselves before our God to seek from him a straight way for ourselves, our children and all our goods.[12] For I was ashamed to ask of the king a band of soldiers and horsemen to help us against the enemy in the way, because we had told the king "The hand of our God is for good upon all that seek him, and the power of his wrath is against all that forsake him." So we fasted and besought our God for this, and he hearkened to our entreaty. (Ezra 8:21-23)

So they departed with 38 Levites and 220 Nethinim (temple-slaves) on the twelfth of the first month (8:31), which in 398 B.C. would have been April 17, and reached Jerusalem on the first day of the fifth month (7:8), or July 31.

After three days the moneys and vessels brought along were delivered at the temple, sacrifices were brought, and the necessary letters were sent to Persian officials. (Some of this must have been attended to en route.)

The first matter said to have been brought to Ezra's attention was that of mixed marriages. If the assumption is correct that Neh. 10 relates to the time of Nehemiah then the oath taken at that time had been poorly kept. Even priests and Levites are accused of such intermarriage. Ezra was grief-stricken; the Chronicler gives him a long penitential prayer (9:6-15). A considerable crowd assembled about him and one man brought forward the suggestion that they expel such foreign wives and their offspring. He urged Ezra to take the matter in hand. This he did and made the priests, Levites, and all Israel swear to act accordingly. He then went for the night to the chamber of Johanan the sons of Eliashib, which was evidently vacant. The reason for this has apparently been preserved

---

[12] Ezra 8:21 served as model for the Pilgrims before they set sail from Holland on the Mayflower, for they held a fast and their beloved minister, John Robinson, preached on this text.

in Josephus' story (*Antiquities*, XI, 7, 1) that Johanan—the high priest to whom the Elephantine Jews had vainly appealed in 410— had slain his brother Jeshua, who with the support of Bagoas, had sought to displace him. The act was committed in the temple and reportedly led to Bagoas' violation of the temple and his punishing of the Jews for seven years. Wherever Johanan may have been he was not at Jerusalem when Ezra was there. The latter thus could occupy the high priest's quarters.

The ensuing action is not directly attributed to Ezra. The command went forth to all those who had (formerly?) returned from the captivity to assemble at Jerusalem on the third day under threat of confiscation of property. By this time it was the twentieth day of the ninth month (December 24, if 398 B.C.) and the cold rainy season was in progress. The motion was made that the matter be handled by the leaders, the individuals concerned summoned gradually, and the divorces processed. This was done. A list of those divorcing is then given. Actually one is surprised to find that the numbers involved were not great: 17 priests, 6 Levites, 1 minstrel, 3 gate-keepers, 86 laymen. But the act of segregation here reported was to ring down through the ages.

For the continuation of the Ezra narrative we must turn to Neh. 8–9. When the seventh month came (it began September 28 in 398 B.C.) the people of the city, including women and children, assembled and requested Ezra to read the book of law which Yahweh had commanded the Israelites. When he opened the book all the people rose and Ezra spoke a word of praise, to which all the people answered "Amen, Amen," raising their hands and then bowing to the ground. The activity of Ezra is, however, lost sight of, for the narrator proceeds to describe how the Levites expounded the law to the people. This no doubt was the regular procedure at later occasions. The people wept as they heard the words of the law, but Ezra (Nehemiah, as noted previously, has been secondarily introduced here in 8:9) *and the Levites* (later custom) told them to be glad on this day which was holy to Yahweh. On the second day the reading was restricted to heads of families, priests, and Levites. Here they learned of the command of Moses to celebrate a feast of Tabernacles in the seventh month. This disrupts the situation, as everybody goes out to build booths. The reading of the law allegedly continued for the entire seven days of the festival, after which came the day of assembly (*Azereth*) "as written in the law." This remark shows that the law presupposed contained the Priestly Code (cf. Num. 29:12–39). The Chronicler has clearly overlaid the Ezra story of acquainting the people with the law with subsequent practice when copies of it were available.

On the twenty-fourth of the seventh month (October 22, 398 B.C.) a fast was held with scripture reading and confession, and praise of God by a group of Levites. Here the Chronicler introduces a long prayer by Ezra, containing a penitent review of Hebrew history, and closing with an utterance that the real Ezra could scarcely have made in view of his indebtedness to the Persian crown —in effect a complaint about suffering under gentile government.

As we have seen the solemn occasion of ch. 10 referred to an event of the time of Nehemiah. The Chronicler uses it with the idea of describing the adoption of the law brought by Ezra. No doubt there was a solemn occasion of a similar nature at this time, too. Whether the book of the law brought by Ezra was the Priestly Code or the whole Pentateuch remains uncertain.

Nehemiah and Ezra, as representatives of the type of Judaism that had developed in the Babylonian captivity, were the men of destiny, who brought about a reconstruction of their prostrate, demoralized, and impoverished country. True, mighty storms were to pass over it in the centuries to come. But their spirit enabled a people that became more and more nurtured in it to withstand all of them and to exist to this very day.

We owe to the Chronicler of *ca.* 300 B.C. the preservation of these materials that are so important for the history of the birth of Judaism. We must now look at the rest of his work, from which Ezra and Nehemiah had been detached. It is called in Hebrew "Words of the Days," a phrase used for the ancient annals of the kings (1 Ki. 14:19, etc.). The Septuagint translators substituted Paralipomena ("things left out," *i.e.*, not given in the older books). St. Jerome substituted "Chronicon," whence comes the familiar name Chronicles. The author was much concerned with the ways of God

in Hebrew history from the standpoint of Deuteronomic doctrine.[13]
People asked, *e.g.*, why the great reformer Josiah had been slain by
Necho, if piety was always rewarded with long life and happiness;
or why so wicked a king as Manasseh was permitted to reign 55
years, longer than any other king, if wickedness was always punished
by disaster and premature death? Such matters constituted problems
for investigation and research (*midrash* as the Hebrew would say).
Even before the Chronicler, answers in the form of stories were
given by scholars and scribes; and various tales and explanations were
collected in a book called "the Midrash of the Book of the Kings."
It is no longer in existence, but it was utilized by the Chronicler, who
refers to it in 2 Chron. 24:27. He also refers to "the Book of the
Kings of Judah and Israel"; to "the Words of Samuel the seer"; "of
Nathan the prophet"; "of Gad the seer"; "of Shemaiah the prophet";
"of Iddo the seer"; "of the Seers"; "the Prophecy of Ahijah the
Shilonite"; "the Vision of Iddo the seer"; "the History of Uzziah by
Isaiah the prophet"; "the Words of Jehu, son of Hanani, which are
inserted in the Book of the Kings of Israel"; and "the Vision of Isaiah
the prophet the son of Amoz in the Book of the Kings of Judah and
Israel." It is uncertain to what extent this reflects real or imaginary
sources.

The Chronicler followed in the footsteps of the Deuteronomist
who had been a pragmatic historian. But his viewpoint was ecclesiastical; in the center of his interest stood Jerusalem and the temple,
and his history was really an "Ecclesiastical Chronicle of Jerusalem."
His work consisted of four parts: a genealogical outline of History
from Adam to the time of Saul (1 Chron. 1–9); 2. the story of David
(1 Chron. 10–29), and that of Solomon (2 Chron. 1–9); 3. The story
of Judah from the Secession to the Exile (2 Chron. 10–36); 4. (originally) the Reconstruction (Ezra–Nehemiah).

The material for the first section he took mainly from the Pentateuch and historical books (1 Sam. 31–2 Ki.) and some lists which
perhaps were from the temple archives.[14] It is significant that he also

[13] The influence of the Priestly document on the Chronicler is not as certain
as formerly believed.

[14] The lists in 1 Chron. 1–9 have been greatly expanded by a later editor or
editors. The section on the clergy (1 Chron. 23:2—27:34) is a whole interpolated unit.

felt impelled to begin his history with Adam; he indicated thereby
that the whole history of the world culminated in the temple at
Jerusalem. He was so greatly interested in the priests and Levites,
the only legitimate ministers of Yahweh, and still more in the
Levitic singers and musicians and their liturgy, that one cannot
escape the conclusion that he himself was one of them.

The story worth telling began for him with David. A comparison
of his treatment of the history of David with that of the Books of
Samuel which forms the basis of his work is most instructive. The
struggle for the kingship was omitted; directly after the death of
Saul,

> Yahweh turned the kingdom to David the son of Jesse. Then all Israel
> gathered themselves to David unto Hebron . . . and anointed David
> king over Israel according to the word of Yahweh by Samuel. (1 Chron.
> 10:14—11:3)

The kingship of Saul's son Eshbaal was completely ignored; David
was Saul's immediate successor. After "all Israel" had helped David
capture the stronghold of Zion, three lists of his adherents are
given, the first (11:10–47) was taken from 2 Sam. 23, the second
and third (12:1–22, 23–40) are characterized by immense numbers,
"a great host, like the host of God" in the second, more than
300,000 in the third, among them 4600 Levites and 3722 priests—
wholly incredible.

> All these, being men of war, that could order the battle array [includ-
> ing the priests and the Levites!] came with a perfect heart to Hebron to
> make David king over all Israel: and all the rest also of Israel were of one
> heart to make David king.

How different all this is from the story in the Book of Samuel.
David's first act after his conquest of Zion, according to the Chronicler, was the bringing of the ark thither, but the tragic death of
Uzzah who had tried to steady the falling ark with his hand was
interpreted as a sign of Yahweh's anger and the ark was left at Obed-
edom's house for the next three months (1 Chron. 13). This time
was filled out with the building of David's palace and his war against
the Philistines, for secular matters were only episodes to the Chronicler (1 Chron. 14). Then David prepared to bring the ark to its ap-

pointed place. Here the Chronicler revels in priests and Levites. David had discovered that

> None ought to carry the ark of God but the Levites, for them has Yahweh chosen to carry the ark of God, and to minister into Him forever. . . . Because ye (the Levites) bore it not at the first, Yahweh our God made a breach upon us, because we sought Him not according to the ordinance.

It makes no difference to the Chronicler that this is in direct contradiction to 2 Sam. 6, which he himself had excerpted in ch. 13 (see vv. 11f.). This was his view of the matter: David appointed Levitic singers and musicians for the festal procession and then the Levites carried the ark to the city into the tent that David had pitched for it. After the offerings had been brought,

> He appointed certain of the Levites to minister before the ark of Yahweh, and to celebrate and to thank and praise Yahweh, the God of Israel,

and a festal psalm, prepared for the occasion by David, was sung by Asaph and his brethren. The ministers of the religious services were then definitely assigned (15f.). The plan of David to build a temple and Yahweh's opposition through Nathan (ch. 17) as well as David's wars are reproduced in the words of the Book of Samuel, but it is noteworthy that everything that reflects badly on David was omitted, the stories of Meribaal and Zibah, of Bathsheba and Uriah, of Tamar and Amnon, of Absalom's rebellion, and of the offering of the sons of Saul. Similarly David's almost disastrous encounter with a Philistine giant was omitted, and the report of 2 Sam. 21:19 that "Elhanan the Bethlehemite slew Goliath" was characteristically harmonized with 1 Sam. 17 by making Elhanan slay "the *brother* of Goliath." In the story of David's census the Chronicler made also certain characteristic corrections of the older report. It was not Yahweh who moved David to number Israel, but "Satan," for God tempts no man to evil. Joab did not count Levi, evidently because the law (Num. 1:49) had forbidden the numbering of Levites, nor Benjamin apparently because the holy city was theoretically located in Benjamin. David paid not 50 shekels for Araunah's threshing floor, but the more royal sum of 600 shekels. The sacredness of this place was not only revealed by the appearance of the angel there, but the divine acceptance of the altar which David built there was accentuated by the Chronicler in the addition,

> And he called upon Yahweh, and He answered him from heaven by fire upon the altar of burnt offering. (21:28)

And yet the Chronicler was too much under the sway of the idea that the tabernacle was the only legitimate place of worship until the temple had been built, not to feel the need of adding the explanation:

> At that time, when David saw that Yahweh had answered him in the threshing-floor of Ornan the Jebusite, then he sacrificed there. For the tabernacle of Yahweh, which Moses made in the wilderness, and the altar of burnt-offering, were at that time in the high place at Gibeon. But David could not go before it to inquire of God; for he was afraid because of the sword of the angel of Yahweh. Then David said, This is the house of Yahweh God, and this is the altar of burnt-offering for Israel. (1 Chron. 21:28—22:1)

Then the Chronicler told how David prepared the temple. He followed here no source, but gave his own ideas of what must have occurred. Everything so far had been leading up to this. David arranged for the workmen and for all the materials that were needed for the building of the temple, for

> David said, Solomon my son is young and tender, and the house that is to be built for Yahweh must be exceeding magnificent, of fame and of glory throughout all countries: I will therefore make preparation for it. So David prepared abundantly before his death.
>
> Then he called for Solomon his son, and charged him to build a house for Yahweh, the God of Israel. And David said to Solomon his son, As for me, it was in my heart to build a house to the name of Yahweh my God. But the word of Yahweh came to me, saying, Thou hast shed blood abundantly, and hast made great wars: thou shalt not build a house to My name, because thou hast shed much blood upon the earth in My sight. Behold, a son shall be born to thee, who shall be a man of rest; and I will give him rest from all his enemies round about; for his name shall be Solomon, and I will give peace and quietness unto Israel in his days. He shall build a house for My name; and he shall be My son, and I will be his father; and I will establish the throne of his kingdom over Israel for ever. (1 Chron. 22:5–10)

Quite differently 2 Sam. 7 (cf. 1 Chron. 17) had explained why David did not build the temple.

After all the preparations were completed, including the appointment of the priests, Levites, doorkeepers, and singers, who were all carefully divided into classes and assigned their offices by lot, and among whom the musicians were treated with special consideration (David himself invented their instruments for them and assumed the final direction)—after all this had been arranged, a great convocation of the leaders of Israel was called together, to whom Yahweh's oracle that Solomon should be the next king and the builder of the temple was unfolded; whereupon the plan of the temple in all its details, sketched by Yahweh Himself, was given to Solomon, accompanied by exhortations to carry out the plan which had been so carefully prepared in every way. After an appeal to the assembled nobles, who contributed liberally for the work, David prayed, and all blessed Yahweh and rejoiced with sacrifices before Him. Then they made Solomon king, "the second time" the Chronicler says (29:22), for David had already made him king in 23:1. The palace intrigue as a result of which Solomon had actually gained the throne was of course omitted. Nothing must mar the picture of the great saint who had built the temple. How much at variance the David of the Chronicler is from the David of the Books of Samuel and Kings! There he is a king and hero, a warrior and statesman, the real founder of the kingdom; here he is the sweet singer of Israel, the founder of the temple, and the author of its liturgy. There he is surrounded by warriors and men of affairs, here by priests and Levites. There we have secular, here ecclesiastical history. The hero has become a saint, the king a liturgist. Which picture is historical and which is not, is manifest at once.

In the first story of Solomon, that of his worship at Gibeon, the difference between the deuteronomistic and the priestly points of view appears quite characteristically. 1 Ki. 3:2–4 had said, in justification of his offering on "the great high place,"

Only the people sacrificed in the high places, because there was no house built for the name of Yahweh until those days. And Solomon loved Yahweh, walking in the statutes of David his father: only he sacrificed and burnt incense in the high places. And the king went to Gibeon to sacrifice there; for that was the great high place: a thousand burnt-offerings did Solomon offer upon that altar. (1 Ki. 3:2-4)

The Chronicler, to whom the tabernacle at Gibeon was the sole legitimate sanctuary, needed no justification for this. He wrote therefore,

So Solomon, and all the assembly with him, went to the high place that was at Gibeon; for there was the tent of meeting of God, which Moses the servant of Yahweh had made in the wilderness. But the ark of God had David brought up from Kiriath-jearim to the place that David had prepared for it; for he had pitched a tent for it at Jerusalem. Moreover the brazen altar, that Bezalel the son of Uri, the son of Hur, had made, was there before the tabernacle of Yahweh and Solomon and the assembly resorted to it. And Solomon went up thither to the brazen altar before Yehweh, which was at the tent of meeting, and offered a thousand burnt-offerings upon it. (2 Chron. 1:3-6)

But he could not use the conclusion of the story in 1 Ki. 3:15, so he wrote for

He came to Jerusalem, and stood before the ark of the covenant of Yahweh, and offered up burnt-offerings, and made a feast to all his servants. (1 Ki. 3:15)

So Solomon came from the high place that was at Gibeon, from before the tent of meeting, to Jerusalem. (2 Chron. 1:14)

Solomon, according to the Chronicler's view, could not have sacrificed in Jerusalem before the temple was built. So he omitted the reference to it. At the beginning he had added that the king was accompanied by an assembly of the notables of Israel in order to enhance the splendor and glory of the scene, and now he followed it by a description of Solomon's immense wealth.

Next the story of the building of the temple was begun. The preparations, including the contract with King Hiram of Tyre, and the description of the temple differ comparatively little from the Book of Kings, but in the dedication the Chronicler elaborated in characteristic fashion the part of the priests and Levites and especially of the singers and musicians. 1 Ki. 8:10f. had only mentioned,

And it came to pass, when the priests were come out of the holy place, that the cloud filled the house of Yahweh so that the priests could not stand to minister by reason of the cloud, for the glory of Yahweh filled the house of Yahweh.

After "the holy place" the Chronicler inserted,

For all the priests that were present had sanctified themselves, and did not keep their courses; also the Levites who were the singers, all of them, even Asaph, Heman, Jeduthun, and their sons and their brethren, arrayed in fine linen, with cymbals and psalteries and harps, stood at the east end of the altar and with them a hundred and twenty priests sounding with trumpets; it came to pass, when the trumpeters and singers were as one to make one sound to be heard in praising and thanking Yahweh; and when they lifted up their voice with the trumpets and cymbals and instruments of music, and praised Yahweh, saying, For He is good; for His loving-kindness endures for ever. (2 Chron. 5:11b–13a)

The statement that Solomon "stood before the altar of Yahweh" was annotated by the explanation that he had made for himself "a brazen pulpit" on which he stood and prayed, for the Chronicler could not believe that the saintly Solomon had arrogated to himself priestly rights. Instead of the blessing of Solomon (1 Ki. 8:54–61), which was again a priestly function, the Chronicler told of fire descending from heaven and consuming the sacrifices, and of the glory of Yahweh filling the whole temple (2 Chron. 7:1–3). The priests' and especially the musicians' part had not been brought out in the old story, so the Chronicler added,

And the priests stood, according to their offices; the Levites also with instruments of music of Yahweh which David the king had made to give thanks to Yahweh (for His lovingkindness endures for ever), when David praised by their ministry: and the priests sounded trumpets before them; and all Israel stood. (2 Chron. 7:6)

Instead of sending the people away on the eighth day, as 1 Ki. 8:66 had done, the Chronicler had them celebrate this day in Jerusalem in accordance with the priestly law of Num. 29:35. In the remaining part of the story of Solomon the Chronicler changed the statement that Solomon had ceded twenty Galilean cities to Hiram into the directly opposite assertion that Hiram had given them to Solomon, who settled Israelites in them; and asserted that Solomon did not subject any Israelite to forced labor in his building operations but only the Hittites, Amorites, Perrizites, Hivites, and Jebusites. The moving of Solomon's queen, the Pharaoh's daughter, from the city of David into Solomon's palace, after it had been completed, was commented upon in this wholly unhistorical but characteristically priestly manner,

> For he said, My wife shall not dwell in the house of David king of Israel, because the places are holy whereunto the ark of Yahweh has come. (2 Chron. 8:11)

The presence of the foreign woman would have a defiling effect! That the Chronicler omitted the darker sides of Solomon's brilliant picture, his polygamy and his building of shrines for the gods of his wives, as well as the rebellions against him, is only what we should have expected from his previous treatment of this saint and prince of peace.

In the succeeding history the Chronicler's two fundamental principles are worked out again and again: the conviction that the law had been in force is Israel from the time of Moses on, and the prophetic-deuteronomic principle of retribution. In light of them the history is not only judged but modified. The Chronicler believed that Judah was the people of the law, Israel had fallen away from Yahweh under Jeroboam I and had lost its position as the people of Yahweh (2 Chron. 11:8–17). Continuity of the legitimate cult of Yahweh was found only in Jerusalem. The history of Israel was therefore omitted, and only when Israel came into contact with Judah and had to be mentioned, was it referred to.

The conclusion of the third part of the Chronicler's history deserves attention. The Jews were carried off to be slaves until Persian rule succeeded the Chaldean,

> To fulfill the word of Yahweh by the mouth of Jeremiah until the land had enjoyed its sabbaths. All the days that it lay desolate it kept sabbath, to fulfill seventy years. (2 Chron. 36:21)

This is not a direct Jeremiah quotation but a combination of his prophecy of the seventy years of exile (Jer. 25:11ff.; 29:10) with Lev. 26:34f. The Chronicler then begins the fourth part of his work, on the Reconstruction, with a renewed reference to the seventy years of Jeremiah (Ezra 1:12; 2 Chron. 36:22). The prophecy was allegedly fulfilled by the edict of Cyrus. It may of course be that the Chronicler overestimated the length of time from 587 to 538. On the other hand there is a real possibility, as we have seen, that the actual return did not take place until 522 and subsequent years. And if one take the date of the completion of the temple as terminus (516, Ezra 6:15) then the seventy years would, indeed, have been fulfilled.

If the Chronicler mirrored the whole life of his time it would indeed have been an age primarily interested in religion, with all reality viewed through a stained glass window. But fortunately we have other light on this age. We will see life through the eyes of the wise men in ch. XIX and of the Psalmists in ch. XX. Here, however, we may turn to a piece of narrative fiction that mirrors Jewish small-town existence, with attention to character as displayed in ordinary human concerns—the Book of Ruth. It is a charming little idyl, which no less a man than Goethe declared to be the loveliest little entity that has been preserved for us among the epics and idyls of the past. It tells of the loyalty of Ruth, the daughter-in-law of Naomi, her diligence and prudence and her great reward. After the death of her husband and her two sons in Moab, where the sons had married the Moabite wives Orpah and Ruth, Naomi decided to go back to her native town of Bethlehem in Judah. In spite of her remonstrances Ruth insisted on going with her, declaring in those beautiful words that have since been repeated by thousands of women in the solemn hour of marriage:

> Whither thou goest, I will go; and where thou lodgest, I will lodge; thy people shall be my people, and thy God my God; where thou diest, will I die, and there will I be buried: Yahweh do so to me, and more also, if aught but death part thee and me. (Ruth 1:16f.)

They arrived in Bethlehem at the beginning of barley harvest and Ruth at once went into the fields to glean after the reapers. She happened on the field of Boaz, who saw her later and invited her to glean only in his field, and gave orders to treat her kindly. To her question, why he should show such favor to a foreigner, he replied,

> It has fully been showed me, all that thou hast done to thy mother-in-law since the death of thy husband; and how thou hast left thy father and thy mother, and thy native land, and art come to a people that thou knewest not heretofore. Yahweh recompense thy work, and a full reward be given thee of Yahweh, the God of Israel, under whose wings thou art come to take refuge. (Ruth 2:11f.)

When Naomi learned of Ruth's good fortune and in whose field she had been gleaning she rejoiced, for Boaz was one of her near kinsmen. And when the harvest came to an end, she had her plan ready, and Ruth obediently carried it out, although it involved no ordinary risk. But Naomi had estimated Boaz's character rightly. When he started up that night from his sleep on the threshing-floor after the joyful harvest meal and discovered Ruth lying at his feet, he treated her with honor and promised to fulfill his kinsman's duty by marrying her, if a still closer relative did not claim her. Richly laden with gifts Ruth returned home to Naomi. On the morrow Boaz offered the kinsman's privilege of buying Naomi's field to the other relative, but when he refused after learning that he must also marry Ruth in addition,[15] Boaz took her as his wife amidst the loud and hearty felicitations of all the people. In due course, Ruth bore a son, and the happy Naomi became his nurse. And this son Obed became later Jesse's father, and Jesse's son was none other than King David.[16]

No lesson is appended, no moral affixed. There is no knowledge of the hatred of foreigners, and particularly that of the Moabites such as was entertained by the cultically and politically minded (Deut. 23:3; Neh. 13:1–3). God looks at the heart and rewards such goodness as Ruth's most richly. One may be certain of his blessing if one is only righteous in his life. Mixed marriages are no problem troubling the author; by having Naomi take the child as her own he has given it full Jewish status. God blessed this child in such a signal fashion that through it Boaz and Ruth became the ancestors of David.

The spirit and purpose of Nehemiah, of making Jerusalem and the Jews so strong that they would be respected by their neighbors,

[15] This obligation is otherwise unreported in connection with Levirate marriage. See Deut. 25:5–10. The custom of taking off the shoe has a more honorable basis in the story than in Deuteronomy. Some use this as argument for an earlier origin of the book. But its Aramaisms point to this era. There were many local village or regional customs in every age.
[16] A later writer added the longer genealogy of Boaz carrying it back to Perez, because he had been mentioned in 4:12. It may be that the Chronicler's mention of Boaz already presupposes the existence of this story (cf. 1 Chron. 2:12). Some scholars think the story has been only secondarily linked with the Davidic ancestry, and that the name of the child originally was not Obed, but one permitting a pun with the name Naomi (cf. Naam or Noam, 1 Chron. 4:15).

must also have continued in certain circles. It was a man of this kind
to whom we probably owe the much discussed chapter, Gen. 14,
which apparently was interpolated in this late period. Whether it is
an extract from a longer historical work or just an individual short
piece, it presupposes the other Pentateuchal sources including P, as
its setting and its diction show. This writer may be regarded as one
of those who had come from Babylonia, where he had obtained
some knowledge about early history. Berossos, the Babylonian priest
who wrote a history of Babylon in Greek about 275 B.C., may well
have had predecessors who wrote in Aramaic. From some such
source this Jew derived an account of a campaign of ancient kings
to Palestine and fitted it into the story of Abraham and Lot. The
latter is carried off as a prisoner from Sodom, thus giving the story-
teller the opportunity to show how Abraham delivered him. With
his small force the latter defeated the Eastern kings. Bearing in mind
that the way back from Damascus to Hebron led via Jerusalem the
author had the inspiration to make Abraham receive the blessing of
Melchizedek king of "Salem" in the name of the Most High God
(cf. Dan. 3:26 etc.), whose priest the ruler was, and pay tithes to
him (with an eye to his descendants in high priestly Jerusalem).
Generously he gives back the recovered property to the liberated
kings of Sodom, disdaining to have it said that they had made
Abraham rich.[17] This story added to the Pentateuch gave every Jew
a lift.

In this period Judaism received a format that it was never to lose.
The Priestly law, superimposed on the Deuteronomic and the instruction in it carried out by the Levites, trained the Jews to separate
themselves from the gentiles. At the same time their success, as
reflected by a man like Nehemiah, led to jealousy of them. In
Babylonia, hatred of the Jews may also have been furthered by the
favor shown them by the Persian rulers or by Jewish conduct at
the time of the diverse revolts of Babylon against Persia. However it

[17] The Dead Sea Scroll written in Aramaic and partially published by
N. Avigad and Y. Yadin, *A Genesis Apocryphon*, 1956, contains a midrashic
rehash of Gen. 14. Amraphel is called king of Babylon, Arioch king of Kptk
(Cappadocia), Tidal "king of nations who is between the rivers." Hobah is
replaced by Helbon (Ezek. 27:18). The King's Valley is explained as the plain
of Beth-haccherem (Jer. 6:2; Neh. 3:14). For translation see Burrows, *More
Light*, 391.

came about, anti-Semitism was born and became a factor in the historical process. It flourished particularly in the Hellenistic capitals of Alexandria and Antioch. In this era when anti-Semitism was already a factor in the West a book appeared that told of how it had failed in the East. That book was Esther.

The tale is told with remarkable literary ability. The beautiful young Jewess [18] Esther is chosen by Xerxes as his queen, after Vashti had been deposed because of her disobedience to the king's command. The king knew nothing of Esther's Jewish origin, for her uncle and foster father Mordecai had forbidden her to speak of it. One day, when he was on duty in the gate of the palace, Mordecai overheard two courtiers plotting the king's death. Through Esther, Xerxes was informed, the plot was foiled, and Mordecai's deed was entered in the royal journal, but went unrewarded at that time. Somewhat later Haman was raised to the position of vizier by the king, and everybody was commanded to bow down and do reverence to him. Only Mordecai refused to do so and incurred thereby Haman's deadly enmity. Discovering that Mordecai was a Jew, Haman determined to wreak his vengeance not only on him but on all his people. He said therefore to the king,

> There is a certain people scattered abroad and dispersed among the peoples in all the provinces of thy kingdom; and their laws are diverse from those of every people; neither keep they the king's laws: therefore it is not for the king's profit to suffer them. If it please the king, let it be written that they be destroyed: and I will pay ten thousand talents of silver into the hands of those that have the charge of the king's business, to bring it into the king's treasuries. (Esth. 3:8f.)

The king gave him at once authority to do with the Jews as he pleased. A royal decree was then issued whereby the 13th day of Adar was set apart all through the empire for the massacre and spoiling of the Jews. In deep distress Mordecai asked Esther to go to the king and intercede for her people. But Esther replied,

> All the king's servants, and the people of the king's provinces, do know, that whosoever, whether man or woman, shall come unto the king into

---

[18] In the version of Josephus, *Antiquities*, XI, vi, 2 she and her foster father lived at Babylon. The king is not Xerxes, but Artaxerxes (I), as in the *LXX*. A Jewish queen is pure fiction; Persian rulers could only select queens from certain families of the aristocracy.

the inner court, who is not called, there is one law for him, that he be put to death, except those to whom the king shall hold out the golden sceptre, that he may live: but I have not been called to come in unto the king these thirty days. And they told to Mordecai Esther's words. Then Mordecai bade them return answer to Esther, Think not thyself that thou shalt escape in the king's house, more than all the Jews. For if thou altogether holdest thy peace at this time, then will relief and deliverance arise to the Jews from another place, but thou and thy father's house will perish: and who knows whether thou art not come to the kingdom for such a time as this? Then Esther bade them return answer to Mordecai, Go, gather together all the Jews that are present in Shushan, and fast ye for me, and neither eat nor drink three days, night or day: I also and my maidens will fast in like manner; and so will I go in to the king, which is not according to the law: and if I perish, I perish. (Esth. 4:11–16)

On the third day, Esther's perilous undertaking succeeded, the king received her graciously and offered at once to fulfill her wish, but she evaded expressing it and invited him and Haman to a dinner that day. When the king asked again at that occasion, she put off her petition and invited him and Haman once more for the following day. Haman, highly elated over this signal honor, met Mordecai on his way home; he again omitted to pay reverence to Haman. Overcoming his anger, he told his wife and friends of all his honor, in which there was only one flaw: the impudence of the Jew Mordecai. They counseled him to have high gallows prepared and to ask the king for permission to hang Mordecai thereon. That night the king could not sleep and had the royal journal read to him. They happened upon Mordecai's discovery of the plot of the assassins. When the king learned that he had not been rewarded for this, he asked Haman, who had just appeared at the court, "What shall be done to the man whom the king delights to honor?" Thinking himself to be the object of such grace, he named the most extravagant of honors; he was then commanded to show them in person to Mordecai! Grief-stricken he went home, where his friends warned him that Mordecai would bring about his fall. At the dinner that day, Esther at last told the king that her own life and that of her people were in peril, and at his angry question "Who is he, and where is he, that durst presume in his heart to do so?" she replied, "This wicked Haman!" This was too much for the king, who went out into the garden to calm himself. Meanwhile Haman implored Esther for his

life and in his fright had fallen upon the queen's couch. When the
king returned and saw him lying there, he misinterpreted the situation. A courtier suggested Haman's high gallows which he had prepared for Mordecai. Thereon he was hanged. His house was given
to Esther who made her uncle her manager. The king even made
him vizier in Haman's place. To undo the wicked plan of Haman,
Esther once more interceded with the king to revoke his decree of
the Jewish massacre. But that was impossible, since a Persian decree
was irrevocable. So he gave authority to Mordecai and Esther to
remedy the matter as best they could. They sent out a royal decree
whereby the Jews were given authority not only to defend themselves on the 13th Adar but "to destroy, to slay, and to cause to
perish, all the power of the people and province that would assault
them, their little ones and their women, and to take the spoil of them
for prey" (8:11). And on that day the Jews massacred 500 men in
Susa alone besides Haman's ten sons, but—they did not take their
spoil! The Jews were not avaricious. At Esther's request the king
set apart the next day for another slaughter and 300 more were
killed in Susa. In the province 75,000 people allegedly lost their lives
at the hands of the Jews on the 13th. Thus the narrator gave his
Jewish readers satisfaction in the imagination, amid the harsh realities
of an age in which they were victims of gentile hatred.

In commemoration of this victory the Jews in Susa celebrated a
festival called Purim on the 15th of Adar (in the villages on the 14th),
spending the day in feasting and sending presents to one another.
Mordecai wrote a letter to all the Jews in all the provinces of the
Persian empire enjoining them to keep this festival. Esther also
wrote a letter "confirming these days of Purim in their appointed
times."

Herein lies the main point of the book. It is seeking to promulgate
a nationalistic festival to strengthen Jewry. The studied avoidance
of any reference to religion and even of the name of God, where it
was naturally called for, is striking. When Mordecai refused to fall
down before Haman, we are not told that it was for religious reasons. When he admonished Esther to rescue her people, else help
would come "from another source," he meant of course from God,
but he did not say so. When Esther fasted three days before her

perilous undertaking, prayer is not mentioned, although fasting and prayer inevitably go together in such cases. When the people celebrated their deliverance, they rejoiced and feasted, but did not thank God. This purely secular character of the story finds its explanation probably not in the author's lack of religion or opposition to it but in the nonreligious character of the festival of Purim, whose origin it describes.

Purim was not one of the ancient yearly festivals commanded in the law. It had arisen in the East, probably in Susa where the story is placed. It may have been an Elamite or Persian festival which the Jews adopted and interpreted to suit their own purpose, after the Hellenistic conquest had changed the old order of things. Which particular festival Purim was, we do not know, for none of the suggestions thus far made is satisfactory.[19] Some see in the names of the leading personages of the tale, Mordecai, Esther, Vashti, and Haman, the names of gods (the most obvious being the Babylonian deities Marduk and Ishtar). They look for a mythological background in the story. But Babylonian names were long, and the theophorous element is put first in them. The tendency of Jews to abridge them could easily have produced such personal names as the ones here given. The links of this story are with folklore rather than mythology.

It may have been some time before a festival of eastern Jews would find acceptance in Palestine. The author of Ecclesiasticus, who wrote around 190 B.C. does not list Mordecai in his praise of famous men (cf. Eccl. 49:13f.), and hence probably did not know the book of Esther. It may even be that Nicanor day, which was celebrated on the 13th of Adar, one day before Purim, in commemoration of the victory of Judas Maccabaeus over the Seleucid general Nicanor in 161 B.C., was instituted as a rival festival in Palestine (1 Macc. 7:49). In any case the oldest allusion to the festival is the remark of 2 Macc. 15:26 (written about 50 B.C.) that Nicanor day was celebrated on the day before Mordecai's day. The colophon of the Greek translation of Esther was written 78–77 B.C.,

---

[19] It gets its name from *pūr*, pl. *pūrīm* "lot," as explained in 9:24-26, cf. 3:7. The word is a loanword from the Akkadian (Asyyro-Babylonian) language, and is explained with the common Hebrew word for "lot."

an indication that the book had been known for some time in Palestine.

During the Maccabean wars for religion and national independence the Book of Esther was bound to become more and more popular, for it expressed the spirit of the people during the latter half of the second century. A strong national self-consciousness and pride had been created in those wars; and the sufferings inflicted by the hated heathen were not forgotten.

Of course the purely secular character of the Book of Esther was to many an evidence that it was not inspired by God, and orthodox scholars fought for a long time against placing it among the sacred writings.[20] The Greek version tried to obviate their objections by inserting a number of religious interpolations, such as prayers of Mordecai and Esther, which, however, breathe the same exclusive, nationalist spirit. Though they were not introduced into the Hebrew text, the book nevertheless overcame all scruples by its great popularity and its intense patriotism, and has ever since been read as the lesson at the yearly festival of Purim.

[20] No scroll of Esther has as yet turned up at Qumran. Opposition to it lasted into the second century A.D. among Jews; and Christians too were slow in accepting it.

XIX

The Wisdom Literature and

the Song of Songs

ONE of the most interesting and important elements in the development of Judaism is the work of the wise men or sages. They take their place beside the priests as teachers of youth in ethics and religion. In a sense they were the successors of the prophets, for they coined their teaching into current change. Neither rising to the lofty conceptions of the greatest prophets nor partaking of their glorious enthusiasm, they yet kept the true balance between form and spirit in an age of growing legalism by their insistence on wisdom as the true norm and guide of life. As pronounced individualists they addressed themselves to individuals, not to the nation. Indeed national interests were not treated by them, not even the Messianic hope, because it was so largely national, while they themselves were cosmopolitan. Thus the author of the dialogue of Job never calls God by His proper Jewish name Yahweh, neither does Ecclesiastes, and if we substitute "God" for "Yahweh" in the Book of Proverbs, the whole book is of universal application. The interest of these wise men was not in Jewish but in human life. Some specimens of their literature are definitely ascribed to non-Jews: Lemuel king of Massa (Prov. 31) and Agur of Massa (Prov. 30). It is quite probable that these chapters were composed by Edomitic authors who might well celebrate the wisdom of Arabian sages. But the real home of the wisdom literature of the ancients was Egypt.[1] Here the style was fixed and the universal spirit governing this literature developed. It was primarily cultivated by scribes, and Hebrew scribes were in the best position to receive stimuli for a similar literary activity from that quarter. We have in our Old Testament three wisdom books, Proverbs, Job, and Ecclesiastes. Another, the Book of Jesus ben Sira (called Sirach in Greek, Ecclesiasticus in Latin and in our translations), is still extant and extremely valuable, but was placed among the Apocrypha.

In the Book of Proverbs we have a number of collections by various writers dating from different times:

1. 1–9 "The Proverbs of Solomon the son of David, king of Israel," a series of connected addresses containing warnings against wickedness and especially against carnal lust, and exhortations to seek wisdom, the most wonderful of all possessions.
2. 10—22:16 "The Proverbs of Solomon," consisting of wise maxims usually in couplet form, entirely different from the first collection.
3. 22:17—24:22 "Words of the Wise," beginning with the exhortation, "Incline thine ear, and hear the words of the wise," mostly in quatrains.
4. 24:23-34 "These also are (sayings) of the Wise," an appendix to the third collection, also in quatrains and longer groups.
5. 25–29 "These also are Proverbs of Solomon, which the men of Hezekiah king of Judah copied." They are mostly in couplets, but also in tristichs, quatrains, or in larger units.
6. 30 "The words of Agur the son of Yakeh of Massa." The first part is tinged by a mild scepticism, the second part contains a number of numerical proverbs.
7. 31:1–9 "The words of King Lemuel of Massa, which his mother taught him," consisting of warnings against women and wine, and of exhortations to righteous administration of justice.
8. 31:10–31 An alphabetical poem in praise of a worthy wife.

The heart of the book is the second collection, "the Proverbs of Solomon," to which were added first "the Words of the Wise" and their appendix (Nos. 3 and 4) and later the other collection of Proverbs of Solomon (No. 5). The last three sections (Nos. 6–8) are

[1] The wisdom of the Babylonians and Assyrians had less immediate influence (see note 4). The Book of Ahikar, partly preserved in Old Aramaic on an Elephantine papyrus and in later versions, hangs together with this Assyrian wisdom. For Ahikar, see *APOT*, II, 715ff. See *ANET*, 427f. for the Old Aramaic.

appendices. To the whole book the first section was prefixed as an introduction; it is the latest in point of time and dates not earlier than the Greek period. No. 3 has been shown to be dependent on the wisdom book of Amenemope, an Egyptian sage.[2]

At the beginning the purpose of the teaching of the sages as well as of this book in particular is stated:

> The Proverbs of Solomon the son of David, king of Israel, (are designed)
>> that one know wisdom and instruction,
>> discern the words of understanding,
>> receive instruction in wise dealing,
>> in righteousness and justice and equity;
>> to give prudence to the simple,
>> to the young man knowledge and discretion;
>> that the wise man hear and increase in learning,
>> and the man of understanding attain unto sound counsels;
>> that one understand a proverb and a figure,
>> the words of the wise and their riddles. (Prov. 1:1–6) [3]

By wisdom the sages meant that sagacity and common sense which enables men to live a happy and a prosperous life. And they taught the young the art of life in brief maxims or long exhortations, by shrewd observations and warm personal appeals. Much of this wisdom is very old and many of the proverbs gathered in these collections had been current among the people for a long time. Their particular form may have been given to them by these sages who were not only collectors but authors. Tradition regarded Solomon as the wisest of the sages and attributed to him 3000 proverbs in which "he spoke of trees, from the cedar that is in Lebanon even unto the hyssop that springs out of the wall: he spoke also of beasts, and of birds, and of creeping things, and of fishes" (1 Ki. 4:32f.).[4] But none of these is preserved. Nevertheless a later age attributed to Solomon at first the second and fifth collections in the

[2] See *ANET*, 421ff. This was first shown by the Egyptologist Adolf Erman in 1924.

[3] If Prov. 1–9 form the introduction to the whole book, then 1:1 does not constitute the title for 1–9 only, but is the beginning of the exposition of the purpose of the proverbs which are given in 10:1ff.

[4] This suggests that there was a book of fables which was attributed to Solomon. This kind of thing is found in Ahikar. The Greek Aesop was stimulated by the eastern fable.

Book of Proverbs, and a still later time even the whole book, although four out of the eight sections are definitely assigned to other authors in their superscriptions. That of the fifth collection (Prov. 25:1): "these also are Proverbs of Solomon, which the men of Hezekiah king of Judah copied out," seems at first to embody a historical tradition. Since the existence of the monarchy is presupposed in 16:12f. and 25:2f. the collection may indeed be preexilic— a compendium made from a larger collection purporting to come from Solomon.

The commonest form of the proverb was the couplet or distich, a verse with two parallel members, in which two things were compared to bring out the likeness, the contrast, or the comparative difference:

> As vinegar to the teeth and as smoke to the eyes,
>> so is the sluggard to them that send him. (10:26)

> A glad heart makes a cheerful countenance,
>> but by sorrow of heart the spirit is broken. (15:13)

> It is better to dwell in the corner of the housetop,
>> than with a contentious woman in a wide house. (21:9)

The tristich is rare:

> As the cold of snow in the time of harvest,
>> so is a faithful messenger to them that send him,
>>> for he refreshes the soul of his masters. (25:13)

But quatrains are frequent:

> A continual dropping in a very rainy day
>> and a contentious woman are alike:
> He that would restrain her restrains the wind,
>> and his right hand encounters oil. (27:15f.)

An example of a five line stanza is:

> To have respect of persons in judgment is not good.
> He that says to the wicked, "Thou art righteous,"
>> peoples shall curse him, nations shall abhor him;
> But to them that rebuke them shall be delight,
>> and a good blessing shall come upon them. (24:23–25)

There are also longer units of six and more lines; the famous description of the drunkard may serve as an illustration:

Who has woe? who has sorrow?
  who has contentions? who has complaining?
Who has wounds without cause?
  who has redness of eyes?
They that tarry long at the wine,
  they that go to try mixed wine.
Look not upon the wine when it is red,
  when it sparkles in the cup,
  when it goes down smoothly:
At the last it bites like a serpent,
  and stings like an adder.
Thine eyes shall behold strange things,
  and thy heart shall utter perverse things.
Yea, thou shalt be as he that lies down in the midst of the sea,
  or as he that lies upon the top of a mast.
"They have stricken me, (shalt thou say) and I was not hurt,
  they have beaten me, and I felt it not:
When shall I awake?
  I will seek it yet again." (23:29–35)

A special form of maxim is represented by the numerical proverbs
which originated from riddles:

For three things the earth trembles,
  and for four, which it cannot bear:
For a servant when he is king,
  and for a fool when he is filled with food;
For an odious woman when she is married,
  and a handmaid that is heir to her mistress. (30:21–23)

The teaching of the wise men dealt with the whole range of life;
with personal affairs, including good manners as well as good morals;
with family relations, including parents, children, and servants; with
social intercourse between friends and enemies, between rich and
poor; with professional and business matters; and with public life
and its interests. There is a wealth of wisdom, of sober and realistic
observation, of sharp epigrammatic characterization, of kindly humor and biting sarcasm, of warm personal exhortation and urgent
appeal that makes the Book of Proverbs a veritable mine of good
counsel for the art of right living. It is a pity that the sages felt so
little the need of grouping their sayings in a systematic manner.

The ideal of the wise man is not high. It is the life of a shrewd, upright man, who knows how to conduct himself wisely so that he may be successful, honored, and happy. The great motive to wise living is always personal happiness. There is no concern about making others happy. Even when the welfare of others is considered, it is always with reference to oneself, as, *e.g.*, in the otherwise so exquisite words:

> Rejoice not when thine enemy falls,
>> and let not thy heart be glad when he is overthrown,
> Lest Yahweh see it, and it displease Him,
>> and He turn away His wrath from him (24:17f.)

or in the famous exhortation:

> If thine enemy be hungry, give him bread to eat;
>> and if he be thirsty, give him water to drink:
> For thou wilt heap coals of fire upon his head,
>> and Yahweh will reward thee. (25:21f.)

Self-interest dominates even these thoughts, as indeed all the counsels of the sages. They never advise goodness for its own sake. Everything is controlled by the idea of selfish gain, whether a good deed is to be done or a virtue to be inculcated, or whether wickedness is to be refrained from. The fundamental principle of morals and religion is that goodness is rewarded, wickedness is punished. The wise will therefore follow the great moral and religious principles in order that he may be happy. The fool will refuse to do so and perish.

The wise men were religious, for they were sure that only thus could they be truly successful and prosperous, honored and happy. But it is significant that they attached little importance in their teaching to the ceremonial law. It is not impossible that it is included in such sayings as,

> He that turns away his ear from hearing the law,
>> even his prayer is an abomination (28:9),

but it is far more probable that the moral law is meant here. The influence of the prophets is strong in the sages. How truly they reflected prophetic thoughts is clear from such maxims as,

The sacrifice of the wicked is an abomination to Yahweh,
> but the prayer of the upright is His delight. (15:8)

By mercy and truth iniquity is atoned for,
  and by the fear of Yahweh men depart from evil. (16:6)

To do righteousness and justice
  is more acceptable to Yahweh than sacrifice. (21:3)

The sacrifice of the wicked is an abomination,
  how much more when he brings it to atone for wickedness! (21:27)

He that covers his transgressions shall not prosper,
  but whoso confesses and forsakes them shall obtain mercy. (28:13)

Prophetic influence is apparent also in the insistence on the inner
man, the character which is to be striven for; the sages emphasized
moral self-discipline and the training of the disposition and will.

The spirit of man is the lamp of Yahweh,
  searching all his innermost parts. (20:27)

Who can say, I have made my heart clean,
  I am pure from my sin? (20:9)

All the ways of a man are clean in his own eyes,
  but Yahweh weighs the spirits. (16:2; 21:2)

The wise men tried to inculcate the principles of a worthy life by
glorifying wisdom as its secret and source. This is especially done
in the first part (1–9), where in beautiful paragraphs wisdom is
personified and shown to be the supreme principle in creation as well
as in the life of man. True living consists therefore in remaining in
harmony with this principle which pervades the universe and reveals
itself to the mind of man. Prov. 1:7; 9:10 declare that "the fear of the
Lord is the beginning (or the chief part) of wisdom." [5]

Agur had tried to understand the secrets of the world only to
come to this conclusion,

I have wearied myself, O God, I have wearied myself, O God,
  and I am consumed.
Surely I am more brutish than any man,
  and have not the understanding of a man;
And have not learned wisdom,
  neither have I the knowledge of the Holy One.

[5] In Job 28:28 religion ("the fear of the Lord") and wisdom are identified.

> Who has ascended up into heaven, and descended?
> Who has gathered the wind in his fists?
> Who has bound the waters in his garment?
> Who has established all the ends of the earth?
> What is his name, and what is his son's name?
> If thou knowest? (Prov. 30:1–4)

No man knows. But God has revealed it in His word,

> Every word of God is tried,
>   a shield for them that take refuge in Him.
> Add thou not to His words,
>   lest He reprove thee, and thou be found a liar. (30:5f.)

To Agur the Holy Scriptures are the source of revelation, but ordinarily the wise men think of God Himself directly revealing wisdom.

It was not enough for them to emphasize the divine source of wisdom. They speculated about wisdom itself, its origin and its relation to man. They thought of wisdom as a divinely created personality which existed before the creation of the world. In an exquisite passage wisdom says,

> Yahweh formed me first of His ways,
>   before His works of old.
> I was set up from everlasting,
>   from the beginning, before the earth was.
> When there were no depths, I was brought forth,
>   when there were no fountains, abounding with water.
> Before the mountains were settled,
>   before the hills was I brought forth:
> While as yet He had not made the earth, nor the fields,
>   nor the beginning of the dust of the world.
> When He established the heavens, I was there:
>   when He set a circle upon the face of the deep,
> When He made firm the skies above,
>   when He fastened the fountains of the deep,
> When He gave to the sea its bound,
>   that the waters should not transgress His commandment,
> When He marked out the foundations of the earth;
>   then I was by Him, as a master workman;
> And I was daily His delight,
>   rejoicing always before Him,
> Rejoicing in His habitable earth;
>   and my delight was with the sons of men. (8:22–31)

Before the creation wisdom existed, and at the creation she was with God as a master workman, the pervading principle of the world. From God she comes down to plead with men, to win the simple and foolish for the true life, to woo them and tempt them by her own beauty and charm that they may love her and thus find life. For wisdom is personified as a wondrously beautiful woman who allures and tempts young men.

> Wisdom cries aloud in the street,
>   she utters her voice in the broad places.
> She cries in the chief place of concourse,
>   at the entering in of the gates,
> In the city she utters her words. (1:20f.)

She has wonderful gifts to bestow, the glory of life is in her.

> Unto you, O men, I call,
>   and my voice is to the sons of men.
> O ye simple, understand wisdom,
>   and ye fools, be of an understanding heart. . . .
> For whoso finds me finds life,
>   and shall obtain favor of Yahweh.
> But he that misses me wrongs himself,
>   all they that hate me love death. (8:4f., 35f.)

What are the blandishments of sin, which is also personified as a beautiful woman, Madam Folly, and all her temptations to one who has seen the glory of the ideal in the wondrous beauty of wisdom, which draws him with irresistible attraction to righteousness and life! Here the sages presented a conception that perhaps was suggested by Egyptian thought.[6]

The Book of Proverbs was the work of men, who assumed that the righteous and wicked are rewarded according to their deserts. But the validity of this belief was challenged and denied by the author of the Poem of Job who could not reconcile it with the facts of life. What heart-burnings it caused to many men who had tried their best to fulfill the commandments of God, when suddenly disaster, misfortune, disease came upon them! The righteous is favored by God, he dies in good old age, only the wicked is over-

---

[6] Compare Maat—truth personified as a goddess.

taken by calamity and cut off in the midst of the years. So they reasoned, and then they would search, and pray to God to help them search their secret hearts to see if there were any hidden sins for which He was punishing them. And if they were not restored to health and prosperity, their friends would declare that they after all had been sinners although they seemed to be righteous, for God who tries the heart knew their wickedness and punished them for it. There was only one cause of suffering: sin! [7]

But now there arose a man who had felt in his spirit the suffering of these righteous souls, had tasted the bitterness of death that is in this dogma, and his heart revolted at the injustice of it. He wrote (*ca.* 400 B.C.) his immortal poem and every word that he wrote had "been fiercely furnaced in the blast of a soul that has struggled in earnest," for he wrote the history of a soul that had suffered and battled, despaired and hoped until it finally gained peace. The story of an ancient eastern magnate (possibly a historical figure originally) who underwent great affliction, served this author's purpose, much as the medieval tale of Dr. Faust served Goethe's. This story made it very clear that Job was absolutely blameless. Yahweh Himself gave him this testimony, "there is none like him on earth, a blameless and upright man, one that fears God and turns from evil." But Satan questioned the unselfishness of his piety, "does Job fear God for nought?" Is there any disinterested religion on earth? Would Job be so profoundly religious, if his devotion were not rewarded by prosperity? Would he still be true to his religion, if he lost everything he possessed, his children included, yea, even his health? If he were afflicted with such a horrible disease as leprosy or elephantiasis, which brands him in the eyes of the world as a wicked sinner? The old story told how Job stood the terrible test. He did not renounce God, and was therefore doubly rewarded for his loyalty in the end.[8]

The author of the poem however was not satisfied with Job's absolute submission as told in the older tale. He introduced three friends Eliphaz, Bildad, and Zophar, who came to visit Job and com-

[7] The tenacity of this doctrine is seen in the Gospels, where Jesus still has to fight against it (cf. John 9:2f.).

[8] The old prose story is contained in Job 1—2:10; 42:10-17.

fort him, thereby creating the possibility of introducing a dialogue.
When they found no words to express their grief Job revealed the
depths of his despair in an opening elegy, in which he went so far
as to curse the day of his birth (3:1ff.).

This elicits a debate, for the friends cannot permit such an irreligious utterance to go unchallenged. Each speaks at length and in
turn assails Job, and to each Job replies. There are thus three cycles
of speeches, which are contained in chs. 3–14; 15–21; 22–27. The third
cycle has suffered damage: parts of the third speech of Bildad, which
is unduly short, and of the third speech of Zophar, which is missing,
may be wrongly attributed to Job in 26:5–14; 27:7–10, 13–23.

The friends represent the accepted teaching that all suffering is
ultimately due to sin. But they had known Job too well to believe
that his terrible suffering could be the result of fearful sins, it could
not be punitive. So they did not question his piety, but tried to comfort him by pointing out the good intentions that God had with
him in this discipline. He need not despair,

> Is not thy fear (of God) thy confidence,
>   the integrity of thy ways thy hope?
> Remember, I pray thee, who (ever) perished, being innocent?
>   or where were the upright cut off?
> According as I have seen, they that plough iniquity,
>   and sow mischief, reap the same.
> By the breath of God they perish,
>   and by the blast of His anger are they consumed. (4:6–9)

No man is sinless, no mortal is just before God (4:17). Let Job remember that, and understand God's gracious plan with him.

> Behold, happy is the man whom God corrects:
>   Therefore despise not the chastening of the Almighty.
> For He makes sore, and binds up,
>   He wounds, and His hands make whole.
> He will deliver thee in six troubles,
>   Yea, in seven no harm shall touch thee. (5:17–19)

This suffering is merely a disciplinary, pedagogical means of God,
intended to refine Job and to make him all the happier afterwards.
So they gave him this advice:

> But as for me, I would seek unto God,
>   and to God would I commit my cause. (5:8)

If thou seek diligently unto God,
   and make thy supplication to the Almighty;
If thou art pure and upright,
   surely, then will He answer thy prayer,
   and compensate thee with the portion due to thy righteousness,
And though thy beginning is small,
   thy latter end He will greatly increase. (8:5–7)

But when Job, stung to the quick by the words of his friends from whom he had expected a different kind of comfort, hotly resents the implications, they charge him with wickedness. His desperate, blasphemous words have revealed to them his true character. And Zophar says to him,

For thou sayest, "My walk is pure,
   and I am clean in Thine eyes."
But oh that God would speak,
   and open His lips against thee,
And that He would show thee the secrets of wisdom!
   for He is manifold in understanding.
Then thou wouldst know that God exacts of thee
   less than thine iniquity deserves. (11:4–6)

And similarly Eliphaz,

When thine iniquity teaches thy mouth,
   and thou choosest the tongue of the crafty,
Thine own mouth condemns thee, and not I,
   yea, thine own lips testify against thee. (15:5f.)

Only in repentance can Job find God's grace returning, let him acknowledge his guilt and he will be saved.

If thou purge thy heart,
   and stretch out thy hands towards Him;
If thou put the iniquity which is in thy hand far away,
   and let not unrighteousness dwell in thy tents:
Surely then shalt thou lift up thy face without spot,
   yea, thou shalt be steadfast and not fear.
For then shalt thou forget thy misery,
   thou shalt remember it as by-gone days. (11:13–16)

At first the friends emphasized the disciplinary, corrective character of suffering, later they insisted on its punitive quality. There is no further development of this theory.

Job shared, of course, at the outset the belief of the friends. While he was still well and happy, it was easy for him to believe that piety and prosperity, sin and suffering go together. But now that he himself has been afflicted, he has in his conscience such a strong opponent of this theory that he denies its truth absolutely. He does suffer, but he knows that he is innocent. To regard his suffering as merely disciplinary and purifying is absurd, it is far too horrible for that, soon he will die the death of ignominy. He does not assert that he is sinless, for no mortal is without sin. But to make man so frail and then punish him for his mortal frailty is unjust.

> If I have sinned, what can I do
>   to Thee, O Thou watcher of men?
> Why hast Thou set me as a mark for Thee,
>   so that I am a burden to Thee?
> And why dost Thou not pardon my transgression
>   and take away my guilt? (7:20f.)

He agrees that no man can be just before God. But the reason for this is that God sets the standard of righteousness: what He declares to be right is right. And if He declares that a man is wrong, as He does with Job, who can hinder Him? He is altogether arbitrary, and He is so wise that no man can prove Him to be wrong, for He can easily entangle a man by His questions into an admission of guilt, even if he is innocent.

Of a truth, I know that it is so:
  but how can a man be just (in an argument) with God?
If he should desire to contend with Him,
  he cannot answer Him one of a thousand.
However wise in heart, and mighty in strength,
  who has (ever) hardened himself against Him with impunity? (9:1-4)

If it is a matter of strength, lo, He is mighty!
  and if it is a matter of justice, who will arraign Him?
Though I am righteous, my own mouth shall condemn me,
  though I am blameless, it shall prove me perverse. (9:19f.)

Job readily admits that God is omnipotent and omniscient, as his friends had declared again and again, but he maintains that His omnipotence and omniscience are not controlled by morality, for

He destroys the righteous and wicked alike and makes no moral distinctions.

> It is all one, therefore I say,
>   He destroys the blameless and the wicked.
> If a scourge slay suddenly,
>   He mocks at the calamity of the innocent.
> The earth is given into the hand of the wicked,
>   He covers the faces of its judges.
> If it is not He, who then is it? (9:22–24)

God has become Job's enemy, He wants to put him in the wrong.

> I know that Thou wilt not hold me innocent.
> I have to be guilty,
>   why then do I labor in vain?
> If I wash myself white as snow,
>   and make my hands never so clean,
> Yet wilt Thou plunge me into the mire,
>   that my own clothes abhor me. (9:28–31)

And yet Job longs to argue his case with God, but that is out of the question.

> For He is not a man as I am, that I should answer Him,
>   that we should come together in judgment.
> Oh, that there were an umpire betwixt us,
>   who might lay his hand upon us both!
> Let Him take His rod away from me,
>   and let not His terror make me afraid:
> Then would I speak without fearing
>   that He is not honest toward me. (9:32–35)

He would ask God why He is persecuting him so terribly, why it is

> That Thou inquirest after mine iniquity,
>   and searchest after my sin,
> Although Thou knowest that I am not wicked. (10:6f.)

Once uttered, this desire to argue his case in open debate with God grows stronger. Job would gladly die, if he only had that chance. And though God should slay him when he dared to argue so fearlessly with Him, the conviction "that a godless man shall not come before Him" (13:16) would be his salvation. But he makes this reservation,

> Only do not two things to me,
>   then will I not hide myself from Thy face:
> Withdraw Thy hand far from me,
>   and let not Thy terror make me afraid.
> Then call Thou, and I will answer,
>   or let me speak, and answer Thou me. (13:20-22)

The friends seek the reason of the suffering in Job. Job seeks it in God. The friends declare that Job is a sinner. Job declares that God is arbitrary, unjust, immoral. The root of the matter is not in him but in God. His language does not stop short of blasphemy.

This is the God of his present experience, unjust and cruel. But there comes into his reasoning a new element: he remembers the God of his past experience and thinks of the wonderful, intimate communion he had with God who showed Himself full of justice and love. A strange conflict of indescribable pathos arises in his soul between the God of the past and the God of the present. Once before, when he spoke of the brief span of life allotted to him before he should go to the land of darkness and death, the little thought had slipped in, that God would come to look for him, but then it would be too late.

> For now shall I lie down in the dust,
>   and Thou wilt seek me diligently, but I shall not be. (7:21)

True enough, Job in the bitterness of his soul interprets his past experience, which is very real to him, in the light of his present experience: God has taken such infinite pains to fashion him and has showed such gracious kindness and love only in order to hide His sinister design, so that He might strike a more deadly blow, when at last he had lulled Job into a sense of security.

> Thou hast granted me life and lovingkindness,
>   and Thy care has preserved my spirit.
> yet these things Thou didst hide in Thy heart,
>   I know that this was in Thy mind:
> If I sin Thou wouldst mark me
>   and not acquit me from mine iniquity.
> If I were wicked, woe unto me,
>   and if I were righteous, yet should I not lift up my head. (10:12-15)

He had been mistaken in the past, when he thought God was just and loving, for God was all the time cherishing a bitter hatred against him and His kindness to him was only a mask for His malicious purpose.

But Job never refers to this interpretation again, the memory of the blessed time of communion had kindled afresh his old conviction of God's righteousness and it reasserts itself most strongly. There is an instance of this, although he himself is not aware of it, in his contention that God cannot be pleased with unjust defenses:

> Will ye speak unrighteously for God,
>   and talk deceitfully for Him?
> Will ye show partiality to Him?
>   will ye be special pleaders for God?
> Would it be well, if He should search you out?
>   or will ye deceive Him as one deceives a man?
> He will surely reprove you,
>   if ye show secretly partiality. (13:7-9)

Here is the old God of truth and righteousness again, although Job does not realize it. But as the struggle goes on in his soul, he comes to feel dimly that God's present attitude toward him does not express His true character. His anger must be a passing mood and so he prays,

> Oh that Thou wouldst hide me in Sheol,
>   that Thou wouldst keep me secret, until Thy wrath is past,
>   that Thou wouldst appoint me a set time, and remember me!
> If a man might die, and live again,
>   all the days of my warfare would I wait,
>   till my release should come.
> Thou wouldst call, and I would answer Thee:
>   Thou wouldst have a desire to the work of Thy hands. (14:13-15)

When Job is overwhelmed again by his unbearable pain, however, he sees in God once more his cruel foe. The conflict in his soul is most moving to behold. He feels very strongly that he will soon die: die innocently, for his death is really a brutal murder committed by God. But as he thinks of his blood so innocently shed, the old, ingrained belief in the righteous heavenly avenger of innocent blood asserts itself so strongly that he appeals to God—against God.

> O earth, cover not my blood,
>   and let my cry have no resting place.

> Even now, behold, my witness is in heaven,
> > and He that vouches for me is on high.
> My friends scoff at me:
> > but mine eye pours out tears unto God,
> That He would maintain the right of a man with God,
> > and of a son of man with his neighbor! (16:18–21)

A strange dualism appears here in Job's thought of God, the God of righteousness over against the God of arbitrary cruelty. One who knows Job will vindicate him. This vindicator must be God Himself, for He is the author of his sufferings and knows therefore that he is innocent. God is arbitrary and cruel indeed, but this very fact shows that the reason of his suffering is in God and not in Job. He can find no refuge with his friends; they will not believe in his innocence, so he is driven in his despair to God, for he cannot get away from the conviction that God is after all truthful. Thus he confidently expects that God will bear witness to him because of His truthfulness. He comes to hope in his vindication; it cannot be far off. Soon he will die, but no matter, God will vindicate him at his grave. How it will be done, he does not say; perhaps he does not know, but he is certain that it will be done. And he is certain also that he himself will see this vindication. The very thought of the vision of God consumes his heart with longing.

> I know that my redeemer lives,
> > and at last He will stand up upon the dust:
> And after (?) my skin has been thus destroyed,
> > then without (?) my flesh shall I see God;
> Whom I shall see on my side,
> > and my eyes shall behold, and not another.
> My heart is consumed within me. (19:25–27) [9]

Job is convinced that God must be righteous in the end! With this the problem, as far as it pertains to Job personally, has received its answer, for Job now knows that God is righteous in spite of His

[9] The text and the interpretation of this famous passage are uncertain. But that Job did not assert his belief in his resurrection or his immortality or prophesy of the Messiah may be safely assumed, for in that case he would have worked this out more fully. Fragments of two manuscripts of Job from Cave IV at Qumran do not give this passage. Cave XI produced fragments of a Targum (Aramaic translation) of Job, of which mention is made in the Talmud.

seeming arbitrariness and that He will acknowledge Job's integrity.

But the problem concerns not only Job but righteous men everywhere, and now the more general question of the problem of the righteous is discussed. Over against the insistence of the friends that the fate of the wicked is fearful, Job proves conclusively that the facts contradict this theory and shows that the wicked prosper and that God does not do anything at all to indicate that He is truly moral in His dealings with men.

> Wherefore do the wicked live,
>   become old, yea, wax mighty in power?
> Their seed is established with them in their sight,
>   and their offspring before their eyes.
> Their houses are safe from fear,
>   neither is the rod of God upon them. (21:7-9)

They are prosperous, lead a life of happiness, and do not care for God.

> They say to God, "Depart from us,
>   for we desire not the knowledge of Thy ways.
> What is the Almighty, that we should serve Him?
>   and what profit should we have, if we pray to Him?" (21:14f.)

The argument that the punishment of the wicked is visited upon their children Job tosses impatiently aside, for to him it does not meet the real question.

> How oft is it that the lamp of the wicked is put out?
>   that their calamity comes upon them?
>   that He distributes sorrows in His anger? . . .
> Let Him not reserve his punishment for his children,
>   let Him recompense it to himself, that he may know it,
> Let his own eyes see his destruction,
>   and let himself drink of the wrath of the Almighty!
> For what cares he for his house after him,
>   when the number of his months is cut off? (21:17, 19-21)

As Job thinks of God's injustice in His dealings with men, his high hope fades, his confidence vanishes. Again he cries out,

> Oh that I knew where I might find Him!
>   that I might come even to His seat!

> I would set my cause in order before Him,
>   and fill my mouth with arguments.
> I would know the words which He would answer me,
>   and understand what He would say to me.
> Would He contend with me in the greatness of His power?
>   if only He would give heed to me,
> He would establish justice and would reason with me,
>   so that I should be delivered forever from judgment.
> Behold, I go forward, but He is not there,
>   and backward, but I cannot perceive Him,
> On the left hand I seek Him, but I cannot behold Him,
>   I turn to the right hand, but I cannot see Him. (23:3-9)

The conclusion of the debate is followed by independent discourses of Job in chs. 27-28, 29-31. The first of these concludes in ch. 28 with a praise of wisdom (cf. p. 344), in a manner that reminds one of Proverbs 1-9. The second begins with a noble elegy in ch. 29-30, and continues with the magnificent "oath of clearance" in ch. 31, that high watermark of Old Testament ethics. Here Job affirms the purity and integrity of his conduct, and dwells on his social-mindedness.

> If I have despised the cause of my man-servant
>   or of my maid-servant, when they contended with me;
> What then shall I do when God takes vengeance,
>   and when He visits, what shall I answer Him?
> Did not He that made me in the womb make him?
>   and did not One fashion us in the womb?
> If I have withheld aught that the poor desired,
>   or have caused the eyes of the widow to fail,
> Or have eaten my morsel alone,
>   and the fatherless has not eaten of it . . .
> If I have seen any perish for want of clothing,
>   or that the needy had no covering,
> If his loins have not blessed me,
>   and if he has not been warmed with the fleece of my sheep;
> If I have lifted up my hand against the fatherless,
>   because I saw my help in the gate:
> Then let my shoulder fall from the shoulder-blade,
>   and mine arm be broken from the bone. . . .
> If I have rejoiced at the destruction of him that hated me,
>   or was triumphant when evil met him:

Yea, I have not suffered my mouth to sin
  by asking his life with a curse. . . .
If after the manner of men I have covered my transgressions,
  by hiding mine iniquity in my bosom,
Because I feared the great multitude,
  and the contempt of families terrified me,
  so that I kept silence and went not out of the door—
                          (31:13-17, 19-22, 29f., 33f.)

Finally Job flings this bold challenge at God:

Oh that I had one to hear me!—
  Lo, here is my signature, let the Almighty answer me!—
And that I had the indictment which mine adversary has written!
Surely I would carry it upon my shoulder,
  I would bind it unto me as a crown:
I would declare unto Him the number of my steps,
  as a prince would I go near unto Him! (31:35-37) [10]

There is the defiance of a titan in these words.

And now God appears and answers out of a whirlwind. He over-
awes Job with His terrible majesty and flings question after question
at him, not one of which he can answer:

Who is this that darkens counsel
  by words without knowledge?
Gird up now thy loins like a man,
  for I will demand of thee and declare thou unto Me.
Where wast thou when I laid the foundations of the earth?
  Declare, if thou hast understanding!
Who determined its measures? if thou knowest!
  or who stretched the line upon it?
Upon what were its foundations fastened?
  or who laid its cornerstone?
When the morning stars sang together,
  and all the sons of God shouted for joy? (38:2-7)

What does Job know about the mighty work of creation and the
marvelous wonders of the world of nature?

Who shut up the sea with doors,
  when it broke forth and issued out of the womb? (38:8)

[10] These verses must be slightly misplaced; they are the appropriate conclusion of Job's monologue.

Hast thou commanded the morning since thy days began,
and caused the dayspring to know its place? (38:12)

Hast thou entered into the springs of the sea?
or hast thou walked in the recesses of the deep? (38:16)

What does he know of the realm of death, of the home of light and
of darkness, of the treasuries of the snow and the hail, or the mysterious coming of the fog and of the rain and the lightning and thunder?
Does he control the forces of the sky, or regulate the constellations'
ordered march, or give commands to all the clouds of rain (38:17–
38)?

Again, what does Job know of the wonders of God's animal
creation? Does he care for the lions? And

Who provides for the raven his prey,
when his young ones cry unto God
and grow faint for lack of food? (38:39–41)

What does Job know of the secrets of the mountain goat, the wild
ass, the wild ox, the horse, the hawk, and the eagle?

Is it by thy wisdom that the hawk soars,
and stretches her wings to the south?
Is it at thy command that the eagle mounts up,
and makes her nest on high? (39:1–12, 26–30)

How can Job dare to criticize God's government of the world and
declare it to be immoral, when he knows so little about it? when he
understands not even one of the mighty riddles of the world? He
thinks that God has nothing else to do but to plague and attack him;
as if he were God's only care. In his self-centered view he thinks
that the whole world revolves around man and everything is
created only for him. But God causes it

To rain on a land *where no man is,*
and on the steppe *where no mortal dwells,*
To satisfy the waste and desolate ground,
and to cause the tender grass to spring forth. (38:26f.)

Likewise many wild animals will never be tamed and be useful
to man.

> Will the wild-ox be content to serve thee?
>   or will he abide by thy crib?
> Canst thou bind with thongs his neck?
>   or will he harrow thy furrows after thee? (39:9f.)

How insignificant is man in view of the vast complexity of the world, and how ignorant is he about its mysteries! But if God's dealings with the world of nature are so mysterious, it is presumptuous to charge Him with immorality in view of the mysteries of the world of men! If the faultfinder thinks that he can rule the world better, more wisely and righteously than God, let him but try it.

> Deck thyself now with excellency and dignity,
>   and array thyself with honor and majesty,
> Pour forth the overflowings of thine anger,
>   and look upon every one that is proud and abase him,
> And look upon every one that is proud and bring him low,
>   and tread down the wicked where they stand.
> Hide them in the dust together,
>   bind their faces in the hidden place,
> Then will I also confess of thee
>   that thine own arm can save thee. (40:10–14)

The great problem of human suffering grows small when it is seen in relation to the whole, when man understands that he is not the center of the universe around whom everything revolves. Before the mighty work of creation and God's wonderful rule of the world of nature, Job is made to feel his own insignificance, becomes conscious of the arrogance of his selfish claims, and confesses,

> I know that Thou canst do all things,
>   and that no purpose of Thine can be restrained.
> Therefore have I uttered that which I understood not,
>   things too wonderful for me, which I knew not.
> I had heard of Thee by the hearing of the ear,
>   but now mine eye sees Thee,
> Wherefore I loathe (my words)
>   and repent in dust and ashes. (40:4f.; 42:2, 3b, 5f.)

God had not answered Job's question as to the reason of his suffering at all. The problem of suffering is as dark as before. And yet in spite of this Job gains peace. He does not know and does not need to know why he suffers, for he has been accorded a vision of God.

The very fact that God has appeared to him, the vision itself is the solution for him. In the course of the debate Job had declared that God does not appear to a wicked man. God's appearance to him implies therefore his vindication. And indeed God did not charge Job with sin; He only pointed out to him his error and presumption, but in appearing to him He showed that Job was still in favor with Him. Job learns that a man may suffer from the most horrible disease, and yet be in favor with God! True piety needs no outward attestation of health, happiness, and prosperity; it does not even need the approval of the righteous, it should rest solely on the witness of conscience. And if problems come that would drive man to despair, let him but trust his own inner voice in the full confidence that, appearances and feelings notwithstanding, God is on his side as his friend. For God is righteous and governs the world righteously, however mysterious His rule may be.

The conclusion of the story of the visit of the three friends, which the author had introduced to make a dialogue possible, is then given (42:7-9). They are rebuked by Yahweh, and told to bring sacrifice and ask Job to intercede for them. It was thus the purpose of the author to take Job's part in the debate. The book then is ended with some folk tale material about how Job's prosperity was restored. "Yahweh blessed the latter end of Job more than his beginning." This can hardly be the original continuation of the story of Job from which 1:1—2:10 was taken, but represents collateral Job legend. In any case it provided the happy ending that ancients liked, as well as moderns do. The poet himself, however, had transcended this solution.

Later generations did not grasp the power of Job's thought nor could they understand his courage; they thought he was presumptuous and considered himself righteous before God. This gave offense; so also did the inability of the friends to answer him convincingly. It seemed incredible to a later poet that Job should have won the debate. So he introduced a new contender named Elihu and added speeches by him (32-37). But Elihu says little that is new, virtually all of it had been said before; he only formulates it more effectively at times. But his speeches interrupt the connection between Job's final challenge (31:35-37) and God's appearance

(38:1ff.). In order to get the original impression and feel the power of the poem we must skip Elihu's speeches, and go directly to the appearance and answer of God to Job.

Another writer inserted in the independent discourses of Job, a beautiful poem on wisdom (28), already mentioned above. In it the question is discussed, whence does wisdom come and where is its home? Only God knows the way to it, only He knows its place. Man does not know. The inference to be drawn is: how then can he hope to understand the mysteries of God's rule?

The splendid pictures of nature in God's answer incited a poet to add vivid descriptions of other remarkable creatures: the ostrich, hippopotamus, and crocodile (39:13–18; 40:15—41:34).

Perhaps a century or more later than the author of Job (*ca.* 300–250 B.C.),[11] another wise man looked on life and its ceaseless round of tasks and inquired into the meaning of it all. It was not only the problem of the suffering of the righteous but of the whole of life that baffled him as he tried to find out its real significance; all his thinking brought to him no answer to his question. He has left a record of his search in the book called "Koheleth" in the Hebrew and by the Greek translators "Ecclesiastes." The word is translated in our Bible as "The Preacher." Originally the name of an office (convener of the *qāhāl* or "assembly"), it came to be used also for the incumbent. The book could be entitled "On the Meaning of Life." It contains a number of discourses, which are not arranged in order nor connected with one another; they contain observations, reflections, and wise sayings by a keen observer and brilliant speaker, who was neither a profound nor a systematic philosopher but merely an old man of much experience and common sense.

He had observed the occurrences in nature and in human life. They were ever the same. One generation of men comes and goes, another comes only to go again. The sun rises and sets, only to rise and set again. The wind blows and circles around, coming back again to its starting point. The rivers run into the sea, day

[11] Fragments of an Ecclesiastes Scroll, believed to date from 200–150 B.C. were found in Cave IV at Qumran, and published by James Muilenburg in 1954. The date of Ecclesiastes therefore cannot be brought down too low.

after day, year after year, yet the sea is never full, and the rivers
well up again from the subterranean ocean to flow again into the sea.

> All things are toiling, no man can speak (of them all),
> The eye is not satisfied with seeing,
> The ear is not filled with hearing. (1:8)

And yet it is ever the same: a ceaseless round of toil and labor with
no progress or aim.

> That which has been is that which shall be,
> And that which has been done is that which shall be done,
> And there is no new thing under the sun. (1:9)

If any one thinks that there is something new, it is only because no
record of it was made in former days so that it has been forgotten.
There is really nothing new, it is always the same. But what then
can be the meaning of this never ending performance? None whatever. Life has no goal and no meaning!

> Vanity of vanities, says Koheleth, all is vanity!

It is not the assertion of a young man in a pessimistic mood, but the
result of long thought on the part of a man who had made as wide an
investigation as possible. It is with profound resignation that the
result is given: "All is vanity and a chasing after wind!" Koheleth
had had unusual opportunities for observing life, and being gifted
with a high degree of intelligence he had probed life in all directions. In order to make his teaching more effective he impersonated
Solomon, for nobody could make the test more complete than this
wisest of all sages, this richest of all kings. He tried to solve the
problem of life, driven thereto by an irrepressible impulse which God
had implanted in his heart as in that of all men, the desire to know
and understand. He observed and learned, but the more he learned,
the sadder he grew.

> I perceived that this also was a chasing after wind. For in much wisdom
> is much vexation, and increase of knowledge increases pain. (1:18)

He tested the pleasures of the world and all the sources of man's
happiness, he undertook great works, built houses and vineyards
and parks with all that belonged to them, kept a large retinue of

servants, had many herds and flocks, got male and female singers and the delights of the sons of men.

> And whatsoever mine eyes desired I kept not from them: I withheld not my heart from any joy, for my heart rejoiced because of all my labor; and this was my portion from all my labor. (2:10)

And then?

> Then I looked on all the works that my hands had wrought, and on the labor that I had labored to do; and behold, all was vanity and a chasing after wind, and there was no profit under the sun! (2:11)

The one thought that takes for him the meaning out of life, that makes wisdom of little value, robs work of its joy, and strips wealth of its power is the thought of death:

> I perceived that one event happens to them all, and I said in my heart, As it happens to the fool so will it happen also to me; and why was I then more wise? How the wise man dies even as the fool! So I hated life, because the work that is wrought under the sun was grievous to me; for all is vanity and a chasing after wind. (2:14ff.)

Nevertheless Koheleth did not throw away life and advise suicide, for to him too, "light is sweet and it is pleasant for the eyes to see the sun" (11:7) and "a living dog is better than a dead lion" (9:4); nor did he scorn wisdom, for he saw that it had an advantage over folly (2:13), and he never maintained that it made no practical difference whether one was a fool or a sage; nor did he despise work, for he had felt too keenly the joy and satisfaction it brings (2:10); nor did he refuse to enjoy wealth and all the pleasures and comfort it bestows. But neither wisdom nor work nor wealth are real ends, the meaning of life is in none of them. For the wise man has the same fate as the fool; the fruit of one's work one must leave to one who has not worked for it and who is perhaps a fool (2:18ff.); one's wealth one may lose by an unlucky adventure (5:13ff.) or one may not have the capacity to enjoy one's riches and honor (6:1ff.).

This is a topsy-turvy world, in which

> The race is not to the swift, nor the battle to the strong, neither yet bread to the wise, nor yet riches to the men of understanding, nor yet favor to men of skill; but time and chance overtake them all. (9:11)

Men are not rewarded according to their deserts. Morality does not control the course of the world.

I saw under the sun, in the place of justice: wickedness; and in the place where the righteous should have been: the wicked (3:16). And again I saw all the oppressions that were done under the sun: and, behold, the tears of such as were oppressed, and they had no comforter, and on the side of their oppressors there was power. (4:1)

There was no just government in the land, the king was capricious and tyrannical and the various officials were corrupt (5:8f.). Righteous men perished and wicked men prospered (7:15). Righteousness did not insure happiness and wickedness did not bring punishment:

There are righteous men to whom it happens according to the work of the wicked; again there are wicked men to whom it happens according to the work of the righteous. (8:14)

There is no moral government in this world. God's rule is not according to righteousness, it is so full of mystery that no man will ever understand it, "although he see no sleep with his eyes day or night." From his fate man can never tell whether God loves or hates him (8:16—9:1). Koheleth did not protest and rebel against this lack of morality in the world. He simply accepted the facts of life as they were, and tried to understand them again and again but all in vain. The greatest riddle to him was death, the common fate of all.

To all there is one event, to the righteous and to the wicked, to the good (and to the bad), to the clean and to the unclean, to him that sacrifices and to him that does not sacrifice; as is the good, so is the sinner, he that swears, as he that fears an oath. This is an evil in all that is done under the sun, that there is one event to all. (9:2f.)

Koheleth knew of the hope that was entertained by some that man would rise again, but he could not believe it.

The misery of man is great upon him, for he knows not that which shall be; for who can tell him how it shall be? (8:7)
That which befalls the sons of men befalls the beasts; the same fate befalls them: as the one dies, so dies the other; yea, they all have one breath; and man has no preëminence above the beasts: for all is vanity. All go to the same place, all are of the dust, and all turn to dust again. Who knows of the spirit of man whether it goes upward, and of the spirit of the beast whether it goes downward to the earth? (3:19f.)

Life to him was bounded by the grave. He had no hope of the future either for the individual or for the nation or for the world.

The Messianic hope with its splendid dream of future national glory was not for him for he was not a nationalist but a cosmopolitan sage. The vision of the regeneration of the world never came to him, for his outlook was individualistic and self-centered. The hope of a resurrection or of immortality he could not make his own, partly from intellectual sincerity, partly from a lack of that deep spiritual passion which made men in his day conquer death in the victorious assurance that their communion with God must be endless no matter what happened. He had no warm, personal faith in God, for God was to him not the living and loving personality, full of righteousness and zeal that He had been to the prophets and to the author of Job. He was not a God with whom man could enter into intimate relation and communion. He had grown distant, He was the ruler of the world and of men, but His government of the world was not that of a righteous God. Koheleth did not deny His existence, but he did deny His moral character: He was inscrutable and His ways were past finding out. No man could understand Him, although man must ever try to do so.

I have seen the travail which God has given to the sons of men to be exercised therewith. He has made everything appropriate in its time: also He has put ignorance in their heart, so that man cannot find out the work that God has done from the beginning even to the end. (3:10f.)

As thou knowest not what is the way of the spirit into the bones in the womb of her that is with child, even so thou knowest not the work of God who makes everything. (11:5)

God has fixed the world order, He has predetermined all events, and no matter what man may do he cannot change them.

For everything there is a fixed season, and an appointed time for every occurrence under heaven. There is a time to be born, and a time to die; a time to plant, and a time to uproot. (3:1f.)

I know that, whatsoever God does, it shall be forever: nothing can be put to it, nor anything taken from it. (3:14)

Consider the work of God: for who can make that straight, which He has made crooked? (7:13)

It is of no use to worry over this and to toil in order to change the unchangeable.

What profit has the worker in that wherein he toils? (3:9)

In the day of prosperity be joyful, and in the day of adversity consider that God has made the one as well as the other, to the end that man should not find out anything that shall be after him. (7:14)

Therefore a man should take life as it is and make the most of it as long as he lives:

There is nothing better for a man than that he should eat and drink and make his soul enjoy good in his labor. (2:24)

> Go thy way, eat thy bread with joy,
> And drink thy wine with a merry heart,
> For God has already accepted thy works.
> Let thy garments be always white,
> And let not thy head lack oil.
> Enjoy life with the wife whom thou lovest
> All the days of thy life of vanity
> Which He has given thee under the sun,[12]

for that is thy portion in life, and in thy labor wherein thou laborest under the sun. Whatsoever thou canst afford with thy substance do, for there is no work, nor planning, nor knowledge, nor wisdom in Sheol, whither thou goest. (9:7–10)

Koheleth advises the young men of his time in the famous passage:

> Rejoice, O young man, in thy youth,
>   and let thy heart cheer thee in the days of thy youth,
> And walk in the ways of thy heart,
>   and in the sight of thine eyes.
> And remove vexation from thy heart,
>   and put away evil from thy flesh,
> Before the evil days come,

---

[12] Cf. also 3:12f., 22; 5:17; 8:15; 11:7–10. There is a striking parallel to this advice in the Babylonian Gilgamesh epic. Tablet X, c. 3, l. 1–13 (see *ANET*, p. 90).

> Why, O Gilgamesh, whither runnest thou?
> The life that thou seekest, thou wilt not find.
> When the gods created man,
> Death they ordained for man,
> Life they kept in their hands.
> Thou, O Gilgamesh, fill thy belly,
> Day and night be joyful!
> Daily be glad!
> Day and night dance and play
> Let thy garments be white,
> Anoint thy head, and purify thyself!
> Cherish the little one holding thy hand,
> Let the wife rejoice in thy bosom.

and the years draw nigh of which thou shalt say,
"I have no pleasure in them";
Before the sun is darkened,
and the light of the moon and the stars,
and the clouds return after the rain;
In the day when the keepers of the house shall tremble,
and the strong men shall bow themselves,
And the grinders cease, because they are few,
and those that look out of the windows be darkened,
and the doors shall be shut in the street;
When the sound of the grinding is low,
and one rises at the voice of the birds
and all the daughters of music are brought low:
Yea, one is afraid of a height,
and terrors are in the way;
And the almond-tree shall blossom,
and the grasshopper shall be a burden,
and the caperberry shall burst,
Because man goes to his everlasting home,
and the mourners go about the streets:
Before the silver cord is snapped,
or the golden bowl is broken,
Or the pitcher is broken at the fountain,
or the wheel is broken at the cistern,
And the dust returns to the earth as it was.
Vanity of vanities, all is vanity. (11:9—12:8)

This must not be understood as a counsel to make happiness the whole aim of life. Koheleth insisted very strongly on the value of work. But not on work by itself, but on work and joy; work without joy is unbearable:

What profit has he that labors for the wind? Especially when all his days he is in gloom and in mourning and much vexation and sickness and wrath? (5:16f.)

Live and enjoy, work and play, not alone but in good fellowship. Fulfill life's duties while it lasts, before it is too late. But do not take things too seriously, neither your work nor your play; be not too conscientious, for it does not pay:

Be not righteous overmuch; neither make thyself overwise: why shouldest thou destroy thyself? Be not overmuch wicked, neither be thou foolish: why shouldest thou die before thy time? It is good that thou shouldest take hold of this, and not withdraw thy hand from that either. (7:16–18)

Koheleth advocated a golden mean! But he never advised licentiousness nor riotous living, for he was not immoral.

Neither was he irreligious. It seemed to him that his advice was in accord with God's plan for man, it was "from the hand of God" (2:24). "That every man should eat and drink, and enjoy good in all his labor is a gift of God" (3:13), it is "his portion" (3:22; 5:19). However little warm personal religion he possessed, however little it influenced his life and thought, he did not deny God's reality or His control of the world, nor did he ridicule religious practices; on the contrary he insisted that they must be performed with true reverence and sincerity (5:1–6).

And yet the whole impression of the book was sceptical. Its heterodoxy and pessimism offended the pious and it would never have found its way into the canon of sacred writings, if it had not been edited and revised in the interest of orthodox religion. By a series of interpolations the offensive passages were reinterpreted and the sceptical implications modified. Thus, *e.g.*, the statement that wickedness was enthroned in the land (3:16) was softened by the addition,

I said in my heart, God will judge the righteous and the wicked, for there is an appointed time for every purpose and for every work. (3:17)

Similarly the observation of Koheleth that the wicked who assembled in the sanctuary far from being scorned for their hypocrisy were praised in the city, was toned down by the reflection:

Because the sentence for an evil deed is not executed speedily, therefore the heart of the sons of men is fully set in them to do evil. But though a sinner do evil a hundred times, and prolong his days, yet surely I know that it shall be well with them that fear God, but it shall not be well with the wicked, neither shall he prolong his days which are as a shadow, because he fears not before God. (8:11–13)

That this was directly opposed to Koheleth's own teaching was not felt by the readers of the revised edition of his book. Neither was the insertion in the famous concluding section (cf. p. 349), where the keen edge of Koheleth's advice to the young man to enjoy life before it is too late, was blunted by the interpolations:

But know thou, that for all these things God will bring thee into judgment. (11:9)

Remember also thy creator in the days of thy youth. (12:1a)

And the conclusion of the whole book now reads in the words of one who wanted the last impression to be one of orthodoxy:

This is the end of the matter, all has been heard.

Fear God, and keep His commandments, for this is the duty of every man. For God will bring every work into judgment, with every hidden thing, whether it be good or evil. (12:13f.)

This class of additions to Koheleth's teaching is easily recognized (cf. also 7:18b, 26b, 29; 12:7b).

There is also another class of additions which seek to counteract the heterodox tendency of the original more indirectly. They elaborate the wisdom of "Solomon." Koheleth had impersonated the wise king. A disciple inserted at those points where proverbs and maxims seemed appropriate a number of wise additions, which were in line with the ordinary wisdom of the time and therefore strengthened the reliability of this book of wisdom, and facilitated its eventual recognition as a sacred writing.[13] They are usually recognized by their interruption of the context. Thus in 4:4 Koheleth had observed that competition and rivalry in work are "vanity and a chasing after wind," and had therefore counselled, "A handful with quietness is better than two handfuls with toil and chasing after wind" (4:6); between these two observations the editor inserted, "The fool holds his hands together and eats his own flesh." (4:5)

These wise additions contain a great deal of shrewd observation and common sense. Only rarely do they change the thought of Koheleth, as for instance in 3:1–9. Koheleth had said,

For everything there is a (fixed) season,
    and an (appointed) time for every occurrence under the sun.
There is a time (appointed) to be born, and a time to die.
There is a time (appointed) for planting, and a time for uprooting.
                                                                    (3:1f.)

That is, in this world everything is predetermined, it occurs at the time that is appointed for it. And the conclusion is drawn, "What

[13] Cf. 4:5; 5:3, 7a; 7:19; 10:1–3, 8–15, 18f.

profit then has the worker in that wherein he toils?" (3:9) What is the use of all his work, since everything that happens is bound to happen, and to happen at the time that is fixed for it? The editor inserted here a number of other illustrations,

> There is a time to kill, and a time to heal;
> A time to break down, and a time to build up;
> A time to weep, and a time to laugh;
> A time to mourn, and a time to dance; etc. (3:3–8)

His intention was evidently to elaborate Koheleth's thought. But he missed the point of it, and the reader now gets the impression that Koheleth meant only that there is an appropriate time for everything.

The conviction that Solomon was the author of the book, and that the saintly and wise king wrote only words fit for edification had much to do in overcoming the objections to its canonization. And yet this Omar Khayyám of the Old Testament would never have received universal recognition had it not been for his friends and admirers who revised and edited his book, so that now along with its pessimism it affirmed the truth of the moral government of the world, the certainty of a righteous judgment, and the supreme duty of the fear of God and of obedience to His Law.

Possibly the author himself or a devoted follower provided the following concluding words to the original unedited book:

It remains to say that Koheleth was a sage; besides, he taught the people knowledge; yea, he tested and examined and arranged many proverbs. Koheleth sought to find out pleasant words, and he wrote uprightness, words of truth. (12:9–11)

Koheleth here views himself or is viewed as a wise man and a popular teacher; also as an author who wrote with fine discrimination and acumen many aphorisms and proverbs, whose style he polished most carefully and whose content was truth. Another early hand added the warning against too much interest in the current flood of wisdom literature:

> Furthermore, my son, be admonished:
> Of making many books there is no end;
> And much study is a weariness of the flesh. (12:12)

This is hardly meant as a reflection on Koheleth's book, but is intended to make the reader regard it as all-sufficient in this department of literature.

The belief in the future life, with resurrection and immortality, which Koheleth could not make his own, gained more and more ground in the following generations [14] and in its light the riddles of human existence could be solved: the apparent injustice of the present life will be righted in the future. The belief in the moral character of God was preserved in this way.

In our English Bibles, as in Luther's translation, Proverbs, Ecclesiastes, and Song of Songs follow the Psalms, the thought evidently being that the books ascribed to Solomon should stand immediately after the Psalms, of which a great many were composed by David. The Song of Songs or Canticles, as it is also called—a name derived from its Latin name *Canticum Canticorum*—mentions Solomon (3:11) and also refers to "the Shulammite" (7:1). The latter designation was already regarded by Church fathers as meaning *Shunamite*,[15] and this suggested that the term refers to the girl from Shunem whose beauty is stressed in 1 Ki. 1:3 and on whose acount Solomon condemned to death his brother and rival, Adonijah (1 Ki. 2:13ff.). The book got into the Old Testament Canon because it was interpreted allegorically as describing the love of Yahweh for Israel and Israel's for Yahweh. If in the parables of Jesus the Kingdom of God is compared with a marriage feast and the king's son, the Messiah, is taken as groom, this also presupposes an influence of the Song of Songs. Very naturally then Christians allegorized the book as referring to Christ's love for the Church and her love for her Lord. In this interpretation the book influenced mysticism and hymnody. It was therefore a considerable shock when a purely secular interpretation came up with Herder and Goethe, who regarded this as poetry fresh from the well-spring of folk literature and celebrating human love. The secular interpretation has terminated the former allegorization. It was recalled, too, that there was dispute

---

[14] See the two Greek wisdom books, "The Wisdom of Solomon" and "The Fourth Book of Maccabees." The former is included in the Apocrypha, the latter among the Pseudepigrapha (see *APOT*, II, 653ff.).

[15] Shunem is called *Solem* by the Arabs—the same dissimilation of *n* to *l*.

among the Jews about receiving the Song of Songs into the Canon as late as the second century A.D., and that poetry like the Rubáiyát of Omar Khayyám and the Divan of Hafiz was only able to survive in the Islamic environment by being allegorized.

While modern study is agreed that the older allegorization must be abandoned there is still a considerable difference in opinion as to how this book is to be understood. Dramatic interpretations keep coming up, and especially that of a background in cult-drama. The ancient nature-religions of the Near East, it is claimed, were wont to celebrate the sacred marriage of the goddess of vegetation (Ishtar, or Astarte) and the resurrected youthful god Tammuz, or Adonis. We have specific allusion to the Tammuz cult at Jerusalem in the period of Babylonian domination (Ezek. 8:14). Some find it significant that the Song of Songs became associated in the Middle Ages with the Passover, a festival that had been linked with the old agricultural festival of Mazzoth in the Persian era. However, there is nothing mythological about these songs. Furthermore, the Egyptian texts of the new kingdom have provided us with love songs that are lyrics pure and simple.[16] They are usually short and associated with joy in the beauties of nature, as is the case with the Song of Songs. As in the Biblical book the lover and the beloved both speak their piece, and refer to each other as brother and sister. This last feature seems to be a sure trace of a connection with Egyptian love poetry. It is reasonable to suppose that the wise men, with their international viewpoint and connections, received Egyptian love songs and developed their own counterparts to them on the basis of this stimulus. We may thus regard the Song of Songs as a collection of small lyrics which have been strung together without any special plan. Some may be old, and of Israelite origin as references to northern areas and places suggest. (Cf. 2:1; 3:9; 4:8f.; 6:4) But the presence of Aramaisms Persian loan words such as *pardēs* (4:13, paradise, or garden) and other linguistic characteristics indicate a third-century date for the collection in its present form.[17]

[16] *ANET*, p. 467ff.
[17] Fragments of scrolls of the Song of Songs were found in Cave IV at Qumran. The presence of such in this community suggests that the allegorization of the book was already in vogue in the first century B.C.

One of the most beautiful of the songs deals with love in the springtime. The maiden describes the coming of her lover, and his invitation.

> Hark, my beloved! behold, he comes,
>   leaping upon the mountains,
>   skipping upon the hills.
> See, there he stands behind our wall.
>   I look through the windows,
>   I glance through the lattice.
>
> My beloved spoke, and said to me,
> Rise up, my love,
>   my fair one, and come away.
> For, lo, the winter is past,
>   the rain is over and gone;
>
> The flowers appear on the earth,
>   the time of singing is come,
>   and the turtle-dove's voice is heard.
> The figtree ripens her fruit,
>   the vines are in blossom,
>   they give forth their fragrance.
> Rise up, my love,
>   my fair one, and come away.
>
> O my dove, that art in the clefts of the rock,
>   in the covert of the steep place,
> Let me see thy countenance,
>   let me hear thy voice;
> For sweet is thy voice,
>   and thy countenance is comely. (Song of Songs 2:8–14)

An interesting feature in the book is the allusion to the lover as king. Ever since the German Orientalist Wetzstein in 1873 reported that in the vicinity of Damascus the bride and groom were treated as king and queen during the seven days of the marriage feast, this has been used to illustrate the Song of Songs. The Syrian couple sat on an improvised throne, all sorts of dances and games were performed in their presence, and love and marriage songs were sung. Among these were songs describing the beauty of the bride and groom. In view of the long persistence of folk customs the assumption that this sort of thing was known in Israel too is not without plausibility. Here it must have taken on the form of identification of the groom with Solomon, and the bride with Abishag of Shunem. This interpretation certainly makes vivid such a statement as:

> Go forth, o daughters of Zion.
>   and behold King Solomon,
> With the crown with which his mother crowned him
>   on the day of his wedding,
>   on the day of the gladness of his heart. (Song of Songs 3:11)

The song that calls upon the Shulammite to return (turn?) for inspection (1:13f.), and starts the description of her charms with:

> How graceful are thy feet in sandals
> O queenly maiden (7:1),

invites illustration with the so-called "parade dance" of the Syrian bride.

For a canonical book the imagery is sometimes rather bold. The fact that the book was not expurgated shows with what conservatism the ancient editors dealt with their text. More serious than the occasional eroticism is the fact that these songs sometimes run counter to sound wisdom instruction, and to propriety as understood by law-abiding Jews (cf. 3:1–5; 5:2–8). In such passages their secular origin becomes apparent.

One great contribution of the Song of Songs is that it brings to life for us the otherwise rather submerged female psyche of Hebrew antiquity. Laws and customs left little room for the marriage of inclination. It is an isolated instance if we hear of Michal's love for David (1 Sam. 18:20). But in the Song of Songs we get the picture of the maiden who idealizes a lover to whom she belongs, soul and body.

> My beloved is mine and I am his,
>   he pastures his flock among the lilies.
> Until the day breathes and the shadows flee,
>   Turn, my beloved, be like a gazelle
>   or a young stag on rugged mountains (Song of Songs 2:16–17)

The pain of love, too, comes to the surface in the repeated warning,

I adjure you, O daughters of Jerusalem
  by the gazelles or the hinds of the field
that you stir not up or awaken love
  until it please (2:7)

The belief that Solomon was the author may be due to the fact
that he was the patron saint of the wise men, and to the report that
he had composed 1005 songs (1 Ki. 4:32). It was called Song of
Songs, not only because it was Solomon's finest, but because it was
regarded as the most beautiful of all songs. The fact that we find
in it only a celebration of the love of man and woman, at best on
the level of a comradeship rooted in physical attraction, does not
make the book unworthy of a place in the canon. Love, this greatest
experience of human life, of which the immortal saying is coined
in 8:6 "Love is strong as death," deserves to be hallowed and viewed
in terms of its relation to God. While the Song does not do that,
but remains on an earthy level, it can be a starting point for thought
about this noble theme. The universally human background in combination with the exotic Oriental imagery that is poured forth here
give the Song an appeal that leads many to consider it the greatest
love poetry in all literature.

XX

The Psalms

POETRY and religion go together. In moments of religious experience, whether the soul is at one with God or seeking Him, its utterances often take poetic form; common prose is not adequate to express its joy or its longing; in rhythmic rise and cadence praise and prayer flow forth, revealing man's deepest feelings and desires. That is why the Psalms are so important, for we have here a singularly profound revelation of the inner life of God's people. Here we "can look into the hearts of all the saints," as Martin Luther said in his Second Preface to the Psalter.[1] Here the hopes and fears of many ages are collected, the longings and yearnings of countless hearts. Here the penitence and grief over sin, the sorrow and anguish over individual and national calamity, the joyful gratitude for forgiveness and restoration, find voice and utterance. Here the passionate plea for revenge on the enemies individual or national, the despair over the apparent injustice of this world order, and the hope of the coming of God's Kingdom, stand side by side. The whole range of human life, its joy and its woe, its light and its shadow, and its daily routine, is treated in the Psalter.

It is apparent that psalms were composed for diverse needs and situations: there are psalms of common worship, pilgrim songs and processional hymns, calls to worship, hymns of praise and thanksgiving for individual or national deliverance, for the harvest and the

[1] The Hebrew name of the Book of Psalms is "Praises" (*tehillīm*). Our title comes via the New Testament (Lk. 24:44, Acts 1:20). A psalm was a song sung to a stringed instrument. In the *LXX* the title is *Psaltērion*—whence our word "Psalter"—a term meaning a harp-like instrument, used symbolically to designate the collection.

joys of nature. There are national psalms, prayers for deliverance from external or internal foes, for national restoration, prayers of trust in national peril and of praise for past deliverance, battle songs, and odes of victory. There are royal psalms, coronation and wedding odes, prayers for the king's just and ideal rule, for God's help in battle or thanksgiving for victory. There are psalms of individual piety with its longings for communion with God and its joy in the experience of it; with its prayers for help and healing, for forgiveness and purification; with its songs of faith and trust and its hymns of thanksgiving and praise. There are didactic psalms, with the warm, insistent teaching of the fear of God, the divine government in the world, retribution for pious and wicked alike; with their warnings against trust in riches, and concerning the vanity and brevity of life; with their teachings of true worship and true sacrifice, of the blessedness of forgiveness, and of charitableness toward others, of the joys of home and of nature and law; and with their lessons from Israel's great history in the past. Out of the heart of life they sprang, and to the heart they speak. Many poets have contributed; some of them were geniuses of poetic power, others were common versifiers. The Psalms are not grouped according to any chronological, topical, or other principle.

The collections we now have in our Psalter date from the period of the second temple. But a number of psalms are older, though it is uncertain whether any go back as far as David, to whom seventy-three are attributed in the titles. It is almost always difficult to tell from what time they come, for they were frequently adapted and revised to the needs of new times. Lines that had reference to particular situations were omitted, as a comparison of two recensions of the same psalm (14 and 53) shows. The psalm thus becomes timeless and better fitted to appeal to all times and to voice the needs of all generations. If Psalm 24:7–10 should go back to the Davidic era it has been provided with a prelude in vv. 1–6 which presupposes the teaching of the great prophets. From the time of the monarchy come the "royal psalms" (2, 18, 20, 21, 45, 72, 101, 110, 132), which have no doubt been preserved only because they were understood as Messianic prophecies. Psalm 46 reproduces the teaching ascribed to Isaiah in the narratives about him emphasizing the power of faith.

The teaching of the prophets regarding sacrifice is seen in others (Ps. 40, 50, 51); and Deutero-Isaiah's influence is felt in many. Not only do we hear the echo of the music of his speech, but also his universal ideas of religion, and his view of nature. Other psalms celebrate the law (Ps. 1, 19:7ff., 119) and show the influence of the legalistic age after the exile, and in their joy over the law they help us to correct our views concerning its burdensomeness. The humanism and individualism of the sages are reflected in still others, in which the problem of retribution is discussed (Ps. 49, 73). Very few psalms bear the stamp of their origin as clearly as Ps. 137, with its sad memory of the Babylonian exile and its fierce cry of hate. Some scholars have held that such Psalms as 74, 79, 83 come from Maccabean times, but this has now become improbable, because there is a Dead Sea Scroll of the Psalms which goes back to that period.[2] In the case of most psalms the clues to their dating are meager.

It was fascinating to some of the ancient editors to give various psalms a biographical background. They gained so much in vividness and interest from such endeavors. Already in late postexilic times such attempts were made and a good many psalms were attributed to certain situations, mostly in the life of David, in which they seemed to have been composed. If a psalmist described his longing for God by "My soul thirsts for Thee . . . in a dry and weary land" (Ps. 63:1), it was set down as "A Psalm of David, when he was in the wilderness of Judah." If a psalmist cried for forgiveness of sin (Ps. 51), it was referred to David's adultery, "A Psalm of David, when Nathan the prophet came to him, after he had gone in to Bathsheba." But these guesses [3] are without historical value, there is not one of them that can be accepted as correct.

The tradition of Davidic authorship of many psalms was established as early as the time of the Chronicler. He believed that David had planned the temple and arranged for the singing and the music in the temple services. To the Chronicler, David was not so much

[2] The first five Caves have produced fragments of some seventeen Psalms manuscripts, the oldest dating from the second century B.C.; and in Cave XI a Psalms Scroll was found that contains forty-four Psalms, including a number that are not in the Hebrew psalter. Three of them are known from ancient translations, but several are new. The scroll was written about 30–50 A.D. according to paleographical indications.

[3] On 14 Psalms: 3, 7, 18, 30, 34, 51, 52, 54, 56, 57, 59, 60, 63, 142.

a mighty warrior as a writer and singer of psalms, and to him and to his chief musicians was therefore attributed the authorship of many of them. How this belief arose is difficult to trace. That David was a musician and poet is certain (Am. 6:5; 1 Sam. 16:16ff.). That he may have written psalms as well as secular poetry (2 Sam. 1:19ff.; 3:33f.) we may easily grant. If he did, some of them may be preserved in our Psalter. But if so, they have been revised and that not a single one can be pointed out which one would immediately recognize as David's—not even Ps. 23, which presupposes the existence of the temple not yet built in his time and the author's close connection with it. When after the postexilic rebuilding of the temple the services were resumed, the old forms and ritual were doubtless in many cases adhered to, although modifications and adaptations were made. A first collection of hymns, old and new, was made; it was called "the Psalms of David." To this gradually were added others. We can still point out the various collections which are now parts of our Psalter:

1. The first David Psalter [4] in Ps. 2–41.
2. The second David Psalter [5] in Ps. 51–72.
3. The Korah Psalter in Ps. 42–49.
4. The Asaph Psalter in Ps. 50, 73–83.
5. An appendix to the Korah Psalter [6] in Ps. 84–89.
6. The Hallelujah Psalter in Ps. 105–107, 111–118, 146–150.
7. The Pilgrim Psalter in Ps. 120–134.
8. Another David Psalter [7] in Ps. 138–145.
9. The hymns in Ps. 93, 95–100 appear to have formed a special collection also.

In the final edition of the Psalter these collections were put together and the whole was divided into five books,[8] each closing with a special doxology. Ps. 150 serves as a doxology for the whole Psalter.

[4] Ps. 2, 10, 33 have no superscription in the Hebrew Bible, but Greek manuscripts attribute Ps. 2, 33 to David, and Ps. 10 is really a part of Ps. 9.

[5] Ps. 66, 67 are not attributed to David in the Hebrew Bible, but Ps. 67 is in the Greek version. Ps. 72 is attributed to Solomon; it was joined to the David Psalter because it was probably taken as a prayer of David *for* Solomon.

[6] Ps. 84, 85, 87, 88 are assigned to the Korahites. Ps. 88 is in addition also assigned to Heman the Ezrahite. Ps. 89 is attributed to Ethan the Ezrahite; Ps. 86 to David. Asaph, Heman, and Ethan were David's chief musicians (1 Chron. 15:17, 19), while Korah was an ancestor of Heman.

[7] Also Ps. 101, 103, 108–110, 122, 124, 131, 133 are assigned to David.

[8] I. Ps. 1–41; II. Ps. 42–72; III. Ps. 73–89; IV. Ps. 90–106; V. Ps. 107–150.

This division coincides with the earlier collections in books I–III, but it is artificial in the last two books. It appears to have been made in imitation of the Pentateuch in order that the five Books of the Law might find their response in the five Books of Praises.[9] Ps. 1 was prefixed to the whole Psalter to emphasize its legal character, and Ps. 2 to emphasize its Messianic character. At one time Ps. 42–83 must have formed a special collection in which the name Yahweh was replaced by Elohim, "God." That this was done editorially is shown by the fact that Ps. 53, which is a duplicate of Ps. 14, still has the original divine name.

The poetic form of the Psalms is worked out carefully, and it greatly enhances their beauty.

The fundamental principle of Hebrew poetry, the so-called parallelism of the members—the balancing of the lines that belong together—makes it possible to perceive much of the poetic beauty of the psalms even in a translation which pays no attention to the rhythm of the original. The important types of this parallelism may be illustrated as follows.

The simplest and most common form is the couplet or distich. In it we find the synonymous parallelism, in which the same thought is expressed in parallel lines,

> The desire of his heart Thou didst grant him,
> and the request of his lips Thou didst not deny (21:2);

the tautological parallelism, in which the same words are exactly or almost exactly repeated,

> Yahweh, how long shall the wicked,
> how long shall the wicked triumph (94:3);

the antithetical parallelism, in which the thought of one line is contrasted with that of the other,

---

[9] The total number of psalms (150) was also artificially established. Originally some psalms, now counted as two, were one, e.g., Ps. 9 and 10, as the alphabetical acrostic form (see p. 147) shows, Ps. 42 and 43 as the refrain in both proves. In other psalms two or more originally unrelated poems are combined, e.g., in Ps. 19, 24, 27, 144. Ps. 108 is a combination of Ps. 57:7-11 and 60:5-12. Ps. 40:13-17 appears as a separate poem in Ps. 70.

The Greek Version counts Ps. 9 and 10 as one, also Ps. 114 and 115, but it divides Ps. 116 and 147 each into two psalms. It has an additional (apocryphal) psalm at the end of the Psalter, Ps. 151. New Testament commentators often quote the Psalms in the numeration of the Septuagint.

> Weeping may tarry for the night,
>> but joy comes in the morning (30:5);

the synthetical parallelism, in which the second line supplements
the thought of the first,

>> I cry unto Yahweh with my voice
>> and He answers me out of His holy hill. (3:4)

The triplet or tristich is not so common,

>> The floods have lifted up, Yahweh,
>> the floods have lifted up their voice,
>> the floods lift up their roaring. (93:3)

The four line stanza is usually a combination of distichs,

>> His mouth was smooth as butter,
>> but war his heart;
>> Softer than oil his words,
>> yet were they drawn swords. (55:21)

The five line stanza is a combination of a distich and a tristich,

>> I am wearied with my groaning,
>> every night make I my bed to swim
>> and my couch I flood with tears.
>> Languid is my eye from grief,
>> it has grown weak from all oppressors. (6:6f.)

The six line stanza is a combination of distichs or tristichs,

>> Yahweh is King; let the peoples tremble:
>> He sits above the cherubim; let the earth be moved.
>> Yahweh is great in Zion:
>> and He is high above all the peoples.
>> Let them praise Thy great and terrible name:
>> Holy is He! (99:1-3)

Here the refrain, "Holy is He," proves that we have a stanza of six
lines.

Larger units also occur, as, for instance, in Ps. 42f., whose three
stanzas of eight or nine lines are clearly marked by the refrain which
is not counted in these eight or nine lines. The refrain is of high
poetic effect. In Ps. 107 a double refrain is used most artistically, the
first is in the middle of the stanzas, where it marks the turning point
of the people's experience,

Then they cried unto Yahweh in their trouble
   and He delivered them out of their distresses (vv. 6, 13, 19, 28),

while the second at the end of the stanzas,

Oh, that men would praise Yahweh for His kindness,
   and for His wonderful works to the children of men (vv. 8, 15, 21, 31),

is always followed by two lines which vary in accordance with the subject of the stanza, *e.g.*, the first described the hunger and thirst of the people in the desert, and thus ends,

Oh, that men would praise Yahweh for His kindness,
   and for His wonderful works to the children of men,
For He satisfies the longing soul,
   and the hungry soul He fills with good. (v. 9)

Far less attractive is the use of the alphabet for binding the lines together either into a single whole, in which successive lines begin with the twenty-two successive letters of the alphabet (Ps. 111f.), or into stanzas in which the first word of each couplet (Ps. 25, 34, 145) or of each tetrastich (Ps. 9, 10, 37) is treated thus. Ps. 119 is the most elaborate and artificial of these, for its twenty-two stanzas consists of eight lines, each one of which begin with the same letter.

The rhythmic movement of the psalms which gives to them their poetic quality in combination with the parallelism of the lines (cf. p. 21) is not easily reproduced in a translation. Unfortunately the great English Versions have laid no stress on it. The frequent alliterations and assonances, which were considered poetic niceties, have not been brought out either.

The psalms that were used in the temple services were sung by the temple choir, accompanied by instrumental music. Responses were probably chanted by another group and sometimes by the people. In Ps. 150 a list of the musical instruments is given. There are also a number of musicological terms in the superscriptions, in the middle, or at the end of many psalms. But their meaning is no longer known—not even that of the familiar selah (Ps. 3:3, 9). It may have indicated use of some instrument, or utterance of a loud cry (customary in some modern Oriental singing at certain points) or may merely be for emphasis of the words just uttered. Sometimes a psalm is given a classifying name. But we can as yet see no difference that would account for designations such as *Miktam, Maskil,* or *Shiggaion.* Babylonian psalmody too has diverse designations for its productions, and there likewise the reasons for the distinctions are not yet understood. Sometimes the direction is given that the psalm is to be sung to the accompaniment of stringed or of wind instruments. Fifty-five psalms have the note *lammenaṣṣeaḥ* which is usually translated "for the chief musician," but which originally appears to have meant "for musical rendering." Sometimes the melody according to which the psalm was to be sung is given (*e.g.,* Ps. 22 is to be sung after the tune of the song "the hind of the morning," Ps. 45, 69 according to *shoshanim* = lilies).

All tradition of the ancient temple music has perished. But this is perhaps not a serious loss, because our sense of tonal harmony is so different from that of the ancients. It would be difficult for us, even if we still had the old music and understood all the directions, to get the same impression from it that the ancient worshipers did when they sang and danced before the Lord. The contents of the Psalms alone remain significant.

To grasp the variety which finds its expression here it is necessary to group those that belong together. We may divide them into three classes: psalms for public worship in the temple, psalms for private worship in the temple, and psalms of a noncultic nature.

1. PUBLIC WORSHIP IN THE TEMPLE

One cannot easily overestimate the importance of temple worship for Judaism. The temple stood in the center of its national and its religious life. The Jews believed that Yahweh dwelt in the innermost part, the holy of holies; here was His home and His throne. The worshipers entered, therefore, literally the presence of God when they went into the temple. There they prayed to Him and thither they turned their faces in their devotions when they were away from the temple.

Three times a year they were expected to go to the temple to attend the great annual festivals. Those were seasons of great joy and festivity. On the given day the cry of the watchmen rang out, "Arise ye, and let us go up to Zion unto Yahweh our God!" (Jer. 31:6), and the bands of pilgrims came from all directions. They were happy throngs, marching to the sound of the pipe (Isa. 30:29) and often singing as they went. We still have in our Psalter a charming collection of Pilgrim songs (Ps. 120–134), which had originally not been written for pilgrimages but which were used by the pilgrims on their march. They are on a variety of subjects. Songs dealing with the history of the nation were favorites, *e.g.*,

> Then the waters had overwhelmed us,
>   the stream had gone over our soul;
> Then had gone over our soul
>   the proud waters.

It may be that the precentor sang first every distich, as he had done with the first line, and the people sang it after him. But now the mighty chorus bursts forth in unison into praise,

> Blessed be Yahweh, who has not given us
>   as a prey to their teeth.
> Our soul is escaped as a bird
>   out of the snare of the fowlers:
> The snare is broken,
>   and we are escaped.
> Our help is in the name of Yahweh
>   who made heaven and earth. (Ps. 124)

The memory of dire national peril lives in this song, but also the joy over God's help.

One of the most beautiful pilgrim songs is Ps. 126 which describes the condition of the returned exiles who had been fired by Deutero-Isaiah's predictions and were disappointed by the different reality; Israel's fate had not really been turned. The glad thanks for the home coming are followed by the humble plea for full deliverance and the confidence that out of the present seed of tears there will yet sprout the harvest of joy:

> When Yahweh turned Zion's fate,
>   we were like them that dream.
> Then was our mouth filled with laughter,
>   and our tongue with singing:
> Then said they among the nations,
>   "Yahweh has done great things for them."

> Yahweh has done great things for us,
> whereof we are glad.
>
> Turn our fate, O Yahweh,
> as the streams in the South land.
> They that sow with tears
> shall reap in joy.
> He that goes forth and weeps,
> when he carries seed for sowing,
> Shall doubtless come home with joy,
> when he brings his (harvest) sheaves. (Ps. 126)

Ps. 124. A solo voice begins, clear and strong,

> If it had not been for Yahweh who was on our side.

This is taken up and repeated by the whole chorus ("Let Israel now say"),

> If it had not been for Yahweh who was on our side,
> when men rose up against us;
> Then they had swallowed us up alive,
> when their wrath was kindled against us:

Sometimes the pilgrims sang *de profundis*, the penitential psalm, which is ageless with its cry of the sinful human soul and its longing for the forgiveness of God:

> Out of the depths have I cried unto Thee, Yahweh,
> O Lord, hear my voice.
> Let Thine ears be attentive
> to the voice of my supplications.
>
> If Thou, Yahweh, shouldst mark iniquities,
> O Lord, who could stand?
> But there is forgiveness with Thee,
> that Thou mayest be feared.
>
> I wait for Yahweh, my soul
> does wait for His word.
> My soul hopes for the Lord
> more than watchmen (hope) for the morning.
>
> Yea, more than watchmen for the morning,
> O Israel, hope for Yahweh;

> For with Yahweh is kindness,
>> and with Him is plenteous redemption.
> And He will redeem Israel
>> from all his iniquities. (Ps. 130)

Songs of homely counsel and wisdom like Ps. 127, 128, 133 or songs of trust like Ps. 125, 131 made the way seem shorter to the pilgrims. Perhaps when they approached the holy city they sang Ps. 121, which is still one of humanity's exquisite treasures:

> I will lift up mine eyes unto the mountains:
>> from whence shall my help come?

The answer is given not by a priest, but by the singing chorus itself:

> My help comes from Yahweh,
>> who made heaven and earth.

> He will not suffer thy foot to be moved:
>> He that keeps thee will not sleep.
> Behold, nor sleeps nor slumbers
>> Israel's keeper.

> Yahweh is thy keeper, Yahweh is thy shade
>> upon thy right hand.
> The sun shall not smite thee by day,
>> nor the moon by night.

> Yahweh will keep thee from all evil,
>> He will keep thy soul.
> Yahweh will keep thy going out and thy coming in
>> from this time forth and for evermore. (Ps. 121)

At last the pilgrims arrived at Jerusalem. Many of them saw for the first time the beautiful city that was sanctified by the temple in which Yahweh dwelt, and glorified by the events of history, of which they had heard so much and whose scenes they now could see with their own eyes. With mingled joy and awe they entered the temple, meditated on the kindness of God, and determined to publish His praise and His righteousness to the ends of the earth. Aye, the joy of all the worshipers! and especially of the pilgrims who had come from distant lands as they now walked about Zion and marked each tower and gate, each bulwark and palace; for each had a story of its own, which they must tell to their friends and especially to their children at home (Ps. 48). Compare also the pilgrim song, Ps. 84, with its ardent longing for the temple and its description of the stations of the procession.

When they set out on their homeward march, they sang Ps. 122, that simple song which tells of the joy with which they received the summons to go up to the temple. They now had been to the holy city which binds all the members of the Jewish people together, by the law which requires all to attend the yearly festivals there, and their hearts were full of good wishes and intentions for her welfare and peace.

We can hardly get an adequate conception of the love that the Jews had for Jerusalem. In passionate devotion a psalmist in exile cries,

> If I forget thee, O Jerusalem,
>   let my right hand wither;
> Let my tongue cleave to the roof of my mouth,
>   if I remember thee not;
> If I prefer not Jerusalem
>   above my chief joy! (Ps. 137:6)

So deeply rooted was the love for Jerusalem, the center of the national and religious life of the people. Here they experienced the power of common worship that bound them together with one another and with God. The great festivals with their processional songs and their hymns, their music and public sacrifices, made a deep and lasting impression on many hearts. With profound devotion they joined in the worship.

With the great festivals, processions were no doubt connected. Of these processional hymns bear witness. As the festal procession marched to the temple the choir called upon the whole earth to sing:

> Make a joyful noise unto Yahweh, all ye lands,
>   serve Yahweh with gladness,
>   come before His presence with singing!
> Know that Yahweh is God,
>   it is He that made us, and we are His,
>   we are His people and the sheep of His pasture.

> Enter His gates with thanksgiving,
>> and His courts with praise:
>>> give thanks unto Him and bless His name!
> For He is good, His kindness is forever
>> and His faithfulness to all generations. (Ps. 100)

The last two lines were taken up as a response. Sometimes the festal procession itself sang the call to worship as it approached the temple:

> Oh come, let us sing unto Yahweh,
>> let us make a joyful noise to the rock of our salvation.
> Let us come before His presence with thanksgiving,
>> let us make a joyful noise unto Him with psalms. . . .
>
> Oh come, let us worship and bow down,
>> let us kneel before Yahweh our Maker:
> For He is our God,
>> and we are the people of His pasture.

With this the procession entered the temple, and a priest now addressed the people, in the name of Yahweh, and earnestly exhorted them to obey His commands with all their hearts, that thus their worship might be truly acceptable to Him.

> Today, oh that ye would hear His voice!
> "Harden not your heart, as at Meribah,
>> as in the day of Massah in the wilderness;
> When your fathers tempted Me,
>> proved Me, and saw My work.
> Forty years long was I grieved
>> with that generation, and said,
> They are people that err in their heart
>> and know not My ways:
> Wherefore I swore in My wrath,
>> that they should not enter into My place of rest." (Ps. 95)

There were many processional hymns, suitable for different occasions. It is significant that the priests endeavored by means of hymn and homily to ethicize the public cult and make it a worship in spirit and truth. This is apparent in the famous processional hymn, Ps. 24, part of which is a liturgy that was used at the annual festival of preexilic times, at which the ark must have been taken from the temple and joyously brought in again.[10] It is now prefaced with a hymnic introduction:

> The earth is Yahweh's, and its fulness,
>> the world, and they that dwell therein.
> For He has founded it upon the seas,
>> and established it upon the floods.

As the procession ascended the temple hill, the question was asked in solemn appeal,

> Who may ascend the hill of Yahweh?
>> and who may stand in His holy place?

To which a priest responded, giving instruction (Heb. *torah*):

> He that has clean hands and a pure heart,
>> who has not lifted up his soul to falsehood,
>> and has not sworn deceitfully.
> He shall receive a blessing from Yahweh,
>> and vindication from the God of his salvation.
> Such is the generation that inquires for Him,
>> that seeks the God of Jacob's face.

No ceremonial requirement is mentioned, the entire stress lies on social morality; not on cultic cleanness but on moral purity! [11] But the endeavor to place the temple services on a moral basis is of the greatest importance: taught by the prophets, the priests had learned that without morality they are valueless. Only men with clean hands and pure and honest hearts may stand in God's sanctuary. The procession now moves on. At the temple gates they break forth into singing,

> Lift up your heads, O ye gates,
>> and be ye lifted up, ye ancient doors,
>>> that the King of Glory may come in!

[10] In Ps. 68:24f. such a procession is described:
> They have seen Thy goings, O God,
>> even the going of my God, my King, into the sanctuary.
> The singers went before, the minstrels followed after,
>> in the midst of the damsels playing with timbrels.

[11] In Ps. 15 we have a striking and somewhat fuller parallel to this: the true worshiper of Yahweh is the righteous citizen. The influence of the prophets is distinctly felt here. In Ps. 15 it stands out in bolder relief, because Ps. 15 is not, like Ps. 24, part of a liturgy.

But from the temple comes the challenge,

> Who is the King of Glory?

At once the answer comes back, clear and strong,

> Yahweh, strong and mighty,
> Yahweh, mighty in battle!

A second time the gates are commanded,

> Lift up your heads, O ye gates,
> yea, lift them up, ye ancient doors,
> that the King of Glory may come in!

Once more the challenging question is asked from within,

> Who is the King of Glory?

And once more the enthusiastic reply is given from without,

> Yahweh, the God of hosts,
> He is the King of Glory!

Doubtless the procession then entered the temple and the sacrifices began.

In Ps. 118 we have a more elaborate processional with a festal liturgy. As the procession starts at the foot of the temple hill the leader (cf. Ps. 42:4) sings,

> Oh give thanks to Yahweh, for He is good,
> and His kindness endures for ever.

The refrain "for His kindness endures for ever" is taken up by "Israel," by "the house of Aaron," and by "them that fear Yahweh," in turn. As the procession marches up the hill, they recount in their song the serious trouble out of which their great and only helper Yahweh had saved them; how they had been attacked by all surrounding nations but how Yahweh had helped them to win the victory over them all; and how therefore

> The voice of rejoicing and victory
> is in the tents of the righteous.

Their suffering had been severe, but full of gratitude and joy the leader declares,

> I shall not die but live,
>   and declare the works of Yahweh.
> Yahweh has chastened me sore,
>   but He has not given me over to death.

By this time the procession has arrived at the temple and the leader of the procession calls to the Levites who keep the gates,

> Open to me the gates of righteousness,
>   that I may enter them and give thanks to Yahweh.

To this demand the Levites respond, stressing the "righteousness" of the gate,

> This is the gate of Yahweh,
>   the righteous may enter it.

The procession now enters singing,

> I thank Thee for Thou hast answered me,
>   and art become my salvation.
> The stone which the builders rejected
>   is become the head of the corner.
> This comes from Yahweh,
>   it is wonderful in our eyes.
> This is the day which Yahweh has made,
>   we will rejoice and be glad in it.

The whole chorus then joins in the plea,

> Save now, we beseech Thee, O Yahweh!
>   O Yahweh, we beseech Thee, send now prosperity!

In the temple court the priests welcome the worshiping throng,

> Blessed be he that enters, in the name of Yahweh:
>   we bless you from the house of Yahweh.

The procession responds,

> Yahweh is God, and has given us light.

Whereupon they are exhorted to perform the sacred dance around the altar (cf. Ps. 26:6), touching the horns of the altar with the branches which they are carrying, for that was from ancient times one of the most significant functions of the ceremony, the formal act of paying reverence to God, by which the immediate contact with the Deity was attained,

> Perform the (sacred) dance with branches,
>> even to the horns of the altar.

The procession marched around the altar in the rhythmic steps of the sacred dance, touching with their branches the horns of the altar and singing,

> Thou art my God, and I will thank Thee,
> Thou art my God, I will exalt Thee.[12]

Whereupon the whole chorus joined in with the refrain with which the psalm had begun,

> Oh give thanks to Yahweh, for He is good,
>> for His kindness endures for ever.

Special festal hymns were sung at the various yearly feasts. Unfortunately the tradition about this matter is meager [13] and apparently not always dependable. According to Jewish tradition Ps. 81 was the New Year's hymn, but it seems more likely that it was originally intended for the Passover. The congregation is gathered in the temple. The choir begins,

> Sing aloud unto God our strength,
>> make a joyful noise to the God of Jacob.
> Raise a song, and strike the timbrel,
>> the pleasant harp with the psaltery.
> Blow the trumpet at the new moon,
>> at the full moon, on our feast-day.
> For it is a statute for Israel,
>> an ordinance of the God of Jacob.
> He appointed it in Joseph for a testimony,
>> when He went out against the land of Egypt. (Ps. 81:1–5)

[12] The use of the first person singular instead of plural in this psalm apparently indicates that the national leader sang those passages, in a representative capacity. It was not he alone who was surrounded by all the nations, nor he alone who was delivered. Although v. 19 says, "I will enter," the priests say in v. 26 "we bless you" (plural).

[13] In the Hebrew Bible Ps. 30 is "a song at the dedication of the House," Ps. 100 "a psalm for the thank-offering," Ps. 38 and 70 are "for (public) confession," Ps. 120–134 pilgrim songs, Ps. 92 is "a song for the Sabbath day." The Talmud mentions also certain psalms that were sung in connection with the extra offerings on the Sabbath and feast days. More important is its tradition that the Great Hallel, Ps. 113–118, was sung on the great festivals. At the Passover Ps. 113–114 were sung before the meal, Ps. 115–118 after the meal. Compare Matt. 26:30 "and when they had sung a hymn, they went out into the Mount of Olives."

Here the choir stops, and a single voice takes up the song: a priest
speaks in the name of Yahweh, like a prophet. He reminds the people
of the deliverance from Egypt, which they are celebrating in this
festival, of the miraculous gift of water at Meribah (cf. Num. 20:13)
and of the legislation at Sinai, and then pleads with them to obey
Yahweh wholeheartedly henceforth,

> Oh that My people would hearken unto Me,
>   that Israel would walk in My ways!

Then they would soon experience His wonderful blessing in their
victory over their enemies and in plentiful harvests (Ps. 81:6–16).
More detailed historical reviews are found in Ps. 78, 105, 106. The
Deuteronomic ordinance had already associated the remembrance of
the saving acts of God with sacrifice (Deut. 26:5–10, see p. 137).

On the great harvest festivals special prayers of thanksgiving for
the harvest were offered. Ps. 67 was one of these. Its scope was not
narrow, for a universal element entered almost inevitably into the
contemplation of the gift of the harvest. Its blessings were not confined to Israel. The God who has provided so plentifully the fruits
of the earth must become manifest to all nations of the world. In
His marvelous blessing of Israel the heathen must see what a wonderful God He is. Let them rejoice in Him and fear Him, for He
will be their guide too. The congregation looks beyond the material
gift of the harvest to the spiritual blessing which Israel is destined
to be for the world, and calls on the nations to join them in praise
and thanksgiving. The prayer begins with the priestly blessing (cf.
Num. 6:25):

> God be gracious unto us and bless us,
>   and make His face to shine toward us;
> That Thy way may be known upon earth,
>   Thy salvation among all nations.
> Let the peoples give Thee thanks, O God,
>   let all the peoples give Thee thanks.
>
> Let the nations be glad and sing for joy;
>   for Thou wilt judge the peoples with equity,
>   and lead the nations upon earth.
> Let the peoples give Thee thanks,
>   let all the peoples give Thee thanks.

> The earth has yielded its increase:
>   may God, even our God, bless us!
> May God bless us;
>   and let all the ends of the earth fear Him. (Ps. 67)

This universal outlook characterizes also the other harvest song, Ps. 65, which is a further proof that the temple cult of the postexilic times was actuated by the high thoughts of prophetic teaching. The ideals of the great prophets, especially of Deutero-Isaiah, were taken over by the psalmists and presented in the public services to the people. The temple worship itself is of course regarded as important and as a means of spiritual satisfaction, yet the God worshiped there is not only the God of the Jews but "the confidence of all the earth and the isles afar off"; to Him "shall all flesh come," and He makes "the outgoings of the morning and the evening to rejoice."

Most hymns were not composed for special occasions, but were suitable for any service of praise. They celebrate God's work in creation and in the processes of nature, or they extol His deliverance of Israel and His righteous rule over them, or they anticipate with great enthusiasm His final judgment of the nations and the establishment of His Kingdom on earth.[14] One of the most enthusiastic of all the hymns or songs of praise, Ps. 148, is taken up almost entirely with the call to the whole creation to praise Yahweh. Heaven with its host, the angels, the sun, moon, and stars, and the heavenly ocean, all must praise Yahweh; the earth and the sea with its sea monsters, fire and hail, snow and fog and storm, mountains and trees, beasts and birds and creeping things, all must praise Him; all mankind, kings and nations, old people and young, all must praise the name of Yahweh,

> For His name alone is exalted,
>   His glory is above the earth and the heavens.

[14] The hymns or songs of praise have a characteristic form. They usually, though not always, begin with "Praise Yahweh," or "Sing unto Yahweh," or "Bless Yahweh," or a similar form. The assembled people, or the priests, Levites and proselytes, or Zion, or the peoples of the earth, or all creation, are addressed to praise Yahweh, and their response is assumed. Then follows the reason for this praise, which differs in accordance with the character of the hymn. It is interesting to note that the shortest song of praise contains these two elements, the hymnal introduction and the reason for the praise (cf. Ps. 117). There are, however, variations from this regular form.

And He has lifted up the horn of His people,
a praise for all His saints,
for the Israelites, the people that is near Him. (Ps. 148)

Here is no narrow view. The psalmist's devotion is not satisfied until the whole wide world resounds with the praise of Yahweh, for His name alone is exalted. It is true, the reason for this praise is the restoration of the national glory of Israel. But this is to the poet the beginning of the salvation of the whole world, which shall come through Israel to all nations, and therefore he may well call on them all to rejoice and to praise Yahweh for this deed, for it redounds to their own redemption. The universal ideas of Deutero-Isaiah are alive in this hymn.

Pure nature hymns are rare, but the few we have are beautiful. It is characteristic that often in the contemplation of nature all narrow, nationalistic thoughts disappear; it is God and man, not God and Jew, that meet in the vast realm of creation. Ps. 8 is an illustration of this. The chorus sings the refrain at the beginning and the end; it is not an exhortation to praise but a praise-song itself. The body of the psalm is sung by a solo voice.

O Yahweh, our Lord, how glorious
is Thy name in all the earth!

Let me sing of Thy glory in the heavens!
out of the mouth of babes and sucklings
Hast Thou founded strength because of Thine adversaries,
to still the enemy and the rebellious.

When I consider Thy heavens, the work of Thy fingers,
the moon and the stars which Thou hast established;
What is man that Thou art mindful of him?
and the son of man that Thou visitest him?

Thou hast made him but a little lower than God,
and crownest him with glory and honor:
Thou makest him to rule over the works of Thy hands,
Thou hast put all things under his feet.

Sheep and oxen, all of them,
yea, and the beasts of the field,

The birds of the heavens and the fish of the sea,
   whatsoever passes through the paths of the seas.

O Yahweh, our Lord, how glorious
is Thy name in all the earth!

Ps. 29 celebrates God's glory in the thunderstorm. In high enthusiasm the poet calls not upon the congregation in the earthly
temple but upon the heavenly beings to adore and glorify Yahweh
in the heavenly temple.[15]

Ascribe unto Yahweh, O ye sons of God,
   ascribe unto Yahweh glory and strength.
Ascribe unto Yahweh the glory due to His name;
   worship Yahweh in holy array.

The voice of Yahweh is upon the waters,
   the God of glory thunders,
      even Yahweh upon great waters.
The voice of Yahweh is powerful,
   the voice of Yahweh is full of majesty.
The voice of Yahweh breaks the cedars,
   yea, Yahweh breaks Lebanon's cedars,
And makes Lebanon to skip like a calf,
   and Sirion like a young wild ox.
The voice of Yahweh cleaves rocks,
   cleaves them with flames of fire.
The voice of Yahweh shakes the wilderness,
   Yahweh shakes the wilderness of Kadesh.
The voice of Yahweh makes the hinds to calve,
   and strips the forests bare,
      and in His temple every one says, "Glory."

Yahweh sat enthroned at the Flood,
   yea, Yahweh sits enthroned as King forever.
May Yahweh give strength to His people,
   may Yahweh bless His people with peace! (Ps. 29)

These are so-called "nature psalms." Ps. 19:1–6 with its powerful
beginning, "The heavens declare the glory of God/and the firmament shows his handiwork," is another. But usually the praise of

[15] Under the impression of the texts from Ugarit (*Ras Shamra*) some hold
this psalm to be an adaptation of a Phoenician one.

God's work in creation is combined with that of His great deeds in history (compare, *e.g.*, Ps. 33, 135, 136). History was always of great importance for the Hebrews, and the great deliverances of Israel formed the theme of many a psalm. Ps. 99 is a hymn of victory in which the hymnal form differs from the usual pattern in that the call to praise comes at the end of the stanzas and the reason at the beginning. It is a very artistic hymn, celebrating Yahweh as the victorious king of the world, the righteous ruler of His people, and their gracious and forgiving God.

> Yahweh reigns; the peoples tremble,
>> He is enthroned above the cherubim; the earth totters.
>
> Yahweh is great in Zion,
>> and high above all peoples.
>
> *Let them praise Thy great and terrible name:*
>> HOLY IS HE!

> A Strong One is King, who loves justice,
>> Thou hast established the right,
>>> Thou hast executed justice and righteousness in Jacob.
>
> *Exalt ye Yahweh our God,*
>> *and worship at His footstool:*
>>> HOLY IS HE!

> Moses and Aaron among His priests,
>> and Samuel among them that call on His name,
>>> they called upon Yahweh and He answered them.
>
> He spoke to them in the pillar of cloud:
>> they kept His testimonies, and the statute that He gave them.
>
> Thou answeredst them, O Yahweh our God,
>> Thou wast a God that forgave them,
>>> and that cleared them of their misdeeds.
>
> *Exalt ye Yahweh our God,*
>> *and worship at His holy hill:*
>>> HOLY IS HE! (Ps. 99)

The response HOLY IS HE! was no doubt sung by the people. Other victory hymns are Ps. 68 [16] and 149.

The experience of God's wonderful deliverance from a terrible national danger stirred a poet to write the great hymn of faith, Ps.

---

[16] A fragment of a commentary on this psalm was found among the Dead Sea Scrolls. The commentary author took it as prophetic of his own time.

46, which gave to Martin Luther the inspiration for his Reformation hymn, "A Mighty Fortress is Our God." There is no exhortation to praise in the psalm, the praise itself is sung directly; three times it reaches its climax in the refrain, in which the whole congregation may have joined.

> God is our refuge and strength,
>   a very present help in trouble.
> Therefore will we not fear, though the earth change,
>   and though the mountains be moved into the heart of the seas;
> Though its waters roar and foam,
>   though the mountains shake at the swelling of its river.
> *Yahweh of hosts is with us;*
>   *the God of Jacob is our high fortress.*
>
> Let the city of God exult and be glad,
>   the holy dwelling place of the Most High.
> God is in her midst, she shall not be moved;
>   God will help her, and that right early.
> Nations were in tumult, kingdoms were moved:
>   He uttered His voice, the earth melted.
> *Yahweh of hosts is with us;*
>   *the God of Jacob is our high fortress.*
>
> Come, behold the works of Yahweh,
>   who has set wonders in the earth:
> Who makes wars to cease unto the end of the earth;
>   He breaks the bow, and cuts the spear in sunder,
>   He burns the war-chariots in the fire.
> "Be still, and know that I am God;
>   I will be exalted among the nations,
>   I will be exalted in the earth."
> *Yahweh of hosts is with us;*
>   *the God of Jacob is our high fortress.* (Ps. 46)

This is one of the most powerful hymns of faith ever sung.

Yahweh's righteous rule was the theme of other hymns. A noble illustration is Ps. 113, where Yahweh, who is exalted above the heavens, is praised for graciously humbling Himself in order to raise the lowest on earth.

> Praise, O ye servants of Yahweh,
>   praise the name of Yahweh.

> Blessed be the name of Yahweh
>   from this time forth and for evermore.
> From the rising of the sun to its setting
>   Yahweh's name is to be praised.
>
> Yahweh is high above all nations,
>   and His glory above the heavens.
> Who is like Yahweh our God,
>   that has His throne on high,
> That humbles Himself to behold
>   the things in heaven and on earth?
>
> He raises up the poor out of the dust,
>   and lifts up the needy from the dunghill,
> That He may set him with princes,
>   even with the princes of His people.
> He makes the barren woman to keep house,
>   and to be a joyful mother of children. (Ps. 113)

When the Jews sang this hymn on the three great yearly festivals, and on the New Moon day and the festival of the dedication of the temple, they thought of Israel as the humble poor who was to be raised to dignity, and the hymn voiced their faith in the certain exaltation of Israel by the omnipotence of Yahweh, the righteous ruler of the world.

But the whole effect of Yahweh's righteous rule is not seen in the present. He is not exercising His Kingship as yet to the full, the nations do not yet acknowledge Him as the only God and King of the whole world. But the time will come, and perhaps quite soon, for had not the prophets foretold the glorious time, when the Kingdom of God would be established on earth? A number of psalmists, under the direct influence of these prophetic convictions, notably as expressed by Isa. 52:7–10, celebrated in their eschatological hymns the enthronement of Yahweh.[17] In their eager anticipation they saw Him

---

[17] Some scholars, following Sigmund Mowinckel's *Psalmenstudien*, I, 1922, do not believe these Psalms to be eschatological. They hold them rather to be cultic, celebrating Yahweh as king at the occasion of His annual festival. The Succoth festival in the autumn is held to have been the one in question. The analogies of the festivals of the ancient Oriental deities are invoked to make this plausible. A recent modification of the theory holds that this supposed enthronization festival arose after the exile, as the substitute for an earlier royal festival celebrating a king's accession.

already going up to His heavenly throne, and broke forth into the
jubilant cry: Yahweh is King! and called upon all mankind, some
even on all nature, to acclaim Him King of all the earth.

> Oh clap your hands, all ye peoples,
>   shout unto God with a ringing cry.
> For Yahweh is most high and terrible,
>   a great King over all the earth.
>
> He subdued peoples under us,
>   and nations under our feet.
> He chose our inheritance for us,
>   the glory of Jacob whom He loved.
>
> God is gone up with a shout,
>   Yahweh with the sound of a horn.
> Sing praises to God, sing praises,
>   sing praises to our King, sing praises.
>
> For God is King of all the earth:
>   sing praises with a skillful strain.
> God has become King over the nations,
>   God has seated Himself upon His holy throne.
>
> The nobles of the peoples are gathered together
>   with the people of the God of Abraham:
> For to God belong the shields of the earth;
>   He is become greatly exalted. (Ps. 47)

The last stanza shows that the subjection of the nations under Israel
which was mentioned as the first effect of Yahweh's assumption of
the government of all nations is not thought of as a mere political
triumph of the Jews, but as a means of establishing the universal
reign of God. Together with Israel the representatives of all mankind are gathered to pay homage to the one and only God, who had
come down to subject the nations but who now has gone up, accompanied by shouts of acclaim, to sit on His heavenly throne as King
of the earth.

   In Ps. 96 the universal teaching of Deutero-Isaiah receives its finest
expression in the Psalter, for this poet's interest centers in Israel's
missionary calling and the salvation of the nations by their recognition of Yahweh, the creator of the heavens, as the only true God.

There is no word of the national exaltation of Israel or the national humiliation of the heathen. On the contrary, all are to come and worship Yahweh in His temple on Zion.

> Oh sing to Yahweh a new song,
>   sing to Yahweh, all the earth.
> Sing to Yahweh, bless His name,
>   proclaim His salvation from day to day.
> Declare His glory among the nations,
>   His marvellous works among all the peoples.
>
> For great is Yahweh, and greatly to be praised:
>   He is terrible above all gods.
> For all gods of the peoples are things of naught,
>   but Yahweh made the heavens.
> Honor and majesty are before Him:
>   strength and beauty are in His sanctuary.
>
> Ascribe to Yahweh, ye families of the peoples,
>   ascribe to Yahweh glory and strength.
> Ascribe to Yahweh the glory of His name:
>   bring presents and come into His courts.
> Oh worship Yahweh in holy adornment,
>   tremble before Him, all the earth.
> Say among the nations "Yahweh has become King!"
>   yea, the world He established that it cannot be moved:
> He will judge the peoples with equity.
>
> Let the heavens be glad, and let the earth rejoice,
>   let the sea roar and its fulness,
> Let the field exult, and all that is in it,
>   then shall all the trees of the wood sing for joy
> Before Yahweh, for He comes,
>   He comes to judge the earth:
> He will judge the world with righteousness,
>   and the peoples with His faithfulness. (Ps. 96)

It is no wonder that the psalmist calls for a new song, the glory is all too great to be expressed by a familiar hymn. Ps. 98 is a companion of Ps. 96 and may have been composed by the same author. Ps. 93 and 97 as well as Ps. 75 and 76 belong to the same class of hymns. Their noble poetic form matches their great prophetic content.

From the poetical point of view the hymns or songs of praise are
the finest in the Psalter. Their power of arousing religious enthusiasm, when they were sung in the temple by the choir to the accompaniment of the temple music, was so great that Jer. 33:11, in predicting the return of joy and happiness to the then forsaken and
ruined city, joins to the happy voices of the bridegroom and the
bride "the voice of them that say, Give thanks to Yahweh, for He
is good, for His kindness endures forever."

Not always did the temple resound with joy. Many were the
occasions when some national calamity, failure of the harvest, epi-
demics of disease, defeat in battle, or humiliation by foreign oppressors brought the people to the temple to plead with Yahweh for
help and deliverance. Instead of music and song there went up
lamentations and prayers, as the people, led by the priests, implored
Yahweh. Sometimes the calamity lasted for years in spite of all
prayers. We may single out in illustration two periods from which
we may date some of these prayers with reasonable assurance, the
time shortly after the return from exile and the time of the Maccabean sufferings.

Among the pilgrim songs which we quoted (pp. 366f.), there is one
prayer, Ps. 126, which reveals the disappointment and suffering
of the exiles in the homeland after their return from Babylon. The
joy over the grace of Yahweh in bringing them back gave way to
sorrow and grief when they found out that He had after all not
yet granted them complete restoration. In sad and plaintive tones
they sang this prayer for the turn of their fate. Compare also the
other pilgrim psalm from this period, Ps. 123, in which the plea for
deliverance from humiliation is voiced in simple but appealing words.

Ps. 85 was sung in the temple service. The choir began by re-
calling God's grace in restoring Israel from captivity:

> Yahweh, Thou hadst become favorable to Thy land,
>   Thou hadst brought back the captivity of Jacob.
> Thou hadst forgiven the iniquity of Thy people,
>   Thou hadst covered all their sin.
> Thou hadst taken away all Thy wrath,
>   Thou hadst turned back the heat of Thine anger.

But this favor did not last long. Conditions set in which seemed to show that Yahweh was still angry, for the people were suffering want and privation. Earnestly the congregation pleads,

> Restore us, O God of our salvation,
>   and cause Thine indignation toward us to cease.
> Wilt Thou be angry with us for ever,
>   wilt Thou continue Thine anger to all generations?
> Wilt Thou not quicken us again,
>   that Thy people may rejoice in Thee?
> Show us Thy kindness, O Yahweh,
>   and grant us Thy salvation.

A solo singer now takes up the song, and declares like one of the prophets that he had listened to Yahweh in this calamity and that he had distinctly heard the divine answer which spoke "peace to His people."

> I will hear what Yahweh will speak:
>   Yea, He speaks peace to His people,
>   and to His godly ones, that they turn not again to folly.
> Surely His salvation is nigh them that fear Him,
>   that glory may dwell in our land.
> Kindness and truth are met together;
>   righteousness and love have kissed each other.
> Truth springs out of the earth;
>   and righteousness has looked down from heaven.
> Yea, Yahweh will give that which is good;
>   and our land shall yield its increase,
> Righteousness shall go before Him,
>   and peace in the way of His steps. (Ps. 85)

It is the message of the great comforter Deutero-Isaiah (cf. Is. 45:8) that the poet had heard in his soul and that he now gives in lines which are quite worthy of his master.

Ps. 90 also comes in all probability from this early postexilic time. It is not so impassioned, but it moves us by its profound sadness. The deep tones of eternity are sounding through its words. God's eternity is contrasted with man's ephemeral existence, and the cause of the latter is laid bare in man's sinfulness. If only man would learn the lesson! Then he would spend his brief life in harmony with God. Life is so short, and without God's grace so unhappy. That God would again have compassion on His servants, remove the years of misfortune, and bless the work of their hands!

Lord, Thou hast been a refuge
   to us in all generations.
Before the mountains were brought forth,
   or the earth and the world were born,
      from everlasting to everlasting Thou art God.
For a thousand years in Thy sight
   are but as yesterday when it is past
      and as a watch in the night.
Thou turnest man back to dust,
   and sayest, "Return, ye children of men."
Thou sowest them year by year,
   they are like grass which shoots up in the morning:
In the morning it blossoms and shoots up,
   in the evening it fades and withers.

For we are consumed in Thine anger,
   and are dismayed in Thy wrath.
Thou hast set our iniquities before Thee,
   our secret sins in the light of Thy countenance.
Thus all our days vanish away in Thy wrath,
   we bring our years to an end as a sigh.
The days of our years are threescore years and ten,
   or if we are in full strength fourscore years.
Yet is their pride but labor and sorrow,
   for it is soon gone and we fly away.
Who knows the power of Thine anger,
   and who fears Thy wrath?
So teach us to number our days,
   that we may get us a heart of wisdom.

Return, O Yahweh, how long?
   and let it repent Thee concerning Thy servants.
Oh satisfy us in the morning with Thy kindness,
   that we may rejoice and be glad all our days.
Make us glad according to the days wherein Thou hast afflicted us,
   and the years wherein we have seen adversity.
Let Thy work appear unto Thy servants,
   and Thy glory upon their children.
And let the gracious kindliness of the Lord our God be upon us;
   and establish Thou the work of our hands upon us;
      yea, the work of our hands establish Thou it. (Ps. 90)

This psalmist has no hope of immortality. This deepens the sadness of his song. But there is a brave manliness in his view of life; and his hope is in God.

A number of psalms were written at a time of great persecution. Some scholars think they came from the oppression under Antiochus IV Epiphanes, *ca.* 165 B.C.; while others doubt that they could be so late in origin. Great calamities were suffered by the Jews in the late Persian and early Hellenistic periods which would provide an equally good background. These psalms were taken over into the public worship because they voiced so well the afflictions of the people and their ardent prayers for help (Ps. 44, 74, 79, 83). They are all in the same strain; Ps. 79 may serve as an illustration.

> O God, the nations are come into Thine inheritance,
>   they have defiled Thy holy temple,
>   they have laid Jerusalem in ruins.
> They have given the dead bodies of Thy servants
>   to be food to the birds of the heavens,
>   the flesh of Thy devoted ones to the beasts of the earth.
> They have shed their blood like water
>   round about Jerusalem, there was none to bury them.
> We are become a reproach to our neighbors,
>   a mockery and derision to them that are round about us.
> How long, O Yahweh, wilt Thou be angry for ever?
>   (how long) shall Thy jealousy burn like fire?
> Pour out Thy fury upon the nations that know Thee not,
>   and upon the kingdoms that call not on Thy name:
> For they have devoured Jacob,
>   and laid waste his homestead.
> Remember not against us our forefathers' iniquities,
>   let Thy compassions speedily come to meet us,
>   for we are brought very low.
>
> Help us, O God of our salvation, for the glory of Thy name,
>   and deliver us and forgive our sins for Thy name's sake.
> Wherefore should the nations say, "Where is their God?"
>   let the vengeance of Thy servants' blood which is shed
>   be made known among the nations in our sight.
> Let the groaning of the prisoner come before Thee:
>   according to the greatness of Thine arm reprieve Thou those that
>   are appointed to die;

And recompense to our neighbors sevenfold into their bosom
  their reproach wherewith they have reproached Thee, O Lord.
So we, Thy people and sheep of Thy pasture,
  will give thanks to Thee for ever,
    we will tell of Thy praise to all generations. (Ps. 79)

A passionate desire for vengeance and a profound conviction of
Israel's innocence are characteristic of these prayers. In Ps. 44:17–22
the innocence of the people is brought out most strongly:

All this is come upon us; yet have we not forgotten Thee,
  neither have we been false to Thy covenant.
Our heart is not turned back,
  neither have our steps declined from Thy way;
That Thou shouldst have crushed us into a place of jackals,
  and covered us with deathly gloom.
If we had forgotten the name of our God,
  or spread forth our hands to a strange god;
Would not God search this out?
  for He knows the secrets of the heart.
Nay, but for Thy sake are we killed all the day long;
  we are accounted as sheep for the slaughter. (Ps. 44:17–22)

The appeal for help is ushered in with an excessive anthropomorphism,

Arouse Thyself! Why sleepest Thou, O Lord,
  awake, cast (us) not off for ever! (Ps. 44:23)

These psalms are interesting from a historical point of view, but
religiously they are distinctly inferior.

The royal psalms form a special group. Among them Ps. 45 is in
a class by itself: it is a wholly secular ode, composed for the occasion of the marriage of an Israelite king to a foreign princess. The
others are of a religious nature; some of them are oracles, others are
prayers for the king. Ps. 110 may have been composed for the
coronation festival of a king in the temple. At a given moment a
priestly prophet announced:

An oracle of Yahweh unto my lord:
"Sit down at My right hand,
  until I make thine enemies
    a stool for thy feet."

> Yahweh has sworn
>   and will not repent:
> "Thou art a priest for ever
>   after the manner of Melchizedek." (Ps. 110)

He is to be high priest as well as ruler. As the monarchy declined the kings were robbed of their ancient role of "supreme bishop." Later this psalm was interpreted as referring to the Messiah.[18]

Ps. 2 also originally referred to a definite king at the time of his accession. It is a psalm of great dramatic power. The king himself speaks, wondering at the rebellion of his subject nations,

> Why do the nations tumultuously assemble,
>   and the peoples devise vain plans?
> The kings of the earth consult with each other,
>   and the rulers take counsel together,
>   against Yahweh and against His anointed:
> "Let us break their bonds asunder,
>   and fling away their cords from us."
>
> He that sits in the heavens will laugh,
>   the Lord will mock at them.
> Then will He speak to them in His wrath,
>   and dismay them in His fiery anger,
> While I am established as His king
>   upon His holy hill of Zion.

The king proceeds to relate the oracle of Yahweh that had been given him

> Let me tell concerning the decree:
>
> Yahweh said to me, "Thou art My son,
>   this day have I begotten thee: [19]
> Ask of Me, and I will give the nations for thy heritage,
>   and the ends of the earth for thy possession.
> Thou shalt break them with a sceptre of iron,
>   thou shalt dash them in pieces like a potter's vessel."

[18] Christians claimed the high priestly office for Christ on the basis of this psalm (cf. Heb. 2:17). But the sect of the Dead Sea Scrolls expected two Messiahs—one with the priestly and the other with the political functions.

[19] Hebrew kings evidently claimed divine sonship as did the Egyptian Pharaohs, but by "adoption" rather than procreation. The adoption must have taken place on the day of accession. We have here the official formula of adoption, frequently found in ancient Oriental legal documents.

So he warns the rebels,

> Now therefore be wise, O ye kings;
>> be admonished ye judges of the earth.
> Serve Yahweh with fear,
>> submit to Him [20] with trembling,
> Lest He be angry and ye perish in the way,
>> for His wrath is quickly kindled.

To this a liturgical addition is appended,

> Blessed are all they that take refuge in Him. (Ps. 2)

The claim of world dominion which is here made by the king of Zion sounds so extravagant that it is no wonder that the psalm was interpreted as messianic already before the time of Jesus (in the Psalms of Solomon, ch. 17). In the days to come heathendom will determine to overthrow the lordship of the Messiah, but it will be in vain.

Ps. 72 shows how far-reaching the hopes and wishes were for the reigning king. It is the most beautiful of these royal psalms. In it the prayers of the people for the new king are voiced. They pray, most probably during the coronation ceremonies in the temple, for righteous government and eternal life, for prosperity and world dominion.

> Give the king Thy judgment, O God,
>> and Thy righteousness to the king's son.
> May he judge Thy people with righteousness,
>> and Thy poor with justice.
> May the mountains bear peace for the people,
>> and the hills righteousness.
> May he judge the poor of the people,
>> save the children of the needy,
>>> and crush the oppressor.

> May he endure as long as the sun,
>> and as the moon, through all generations.
> May he come down like rain upon the mown grass,
>> as showers that water the earth.
> May righteousness flourish in his days,
>> and abundance of peace, till the moon be no more.

[20] The text originally must have read, *Kiss his feet,* according to a widely accepted conjecture of Alfred Bertholet.

May he have dominion from sea to sea,
  and from the River to the ends of the earth.
Let his adversaries bow before him,
  and his enemies lick the dust.
Let the kings of Tarshish and of the isles render tribute,
  the kings of Sheba and Saba offer gifts.
Yea, let all kings fall down before him,
  all nations serve him. . . .

So may he live, and may men give him of the gold of Sheba,
  and pray for him continually,
    and bless him all the day long. . . . (Ps. 72)

Here again it was easy to interpret the psalm of the great ideal world ruler, the Messiah who was to come. But that was not its original meaning.

We have also a prayer for success in battle before the king went forth to war (Ps. 20), and a thanksgiving for victory after his return (Ps. 21), besides other prayers for him in Ps. 61, 89, 132, 144.

2. PRIVATE WORSHIP IN THE TEMPLE

Along with the public worship for the whole community there were certain occasions for the individual worshiper when he poured forth his thanksgiving or his petition in the temple.[21] Under the stress of danger or severe illness or other calamities men prayed to Yahweh and vowed to bring offerings of thanksgiving, if He would hear them.[22] If then God granted deliverance, the worshiper came to the temple with his family and friends to offer the sacrifice which he had vowed in accordance with his need and his ability, ordinarily a blameless bullock, sheep, or goat (Lev. 22:17ff.) and unleavened cakes with oil (Lev. 7:11ff.). Anyone that happened to be in the temple, especially the poor, joined the party, for the sacrificial animal had to be eaten that same day [23] and nothing must be left.

[21] The question whether the "I" of the Psalms is to be taken individually or collectively has been the subject of much controversy. The former is usually the more satisfactory interpretation.

[22] This was done in earlier as well as in later times. Hannah, the mother of Samuel, was not the only one, even in early times, who prayed in the temple alone and made a vow, if God would grant her petition (1 Sam. 1:9ff.). It was her silent prayer that astonished Eli the priest, for ordinarily people prayed aloud.

[23] The later law (Lev. 7:16ff.) permitted the eating of special and freewill offerings also on the second day to meet the exigencies of the occasions.

Songs of thanksgiving were sung on such occasions. Ps. 66 is one of these. The temple choir began with a hymn,

> Make a joyful noise to God, all the earth:
>> sing forth the glory of His name;
> Make His praise glorious,
>> say unto God, How terrible are Thy works!
> Through the greatness of Thy strength shall Thy enemies
>> come cringing to Thee,
> All the earth shall worship Thee,
>> and shall sing to Thee, shall sing to Thy name.

This hymnal praise continued, one part of the choir singing the second stanza (vv. 5–7), another part taking up the third (vv. 8–12). Then the worshiper who brought the sacrifice stepped forth and sang,[24]

> I come into Thy house with burnt-offerings,
>> I will pay Thee my vows,
> Which my lips uttered,
>> and my mouth spoke when I was in distress.
> I will offer unto Thee burnt-offerings of fatlings,
>> with the sweet smoke of rams;
> I will offer bullocks with he-goats.

With this he turned to the assembled party and told what God had done for him:

> Come, and hear, all ye that fear God,
>> and I will declare what He has done for my soul.

The sentences that follow lack the concrete description of the individual distress and deliverance, because the psalm was to be used by anyone bringing a votive offering.

> I cried unto Him with my mouth,
>> and high praise was under my tongue.
> If I had had iniquity in view in my heart,
>> the Lord would not hear.
> But verily God has heard,
>> He has attended to the voice of my prayer.
> Blessed be God, who has not turned away my prayer,
>> nor (withheld) His kindness from me. (Ps. 66)

[24] Cf. Job 33:27f.

The insistence on the absence of any secret evil intention in connection with the prayer must not be overlooked. It shows again the endeavor to ethicize the cultic functions in the temple.

Sometimes men took refuge in the sanctuary, where God dwelt and where their prayers for help seemed so much more effective. This seems to have been so especially in cases of accusation, in persecutions by enemies, and in sickness. Ps. 26 was probably used in connection with clearing oneself of an accusation. Just of what the psalmist was accused is not said. The early law demanded that in certain cases the defendant had to clear himself in the temple by an oath (Ex. 22:8, 11) and the later law still has an ancient rite by which a woman suspected of adultery was either vindicated or found guilty and punished (Num. 5:11ff.). This is the underlying idea also in the ceremony for which Ps. 26 is intended. The psalmist had gone to the temple with his accusers, and began by calling upon God, loudly protesting his innocence:

> Judge me, Yahweh, for I have walked in mine integrity,
>   and in Yahweh have I trusted without wavering.
> Try me, Yahweh, and prove me,
>   test my heart and my mind.
> For Thy kindness is before mine eyes,
>   and I have walked in Thy truth.
> I have not sat with insincere persons,
>   neither do I go with dissemblers.

After this prayer followed the symbolic ceremony of the washing of his hands, which was accompanied (we may assume, although it is not stated) with a solemn oath by Yahweh who tests the heart and mind,

> I wash my hands in innocency. (cf. Matt. 27:24)

The priest thereupon pronounced him free of the accusation, and the man began the cultic dance around the altar, on which a sacrifice had been brought, and thanked and praised Yahweh,

> I will go around Thine altar, Yahweh,
> That I may make loud thanksgiving to be heard,
>   and tell of all Thy wondrous works:

> Yahweh, I love the habitation of Thy house,
> and the place where Thy glory dwells.

With a look upon his accusers, the psalmist then prays to God,

> Take not away my soul with sinners,
> nor my lip with men of blood;
> In whose hands are wicked devices,
> and their right hand is full of bribes.

He himself will maintain his upright life with God's help,

> But as for me, I will walk in mine integrity,
> redeem me, and be merciful unto me.
> My foot stands in an even place:
> in full assemblies will I bless Yahweh. (Ps. 26)

Then "this man went down to his house justified" (cf. Luke 18:14), cleared of the accusation, able to take his part afresh in the life of the people.

It is amazing how much distress was caused by the animosity of personal enemies, how bitter were the complaints, and how terrible the calls for vengeance upon them. Most of the prayers for protection from the enemies and for their punishment were originally intended for private use and they could be prayed anywhere. But some of them accompanied the sacrifices in the temple. For instance, Ps. 5 was the morning prayer of a devoted worshiper in the sanctuary.

> Give ear to my words, Yahweh,
> consider my meditation.
> Hearken unto the voice of my cry,
> my King and my God,
> For unto Thee I pray in the morning,
> mayest Thou hear my voice.
> In the morning I arrange (my sacrifice) and look out.

He knows that wicked people are not permitted in Yahweh's temple (cf. Ps. 15),

> But I, through the abundance of Thy kindness
> may come into Thy house:
> I may worship toward Thy holy temple
> in the fear of Thee, Yahweh.

Now comes his prayer,

> Lead me, Yahweh, in Thy righteousness,
>   because of mine enemies,
>   make Thy way even before my face.
> For there is no steadfastness in their mouth,
>   their inward part is a yawning gulf,
> Their throat is an open sepulcher,
>   while they flatter with their tongue.
> Declare them guilty, O God,
>   let them fall by their own counsels;
> Thrust them out for the multitude of their transgressions,
>   because they have been defiant against Thee. (Ps. 5)

But let the righteous rejoice over the effective protection of God from their enemies, who are also God's enemies in the psalmist's estimation. There is no pity, much less love for them, but only a relentless spirit of vengeance. It is true enough that when this psalm and similar ones were taken into the public cult of the temple, it was not the personal enemies but the opposing party of the worldly minded and ungodly Jews for whom the pious party had these "pious" wishes. But originally they were meant for the personal enemies of the individual worshiper. In either case these imprecatory psalms are vitiated for us by the spirit of vengeance. One of the worst of them is Ps. 109 with its fearful curses upon the enemies, which was used in the public worship as a "sacred" song!

In most of the prayers of the sick there is also a complaint over heartless people who had been friends before, but who have turned against the sick, strikingly enough just because of his sickness. It seems incredible to us that one should deny sympathy and help to the sick. But this was due to the doctrine that health and prosperity are the reward of piety, but disease and misfortune the result of wickedness. Disease was therefore an indication of sinfulness, as Job's friends too assumed. The old man who prays for deliverance from his extraordinary sufferings in Ps. 71 complains,

> Mine enemies speak concerning me,
>   and they that watch for my life take counsel together,
> Saying, "God has forsaken him:
>   pursue and take him, for there is none to deliver." (Ps. 71:10f.)

In Ps. 41 the psalmist laments,

> Mine enemies speak evil of me,
> "When will he die, and his name perish?"
> And if one come to see me, he speaks insincerity:
> his heart gathers malice to itself;
> when he goes abroad, he speaks of it.
>
> All they that hate me whisper together against me,
> they imagine evil for me:
> "Some deadly thing has fast hold of him,
> and now that he lies, he will rise up no more."
> Yea, mine own intimate friend in whom I trusted,
> who ate my bread has lifted up his heel against me. (Ps. 41:5-9)

The suffering from the disease may have been terrible, especially when the sick person was covered with loathsome and festering wounds, when his body was racked with fever, and his strength was fast ebbing away, but the bitterness of being forsaken even by his close relatives was more terrible still.

> My lovers and friends stand aloof from my plague;
> and my kinsmen stand afar off. (Ps. 38:11)

It is easy to understand that some of these sufferers long for an opportunity to pay them back for their cruel behavior.

> But Thou, Yahweh, be gracious to me and raise me up,
> that I may requite them. (Ps. 41:10)

Nevertheless these psalmists themselves also had the belief that their suffering was the result of their sin, and often confessed it with penitent sorrow:

> O Yahweh, reprove me not in Thy wrath,
> neither chasten me in Thy displeasure. . . .
> For mine iniquities are gone over my head,
> as a heavy burden they are too heavy for me. . . .
> I declare mine iniquity,
> I am sorry for my sin. (Ps. 38:1, 4, 18)

But occasionally a psalmist was not conscious of any deliberate sin that should deserve such punishment as his serious sickness constituted. Then he pleaded for light on the reason of his suffering,

> Yahweh, why castest Thou off my soul?
> why hidest Thou Thy face from me? (Ps. 88:14)

Or like the sufferer of Ps. 22, who had been so brutally wounded by his enemies, he cried out,

> My God, my God, why hast Thou forsaken me?
> why art Thou so far from helping me,
> from the words of my groaning? (Ps. 22:1)

3. PSALMS OF A NONCULTIC NATURE

There are some psalms that have no trace of the sacrificial cult in them. They seem to express the deep, personal piety of the psalmist quite independently. Here the heart speaks out of its depths, prays for help and forgiveness, thanks for God's grace and sings His praise.[25] In some of them there is even a distinct reaction against the sacrificial system, e.g., in that greatest of all the penitential psalms, Ps. 51, that still moves men's hearts to repentance, and voices for them their deep need of forgiveness and purification, and the renewing and steadying of their will.

> Have mercy upon me, O God, according to Thy kindness:
> according to the multitude of Thy tender mercies
> blot out my transgressions.
> Wash me thoroughly from mine iniquity,
> and cleanse me from my sin.
>
> For I know my transgressions;
> and my sin is ever before me.
> Against Thee, Thee only, have I sinned,
> and done that which is evil in Thy sight;
> That Thou mayest be justified when Thou speakest,
> and be clear when Thou judgest.
> Behold, I was brought forth in iniquity;
> and in sin my mother conceived me.
> Behold, Thou desirest truth in the inward parts (?);
> and in the hidden part make me to know wisdom.

[25] It seems unlikely that there was any private worship in our sense. The authors of psalmody were no doubt members of the Levitic minstrel families listed in 1 Chron. 25. Psalms need not always betray by their words the cultic use made of them. Some fine Babylonian psalms have come down in magical incantation texts, for which they were not originally written. The injection of prophetic ideas, as in the so-called antisacrificial psalms, is not wholly impossible within the framework of the cult, according to some scholars.

Purify me with hyssop, that I may be clean:
　　wash me, that I may be whiter than snow.
Make me to hear joy and gladness,
　　that the bones which Thou hast crushed may rejoice.
Hide Thy face from my sins,
　　and blot out all mine iniquities.

Create in me a clean heart, O God;
　　and renew a steadfast spirit within me.
Cast me not away from Thy presence;
　　and take not Thy holy Spirit from me.
Restore to me the joy of Thy salvation;
　　and uphold me with a willing spirit.
Then will I teach transgressors Thy ways;
　　and sinners shall be converted to Thee.

Deliver me from (the land of) silence, O God, Thou God of my
　　　salvation;
　　and my tongue shall sing aloud of Thy righteousness.
O Lord, open Thou my lips;
　　and my mouth shall show forth Thy praise.
For Thou delightest not in sacrifice; else would I give it:
　　Thou hast no pleasure in burnt-offering.
My sacrifice, O God, is a broken spirit:
　　a broken and a contrite heart, O God, Thou wilt not despise.
　　　　　　　　　　　　　　　　　　　　(Ps. 51:1–17)

The influence of the great prophets is so unmistakable here, that we
read with surprise the incongruous, later addition in v. 18f. which
prays for the restoration of Zion and tells of the sacrifices that will
then be offered again in the temple. To our psalmist animal and
cereal sacrifices were of as little value as to Ps. 40, which says,

　　Sacrifice and offering Thou hast no delight in;
　　　mine ears hast Thou opened:
　　Burnt-offering and sin-offering Thou hast not required. (Ps. 40:6)

Ps. 50, where God is introduced as appearing in a theophany and
as addressing the people Himself, makes it plain that their zeal for
sacrifices is mistaken.

　　　Hear, O My people, and I will speak,
　　　　O Israel, and I will protest unto thee:
　　　I am Yahweh, thy God,
　　　　[who brought thee out of the land of Egypt].

> I will not reprove thee for thy sacrifices;
>   thy burnt-offerings are continually before Me.
> I will take no bullock out of thy house,
>   nor he-goats out of thy folds.
> For every beast of the forest is Mine,
>   and the cattle on the hills of God.
> I know all the birds of the mountains
>   and that which moves in the field is Mine.
>
> If I were hungry, I would not tell thee:
>   for the world is Mine, and its fulness.
> Do I eat the flesh of bulls,
>   or drink the blood of goats?
>
> Offer to God the sacrifice of thanksgiving,
>   so wilt thou pay thy vows to the Most High;
> And call upon Me in the day of trouble:
>   I will deliver thee, and thou shalt glorify Me. (Ps. 50:7-15)

Genuine thanksgiving and heartfelt prayer are the real offerings
that please God, and their sincerity must be attested by a righteous
life.

> Whoso offers the sacrifice of thanksgiving glorifies Me,
>   and to him that keeps My way
>   will I show the salvation of God. (Ps. 50:23)

The spiritualization of sacrifice has begun. Ps. 141 prays,

> Let my prayer be set forth as incense before Thee,
>   the lifting up of my hands as the evening sacrifice. (Ps. 141:2)

A psalmist who can say of himself, "the zeal of Thy house has eaten
me up" (taken in a future sense in John 2:19), nevertheless declares,

> I will praise the name of God with a song,
>   and magnify Him with thanksgiving;
> And it will please Yahweh better than an ox
>   or a bullock that has horns and hoofs. (Ps. 69:30f.)

And so we find in the Psalter a number of hymns in which the
religion of the heart pours itself forth in praise and thanksgiving
without any ceremonial trace whatsoever. The most famous of these
personal hymns or songs of praise is Ps. 103.

Bless Yahweh, O my soul;
  and all that is within me, bless His holy name.
Bless Yahweh, O my soul,
  and forget not all His benefits:
Who forgives all thine iniquities;
  who heals all thy diseases;
Who redeems thy life from the pit;
  who crowns thee with kindness and compassion;
Who satisfies thy desire with good things,
  so that thy youth is renewed like the vulture's.

Yahweh executes righteous acts,
  and judgments for all that are oppressed.
He made known His ways to Moses,
  His doings to the children of Israel.
Yahweh is merciful and gracious,
  slow to anger, and abundant in kindness.
He will not always contend;
  neither will He keep His anger for ever.
He has not dealt with us after our sins,
  nor rewarded us after our iniquities.
For as the heavens are high above the earth,
  so great is His kindness toward them that fear Him.
As far as the east is from the west,
  so far has He removed our transgressions from us.
Like as a father pities his children,
  so Yahweh pities them that fear Him.
For He knows our frame;
  He remembers that we are dust.
As for man, his days are as grass;
  as a flower of the field, so he blossoms.
For the wind passes over it, and it is gone;
  and its place knows it no more.
But the kindness of Yahweh is for ever,
  and His righteousness unto children's children;
To them that fear Him, that keep His covenant,
  and to those that remember His precepts to do them.

Yahweh has established His throne in the heavens;
  and His kingdom rules over all.
Bless Yahweh, ye His angels,
  that are mighty in strength, that fulfil His word,

> Bless Yahweh, all ye His hosts,
>   ye ministers of his, that do His pleasure.
> Bless Yahweh, all ye His works,
>   in all places of his dominion:
> *Bless Yahweh, O my soul.* (Ps. 103) [26]

Among the individual psalms there are not only prayers for help and forgiveness and hymns of praise, but also many spiritual songs and meditations on fundamental themes, which throw light on the religious life of the people, especially in postexilic times. We may consider first some psalms on the omnipresence of God, His providence, and His righteous rule. Ps. 139 is a meditation on God's omnipresence and omniscience. This psalm is unique in the Psalter. It shows that the belief in monotheism necessitated an understanding of the problems connected with it. There is real philosophical thinking in this meditation, although the form is not speculative but poetic: the poet sinks down in adoration of the great wonder of the one omnipresent and omniscient God who is not bound by space and time, and his meditation becomes a hymn.

> O Yahweh, Thou hast searched me, and known me,
>   Thou knowest my downsitting and mine uprising;
>   Thou understandest my thought afar off.
> Thou searchest out my walking and my lying down,
>   and art acquainted with all my ways.
> For there is not a word in my tongue,
>   but, lo, O Yahweh, Thou knowest it altogether.
> Thou hast beset me behind and before,
>   and laid Thy hand upon me.
> Such knowledge is too wonderful for me;
>   it is high, I cannot attain to it.
>
> Whither shall I go from Thy Spirit?
>   or whither shall I flee from Thy presence?
> If I ascend up into the heaven, Thou art there:
>   if I make my bed in Sheol, behold, Thou art there.

[26] The companion psalm, Ps. 104, celebrates God's glory in the work of creation. It has such close affinities to the solar hymn of Pharaoh Amenhotep IV (*ca.* 1370 B.C.) that it would seem that the psalm was deliberately patterned after the Egyptian hymn. For a translation see *ANET*, p. 365. But here as elsewhere the peculiar genius of Israel shows itself in such a complete assimilation of the foreign material that the psalm appears as a thoroughly Jewish composition with all the distinctive Israelite belief in the personal Creator.

> If I choose the wings of the dawn,
>   and dwell in the uttermost parts of the sea;
> Even there would Thy hand seize me,
>   and Thy right hand would hold me.
> If I say, Surely the darkness shall screen me,
>   and the light about me shall be night;
> Even the darkness is not too dark for Thee,
>   but the night shines as the day:
>   the darkness and the light are both alike to Thee. (Ps. 139:1–12)

After considering the divine mystery of his own formation and birth the psalmist exclaims, overwhelmed by the wonder of it all,

> How precious are Thy thoughts to me, O God!
>   how great is the sum of them!
> If I should count them, they are more in number than the sand,
>   were I to come to the end I would still be with Thee (139:17f.)

Then suddenly he bursts forth into an almost unaccountable denunciation of the enemies of God, whom he hates as if they were his own personal enemies too. In his fanatic devotion to God it seems incomprehensible to him that anyone should not worship and serve Him, that anyone should persist in wickedness and defy Him. He wants all such to be destroyed, in order that God may be everywhere glorified:

> Oh that Thou wouldst slay the wicked, O God!
>   and that bloodthirsty men would depart from me!
> Who defy Thee with wicked intent,
>   and take Thy name in vain.
> Do not I hate them, O Yahweh, that hate Thee?
>   and do not I loathe them that rise up against Thee?
> I hate them with a perfect hatred:
>   they are become mine enemies. (139:19–22)

So completely has he identified himself with God's cause that he hates God's enemies as his own. And so little does he realize the essential heinousness of his fanaticism that he prays to God with utter sincerity,

> Search me, O God, and know my heart,
>   try me, and know my thoughts;
> And see if there be any wicked way in me,
>   and lead me in the way everlasting. (139:23f.)

The thought never occurred to him that his hatred was a wicked way, which must lead to sorrow and pain. He was still far from the teachings of Him who said, "Love your enemies . . . that ye may be sons of your Father who is in heaven," for He loves His enemies too (Matt. 5:44f.).

Ps. 91 is a meditation on the providence of God. After a forceful introductory statement of the theme (vv. 1f.) the poet addresses and instructs the believer by celebrating the security enjoyed by him that trusts in God in the midst of danger (vv. 3–43). At the conclusion Yahweh Himself speaks and confirms this magnificent exposition with a personal promise (vv. 14–16).

> He that dwells in the secret place of the Most High,
>   that abides under the shadow of the Almighty,
> Shall say to Yahweh, "My refuge and my fortress;
>   my God, in whom I trust."
>
> For He will deliver thee from the snare of the fowler,
>   and from the pit of destruction.
> He will cover thee with His pinions,
>   and under His wings shalt thou take refuge,
>   His truth is a shield and a buckler.
> Thou shalt not be afraid for the terror by night,
>   nor for the arrow that flies by day;
> For the pestilence that walks in darkness,
>   nor for the destruction that wastes at noonday.
> Though a thousand fall at thy side,
>   and ten thousand at thy right hand;
>   it shall not come nigh thee.
> Only with thine eyes shalt thou behold,
>   and see the reward of the wicked.
> For as for thee, Yahweh is thy refuge,
>   thou hast made the Most High thy stronghold;
> There shall no evil befall thee,
>   neither shall any plague come nigh thy tent.
> For He will give His angels charge over thee,
>   to keep thee in all thy ways.
> They shall bear thee up in their hands,
>   lest thou dash thy foot against a stone.
> Thou shalt tread upon the lion and adder:
>   the young lion and the serpent shalt thou trample under foot.

> Because he has set his love upon Me, I will deliver him:
>> I will set him on high, because he has known My name.
> He shall call upon Me, and I will answer him;
>> I will be with him in trouble:
>> I will deliver him, and honor him.
> With long life will I satisfy him,
>> and show him My salvation.

It is a religious quietism that is celebrated here, the passive trust in God's protection and care, rather than the active overcoming of danger and the conquest of evil. This is the ideal of the meek and the poor, the quiet in the land, who trust in God for everything.

There are, of course, also songs of virile strength, such as Ps. 101, where a man of high authority, a ruler, promises to God not only a personal life of integrity but also a righteous administration of the city of Jerusalem, which favors the just and punishes the wicked:

> Morning by morning will I destroy
>> all the wicked of the land;
> To cut off from the city of Yahweh
>> all the workers of iniquity. (Ps. 101:8)

But ordinarily the establishment of righteous conditions is only expected from the divine intervention (cf. Ps. 58). In the so-called eschatological hymns we witnessed the eager anticipation of Yahweh's assumption of the government of the world. The poet of Ps. 82 saw Yahweh standing among the unjust judges of the earth and rebuking them:

> How long will ye judge unjustly,
>> and respect the persons of the wicked?
> Judge the poor and fatherless,
>> do justice to the afflicted and destitute!
> Rescue the poor and needy,
>> deliver them out of the hand of the wicked!

But these judges have so little ethical discernment that the moral foundations of the earth are endangered. Yahweh must therefore intervene, and in passionate plea the psalmist prays,

> Arise, O God, judge the earth,
>> for Thou art the heir [27] of all nations. (Ps. 82)

[27] *I.e.*, the rightful lord.

Only thus can righteousness be established in the world.

Righteousness was the fundamental requirement of Yahweh for all. Its paramount importance was brought out in a number of psalms. We saw how as a result of the prophetic emphasis on righteousness the sacrificial cult in the temple was ethicized by some psalmists, and how the prophetic Ps. 50 criticized the whole sacrificial system. In Ps. 15 we have a song which has sometimes been called a catechism for the proselytes, but which was later taken into the public cult (cf. Ps. 24). It answers the question of the conditions of true communion with God by an exclusive emphasis on social morality:

> Yahweh, who may be a guest in Thy tent?
>   who may dwell in Thy holy hill?
>
> He that walks uprightly, and works righteousness,
>   and speaks truth in his heart;
> He that slanders not his neighbor,
>   nor does evil to his friend,
>   nor takes up a reproach against his neighbor,
> In whose eyes a reprobate is despised,
>   but who honors them that fear Yahweh.
> He that swears to his own hurt, and changes not,
>   he that puts not out his money to interest
>   nor takes a bribe against the innocent.
> He that does these things without ever wavering. (Ps. 15)

Quite justly did an eminent Jewish commentator remark on this psalm: "If Israel had accepted this conception . . . the religion of Yahweh would have become the religion of the world" (Ehrlich).

But it was not accepted, the law became supreme, the religion of Yahweh became legalistic, and no legalistic form of religion, however exalted its ethics, can ever be a true expression of the religion of the spirit. Moreover, the Jewish law insisted on ceremonies as well as on morals. Besides the danger of externalizing religion there was also the danger of placing the primary, fundamental moral requirements on the same level with the ceremonial. And the wearisome burden of this mass of legal details, which never allowed one to

gain peace, rested as a heavy yoke upon many people. It required
much knowledge too; one had to study the law day and night, as
Ps. 1 says, if one intended to be truly righteous. We therefore find
in the Psalter such legal psalms as Ps. 19:7ff. and especially the long
alphabetical Ps. 119, with their praises of the law.

> The law of Yahweh is perfect, refreshing the soul:
>> The testimony of Yahweh is trustworthy, making wise the simple.
> The precepts of Yahweh are right, rejoicing the heart:
>> The commandment of Yahweh is pure, enlightening the eyes.
> The fear of Yahweh is clean, enduring for ever:
>> The ordinances of Yahweh are true and righteous altogether.
> More to be desired are they than gold, yea, than much fine gold:
>> Sweeter also than honey and the droppings of the honeycomb.
>> (Ps. 19:7-10)

> Oh how love I Thy law!
>> it is my meditation all the day. (Ps. 119:97)

> How sweet are Thy words to my palate!
>> sweeter than honey to my mouth! (Ps. 119:105)

This intense love of the law was due to the fact that it had become
to these earnest men a guide to God. In the study of it they experienced a fellowship with Yahweh, who had here expressed His will.

The law became to them a means of direct communion with God.

The longing for fellowship with God has found tones so deep and
so human in some psalms of intimate communion that they still
touch responsive chords in human hearts. The condition of the
exiled singer who wrote Ps. 42f., harassed by enemies and pained
by his own bitter grief, may be quite his own; his delight in the festal
procession and the worship in the temple may even be quite foreign
to us, yet his cry for the living God comes out of the far depths of
the soul and seems like the cry of our own souls, whose yearning it
has awakened.

> As the hind cries for the water brooks,
>> so cries my soul for Thee, O God.
> My soul thirsts for God, for the living God,
>> when shall I come and appear before God?
>> (Ps. 42:1f., cf. also Ps. 63:1f.)

The sorrow over interrupted fellowship with God pervades the penitential psalms. And the blessedness of forgiveness is sung in Ps. 32,

> Blessed is he whose transgression is forgiven,
>   whose sin is covered.
> Blessed is the man to whom Yahweh imputes not iniquity,
>   and in whose spirit there is no guile. (Ps. 32:1f.)

Happy is he who can sing with all his heart the shepherd psalm, that most beloved of them all:

> Yahweh is my shepherd; I shall not want.
>   He makes me to lie down in green pastures:
> He gently guides me unto still waters.
>   He refreshes my soul.
> He leads me in paths of righteousness
>   for His name's sake.
>
> Yea, though I walk through a valley of deep gloom,
>   I will fear no evil,
> For Thou art with me. Thy rod and Thy staff,
>   they comfort me.
>
> Thou preparest a table before me
>   in the sight of mine enemies: [28]
> Thou hast anointed my head with oil,
>   my cup is well filled.
>
> Only goodness and kindness shall follow me
>   all the days of my life;
> And I shall dwell in the house of Yahweh
>   for length of days. (Ps. 23)

In the strength of this personally experienced communion with God some psalmists faced the hardest problems of life and solved them: death was the one, God's moral government of the world the other. We saw how long it took the Jews to arrive at a satisfying conception of the life after death. The psalmists too remained on the older level of thought where one might say

> There is no remembrance of Thee in death,
>   who shall give Thee thanks in Sheol? (Ps. 6:5, cf. also 30:8f.)

[28] The mention of enemies mars the beauty of this psalm. This and the close connection of religion with the temple are limitations of the psalmist.

But there were some who through the inherent power of their experience of divine fellowship transcended death by their victorious faith that this communion could never be broken. The author of Ps. 49—a didactic poem, teaching that the rich, in spite of their wealth and glory, cannot escape death—expresses the faith for himself

> But God will redeem my soul from the power of Sheol,
>   for he will receive me. (Ps. 49:15)

Similarly the believer of Ps. 16, to whom God was his highest good, was so secure in the joy and peace of his intimacy with God that it seemed utterly incredible to him that this should ever come to an end. He knows that death must come, and he sees no way of escape, but he is nevertheless serene,

> For Thou wilt not leave my soul to Sheol,
>   neither wilt Thou allow Thy devoted one to see the pit.
> Thou wilt show me the path of life:
>   in Thy presence is fulness of joy;
>   in Thy right hand there are pleasures for evermore. (Ps. 16:10f.)

He has no clearly thought out doctrine of resurrection or immortality. He does not know the way, but God will show it to him. If he were the author of Ps. 17, as is not unlikely, the great test of suffering came to him also, but it did not shake him in his faith:

> As for me, I shall behold Thy face in righteousness,
>   I shall be satisfied, when I awake, with (beholding) Thy form.
>   (Ps. 17:15)

He had experienced the grace and love of God too profoundly, and he believed in His righteousness too implicitly to doubt that he is God's forever.

The righteousness of God, however, constituted for some a serious problem. They could not harmonize the experiences of life, the prosperity of the wicked, and the suffering of the righteous with their faith in God's moral government of the world. There were some, indeed, who would quiet the misgivings of the thoughtful with a strong reiteration of the old doctrine of retribution, e.g., the aged, wise, and orthodox saint in Ps. 37, who tried to steady the doubters by his counsel in the manner of the wisdom literature,

> Fret not thyself because of evil-doers,
>   neither be envious against them that work unrighteousness.
> For they shall soon be mown down like the grass,
>   and wither as the green herb.
> Trust in Yahweh, and do good;
>   dwell in the land, and follow after faithfulness:
> So shalt thou have thy delight in Yahweh,
>   and He will give thee the desires of thy heart. (Ps. 37:1–4)

For this is the result of his prolonged observation,

> I have been young and now I am old,
>   yet have I not seen the righteous forsaken,
>   nor his seed begging bread. (Ps. 37:25)

But others had different experiences; notably the author of Ps. 73. At the very beginning he states the outcome of his struggle:

> Surely God is good to the upright,
>   to such as are pure in heart.

Now he knows this, now he is certain of it, but for a while this seemed to him incredible. The facts of life were so strongly opposed to it, that he had almost suffered shipwreck in his faith. The good fortune of the wicked, their security, arrogance, and brazen denial of any divine government of the world were so impressive to him who had to suffer so much in spite of his passionate devotion to righteousness that he almost came to the conclusion,

> Surely in vain have I cleansed my heart,
>   and washed my hands in innocency;
> For all the day long have I been plagued,
>   and chastened every morning. (Ps. 73:13f.)

It was only his regard for the pious community that kept him from uttering these thoughts; he must be loyal to his friends, for they must not suffer through his scepticism. But the problem pressed all the harder upon his mind and seemed completely insoluble, until he went into the sanctuary where he received the solution in a spiritual illumination. He considered the fate of the wicked and understood.

Surely Thou settest them in slippery places;
  Thou castest them down to destruction.

How are they become a desolation in a moment!
　　they are utterly brought to an end by sudden terrors! (Ps. 73:18f.)

He had not seen this before, he had suffered all this mental agony
because of his own stupidity. It is somewhat amazing that he should
have regarded this as a tenable solution of his problem. To us, as
well as to the author of Job, this is totally unsatisfactory. But it is
not the whole of the poet's illumination. He realizes with sudden
gladness that he, in striking contrast to the wicked, has found in his
communion with God the solution of life, a compensation for all its
sorrows.

> Yet I am continually with Thee;
> 　Thou holdest my right hand.
> Thou wilt guide me with Thy counsel,
> 　and afterward receive me with glory.
> Whom have I in heaven but Thee?
> 　and having Thee, there is naught on earth that I desire.
> My flesh and my heart fail:
> 　but God is the strength of my heart
> 　and my portion forever.

Those who faithlessly depart from God are destroyed,

> But as for me, to draw near unto God is good for me;
> 　I have made the Lord my refuge,
> 　that I may tell of all Thy works. (Ps. 73:23–28)

The intellectual solution by the terrible end of the wicked is untenable, but the practical solution by his communion with God is as
true today as ever. Faith triumphs over doubt because of its experience of direct fellowship with God. Here are the roots out of which
the belief in immortality could grow. When communion with God
was combined with the brave sense of righteousness, so characteristic of Israel, it was bound to develop into this hope. Without the
one or the other of these a vital faith in an eternal life of union with
God is difficult to attain. These psalmists may not have reached a
doctrine of immortality, but they were not far from it, for they
experienced, what the author of the fourth Gospel so clearly defined, that knowledge of God is eternal life (cf. John 17:3).

　It is just this element of profound trust that makes the Psalter
so full of spiritual power: a trust so deep that it can say,

Yahweh is my light and my salvation,
  whom shall I fear?
Yahweh is the strength of my life,
  of whom should I be afraid? (Ps. 27:1);

a trust so strong that it can burst into the powerful Ps. 46; a trust
so serene that it can sing the shepherd Ps. 23; a trust so jubilant that
it can cry,

Whom have I in heaven but Thee?
  and having Thee there is naught on earth that I desire. (Ps. 73:25)

Not all of the Psalter is of value for us today; and yet there is so
much of it that still voices deep human longings, that kindles the
inner life, that teaches pure moral religion, so much of it that is of
such poetic excellence and spiritual insight that it still deserves, in
spite of its imperfections, crudities, and barbarities, to be used, with
discrimination, as a book of public and private devotion.

Psalmody had accompanied Israel through the centuries, and its
flow did not cease in the third century B.C. Among the Dead Sea
Scrolls has been found a new collection of Hebrew hymns of the
Maccabean period: the thanksgiving hymns (*Hodayoth*) from Cave
1.[29] We also have in Greek translation a collection of psalms composed shortly before and after Pompey's capture of Jerusalem in
63 B.C., which is called "Psalms of Solomon." [30] The *Magnificat* and
Benedictus in the Gospel of Luke (1:46–55, 68–79) are so thoroughly
psalm-like in form and content and so Jewish in character, that they
must have been adapted from some Jewish collection.

[29] See M. Burrows, *The Dead Sea Scrolls*, pp. 400–415 for translations.
[30] Cf. *APOT*, II, pp. 625–652.

XXI

The Later Postexilic Prophets

HOW profoundly the priests influenced religious life and thought after the exile we have witnessed more than once even among the prophets. In Joel we meet a prophet in whose case this is particularly evident. He even stresses the importance of sacrifices (cf. 1:9, 13; 2:14).

The editors of the Book of the Twelve put Joel between Hosea and Amos and thus regarded the author as an eighth-century prophet. But the numerous Aramaisms in the language and the lack of any indication of the existence of the monarchy point to postexilic times for the basic chs. 1–2. We may date the prophet in the late fifth or early fourth century.

A great locust plague, worse than anything the oldest inhabitant could remember, roused Joel to his prophetic activity. In a vivid manner he describes the vast army of locusts, names them in the various stages of their entomological development, pictures their rapid advance and their destructive activity. Through injected references to the Day of Yahweh, this terrible foe takes on mythical apocalyptic features.[1] These allusions were formerly regarded as later additions, but are now widely held to be original; old Canaanitic phraseology in the mythological texts from Ugarit (*Ras Shamra*) has been adduced for comparison. The plague was accompanied by a drought which made matters worse. The country faced ruin, and the cult was threatened with cessation. "The meal-offering and the drink-offering" the prophet complains, "Are cut off from the house of Yahweh." (1:9)

[1] Utilized in Rev. 9:3f.

In these circumstances Joel calls upon the priests to arrange a day for fasting and mourning and for a penitential assembly of the entire population in the temple at Jerusalem, and provides a suitable lamentation for the occasion. In 2:1–14 the locusts come against Jerusalem itself, like an invading army. Yahweh promises to relent if repentance is in evidence, and the prophet calls for it. He then repeats the demand for a fast-day, describes how it was thereupon conducted and gives the petition uttered by the priests. Prophetically he envisions Yahweh's act of mercy and His promise to remove "the northerner" and give new fertility (2:15–20, 25–27). In the midst of Yahweh's speech the prophet burst forth into beautiful strains of joy (2:21–24).

Perhaps this is all that Joel wrote. If so, it gives us an interesting picture of a prophetic activity in connection with an actual situation of calamity of nature. His clear and fluent style, his rhythmic lines so swift and beautiful, his graphic and dramatic descriptions, and his stirring appeals mark him as also a poet and an orator.

It is a moot question whether Joel extended his prophecy and wrote of the awful judgment day of Yahweh on the world in 2:28f. The prophetic author of that passage first foretold the great excitement that would seize all classes:

> And it shall come to pass afterwards,
>   that I will pour out My Spirit upon all flesh;
> And your sons and your daughters shall prophesy,
>   your old men shall dream dreams,
>   your young men shall see visions:
> And also upon the servants and upon the handmaids
>   in those days will I pour out My spirit. (Joel 2:28–29)

The contents of their inspiration, we must assume, concerned the coming day of Yahweh. Young and old, male and female, high and low among the Jews (for only they are meant by "all flesh") will experience the prophetic urge.[2]

Then come the eschatological portents

---

[2] Joel has sometimes been called the Prophet of Pentecost, and indeed Peter quotes this passage in his sermon in Acts 2:17f. But Joel did not predict the fuller illumination or spiritual transformation, which Christians associate with the coming of the Spirit.

> And I will show wonders in the heavens and in the earth,
> blood, and fire, and pillars of smoke.
> The sun shall be turned into darkness,
> and the moon into blood,
> Before the great and terrible day
> of Yahweh comes. (2:30-31)

But those that call on Yahweh's name shall be delivered, whether they are in Jerusalem and Judah, or elsewhere (2:32).

Another prophecy (3:1-3) describes the judgment on the nations at the time when Yahweh restores the fortunes of Judah and Jerusalem. Yahweh will gather them into the valley of "Jehoshaphat," no doubt named after the king of Judah who established a supreme court at Jerusalem. (2 Chron. 19:4f.) Since the name means "Yahweh judges" the place bearing it seemed particularly suitable for the purpose in view here. This prophecy seems to be continued in Joel 3:9-17. All people will be summoned to prepare for war, "Beat your plowshares into swords, and your pruninghooks into spears!" Come all of you to the Valley of Jehoshaphat, "for there will I sit to judge all the nations round about." Then the command will be given to the heavenly reapers to put in the sickle and reap the harvest and tread the winepress of the nations. Thereafter Yahweh will forever protect his people against foreign invaders.

It seems that a later hand inserted 3:4-8 in the prophecy of the judgment in the Valley of Jehoshaphat. It is an oracle against Tyre, Sidon, and the Philistines, for whom the author expected particular retribution because they carried off Yahweh's rich treasures to their temples, and sold Jewish captives to the Greeks. Yahweh will sell their sons and daughters to the Jews, who in turn will sell them to the distant Sabeans of South Arabia.

An editor added at the end of the book a colorful, though not original, description of the future fertility of Judah and the wonderful spring that would flow out of the temple, watering the Valley of Shittim, and predicted, quite in the manner and spirit of Trito-Isaiah and Isaiah 34f., the ruin of Egypt and Edom on account of pogroms that had taken place in their land (3:18ff.).[3]

[3] The chapter and verse count unfortunately differs in the English and Hebrew after 2:27. We have adhered to the English.

To the late Persian era belong very probably two oracles, which are now preserved in the Book of Isaiah, the one against Sidon (Isa. 23:1–14), the other against Egypt (Isa. 19:1–15). The former seems to reflect the terrible destruction of Sidon by Artaxerxes III in 348 B.C. The poem paints the dismay in the great commercial centers over the fall of that "mart of nations," the ancient joyful city, "whose feet carried her afar off to sojourn."

> Yahweh of hosts has purposed it,
>   to stain the pride of all glory,
>   to bring into contempt all the honorable of the earth. (Isa. 23:9)

Later on, after Alexander the Great's capture and destruction of Sidon's sister city Tyre in 332 B.C., this poem was augmented by vv. 15–18 and interpreted as referring to the fall of both Sidon and Tyre. For seventy years Tyre will be forgotten, but then Yahweh will visit her again and she will be the great merchant of the world once more.

> And her merchandise and her hire shall be holy to Yahweh; it shall not be treasured nor laid up; for her merchandise shall be for them that dwell before Yahweh, to eat sufficiently, and for durable clothing. (Isa. 23:18)

This means that the profit of her commerce shall go to the Jews! There is no hint of any spiritual relation of Tyre to Yahweh or of any spiritual benefit for her. Political dependence on the Jews is expressed by the figure of her income being holy to Yahweh.

In Isa. 19:1–15 the writer predicted an invasion of Egypt. She will be forsaken by all her idols.

> And I will give over the Egyptians
>   into the hand of a cruel lord,
> And a fierce king shall rule over them,
>   says the Lord, Yahweh of hosts. (Isa. 19:4)

This fierce king was in all probability Artaxerxes III, who marched against Egypt in 343 B.C. The Nile will be dried up and all Egyptian industries will be ruined. The princes and counsellors will not know how to advise the Pharaoh.

> Neither shall there be for Egypt any work, which head or tail, palm-branch or rush (*i.e.*, high or low) may do. (Isa. 19:15)

Perhaps we may include here the prophecy of Isa. 33, which cannot be attributed to that ancient prophet. It is really a "prophetic liturgy," in which diverse literary forms are employed.[4] It was no doubt written for a definite situation, details of which are preserved. The following words hardly permit any other construction.

> Behold, the valiant ones cry without,
>   the ambassadors of peace weep bitterly.
> He has broken the covenant, despised the cities,
>   and regarded not man. (Isa. 33:7f.)

In view of the Dead Sea Isaiah Scroll it seems unlikely that this refers to events of Maccabean times. It is more probable that history of the third or fourth century B.C., about which our information is meager, holds the key to the background. A woe had already been pronounced upon the treacherous tyrant, but now Yahweh declares that He will rise and consume the peoples. Then the sinners in Zion will be afraid, because they will realize that they cannot live in the presence of the devouring fire, the eternal burnings of Yahweh's appearance. Only the righteous may dwell in His presence, and will be protected and provided for by Yahweh. A little while before the defender of the temple had to capitulate, but soon,

> His place of defence shall be the fortresses of rocks,
>   his bread shall be given him, his waters shall be sure. (Isa. 33:16)

Then the golden time will come.

> Thine eyes shall see the King in His beauty,
>   they shall behold a land that reaches far.
> Thy heart shall muse on the terror;
>   where is he that counted, where is he that weighed?
> Zion shall be a quiet habitation, which shall never again be disturbed,
> For Yahweh is our judge, Yahweh is our lawgiver,
>   Yahweh is our King; he will save us. (Isa. 33:17f., 22)

To this general period also may be assigned the so-called Isaiah Apocalypse (Isa. 24–27). The author had his predecessors in Ezekiel and Zechariah. He saw, as they had seen, the hidden secrets of the heavenly realm and revealed the spiritual forces that were shaping the destiny of the world according to God's plan. He looked to the

[4] Micah 7:7-20 is another prophetic liturgy of the late Persian or early Greek period.

future, for it held the key that unlocked all problems, solved all the
mysteries and inequalities, and harmonized all contradictions. Different from the prophets, these apocalyptists were not orators who
appeared before the people and gave to them the divine revelation
with the full backing and responsibility of their own personality,
but writers who unfolded the great panorama of the future, as it had
come to them by study, meditation, and vision. They remained, as
a rule, anonymous, or used pseudonyms, frequently the great names
of antiquity, in order to enhance the authority of their writings.
The author of Isa. 24–27 was one of these nameless apocalyptic
writers. The theme of his booklet is the Judgment of the World and
the Kingdom of God. There is a mixture in it of prophetic and song
elements. The prophetic passages are 24:1–3, 13, 17–23; 25:6–8;
27:1, 12–13.

The whole earth will be laid waste and turned upside down and
all classes of people will be affected. They have broken "the eternal
covenant" which God had made with men at the time of Noah
(cf. Gen. 9:1ff.), in which certain fundamental laws were laid down
as binding on all mankind, among them especially the prohibition of
murder. The symptoms of the coming catastrophe are already visible
in the general fading and weariness of the world: all lose their vital
power and joy of living; only few will be left in the general up-
heaval. Some indeed are full of good cheer because of some event,
which we unfortunately cannot identify, which makes them rejoice
and sing: "Glory to the righteous!" But our prophet feels differently:

> I said, I pine away, I pine away, woe is me!
>> the treacherous have dealt treacherously,
>> yea, the treacherous have dealt very treacherously.
> Fear, and the pit, and the snare
>> are upon thee, O inhabitant of the earth. (Isa. 24:16)

And now begin the terrible convulsions that will introduce the great
judgment.

> The windows on high are opened,
>> and the foundations of the earth tremble.
> The earth is utterly broken,
>> the earth is rent asunder,
>> the earth is shaken violently.

The earth shall stagger like a drunken man,
    and shall sway to and fro like a hammock.
And its transgression shall be heavy upon it,
    and it shall fall and not rise again. (Isa. 24:18–20)

The picture is painted in a most impressive way in the original, where the word-pictures and assonances heighten the power of the colossal convulsions, till finally the moral cause of this chaos is laid bare.

The first act of the judgment will be the imprisonment of the heavenly patrons and of the earthly kings of the nations, both of whom direct their peoples' affairs. Their imprisonment in the subterranean pit will last a long time before they are finally judged.[5] This imprisonment and judgment of the angels is elaborated in later apocalypses, e.g., that of Enoch. In our apocalypse there follows directly the beginning of the Kingdom of God in Zion in visible glory. The sun and moon will pale before His glory, and as in days gone by the elders saw the glory of God on Mount Horeb, so they shall see it on Mount Zion. There is no mention of a Messiah. God Himself is enthroned.

In connection with His assumption of universal sovereignty Yahweh will give a coronation feast on Mount Zion to which all peoples without exception are invited:

And Yahweh of hosts will make
    to all peoples in this mountain
A feast of fat things, a feast of wines on the lees,
    of fat things full of marrow, of wines on the lees well refined.
And He will destroy in this mountain
    the face of the covering that covers all peoples,
And the veil that is spread over all nations.
    He has swallowed up death forever; [6]
And the Lord Yahweh will wipe away tears
    from off all faces;
And the reproach of His people will He take away
    from off all the earth:
For Yahweh has spoken it. (Isa. 25:6–8)

Great joy will prevail at the banquet, where all will be in direct communion with God. All the secret tears will be dried by Yahweh

---

[5] Later, e.g., in the Revelation of John, the time was specified as a thousand years, the millennium, for to God a thousand years are like a day; cf. Ps. 90:4.

[6] In 1 Cor. 15:54 the Hebrew word for "forever" is translated, under the influence of Aramaic, by "in victory."

Himself, never again shall the people weep, for death itself will be
destroyed and eternal felicity will rule in all hearts. This is one of
the most beautiful passages in the Old Testament. Its large-hearted
catholicity and human tenderness single it out. Its music has sung
itself into the sorrowing heart of mankind. Zion, it is true, is still
the center of the world, and the Jews are still considered especially
by Yahweh, yet not in order to give them a higher place. It is surprising, however, to notice how little stressed, how incidental is the
significant idea of the abolition of death. As if it were by no means
new and astounding. Perhaps it was not so new to the people as we
think. The author does not speak of the resurrection of the dead,
but of the immortality of the living.

The final judgment of mankind and of the heavenly host is still
to come, if indeed the order of the text is chronological. But His
people are called by Yahweh to hide themselves "for a little moment,
until the indignation is overpast."

> For behold Yahweh comes out of His place
>   to punish the inhabitants of the earth for their iniquity:
> The earth also shall disclose her blood,
>   and shall no more cover the slain.
> In that day will Yahweh punish
>   with His hard and great and strong sword
> Leviathan the swift serpent,
>   and Leviathan the crooked serpent,
> And He will slay the monster that is in the sea. (Isa. 26:21—27:1)

The coming intervention of the deity is described in terms of his
primeval conflict with the monster of the deep at the time of Creation. This hydra-headed creature (Ps. 74:14) is called Leviathan.
Surprisingly the old Canaanite texts from Ugarit (*Ras Shamra*) also
allude to Leviathan, but with a more contracted name-form, *Ltn:*

> When thou strikest *Ltn*, the swift serpent,
> Thou wilt finish the crooked serpent,
> The powerful one with seven heads.

Some of the same words appear here as in Isa. 27:1, thus revealing
how the Hebrew writers received stimulation from the Canaanite
or perhaps the Phoenician elements in the Palestine of this period.

After this is past, the gathering of every one of the dispersed Jews
takes place. A trumpet will be blown,

And they shall come that were ready to perish in the land of Assyria,
    and they that were outcasts in the land of Egypt.
And they shall worship Yahweh
    in the holy mountain at Jerusalem. (Isa. 27:13)

This had become one of the tenets of the Jewish hope of the future,
and even this author could not help emphasizing it. But he had felt
the sorrow and suffering of humanity and voiced the hope of the
final joy of all mankind so beautifully that in their sorrow men still
turn to his words and read of the time when there shall be no more
tears.

In one of the poems which have been combined with the apocalypse and in which the historical allusions are so tantalizingly elusive
that we cannot make out their date, there is a passage of great
significance in which the hope of the resurrection is expressed. Although there had been some events that had raised the spirit of the
people, the death of some overlords and the enlargement of the country, yet in all the pains and efforts of bringing something new to life
they had failed, "we have not wrought deliverance in the land,
neither have inhabitants of the world been born." The smallness of
the population of the country worried the poet, but he gives voice to
this hope,

    Thy dead shall live,
       their corpses shall arise;
    They that dwell in the dust
       shall awake and sing,
    For Thy dew is as the dew of lights,
       and the earth shall bring forth the shades. (Isa. 26:19)

Yahweh's dead, faithful saints will be raised, their actual bodies will
come back, not only their ghosts. Yahweh has a life-giving dew,
the dew of lights, which will be dropped down on the graves and
revivify the corpses. It is not the resurrection of all that is hoped
for here, only the resurrection of Yahweh's dead, perhaps of the
martyrs and other saints. At last this hope had come. The brief
reference to it here suggests that it was not entirely new among the
people for whom the author wrote.

The large-hearted catholicity of the apocalyptist of Isa. 24–27
has filled us with grateful admiration. Fortunately, he was not the
only one of those universal spirits among the Jews that understood

the full import of monotheism. One was even greater than he. Sometime during the Greek period, perhaps between 300–200, he wrote the story of Jonah, which belongs to the finest and highest that the Old Testament writers have produced and which reveals the prophetic spirit in the purest and truest way. Most deservedly was it included among the prophetical books of the canon, although it was not a prophecy of Jonah, but a story about the prophet. Long ago, in the time of Jeroboam II of Israel (784–744), Jonah had lived and prophesied victory and national aggrandizement to that brilliant king (2 Ki. 14:25). None of his prophecies are preserved, but he was most probably a thoroughly nationalistic prophet. The author of the present book used him as the representative of the narrow, nationalistic tendency among the Jews, according to which they alone were Yahweh's peculiar people and the sole object of His love and care, while the heathen were not only their enemies but also Yahweh's and merited nothing but punishment and destruction. This viewpoint is one that he gently tries to prove unworthy.

Yahweh had commanded Jonah to go to Nineveh and prophesy God's punishment on account of her wickedness, but the prophet refused to go and fled from Yahweh's presence, *i.e.*, from the land of Israel, taking a ship at Joppa, to escape Yahweh's anger. But Yahweh sent a terrific storm, which the mariners at first tried to calm by prayer, while Jonah slept. When this proved of no avail, Jonah was discovered, rudely awakened from his sleep, and ordered to pray to his God. Then the lot was cast to find out on whose account God had sent the storm, and it fell on Jonah. He confessed that he had fled from Yahweh and advised them to cast him into the sea. But only after renewed endeavors to save the ship had been in vain and after an earnest prayer for Yahweh's mercy did they throw him into the sea, which at once became calm; whereupon the sailors, overcome by awe, offered a sacrifice and made vows to Yahweh.

Meanwhile a great fish had been ordered by Yahweh to swallow Jonah, who spent three days and three nights inside of the fish before he was ejected upon the dry land.[7] This part of the story has caused much difficulty to those who foolishly seek to defend its

---

[7] A pious reader missed the prayer which Jonah had uttered in the fish and so inserted a psalm (2:2–9).

historicity. Such tales of miraculous deliverance, with many variations of detail, occur in folk tales the world over; maritime people spoke of a huge fish or a sea monster, inland people of a wolf or a dragon or bear. At Joppa, the very embarkation point of Jonah, the Greeks located the story of Perseus and Andromeda, with his fight inside of the sea monster. The author took this bit of folklore and used it as a means of transporting Jonah back to the land.

At Yahweh's renewed command a chastened Jonah now went to Nineveh, which is imagined as having been an immense city of three days' journey in diameter. Going in a day's journey he cried to the astonished Ninevites, "Yet forty days, and Nineveh shall be overthrown!" At once they repented, proclaimed a fast, and sat in sackcloth and ashes. Even the king joined them and published a decree of fasting in his own and his nobles' name, calling upon the people to repent and turn from their evil ways in order to gain God's favor. And they all fasted and repented. Surely, this was a more astounding miracle than the miracle of the fish! Moved by their penitence Yahweh did not execute His threat. This angered Jonah, who remonstrated with Him: he had known that Yahweh was too gracious to carry out His threat; that was why he had refused to go on His mission and had fled to Tarshish. "Therefore now, O Yahweh, take my life from me, for it is better for me to die than to live."

But Yahweh in a most effective way taught him the superlative folly of his behavior. A kindly humor without sting or bitterness runs through the rest of the tale. Jonah had made a booth for himself outside of the city, where he had waited for the destruction of Nineveh. There Yahweh caused a gourd to grow, whose shade was highly welcome to the prophet. But Yahweh destroyed the gourd through a worm and sent one of those terrible sultry east winds, which with the scorching sun made Jonah so faint that he asked again for his death. So angry was he over the withering of the gourd! But Yahweh said to him,

Thou hast had regard for the gourd, for which thou hast not labored, neither madest it grow, which came up in a night and perished in a night; and I should not have pity on Nineveh, that great city, in which are more than 120,000 persons that cannot discern between their right hand and their left; and also much cattle? (Jonah 4:10f.)

With this question the story closes. The author does not tell whether Jonah was convinced by the irresistible argument. It is not Jonah, but every reader that must answer the question. All must learn that Yahweh is not the God of the Jews only but the God of all men, who pities and cares for all, even for Israel's worst enemies and who wants all to repent and be forgiven. This was noble religious thought.

If the Jews had but listened to this appeal, they would have become the great missionaries of the world carrying the gospel of the one God to all the world until they had established the universal religion. That was Deutero-Isaiah's vision and this writer's hope.

Perhaps about the same time in the Greek period, other Jewish voices spoke up in the liberal spirit. It is with delight that we come upon such prophecies as those that were interpolated to the oracle against Egypt in Isaiah 19:1–15, of which the first addition vv. 16–18 predicted,

In that day there shall be five cities in the land of Egypt that speak the language of Canaan, and swear by Yahweh of hosts; one shall be called the city of the sun. (Isa. 19:18)

The allusion is clearly to Palestinian communities in Egypt—that of Heliopolis being singled out for mention. When the Jewish temple at Leontopolis was founded by the fugitive high priest Onias in the first half of the second century this prophecy was quoted in justification of it (Josephus, *Antiquities*, XIII, 3, 1). If the report is reliable the prophecy must certainly be somewhat older.

The second prediction refers to an existing altar of Yahweh in Egypt, hardly the one at Elephantine of which the Aramaic papyri tell, which was destroyed at the beginning of the fourth century, but a later one farther to the north. The oppression of the Jews here referred to may well be the enslavement of the Jews carried off to Egypt by Ptolemy I, and the "savior" mentioned may be Ptolemy II Philadelphus who set them free (see Josephus, *Antiquities*, XII, 1–2).

In that day shall there be an altar to Yahweh in the midst of the land of Egypt, and a pillar at its border to Yahweh. And it shall be for a sign and for a witness to Yahweh of hosts in the land of Egypt; for they shall cry to Yahweh because of oppressors, and He will send them a savior, and a defender, and He will deliver them. And Yahweh shall be known to

Egypt, and the Egyptians shall know Yahweh in that day; yea, they shall worship with sacrifice and oblation, and shall vow a vow to Yahweh, and shall perform it. And Yahweh will smite Egypt, smiting and healing; and they shall return to Yahweh, and He will be entreated of them, and will heal them. (Isa. 19:19–22)

The third prophecy reflects friendly relations between Ptolemaic Egypt and Seleucid Syria (successor state of ancient Assyria).

In that day shall there be a highway out of Egypt to Assyria, and the Assyrian shall come into Egypt, and the Egyptian into Assyria; and the Egyptians shall worship with the Assyrians. (Isa. 19:23)

The fourth prediction gives the Jewish community of Palestine an important central role in the alliance.

In that day shall Israel be the third with Egypt and with Assyria, a blessing in the midst of the earth; because Yahweh of hosts has blessed them, saying, Blessed be Egypt My people, and Assyria the work of My hands, and Israel Mine inheritance. (Isa. 19:24f.)

Other universal prophecies, which looked forward to a restoration of the nations, were inserted in the prophetic books. For instance, Zephaniah 3:9f. contains now a beautiful utterance of hope, not shared by that prophet of the coming day of wrath.

> For then will I turn to the peoples
> a pure language,
> That they may all call upon the name of Yahweh,
> to serve Him with one consent. (Zeph. 3:9)

In Jeremiah 12:14–17 Yahweh now says after the punishment of the "evil neighbors" of Israel,

I will return and have compassion on them; and I will bring them again, every man to his heritage, and every man to his land. And it shall come to pass, if they will diligently learn the ways of My people, to swear by My name, As Yahweh lives; even as they taught My people to swear by Baal; then shall they be built up in the midst of My people. But if they will not hear, then will I pluck up that nation, plucking up and destroying it, says Yahweh (Jer. 12:15b–17).

The last two passages never were independent prophecies, but were written for these particular places and inserted by editors.

When Alexander the Great entered upon his mighty career in 332 and conquered the Persian empire, the Jews were deeply stirred and the hope of future glory sprang up afresh. A prophet, whose prophecies are preserved in Zechariah 9–11, and whom we may therefore call the Second or Deutero-Zechariah, voiced such hopes at this time.[8] He saw all Syria, Phoenicia, and Philistia subjected and part of the Jewish domain.

> Yahweh is [9] in the land of Hadrach,
>   and Damascus is His resting place,
> For the cities of Aram belong to Yahweh,
>   Hamath also which borders thereon,
>   Tyre and Sidon, because they are very wise. (Zech. 9:1f.)

Yahweh has already occupied all these lands. The strong fortifications of Tyre and her wealth cannot save her from it. The Philistine cities also are conquered and incorporated in the domain of Judah.

> And I will take away his blood out of his mouth,
>   and his abomination from between his teeth;
> And he also shall be a remnant for our God;
>   and he shall be as a clan in Judah
>   and Ekron as a Jebusite. (Zech. 9:7)

The incorporation of Philistia in Judah involves the acceptance of the laws concerning clean and unclean food and especially concerning the eating of blood. One misses the insistence on circumcision as one of the conditions, inasmuch as the Philistines had always been contemptuously referred to as the uncircumcised. But it is not a religious and certainly not a moral and spiritual conversion to which our author looks forward, but a political subjugation, which insisted on conformity to certain external ritual requirements, in the spirit of the Priest Code.

The Messianic hope is aroused in the prophet. He knows that Yahweh will defend His own city against all attacks by foreign foes, but he looks forward to an ideal king, Yahweh's agent and vice-regent in Jerusalem, whom he then predicts

> Rejoice greatly, O daughter of Zion,
>   shout, O daughter of Jerusalem;

[8] He appears to have used an older oracle as the basis of his own in 9:1–8. Aram and Hadrach were political realities of the Assyrian era, not of the fourth century.

[9] The text here must be restored conjecturally.

> Behold, thy king comes to thee,
>   he is vindicated and victorious;
> Lowly, and riding upon an ass,
>   even upon a colt, the foal of an ass. (Zech. 9:9)

As a victorious conqueror he returns from the war in which Yahweh
has vindicated his cause and saved him. But the ideal king is not
only a brilliant warrior, but a prince of peace. He does not come
back on his battle-horse, but on an ass that had never yet been used,
for he belongs to the pious, devoted adherents of Yahweh, the lowly.
And as such he will reign:

> He will cut off the chariot from Ephraim,
>   and the horse from Jerusalem;
> And the battle bow shall be cut off;
>   and he shall dictate peace to the nations:
> And his dominion shall be from sea to sea,
>   and from the River to the ends of the earth. (Zech. 9:10)

It is a thoroughly national idea, involving a world empire and its
peaceful enjoyment for Israel.

Still another poem (Zech. 9:11–17), predicts the return of the
exiles. Yahweh has regard for the blood of the covenant, by which
Israel is bound to him, and calls on "the prisoners of hope" to return,
for the Israelites and Judeans together will fight against the Greeks.

> And Yahweh shall be seen over them,
>   and His arrow shall go forth as the lightning;
> And the Lord Yahweh will blow the trumpet,
>   and will go with the whirlwind of the south. (Zech. 9:14)

Thus aided by the ancient war god, they will gain a decisive victory,
which is described in bloodthirsty fashion much like that of Ps. 149.
A third brief poem (Zech. 10:1–2) urges prayer for rain, and rails
against the teraphim, which give false augury. In a fourth poem,
Zech. 10:3—11:3, in which the figure of Yahweh's flock is abandoned
for that of the steed on which he rides, the battle is once more described, and the return of the exiles from Egypt and Assyria predicted. It is remarkable that the hope of a return of the northern
tribes finds expression here. After obscure allusions to the fall of a
cedar and of an impenetrable forest the poem concludes with

> Hark the wail of the shepherds,
> for their glory is despoiled.
> Hark the roar of the lions,
> for the jungle of the Jordan is laid waste. (Zech. 11:3)

Events of the Hellenistic era may have elicited these prophecies.

Of very different nature is Zech. 11:4–17. It is a narrative piece, which reflects certain historical events to which the key is lost. The prophet is told to enact two allegories in the presence of the people. First he is to act the part of the shepherd, *i.e.*, the ruler of his oppressed people, who are a veritable "flock of slaughter," sold and killed. His two policies of government are represented by two staffs, the one symbolizing "graciousness" or friendship, the other "union" or harmony. But soon he becomes impatient. He will no longer rule them with "graciousness," and leaves them to their fate. He breaks the staff "graciousness" and demands his wages from the traffickers of the people whose hired "shepherd" he had been. They give him the paltry sum of thirty shekels, which Yahweh commands him to cast into the temple treasury. Then he breaks the other staff "union," symbolizing that the union between Israel and Judah is at an end. The whole is enigmatic. The last mentioned item may reflect the break between Jews and Samaritans.

In the second allegory the prophet acts the part of the "foolish shepherd," who does not care for his sheep but maltreats and devours them." [10] It seems probable that events and personages of the third century stand in the background, but their identification is well nigh impossible owing to the paucity of our knowledge of what went on in Judea in those times.

The remaining chapters of the Book of Zechariah (12–14) may be called the Third or Trito-Zechariah.[11] In ch. 12 the prophet foresees that all the surrounding peoples and even the country of Judah (perhaps the portion of Judah not in Jewish hands) will take part in a siege of Jerusalem. But the city will prove too strong, the besiegers will be repulsed. Then the Judean chieftains will perceive that Yahweh is with Jerusalem and they will turn against the invaders,

---

[10] Some scholars draw 13:7–9 into this connection as misplaced, but this is not necessary.

[11] This designation is only for convenience. There is no certainty that the successive prophecies are from the same hand.

and defeat them and thus save Jerusalem. Through this it will come about "that the glory of the house of David and the glory of the inhabitants of Jerusalem be not magnified above Judah." The Jerusalemites could have succeeded even without the help of their countrymen, "for he that is feeble among them at that day shall be as David; and the house of David shall be as God, as the angel of Yahweh before them," so strong and so powerful!

After the successful defense of the city, "the house of David and the inhabitants of Jerusalem" will engage in solemn and bitter mourning for a certain individual who had been murdered. The mourning will be like that for Hadadrimmon in the plain of Megiddo. They shall mourn in groups, the women separately in each group.

In ch. 13:1–6 it is prophesied that the sin of the Davidic house [12] and of the people will be washed away in a fountain that will be opened in Jerusalem; all idolaters and prophets and the unclean spirit itself will be removed.

The propaganda against prophets is peculiar since the author himself speaks as a prophet. Perhaps he aspired to be the final member of that noble order.

And it shall come to pass that, when any shall yet prophesy, then his father and his mother that begat him shall say to him, "Thou shalt not live; for thou speakest lies in the name of Yahweh;" and his father and his mother that begat him shall thrust him through when he prophesies. And it shall come to pass in that day, that the prophets shall be ashamed every one of his vision, when he prophesies; neither shall they wear a hairy mantle to deceive: but he shall say, "I am no prophet, I am a tiller of the ground; for I have been made a bondman from my youth." And one shall say to him, "What are these wounds between thine arms?" Then he shall answer, "Those with which I was wounded in the house of my friends." (Zech. 13:3–6)

In the brief piece 13:7–9 the sword is invoked against a shepherd referred to as "this man that is my fellow," and hence perhaps a high

---

[12] The frequent mention of the house of David is striking in chs. 12–13. When it was exterminated is not clear—perhaps in Persian, or in Maccabean times. The persecutions attributed to Vespasian and Domitian (Eusebius, *Ecclesiastical History*, III, 12 and 19) were no doubt concerned with new claimants. In view of the polygamy of the Judean kings there naturally were a great many who could assert descent from David, when it was expedient to do so.

priest (cf. Zech. 3:7). The people will suffer terribly but out of this punishment will come a purified remnant.

In ch. 14 we have a continuation of the highly imaginative prediction we first encountered in Ezekiel. The prophet predicts that the attack of the nations will at first be successful, Jerusalem will be captured and one half of her population will be carried into exile. But then Yahweh Himself will appear to fight against the enemies. He will stand on Mount Olivet, which will be split, and through the the chasm thus formed the people will escape. Thereupon Yahweh will enter Jerusalem with His holy angels and the Kingdom of God on earth will begin. The climate will be changed, so that there will be no more extremes of temperature, "neither heat nor cold nor frost." Perpetual light will shine, night shall never come again, even "at evening time there will be light." Perennial streams will flow from Jerusalem eastward and westward, irrigating the whole country, which will become a veritable paradise. The sovereignty of Yahweh will be recognized by the whole earth; and the political unity of the world under a theocracy, Yahweh being the sole king, will be combined with the religious unity of the world in the recognition of Yahweh as the one God.

Yahweh shall be King over all the earth: in that day shall Yahweh be one, and His name one. (Zech. 14:9)

The spiritual preeminence of the religion of Jerusalem will be accompanied by the physical elevation of the city. The whole country is to be levelled down to a plain as low as the Jordan valley, but Jerusalem will be on a high mountain visible from everywhere.

After the nations that had attacked the holy city have been destroyed by an appalling plague and by a panic in which they will fight against one another, their remnant shall come to recognize Yahweh and make a yearly pilgrimage to the universal sanctuary at Jerusalem, the religious center of the world, to pay homage to the King of the world by celebrating the great harvest thanksgiving festival, the feast of tabernacles, in Jerusalem. That will be their stern duty. If any do not come, they will be punished by Yahweh with drought, or if it should be Egypt, with the plague, since Egypt did not depend on rain for its harvests. It is not the love of God that has conquered their hearts, it is not the free, spontaneous worship of their spirits that they bring, but the outward acknowledgment of Yahweh's deity and kingship. When they all come, "in that day there shall be upon the bells of the horses 'Holy unto Yahweh,'" for they will be consecrated, since they bring pilgrims not warriors. And there will be so many thousands of worshipers that the temple vessels will not suffice, and

Every pot in Jerusalem and in Judah shall be holy to Yahweh of hosts, and all they that sacrifice shall come and take of them, and boil therein (their sacrificial meals). And in that day there shall be no more a trader in the house of Yahweh of hosts. (Zech. 14:21)

Ritual sanctity is this prophet's ideal. There is not much left of the great teaching of the preexilic prophets. How far we have traveled from Amos and Hosea, Isaiah and Micah and Jeremiah. How external the universal ideal of Deutero-Isaiah has become, and how exclusive his monotheism in the messages of these prophets.

The activity of the editors of the prophetic books was of great significance and far-reaching influence. None of the books has escaped editorial revision. The words of the prophets were not their own but Yahweh's. His authorship was paramount, even if there had already been a conception of the rights of the authors of literary works. Thus there were bound together with the Book of Isaiah not only the Books of the Second and Third Isaiah (Isa. 40–55; 56–66), but also the apocalypse in Isaiah 24–27, and many other single chapters of passages. To the Book of Zechariah were added the Books of the Second and Third Zechariah (Zech. 9–11 and 12–14), originally, also the Book of Malachi. Many prophecies by men of various times, whose names had been forgotten, were circulating among the people. They were put into the prophetic collection, to which they seemed to belong according to their subject, if not by their authorship. Thus a number of anonymous Oracles against the Nations were collected with Isaiah's Oracles against the Nations in one book (Isa. 13–23), another series of such prophecies with Jeremiah's in another book (Jer. 46–51). Prophecies of hope were gathered together in a Little Book of Comfort with Isaiah's (Isa. 32–35) or with Jeremiah's prophecies of hope (Jer. 30–33) as a nucleus. It happened that such booklets were not always inserted in the same place and order in the various manuscripts so that, *e.g.*, Jeremiah's Book of Oracles against the Nations (Jer. 46–51) is in a different place in the Greek Bible, which inserts it after 25:13.

But all this is but one phase of the editorial activity of the Jews. God had a message for every age. He still spoke through His prophets of old, but the times changed and the needs varied. So with changing times and varying needs these books were constantly adapted to the new conditions. We saw how Judean editors brought the books of Amos and Hosea up to date in order that they might serve as guides and warnings to Judah, lest it also be engulfed in ruin. After the Babylonian exile had brought the fearful catastrophe which the prophets had predicted, and new prophets, especially the great Deutero-Isaiah, had written their predictions full of hope and glory, the earlier prophets were edited afresh and words of hope and restoration were added. It seemed not quite true in the light of events that Amos should have predicted nothing but absolute destruction for all Israel, so there was added in 9:8–10,

> Save that I will not utterly destroy the house of Jacob, says Yahweh. For, lo, I will command, and I will sift the house of Israel among all the nations, like as grain is sifted in a sieve, yet shall not the least kernel fall upon the earth. All the sinners of My people shall die by the sword, who say, The evil shall not overtake nor meet us.

Similarly in Jeremiah the little clause was inserted, "yet will I not make a full end" (4:27; 5:10, 18). But not only sentences and clauses but whole new oracles were added. Thus the glowing prediction at the end of the Book of Amos (9:11–15; cf. p. 96), which totally modified the impression of the message of that powerful prophet of doom, is to be regarded as supplementary.

The restoration of Israel in its various aspects forms the theme of many such additions (*e.g.*, Mic. 7:8ff.; Zeph. 3:14ff.). Sometimes a nucleus was expanded as in Obadiah and Joel, sometimes the whole was new. Again and again there were inserted the hopes of the return of the scattered people from exile (*e.g.*, Mic. 2:12f.; 4:6–8; Jer. 23:3f.), of the reunion of Israel and Judah under the leadership of a Davidic king (*e.g.*, Hos. 1:10f; 3:5, the single phrase "and unto David their king"), of the larger city (Jer. 31:38ff.), of the reconquest of all the former territory (*e.g.*, Zeph. 2:7a, 9b; Ob. 18–21), of Yahweh's visible dwelling in Zion (Isa. 4:5f.), of the punishment of the nations (Isa. 19:16f.), of Israel's lordship over the heathen (Isa. 14:1–4a), occasionally of the restoration of the nations (Zeph. 3:9f.; Jer. 46:26b; 48:47; 49:6, 39).

Sometimes it was liturgical matter that was inserted, *e.g.*, the little poems on Yahweh's greatness in nature in Amos 4:13; 5:8f.; 9:5f. to enhance the power of the prophetic appeal, or a psalm was added to furnish a suitable ending for a book, *e.g.*, Isa. 12, or poems were inserted as in Isa. 25–27, or a prayer where it seemed to be called for (*e.g.*, Jer. 32:17ff.), or a call to reverent silence in worship (Hab. 2:20).

Again, didactic portions were supplied especially on the folly of idolatry (Hab. 2:18; Jer. 10:1ff.) and appeals to the wise and reasonings with them (Hos. 14:9; Jer. 9:12ff.).

To the Books of Isaiah and Jeremiah historical chapters were affixed (Isa. 36–39, taken from 2 Ki. 18:13—20:19; Jer. 52).

By all this the appearance of the original books of the prophets was modified considerably. Rarely was a prophetic text itself changed as in Zech. 6:9ff., where the royal oracle was altered into a priestly one (cf. p. 253). This was more frequently done by additions as in Jeremiah 33:18–22. An eager and intensive study of the prophetic books is revealed by this editorial activity of so many earnest men. In Mic. 3:5 there is an interesting illustration of an addition which is based on a study of the Immanuel passage in Isa. 7:1ff. It is interpreted messianically. Immanuel (with us is God) and Shearjashub (a remnant shall return) are utilized here.

These editors were sure that God spoke through the prophets to their time in ever fresh manner and that He had kindled His light in their own souls too. But not all of them understood the greatness and originality of the prophets. The law had gained its dominant place, God's will was revealed through it. He sent no more His living original spokesmen. So a writer added at the end of the Book of Malachi, "Remember ye the law of Moses My servant." (4:4) To him the prophets had been nothing but interpreters of the law. Another added a further very important postscript, an oracle predicting that one other prophet might be expected before the great day of Yahweh: Elijah, who would return from heaven, and reconcile the divided older and younger generations to forestall destruction of the land by Yahweh (4:5–6).

XXII

Daniel and the Greek Peril

AFTER a century-long conflict between the Seleucid kings of Syria and the Ptolemies of Egypt, Palestine had finally come into the hands of Antiochus III the Great through his victory at Paneas in 198 B.C. Under his reign Hellenistic civilization with its ideas and practices influenced the Jews in Judea more profoundly than before. The rich and cultured Jews especially felt the irresistible attraction of the Hellenistic view and mode of life. The conflict between them and the followers of the law became more bitter all the time. At last the very life of Hebrew religion seemed to the faithful to be at stake, when Antiochus IV Epiphanes (175–164 B.C.) tried to force Hellenistic culture and religion upon the Jews.[1] A strife for the high priesthood brought about his interference in Jewish affairs, and led to the Maccabean wars. Jason, the brother of the high priest Onias III, a Hellenizer as his Greek name shows, had succeeded in persuading Antiochus by the promise of large sums of money to give to him the high priesthood. Onias had to flee. Jason began at once with his Hellenistic schemes; a Greek gymnasium was built in Jerusalem, and Greek customs were introduced. Two years later Jason was displaced by Menelaus, who had promised the king even greater sums, which he took out of the temple treasury after his appointment.

[1] The events from here on are related in the apocryphal book of 1 Maccabees.

Antiochus was at this time warring in Egypt, and the rumor came to Jerusalem that he had fallen in battle. Jason tried to regain the high priesthood and a sanguinary fight took place in the city. Menelaus fled to Antiochus, for the rumor was false, and Antiochus returned to reinstate Menelaus and to punish the city (170 B.C.). The temple treasury was looted and the costly furniture, including the golden candlestick and table, was taken. When two years later Antiochus marched once more against Egypt, Rome interfered through her legate Popilius Laenas, who commanded him peremptorily to withdraw on peril of war with Rome. He retreated in an ugly mood and now determined to proceed with his program of Hellenizing the Jews in earnest. On its homeward march his army stopped awhile in Jerusalem. After an ostensibly peaceful entrance they attacked the people, killed some, and then began to plunder. The city walls were razed, and a Syrian garrison was placed in the strongly fortified Akra.

Soon other measures were taken. The observance of the Sabbath and of circumcision was forbidden, the temple services and sacrifices were stopped, the sacred books were destroyed, and much damage was done to the temple. Even this was not enough. On the 15th day of Kislev (December 23) 168 there was planted to the horror of the Jews a symbol of the god *Baal-shamayim*,[2] the God of Heaven (whom the Greeks identified with Zeus), on the sacred altar of burnt-offering, and on the 25th of the month (our January 2, 167) a sacrifice of swine was brought to this heathen deity in Yahweh's temple! Everywhere in the country altars and images were erected and the Jews were ordered to pay homage to them and to sacrifice swine.

In the little country town of Modeïn Mattathias, a priest, according to tradition, slew the law-enforcement officer who came to compel obedience. This sparked a revolt in which his sons, chief among them the Judas Maccabaeus, carried on a guerrilla activity and in the

---

[2] Jewish loathing expressed itself in calling it *shiqqūṣ meshōmēm*, which form appears in Dan. 11:31; 12:1, and in the Greek of 1 Macc. is rendered "abomination of desolation," as also in Mark 13:14; Matt. 24:15. "Abomination" is a frequent designation for idols or heathen symbols in the Old Testament, here of *Baal*, while *meshōmēm* is a twisting of *shāmayim* "heaven." The object may have been a small altar.

next few years won victories which are described as "a little help" (Dan. 11:34). In 165, Jerusalem, except the citadel, was in their hands, and on the 25th of Kislev (December 24) 165 the temple was cleansed and rededicated. But after all, how could the small bands withstand in the long run the power of a world-empire like Syria? It seemed impossible, and in many hearts hope died and the look of despair came into many eyes.

Just at this crisis there appeared the Book of Daniel throbbing with the power of an unconquerable faith. Like a trumpet it sounded the call to loyalty and trust. Hold fast, be faithful to your God! The time of salvation is at hand! Soon, very soon complete and glorious deliverance will be yours!

Using and slightly pointing up a book of old Eastern tales, probably written in the third century in the Aramaic language (2:4b–6), the author told of men who in like perilous situations had been loyal to Israel's religion: of Daniel and his three friends, who kept the ritual laws concerning food and drink and became fairer, wiser, and more honored than others (ch. 1); of Shadrach, Meshach, and Abednego, who refused to worship the golden image of Nebuchadrezzar and were thrown into the fiery furnace, where they were shielded by God's angel (ch. 3); of Daniel, who fearlessly performed his daily prayers and was thrown into the lions' den, but wonderfully saved by the angel of God (ch. 6). So gloriously did God help His faithful saints that even the heathen kings were astounded and compelled to bless the God of these men, "who had sent His angel and delivered His servants that trusted Him," and to declare,

He is the living God, and steadfast forever. . . . He delivers and rescues, and He works signs and wonders in heaven and in earth, who has delivered Daniel from the power of the lions. (Dan. 6:26f.)

God helped His faithful saints most marvelously out of the direst perils. Will He not do so still? Only trust in Him and be loyal to Him and to His cause! And as for the tyrant? Read what God did to King Nebuchadrezzar, when in godless pride he boasted, while walking on the roof of his palace:

Is not this great Babylon, which I have built by my mighty power as a royal residence and for the glory of my majesty? (Dan. 4:28)

He reduced him to the level of a beast, that ate grass in the open field, where "his body was wet with the dew of heaven, till his hair was grown like eagles' feathers, and his nails like birds' claws," until he finally came to acknowledge the sovereignty of God (ch. 4). Or listen to what He did to "King Belshazzar" (who actually was only the crown prince), when he mocked Him by drinking from His sacred temple vessels at one of his banquets, how that awful mysterious hand wrote *mene, mene, tekel, upharsin* [3] upon the wall, which Daniel interpreted as meaning,

Mene, God has numbered thy kingdom, and brought it to an end;
Tekel, thou art weighed in the balances, and found wanting;
Peres, thy kingdom is divided, and given to the Medes and Persians.
(Dan. 5:26ff.)

In the same night Belshazzar was slain! God is not mocked with impunity. Do you think that Antiochus, who has plundered the temple and taken the sacred vessels (1 Macc. 1:21-24), will escape without punishment? The author does not say this with so many words, but he wants his readers to infer it. Yahweh alone is God, and He alone is King. The various kings have their kingdoms only by His grace. So far He has given the dominion of the world to different nations in turn, but the time is at hand when He will give it to His saints. There is a definite divine plan in the history of the world. The heathen sages do not understand it, but God has revealed it to His servant Daniel in dreams and visions.

That the stories contained in the book of Daniel have undergone evolution has long been suspected. Especially is this the case with the one of ch. 4 about Nebuchadrezzar's dwelling with the beasts of the field for seven "times" (*i.e.*, years). Ever since the Babylonian text called *A Verse Account of Nabonidus* was published by S. Smith in 1934 (see *ANET*, 312f.)—which reported that Nabonidus, the last king of Babylon, went to Teima (in Arabia) for seven years—

---

[3] The writing consisted only of consonants, the words involved being *mn'*, *tql*, *prs*. The business-conscious Babylonian would think at once of the familiar monetary units mina, shekel, and half mina. This made no sense. But the wise Daniel pointed out that the words could be pronounced and interpreted differently, namely as forms of verbs meaning number, weigh, divide. The longer form of the inscription in v. 25 is not heeded in v. 26f. *Upharsin* could be rendered "and divisions."

it has been suspected that this event has here been transferred to the more celebrated Nebuchadrezzar. Recently the Dead Sea Scrolls have fully confirmed this critical inference, for among them has turned up a fragment of a *Prayer of Nabonidus* from Cave IV.

The words of the prayer which Nabonidus king of Assyria and of Babylon, the great king, prayed when he was smitten with a severe inflammation by the command of the Most High God, in the city of Teima: I was smitten for seven years and I was put far from men. But when I confessed my trespasses and sins he left me a seer. He was a Jew of the exiles in Babylonia. He gave his explanation and wrote that honor should be given and great glory to the Most High God. And he wrote thus: When you were smitten with a severe inflammation in the city of Teima by the command of the Most High God you prayed to the gods made of silver and gold, of bronze, of iron, of wood, of stone, of clay—

No doubt the Jewish seer's [4] advice led to the cure of Nabonidus and to his consequent praise of the Most High. In the Daniel version the sickness motif was dropped and replaced with the curious one of living among the beasts and eating grass.

The first revelation of consequence for the crisis of 165 B.C. was allegedly given in a dream to Nebuchadrezzar (ch. 2) which Daniel was able to interpret. The king dreamt of an image whose "head was of fine gold, whose breast and arms were of silver, whose belly and thighs were of brass, its legs of iron, its feet part iron and part clay." It was broken in pieces by "a stone cut out without hands," which "became a great mountain, and filled the whole earth." The image represented the four world-empires, the Babylonian, Median, Persian, and Greek. The Babylonian is the head of gold, the Greek composed of iron and clay, strong in part, weak in part, not firmly welded together. The stone is Israel.

In the days of those kings (*i.e.*, the Greek kings) shall the God of heaven set up a kingdom which shall never be destroyed, nor shall its sovereignty be left to another people; but it shall break in pieces and consume all these kingdoms, and itself shall stand forever. (Dan. 2:44)

At the time when this book appeared, men were living in the fourth kingdom, in the Greek period. How soon will its end be here?

[4] His anonymity suggests that the Daniel stories have only been transferred to Daniel secondarily. The text was published by Milik in 1956.

Will it be soon or will it be delayed? This question is answered in the visions of Daniel, chs. 7–12.

To the older materials of 1–6, the author of Daniel added another Aramaic chapter, ch. 7., Daniel's vision of the four beasts. There, only the fourth or Greek kingdom is described more in detail and the final judgment on Antiochus IV Epiphanes is foretold. Of the four great beasts that Daniel saw coming out of the sea the lion with eagle's wings represented the Babylonian, the bear the Median, the leopard with four bird wings on its back the Persian, and the terrible, strong beast with iron teeth and ten horns the Hellenistic kingdoms.[5] The ten horns represented the ten kings of Syria from Alexander the Great to Demetrius.[6] The other horn, which came up as the prophet looked, the "little one before which three of the first horns were plucked up by the roots," was no one else but Antiochus Epiphanes, who had "a mouth speaking great things." The three horns were his immediate predecessors, Seleucus IV, Heliodorus, and Demetrius, who "were plucked up by the roots" in 176 B.C. With Antiochus IV the end is reached.

I beheld till thrones were placed, and one that was ancient of days sat down: His raiment was white as snow, and the hair of His head like pure wool; His throne was fiery flames, and its wheels burning fire. A fiery stream issued and came forth from before Him: thousands of thousands were ministering to Him, and ten thousand times ten thousand were standing before Him: the judgment (the judge) was seated, and the books were opened. I beheld at that time because of the voice of the great words which the horn spoke; I beheld even till the beast was slain, and its body destroyed, and it was given to be burned with fire. And as for the rest of the beasts, their dominion was taken away: yet their lives were prolonged for a season and a time.

I saw in the night-visions, and, behold, there appeared coming with the clouds of heaven one like a son of man, and he came even to the ancient of days, and they brought him near before Him. And there was given him

---

[5] Hybrid monsters are ancient in art, particularly in Babylonia and Assyria. But with a total lack of artistic capacity this Jewish apocalyptist invents weird creatures. He is governed by the desire to introduce numerous facts in symbolic form.

[6]
Alexander 336–323	Seleucus III 226–222
Seleucus I 312–280	Antiochus III 222–187
Antiochus I 280–261	Seleucus IV 186–176
Antiochus II 261–247	Heliodorus 176
Seleucus II 246–226	Demetrius 176

dominion, and glory, and a kingdom, that all the peoples, nations, and languages should serve him: his dominion is an everlasting dominion, which shall not pass away, and his kingdom that which shall not be destroyed. (Dan. 7:9–14)

In the interpretation which the angel gave to Daniel "the one like a son of man," who came with the clouds of heaven and to whom was given eternal dominion, is interpreted as the representative of the kingdom of the saints of the Most High.

These great kings, which are four, are four kings that shall arise out of the earth. But the saints of the Most High shall receive the kingdom, and possess the kingdom for ever, even for ever and ever. (7:17f.)

It may be that "the one like a son of man" was Israel's patron angel and representative Michael (Dan. 12:1), who is the conqueror of the dragon in Rev. 12:7. In any case, our author does not seem to identify him with the Messiah. That, however, is done in the pseudepigraphic Book of Enoch (chs., 46, 48, 63, 69), which was written before 64 B.C., and in the apocryphal Second Book of Esdras (ch. 13) of the time of Domitian (81–96 A.D.).[7] Daniel was especially interested in the little horn which represented Antiochus IV, although of course he never mentioned him by name. This cryptic veiling in the unveiling is characteristic of apocalypses.

Thus he said, The fourth beast shall be a fourth kingdom upon earth, which shall be different from all the kingdoms, and shall devour the whole earth, and shall tread it down, and break it in pieces. And as for the ten horns, out of this kingdom shall ten kings arise: and another shall arise after them; and he shall be different from the former ones, and he shall put down three kings. And he shall speak words against the Most High, and shall afflict the saints of the Most High; and he shall think to change the times and the law; and they shall be given into his hand until a time and times and half a time. But the judgment shall be seated, and they shall take away his dominion, to consume and to destroy it unto the end. And the kingdom and the dominion, and the greatness of the kingdoms under the whole heaven, shall be given to the people of the saints of the Most

---

[7] If Jesus calls himself Son of Man in the Gospels this presupposes the messianic interpretation of the figure in Daniel's vision. Whether the Enoch passages are pre-Christian has long been a matter of dispute. Since the section of the book in which they occur (chs. 37–71, the so-called *Similitudes*) is not contained in the Enoch manuscripts found at Qumran, their antiquity has become doubtful.

High: his kingdom is an everlasting kingdom, and all dominions shall serve and obey him. (Dan. 7:23–27)

With the seventh chapter the Aramaic portion of Daniel which began in 2:4b ends and the rest of the book is in Hebrew. The vision of the ram and the he-goat with the four horns out of which came a little horn (ch. 8) is a variation of the preceding vision. The ram with the two horns is definitely explained as the Medo-Persian empire, the he-goat as Alexander the Great.

The ram which thou sawest, that had the two horns, they are the kings of Media and Persia. And the rough he-goat is the king of Greece, and the great horn that is between his eyes is the first king (*i.e.*, Alexander the Great). And as for that which was broken, in whose place four stood up, four kingdoms shall stand up out of the nation, but not with his power. (Dan. 8:20–22)

They were the kingdoms of Alexander's successors, (1) Cassander's in the west, Macedonia and Greece, (2) Lysimachus' in the north, Asia Minor as far as Pontus and Paphlagonia, (3) Seleucus' in the east, Asia as far as the Indus but with Asia Minor excepted, and (4) Ptolemy's in the south, Egypt with Phoenicia and Coelesyria.

But in the latter time of their kingdom, when the transgressors are come to the full, a king of fierce countenance, and understanding dark sentences shall stand up,

that is, Antiochus Epiphanes. He is the "little horn."

And out of one of them came forth a little horn, which waxed exceeding great, toward the south, and toward the east, and toward the beauteous land. And it waxed great, as far as the host of heaven; and some of the host and of the stars it cast down to the ground, and trampled upon them. Yea, it magnified itself, even to the prince of the host; and it took away from him the daily sacrifice, and the place of his sanctuary was cast down. And the temple service was abandoned together with the daily sacrifice through transgression; and truth was cast down to the ground, and it (the horn) carried out its purpose successfully. (Dan. 8:9–12)

And his power shall be mighty, but not by his own power; and he shall utter astonishing things and shall accomplish his purpose, and he shall destroy the mighty ones, and against the holy ones in his policy, he shall succeed by means of deceit, and he shall magnify himself in his heart, and unawares shall he destroy many: he shall also stand up against the prince of princes; but he shall be broken by no (human) hand. (Dan. 8:24f.)

But how soon will his end come?"

Then I heard a holy one speaking; and another holy one said unto the one who spoke, How long shall the vision be that the daily sacrifice shall be taken away and an appalling transgression be set up and the sanctuary and the temple service be trodden under foot? And he said to me, For two thousand and three hundred evenings and mornings; then shall the sanctuary be restored to its rightful use. (Dan. 8:13f.)

As we have seen, the altar in the temple at Jerusalem had been defiled in 168; on the same day three years later, 165, the temple was cleansed and rededicated. Two thousand-three hundred evenings and mornings (or one thousand one hundred and fifty days) are 3 years and 55 days. Had the author already witnessed the rededication? If so, he wrote in December, 165, or January, 164. But this is not quite certain. That he expected "the end" early in 164 he says unmistakably.

The question of the exact time of the end gave him no rest. He studied the writings of the older prophets and found in Jeremiah's book the prophecy of the seventy years. After much fasting and prayer the correct understanding of this prediction was given to him by the angel Gabriel. The seventy years are not simply years, but weeks of years, *i.e.*, 490 in all.

Know therefore and discern, that from the going forth of the commandment to restore and to build Jerusalem unto the anointed one, the prince, are seven weeks, and threescore and two weeks: it shall be built again, with street and moat. And at the end of times, even after the sixty-two weeks [8] shall the anointed one be cut off, without judicial trial, and the city and the sanctuary shall be destroyed together with a prince and the end shall come with a flood, and even unto the end shall be war . . . and the covenant shall be annulled for many for one week: and in the midst of the week shall the sacrifice and the oblation cease; and in its place shall be an appalling abomination until the determined ruin shall be poured out upon the appalling thing. (Dan. 9:25–27)

The end is due in June, 164.

The most elaborate and detailed vision is given in ch. 10f., in which the history of the Greek kingdoms and especially of the time

---

[8] The author makes here a mistake of about 70 years, for 62 weeks are 434 years, which would give the year 103, if deducted from 537. A Hellenistic-Jewish writer, Demetrius (*ca.* 200 B.C.), and Josephus made a similar mistake in their chronology of this period.

of Antiochus IV is given so accurately that ch. 11 can be used as a historical source of the period. This knowledge contrasts strangely with the author's ignorance about the time of Nebuchadrezzar and his successors, in which Daniel is supposed to have lived. He is so poorly informed that he commits serious historical blunders. He is hazy about the time of Alexander and the Diadochi, but knows a good deal about the third and second centuries. He gives interesting and reliable details of the conflict of the Seleucids with the Ptolemies, of their wars and their marriages, until he finally comes to the accession of Antiochus Epiphanes.

And in his place shall stand up a contemptible person, to whom they had not given the majesty of the kingdom: but he shall come unawares, and shall obtain the kingdom by intrigues. And the forces shall be completely overwhelmed from before him, and shall be broken; yea, also the prince of the covenant. And after the league made with him he shall work deceitfully; and he shall come up, and shall become strong, with a small people. Unexpectedly shall he come even upon the fattest places of the province; and he shall do that which his fathers have not done, nor his fathers' fathers; he shall scatter among them prey, and spoil, and substance: yea, he shall devise his devices against fortresses and that until a time. And he shall stir up his power and his courage against the king of the south with a great army; and the king of the south shall war in battle with an exceeding great and mighty army; but he shall not stand; for they shall devise devices against him. Yea, they that eat of his delicacies shall destroy him, and his army shall be swept away; and many shall fall down slain. And as for both these kings, their hearts shall be to do mischief, and they shall speak lies at one table: but it shall not prosper; for yet the end shall be at the time appointed.

And he shall return into his own land with great substance; and his heart shall be against the holy covenant; and he shall execute his purpose, and return to his own land. At the time appointed he shall return, and come into the south; but it shall not be in the latter time as it was in the former. For ships of Kittim shall come against him; therefore he shall be cowed, and return, and have indignation against the holy covenant, and shall execute his purpose: he shall even return, and have regard unto them that forsake the holy covenant. And forces sent by him shall stand, and profane the sanctuary, even the fortress, and shall take away the daily sacrifice, and they shall set up the appalling abomination. And such as do wickedly against the covenant shall he pervert by flatteries; but the people that know their God shall be strong, and do exploits. And they that are wise among the people shall instruct many; yet they shall fall by the sword and by flame, by captivity and by spoil, many days. Now when they shall fall, they shall be helped with a little help; but many shall join themselves to them with false protestations. And some of them that are wise shall fall, to refine them, and to purify, and to make them white, even to the time of the end; because it is yet for the time appointed.

And the king shall do according to his will; and he shall exalt himself, and magnify himself above every god, and shall speak astonishing things against the God of gods; and he shall prosper till the indignation be accomplished; for that which is determined shall be done. Neither shall he regard the gods of his fathers, nor the desire of women, nor regard any god; for he shall magnify himself above all. But in his place shall he honor the god of fortresses; and a god whom his fathers knew not shall he honor with gold, and silver, and with precious stones and costly things. And he shall procure for the strongest fortresses adherents of a foreign god: whosoever acknowledges him he will increase with glory; and he shall cause them to rule over many, and shall divide the land for a reward. (Dan. 11:21–39)

So far the author is in strict accord with history. But now he begins to predict, and here he proves to be mistaken, for he believed that Antiochus would make another campaign against Egypt and lose his life there. In reality he died in Persia in 164. The author was right, therefore, as far as the year of Epiphanes' death is concerned. But was he right also in regard to the end? Did it come at that time? Let us see what he says about this.

And at that time shall Michael stand up, the great prince who stands for the children of thy people; and there shall be a time of trouble, such as never was since there was a nation even to that same time: and at that time thy people shall be delivered, every one that shall be found written in the book. And many of them that sleep in the dusty ground shall awake, some to everlasting life, and some to shame and everlasting abhorrence. And they that are wise shall shine as the brightness of the firmament; and they that turn many to righteousness as the stars for ever and ever. (Dan. 12:1–3)

This is the most important passage concerning the resurrection in the Old Testament. Not all the dead will be raised, only many, most probably the martyrs and the especially wicked, the ones to eternal life, the others to eternal shame and contempt. Let the people but be loyal to Yahweh, even if they should be killed for their faithfulness, for they will be raised and enjoy eternal felicity! But "how long shall it be to the end of these wonders?" The answer is given, "for a time, two times and a half" which means three years and a half, *i.e.*, till June, 164.

There is a fire burning in this book, a faith throbbing in its pages of such intensity and power, that we must believe that it met with instantaneous acceptance. But a question was certainly going to be asked when it appeared, unless the author anticipated it. The book went out under the name of the ancient saint Daniel, of whom Ezekiel had spoken as one of the great holy figures of the past in conjunction with Noah and Job.[9] Our author believed that Daniel lived in the latter part of the Babylonian exile and in the following years. If that was so, why then had nobody ever heard of his book or seen it before? Because Yahweh had commanded that it should be kept secret until the time of the end and that was now!

"Shut thou up the vision, for it belongs to many days to come" (8:26), and "go thy way, Daniel, for the words are shut up and sealed till the time of the end." (Dan. 12:9)

Why did the author resort to this fiction? Because he would never have gained a hearing for his great and stirring message which burnt in his soul, if he had appeared in person before the people or had sent out his book under his own name. For the time of the prophets was at an end, the law was the revelation of God's will, the people believed that prophetic inspiration had ceased. So he used this literary device not in order to deceive, but in order to make his book a real vehicle for his message. That men did not think that this was a fraud is clear from the fact that most apocalypses used this same device after him.

There was an astonishing boldness in a faith that dared to fix the exact time of the end in the immediate future. But the popularity and influence of the book was such that even when the calculated time had passed, it survived. The author himself added, by new calculations, at first half a month, 1290 days instead of 1277, and again a month and a half, 1335 days instead of 1290 (12:11-12). Finally he closed with the resigned statement put in the mouth of his heavenly mentor, "but go thou thy way till the end be, for thou

[9] The Daniel of this book cannot be identical with the Daniel of Ezekiel. The latter's Daniel is an old Canaanite king *Danel,* a legend about whom came to light in the *Ras Shamra* texts in 1936.

shalt rest and stand in thy lot, at the end of the days" (12:13), *i.e.*, he shall participate in the final bliss. Later, after the Hellenistic kingdom of Syria had been overthrown, the fourth kingdom was interpreted as referring to Rome (cf. *The Apocalypse of Baruch*, ch. 36–40, a pseudepigraphic book of *ca.* 90 A.D.), and still later, under the theory that the empires were extensions of Rome's, it was ever again adapted to new times by new interpretations of the figures and symbols. Dogma held it impossible that the prophet could have been mistaken.

An unsolved riddle of the book is its bilingual character. It begins in Hebrew (1:1—2:4a), continues in Aramaic with the prefatory remark of an editor *"arāmīth,"* and returns to Hebrew in ch. 8. Perhaps two versions had to be used to set up the text, the only available manuscript of the Hebrew one may have lacked 2:4b—7:28, which then was taken from an Aramaic one. This is only mentioned as a possibility, for other explanations can be adduced.

Fragments of several manuscripts of Daniel have been found at Qumran in Cave IV. One is a copy written only half a century after the original publication of the book! The text is said to vary widely from the canonical one, suggesting that it may not yet have been regarded as sacred literature. From the Septuagint we know that the text underwent expansions, which the manuscripts used by the editors of the Palestinian Daniel did not contain. These additional materials have been put among the Old Testament Apocrypha. They are

1. the *Story of Susanna,* a woman falsely accused of adultery, which is prefixed to the book, and thus has no organic place in it. It is a separate legend about Daniel's inspired wisdom, which was not suited to the spirit and purpose of the author of the canonical book, if it existed in his time.

2. *The Song of the Three Holy Children,* put after Dan. 3:23; it is a Jewish psalm of thanksgiving, tranlsated from the Hebrew.

3. The story of *Bel and the Dragon;* this was put at the end of the book and thus likewise has no organic place. It tells how Daniel discredited the priests of Babylon in the eyes of Cyrus, uses the motif of Daniel in the lions' den (ch. 6), and relates the curious legend of how the prophet Habakkuk was miraculously transported

to Babylon to bring Daniel food in that situation. Romancing about Daniel was evidently something quite independent of, and indeed more original than, the use of his personage as apocalyptist.

The story of the influence that has gone forth from the book of Daniel has not been written and much of it can no longer be recovered. To what extent was Jesus himself governed by Daniel's prophecy? Was it early Christian thinking that first applied the prediction of 7:13 to him? What role did the Book of Daniel play in the Jewish revolts of 68–70 A.D. and in the Barcocheba uprising of 132? More visible is the proliferation of apocalyptic literature for which this book set the pattern. It may even be that the Habakkuk and Nahum commentaries of the Dead Sea Scrolls were stimulated by Daniel. The book of Revelation in the New Testament received and gave forth anew the thought and spirit of Daniel. The story of their combined impact on Christian history is one of human zeal, error, and disappointment offset by incredible courage in the face of discouragement and persecution. Much of the Christian travail would have been avoided had the words which the author of Acts, with an eye on Daniel, attributed to the risen Lord been heeded: "It is not for you to know times or seasons which the Father has fixed by his own authority." (Acts 1:7)

One great intellectual contribution of this book must not be overlooked. In it the mind of man for the first time gazed as from above on the whole process of human history and gave it an interpretation. The stimulus thus provided has induced innumerable others to do likewise with very different means and results. The pessimistic interpretation of the present, with the world empires viewed as beasts—the one under which the author was living being the most terrible of all—was offset by his faith in God's government and his optimism concerning the future. The moral lesson he taught his contemporaries is unforgettable: there may be nothing that men can do in the face of tyranny and persecution except to stand ready to die for their faith, but that is enough, if they will firmly believe, "His kingdom is forever."

XXIII

Canon and Text

WHY were only the books which are at present in the Old Testament included in the final collection? The Old Testament was meant to contain only sacred writings, secular books were therefore excluded on principle; if some were nevertheless admitted, as the Book of Esther and the Song of Songs, they had to be interpreted in a religious or allegorical manner in order to be acceptable. But there were other religious books, some of them of high value and even written in the sacred Hebrew language, that were not admitted. What was the reason for this apparently strange procedure? A brief survey of the formation of the canon will show this.

I. THE CANON

The canon of the law, containing the so-called five books of Moses, had been fixed between the time of Ezra and the founding of the Samaritan church, for when the rival organization on Mount Gerizim was established, probably in the latter part of the fourth century, the Pentateuch was taken over by the Samaritans as their sacred book. The principle of canonization was divine inspiration, *i.e.*, these books were regarded as sacred, because they contained the word of God; and as such they were the final authority, the fundamental law of the Jewish community. Moses had been merely God's spokesman, His mouthpiece, nothing else; the real author was God. There had been several stages in the process of canonization; the most notable were the adoption of the Deuteronomic law at the time of Josiah's reformation and the recognition of the Priestly law or perhaps of the whole Pentateuch at the time of Ezra. The canon of the law, the Torah, now was complete. It has remained the highest Jewish authority ever since.

The canon of the prophets, comprising the so-called "Former Prophets," the Books of Joshua, Judges, Samuel, and Kings; and the "Latter Prophets," Isaiah, Jeremiah, Ezekiel, and the Twelve, must have come up after the Samaritan schism. It was fixed by 200 B.C., but its authority was never as great as that of the law. The prophets had, indeed, been God's spokesmen too, and this gave their words divine sanction. But after the formation of the canon of the law, they were regarded as mere expounders of the law, and not in the same class with Moses (cf. Num. 12:6f.). The Book of Ezekiel even had difficulty in gaining admission to the canon because it contained some statements which could only with difficulty be harmonized with the law.

The canon of the prophets was already closed when the Book of Daniel appeared, so that it could not be included in it. It was placed in the third collection, "the writings" or "hagiographa." A number of religious books, some of which were in existence before the canon of the prophets was closed, also could not be put among the prophets on account of their character. But they were much used and appealed to as authoritative along with the law and the prophets. The Palestinian Jews of the first century believed that the period of divine inspiration had come to an end with Ezra and Nehemiah. And when they finally fixed the extent of the canon or of the authoritative collection of Holy Scripture, an all-important question was whether a book was written or believed to have been written before this time. Any book which on the face of it was composed later, as for example the extremely worth-while book of Ecclesiasticus or Sirach, could not be admitted. Only the Psalms, Proverbs, Job, Song of Songs, Ruth, Lamentations, Ecclesiastes, Esther, Daniel, Ezra-Nehemiah, and Chronicles found their way into the third division of the Canon. There was dispute about Song of Songs, Ecclesiastes, and Esther. At a gathering of Rabbis at Yamnia (Yabneh in the Old Testament), ca. 100 A.D., this canon of the writings was endorsed, but it was not until the second and third centuries that opposition to the three controversial books ended.

The Greek-speaking Jews of Alexandria had brought about a

translation of the Hebrew sacred books from about the middle of
the third century B.C. It was one of the most important achievements
in religious history, for by this means numerous gentiles became
familiar with these writings and were attracted to the Jewish religion. This paved the way for Christianity; and in the New Testament this Greek translation is authoritative Holy Scripture. A
legendary account of how the translation was made by a group of
70 (72) men [1] is given in the *Letter of Aristeas*.

The Septuagint contained books which were not received by the
Palestinian Rabbis into the canon. When Jerome (*ca.* 400) made his
Latin translation, later called the Vulgate, and took cognizance of
the fact that these were not found in the Hebrew scriptures he called
them "apocrypha," probably in translation of a Hebrew word, and
meaning that they should be kept under cover and not flaunted
before the world. In the early centuries they had been valued very
highly in the Church for religious instruction. Jerome left them
dispersed among the canonical books and did not group them. This
was first done by Martin Luther, who relegated them to the end
of the Old Testament as "The Apocrypha." He eliminated our 1
and 2 Esdras (more correctly called IV Ezra), even casting his copy
of the latter into the Elbe River. The rest he regarded as "books
that are not equally esteemed with Holy Scripture, but nevertheless
are profitable and good to read." The *AV*, however, retained 1 and
2 Esdras, though following Luther in grouping the Apocrypha.

The Roman Church defined its position at the Council of Trent
(1546) and maintained the canonicity of the Apocrypha. They thus
are part of the Catholic Bible to this day. The Westminster Assembly
in 1643, following earlier Reformed precedent, denied the Apocrypha any recommended status. The full consequence of this was drawn
in England in 1827, when the British and Foreign Bible Society after
a severe controversy decided to exclude from its Bibles "those un-
hallowed productions of the wisdom and folly of men that have
been so presumptuously associated with the sacred oracles of God."
The consequence of this unjust stricture has been that few people

---

[1] Hence Latin *septuaginta*, in Roman numerals *LXX*, came to be used as its
name. Septuagint studies are a field in themselves. New material found in
Egypt, in Cave IV at Qumran and at Wadi Murabba'at, is of importance. For
the letter of Aristeas see p. 462.

possess a copy of the Apocryphal books, which are interesting in themselves and extremely valuable for the glimpses they give of changing times after the close of the Old Testament canon. For a list of them and other books of a similar nature see pp. 461f.

2. THE TEXT

The alphabetic writing of the Semitic peoples was purely consonantal. If the reader will have someone write out for him a sentence in English, omitting all vowels, and then seek to read it he may not find this easy to do quickly if the subject matter is not clear to him. All Semitic languages (except the Assyro-Babylonian) were written in this shorthand manner. From the sixth century men called *Masoretes* provided the Biblical text with vowel-points and with *Masorah* (remarks in the margins and at the end of a book). There were several systems of vocalization—the Babylonian supralinear one and the Tiberiensian mixed one; the latter of which became dominant in the end and is used in printed Hebrew Bibles. The oldest known Masoretic codices, as established through the researches of Paul Kahle, are the one of the prophets of 895 in Leningrad, and those in Cairo and Aleppo dating from the beginning of the tenth century. They were all written by members of the Masoretic family of Ben Asher.[2] This family was rivaled by that of Ben Naphthali, which notably is represented by a codex of 1105 A.D. that bears the name of the great Humanist, Reuchlin. The printed Hebrew Bibles (the first appeared at Soncino in 1488) until the 1937 edition of R. Kittel's *Biblia Hebraica*, in which Kahle used a pure Ben Asher manuscript of 1008 from Leningrad, represented a mixture of both.

Once a literature becomes canonical and therewith sacred its text is carefully guarded. The Masoretes did not even change patent errors but provided a directive "read": (*qerē*) in the margin. The Hebrew manuscripts that have come from the Middle Ages were standardized to such a degree that it became very reasonable to suppose that a single manuscript was the parent of them all, and that manuscripts which exhibited important variations were allowed

---

[2] In the Ben Asher manuscripts there is no *o* vowel in the vocalization of *w* (see p. xiii, note 1), only *e* and *a*. This may have suggested Aramaic *shemā*, "the name."

to perish. When every manuscript shows such an idiosyncrasy as the raised letter *n* in M^{n}shh in Judg. 18:30—a correction obviously intended to shield Moses (Heb. *Mosheh*) by urging one to read *Menasheh* (Manasseh)—the dependence on an archtype becomes plain. At the same time the change made in this instance is so conservative that one can see that it was done when the text was considered too sacred to alter.

There are bolder changes discernible, which perhaps were made earlier. Indelicate expressions were removed and euphemisms were substituted; religiously objectionable statements were changed. Thus in 1 Sam. 25:22 it seemed improper to let David curse himself in his oath, so *the enemies* of David were inserted, "God do so to (*the enemies of*) David, and more also, if I leave of all that pertain to him by the morning light so much as one man-child." Cf. also 2 Sam. 12:14.

Hosea's declaration, "I will take away the names of the Baalim out of her mouth, and they shall no more be mentioned by their name" (Hos. 2:17), was taken quite literally later on and applied to the occurrences of Baal even in proper names. Instead of reading *baal* they read *bōsheth = shame*. Thus the name of Saul's son Eshbaal, as it is still given in 1 Chron. 9:39, was changed to *Ishbosheth* in 2 Sam. 2:8, etc.; the name of Jonathan's son Meribbaal (1 Chron. 9:40) was read *Mephibosheth* in 2 Sam. 9:6; and even Gideon's name Jerubbaal (Judg. 6:32) became *Jerubbosheth* in 2 Sam. 11:21.

In view of the hostility existing between Jews and Samaritans in the time of Christ and earlier it was embarrassing to the Jews that the Samaritans could point to Deut. 27:4, where Mt. Gerizim was mentioned as the place where Yahweh had commanded an altar to be built, whereas nowhere in the whole book of the law was Jerusalem named as the sole place of worship. The Jews were not above falsifying the text of the passage by substituting the name *Ebal* (the mountain of the curses) for Gerizim, and later even claimed that Ebal and Gerizim lay in the vicinity of Jericho—a transfer that is already reflected in the Copper Scroll from Qumran.[3]

But still earlier changes of text are discernible—changes which

[3] On the Copper Scroll, see the book of John Allegro, *The Treasure of the Copper Scrolls* (1960), in which a translation may be found.

would not have been made by late editors. For instance in the interest of a theological trend of a certain time, *Elohim* = *God* was sometimes substituted for Yahweh. The most significant illustration of this is the Elohistic section of the Psalter, Ps. 42–83. Other dogmatic changes too were made, *e.g.*, in Hab. 1:12 the prophet had said, "Art Thou not from everlasting, O Yahweh my God, my Holy One *that shall not die?*" It seemed blasphemous even to utter such a thought, and so the text was slightly changed (only one letter is involved) to *"we shall not die."*

More important than all such changes are corruptions suffered and minor additions made somewhere along the line before the text was guarded. The corruptions and their causes are only of interest to the Hebraist.[4] Many small additions were due to incorporation into the text of something that had been written in the margin. Thus someone annotated Isa. 7:17, "Yahweh will bring upon thee and upon thy people, and upon thy father's house, days such as have not come, since the day that Ephraim departed from Judah," with *the king of Assyria*. This is correct, of course, and the Dead Sea Isaiah Scroll has it; but it certainly was not written by Isaiah himself. Similarly, somebody noted on Ezek. 4:1, "Thou also, son of man, take thee a tile, and lay it before thee, and portray upon it a city," *Jerusalem*. This is again quite correct, but the construction in Hebrew shows that it is an addition in the text.

In view of what could be detected of textual corruption and change, the question whether one could get back to an older text than that on which the Massoretic manuscripts rested loomed important. Here scholarship had only the ancient versions, above all the Septuagint, to turn to for clues to different readings. However, the text of the Septuagint itself requires intensive research, and is of unequal value in the different Biblical books.

Then in 1947 came the find of the Dead Sea Scrolls in a cave at Khirbet Qumram. Large-scale cave explorations by Beduin and by accredited exploration parties followed in succeeding years, resulting in the discovery of more caves and of a vast amount of manuscript materials, though mostly in the form of fragments. Cave IV alone is said to have produced "tens of thousands," of fragments repre-

[4] See the previous edition of this book, pp. 430–433.

senting hundreds of different manuscripts, most of them Biblical. An international team of scholars has been assorting them and trying to piece them together in one of the greatest "picture-puzzle" operations of all time. It will be years before all this material is completely published, and then its application to the restoration of the text of the Old Testament will be a long process.

The prize Biblical manuscript among those hitherto published has been the large Isaiah Scroll [5] from Cave I, since it is completely preserved except for a few *lacunae*. Owing to the paucity of surviving ancient materials written in Hebrew there initially was much dispute about the age of the manuscript; but thanks to the Qumran excavations which dated the settlement, and all the further finds, including those of Cave IV and of the Wadi Murabba'at caves farther to the south, a science of Hebrew palaeography has blossomed forth. Most manuscripts can now be approximately dated, and ere long they may become datable to a decade. Writing keeps changing, as anyone can convince himself by looking at English letters or manuscripts written in different generations. The Isaiah manuscript, the first Scroll to be published, was written in the late second or early first century B.C.

Here for the first time men saw a Hebrew Biblical book as it was handed down in pre-Christian times. The manuscript was made of seventeen pieces of prepared leather, approaching the parchment stage, sewn together to form a band 24½ feet long and 10⅝ inches high. Fifty-four vertical columns of writing were required to copy Isaiah—a little less than one to a chapter of our chapter division. Faintly ruled lines on the reverse, made with a sharp instrument, were sufficiently visible on the obverse for guidance. The scribe often made mistakes and corrected them himself. Sometimes he corrected a letter directly by writing over it; anon he inserted an omitted letter, word, or phrase above the line. Later hands also made corrections. The text has paragraphing, but begins the new line without indentation. Within the paragraph, breaks are made where the subject matter warrants. There are also marginal signs, which are held to be of later origin.

In contents the Isaiah manuscript exhibits many variations from

[5] *The Dead Sea Scrolls of St. Mark's Monastery,* I, ed., Millar Burrows (1950).

the Masoretic text, though most of them are of a minor nature. The situation is somewhat like that of a copy of the *AV* as printed a few hundred years ago and one printed today, in which archaic spellings and verb forms have been modernized. The Isaiah manuscript has older grammatical forms, which were abandoned before the text that came down to the Masoretes was established. A surprising amount of use is made of the letters *w* and *y* as vowel indicators. This can be perplexing, as when a word that is always spelled *bmh* (*bāmāh* "high-place") in the Masoretic text is written *bwmh*, suggesting a pronunciation *bōmāh* or *būmāh*. In some cases the vocalizer shows surprising knowledge. Thus the title of the Assyrian officer of Isa. 20:1, which the *MT* vocalizes Tartan as does the Septuagint), is here written *twrtn*, indicating a pronunciation *Turtan*—a form that appears in the Assyrian inscriptions. The name Ararat in Isa. 37:38 appears as *Ḥwrrt;* leaving aside the matter of the change of initial consonant this spelling indicates that the first vowel was *u*, and this is correct, because in the Assyrian inscriptions the name is *Urartu*. Some think that the text editor must have been a Jew from Babylonia to be aware of such things. But he does not solve for us the puzzle of the corrupt god-name Nisroch in Isa. 37:38.

The actual variants in meaning in the Isaiah manuscript are of controversial nature.[6] Some scholars hold the Masoretic text is superior in the instances that have been brought forward. But there are real contributions. Thus in Isa. 49:12 the land of *Sinim* is mentioned in the *MT* as an area from which exiles are to return; the Scroll reads *swnyym* thereby confirming the suggestion that this means "people of Sewen" (the name is so written in Egyptian and in the Aramaic papyri; cf. also Ezek. 29:10; 30:6; today Assuan). In Isa. 36:19; 37:13 the *MT* has a city or principality called Sepharvaim; the scroll here reads *spryym*, inviting the explanation of the name as "the *Shuprians*" or inhabitants of Shupria (pronounced Supria by the Assyrians), a region southwest of Lake Van. Instead of the city Henaʿ of 37:13 the scroll has "and Nʿ" which raises new possibilities for the identification of the name.

The first impression of some scholars was that the Dead Sea

---

[6] See Burrows, *Dead Sea Scrolls*, p. 301ff. *More Light*, p. 146ff.

Scrolls confirmed the excellence of the Masoretic Text. But the fragments of nearly a hundred Biblical scrolls from Cave IV compelled a modification of opinion. Here were some manuscripts that differed considerably from the *MT* and, surprisingly, agreed very often with the Septuagint. An archaic scroll of the Books of Samuel written no later than 200 B.C. has proved particularly important, even giving readings that are superior to the manuscript used by the Septuagint translator. The later manuscripts, especially those from the second century A.D. from Wadi Murabba'at, agree so closely with the *MT* that one must assume that the consonant text of the Old Testament was already established by the time of the Barcocheba revolt of 132 A.D. from which those finds date. That is exactly what one should expect in view of the finalization of the Canon, *ca.* 100 A.D. The Masoretic editors only worked over this text to make sure that it was read and understood properly and uniformly. It was known from ancient Hebrew inscriptions that the script in which all but the youngest materials in the Old Testament must have been written was the one also used by the Phoenicians and Moabites. However, the Jews under the influence of Aramaic adopted the use of a cursive script, and it is in this script that the Isaiah Scroll is written. The Samaritans, who took over the Pentateuch as their sole Sacred Book (perhaps in cursive script), apparently replaced it with a manuscript of Maccabean times, written in the ancient script Hebrew, which they continued to use for their own writings. The Qumran finds have brought some manuscript materials to light that are written in the palaeo-Hebrew script antedating the Maccabean age.[7] In some manuscripts using the cursive script, for instance in the Habakkuk commentary, the name Yahweh is written in the old Hebrew characters. Perhaps this means that a substitute word was already used for it; the archaic writing made the name stand out and prevented utterance of it by mistake. A Greek translation of Leviticus from Cave IV, written on papyrus in the last century B.C., instead of substituting the word *kyrios* "Lord" for the divine name, as does the received

---

[7] The greatest amount of "inside information" about the scrolls accessible to the general reader is found in Frank M. Cross, Jr., *The Ancient Library of Qumran,* (1958). According to him the chief importance of the scrolls lies in the data they yield for the reconstruction of the textual history of the Old Testament (p. 125).

Septuagint text, transcribes the name as IAŌ (ch. *Yeho* in Hebrew names such as *Yehoram* or in traditional spelling Jehoram; and the *Yahu* or *Yaho* of the Elephantine papyri).

It is unlikely that even the Dead Sea Scrolls will solve every difficulty of the Old Testament text. Books written much earlier than the second or first century B.C. had by this time a long history of transmission, in which numerous mistakes may have crept in. Often critical conjecture is needed to restore the sense and such attempts can rarely be made convincing.

For practical purposes this is not as serious as it sounds, for in spite of numerous mistakes in the Hebrew text and many mistranslations in ancient and modern versions, the Old Testament has exerted its living power and will continue to exert it as long as men, thirsting for the revelation of the living God, read the pages of this book, which together with the New Testament has become The Bible of Mankind, Israel's priceless literary bequest to the world.

Appendix

CHRONOLOGY OF OLD TESTAMENT LITERATURE

1. THE PREMONARCHIC PERIOD, before *ca.* 1000 B.C. (topically arranged):
    - (*a*) *Early Poems:* Song of Lamech (Gen. 4:23f.). Song of Miriam (Ex. 15:21). War with Amalek (Ex. 17:16). Incantations to the Ark (Num. 10:35f.). List of Stations (Num. 21:14f.). Song of the Well (Num. 21:17f.). Taunt Song on the Amorites (Num. 21:27-30). Joshua's Appeal to the Sun and the Moon (Josh. 10:12f.). Song of Deborah (Judg. 5).
    - (*b*) *Proverbs, riddles, and fables:* David's Proverb (1 Sam. 24:13). Samson's Riddles (Judg. 14:14, 18) and Taunt (Judg. 15:16). Jotham's Fable (Judg. 9:7-15).
    - (*c*) *Prophetic blessings and oracles:* The Blessing of Noah (Gen. 9:25-27) and of Jacob (Gen. 49). The Oracles of Balaam (Num. 23f.).
2. THE TIME OF DAVID, SOLOMON, AND JEROBOAM I, from *ca.* 1000-900 B.C.:
    - (*a*) *Poems:* Paean over David's victories (1 Sam. 18:7 etc.). Sheba's War Cry (2 Sam. 20:1). David's Lamentation over Saul and Jonathan (2 Sam. 1:19ff.), and over Abner (2 Sam. 3:33f.). Nathan's Parable (2 Sam. 12:1-4). Solomon's Dedication of the Temple (1 Ki. 8:12f.). The Books of Yashar and of the Wars of Yahweh. The Blessing of Moses (Deut. 33). The Song of Moses (Deut. 32).
    - (*b*) *Narratives:* The Story of the Ark (1 Sam. 4:1—7:1; 2 Sam. 6); Narratives of Saul's Rise (1 Sam. 9—10:16; 11; 13; 14); Narratives of David's Rise (1 Sam. 6:14—2 Sam. 5:8); the Davidic Succession Narrative (2 Sam. 9—20; 1 Ki. 1-2). The Book of the Acts of Solomon (1 Ki. 3-11 in part). Beginnings of the Royal Annals and of temple records.
    - (*c*) *Laws:* The Book of the Covenant (Ex. 20:23—23:19). The so-called Cultic Decalogue of Ex. 34.

3. THE NINTH AND EIGHTH CENTURIES:

The Elijah Stories (1 Ki. 17–19, 21). The Elisha Stories (2 Ki. 2–8 in part, 13:14–21). Narratives of the Rise and Fall of the Dynasty of Omri (1 Ki. 20, 22; 2 Ki. 3, 6:24—7:20, 8:7–15, 9, 10). The Yahwist (*ca.* 900 B.C.). The Elohist (*ca.* 800 B.C.). Amos (*ca.* 750). Hosea (from *ca.* 745–725). Isaiah (from 738–700 and perhaps later). Micah (*ca.* 725–700).

4. THE SEVENTH CENTURY:

Combination of the Yahwist and the Elohist by the Jehovist. Deuteronomy (published in 621 B.C.). Zephaniah (*ca.* 627–626). Jeremiah (from 626 on.) Nahum (*ca.* 606).

5. THE SIXTH CENTURY:

Jeremiah (continued till after 586). Habakkuk (between 600 and 590). Ezekiel (593–571). The Holiness Code (Lev. 17–26). Lamentations (586–550). Isaiah 63:7—64:12. The Deuteronomistic Historical Work (*ca.* 550). Isaiah 13:2–22; 14:4–21; 21. Deutero-Isaiah (Isa. 40–55, between 546 and 539). Haggai (520). Zechariah 1–8 (520–518). Isaiah 56:9—58:12; 59:1–15a; 65:1–16; 66:1–6, 5–18a, 24 (from 520 on). The Priestly Document (*ca.* 500 or later).

6. THE FIFTH CENTURY:

Isaiah 59:15b—63:6; 65:17–25; 66:7–14, 18b–23. Jeremiah 3:14–18. Isaiah 34–35. Obadiah. Isaiah 15–16. Amos 9:8b–15. Zephaniah (later elements). Isaiah 11:10–16. Malachi (*ca.* 460). The Memoir of Nehemiah (after 432). Joel (*ca.* 400).

7. THE FOURTH CENTURY:

Combination of the Priestly Document with the Jehovist. Separation of Deuteronomy from the Deuteronomistic Historical Work, and combination with the Priestly-Jehovistic work to form the Pentateuch. The Memoir of Ezra. Joel (later elements). Isaiah 19:1–15; 23:1–14. Proverbs (older portions, especially 22:17—23:12). Job. Isaiah 24–27. Zechariah 9:1–10. The Aramaic History of Jerusalem (Ezr. 4:6—6:18). The Chronicler's Historical Work. (Chronicles, plus Ezra-Nehemiah, *ca.* 300). The Book of Ruth.

8. THE THIRD CENTURY:

Completion of the Psalter. Song of Songs. Proverbs 1–9, 30–31. Jonah. Isaiah 19:16–25. Ecclesiastes (*ca.* 300–250). Zechariah 9–11. Zechariah 12–14. Isaiah 33. Minor additions to the prophetic books. Aramaic Daniel Narratives (*ca.* 200). Genesis 14. Esther.

9. THE SECOND CENTURY:

Daniel (165–164).

THE APOCRYPHA

The Book of Ecclesiasticus or Sirach, *ca.* 190 B.C. A wisdom book in the manner of Proverbs. The Greek translator notes that he came to Egypt under King Euergetes (meaning Ptolemy VII) in the ruler's 38th year (132 B.C.) and translated the book of his grandfather Jesus the son of Sira. The book was only known in Greek and versions made from it, but from the Genizah of a Cairo Synagogue fragments of manuscripts were salvaged permitting recovery of two-thirds of the Hebrew (since 1896). The Qumran finds of Cave II have reportedly produced some fragments of the Hebrew, thus proving that the book was known and valued by the Dead Sea community.

The Book of Tobit, *ca.* 175 B.C. Preserved only in Greek, but the Qumran finds have produced Aramaic and Hebrew fragments. It probably was written in Aramaic. Has story interest similar to Esther.

The Book of Judith, *ca.* 150 B.C. The tale of Judith and Holofernes is composed with an eye to the Syrian oppressors of the author's time. There seems to be no trace of it at Qumran.

First Maccabees, *ca.* 100 B.C. The great story of the Maccabean period from a source in sympathy with this family.

Second Maccabees, *ca.* 50 B.C. Based in part on Jason of Cyrene's history of the happenings. One gets an entirely different picture of the Maccabees.

The Wisdom of Solomon, first century B.C. In it Judaism takes on a Hellenized character. Of importance for early Christianity, having points of contact with the New Testament. Included in the Muratorian Canonical list of the second century A.D. as part of the New Testament. A Fragment of it was discovered in the Dead Sea Scrolls explorations at *Khirbet Mird*.

First Esdras (III Ezra in the Vulgate). Really a translation of the close of Chronicles, Ezra, and a piece of Nehemiah, with interpolation of the story of the three pages of Darius in chs. 3:1—5:3 (probably an original Greek production, not a translation). It was made in the late second century. It is of importance for the study of Ezra-Nehemiah.

The Epistle of Jeremiah, second century B.C. Placed after the Lamentations in the Septuagint, but in the Vulgate appended to the Book of Baruch.

The Book of Baruch. Follows Jeremiah in the Septuagint. Originally written in Hebrew, about the middle of the first century.

The Additions to Esther. See p. 320.

The Additions to Daniel: Song of the Three Holy Children; History of Susanna; Bel and the Dragon. See p. 446.

The Prayer of Manasses. This comes from a collection of psalms scattered through the Bible and called *The Odes*. The collection is found in the Septuagint after the Psalms. The final selection, the Prayer of Manasses, however, is an original Greek composition, written for the situation of 2 Chron. 33:12–13, but not inserted there in any known manuscripts. It dates from the first century A.D.

Second Esdras (So-called only in the English translations. In the *LXX*, Second Esdras is the name of our canonical Ezra-Nehemiah, treated as one book.) Generally called IV Ezra, after the Vulgate in which it and III Ezra (our and the Septuagint's First Esdras) are put after the New Testament. IV Ezra is preserved only in Latin, Syriac, and Ethiopic translations. It was written originally in Hebrew in the time of Domitian, *ca.* 95 A.D., and is thus a Jewish counterpart to the Revelation of John.

THE PSEUDEPIGRAPHA

Third Maccabees, *ca.* 25 B.C. Has nothing to do with the Maccabees. It tells of Ptolemy IV Philopator's violation of the temple in 217 B.C.; of his persecution of Jews in Egypt; his change of heart; and of a festival commemorating the deliverance. It was written in Greek.

Fourth Maccabees. Likewise has nothing to do with the Maccabees. It is a philosophical tract written at the end of the first century B.C. or early in the first century A.D.

The Psalms of Solomon. Preserved in Greek, but originally written in Hebrew, *ca.* 30 B.C. Important for the insight they give into life and thought in Palestine before Christ. The Messianic 17th Psalm is especially noteworthy.

The Letter of Aristeas, *ca.* 100 B.C. Tells the legend of the origin of the Septuagint Bible translation. Contains valuable information.

Enoch. This great corpus of material has only come down in complete form in an Ethiopic translation made from a Greek version. Copies of it in Hebrew and Aramaic existed in the Qumran community. At that time however, it evidently did not contain the much discussed Similitudes (1 Enoch, 37–71). The oldest elements in the book are pre-Maccabean. It is quoted in the New Testament in Jude vv. 14–15.

The Testaments of the Twelve Patriarchs. This work, which is preserved in Greek and some versions, has evidently evolved from separate testaments of the individual sons of Jacob. From Qumran now has come knowledge of Testaments of Levi and Naphtali in Aramaic. No doubt the material is largely second century B.C.

The Book of Jubilees, *ca.* 100 B.C. Fragments in Hebrew have been found in Qumran. The work reflects the use of the solar calendar that was also used at Qumran.

Besides these there are: the Assumption of Moses, the Syriac Apocalypse of Baruch, the Greek Apocalypse of Baruch, the Martyrdom and Ascension of Isaiah, the Sibylline Oracles and the Life of Adam and Eve. These books, however, were edited in the early centuries of the Christian era.

Pseudepigraphic writings enumerated, including the late ones, will be found in *APOT*, vol. II, except 3 Maccabees, which is given in vol. I. *APOT* also includes The Story of Ahikar and the Zadokite fragments.

SOME NEWLY DISCOVERED JEWISH WRITINGS

(For translations see Bibliography p. 479.)

The Damascus document or Zadokite fragments. Found in a late Hebrew manuscript in the Cairo Genizah, it was quickly recognized as pre-Christian. Fragments of the work have turned up at Qumran, and it is evidently a product of that community. Its date is in dispute—some think it goes back to the Maccabean age. It seems to be younger than the document next mentioned.

The Rule of the Community, originally labeled Manual of Discipline. An extremely important document. First published in 1951 from the finds of Cave I at Qumran.

The Rule of the Congregation. Material related to the preceding and published in 1955. From Cave I.

The Habakkuk Commentary. From Cave I, published in 1950.

The War of the Sons of Light with the Sons of Darkness. From Cave I. Published in 1954, after earlier partial publication.

The Thanksgiving Psalms. Also published completely in 1954. This and the preceding work belonged to the materials that came from Cave I and were acquired for the Hebrew University.

The Genesis Apocryphon. Partially published in 1956. From Cave I.

Selected Bibliography

IN conformity with the general character of the book, the following bibliography is for the student and general reader rather than the specialist.

BIBLE TRANSLATIONS, TEXTS, REFERENCE BOOKS

TRANSLATIONS

The Bible. A New Translation by James Moffatt. New York, Geo. H. Doran, 1924.

The Complete Bible, an American Translation. Edited by J. M. Powis Smith and Edgar J. Goodspeed. Chicago, University of Chicago Press, 1935.

The Holy Bible. Edited with various renderings and readings by T. K. Cheyne, S. R. Driver, R. I. Clarke, A. Goodwin, and W. Sanday (the so-called Variorum Bible). Third edition. London, Eyre and Spottiswoode, 1891.

The Holy Bible. Revised Standard Version. New York, Thomas Nelson, 1952.

The Septuagint Bible. Translated by Charles Thomas. Edited, revised, and enlarged by C. A. Muses. Indian Hills, Colo., Falcon's Wing Press, 1954.

Biblia Hebraica. Edited by Rudolf Kittel, A. Alt, O. Eissfeldt. Masoretic text by Paul Kahle. Seventh Edition. Stuttgart, Privilegirte Württembergische Bibelanstalt, 1952. (The critical footnotes, giving readings of versions and emendations, make this the most helpful edition for study purposes.)

Die Septuaginta. Two volumes. Edited by Alfred Rahlfs. Stuttgart, Privilegirte Württembergische Bibelanstalt, 1935.

CONCORDANCES

Analytical Concordance to the Bible. Robert Young. New York, Funk and Wagnalls, 1955.
Exhaustive Concordance of the Bible. James Strong. Nashville, Abingdon Press, 1955.
Nelson's Complete Concordance to the Revised Standard Version. New York, Thomas Nelson, 1957.
Unabridged Concordance to the Bible. Alexander A. Cruden. Westwood, N.J., Revell, 1953.

BIBLE DICTIONARIES

Dictionary of the Bible. Five volumes. Edited by James Hastings and J. A. Selbie. New York, Scribner, 1905.
Encyclopedia Biblica. Four volumes. Edited by T. K. Cheyne and J. S. Black. London, Black, Ltd., 1899–1903.
The Interpreter's Bible Dictionary. Four volumes. Nashville, Abingdon Press, 1962.

ONE VOLUME BIBLE DICTIONARIES

Dictionary of the Bible. Edited by James Hastings. Revised by H. H. Rowley and F. C. Grant. New York, Scribner, 1962.
An Encyclopedia of Bible Life. Third edition, M. S. Miller and J. L. Miller. New York, Harper, 1962.
Harper's Bible Dictionary. Sixth edition, M. S. Miller and J. L. Miller. New York, Harper, 1961.
Seventh Day Adventist Bible Dictionary with Atlas. Edited by Siegfried H. Horn. Washington, D.C., Review and Herold, 1960.
Unger's Bible Dictionary. Third edition, Merrill F. Unger. Chicago, Moody Press, 1960.
Westminster Dictionary of the Bible. Edited by J. D. Davis. Revised by H. S. Gehmann. Philadelphia, Westminster Press, 1944.

Biblisch-Historisches Handwörterbuch. Three volumes. Bo Reicke and Leonhard Rost. Göttingen, Vandenhoeck und Rupprecht, 1962 ff.
Biblisches Reallexikon. Kurt Galling. Tübingen, J. C. B. Mohr, 1937. (*Handbuch zum Alten Testament.* Edited by Otto Eissfeldt. Erste Reihe, I.)
Calwer Bibel-Lexikon. Fifth edition, Theodor Schlatter. Stuttgart, Calwer Vereinsbuchhandlung, 1961.
Protestantische Realenzyklopädie. Twenty-four volumes. J. J. Herzog. Third edition, Albert Hauck. Leipzig, Hinrichs, 1896–1913.
Die Religion in Geschichte und Gegenwart. Six volumes. Third edition, Kurt Galling, et al. Tübingen, J. C. B. Mohr, 1956–1962.

Lexikon zur Bibel. F. Rienecker. Wuppertal, Brockhaus, 1960.

GENERAL ORIENTATION

BIBLE HANDBOOKS

Manson, Thomas W., editor. *A Companion to the Bible.* Edinburgh, T. Clarke, 1950.

Neil, William, editor. *The Bible Companion.* New York, McGraw-Hill, 1960.

RECENT DEVELOPMENTS

Peake, Arthur S. *The People and the Book: essays on the Old Testament.* Oxford, Clarendon Press, 1925.

Robinson, H. Wheeler, editor. *Record and Revelation: essays on the Old Testament.* Oxford, Clarendon Press, 1938.

Rowley, Harold H., editor. *The Old Testament and Modern Study: a Generation of Discovery and Research.* Oxford, Clarendon Press, 1951.

Willoughby, Harold R., editor. *The Study of the Bible Today and To-morrow.* Chicago, University of Chicago Press, 1947.

HISTORY OF CRITICISM

Hahn, Herbert F. *The Old Testament in Modern Research.* Philadelphia, Muhlenberg Press, 1954.

Kraeling, Emil G. *The Old Testament Since the Reformation.* New York, Harper, 1955. (An account of the theological debate concerning the authority of the Old Testament as this was brought on by the rise of criticism.)

Kraus, Hans Joachim. *Geschichte der historish-kritischen Erforschung des Alten Testaments von der Reformation bis zur Gegenwart.* Neukirchen, Erziehungsverein, 1956.

INTRODUCTION AND HISTORY OF LITERATURE

Anderson, Bernard W. *Understanding the Old Testament.* New York, Prentice Hall, 1957.

Anderson, George W. *A Critical Introduction to the Old Testament.* London, Duckworth, Ltd., 1959.

Bentzen, Aage. *Introduction to the Old Testament.* Second edition. Copenhagen, G. E. C. Gad, 1952.

Cook, Stanley A. *Introduction to the Bible.* Harmondsworth, Middlesex, Penguin Books, 1945.

Driver, Samuel R. *Introduction to the Literature of the Old Testament.* Ninth edition. Edinburgh, T. Clarke, 1913.

Kuhl, Curt. *The Old Testament: its Origin and Composition.* Translated by C. M. T. Herriott. Edinburgh, Oliver and Boyd, Ltd., 1961.

Moore, George Foote. *The Literature of the Old Testament.* Second edition, C. H. Brockington. Oxford, Oxford University Press, 1948.

Nielsen, Eduard. *Oral Tradition: a Modern Problem in Old Testament Introduction.* London, SCM (Student Christian Movement) Press, 1954.

Oesterley, William O. E. and Theodore H. Robinson. *Introduction to the Books of the Old Testament.* New York, Macmillan, 1935.

Pfeiffer, Robert H. *Introduction to the Books of the Old Testament.* New York, Harper, 1957.

—— *Introduction to the Old Testament.* New York, Harper, 1948.

Robinson, H. Wheeler. *The Old Testament: its Making and Meaning.* London, University of London Press, 1956.

Robinson, Theodore H. *The Old Testament: a Conspectus.* London, Duckworth, Ltd., 1953.

Rowley, Harold H. *The Growth of the Old Testament.* London, Hutchinson, 1950.

—— *The Rediscovery of the Old Testament.* Philadelphia, Westminster Press, 1946.

—— *The Servant of the Lord.* London, Lutterworth Press, 1952.

Weiser, Artur. *The Old Testament: its Formation and Development.* Translated by Dorothea M. Barton. New York, Association Press, 1961.

Budde, Karl. *Geschichte der Althebräischen Literatur.* Second edition, Leipzig, 1909.

Eissfeldt, Otto. *Einleitung in das Alte Testament.* Second revised edition. Tübingen, J. C. B. Mohr, 1956. (The foremost book for the scholar.)

Gunkel, Hermann. "Die Israelitische Literatur." *Kultur der Gegenwart,* Vol. I. P. Hinneberg. Leipzig, Teubner, 1906. (Pioneer outline of the form-critical approach.)

Hempel, Johannes. *Die Althebräische Literatur und ihr Hellenistisch-Jüdisches Nachleben.* Potsdam, Athenaion, 1930. (Form-critical and archaeological.)

Lods, Adolphe. *Histoire de la littérature Hebraique at Juive.* Paris, Payot, 1950.

Meinhold, Johannes. *Einführung in das Alte Testament.* Third edition. Giessen, Töpelmann, 1932.

Sellin, Ernst. *Einleitung in das Alte Testament.* Ninth edition, Leonhard Rost. Heidelberg, Quelle-Meyer, 1959.

Steuernagel, Carl. *Lehrbuch der Einleitung in das Alte Testament.* Tübingen, J. C. B. Mohr, 1912.

CANON AND TEXT

Ap-Thomas, D. R. *A Primer of Old Testament Text-Criticism.* London, Epworth Press, 1948.

Bruce, Frederick F. *The Books and the Parchments.* London, Pickering and Inglis, Ltd., 1950.

Flack, Elmer E. and Bruce Metzger, editors. *The Text, Canon and Principal Versions of the Bible.* Grand Rapids, Michigan, Baker Book House, 1956.

Kahle, Paul. *The Cairo Geniza* (Schweich Lectures). London, British Academy, 1948.

Kenyon, Sir Frederick C. *Our Bible and the Ancient Manuscripts.* Revised by A. W. Adams. New York, Harper, 1958.

—— *Recent Developments in Textual Criticism of the Greek Bible.* London, Oxford University Press, 1933.

—— *The Text of the Greek Bible.* London, Duckworth, Ltd., 1949.

Margolis, Max L. *The Hebrew Scriptures in the Making.* Philadelphia, Jewish Publication Society, 1922.

Ostborn, Gunnar. *Cult and Canon, a Study in the Canonization of the Old Testament.* Uppsala, Lundequist, 1955.

Price, Ira M. *The Ancestry of Our English Bible.* Edited by W. A. Irwin and A. P. Wikgren. New York, Harper, 1956.

Roberts, B. J. *The Old Testament Texts and Versions.* Cardiff, University of Wales, 1951.

Robinson, H. Wheeler, editor. *The Bible in its Ancient and English Versions.* Second revised edition, W. D. McHardy. Oxford, Clarendon Press, 1954.

Ryle, Herbert E. *The Canon of the Old Testament.* Second edition. New York, Macmillan, 1904.

Smith, W. Robertson. *The Old Testament in the Jewish Church.* Third edition. New York, Macmillan, 1926.

Swete, Henry B. *Introduction to the Old Testament in Greek.* Third revised edition, R. R. Ottley. Cambridge, University Press, 1914.

Würthwein, Ernst. *The Text of the Old Testament; an Introduction to Kittel-Kahle's Biblia Hebraica.* Translated by Peter R. Ackroyd. New York, Macmillan, 1957.

Zeitlin, Solomon. *An Historical Study of the Canonization of the Hebrew Scriptures.* Philadelphia, Jewish Publication Society, 1933.

Buhl, Frants. *Kanon und Text des Alten Testaments.* Leipzig, 1891.

Geiger, Abraham. *Urschrift und Übersetzungen der Bibel.* Second edition. Frankfurt, W. A. Wahrmann, 1928.

Hölscher, Gustav. *Kanonisch und Apokryph*. Naumburg, 1905.
Kahle, Paul. *Der Hebräische Bibeltext seit Franz Delitzsch*. Stuttgart, W. Kohlhammer, 1960.
Noth, Martin. *Die Welt des Alten Testaments*. Third edition. Berlin, Töpelmann, 1957.

COMMENTARIES

Kent, Charles F., editor. *The Student's Old Testament*. Six volumes. New York, Scribner, 1904–1927.
Kautzsch, Emil, editor. *Die Heilige Schrift des Alten Testaments*. Third edition, two volumes, Alfred Bertholet. Tübingen, J. C. B. Mohr, 1922–1923.

ONE VOLUME COMMENTARIES

Alleman, Henry G. and Elmer E. Flack, editors. *Old Testament Commentary*. Philadelphia, Muhlenberg Press, 1951.
Clarke, W. K. L. *Concise Bible Commentary*. London, S.P.C.K., 1952.
Davies, G. H., editor. *Twentieth Century Bible Commentary*. Second edition, A. Richardson and C. L. Wallis. New York, Harper, 1955.
Dummelow, John R., editor. *A Commentary on the Holy Bible*. New York, Macmillan, 1947.
Eiselen, Frederick, and E. Lewis, D. C. Downey, editors. *The Abingdon Commentary on the Bible*. Nashville, Abingdon Press, 1929.
Gore, C., and H. H. Goudge, A. Guillaume, editors. *New Commentary on the Holy Scriptures Including the Apocrypha*. New York, Macmillan, 1928.
Peake, Arthur S., *Commentary on the Bible*. New York, Thomas Nelson, 1961.

COMMENTARY SERIES

The Cambridge Bible for Schools and Colleges. Cambridge, Cambridge University Press, 1895 ff.
The Expositor's Bible. London, Hodder and Stoughton, 1892 ff.
Harper's Annotated Bible Series. New York, Harper, 1956 ff.
The International Critical Commentary. New York, Scribner, 1895 ff. (Only useful to persons who have studied Hebrew and Greek; the most learned commentary in English.)
The Interpreter's Bible. Six volumes. Nashville, Abingdon Press, 1952 ff.
The New Century Bible. Edinburgh, 1904 ff.
Torch Bible Commentaries. London, SCM Press, 1950 ff.
The Westminster Commentaries. London, Methuen, 1904 ff.

Das Alte Testament Deutsch. Twenty-five volumes. Göttingen, Vandenhoeck und Ruprecht, 1949 ff.
Biblisher Kommentar: Altes Testament. Neukirchen, Eziehungsverein, 1962 ff.
Handbuch zum Alten Testament. Tübingen, J. C. B. Mohr, 1935 ff.
Handkommentar zum Alten Testament. Göttingen, Vandenhoeck und Ruprecht, 1892 ff.
Kommentar zum Alten Testament, Leipzig, A. Deichert, 1913 ff.
Kurzer Handkommentar zum Alten Testament. Tübingen, J. C. B. Mohr, 1897 ff.
Die Schriften des Alten Testaments in Auswahl. Seven volumes. Göttingen, Vandenhoeck und Ruprecht, 1921 ff. (Representative of the school of comparative religion.)

PENTATEUCH

Carpenter, Joseph E. and G. Harford-Battersby. *The Hexateuch According to the Revised Version.* Two volumes. New York, Longmans, Green, 1900.
Mowinckel, Sigmund. *The Two Sources of the Predeuteronomic Primeval History (JE) in Gen. 1–11.* Oslo, J. Dybwad, 1937.
Rad, Gerhard von. *Studies in Deuteronomy.* Translated by David Stalker. London, SCM Press, 1953.
Simpson, Cuthbert A. *The Early Traditions of Israel.* Oxford, Blackwell, 1949.
Simpson, David C. *Pentateuchal Criticism.* Second edition. London, Oxford University Press, 1924.
Smith, John M. Powis. *The Origin and History of Hebrew Law.* Chicago, University of Chicago Press, 1931. (With translations of ancient Oriental codes.)
Welch, Adam C. *The Code of Deuteronomy.* London, Clarke, 1924.
—— *Deuteronomy; the Framework of the Code.* London, Oxford University Press, 1932.

Alt, Albrecht. *Die Ursprünge des Israelitischen Rechts,* 1934. See Alt, *Kleine Schriften zur Geschichte Israels,* I, 278–332. München, Beck, 1953.
Beyerlin, Walter. *Herkunft und Geschichte der ältesten Sinaitraditionen.* Tübingen, J. C. B. Mohr, 1961.
Eissfeldt, Otto. *Die ältesten Traditionen Israels.* Berlin, Töpelmann, 1950.
—— *Hexateuchsynopse,* Leipzig, Hinrichs, 1922.
—— *Die Genesis der Genesis.* Tübingen, J. C. B. Mohr, 1958.

Gressmann, Hugo. *Mose und seine Zeit; ein Kommentar zu den Mose-sagen.* Göttingen, Vandenhoeck und Ruprecht, 1913.

Jepsen, Alfred. *Untersuchungen zum Bundesbuch.* Stuttgart, Kohlhammer, 1927.

Jirku, Anton. *Das weltliche Recht im Alten Testament.* Gütersloh, Bertelsmann, 1927.

Kock, Klaus. *Die Priesterschrift von Exodus 25 bis Leviticus 16.* Göttingen, Vandenhoeck und Ruprecht, 1959.

Kornfeld, Walter. *Studien zum Heiligkeitsgetz.* Wien, Herder, 1952.

Noth, Martin. *Die Gesetze im Pentateuch, ihre Voraussetzungen und ihr Sinn.* Halle, M. Niemeyer, 1940.

—— *Überlieferungsgeschichte des Pentateuch.* Stuttgart, W. Kohlhammer, 1948.

—— *Überlieferungsgeschichtliche Studien I, Die sammelnden und bearbeitenden Geschichtswerke des Alten Testaments.* Halle, M. Niemeyer, 1948.

Rad, Gerhard von. *Das formgeschichtliche Problem des Hexateuchs.* Stuttgart, W. Kohlhammer, 1938.

—— *Die Priesterschrift im Hexateuch literarisch untersucht und theologish gewertet.* Stuttgart, W. Kohlhammer, 1934.

Rendtdorff, Rolf. *Die Gesetze in der Priesterschrift.* Göttingen, Vandenhoeck und Ruprecht, 1954.

Smend, Rudolph. *Die Erzählungen des Hexateuch auf ihre Quellen untersucht.* Berlin, G. Reimer, 1912.

—— *Das Mosebuch von Heinrich Ewald bis Martin Noth.* Tübingen, J. C. B. Mohr, 1959.

Volz, Paul and Wilhelm Rudolph. *Der Elohist als Erzähler. Ein Irrweg der Pentateuchkritik.* Giessen, Töpelmann, 1933.

Cazelles, Henri. *Étude sur le code de l'alliance.* Paris, 1946.

Mowinckel, Sigmund. *Le Décalogue.* Paris, Felix Alcan, 1927.

HISTORICAL BOOKS

Garstang, John. *Foundations of Bible History: Joshua and Judges.* New York, Richard Smith, 1931.

—— *The Heritage of Solomon.* London, Williams and Norgate, 1934.

Hoshander, Jacob. *The Book of Esther in the Light of History.* Philadelphia, Dropsie College for Hebrew and Cognate Learning, 1923.

Kapelrud, Arvid S. *The Question of Authorship in the Ezra Narrative.* Oslo, J. Dybawd, 1944.

Myers, Jacob M. *The Linguistic and Literary Form of the Book of Ruth.* Leiden, E. J. Brill, 1955.

Simpson, Cuthbert A. *Composition of the Book of Judges.* Oxford, Blackwell, 1957.

Torrey, Charles C. *The Chronicler's History of Israel; Chronicles-Ezra-Nehemiah Restored to its Original Form.* New Haven, Yale University Press, 1954.

—— *Ezra Studies.* Chicago, University of Chicago Press, 1910.

Welch, Adam C. *The Work of the Chronicler; its Purpose and Date* (Schweich Lectures). London, British Academy, 1938.

Eissfeldt, Otto. *Die Komposition der Samuelisbücher.* Leipzig, Hinrichs, 1931.

—— *Die Quellen des Richterbuches.* Leipzig, Hinrichs, 1925.

Fohrer, Georg. *Elia.* Zürich, Zwingli-Verlag, 1957.

Gunkel, Hermann. *Elias, Jahve und Baal.* Tübingen, J. C. B. Mohr, 1906.

—— *Esther.* Tübingen, J. C. B. Mohr, 1916.

—— *Geschichten von Elisa.* Berlin, Curtius, 1922.

Jepsen, Alfred. *Die Quellen des Königsbuches.* Halle, M. Niemeyer, 1953. (Valuable also for chronology.)

Rost, Leonhard. *Die Überlieferung von der Thronnachfolge Davids.* Stuttgart, Kohlhammer, 1926.

Schäder, Hans Heinrich. *Esra der Schreiber.* Tübingen, J. C. B. Mohr, 1930.

Täubler, Eugen. *Biblische Studien; Die Epoche der Richter.* Tübingen, J. C. B. Mohr, 1958.

Rad, Gerhard von. *Das Geschichtsbild des Chronistischen Werkes.* Stuttgart, W. Kohlhammer, 1930.

THE PROPHETIC BOOKS

Graham, William C. *The Prophets and Israel's Culture.* Chicago, University of Chicago Press, 1934.

Guillaume, Alfred. *Prophecy and Divination among the Hebrews and other Semites.* New York, Harper, 1938.

Haldar, Alfred. *Associations of Cult Prophets among the Ancient Semites.* Stockholm, Almqvist and Wiksells, 1945.

Heaton, Eric W. *The Old Testaments Prophets.* Harmondsworth, Middlesex, Penguin Books, 1958.

Henshaw, Thomas. *The Latter Prophets.* London, Allen and Unwin, 1958.

Howie, Carl O. *The Date and Composition of Ezekiel.* Philadelphia, Society of Biblical Literature, 1950.

Hyatt, James P. *Jeremiah the Prophet of Courage and Hope.* New York, Abingdon Press, 1958.

Irwin, William A. *The Problem of Ezekiel.* Chicago, University of Chicago Press, 1943.

James, Fleming. *Personalities of the Old Testament*. New York, Scribner, 1936.

Johnson, Aubrey R. *The Cultic Prophet in Ancient Israel*. Cardiff, University of Wales, 1944.

Knight, Harold. *The Hebrew Prophetic Consciousness*. London, Lutterworth Press, 1947.

Kuhl, Curt. *The Prophets of Israel*. Translated by R. J. Ehrlich. Edinburgh, Oliver and Boyd, 1960.

Leslie, Elmer A. *Jeremiah Chronologically Arranged, Translated and Interpreted*. Nashville, Abingdon Press, 1954.

Lindblom, Johannes. *The Servant Songs of Deutero-Isaiah*. Lund, C. W. K. Gleerup, 1951.

—— *A Study on the Immanuel Section in Isaiah*. Lund, C. W. K. Gleerup, 1958.

Lods, Adolphe. *The Prophets and the Rise of Judaism*. Translated. London, Kegan Paul, 1937.

Mattuck, Israel I. *The Thought of the Prophets*. London, Allen and Unwin, 1953.

Milley, Charles R. *The Prophets of Israel*. New York, Vision, 1960.

Mowinckel, Sigmund. *Prophecy and Tradition*. Oslo, J. Dybwad, 1946.

—— *He that Cometh*. Translated by G. W. Anderson. Nashville, Abingdon Press, 1956.

North, Christopher R. *The Suffering Servant in Deutero-Isaiah*. London, Oxford University Press, 1948, 1956.

Paterson, John. *The Goodly Fellowship of the Prophets*. New York, Scribner, 1948.

Peake, Arthur S. *The Servant of Yahweh and Other Lectures*. Manchester, Manchester University Press, 1931.

Robinson, H. Wheeler. *Two Hebrew Prophets: Studies in Hosea and Ezekiel*. London, Lutterworth Press, 1948.

Robinson, Theodore H. *Prophecy and the Prophets in Ancient Israel*. New York, Scribner, 1923.

Rowley, Harold H. *Darius the Mede and the Four World Empires in the Book of Daniel*. Cardiff, University of Wales, 1935.

—— *The Relevance of Apocalyptic*. London, Lutterworth Press, 1944.

Scott, Robert B. Y. *The Relevance of the Prophets*. New York, Macmillan, 1944.

Skinner, John. *Prophecy and Religion, Studies in the Life of Jeremiah*. Second Edition. Cambridge, University Press, 1922.

Smith, George Adam. *Jeremiah*. Fourth edition. New York, Harper, 1929.

Smith, John M. P. *The Prophets and Their Times*. Second edition revised, W. A. Irwin. Chicago, University of Chicago Press, 1941.

Smith, Sidney. *Isaiah Chapters XL–LV: Literary Criticism and History* (Schweich Lectures). London, British Academy, 1940.

Torrey, Charles C. *Pseudo-Ezekiel and the Original Prophecy. A New Interpretation.* New Haven, Yale University Press, 1930.

—— *The Second Isaiah.* New York, Scribner, 1928.

Welch, Adam C. *Jeremiah, His Time and His Work.* New York, Macmillan, 1956.

—— *Kings and Prophets of Israel.* Edited by N. W. Porteous. London, Lutterworth Press, 1952.

—— *Prophet and Priest in Old Israel.* New York, Macmillan, 1953.

—— *Visions of the End: a Study in Daniel and Revelation.* New edition, N. W. Porteous. London, J. C. Clarke, 1958.

Widengren, George. *Literary and Psychological Aspects of the Hebrew Prophets.* Uppsala, Lundequist, 1948.

Wolfe, Roland E. *Meet Amos and Hosea.* New York, Harper, 1945.

Beyerlin, Walter. *Die Kulttraditionen Israels in der Verkündigung des Propheten Micha.* Göttingen, Vandenhoeck und Ruprecht, 1959.

Birkeland, Harris. *Zum Hebräischen Traditionswesen. Die Komposition der Prophetischen Bücher des Alten Testaments.* Oslo, J. Dybwad, 1938.

Budde, Karl. *Jesaja's Erleben.* Gotha, L. Klotz, 1928.

Duhm, Bernhard. *Israels Propheten.* Second edition. Tübingen, J. C. B. Mohr, 1922.

Elliger, Karl. *Deuterojesaja in seimen Verhältnis zu Tritojesaja.* Stuttgart, W. Kohlhammer, 1933.

—— *Die Einheit des Tritojesaja* (55–66) Stuttgart, W. Kohlhammer, 1928.

Fohrer, Georg. *Die Hauptprobleme des Buches Ezechiel.* Berlin, A. Töpelmann, 1952.

Gressmann, Hugo. *Der Messias.* Göttingen, Vandenhoeck und Ruprecht, 1929.

Grunneweg, Antonius. *Mündliche und schriftliche Tradition der vorexilischen Prophetenbücher als Problem der neueren Prophetenforschung.* Göttingen, Vandenhoeck und Ruprecht, 1959.

Gunkel, Hermann. *Die Propheten* (reprint from *Die Schriften des Alten Testaments*). Göttingen, Vandenhoeck und Ruprecht, 1917.

Hänel, Johannes. *Das Erkennen Gotte bei den Schriftpropheten.* Berlin, W. Kohlhammer, 1923.

Hentschke, Richard. *Die Stellung der vorexilischen Schriftpropheten zum Kultus.* Berlin, A. Töpelmann, 1957.

Herntrich, Volkmar. *Ezechielprobleme.* Giessen, A. Töpelmann, 1929.

Hertzberg, Hans W. *Prophet und Gott: eine Studie zur Religiosität des vorexilischen Prophetentums.* Gütersloh, C. Bertelsmann, 1923.

Hölscher, Gustav. *Hesekiel, der Dichter und das Buch.* Giessen, A. Töpelmann, 1924.

—— *Die Profeten.* Leipzig, Hinrichs, 1914.

Jenni, Ernst S. *Die politischen Voraussagen der Propheten*. Zürich, Zwingli-Verlag, 1956.

Jepsen, Alfred. *Nabi*. München, Beck, 1934.

Kraus, Hans Joachim. *Die prophetische Verkündigung des Rechts in Israel*. Zollikon, Evangelischer-Verlag, 1957.

Lindblom, Johannes. *Die Jesaja-Apokalypse*. Lund, C. W. K. Gleerup, 1938.

Messel, Nils. *Ezechielfragen*. Oslo, J. Dybwad, 1945.

Norden, Eduard. *Die Geburt des Kindes*. Leipzig, B. G. Teubner, 1924.

Quell, Gottfried. *Wahre und Falsche Propheten*. Gütersloh, C. Bertelsmann, 1952.

Schmidt, Hans. *Jona*. Göttingen, Vandenhoeck und Ruprecht, 1906.

Volz, Paul. *Prophetgestalten des Altes Testaments*. Stuttgart, Calwer Vereinsbuchhandlung, 1938.

Weiser, Arthur. *Die Prophetie des Amos*. Giessen, A. Töpelmann, 1929.

POETRY AND THE POETIC BOOKS

Gray, George B. *The Forms of Hebrew Poetry*. London, Hodder and Stoughton, 1915.

Oesterley, William O. E. *Ancient Hebrew Poems*. New York, Macmillan, 1938.

Robinson, Theodore H. *The Poetry of the Old Testament*. London, Duckworth, Ltd., 1947.

Rothstein, J. W. *Grundzüge des Hebräischen Rhythmus und seiner Formenbildung nebst lyrischen Texten*. Leipzig, J. C. Hinrichs, 1909.

PSALMS

Birkeland, Harris. *The Evildoers in the Book of Psalms*. Oslo, J. Dybwad, 1955.

James, Fleming. *Thirty Psalmists*. New York, Putnam, 1938. (An introduction to Gunkel's form-critical method.)

Mowinckel, Sigmund. *The Psalms in Israel's Worship*. Two volumes. Translated by Ap-Thomas. Nashville, Abingdon Press, 1962.

Oesterley, William O. E. *A Fresh Approach to the Psalms*. New York, Scribner, 1937.

Paterson, John. *The Praises of Israel: Studies Literary and Religious in the Psalms*. New York, Scribner, 1950.

Simpson, David C., editor. *The Psalmists*. Oxford, Oxford University Press, 1926.

Smith, John M. P. *The Religion of the Psalms*. Chicago, University of Chicago Press, 1922.

Snaith, Norman H. *Hymns of the Temple*. London, SCM Press, 1951.

—— *Studies in the Psalter*. London, Epworth Press, 1934.

Terrien, Samuel. *The Psalms and Their Meaning for Us Today.* Indianapolis, Bobbs-Merrill, 1952.
Welch, Adam C. *The Psalter in Life, Worship and History.* Oxford, Clarendon Press, 1926.

Balla, Emil. *Das Ich der Psalmen.* Göttingen, Vandenhoeck und Ruprecht, 1912.
Birkeland, Harris. *Die Feinde des Individuums in der Israelitischen Psalmenliteratur.* Oslo, 1933.
Gunkel, Hermann, and Johannes Begrich. *Einleitung in die Psalmen,* volume one of Gunkel's commentary in the *Handkommentar.* Göttingen, Vandenhoeck und Ruprecht, 1933. (Invaluable work for form criticism.)
Jansen, H. Ludin. *Die spätjüdische Psalmendichtung.* Oslo, J. Dybwad, 1937.
Mowinckel, Sigmund. *Psalmenstudien I–VI.* Kristiania, J. Dybwad, 1921–1924. (A work that provided much stimulation for cultic interpretation and the search for the cultic element in the Old Testament.)
Quell, Gottfried. *Das kultische Problem der Psalmen.* Stuttgart, W. Kohlhammer, 1926.
Schmidt, Hans. *Das Gebet der Angeklagten in Alten Testament.* Giessen, A. Töpelmann, 1928.
Westermann, Claus. *Das Loben Gottes in den Psalmen.* Berlin, Evangelische Verlagsanstalt, 1953.

SONG OF SONGS

Jastrow, Morris. *The Song of Songs.* Philadelphia. Lippincott, 1922.
Rowley, Harold H. *The Servant of the Lord and Other Essays on the Old Testament.* London, Lutterworth Press, 1952.
Waterman, Leroy. *The Song of Songs, Translated and Interpreted as a Dramatic Poem.* Ann Arbor, University of Michigan Press, 1948.

Kuhn, Gottfried. *Erklärung des Hohen Liedes.* Leipzig, A. Deichert, 1926.
Schmökel, Hartmut. *Heilige Hochzeit und Hoheslied.* Wiesbaden, Steiner, 1956.

LAMENTATIONS

Gottwald, Norman K. *Studies in the Book of Lamentations.* Chicago, A. Allenson, 1954.

THE WISDOM BOOKS

Ginsberg, Harold L. *Studies in Koheleth.* New York, Jewish Theological Seminary of America, 1950.
Gordis, Robert. *Koheleth, the Man and His World.* Second edition. New York, Jewish Theological Seminary of America, 1951, 1955.

Jastrow, Morris. *A Gentle Cynic*. Philadelphia, Lippincott, 1919.

Jung, Carl G. *Answer to Job*. London, Routledge and Paul, 1954.

Kraeling, Emil G. *The Book of the Ways of God*. New York, Scribner, 1939.

Macdonald, Duncan. *The Hebrew Philosophical Genius*. Princeton, Princeton University Press, 1936.

Odeberg, Hugo. *Qohaeleth*. Stockholm, Almqvist and Wiksells, 1929.

Oesterley, William O. E. *The Wisdom of Egypt and the Old Testament*. London, Society for Promoting Christian Knowledge, 1927.

Power, Arnold D. *Sidelights on the Book of Proverbs*. London, Longmans Green, 1950.

Rankin, Oliver S. *Israel's Wisdom Literature*. Second edition. Edinburgh, T. Clarke, 1954.

Ranston, Harry. *Ecclesiastes and the Early Greek Wisdom Literature*. London, Epworth Press, 1925.

—— *The Old Testament Wisdom Books and Their Teaching*. London, Epworth Press, 1930.

Ringgren, Helmer. *Word and Wisdom: Studies in the Hypostatization of Divine Qualities and Functions in the Ancient Near East*. Lund, 1947.

Robinson, H. Wheeler. *The Cross in the Old Testament*. Philadelphia, Westminster Press, 1955.

Robinson, Theodore H. *Job and His Friends*. London, SCM Press, 1954.

Rowley, Harold H. *The Book of Job and Its Meaning*. Manchester, Manchester University Press, 1958.

Rylaarsdam, John C. *Revelation in Jewish Wisdom Literature*. Chicago, University of Chicago Press, 1946.

Stevenson, William B. *The Poem of Job: a Literary Study with a New Translation*. Second edition. London, British Academy, 1947, 1948.

Terrien, Samuel. *Job, Poet of Existence*. Indianapolis, Bobbs-Merrill, 1957.

Baumgärtel, Friedrich. *Der Hiobdialog. Aufriss und Deutung*. Stuttgart, W. Kohlhammer, 1933.

Boström, Gustav. *Proverbiastudien: die Weisheit und das fremde Weib in Sprüche 1–9*. Lund, C. W. K. Gleerup, 1935.

Eissfeldt, Otto. *Der Maschal im Alten Testament*. Giessen, A. Töpelmann, 1913.

Fichtner, Johannes. *Die Altorientalische Weisheit in ihrer Israelitisch-Jüdischen Ausprägung*. Giessen, A. Töpelmann, 1933.

Galling, Kurt. *Die Krise der Aufklärung in Israel*. Mainz, Gutenberg, 1951.

Gressmann, Hugo. *Israels Spruchweisheit im Zusammenhang der Weltliteratur*. Berlin, K. Curtius, 1925.

Kuhn, Gottfried. *Beiträge zur Erklärung des Salomonischen Spruchbuchs*. Stuttgart, W. Kohlhammer, 1931.

Meinhold, Johannes. *Die Weisheit Israels in Spruch, Sage und Dichtung.* Leipzig, Quelle and Meyer, 1908.

Rudolph, Wilhelm. *Vom Buche Kohelet.* Münster, Aschendorff, 1959.

Thilo, Martin. *Der Prediger Salomo.* Bonn, Marcus und Weber, 1923.

Westermann, Claus. *Der Aufbau des Buches Hiob.* Tübingen, J. C. B. Mohr, 1956.

Zimmerli, Walther. *Die Weisheit des Predigers Salomo.* Berlin, A. Töpelmann, 1936.

APOCRYPHA AND PSEUDEPIGRAPHA

TRANSLATIONS

The Apocrypha. Revised Standard Version. Thomas Nelson, 1957.

Ball, C. J. The Variorum Apocrypha. London, Eyre and Spottiswoode.

Charles, R. H., editor. The Apocrypha and Pseudepigrapha of the Old Testament in English. Two volumes. Oxford, Clarendon Press, 1913. (An immense work with commentary; chiefly for the professional.)

Goodspeed, Edgar J. The Apocrypha. An American Translation. Chicago, University of Chicago Press, 1938.

Kautzsch, Emil, editor. *Die Apokryphen und Pseudepigraphen des Alten Testaments.* Two volumes. Tübingen, J. C. B. Mohr, 1900.

Riessler, Paul. *Altjüdisches Schrifttum ausserhalb der Bibel übersetz und erläutert.* Augsburg, Filser, 1928. (Includes Hellenistic Jewish texts and late Pseudepigrapha.)

INTRODUCTION AND HISTORY

Brockington, L. H. *Critical Introduction to the Apocrypha.*

Dentan, Robert C. *The Apocrypha: Bridge of the Testaments.* Greenwich, Conn., Seabury Press, 1954.

Jewish Apocryphal Literature Series. Commentaries on various books. New York, Harper.

Oesterley, William O. E. *An Introduction to the Books of the Apocrypha.* New York, Macmillan, 1935.

Metzger, Bruce M. *An Introduction to the Apocrypha.* London, Oxford University Press, 1957.

Pfeiffer, Robert H. *History of the New Testament Times with an Introduction to the Apocrypha.* New York, Harper, 1949.

Torrey, Charles C. *The Apocryphal Literature.* New Haven, Yale University Press, 1945.

Bousset, Wilhelm. *Die Religion des Judentums in neutestamentlichen Zeitalter.* Third edition, Hugo Gressmann. Tübingen, J. C. B. Mohr, 1926.

Schürer, Emil. *Geschichte des Jüdischen Volkes im Zeitalter Jesu Christi.*
Three volumes. Third and fourth edition. Leipzig, Hinrichs, 1901 ff.

DEAD SEA SCROLLS

Allegro, John M. *The Dead Sea Scrolls.* Harmondsworth, Middlesex,
Pelican Books, 1956.
Burrows, Millar. *The Dead Sea Scrolls.* New York, Viking Press, 1955.
(Also gives translations and exhaustive Bibliography.)
—— *More Light on the Dead Sea Scrolls.* New York, Viking Press, 1958.
Cross, Frank M. *The Ancient Library of Qumran and Modern Biblical
Studies.* Garden City, Doubleday, 1958. (The most precise information
on unpublished material.)
Dupont-Sommer, A. *The Essene Writings from Qumran.* Translated by
G. Vermes. Cleveland, 1962 (Meridian Book).
Gaster, Theodore H. *The Dead Sea Scriptures in English Translation.*
Garden City, Doubleday, 1956 (Anchor Book).

MISCELLANEOUS

GEOGRAPHY AND HISTORY

Baly, Dennis. *The Geography of the Bible.* New York, Harper, 1957.
Beek, M. A. *History of Israel from Abraham to Barcochba.* New York,
Harper, 1962.
Bright, John. *History of Israel.* Philadelphia, Westminster Press, 1959.
Kraeling, Emil G. *Rand McNally Bible Atlas.* Chicago, Rand McNally,
1956. (Hebrew history reviewed with particular attention to topogra-
phy and archaeology.)
—— *Rand McNally Historical Atlas of the Holy Land,* 1960. (The
maps of the preceding work, with brief text.)
Noth, Martin. *History of Israel.* Second edition, P. R. Ackroyd. New
York, Harper, 1960.
Wright, G. Ernest and Floyd V. Filson. *The Westminster Historical
Atlas to the Bible.* Philadelphia, Westminster Press, 1956.

ARCHAEOLOGY

Albright, William F. *The Archaeology of Palestine.* Revised edition.
Harmondsworth, Middlesex, Pelican Books, 1960.
Finegan, Jack. *Light from the Ancient Past.* Second edition. Princeton,
Princeton University Press, 1959.
Price, Ira M. *The Monuments and the Old Testament.* Revised edition,
O. R. Sellers and E. L. Carlson. Philadelphia, Judson, 1958.

Pritchard, James B. *Ancient Near East in Pictures Relating to the Old Testament*. Princeton, Princeton University Press, 1955.
—— *Ancient Near Eastern Texts Relating to the Old Testament*. Second edition. Princeton, Princeton University Press, 1950.
Wright, G. Ernest. *Biblical Archaeology*. Philadelphia, Westminster Press, 1957.
Vaux, Roland de. *Ancient Israel: Its Life and Institutions*. New York, McGraw-Hill, 1962.

RELIGION AND THEOLOGY

Albright, William F. *From the Stone Age to Christianity*. Baltimore, Johns Hopkins Press, 1957.
—— *Archaeology and the Religion of Israel*. Third edition, Baltimore, Johns Hopkins University Press, 1954.
Jacob, Edmond. *Theology of the Old Testament*. New York, Harper, 1958.
McCown, Chester C. *Man, Morals and History*. New York, Harper, 1958.
Muilenburg, James. *The Way of Israel*. New York, Harper, 1961.
Pedersen, Johannes. *Israel: Its Life and Culture*. Two volumes. London, Milford, 1926–1940.
Rad, Gerhard von. *Theology of the Old Testament*. Two volumes. Philadelphia, Westminster Press, 1961 f.

Index of Biblical Passages

General Index